CABELL COUNTY ANNALS AND FAMILIES

By GEORGE SELDEN WALLACE

MCMXXXV
GARRETT & MASSIE, PUBLISHERS, RICHMOND

This volume was reproduced from
An 1935 edition located in the
Publisher's private library,
Greenville, South Carolina

All rights reserved. No part of this publication may be reproduced,
stored in a retrieval system, transmitted in any form, posted
on to the web in any form or by any means without the
prior written permission of the publisher.

Please direct all correspondence and orders to:

www.southernhistoricalpress.com
or
SOUTHERN HISTORICAL PRESS, Inc.
PO BOX 1267
375 West Broad Street
Greenville, SC   29601
southernhistoricalpress@gmail.com

Originally published: Richmond, VA 1935
Copyright 1935
By: Frances G. Wallace
Reprinted by: Southern Historical Press, Inc.
Greenville, SC
ISBN #0-89308-950-8
All rights Reserved.
Printed in the United States of America

TO

JOHN JACOB CORNWELL

GOVERNOR, 1917-1920

WHO IS THE EXEMPLIFICATION

OF ALL THAT IS BEST

IN PRIVATE AND PUBLIC LIFE

THIS VOLUME IS RESPECTFULLY DEDICATED

FOREWORD

THIS work is to record for future generations an account of the men and women and their problems from the beginning of Cabell County. I had the use of the digest of the records of the County Court and of the Circuit Superior Courts of Law and Chancery from 1809 to 1873 which were made up by R. S. Douthat and from these records secured the dates and data on which most of this work is based. I desire to express to Mr. Douthat my appreciation for the use of his digest and to compliment him on its accuracy. Franklin L. Burdette, Senior, has been most useful. His accurate knowledge of the history of this county is not equalled.

The author is indebted to W. H. Newcomb and Miss Ethel Nash for their assistance in securing material; to C. E. King, Deputy Circuit Clerk and Joseph L. Shifflette, for their active assistance in running records; to G. C. Wofford for making photographs of many of the old houses; to P. Walker Long for putting at his disposal the records of the Huntington Publishing Company; and to his efficient secretary, Miss Marie Gengenbacher, who not only typed the history but was alert and helpful in detecting errors in names and dates.

In addition to the foregoing there have been many others who have been helpful and to these the author is most grateful.

GEORGE SELDEN WALLACE.

August, 1935.

CONTENTS

	PAGE
I. CABELL COUNTY	1
THE SAVAGE GRANT	2
II. GREENBOTTOM	5
III. PREHISTORIC SETTLERS	8
IV. FORMING OF THE COUNTY	10
V. ORGANIZATION OF THE COUNTY	17
SUPERIOR COURTS OF LAW AND CHANCERY	17
THE COUNTY COURT	18
GENTLEMEN JUSTICES	18
SHERIFFS	20
PROSECUTING ATTORNEYS	20
DELEGATES	20
CURRENT EVENTS PRIOR TO 1860	22
SAMPSON SANDERS	32
PROHIBITION BEFORE THE EIGHTEENTH AMENDMENT	32
VI. THE FATEFUL YEARS, 1860-1871	34
COURT ACTIONS GROWING OUT OF THE WAR	42
THE COUNTY UNDER THE NEW STATE	43
VII. COUNTY POLITICS SINCE 1872	48
THE NARRATIVE SINCE THE CIVIL WAR	52
COMMON PLEAS COURT	59
DOMESTIC RELATIONS COURT	61
GRIST MILLS	61
TOBACCO	65
OIL AND GAS	66
VIII. GRAVEYARDS AND CEMETERIES	68
PAT'S BRANCH GRAVEYARD	68
BUFFINGTON GRAVEYARD	69
PRIVATE GRAVEYARDS	69
IX. SOLDIERS OF THE REVOLUTION	70
X. THE WAR OF 1812	74
XI. THE WAR WITH MEXICO	75

CONTENTS

	PAGE
XII. THE GREAT TRAGEDY	77
Troop Movement in Cabell, 1861-65	85
On the Union Side	87
XIII. THE WAR WITH SPAIN	91
First West Virginia U. S. Volunteer Infantry	91
Second West Virginia U. S. Volunteer Infantry	92
Philippine Insurrection	92
XIV. THE WORLD WAR	94
XV. THE MILITIA	97
XVI. THE NATIONAL GUARD	102
XVII. UNITED STATES ENGINEERS	110
United States Recruiting Officers	111
XVIII. THE ORGANIZED RESERVES	112
XIX. UNITED STATES NAVAL COMMUNICATION RESERVES	113
Roads	114
Road to the Big Sandy	117
Guyan Valley Road	118
Lincoln County Pike	118
Mason County Road	119
McCoy Road	119
Waterways	120
The Ohio River	123
XX. RAILROADS	125
XXI. SCHOOLS	130
XXII. HUNTINGTON SCHOOLS	139
The Schoolmaster	147
Marshall College	150
Morris Harvey College	163
The Prichard School	165
Early Doctors	165
XXIII. STATE INSTITUTIONS	168

CONTENTS

		PAGE
XXIV.	THE CITY OF HUNTINGTON	170
	THE JESSE JAMES ROBBERY	180
XXV.	CURRENT EVENTS, 1871-1893	201
XXVI.	THE CITY ATTAINS ITS MAJORITY	219
XXVII.	HUNTINGTON LAWYERS	245
	POLITICAL LEADERS	246
XXVIII.	TO CONTINUE THE STORY	248
XXIX.	MANUFACTURERS AND WHOLESALERS	258
XXX.	PARKS AND PLAYGROUNDS	267
XXXI.	THEATRES	272
XXXII.	PUBLIC UTILITIES	274
	STREET RAILWAYS	274
	ARTIFICIAL GAS	278
	WATER COMPANY	278
	TELEPHONES	279
	NATURAL GAS	282
	ELECTRIC LIGHTS	284
XXXIII.	CHURCHES	286
	BAPTIST	286
	CATHOLIC	293
	CONGREGATIONAL	296
	METHODISTS	299
	OHEV SHOLOM	306
	PRESBYTERIANS	307
	PROTESTANT EPISCOPAL CHURCH	309
XXXIV.	THE TOWN OF BARBOURSVILLE	316
XXXV.	CENTRAL CITY	322
	NEUTRAL STRIP	324
XXXVI.	CULLODEN	325
XXXVII.	THE TOWN OF GUYANDOTTE	326
XXXVIII.	HARVEYTOWN	337
XXXIX.	THE LOST CITY	338

CONTENTS

	PAGE
XL. MILTON	340
XLI. ONA	342
XLII. SALT ROCK	343
XLIII. SAINT CLOUD	344
XLIV. FAMILIES	346
ABBOTT	346
MONSIGNOR HENRY B. ALTMEYER, LL.D.	347
ARCHER	348
BEUHRING	349
BILLUPS	355
BOSTICK	357
BRADSHAW	357
BROH	359
DOUGLAS WALTER BROWN	360
JAMES HENRY BROWN	363
BUFFINGTON	373
BURDETTE	375
CAMPBELL	377
COX	378
DARLINGTON	379
DAUGHTERS OF THE AMERICAN REVOLUTION	380
DOUTHAT	383
EVERETT	384
B. W. FOSTER	386
FRAMPTON	388
FRANCIS	389
FREEMAN	390
GALLAHER	391
GIBSON	392
EUSTACE GIBSON	393
GIDEON	394
HALL	395
HAMPTON	396
HANNAN	398
HARRISON	399
HARSHBARGER	401
HENRY DRURY HATFIELD	403

CONTENTS

	PAGE
ADAM HATFIELD	404
HAWORTH-CAMMACK-MATHEWS	405
HITE	409
HOLDERBY	410
HOLLENBECK	415
HULL	416
JENKINS	416
JAMES JOHNSTON	419
SAMUEL WOODROW JOHNSTON	420
KAIL	420
KILGORE	422
KYLE	423
LAIDLEY	425
LANE	429
LAYNE	429
LE SAGE	431
LONG	435
LOVE	439
GEORGE MARSHALL LYON	442
MARCUM	444
MARTIN	446
MAUPIN	446
MCCOMAS	447
MCCORMICK	448
MCGINNIS	449
MEEK	450
GEORGE F. MILLER	452
JOSEPH S. MILLER	453
MOORE	454
BISHOP THOMAS ASBURY MORRIS	456
MORRIS	458
NAGLEE	462
NASH	462
NEAL	463
DR. W. E. NEAL	465
JOHN HUNT OLEY	466
PAGE	468
PAINE	469
PANCAKE	470

CONTENTS

	PAGE
Pine	471
Poage	471
The Rt. Rev. Msgr. Thomas A. Quirk	471
Richmond	473
Ricketts	474
Rolfe-McLaughlin	475
John Hooe Russel	476
Jeffrey Russell	479
Mark Russell	479
Rutherford	480
Samuels	480
Samworth	481
Scales	481
Scherr	482
Scott	483
Seamonds	484
Shepherd	485
Shoffstall	486
Sikes	488
Simmons	489
Spurlock	489
Staley	496
Switzer	497
Taylor	499
Thornburg	501
Tynes	504
Vinson	505
Walton	508
Wallace	510
George Selden Wallace	510
Wellman	510
Reverend John W. Werninger	512
Wiatt	513
Wilson	515
XLV. THE SAVAGE GRANT	518
Owners of the Savage Grant	521
XLVI. COUNTY, STATE, AND FEDERAL OFFICIALS	522
Cabell County Men in the Federal Government	522

CONTENTS

	PAGE
CIRCUIT COURT JUDGES	522
SHERIFFS	522
CIRCUIT CLERKS	524
COUNTY CLERKS	524
PROSECUTING ATTORNEYS	525
MEMBERS OF THE GENERAL ASSEMBLY OF VIRGINIA	525
MAYORS OF HUNTINGTON	527

XLVII. MUSTER ROLLS 528
    ROLL OF JOHN SIMMONS' COMPANY 528
    CONSOLIDATED MUSTER ROLL OF CAPTAIN
      E. W. MCCOMAS' COMPANY C 533
    CONSOLIDATED MUSTER ROLL OF CAPTAIN
      GEORGE W. CHAYTOR'S COMPANY F 537
    THE BORDER RANGERS, COMPANY E 539
    OFFICERS OF 2D INFANTRY, HUNTINGTON 545
    COMPANY G, 2D INFANTRY, HUNTINGTON 545
    COMPANY H, 2D INFANTRY, HUNTINGTON 546
    COMPANY I, 2D INFANTRY, HUNTINGTON 546
    ROSTER, COMPANY F, 2D INFANTRY, MILTON... 546
    BAND, 2D INFANTRY, HUNTINGTON 546
    HEADQUARTERS COMPANY, 150TH INFANTRY, HUNTINGTON 546
    HEADQUARTERS, 3D BATTALION, 150TH INFANTRY, HUNTINGTON 547
    HEADQUARTERS COMPANY, 3D BATTALION, 150TH INFANTRY, HUNTINGTON 547
    MEDICAL DEPARTMENT DETACHMENT, 3D BATTALION, 150TH INFANTRY, HUNTINGTON. 547
    COMPANY I, 150TH INFANTRY, HUNTINGTON.. 547
    COMPANY K, 150TH INFANTRY, HUNTINGTON.. 547
    MEN COMMISSIONED FROM THE FIRST TRAINING CAMPS, 1917 547
    MEDICAL OFFICERS 1917-1919, DOCTORS AND DENTISTS 548
    CABELL COUNTY'S HONOR ROLL, 1917-1919.... 548

INDEX 551

LIST OF ILLUSTRATIONS

	PAGE
Governor W. H. Cabell	Frontispiece
Albert Gallatin Jenkins Home	6
Old Courthouse at Barboursville	12
The First Courthouse in Huntington	14
The Present Courthouse	16
Judge John Coalter	19
Forrest Hill, Home of P. C. Buffington	21
The Thomas Buffington House	21
Lamartine, the Home of John Laidley	23
Lombardy Lawn, the Home of Judge W. H. Hagen	23
Elisha McComas House	28
Home of James Holderby	31
James Gallaher's House	31
Martin Hull House	45
James Johnston Home	45
Dudley Irvin Smith, Sheriff	49
Albert Gallatin Jenkins	78
Suspension Bridge, Guyandotte	80
J. K. (Doc) Suiter	84
The Adam Black House	116
Wharfboat	122
Chesapeake and Ohio Passenger Station	126
Baltimore and Ohio Passenger Station	128
Looking North on 13th Street from Oley School	142
Faculty at Marshall College, 1869	158
Marshall College in the 80's	160
Collis P. Huntington	171
Peter Cline Buffington, First Mayor of Huntington	173
North Side of 3rd Avenue	176
South Side of Fourth Avenue	178
2nd Avenue, Between 7th and 8th Streets	182
Laidley and Johnston's Grocery	185
South Side 3rd Avenue	188
Northeast Corner 9th Street and 4th Avenue	190
North Side 3rd Avenue	192
The 1913 Flood	194
The 1884 Flood, South Side 3rd Avenue	196
3rd Avenue During 1913 Flood	198

LIST OF ILLUSTRATIONS

	PAGE
North Side of 4th Avenue During 1913 Flood	204
Ely Ensign	206
The 1884 Flood, 3rd Avenue, West from 10th Street	208
The New City Hall and Fire Station	211
Chamber of Commerce Group	214
Hotel Adelphi	216
Florentine Hotel	218
Dan Hill, the Early Cab Driver	220
Officials of the Chesapeake and Ohio Railroad	222
Delos W. Emmons	225
Valentine-Newcomb Store	227
Via's Restaurant	230
J. L. Crider's Drug Store	232
Ward Building	235
Peter Baer and Wife	238
D. W. Emmons and Wife	254
Log Cabin of John Q. and Eliza Adams	262
The First Street Car	275
Bicycle Club	280
Churches of Huntington, 1900	288
The Methodist Episcopal Chapel	302
5th Avenue Looking West	310
Trinity Episcopal Church	313
Barboursville, 1861	317
Thomas Thornburg's Store House at Barboursville	320
J. L. Caldwell	333
Slave Quarters, Built About 1830	339
Old Mud River Bridge Near Milton	339
H. Chester Parson's House	345
Frederick G. L. Beuhring and Frances Dannenberg Beuhring	350
Dr. Henry Brown House	362
Matilda Scales, Wife of Dr. Benjamin Brown	365
J. H. Brown	367
The Elms, Home of Judge James Henry Brown	368
Nancy Scales Buffington and William Buffington	374
The Daughters of the American Revolution Cabin	382
Bradley Waters Foster	385
James Holderby	411
Robert Holderby Home	412

LIST OF ILLUSTRATIONS

	PAGE
Robert Holderby, Sr.	413
Susan Ann Chapman, Wife of Robert Holderby	414
Samuel W. Johnston House	418
John Laidley and His Wife, Mary Scales Hite	426
Le Sage House, Le Sage	433
George F. Miller, Jr.	451
John Hunt Oley	467
John Hooe Russel	477
Burwell Spurlock, the Great Preacher	493

I: CABELL COUNTY

THE territory which we now know as Cabell County has been successively a part of the counties of Orange, Augusta, Botetourt, Fincastle, Montgomery, and Kanawha. The first territorial organization of the Colony of Virginia was the eleven plantations which sent delegates to the Assembly of 1619. Then the original eight shires or counties were organized. Other counties followed but these were in the territory east of the Blue Ridge Mountains. Orange County which was formed from Spotsylvania is the first county from which Cabell can trace a legitimate descent. Orange was formed from Spotsylvania, and its western limits were fixed "westerly by the utmost limits of Virginia." Augusta was cut off from Orange and was defined as the territory "lying on the other side of said line beyond the top of the Blue Ridge." Botetourt was formed from Augusta in 1769 and its western limits were fixed "as far west as the county court cared to extend them," with the proviso that the inhabitants of that part of the county which lay on the Mississippi River should be exempt from any levies to be laid for the purpose of building a court house and jail. Fincastle was organized in 1772 but four years later was divided and Montgomery County was formed with its northern boundary along the Great Kanawha and included what is now Cabell County. Kanawha was formed in 1789 from parts of Augusta and Montgomery and its western boundary was definitely fixed on the Ohio River.

What white man first saw Cabell County is not known. LaSalle discovered the Ohio River about the middle of the seventeenth century but whether he reached its waters by the way of the Allegheny or Wabash River is not known.

On the 14th day of June, 1671, at Sault Ste. Marie, Daumont de Saint Lusson, surrounded by a small group of Frenchmen, all dressed in gorgeous colorings of silk and velvet, except the Jesuit Fathers, and in the presence of representatives of some fourteen Indian tribes erected a huge cross and placed on a post a metal plate bearing the royal arms of France. He then with drawn sword in hand read a proclamation to the nations of the world announcing that he took possession in the name of Louis XIV, King, etc.

I take possession of this place * * * and all rivers, lakes and streams contiguous and adjacent thereunto, both those which have been discovered and those which may be discovered hereafter . . . bounded on the one side by the seas of the North and of the West, and on the other by the South Sea.

[1]

In 1749 the Governor General of Canada sent an expedition from Quebec under the command of Captain Celoron down the Ohio River to establish monuments of France's renewal of possession of this territory. In the execution of his mission he buried plates at the mouth of its principal tributaries. These plates bore an inscription asserting France's claim to the great valley. One of them was dug up at the mouth of the Great Kanawha in 1846. Captain Celoron and his party passed along what is now Cabell County.

The English in support of their claim to the same territory show that in 1671 Thomas Batts and Robert Fallom were commissioned by Major General Wood to find the ebb and flow of the western waters on the west side of the mountains in order to discover the South Sea. Under this commission they set forth from Appomattox town at 8:00 A.M., Friday, September 1, 1671. On September 8th they came upon a tree marked with coal—M. A.N.i. Five days later after they crossed the mountains they came upon two other trees marked with coal—MANI—and one M.A.—and several other scratchments. These men had reached the waters of New River and were travelling west. On September 14th they came on a clear place and "saw lying southwest curious prospect of hills like waves raised by gentle breeze of winds rising one upon another. Mr. Batts supposed we saw sayles but I rather think these to be white cliffs." Six days later they saw again what "we supposed to be a great bay." On September 17, 1671, they found four trees on the west side of the mountain and marked these with marking irons and solemnly made claim to the country in the name of Charles II, King, etc.

Just how far west these two travellers reached is not known but from the fact that these adventurers found markings on the trees it is asserted that many Englishmen had reached the Ohio River prior to its discovery by the French. We know that in 1755 Mary Ingles, after her escape from the Indians at Big Bone Lick in Kentucky, traversed the south side of the Ohio River to the mouth of the Great Kanawha River, so she must have passed through this territory. Whatever the facts may be as to the priority of discovery, the English and the Colonists were successful in the war which we know as the French and Indian War, and New France became English by the Treaty of Paris in 1763.

THE SAVAGE GRANT

On December 15, 1772, Governor Dinwiddie made a grant of 28,628 acres to John Savage and sixty other persons for military services in the French and Indian Wars. This boundary of land extended along the Ohio River from a point below the mouth of the Big Sandy to a point above the mouth of Nine Mile, and up both sides of the Sandy to the forks. It has since been known as the Savage Grant. In 1775 some of the grantees under this patent met on the land and by verbal agreement proceeded to divide a portion of it among themselves and other part owners. At this time this land was valued at 49 cents an acre.

In 1809, a number of other part owners instituted a suit in the Superior Court of Chancery at Staunton insisting that the partial division of 1775 was unjust and prayed that it should be set aside. The court named William Sterrett, John Henderson, Andrew Parks, George Summers, and Lewis Summers, gentlemen, as commissioners to divide the lands in the Savage Grant, having respect as far as possible to the division of 1775 and to ascertain the difference between the values of the several lots in order that they might be equalized. These gentlemen secured the services of General Edward W. Tupper "a skillful mathematician and land surveyor who under their direction and superintendence made the necessary surveys." These commissioners completed the work and the division made by them was confirmed by an order made on the 8th day of December, 1818. From this report as well as a statement which appears in the case of Commonwealth, vs. Hite, reported in the 6th Leigh, page 588, it seems that some of the grantees and part owners at the time of the division in 1775 took possession of their respective parts and had continued in the possession and enjoyment thereof but who these persons were or what portion they settled on is not stated. George Washington came down the Ohio River in 1770 to the mouth of the Great Kanawha but there is no record of his having been in Cabell County. One or more stones marking the exterior boundaries of the Savage Grant are marked G. W. and this has given rise to the story that George Washington himself made the survey. This is not according to the fact. The survey was made by Colonel William Crawford, afterwards burned at the stake in Northern Ohio by the Indians, and the use of the initials simply indicate that it was George Washington or military land.

William Buffington of Hampshire County purchased lot 42 of the Savage Grant from John Savage and willed this tract to his two sons, Thomas and William Buffington, who by the decree of December 8, 1818, were confirmed in its possession. Thomas Buffington and his brother, Jonathan, came to Cabell County about 1796 and at that time found Thomas Hannon settled on the Little Guyan, and Hannon is regarded as the first settler in this county. He is buried in Mason County just beyond the Cabell line and his gravestone records the fact that he was a soldier in the Revolutionary War. Thomas Buffington built on the point on the Ohio River just below the mouth of the Guyandotte and this house, with some additions, was the home of the late D. W. Emmons.

II: GREENBOTTOM

A SHORT distance above the Savage Grant is Greenbottom which contains 4,441 acres and fronts eight miles along the Ohio River. It was patented to Joshua Fry but the patent is not of record in either Botetourt or Augusta counties and the land office in Richmond can give no information concerning it. But as Fry was colonel of the regiment in which Washington was lieutenant colonel in the French and Indian War it is logical to assume that the grant was to Fry for this service. Joshua Fry* who describes himself as of the county of Mercer, State of Kentucky, by deed dated July 9, 1805, and of record in Mercer County, Kentucky, and Kanawha County, West Virginia, conveyed to Peyton Short of Woodford County, Kentucky, the lower moiety, twenty-five hundred acres, of Greenbottom survey (the upper half of which had been sold to Wilson C. Nicholas, but the deed is not of record) but reserved to —— Spurlock the right to live in the "tenement on which he has settled" for the term of seven years from March 1, 1805. Short by deed dated September, 1811, conveyed this moiety to Nicholas.

Wilson Cary Nicholas who was governor of Virginia from 1814 to 1816 conveyed the entire tract to William Wirt and Robert Gamble, trustees, by deed of trust dated July 19, 1819, to secure William H. Cabell, one time governor of Virginia, and for whom this county was named, as an endorser on some $23,000.00 of paper. The trustees sold the property at the front door of the Eagle Tavern in Richmond, Virginia, to Governor Cabell for $13,000.00. Cabell afterwards conveyed this property to John Coalter, who held the first court in this county—and John H. Cocke, trustees, to secure certain indebtedness. They in turn sold this property to Captain William Jenkins for $15,000.00 and conveyed it to him by deed of September 20, 1825.

Captain Jenkins moved on the place at once and farmed it on a large scale. It was the finest estate in the county. At Captain Jenkins' death it was devised to his three sons—General Albert Gallatin Jenkins, the upper portion; Major Thomas Jefferson Jenkins, the middle part; and Dr. William Jenkins, the lower end. The last of this land passed out of the hands of the last Jenkins some years ago and the whole tract is now divided into a number of small farms.

---

*Colonel Joshua Fry died at Fort Cumberland, Maryland, May 30, 1754. The grantor in the above deed was a grandson of the original patentee and migrated from Albemarle County to the State of Kentucky about the beginning of the nineteenth century.

Albert Gallatin Jenkins home, Greenbottom

The Hon. Elliott Northcott, Judge of the United States Circuit Court of Appeals, owns the greater part of the General Albert Gallatin Jenkins' portion and has built a handsome home on it.

The Greenbottom Grant and the Savage Grant covered all of the Ohio River bottoms which are the best lands in the county.

III: PREHISTORIC SETTLERS

WHEN the first white settlers came the land was covered by forests, but at Greenbottom they found well defined evidence of streets laid out at regular intervals and intersected at right angles with other streets. In the bottoms on which Huntington now stands were numerous mounds all of which have been leveled, and on the hills in the southern part of the city still may be seen four fire pits which were probably used for signal fires. These pits are located on commanding sites and are in about the same condition as when their makers left them. Indian relics were plentiful and a few years ago the workmen excavating a cellar on 11th Street near 3d Avenue came upon the unfinished work of an arrowmaker. In the ravine in front of Marshall College near the Ohio River bank there were found large quantities of Indian pottery and this was explained by the fact that on the opposite side of the Ohio River at the mouth of the Indian Guyan Creek was an Indian village and that this was the point at which these Indians landed and made camp on their trips to West Virginia. The country abounded with game and the county at the very beginning paid a bounty for wolf scalps ranging from four to eight dollars for old wolves and from two to four dollars for young ones. The last bounty paid was eight dollars for an old wolf scalp in 1850. Bounties for fox scalps continued until 1860. Deer continued plentiful until 1872 when they were killed out by an epidemic of black tongue. Persons now living have heard from their elders how the streams were stocked with fish which might be caught with their hands. There is no authentic account of any Indian raids within the present limits of Cabell County but Indian raids along the Sandy River were numerous, and Jennie Wiley was taken through what is now Mingo and Wayne counties, which territory at that time was a part of the original Cabell County. Howe in his *History of Lawrence County, Ohio,* relates that in 1791 James Kelly and William Kelly on account of Indian troubles were returning from Maysville, Kentucky, to their home in Westmoreland County, Pennsylvania. They embarked in a large canoe with two men to assist in navigating the boat with Mrs. Kelly, wife of James, and two children, a boy James, five years of age and an infant girl named Jane. About a mile below the mouth of the Guyandotte, and near the Virginia shore, they were fired upon by a party of Indians secreted behind trees on the Virginia side. The two Kellys were killed but the other two men landed the boat on the Ohio side where one of the men ran away and was not heard of. Almost immediately after landing Mrs. Kelly was bitten by a rattlesnake and the other man went on foot to Gallipolis to secure relief which he did and returned four or five days later. Mrs. Kelly survived and both of her children grew up and lived in Ohio.

Jonathan Buffington who came with his brother, Thomas, to the Savage Grant about 1796 or shortly thereafter, built a home on the east side of the Guyandotte River somewhere above its mouth. One day in a year not fixed but said by the Buffington descendants to have been a short time after he came there, Jonathan returned to his home after a brief absence and found it burned, all of his family except one girl murdered and scalped. The girl had been carried off by the Indians and Jonathan started at once in pursuit. He did not recover his daughter but he was captured by the Indians and made to run the gauntlet. However, his life was spared and he returned home. At the Pan-American Exposition in Buffalo, New York, in 1901, there was an Indian Chief named Jonathan Buffington. Is it possible the captive girl gave her name to her Indian children?*

---

*The Hagen family say this occurred in Cabell County but P. C. Buffington, II, thinks that it was in Randolph County.

IV: FORMING OF THE COUNTY

CABELL COUNTY was formed in 1809 from a part of Kanawha County and its boundary included all of the present counties of Wayne and Mingo and a portion of Logan, Boone, Putnam, and Lincoln. Its present area is 261 square miles and it fronts along the Ohio River for a distance of twenty-five miles and is drained by the tributaries of that stream and by the Mud and Guyandotte rivers, Twelve Pole Creek, and a number of other large creeks. Except along the river the land is hilly and broken and was originally covered with timber, all of which has now been cut over. Most of the county is underlaid with coal but not of a sufficient thickness to have any commercial value. It produces some oil and considerable quantities of gas. The river bottoms are good farm lands and the hills are especially good for fruit growing. At the time the county was organized it was sparsely settled and the larger portion of its population was along the rivers.

The county was named for William H. Cabell, who was governor of Virginia from 1805-1808. The county government was organized by Judge John Coalter in April, 1809, in the house of William Merritt which was located at or near the present town of Barboursville. The act creating the county named a commission to locate a county seat and a place for the public buildings. On May 9, 1809, the commissioner reported as follows:

We, John Shrewsbury, William Clendennin, John Reynolds, Jesse Bennett and David Ruffner, appointed to locate the public buildings under the act, etc. taking into consideration the convenience and inconvenience of the population, and interest of the country, do fix the mouth of the Guyandotte, on the upper side, in the middle of a field occupied by William Holderby, as the most practicable place for said public buildings, etc.

The middle of the field referred to in the report above is a square 100 feet on each side of what is now Bridge Street and extending back from the west line of Main Street to the alley between Main and Guyan streets and includes Bridge Street itself. As late as 1910 the older people in Guyandotte referred to this area as the courthouse square. Of course, there was trouble about locating the public buildings. There always is. But let W. S. Laidley tell you about the report of these commissioners:

They reported that they had selected a place in the middle of a field at the mouth of the Guyandotte, on the upper side, which field was occupied by William Holderby. No mention of any town was made as being there then.

FORMING OF THE COUNTY

In the report of Virginia cases, page 176, there is a case of Commonwealth vs. Morris. John Morris was indicted for making the charge publicly against Thos. Ward, Sheriff, that he, Ward, had circulated a petition among the citizens, obtaining their signatures, asking the Legislature to locate the county seat of the new county of Cabell on his plantation, where it was first held, and Morris says that Ward circulated this petition secretly and the sheriff secured signatures by promising not to be over strenuous in collecting taxes. Morris said that Ward's plantation was no suitable place, that it was among the hills and mountains, not near the center of population or territory, but the most inconvenient place that could be thought of.

There was a question of law in the case raised, whether Morris would be allowed to prove the truth of his charges, and it was held by the general court that he could. We imagine this explains why the commission of men from other counties was appointed to locate the court house, but it is said that the court had been held on Ward's plantation, and in the house of William Merritt. Judge Coalter's court was held in April, 1809, and the court house was located in May, 1809.

From all which we should judge that when the application was made to the Legislature for the establishment of the county of Cabell that there was no mention made of the location of the court house and perhaps it was left to the court. And then Major Thos. Ward sent in his petition to have it located on his plantation and John Morris, Jr. learned thereof and he talked plainly and sent his reply to the Legislature, for which he was indicted, and the commission was appointed to locate the county seat.

We imagine that Ward's plantation was either where Barboursville was located or near there, and we also surmise that William Merritt's house was either near his mill, near the mouth of Mud, or in Barboursville, and that Judge Coalter held his court there for the reason that he had not learned of any buildings suitable in the middle of Holderby's field at the mouth of Guyandotte.

We confess that this explanation is not entirely satisfactory. We do not know when the court house was removed to Guyandotte, or when it was removed therefrom, nor to what locality it was taken. We find that Guyandotte was made the court house in 1809, and established as a town in 1810, which looks as if it was growing backward.

We take it for granted that Holderby's field was in Guyandotte from the description, although it is not so stated, and small towns do not often have large fields therein.

The courthouse continued at Guyandotte until 1814 when it was removed to Barboursville where it remained until 1863, when the record discloses that at a County Court held at Barboursville, on Monday, January 5, 1863, there was present Samuel A. Childers, Roland Bias, John M. Blake, and John Ferguson, gentlemen justices. The following preamble and resolution was adopted:

Whereas, the county of Cabell is exposed to the marauding incursions of the rebels; that the authorities have been unable to hold court in Barbours-

Old courthouse at Barboursville, built 1850

ville without procuring from the United States troops a guard, and as they are advised that the Commissioner of the Revenue, on Saturday, last, while engaged in the Clerk's office, a part of the court house, forceably took the books from the officer, and from the fact that protection can be more conveniently had to attend court in Guyandotte, it is ordered to be certified to the Governor to request him to issue his proclamation authorizing the courts of Cabell County to be held in the Town of Guyandotte, until further orders. Signed. S. A. Childers.

Francis H. Pierpont, Governor on the —— day of February, 1863, issued his proclamation and authorized the courts of Cabell County to be held in the town of Guyandotte. Under the authority of this proclamation the Circuit Court convened in the town of Guyandotte on Friday, March 27, 1863, and continued there until 1865.

Judge J. H. Brown was the circuit judge under the restored State. After the new State was formed H. J. Samuels was appointed judge of this circuit and held the first term at Guyandotte in the early part of November, 1863, with the following attorneys present: Hon. Laban T. Moore of Kentucky; Ralph Leete of Ironton, Ohio; E. M. Fitzgerald, prosecuting attorney Charles Moore, Thomas B. Kline of Point Pleasant, and B. D. McGinnis. An account of this term of court given in the *Ironton Times* of November 16, 1863, follows:

The crowd of suitors, witnesses and jurors is about the same as in former years when they used to assemble at the court house at Barboursville before the rebellion. The youthful appearance of the judge, the clerk and the members of the bar is in remarkable contrast with the old officers and members of the bar constituting the Cabell circuit court of former times, and indicates the change made by the civil troubles. The grave and solemn visages of old Judge McComas, John Laidley and John Samuels are not here. For more than thirty years these three men have formed the central figures of the circuit court. . . .

The old lawyers—Fisher, Summers and Mansfield—are all gone. It will be remembered that Mansfield received a wound in the skirmish at Barboursville in July, 1861, from which he died. Fisher is somewhere in Dixie and Summers does not come this way.

The court docket is much larger than I expected to find it, and presents a heavy show of business, both civil and criminal. Suitors in rebellion were called and their cases dismissed; the judges remarking at the time that those seeking the subversion of the laws and of the authority under which the court was sitting, could not use the authority of his court to aid the cause of the rebellion. Under this rule the action of his brother in the Confederate service was dismissed.

. . . The grand jury returned a large number of presentments and indictments, I think some seventy in all. One man is indicted for refusing to list his property for taxation under the new State government, he still adhering to the seceded State of Virginia. Another is indicted for feeding armed rebels,

The first courthouse in Huntington, 9th Street and 4½ Alley

and sundry others for taking horses and cattle, not their own, for the use of the rebels.

The County Court held its first meeting in Guyandotte on March 2, 1863, and continued to meet there until July 6, 1863, which is the last record of its meetings. The County Court was abolished by the Constitution of 1863 and the board of supervisors succeeded to its police and fiscal jurisdiction. The first meeting of this board was held on July 30, 1864, but the place of meeting is shown as the recorder's office without designating its location. On its next meeting on August 9, 1864, it made the following order:

It appearing to the Board that the Court House of this county is in the possession of the military authorities and not in a suitable condition to enable the Board to hold their meeting therein, IT IS ORDERED That the meetings of this Board be held in the office of the recorder of Cabell County in the town of Guyandotte until otherwise ordered.

From that date on the board met at Guyandotte until the 22d day of August, 1865, when it adjourned to meet, and did meet, at Barboursville on September 2, 1865. On its records appears a minute to the effect that the board had made a verbal contract with W. O. Wright for the use of his house in the town of Guyandotte from the first day of November, 1864, to the first day of June, 1865, for the Circuit Court and clerk's office, Wright to have a courtroom and two jury rooms suitably prepared and ready for use by the first day of the November term, and was to be paid $65.00 rent.

The courthouse was returned to Barboursville in September, 1865, and remained there until December 26, 1887, when it was moved to Huntington and located in the city building on the east side of 9th Street between 4½ Alley and 5th Avenue. It remained in this location until 1901 at which time the new courthouse was completed in the square between 7th and 8th streets, and 4th and 5th avenues, and it was then removed into the new building. In 1924 the building was remodeled and a western wing added.

The present courthouse, 1901

V: ORGANIZATION OF THE COUNTY

THE county was organized by Judge John Coalter of the Superior Court of Law on the second Monday in May, after the fourth Monday in April, 1809, who then held a term of court at the home of William Merritt. Judge Coalter appointed Edmund Morris as clerk and admitted James Wilson to the Bar and named him prosecutor for the commonwealth.

Thomas Ward was the first sheriff and Elisha McComas was named as foreman of the first grand jury. Four persons, A. Porter, Steven Kelly, Isom Garrett, and Robert Tabor were fined for not attending as grand jurymen. The grand jury returned sixteen indictments, nine of which were for selling liquor without a license. The term lasted one day and the prosecuting attorney was allowed five dollars for his service, the clerk ten dollars, and the sheriff eight dollars. This court continued to be held in the home of William Merritt until after the 9th day of May, 1810. The regular September term convened on October 8, 1810, at the courthouse in Guyandotte. The following persons were admitted to the Bar: David Cartmill, Henry Hunter, William H. Cavendish, John Mathews, Ballard Smith, Lewis Summers, and Sylvester Woodward.*

The county government at this time consisted of the Superior Court of law, the County Court, justices of the peace, the sheriff, the prosecuting attorney and some minor officers. All county officers were appointed until after the adoption of the constitution of 1851 when county officers with the exception of the circuit clerks were made elective. Delegates to the Legislature were elected from the beginning. All elective and appointive officers were required to take the oath to suppress duelling.

SUPERIOR COURTS OF LAW AND CHANCERY

When the county was organized the administration of law and equity was separate. There was one Superior Court of Chancery which was divided into four districts and presided over by four chancellors, two of whom were assigned to the territory west of the mountains, and sessions of this court were held at Clarksburg and Lewisburg. There was a Superior Court of Law held by a single judge twice a year in each county. In 1819 Cabell County was placed

---
*Sylvester Woodward was the first Prosecuting Attorney of Mason County and afterwards Attorney General of New York State.

in the 14th circuit composed of Lewis, Harrison, Mason, Cabell, and Kanawha counties. This system continued until 1831 when the courts were reorganized and the common law and equity jurisdiction was combined in a single judge and the court was denominated Circuit Superior Court of Law and Chancery. All of the circuit judges were members of the general court. In 1851 the name of this court was changed to the Circuit Court which has continued to this date.

David McComas of Cabell County was appointed judge of this court in 1843 and served until 1852. In that year he was a candidate for this office but was defeated by George W. Summers of Kanawha. Summers resigned and David McComas was appointed to fill out his term and served from 1858 to 1862, when he went with the Confederacy. James H. Brown, born in Cabell County but who lived in Kanawha, served 1862-1863, when he went on the Supreme Court bench. Judge Brown was succeeded by Henry J. Samuels of Cabell who was the first judge of Cabell County, West Virginia, served 1863-1866, and was succeeded by Judge William L. Hindman.

THE COUNTY COURT

The County Court is strictly a Virginia institution and found its beginning in the monthly courts of the Colony. At the time the county was organized the County Court was composed of four justices of the peace who were denominated as the gentlemen justices. It had common law and chancery jurisdiction, limited criminal jurisdiction, and police and fiscal jurisdiction. These justices were first appointed by the governor for indefinite terms but under the Constitution of 1851 their terms were fixed for four years. Under the first Constitution of West Virginia the county courts were replaced by the board of supervisors which had only police and fiscal jurisdiction. By the Constitution of 1872 the county courts were restored and were composed of a president and two justices of the peace and this continued until the first of January, 1881, when the judicial power was taken away from the court and its members became commissioners of the county court and their jurisdiction limited to the administration of internal and fiscal affairs of the county.

GENTLEMEN JUSTICES

Any attempt to list the gentlemen justices who made up the county court from the time of the organization until the Constitution of 1863 is a roster of the names of families which are still well known

Judge John Coalter, who organized the county

and respected in this county. William Buffington and Elisha McComas appear to have served longer than any of the others, but in the list of those who served more than one term must be included the names of:

Elisha McComas, Mark Russell, James and Absolom Holderby, Edmund, James, and Allen McGinnis, John Hannon, Levi McCormack, Solomon Thornburg, Patrick Keenan, Benjamin Drown, F. G. L. Beuhring, Samuel Short, William Buffington, Manoah Bostick, Thomas Kilgore, Jesse Spurlock, Noah Scales, John Everett, Jr., Hugh Bowen, William Fullerton, Benjamin Brown, John Samuels, Sampson Sanders, John W. Hite, and Abia Rece.

SHERIFFS

At first three persons were nominated by the County Court to the governor for the office of sheriff and one of these was named for the term of one year. Later these nominations were limited to members of the County Court and the practice prevailed of naming the senior justice as sheriff. Henry Brown was one of the first justices of Cabell County and he was appointed the second sheriff. He is supposed to have been killed as his horse and hat were found but no trace of his body. To name all of the men who served in the office of sheriff from 1809 to 1860 would make this too voluminous. Suffice to say, many names which are still household words appeared in this list: Samuel Short in 1814, Mark Russell in 1815, Elisha McComas in 1816, 1840, and 1841; John Hannon in 1817 and 1844, James Holderby in 1819, Frederick G. L. Beuhring in 1849 and 1851, Solomon Thornburg in 1842, and John Everett, Jr., in 1836 and 1837. The first sheriff elected was Enoch Underwood who served from 1852 to 1855 and who was followed by William B. Moore who served from 1856 to 1860.

PROSECUTING ATTORNEYS

James Wilson, prosecutor of the commonwealth, served as prosecutor from 1809 to 1817 when he resigned and was succeeded by John Laidley who served continuously from 1817 to 1860.

DELEGATES

This office was elective and from 1809 to 1830 Cabell County was entitled to two delegates; from 1831 to 1842 was entitled to one delegate; and from 1842 Cabell was from time to time in a delegate district. The honor of representing Cabell in the General Assembly

Top—Forrest Hill, home of P. C. Buffington. (The wing on the left has been added.) *Bottom*—The Thomas Buffington house after it had been added to and became the home of D. W. Emmons. D. W. Emmons (left); C. W. Smith, General Manager, Chesapeake and Ohio (right).

must have been a coveted one for the records show more than one contested election for this office. The first of such contests appears in May, 1821, when the County Court named commissioners to take evidence in the contest between Elisha McComas, Edmund McGinnis, Andrew Barrett, and Alexander Catlett, Jr. During this period the following persons served as delegates more than one term: Elisha McComas, twelve; John Everett, Jr., seven; Edward McGinnis, six; Solomon Thornburg, five; John Morris, F. G. L. Beuhring, four each; Manoah Bostick, John Laidley, William Spurlock, and Frederick Moore, three each; Dr. Henry B. Maupin, two; and Thomas Thornburg made his debut for one term in 1857.

CURRENT EVENTS PRIOR TO 1860

From the formation of the county to 1860 there was no crisis in the affairs of the people. It is true there was the War of 1812-1814 and the Mexican War and in both instances Cabell County sent its full quota of men but the war was not brought close home to them.

The farms along the river bottom were improved and these farmers became prosperous and as evidence there was built along the river these two-story brick houses with an ell which represented the high-water mark of the farmer's prosperity, beginning with the Jenkins' home at Greenbottom and ending with the Frampton home on Four Pole.

The County Court records prior to May 3, 1814, have been lost and as a consequence there is no record dealing with the construction of the first courthouse, and the only reference to it is an order showing that the courthouse and jail was completed and that on the 29th day of August, 1812, the commissioners accepted the work from Thomas Ward the contractor and certified that "they had been in their opinion, done equal to the contract." There is an order made on May 3, 1814, in which it is stated that the commissioners who had been appointed to sell the courthouse, jail, and public square in the town of Guyandotte returned the bond of George Ward and his security for the purchase price of this property but no deed is of record for this property. There is no record dealing with the construction of the new courthouse at Barboursville and the first court reference to this structure is an order made on May 2, 1815, appointing commissioners to let the contract to the lowest bidder for the construction of the public stocks and pillory to be erected on the public square near the jail.

Top—Lamartine, the home of John Laidley. *Bottom*—Lombardy Lawn, the home of Judge W. H. Hagen.

It is interesting to remember that at this time the jail was for the safekeeping of the prisoners and debtors, and that there was a general law which required the justices to mark and lay out the "bounds and rules" of the county not exceeding ten acres adjoining the jail where every prisoner not committed for treason or felony who gave security to keep the rules had the right to walk for the preservation of his health. On February 25, 1817, the "rules and bounds" were fixed as follows:

From the alley between John Laidley's and Rufus Maynards, to include all the Town of Barboursville from said alley, so as to include the house of Philip Baumgardner, the Court House, Jail and all the houses and cross streets.

From the beginning the County Court named some person to look after the Guyandotte River banks at its mouth. Just what this man was to do is not clear but this position was continued for a great many years.

In November, 1817, we find an entry that John Laidley was allowed an expense account for travel to Kanawha Courthouse a distance of forty miles to compare the Congressional polls of this district, crossing three ferries and returning, all for five dollars and forty-nine cents.

As early as 1818 we find that Jeremiah Ward, for extraordinary service, liberated a slave, a *woman of color* named Pig alias Margaret, which became effective after his death and she was given liberty to live and reside in Cabell County. Pig apparently could not support herself as is evident by an order made on September 27, 1824, directing the sheriff to distrain and sell so much of the estate of Jeremiah Ward, deceased, which would be sufficient to maintain Pig, a woman of color, who was liberated by Jeremiah Ward as the persons to whom Ward's estate was bequeathed refused to support her. There were a number of other cases in which slaves were freed but the outstanding instance was the case of Sampson Sanders which will be told in another chapter.

When slaves were emancipated it was necessary for the freed man to apply to the County Court for permission to remain in the county and there are a number of records of these cases in the county. Sometimes there were people of mixed blood who were embarrassed by their color. A case in point is as follows: On February 22, 1836, there is an entry that a number of persons named in the order who were free persons of mixed blood and resided in Cabell County but who

ORGANIZATION OF THE COUNTY 25

were not white persons, nor freed negroes or mulattos, had made an application to the court for a certificate under the act of February 25, 1833, and the applicants produced satisfactory evidence of white persons before the court which made an order certifying that the applicants were citizens of Cabell County and that they were not, nor either of them freed negroes or mulattos and that they were to be protected and secure from and against all the pains and penalties, disabilities, and disqualifications imposed by law upon freed negroes or mulattos.

In May, 1821, William Wilson was indicted for issuing a challenge to a duel.

John Laidley represented the county in the Virginia Constitutional Convention, October, 1829, to January 1, 1830.

In 1833 Philip Rootes Thompson, who was the grandfather of William Rootes Thompson, now a member of the Huntington Bar, was admitted to practice in the courts of Cabell County.

In 1837 the Barboursville people were given permission to keep school in the courthouse.

By 1838 the stocks and whipping posts at the jail were in disrepair and an appropriation was made to have them repaired.

On March 25, 1839, one J. H. Ferguson was appointed jailer and took the several oaths required by law. On September 4, 1840, this same J. H. Ferguson, along with Evermont Ward was admitted to practice law. Both of these men were out of the ordinary. James H. Ferguson had begun life as a shoemaker. He married Elizabeth Derton (or Derting) in the early 40's and after he was admitted to practice he located at Logan Courthouse, where five children were born to this marriage. The second child, William Ferguson, enlisted in the Confederate Army and was killed in service. At a date not definitely fixed, J. H. Ferguson disappeared from Logan Courthouse and was gone for a number of years. Where he was and what he did during those years remains a mystery. Tradition says that he went to Utah and was the same J. H. Ferguson who was attorney general under Brigham Young, but of this there is no proof. Captain William Hovey, grandfather of T. W. Peyton, who was a captain in the Federal Army and lived at Barboursville for many years, met Ferguson in Ironton during the Civil War and spoke to him, but Ferguson denied his identity. Hovey insisted that he was James H. Ferguson and Ferguson then admitted it and returned to his home and resumed the practice of law in Cabell County. Ferguson was a staunch

Union man; was attorney for the several plaintiffs in the suits brought against Buffington, Jenkins, and others; was a captain in the home guard company for a month in April and May, 1865; served as a delegate in the Legislature; prepared the Code of 1868; defeated Hindman for circuit judge, and served as circuit judge for about two years. Later he was defeated for delegate to the Constitutional Convention of 1872 by Evermont Ward. Judge Ferguson was easily the most commanding figure in the county at this time and continued a successful practitioner until he was a very old man.

During Judge Ferguson's absence his wife returned to Barboursville with the four living children and died at the beginning of the Civil War. Her children were taken by their maternal relatives and one, Mary Yenthus Ferguson was taken into the home of William P. Yates and his wife who were then well advanced in years, where she remained until the return of her father. Judge Ferguson married a second time, Elizabeth Ong, and he and his second wife took the two single daughters into their home and reared them. Judge Ferguson remained at Barboursville for a number of years and later moved to Charleston where his second wife died. On July 24, 1879, Ferguson married Elizabeth A. Creel of Barboursville.

Evermont Ward was famous as the inventor and owner of a proprietary medicine known as "Ward's Magic Relief." He practiced law for many years and in 1872 defeated Judge Ferguson for delegate to the Constitutional Convention, was afterwards elected and served as judge of the Circuit Court which included Cabell County for the years 1873 to 1880.

On August 4, 1841, Turner Thurman and Peyton Newman engaged in a fight within the "verge" of the court. Newman was required to give bond to keep the peace for three years and Thurman was imprisoned in the public jail until twelve o'clock of Saturday next and paid the cost.

During this period the court fixed the tavern fees and rates for ferryage from time to time and a fair sample of these tavern rates were: For whiskey, apple and peach brandy, per gallon $2.00; rum, wine and French brandy, per gallon $4.00; breakfast, dinner and supper, each 25c; lodging per night $12\frac{1}{2}$c; oats and corn, per gallon, $12\frac{1}{2}$; horse at hay or pasture, per night, $12\frac{1}{2}$; provided, that at the houses where the mail stages may call, the tavern keepers shall have the liberty to add fifty per cent upon the above charges, on all such as travel on stages.

ORGANIZATION OF THE COUNTY

In 1842 the county records disclose that certain debtors had been imprisoned in the public jail and that the court house and jail were in disrepair and the Circuit Court issued a rule against the gentlemen justices to show cause, if any they could, why they should not be fined and punished for failing to keep a good and sufficient jail and courthouse. The justices evidently excused themselves as we find no record of any punishment.

At the March term, 1849, William C. Miller, Enoch Underwood, Edmund Rece, and Daniel Love were named commissioners to report a plan and the probable cost of a new courthouse and clerk's office. This commission reported and on May 14, 1849, a vote was taken whether a new courthouse and clerk's office under one roof should be erected and the motion carried by one vote. A number of commissioners were named to take bids on the work and report at the September term, and on September 10, 1849, a new set of commissioners were appointed, viz: William McComas, Solomon Thornburg, Lewis Roffe, Daniel Love, and Sidney Bowden, to superintend the building of the new courthouse and to enter into a written contract with such person or persons as they or a majority of them deemed proper and best to do the work. This was done and the building was completed at a date not shown, but in 1851 the old courthouse and clerk's office was offered for sale at public auction. Apparently there was no bidding and later the court ordered these buildings pulled down.

Elisha McComas died November 12, 1849, and the court made the following order:

Whereas, it being represented to the Court that General Elisha McComas, the Presiding Justice of this county, departed this life at his residence in this county on the twelfth instant (November 12, 1849) the following testimonial is ordered to be placed upon the Order Book of this court:—That the members of this Court have heard, with deep regret, of the death of the said Presiding Justice and take great pleasure in bearing testimony to the uniform, independent and gentlemanly deportment of the deceased upon this Bench, and his kind, courteous and affable conduct in all the various relations of life and that the past public services of the deceased, as representative for the county in the Legislature of the State, and other public stations, have been characterized by faithfulness and efficiency. And further, that we condole with the bereaved relatives of the deceased and beg to mingle our sorrows with theirs, the deceased having been a member of this Court from the organization of the county, for upward of forty years. The Press and the Bar and the citizens of the county, now present, upon motion, are included in the foregoing testimonials of respect and add their regrets and condolence to that of the court.

Elisha McComas house, circa 1835

Elisha W. McComas served in the Virginia Constitutional Convention from October 14, 1850, to August 1, 1851.

An act of the General Assembly passed April 2, 1852, required the county to be laid off into districts for the election of magistrates and constables and the court named Daniel Love, George F. Miller, G. W. Summers, Charles Lattin, Solomon Midkiff, Jeremiah Witcher, and Francis G. L. Beuhring, as commissioners to make this division. The report of these commissioners was adopted and the county was divided into five magisterial districts which were described substantially as follows:

DISTRICT 1: Which began at the mouth of Four Pole Creek and the Ohio River and ran by courses and calls and which the committee called the Lower Guyan District and had two places of voting, one at the town hall at Guyandotte and the other at Albert Laidley's store on the Turn Pike.

DISTRICT 2: Began at File's Branch and thence up the Ohio River to James Knight's Ferry and then by courses and calls, one of which touched the Wayne County line and which was called Barboursville District with a voting place at the Court House.

DISTRICT 3: Began at James Knight's ferry and was east of District 2. This was called Mud River and Ohio District and had a voting place at Captain Daniel Spurlock's and one at the Doolittle Mill.

DISTRICT 4: Began at the junction lines of District 3 and the Mason County line and one of its calls ran with the ridge to the Logan and Boone line and this district was called Valley and Upper Mud District and had two election precincts, one at the widow Thos. Kilgore's and the other not named.

DISTRICT 5: Began at the old Carson's place where Emerson Turley then lived and was run by courses and calls and this District was called the Upper Guyan District. It had two places of voting, one at Andrew McComas's and one at "Nine Mile," William McComas's.

Under the county organization of 1863 these districts were designated as townships and in 1867 when Lincoln County was cut off, most of Carroll district was included in the new county, and the remaining districts were referred to as Barboursville, Grant, Guyandotte, McComas and Union. These names have continued with the exception that Guyandotte district on March 28, 1928, was divided into three districts and the portion of the old district outside the city of Huntington continued as Guyandotte district and the portion inside the limits of the city of Huntington was named Gideon and Kyle districts.

Shortly after the completion of the new courthouse in 1852 the court directed W. C. Miller to buy a lightning rod for the courthouse and the necessary coarse carpet for the court room and two dozen good split bottom chairs and the sheriff was directed to have glass put in the courthouse windows, the dirt removed from the floor, new straw put under the carpets, and blinds put on the windows.

In 1852 a new jail was erected.

Prior to 1853 there were overseers of the poor for the several districts and it was the practice to board the paupers with the people who would keep them at the lowest figure. In 1853 the County Court purchased a farm from Richard McAllister and established thereon a poor house for the use of the poor of the county. This poor farm continued as a county institution until some time during the Civil War when the man who was in charge of it disposed of all the personal property thereon and the court had some difficulty in getting a settlement with him. The court made an effort to dispose of the farm but was unable to do so. It thereupon advertised to rent the farm to the highest bidder and the renter to board the paupers. The best bid was the one made by A. F. McKendree who offered to pay $135.00 rent for the farm and to board the paupers for $6.25 per month, each. This bid was accepted and Mr. McKendree was awarded the contract to rent the farm and keep the paupers for the year beginning March 1, 1870. This arrangement was continued through Mr. McKendree's lifetime and after his death his son, William McKendree, had the contract for keeping the Cabell County poor up to the year 1928. This arrangement could not, of course, have been a good one, but both of the McKendrees were good men and they faithfully performed their duties as is evidenced by the fact that they continued to have these contracts all of these years. On December 5, 1927, T. H. Nash then and now the president of the Cabell County Court brought about the purchase of the Everett farm of 156 acres at Ona, and established thereon a home for the aged and infirm white people of Cabell County. Good buildings were erected and the farm has been cultivated with a high degree of efficiency with the result that it is operated at a profit and the institution is one that the county may well be proud of.

At the election held in June, 1858, Horatio H. Wood was elected circuit and county clerk and presented his certificate of election to the court and asked to qualify, but his election was challenged. At the next term some of the challengers asked that their names be withdrawn from the petition against Wood and he was permitted to qualify. In the same year the County Court for the first time availed

Top—Home of James Holderby. *Bottom*—James Gallaher's House, later occupied by his son-in-law, J. H. Poage, fronting the old pike between 12th and 13th Streets.

itself of the Virginia law and appointed patrollers, one set for Guyandotte and two for the county. These appointments emphasized the fact that the slavery question was being agitated and brings out in bold relief the name of Sampson Sanders.

SAMPSON SANDERS

About the turn of the nineteenth century a widow, Martha Sanders, with her two children, Sampson, a son, and Hetty, a daughter, came to Cabell County from the east. The daughter married Thomas Kilgore. In 1802 Thomas Kilgore sold Martha Sanders 250 acres of land on Mud River, a part of the Duval Patent. Sampson Sanders was reared on this place and is buried in a graveyard on it, which lies on a ridge north of the Midland Trail at the bridge west of Milton. One of the earliest mentions of Sampson Sanders in the records of this county is when he and Thomas Wiatt were on the 23d day of March, 1829, fined for failing to appear as petit jurors. Tom Wiatt, uncle of the Tom of our own day, evidently talked them out of it as his fine was remitted—but the record is silent as to Sampson. The record, however, speaks volumes about Sampson Sanders during the remainder of his life and at his death he owned many thousand acres of land scattered all over the county. He was the largest slave owner in the county and perhaps the richest man in it. He had never married. He died in July, 1849 and his will was probated on July 9th, of that year and the court required his executors to give a bond of $60,000.00. Under the terms of his will he directed that all of his slaves, some sixty in number, be made free and bequeathed $15,000.00 to his executors to be used to purchase homes for the slaves in the state of Indiana or some other free state and directed how the younger slaves were to assist the older and infirm ones. Before this was done Indiana enacted a law prohibiting the settlement of freed men in that State and these people were located in Michigan, and tradition says that the climate did not suit them and they had a hard time in their new homes.

PROHIBITION BEFORE THE EIGHTEENTH AMENDMENT

In the debates which preceded the repeal of the Eighteenth Amendment many references were made to the halcyon days of yore when whiskey licenses could be had for the asking, and the truth is that in Cabell County licenses to sell whiskey were obtained without difficulty. Opposition to the licenses began to develop early and at

ORGANIZATION OF THE COUNTY

a meeting of the County Court held on May 22, 1854, the court made an entry that one James H. Vandiver made an application to keep an ordinary in the town of Guyandotte at the end of the stage line which runs from Staunton. John Laidley opposed the granting of the license and the applicant challenged the right of Laidley to be heard for the reason that he was the public officer and was not responsible or liable for costs. The court overruled the objection and thereupon the applicant challenged the right of one of the justices to sit on the grounds that he was a member of the Sons of Temperance and had no right to vote on the application. This objection was likewise overruled and the court refused the license and said that it was not refusing it on any other ground but that they believed they had the uncontrollable power to grant or withhold licenses at their own will and pleasure; that they did not grant any license to any other persons under any circumstances whatever to sell liquor in Cabell County, and that they took this action at the request of the citizens of the county and in respect to adjoining counties which had all refused the granting of licenses for the year 1854. In 1860 the court again refused to grant licenses. In 1870 we find both the citizens of Barboursville and of Guyandotte petitioning the court to refuse licenses in their respective villages. The petition was granted to Barboursville which was dry but was refused at Guyandotte. S. R. Thompson, principal of Marshall College for the year 1870 requested that liquor be not sold within a mile of the college and the court granted that request but spelled Marshall "Martial." The court made an order not to grant any license within three miles of the Chesapeake and Ohio Railway Company station, and it is of interest to call attention to the fact that in these good days the first term of the grand jury held in 1809 returned nine indictments for unlawful retailing. At the February, 1869, term, there were eighty-eight indictments returned, eighty-one for unlawful retailing.

VI: THE FATEFUL YEARS 1860-1871

IT IS difficult to appraise political opinion on the momentous questions which confronted the people of Cabell County in the years 1860 and 1861. The vote for presidential electors in this county was as follows: Bell (Union) 316; Breckinridge (Democrat) 161; Douglas (Democrat) 407; making a total of 884 votes cast. There was not a single vote cast for Abraham Lincoln.

After the election of 1860 the country was much distraught and Governor Letcher called an extra session of the General Assembly to meet on January 7, 1861. Seven days later the General Assembly passed an act providing for a convention of the people of Virginia, the delegates to which to be chosen in the same manner as the members of the General Assembly.

William McComas, one time member of Congress, was elected delegate from Cabell County. The convention convened on February 13, 1861, and on April 17, 1861, adopted an Ordinance of Secession by a vote of eighty-eight yeas and fifty-five nays. William McComas voted against the ordinance. This ordinance was submitted to the vote of the people on May 23, 1861, and was adopted by a majority vote. Cabell gave a majority of 650 against secession but the correspondent of the Wheeling *Intelligencer* wrote that "Guyandotte was a hot bed of secession and the southern folks do about as they please."

Shortly after the Ordinance of Secession was adopted there was a mass meeting held at Clarksburg which sent out a call for a convention to be held at Wheeling. In response to this call, a convention met at Wheeling on May 13, 1861, which is known as the First Wheeling Convention. Cabell County did not send delegates, but the delegates from Harrison County acting under the authority of a convention said to have been held at Barboursville represented Cabell County.

In justification of recognizing the Harrison County delegates as alternates for Cabell County, Robert Hager of Boone made the following remarks: "I am informed by the delegate from Wayne, notwithstanding Zeigler had a regiment there, that all elections had to be guarded by his regiment. I do not know how many elections were held in Cabell County. However, they held one somewhere and the county is represented. If it requires a military force to hold an election, if Wayne County which borders on the Ohio River had to have a military force to hold an election at two points; if a detachment went up and held an election there (Boone) and got into a corner of Raleigh and held an election there, with what difficulty are the counties represented."

The convention was in session three days and adopted some fourteen resolutions the first of which asserted that the Ordinance of Secession passed on the 17th day of April, 1861, was unconstitutional, null and void, and recommended to the counties there represented and other persons who entertained the same views to meet on the 4th day of June and select delegates to a convention to meet on the 11th day of that month and named a central committee to arrange details. The second convention assembled at Wheeling on June 11, 1861. Albert Laidley who had been elected to represent Cabell County in the General Assembly at Richmond appeared at Wheeling but did not take a seat in the convention. He later went to Richmond where he took a seat in the General Assembly session beginning December 2, 1861, as a delegate from Cabell County.

On Friday the 14th day of June the convention known as the Second Wheeling Convention adopted an ordinance which provided for the organization of what has since been known as the Restored Government of Virginia. This ordinance also provided for the appointment of a governor and lieutenant governor by the convention to hold their offices for six months or until their successors were elected and qualified; for a council of five members to be appointed by the convention to advise with the governor; for the election of a legislature, and finally prescribed an oath to be taken by all state and county officers.

Francis H. Pierpont was elected governor without opposition and he thereupon called the Assembly in extra session on June 1, 1861. This was the first General Assembly of the Restored Government at Wheeling. Cabell was represented in the Senate as a part of the seventh senatorial district composed of the counties of Mason, Jackson, Cabell, Wayne, and a part of Roane, by Andrew Flesher, and was represented in the lower house by Edward B. Wright.

It will now be seen that Cabell County had two state governments, or to state it differently, there was a state government of Virginia which functioned east of the mountains with its capital at Richmond, and the Restored Government of Virginia with its capital at Wheeling. The boundary lines between the two governments changed with the military operations. Albert Laidley's term as delegate ended

March 31, 1862, and he returned to Cabell in May, 1865. It is interesting to note that the first oath of allegiance found of record is the oath that was taken by Mr. Laidley before the Provost Marshal at Charleston, West Virginia, on May 5, 1865.

P. C. Buffington who had been county surveyor and served in the sessions 1840-1, represented Cabell County as a delegate in Richmond in the session beginning December 7, 1863, and ending March 10, 1864.

The General Assembly met in regular session in December, 1861, and passed an act on January 17, 1862, which provided for an election to be held on the 22d day of the succeeding May to elect a governor, a lieutenant governor, and an attorney general. An election was held on this date and Pierpont was elected governor, but there is no record of any vote taken in Cabell County at this election.

The division of the State of Virginia had been much discussed by the people living west of the mountains and as early as 1776 David Rogers and a group described as "a number of malcontents" had, in the House of Burgesses at Williamsburg, proposed such a division. In the Second Wheeling Convention which assembled on June 11, 1861, the division of the State was to the fore. Many of the delegates were advocating a new Virginia and the Union. On August 7, 1861, a committee on a division of the state was appointed. This committee on August 13th reported an ordinance for the division of the state and this ordinance was adopted on August 20, 1861. It provided that the governor call an election and submit to the people the proposal to form a new state to be called the State of Kanawha, and to elect delegates to a Constitutional Convention to be held in the city of Wheeling on November 26th, following. The vote on this ordinance was taken on October 24, 1861, and the vote reported was 18,408 for and 781 against.* Thereupon the governor called the convention to meet on the 26th day of November, 1861. Cabell County was represented by Granville Parker, who was born in Massachusetts. He was a lawyer who lived at Guyandotte, and was the local representative of the Guyandotte Land Association. He did not remain in Cabell County after the war. This convention adopted a Constitution and adjourned, but reconvened on February 12, 1863, for the purpose of making certain changes required by Congress regarding extinguishing slavery before West Virginia would be ad-

---

*The county records do not show the vote in Cabell but the State records show the vote 200 for and none against.

mitted as a State. This Constitution was submitted to the vote of the people and the returns showed that Cabell County cast one hundred and six votes for and none against. The result of this vote was certified to the President of the United States who issued a proclamation declaring that sixty days thereafter, to-wit, on June 20, 1863, West Virginia should be admitted as a State.

In the early part of 1863 it was certain that West Virginia would be admitted into the Union, and this made it necessary to select officers for the new State. On February 19, 1863, the Constitutional Convention which was still in session adopted a resolution recommending to the people of the counties which were to be included in the new state to appoint delegates to a convention to be held at Parkersburg on the first Wednesday after the expiration of ten days from the date of the proclamation by the President declaring West Virginia a State in the Union. This convention which was denominated as the Unconditional Union Convention assembled at Parkersburg on May 6, 1863, and nominated state officers. W. H. Copley, a merchant of Guyandotte was the delegate from Cabell County. On the 12th of May the executive committee of the Constitutional Convention issued a proclamation fixing May 28th as the date on which the election was to be held. The official returns of this vote do not include any vote from Cabell County.* Arthur I. Boreman was elected the first governor of West Virginia.

The first Legislature of the new State convened at Wheeling June 20, 1863. William H. Copley was the senator from the 8th Senatorial District which included Cabell. E. D. Wright of Guyandotte was the delegate from Cabell, and Edmund Kyle later to be prominent in Cabell County politics was the sergeant-at-arms. The second Legislature convened on January 19, 1864. Copley was still the senator and Samuel A. Childers of Guyandotte was the delegate. The third Legislature convened on January 17, 1865, and Edward D. Wright of Guyandotte was the senator and James H. Ferguson was the delegate.

One of the first acts of the Second Wheeling Convention was the adoption of an ordinance which required state and county officials to take an oath to the Restored State of Virginia. This oath was substantially in form the oath now required from public officers. The first legislature of the new state of West Virginia on November 13, 1863, passed an act declaring:

---

*Unofficial returns say 106 for and none against.

> Every person who aided or abetted the so called Confederate States of America . . . in any invasion of this state or hostile action against the same . . . or who shall accept, hold or exercise any official commission or authority under the said Confederate States

an enemy of the state and that all estate real and personal belonging to such persons found in the state would be forfeited to the state.

On November 16, 1863, an act was passed requiring a test oath from all public officers and this oath contained the following provisions:

> That I had never voluntarily borne arms against the United States; that I had voluntarily given no aid or comfort to persons engaged in armed hostilities thereto * * * that I have not sought, accepted or attempted to exercise the function of any office whatever, under any authority in any way hostile to the United States. . . .

Later this act was extended and teachers, physicians, and all persons whose business was done under a license from the state were required to take such an oath.

Another act was passed known as the Suitors Test Act which gave either the plaintiff or the defendant the right to suggest that the opposite party was a public enemy and if he did not promptly meet the accusation with an oath establishing his loyalty judgment was rendered against him.

In 1865 there was submitted to the vote of the people a Constitutional Amendment which disfranchised all persons who since June 1, 1861, had given voluntary aid to the rebellion. A vote was taken on this amendment on October 25, 1865, the vote in Cabell County being 295 for and 163 against. The majority vote in the state was favorable to the amendment and it became a part of the Constitution on February 13, 1866.

In addition to this Constitutional Amendment the Legislature passed the following acts: first, the act of February 5, 1865, which required voters to swear that they had never borne arms against the Federal government; second, the act of February 11, 1865, which required the defendant in a civil case against whom a judgment had been taken on an order of publication to take the oath of November 16, 1863, before he could set aside the judgment and have a rehearing; third, the act of February 23, 1865, which required an oath of allegiance from persons who had served the Confederacy; fourth, act of February 14, 1866, which required attorneys to take the oath of November 16, 1863; fifth, act of February 26, 1866, requiring voters to take the oath before they could be registered.

THE FATEFUL YEARS 1860-1871 39

With this political and legislative background we will recount the events as they took place during this period as shown by the court records.

Cabell County was Southern in its sympathies and many of its prominent citizens and largest property owners were out and out secessionists. Some of these men left the county and cast their lot with the Confederacy. After the beginning of hostilities Federal forces occupied Cabell County and continued therein until after the war. The presence of these soldiers and the changes in the government put the Union element in full and complete control of the county government. At the election held on November 8, 1864, there were 187 votes cast for Lincoln electors and not a single vote cast for McClellan.

In 1860 H. H. Wood, familiarly known as "Race" was county and circuit clerk and had four years then to serve. Ira J. McGinnis was elected prosecuting attorney in May of that year for a term of two years beginning on July 1st, following. John S. Wilkinson was elected sheriff at the same time for the same term. All three of these men were strong Southern sympathizers and it is interesting to see how their term of office was ended. The records are silent about H. H. Wood but it is said that he retired to the home of some of his relatives in Kanawha County and resided there until his death. On June 2, 1862, the County Court made an allowance to J. Witcher as clerk of that court but there is nothing to indicate how Witcher was appointed. On July 7, 1862, there is an entry in the order books of the County Court that upon motion of J. S. Witcher, clerk of that court Thomas J. Merritt was on that day appointed a deputy clerk. On October 2, 1862, John S. Witcher appears as clerk of the Circuit Court. On December 13, 1862, Witcher was commissioned a second lieutenant in the Third Regiment of West Virginia Cavalry but when he joined his regiment or gave up his clerkship is not shown. In June, 1863, the County Court made the following order:

It appearing to the court that John S. Witcher who was formerly clerk of this court, did receive a payment and is receiving an emoulent of an officer in the United States Army on or about the first day of November, 1862, whereat he vacated his office as clerk and T. J. Merritt has performed all of the duties as clerk since that time. It is now ordered that T. J. Merritt be allowed $40.00 for his exofficio service and $28.00 for the fuel and stationery to be paid by the sheriff and deducted from the allowance made to the said J. S. Witcher by this court in June, 1862.

This is the last record of the County Court and the next record begins with the board of supervisors on July 30, 1864. The Circuit Court on March 27, 1863, appointed Thomas J. Merritt as clerk pro tem until a clerk could be elected. He was elected on May 28, 1863, for a four year term, but died in May, 1864, and William Merritt, his deputy, acted as clerk and was afterwards elected in May, 1865, for the unexpired term. William Merritt resigned on August 11, 1869, and was succeeded by Joseph S. Miller who was appointed to fill out the unexpired term. Miller was elected on October 27, 1870, for a four year term.

John S. Wilkinson, the sheriff, lived on a farm in what is now Lincoln County. His son, the Hon. D. E. Wilkinson says his father resigned and retired to his farm and that John B. Alford who had been a deputy was named, but this is not borne out by the records. Alford in 1864 sued General Jenkins and others, and in his declaration set out the fact that he was captured in November, 1861, and taken to Richmond where he was kept in prison for one year. Under date of April 7, 1862, there is an entry in the County Court records which refers to Wilkinson as the late sheriff, and following this entry pages 361 to 405 have been cut from the record book and the next entry bears date April 8, 1862.* We have a feeling that the entry of April 8th was written subsequently to that date. At all events under date of April 11, 1862, there is an entry that David P. Ferguson who had been elected sheriff on the 26th day of December, 1862 —the last figure has been scratched and might be and probably was intended to be 1861—appeared and gave bond and took the several oaths including the oath prescribed by the convention of June 11, 1861. What became of Ferguson? In March, 1863, Solomon Hatton was acting sheriff and afterward there is no further mention of him.

John B. Alford was elected sheriff in 1863. John Harshbarger was elected in 1866 for a four year term and he was succeeded by D. I. Smith who was elected in 1870.

Ira J. McGinnis who had been elected prosecuting attorney in May, 1860, for a term of two years resigned and went over to "Dixie," entered the Confederate service and remained until the end of the war. The court record dated May 2, 1862, states that John Laidley, Jr., had been elected to fill the vacancy caused by the resignation of Ira J. McGinnis. On the 2nd day of March, 1863, B. D. McGinnis, a Union man and a cousin of Ira J. McGinnis was named to fill out

---

*The record book of the circuit court has a number of pages cut out and an entry is made April 3, 1861; the next entry is November 20, 1862.

the unexpired term of Ira J. McGinnis. On May 28, 1863, the records of the Circuit Court disclose that E. M. Fitzgerald produced satisfactory evidence that he had been elected prosecuting attorney. At the November term, 1864, Fitzgerald was absent and B. D. McGinnis was appointed pro tem. In 1864 McGinnis was elected prosecuting attorney for a term of two years beginning January first.

On March 12, 1866, the board of supervisors made an order that the clerk notify McGinnis to employ Sam Capehart, attorney to assist him in prosecuting all cases of felony and every other misdemeanor for which indictments have been or might thereafter be made by the grand jury of the county. McGinnis was reëlected in October, 1868, but resigned February 1, 1869. He was a candidate in 1870 but was defeated.

To take care of such unsettled conditions the Legislature of the Restored State passed an act which gave the auditor power to appoint a tax collector to collect State taxes in any county in which there was no sheriff. On March 2, 1863, an order was made reciting that in the absence of the sheriff, J. B. Baumgardner was appointed to the office of collector of taxes for county purposes for 1861 and 1862. Baumgardner qualified and on June 2, 1863, he was commissioned to the same office by the auditor to collect State taxes. He was given the tax tickets for 1861 and 1862. "Fatty" as he was called, kept a hotel at Barboursville. He was a large man of exceedingly good nature, but made enemies in his efforts, or perhaps his methods, of collecting taxes. On one occasion he was fired on by someone near the Everett place near Ona and the record shows that "Rebel" Spurlock relieved J. M. Smith, who was Fatty's deputy of $2,247.23. The Legislature found it necessary to pass three separate acts dealing with Fatty's office. The first act gave Fatty credit for the amount taken by "Rebel" Spurlock, the second was an act of indemnity holding him harmless from any court action by reason of his activities, and the third act passed February 28, 1865, required him to turn over to the then sheriff the tax tickets for 1861 and 1862, directing the auditor not to make a settlement with him until he did.

In 1863 Greenville Harrison was commissioner of revenue and while he was at work in the courthouse a band of "rebels" swooped down on him and took away his tax books. Who these "rebels" were is not known but the incident brought about the removal of the courthouse to Guyandotte.

COURT ACTIONS GROWING OUT OF THE WAR

At the November, 1862, term the grand jury returned misdemeanor indictments against Lieutenant Bush, P. C. Buffington, E. H. Walter, John Shelton, A. G. Jenkins, John Clarkson, James Wolford, Thomas J. Jenkins, and George S. Holderby. No copy of these indictments can be found in the clerk's office but as all of the defendants were Southern men and A. G. Jenkins was then lieutenant colonel and John Clarkson, colonel of the 8th Virginia Cavalry, C. S. A., it is fair to assume that these indictments grew out of some of their military activities in this county.

At the November term, 1863, in the case of R. S. Bias vs. James Parrish, the defendant appeared and represented to the court that the plaintiff was a public enemy of the United States government and the court made an order dismissing the suit.

In 1864, Julius Freutel, J. B. Alford, Thomas Kyle, C. Dusenberry, and Robert Ross brought separate suits against Thomas J. Jenkins, George W. Holderby, Peter C. Buffington, Robert Holderby, John Chapman, Hurston Spurlock, Milton J. Ferguson, John N. Clarkson, Warren P. Reece, Calwellsy Simmons, Joseph W. Morris, Wilson B. Moore, Henry Buffington, John N. Buffington, Leander Gilkerson, James Ferguson, Burwell Spurlock, Vincent A. Witcher, James R. Morris, John Plymale, Henry Everett, John S. Everett, James Everett, Peter Everett, Henry C. Poteet, V. R. Moss, Charles K. Morris, Charles L. Roffe, Godfrey Sights, William A. Jenkins, and Charles Shelton, and levied attachments on the lands of P. C. Buffington and the Jenkins. Service was had upon the defendants by an order of publication published in a Point Pleasant paper. The declarations in each case charged that the defendants had conspired together and were making war against the government, and in the first three cases alleged that the plaintiffs had been arrested and taken to Richmond, Virginia, and in the last two cases the declaration alleged that the defendants had destroyed their property and had taken in the Ross case his hogs, sheep, cattle and bacon. In the Dusenberry case the jury returned a verdict in his favor for $10,000 and in each of the other cases the jury returned a verdict in favor of the plaintiff for $30,000.00.

On January 11, 1870, the lands belonging to T. J. Jenkins, W. A. Jenkins, and P. C. Buffington were sold to satisfy these judgments. Later the defendants appeared and filed a motion for a rehearing but the court refused to permit the defendants to plead because they could not take the test oath and an appeal was taken to the Supreme Court which held the test oath unconstitutional and permitted the defendants to plead.

THE COUNTY UNDER THE NEW STATE

Under the Constitution of the new State the County Court was abolished and the board of supervisors was given control of the police and fiscal affairs of the county. The first election for members of this board was held on July 30, 1864, and the following persons were elected and attended the first meeting on August 8, 1864: Silas M. Clark, Thomas Joy, and Julius Freutel, who was the same person who had been taken as a hostage in 1861. The board organized and elected Silas M. Clark president, and Thomas J. Hayslip clerk. One of the first actions of this board was to notify the James River and Kanawha Turnpike Company that it accepted the relinquishment of as much of their road as was in Cabell County and at the meeting held on October 4, 1864, they included in the levy the sum of $1,500.00 for the support of soldiers' families. At the November election Thomas J. Hayslip was elected county recorder and there was a contest before the board over the office of circuit clerk between Curry and Merritt; Merritt was seated. This board laid the county off into townships. At a meeting held on February 9, 1865, it was recited that under the President's call for 300,000 men Cabell County's quota was seventeen men and it was resolved that a levy be made on the real estate of the county for $10,000 to relieve the county of the impending draft. At the meeting of February 26th it was resolved to give each volunteer that might be credited to Cabell County in the coming draft a county order for $400.00 payable to such volunteer or his assignee whenever such volunteer should present to the president and clerk of the board a certificate from the Provost Marshal that he had been accepted and credited to this county.

Julius Freutel was authorized to borrow $6,800.00 from some bank or individual on the credit of the county to make these payments but the war ended and the draft was not made. Freutel went to Ironton and Point Pleasant on this mission and was allowed an expense account for the trip and for taking recruits to Point Pleasant. In the fall election of 1865, John S. Witcher defeated James H. Ferguson for delegate, and Thomas Thornburg who ran as the Conservative candidate for State Senate received only one vote. In the following year the Union ticket was again successful and John S. Witcher was elected secretary of state, James H. Ferguson was elected delegate and William L. Hindman was elected judge of the 8th circuit of which Cabell County was a part. Sectional feeling was still high and notwithstanding that the Supreme Court of the United States on January 14, 1867, in the case of ex parte Garland, held the test oath unconstitutional, we find that in 1868 the Legislature removed William L. Hindman, judge of the circuit court, on the grounds of misconduct in office, incompetency and neglect of duty. The facts on which this finding was based were that it was shown that Judge Hindman sitting in Cabell County had on November 19, 1867, permitted Samuel A. Miller described as an active and influential partisan in the rebellion against the United States, a quartermaster in the so-called Confederate service, and a member of the so-called Confederate Congress, and David S. Hounshell, described as an active partisan in the rebellion and a colonel in the so-called Confederate service (Colonel 4th Regiment Virginia State Line) to be admitted to the Bar and to practice as attorneys and counsellors-at-law in the Circuit Court of Cabell County without requiring them to take the oath required by the Act of February 14, 1863, commonly called the "Attorney's Test Oath."

In 1867 for reasons not very clear the board of supervisors refused to permit the churches to use public schools. In the same year Lincoln County was formed and Carroll Township became a part of that county and a portion of this district which remained in Cabell County became Grant and the name of Grant Township appears for the first time. In this year the county purchased Marshall Academy, of which we tell elsewhere, and voted upon the proposal to subscribe $150,000.00 worth of stock in the Chesapeake and Ohio Railway Company. The resolution submitting this vote is interesting in that it permitted all qualified voters and

all other white males thereof who are neither minors . . . or under a conviction of treason * * * and who have been a resident of the state for a year and of the county thirty days and are assessed with a tax therein for the year 1867 to vote.

Apparently Confederate soldiers who owned property were permitted to vote.

An order was made April 11, 1867, not to "pay any county orders until all orders issued in favor of county officers for their services be paid and that in all cases the orders drawn in favor of the county

Top—Martin Hull House, corner 14th and Washington
Bottom—James Johnston home, Jefferson Avenue and 7th Street, West, built about 1835

officers shall have preference over any other order drawn on the treasurer."

The board of commissioners was lectured by B. D. McGinnis, the prosecuting attorney, upon the manner of holding court. They were apt scholars and we find that it ordered:

That the members of this board including the clerk and the prosecuting attorney is prohibited from holding conversations with anyone while the board is in session.

The prosecuting attorney and sheriff were fined for failing to attend a meeting of the board held on July 4, 1870, but this fine was later remitted.

In the election of 1868 the parties were again Union and Conservatives. Judge Hindman sought vindication at the polls and was a candidate for circuit judge on the Conservative ticket. J. H. Ferguson was his opponent on the Union ticket. Ferguson was elected. The vote on the National ticket was Grant and Colfax 251 votes, Seymour and Blair 148 votes, or a Union majority of 103 votes. John S. Witcher was elected to Congress and D. I. Smith, Conservative, was defeated for county recorder.

In 1869 John S. Wilkinson, one time sheriff and a Conservative, was elected delegate.

The board of supervisors elected J. W. Church clerk of the board for the years 1867 and 1868, and elected Joel K. Salmon to the same office, 1869 to 1872.

In the year 1870 Frank Hereford defeated Witcher for Congress. Ferguson was again elected delegate and T. J. Hayslip was elected recorder, but the Conservatives, or Democrats, elected D. I. Smith, sheriff, Jas. S. Miller, clerk of the Circuit Court and W. H. Tomlinson, prosecuting attorney.

On February 28, 1870, the Legislature proposed an amendment to Section 1, Article 3 of the Constitution which eliminated from this section the paragraph which denied the right to vote to persons who had participated in the rebellion and by an act passed February 14, 1871, this amendment was submitted. The act provided that if it received a majority vote the governor should declare it a part of the Constitution and in force from April 27th, 1871. This amendment was known as the Flick Amendment and was adopted at an election held April 27, 1871. The vote in Cabell County was 431 for and 52 against. This amendment removed the disability of soldiers and marks the end of the epoch.

The legislature of 1870 repealed the suitor's oath and changed the oath of an attorney-at-law and teachers to their present form.

On February 23, 1871, the Legislature submitted to the people the question of calling a Constitutional Convention and passed an act that no persons who aided in the late war should be civilly or criminally liable or have his property taken because of any action done according to usages of civilized warfare.

The proposal to call the Constitutional Convention was carried and in the election held on October 26, 1871, James H. Ferguson was defeated as a delegate. Evermont Ward and Thomas Thornburg were elected delegates to this convention which afterwards framed the Constitution of 1872, the present Constitution of this state. In the election of 1871 W. H. Hagen was elected a member of the board of supervisors, and on January 2, 1872, was elected president of the board.

VII: COUNTY POLITICS SINCE 1872

THE Constitution of 1872 was submitted to a vote of the people on August 22, 1872. The ordinance submitting it provided an election should be held at the same time for all state and county officers; that if the Constitution were adopted by a majority vote the officers elected should with certain exceptions take office on January first, following. One of the exceptions was members of the Legislature who took office at once and the Legislature met in November following at which time it passed an act fixing the term of office of the several state and county officers which had been elected. This was done by saying that these officers should hold office until their successors were elected and qualified and fixing the date when the first successor should be elected and the term of his office thereafter.

At the August, 1872 election, Cabell elected the full Democratic ticket as follows:

Clerk of Circuit Court: M. S. Thornburg,
Clerk of County Court: Jos. S. Miller,
Sheriff: D. I. Smith,
Prosecuting Attorney: L. C. Ricketts,
Presiding Justice, County Court: W. H. Hagen,
Assessor, First District: Dyke Bowen,
Assessor, Second District: Peter Everett,
For ratification of Constitution: 1,010,
Against ratification of Constitution: 660.

From 1872 to 1896 the county was Democratic except for some minor upsets. In 1878 Thomas Harvey, Democrat, on the Greenback ticket, defeated Eustace Gibson, Democrat, for the Legislature. In 1880 there was a bitter primary over the nomination between D. I. Smith and E. Kyle, for sheriff. Kyle, however, was nominated and elected sheriff. In 1894 the Republicans elected a member of the County Court.

In 1896 the Democrats held a primary for the nomination of county officers, and there was a bitter contest between F. F. McCullough and Garland Buffington for the nomination of county clerk. Buffington won the nomination. W. W. Marcum of Wayne County opposed Judge Thomas H. Harvey for the Democratic nomination for circuit judge. Both men were ex-Confederate soldiers. The contest was bitter and in Cabell County mass conventions were held to

Dudley Irvin Smith, Sheriff, 1871-1876; member County Court 1903-1920

select delegates. The Guyandotte district convention resulted in a split and there were two sets of delegates. The judicial convention which followed was marked by great disorder. Judge Harvey was nominated on the regular Democratic ticket but Marcum ran on an independent ticket. The Republicans nominated Edward S. Doolittle but the district was largely Democratic and at the time he was nominated the chances to win were not bright. However, in the landslide that followed he was elected and served two terms. There has been no Democratic judge in this circuit since Judge Harvey.

While the Democrats were amusing themselves in these contests the Chicago Convention nominated William Jennings Bryan for president and adopted a free silver platform. This brought about the greatest division in party alignment since the momentous days of 1860. Bryan made a great appeal to the masses everywhere and particularly in the rural sections. The Bryan people wore silver hats and the Republicans and Democrats who were supporting the Palmer and Buckner tickets were called "Gold Bugs." A big meeting was held in Huntington and Bryan spoke from a platform on the corner of 5th Avenue and 9th Street where the postoffice now stands. People flocked into the city from every direction. The driving park at 31st Street and 3d Avenue was turned into a camping ground and many people from adjoining counties made a camp there the night before and the night after the speaking. A cavalcade of horsemen came in from Lincoln, Boone and other counties. The crowd was the largest that ever attended a Huntington political meeting. The railroad influence was for McKinley, and M. E. Ingalls who was then the president of the Chesapeake and Ohio Railway Company came to Huntington and made a personal appeal to the railroad employees to vote against free silver. As a result of his effort many stalwart Democrats followed his advice and in the election the county went Republican except for R. W. McWilliams, circuit clerk. Sam Gideon was elected to the County Court and this gave the Republicans control of the court which continued, except for the period of 1903 and 1904, until 1910 in which year the Democrats took control and have continued in control except for the two years of 1921 and 1922.

In the decade beginning in 1900 the county gave a Democratic majority of approximately 500 and the city had a normal Republican majority of something in excess of that number. This made political contests close with Republicans usually victorious. During this whole time an increasing number of independent voters appeared as is shown by the fact that in 1904 Theodore Roosevelt carried the county by something like 600 majority and the Democrats elected W. S. Spencer, sheriff, and George S. Wallace, prosecuting attorney. In 1912 and 1916 the county went Democratic; in 1920 Harding carried the county over Cox; in 1924 Davis carried the county over Coolidge; in 1928 Hoover defeated Al Smith, and in the following election was overwhelmed by Franklin Delano Roosevelt. During most of this time the poll of the county showed a Democratic majority but when the vote was taken the voters did not follow the party label. This fact is distressing to party managers but it makes for good government.

In 1912 William Rootes Thompson was given the Democratic nomination for governor by acclamation. George I. Neal was still the dominant factor in Democratic politics. In the next year after Woodrow Wilson became President, William E. Chilton, who was unfriendly to Neal, distributed the patronage and in a few instances he was able to alienate one or more of the Neal henchmen, but despite the lack of patronage, Neal continued in control for a number of years.

But to return to the County Court. While the court can be regarded as the political barometer of the county yet we must not forget the tremendous responsibilities and arduous duties which have been imposed on them from the beginning. Always made up of laymen it is not too much to say that the gentlemen justices who made up the County Court and afterwards the board of supervisors which served in the place of the County Court in the years 1863 to 1872, and the county commissioners who served on the County Court since 1873, have been men of sterling worth and have served their people faithfully. A roster of the men who served as gentlemen justices from 1809 to 1863 would be a roster of representative families in the county. Those who have served in more recent years have measured up to the best traditions. The older residents of this county remember W. H. Hagen, a man of real worth and long a member of the court; B. H. Thackston who began the construction of the present courthouse; Sam Gideon the most progressive man of his day. The present generation knew D. I. Smith (Irving as he was familiarly called) who regarded the county interests as his own; Major T. McK. Hays, a conservative, splendid business man, and T. H. Nash now president of the court and a most energetic and capable man.

We have given some of the political history of the county but will return now to the more commonplace things in the county life.

THE NARRATIVE SINCE THE CIVIL WAR

The close of the Civil War found the county demoralized and the people were presented with many problems in addition to the political ones about which we have spoken.

The James River and Kanawha Turnpike Company in 1866 in anticipation of the completion of the Chesapeake and Ohio Railway, with the permission of the County Court abandoned so much of the pike as lay within Cabell County and the County Court took over this road. The suspension bridge at Guyandotte was owned by a corporation and the State of Virginia owned a large block of this stock. Upon the division of the State the stock owned by Virginia became the property of the State of West Virginia which in turn vested it in the county.

On April 5, 1869, the county began to take an active interest in the bridge company and a few years later, during the time D. I. Smith was sheriff, it purchased the stock belonging to the individual stockholders and the bridge was made a free one.

The coming of the Chesapeake and Ohio Railway was destined to change Cabell from a purely agricultural county to an industrial and commercial one, and in a few years Huntington was to be the center of population and happenings of importance were to take place in that city. We will record here events which are of countywide interest.

In the late 60's the board of supervisors were having trouble with the county press about the cost of publishing financial statements and other items and they passed a resolution refusing to make the payments demanded. They eventually felt the power of the press and on July 5, 1869, an order was made agreeing to pay the Cabell County press $12.00 per column for publishing items of interest for the County Court.

In the summer of 1873 the *John Porter*, a tow boat, left New Orleans with a tow of eighteen barges for Pittsburgh. After the boat reached the Ohio River one of the crew was stricken with cholera, and the crew became panic stricken. Word of the cholera preceded the boat and it was not permitted to land. The disease grew worse and most of the crew died. At Gallipolis Island the rocker arm broke and the boat drifted ashore. The epidemic broke out in Gallipolis and sixty-six persons died. Dan Wormeldorff of Guyandotte was stricken with the dread malady and died, and on June 30th, the Rev. John Fox, a Methodist minister who had been presiding elder for three years but in 1872 had taken charge of the churches in Barboursville, Guyandotte and Holderby Grove, preached the funeral. Mr. Fox appeared in the best of health and went to his friend, A. J. Keenan's home in Guyandotte to spend the night. During the night he was stricken and died the next day, July 1, 1873. These were the only cases of cholera in the county. How the first one was contracted is still a mystery.

In 1876 Ed. Williams and Matilda Meehling murdered Charles P. Meehling the husband of Matilda. While they were confined in the jail at Barboursville an infuriated mob lynched Williams in the courthouse yard. The Meehling woman was convicted of murder on March 8, 1876, and sentenced by Judge Ward to life imprisonment. Judge Ward in imposing the sentence said:

Matilda Meehling, you have been indicted, tried by a jury of your country and convicted of murder in the first degree. Murder with malice aforethought; of wilful, deliberate, premeditated murder. Of the correctness of this verdict there is not only no reasonable doubt, but not even the shadow of a doubt.

The atrocity of your crime is almost without a parallel. The deed of which you have been convicted is one of the foulest that blackens the annals of time. You were a poor girl, in the humblest walks of life. An honest, industrious young man, with no fortune but his own strong right arm and manly resolves, led you to the altar. You there gave him your hand, and, he supposed, your heart. He vowed to love protect and cherish you and forsaking all others cleave alone unto you, and he paid this vow to the Most High. He made you the partner of his bosom and the mother of his children, and provided you with reasonable comforts. He purchased a handsome little farm, on time, payable in numerous small installments; improved it; stocked it and had paid all but a small pittance of the purchase money. He doubtless looked forward with bright expectancy to an early period in the future when he could have a comfortable little home for his loved ones and owe no man anything. But alas for human expectations, he employed Williams as a laborer, not dreaming that he was taking an adder into his bosom—a serpent into his Eden, to mar his happiness and destroy his life—but it was so.

Williams dishonored his house, defiled his bed, and with his bloody-minded and adulterous wife conspired his death. After the intimacy between yourself and Williams commenced the presence of your lawful husband could no longer be brooked. He became a "Mordicai the Jew at the Kings gate." You could not consent to have your pleasures broken or circumscribed.

Twice you attempted to poison him, and twice you failed, by administering overdoses, and although you witnessed the terrible suffering he had to undergo on account of your cruel and inhuman act, your iron heart never felt the soft touches of pity. You saw his hands withering, his limbs paralyzing and his frame wasting from the effects of the poison. Grim Death was slowly and certainly doing his work, but too tardily for your impatient spirit. You could not leave to time his taking off, but you urged your associate to speedy work—the deed must be done this night—this very night. You could not let the hallowed Sabbath pass. He follows your evil counsels and in a few hours afterwards, the dreadful deed was done. A deed which time cannot erase or the ocean's waters wash out. A deed as deep, as foul, as black as any recorded on history's pages. Whilst your poor husband is sitting by the fire, all unconscious of impending evil, he sees the uplifted axe, and has but time to say: "Oh! don't kill me!" and blow after blow falls on his head, mashing it as if it were to a jelly. Next the head is almost severed from the body with a butcher's knife.

The evidence does not show how he obtained this knife, but your little boy of too tender years to be sworn, whilst sitting on my knee told me that you gave him the knife. He is now taken by the head and heels and buried in the dung and filth of the stable and animals are turned in to trample upon his already mangled remains. You return wash up the blood and you and your associate inaugurate a new administration; take the superintendence of affairs and all goes merrily, although within sixty or seventy yards of this horrid spectacle. In a few days your husband is missing—an alarm is felt by the neighbors, but none by yourself and Williams. Suspicions, however are aroused and fall in the right direction. Williams and yourself are arrested and committed to jail. All turn out to make search, and in the stable, buried in the dung, trodden over by the horses, there is found the mangled remains of a man who had lived amongst them, and commanded their respect and esteem, exhibiting a spectacle the very thought of which is sickening to the human heart. They were justly indignant, but let feeling carry them too far, they did not wait for the sentence of the law but took judgment into their own hands. This was wrong. The law should have been permitted to take its course, for while it reveals its terrors to the guilty offender, it is, at the same time, the staff of honesty and the shield of innocence.

They came in mass to the jail, took Williams and hung him. You were then brought and the vote taken in your case, and at first there was no dissenting voice. But after a moment's pause, some noble and manly-spirited fellow said "No, Gentlemen, no—she is a woman; for the honor of her sex spare her, forbear and let the law take its course." Every soul yielded silent acquiescence, the crowd dispersed and you were returned to your cell and now the law has taken its course; its sentence is written and it becomes my painful duty to pronounce it upon you.

And now, twice has your life been saved solely on account of your sex. You are a woman, and woman is Heaven's best, divinest gift to man. She is his acknowledged superior in all of the excellencies and refinements of life. She is pure. She is tender. She is kind. She is affectionate and loving, and man masculine, not only loves, but adores her, and the more so, as she is part and parcel of his own being; taken from his side to be his own equal—under his arm to receive his protection—from near his heart to be loved. He regards her as a being dwelling in an atmosphere pure and serene, and made a little lower than the angels. But like the angels who kept not their first estate, she sometimes becomes fallen, and when she falls great is the fall. When she once turns fiend, she becomes a fiend incarnate.

Twice, I repeat, your life has been spared because you are a woman; once by the mob and once by the jury. I do not condemn but appreciate this feeling. Mercy is the darling attribute of the Ever Living and Just. But this mercy was not shown on account of your supplications for it—not in answer to your imploring cry of "That mercy I to others show, that mercy show to me?" but simply on account of your sex. It may be mercy to you to have your days prolonged as it gives greater opportunities for a preparation to meet the Judge of all the earth; but still your fate is hard, very hard indeed. You are to be excluded from society and housed with its outcasts, without regard to race, color or previous condition, and doomed to hard labor and coarse diet all the days of your life.

It is no small matter to give up our worldly enjoyments, but with you they are pretty much at an end. Your neighborly visits. Your social meetings and your church goings are now things of the past. When you leave this place, you will have gazed perhaps for the last time upon the features of your aged father, and your little children whom you leave in the world without a mother's oversight, and with no father, save the Father in Heaven, who (thanks to His holy name) will ever be a Father to the fatherless. When you leave us, you leave us no more to return amongst us. Your counsel, in his eloquent appeals for mercy in your behalf begged that you might be permitted to return, even though it be when your locks were whitened by time and your frame bent with age and infirmity. This cannot be; but were it possible, there would then be nothing to interest you. All things would be strange—passingly strange. The farms and roads would be changed, the little saplings would be trees, the old people gone and the young people old. They could afford you no pleasure; but if they could, that pleasure is forfeited. Your body must remain in the damp cells of the penitentiary until it is consigned to the colder chamber of the grave. And Matilda, when your earthly imprisonment ends, you will still have another trial to undergo before the Great Judge, the righteous and unerring Judge, whose eye extends over all the transactions of the children of men, and "without whose knowledge not a sparrow falleth to the ground." He will judge without jury or witnesses and from his sentence there is no appeal. Oh, Matilda! Prepare to meet thy God. Give up all hope or expectation of worldly pleasure. Such hopes will prove delusive and false, and the veriest of vanities. Send your petition to the Throne of the Heavenly Grace. Rely not on your own merits, for we are all without merit; but plead the Merits of One whose atoning virtues are sufficient to blot out the sins of the whole world. The sentence of the Law is, that you be taken to jail, and the sheriff of this county convey you from thence to the public jail and Penitentiary House of the State and that you be therein confined during your natural life. And may you there learn to unlearn what you have learned amiss.

A few years after this event an unknown negro made an assault upon a child and after his arrest he was taken from the jail at Barboursville and lynched in the courthouse yard.

In 1876 George F. Miller was elected sheriff. He was a native of Germany and the first foreign-born citizen to hold this office. His son, George F. Miller, Jr., was the most outstanding business man this county ever had.

On March 30, 1888, the east span of the Guyandotte Bridge was knocked loose by a train on which C. W. Kilgore was conductor and W. S. Richardson was engineer, and on November 27th of the following year the western end of the same bridge went down with engine 263 on which Vallery Freeman, father of Judge C. W. Freeman, was the engineer, and was killed in the accident.

In December, 1892, the county bought a city block in Huntington on which to erect a new courthouse and jail. The purchase of this property occasioned much debate within the city. Some of the people felt that the location was too far out and others asserted that the block was too much ground for a courthouse. Both groups were wrong and the county in the next year began the construction of a new jail which was completed in 1894 and in the next year the foundations were dug for the courthouse. The construction of the courthouse was slow but was finally completed on the —— day of December, 1901, and the county offices moved therein. In 1924 a west wing was added, and the present facilities are not sufficient to accommodate the needs of the county.

Cabell County like the rest of the country suffered severely in the Cleveland panic but something will be told about this in the chapter entitled "City of Huntington." Suffice to say that economic conditions continued to be bad until the beginning of the new century, when an unprecedented era of prosperity began and continued for a quarter of a century.

In 1898 the Spanish-American War came and went and a number of Cabell's sons responded to the call but the war did not last long enough to disturb the lives of the community.

In December, 1899, the Circuit Court of Logan County transferred to Cabell for trial the case of the State vs. Robert Hatfield which was one of the cases that grew out of the Hatfield-McCoy feud. This case was tried before Judge E. S. Doolittle on December 5, 1899, with a jury of which James A. Walkinshaw was foreman, E.

E. Williams was prosecuting attorney and H. T. Lovett, the assistant. The jury found Hatfield "not guilty."

In 1902 the county authorized the first bond issue for $300,000.00 for hardsurfacing the county roads. This was followed by two other bond issues, one for $600,000.00 in 1915, and one for $1,000,000.00 in 1920, making a total of $1,900,000.00 bonds the proceeds from which were used to hardsurface the primary roads of the county. These roads were taken over by the State Road Commission in the year 1922. The Cabell County roads about which we have spoken in another chapter had been hardsurfaced and the State Road Commission has completed this work and is now working on the secondary roads. At this writing Cabell County has fifty-three miles of hardsurfaced roads which is in striking contrast to the frontier county organized in 1809 and for fifty years after its organization paying a bounty for wolf scalps.

In 1903 slot machines were being operated in the city of Huntington and then, as now, the group who was responsible for the operation represented considerable political power. Judge D. E. Mathews of the Criminal Court instructed the grand jury that slot machines were prohibited by the statute which made it unlawful to keep or maintain a gaming table "commonly called an A.B.C. or E.O. table . . . or tables of like kind under any denomination whether . . . played with cards . . . or otherwise." Judge E. S. Doolittle, then circuit judge, within the same week instructed the grand jury in Wayne County that slot machines did not fall within the inhibitions of the statute. The grand jury in the criminal court returned a number of indictments against the owners of the slot machines. Most of these machines were hidden before they could be seized but on the trial which followed the owners were convicted and sentenced. The defendants appealed to the Circuit Court who reversed the criminal court. Judge Doolittle wrote a lengthy opinion in which he emphasized the fact that the word "table" used in the statute was the controlling word and then he defined a table and demonstrated that the shape of a slot machine would not bring it within the definition of a table. The slot machine evil had spread to other counties, and in Marion County there was a conviction and an appeal taken to the Supreme Court and that court, in June 1904, held that slot machines were within the inhibition of the statute and that the statute was directed against games of the kind referred to and not the form of table or instrumentality on which the game was played. This decision continues to be the law.

In the summer of 1910 the first aeroplane came. It was operated by a man named Walsh and landed in League Park at 7th Street West. It remained in Huntington for several days.

January 1, 1913 the Chesapeake and Ohio bridge over the Guyandotte River again went down with engine No. 822. Engineer Charles Webber was thrown into the river and eight persons were killed. In March of this year came the unprecedented flood. Four years later came the World War and for two years Cabell countians lived, thought and acted in terms of war.

In June, 1920, Bob Shank, who had been an instructor in flying during the period of the war, and for two years following the war had been a mail pilot of Washington, returned home and leased a part of the Kyle farm at Little Seven Mile and established a flying field. An unsuccessful attempt was made to make this a permanent venture. Later a flying field was established on the Ohio side of the river.

The bed and banks of the Ohio River to the low water mark on the Ohio side are part of the state of West Virginia and the Cabell County line extends to the low water mark on the Ohio side. Events which took place on this river within the boundary of the county may be properly regarded as a part of Cabell County's history. In the river opposite 28th Street in the city of Huntington are rocks known as the Guyandotte or California Rocks. The name is derived from the fact that a boat named the *California* was sunk at this point about the middle of the nineteenth century. Afterwards the *John Brown* was wrecked at that point about 1885. About 9:30 p. m. on January 1, 1905, the boiler on the towboat, the *Defiance,* which was owned by the Monongahela River Coal and Coke Company, in charge of Captain James Woodard, exploded and killed eight of the crew and set fire to the boat. P. V. Daniels of Bradrick with a motorboat was the first man on the scene and was active in the rescue work. A sister boat, the *Exporter,* was coming down the river with a tow of barges and tied up at Curryville and helped with the rescue work. It was noon of the next day before the fire was extinguished and the bodies recovered.

On February 2, 1916, at 9:00 a. m. the *Sam Brown,* a towboat which belonged to the Pittsburgh Coal Corporation had come out of the Kanawha River with fifteen loaded barges. It had picked up some barges at the Island Creek Tipple and then dropped down the river and tied up opposite First Street, East, when the boiler exploded and the whole upper works were hurled into the air. The explosion shook the entire city. Of the crew of thirty-four persons only twenty escaped injury. One man was blown 300 feet in the air and thrown into the river. The cook went mad and had to be overpowered and taken to a hospital where he later died.

On July 14, 1924, the Huntington and Ohio Bridge Company was organized and entered upon the construction of a toll bridge across the Ohio River at 6th Street which was completed on May 23, 1926.

In November, 1925, Peter de Lang, Boyd L. Singles and Jack Westley held up and robbed the Guyandotte Bank of $7,500.00. They were promptly arrested, indicted, tried and convicted and each given a sentence of twenty-five years imprisonment in the penetentiary.

Boyd Jarrell died August 6, 1931. He was born on Mill Creek in Wayne County in 1870. Educated in the common schools of Wayne County and with some work at the West Virginia University, he taught school for a time in his native county, then took a position on the *Wayne News* under W. L. Mansfield. In 1904 he came to Huntington with the *Dispatch* and four years later joined with the *Advertiser* where he remained two years when he went over to the *Herald* where he remained until his death. His was a commanding personality. He had many friends and was easily the outstanding newspaper man in the tri-state region.

John Herriman Holt died December 10, 1933. He had been counsel for the Norfolk and Western Railway Company and of counsel in the Virginia Debt case. He was the Democratic nominee for judge of the Supreme Court of Appeals in 1896, for governor in 1900 and had placed John W. Davis in nomination for candidate for president on the Democratic ticket in 1924. Holt was one of the greatest lawyers of his day.

COMMON PLEAS COURT

In 1893 the Criminal Court of Cabell County was established and given criminal jurisdiction. Afterwards in 1917 its name was changed to the Common Pleas Court and its jurisdiction was enlarged and included civil appeals from justices of the peace. The first judge of this court was William T. Thompson, 1893-94. He was admitted to the Bar August 23, 1870; was prosecuting attorney January 1, 1877, and served a second term 1881-1884; was state treasurer 1886-1892. Many stories survive as to his eccentricities. He advocated the sterilization of criminals and wrote an article on the subject. When he felt his end approaching he made his preparations to go, provided himself with a vault on which he inscribed the date of his birth and the year of his death. He then purchased a coffin and when the undertaker did not deliver the kind ordered he refused to take it and successfully defended a law suit growing out of such refusal.

In 1894 B. D. McGinnis, who had been prosecuting attorney during the Civil War but who had not been in practice for many years, was elected to succeed Judge Thompson. During his term George S. Wallace, then a young lawyer, was employed to defend a prisoner who was confined in the jail, and he went to the jail to interview his client. Frank H. Richardson, who was then jailer, refused the lawyer the right to hold a private conference with his client. Wallace appealed to Judge McGinnis who promptly made an order directing the jailer to permit him to have a conference with his client outside the hearing of the jailer or the turnkey. Judge McGinnis was defeated for the nomination for a second term and the jailer took great credit for his defeat.

D. E. Mathews succeeded Judge McGinnis in 1900 and served until November, 1906, when he resigned to accept a place in the attorney general's office and J. P. Douglas was appointed to fill out the unexpired term. Judge Mathews is the son of Welsh parents and a self-educated man. He is the kindest man imaginable and patient in the highest degree, but under it all is a man of firmness of character and honesty of purpose. There is a joke he tells how, on one occasion, a colored man was indicted for some offense and was in court awaiting trial. His case was not reached as promptly as the colored man wished so he went up to the Judge and said: "I works at the Chesapeake and Ohio shops and I's got a good job and I ain't got no time to be foolin' around this court so I'll give you ten dollars and you let me go." The judge smiling, told the darky that his proposal could not be accepted and that he must wait and be tried. The darky did wait, was tried, but was acquitted and as he left the court room he told the judge that he had lost ten dollars by not accepting his proposition. Judge Mathews was defeated in 1906 by Judge Thomas W. Taylor, but he defeated Judge Taylor in 1918 and served until 1924.

Judge Thomas W. Taylor who served from 1907 to 1918, both

COMMON PLEAS AND DOMESTIC RELATIONS COURTS

years included, was educated at the University of North Carolina and the University of Virginia. He served in the Confederate Army and came to Huntington in its beginning, was a justice of the peace and served in the City Council. He was an ardent Presbyterian and while a kind man he had the courage of his convictions and could not be swayed from any course he thought right. In 1917 John Hill, alias Gigger Hill, was indicted for first degree murder for killing George Church. Hill pleaded guilty to murder in the first degree and Judge Taylor accepted the plea and remanded the prisoner to jail to await sentence. A few days later Judge Taylor sentenced Hill to be hanged. The crime was a cold-blooded one and so far as anyone then or now knows there were no extenuating circumstances. Almost immediately an effort was made to get the judge to change his sentence and it was urged that somebody not named had told the prisoner that if he confessed that it might be better for him. The judge investigated this statement and found no evidence to support it so he declined to change his sentence. An appeal was made to the governor who commuted the sentence to life imprisonment. Judge Taylor lived to a ripe old age, and retained his faculties to the end. He died respected by the entire community.

Judge H. C. Warth who succeeded Judge Mathews, January 1, 1925, is still on the bench. He has a fine presence, splendid judicial manners, and commands the respect of the Bar and the public.

DOMESTIC RELATIONS COURT

This court was created by the acts of 1921. It has jurisdiction of divorce and juvenile cases. The first judge of this court was George R. Heffley, who was appointed by Governor Morgan and served until the next general election, 1922, when L. D. Isbell was elected and served a full term of eight years. Judge Isbell was killed by an automobile after his successor, Judge Ira P. Baer, had been elected. Judge Baer is the present judge of this court.

GRIST MILLS

When the settlers went into a new county it was not unusual for the man of the family to go on ahead and put in a corn crop and then return for his family. After the crop was harvested the problem was to grind the grain. Just how primitive the methods adopted in Cabell County were we cannot now say but we do know that the querne mill, hand and horsepower mills were used and waterpower mills followed. If we should say that the mills were the first public utility in the county some of our folks would stare. But such is the fact. At the time of the organization of this county the Virginia law provided for the condemnation of land for mill sites, prohibited the taking of toll by millers except in mills established by order of court, required the miller to "well and sufficiently grind the grain" and in due turn fixed the toll at ⅛ for grain ground into meal, 1/16 of grain ground into hominy or malt. But the miller had compensations—he was exempt from military services and until 1919 "the owner or occupier of a water grist mill" was ineligible to serve as a member of a grand jury. The miller was the butt of many jokes. One saying which is still current is "the miller's hogs are fat but nobody knows whose grain they eat." Perhaps the miller was not always careful in taking his toll.

In all events the mills and the miller were important in the community. It was a familiar sight until a recent date to see a man or boy mounted on a horse, with a sack of grain slung on behind, going to the mill. So the location of these mills are of interest. Just when the first grist mills were erected in this county is hard to say. Merritt's Mill near the mouth of Mud River was there at an early date, perhaps before the county was organized.

In 1816 in giving the lines of an election precinct there is a reference in the county records to Jordan's Mill.

In 1817 Richard and Benjamin Brown, Peter Scales, and William Buffington were given leave to build a mill dam on Four Pole on their property. Just where that was is not now known but the Browns owned a tract of land which extended from about 7th to 9th Street, East.

Phil Wintz was given permission to build a mill on Nine Mile in January, 1818.

The Dundas Mill at the falls of Mud River was built by John Dundas shortly after he came to this county, probably about 1820. Just before the war this mill was purchased by David Harshbarger, father of the present sheriff and was operated by him until some time during the Civil war when it was destroyed by fire. Ten years later a smaller mill was built on the same site by Mr. Graham but it did not prove profitable.

Howell's Mill is perhaps the best known in the county. It has been known as the Hilliard, Herndon, Doolittle, and Howell Mill, and is said to be the largest structure and perhaps the most profitable mill in the county before the Civil War. It had its beginning with John Hilliard when he built a small mill in the beginning of the last century and operated it until 1819. The mill property was then sold to Valentine Herndon and the grist, flour and small saw mill was operated by him until about 1829, when it was sold to Ambrose Doolittle. A short time after this purchase Mr. Doolittle built a modern mill, thoroughly equipped for the day and time, which he operated with waterpower. He rebuilt the saw mill, built an addition for a carding machine, and established a furniture factory. He also made a venture into the silk raising industry. After the death of Ambrose Doolittle which occured a short time before the Civil War, the mill was operated by his sons-in-law, Jonathan Switzer and Armistead B. Howell, who had come from Buckingham County, Virginia. Later this mill became the property of A. B. Howell.

On July 27, 1829, John Morris who owned the land on both sides of Kilgore Creek was given permission to establish a mill.

The Adam Black mill was located on Mud River above the Howell Mill and near the present Yates crossing but the dam of the Howell Mill prevented its successful operation, and brought about some litigation between the owners, and this mill was abandoned.

In 1827 Sampson Sanders was given permission to erect a dam and a mill and later was given permission to raise his dam to seven feet but was required to build locks. This mill later was known as the Dusenberry Mill, and was operated to a comparatively recent date.

Joseph Marcum was given permission to build a dam in 1827 on Mud River but the location is not known.

The Porter Mill on Mud River was established in 1832, and continued in operation for many years and finally fell into non-use.

In 1832 there is a reference to the Asher Mill, and John Hannon had a mill near Greenbottom in 1841.

Martin's Gazetteer of 1835 records the fact that at that date in Guyandotte there was a steam grist and saw mill and a carding machine propelled by the same power. The location of this mill or how long it stood is not known, but not many years afterward Thomas Buffington and Company, composed of Thomas Buffington, T. J. Jenkins, Addison J. Buffington, and Charles W. Hannon, built an up-to-date three-story mill on the corner of Water and Buffington Streets, which was burned in 1861, the chimney of which still stands. This mill did a big business and Buffington and Company had a steamboat which was named *Dr. Buffington* on which they shipped flour to various river points. Dr. Buffington built the old brick house on Main Street which is now owned by Mrs. Jennie Stewart.

Charles Cummings had a mill on the right fork of Mud River in 1846.

Albert Pine was given permission to build a mill on Four Pole Creek in 1846 which was located at about 12th Street, West. Pine sold out, moved to Texas, and J. L. Thornburg became the owner of the mill, a combination grist and sawmill, and operated it for a number of years. The remains of the old dam could be seen until a few year ago.

There was another mill on Four Pole Creek on what we know as the Lincoln Pike which has been known successively as the Graham, Patten and Wooten mill. It continued in operation until after the Civil War. The last sign of this mill was washed away in 1905.

John Hensley had a mill on Heath's Creek in 1850.

William Gill had a mill at Salt Rock about the time of the Civil War which ran for a number of years.

The first mill in the city of Huntington was the one built on 4th Avenue between 9th and 10th Streets and named the Albert Mills in honor of Albert Laidley. This was a two-burr mill, one for corn and one for wheat. It was built about 1875 and continued for ten years. Robert Wilson built a burr mill on the southwest corner of 9th Street and 4th Avenue in 1879 and operated it for a while but had a boiler explosion which destroyed the mill. Dr. A. J. Beardsley and his brother-in-law, George N. Biggs, took over the property and put up a three-story roller mill which operated successfully and put the Albert Mill out of business. This Beardsley Mill, as it was called, was later burned.

In 1889 W. W. Gwinn and O. E. Gwinn had a mill at Glenwood, West Virginia, but moved to Huntington and built what was then a modern roller mill on its present location. In the beginning it employed ten persons and manufactured flour, meal, and feed. The business has prospered from the start and after a time it was incorporated as Gwinn Brothers and Company. From time to time the mill has been enlarged and is now a modern 500-barrel mill and employs fifty people. D. B. Gwinn is president, and its products are marketed in West Virginia, Ohio, Kentucky, Virginia, and the Carolinas.

In 1916 the Keister Milling Company was organized and erected a roller mill on 15th Street and 2½ Alley. The mill has a capacity of

150 barrels per day and continued under this name until about 1932 when it went through a reorganization and is now owned by the above-named company, i.e., the Huntington Milling Company. The mill has a capacity of 150 barrels flour, 500 bushels meal, and 40 tons feed.

Martin's Gazetteer of Virginia, 1835, reports a mill at Barboursville. This, no doubt, was Merritt's Mill at the mouth of Mud River. There is a roller mill now in the village that was erected about 1901 by J. H. Lloyd who operated it a few years when it was taken over by G. R. Ayres who operated it successfully for many years. After Mr. Ayres' death the mill became the property of W. F. May.

In 1874 John Harshbarger and Mit Newman were partners in the milling business and operated a sawmill. They concluded to and did erect a two-burr steam mill at Milton. The partnership continued for several years when Harshbarger took the flour mill and Newman took the sawmill. In 1888 Ira J. Harshbarger became a partner with John Harshbarger and rollers were put in the mill. In 1890 George W. Harshbarger bought out John's interest, and the business continued as Harshbarger Brothers until 1902 when it was incorporated as the Harshbarger Milling Company, under which name it now operates. The mill is operated by electrical power and has a capacity of 150 barrels per day.

TOBACCO

As early as 1873 the record discloses there was a tobacco warehouse on the hills south of the city and in 1875 the Legislature passed an act providing for the inspection of tobacco and the establishment of state tobacco warehouses at Huntington and Parkersburg. The act provided for a state superintendent for tobacco warehouses and an inspector of tobacco for each warehouse. Dr. P. H. McCullough was appointed superintendent and C. H. Summerson of Guyandotte was named inspector for the Huntington warehouse. The first warehouse was located in a brick building on 3d Avenue near 7th Street. The production of tobacco in this county was small and this warehouse did not justify its existence, and after a year or two it was abandoned. At the beginning of the century the American Tobacco Company put a number of field buyers in the tobacco growing counties which included Cabell and this gave a stimulus to tobacco growing. The Harshbargers built a receiving house at Milton and a tobacco buyer was located there. This house has been in continuous operation since that date, but the county buying has been discontinued.

In 1910 some local people organized the Warehouse Land Company and purchased a tract of land on the Ohio River between 26th and 27th Streets between First Avenue and the River, on which was located an old stove foundry. The company converted this foundry into a tobacco auction warehouse and leased it to M. L. Kirkpatrick and H. E. Spilman who in turn conveyed the lease to the Huntington Tobacco Warehouse Company. An auction tobacco sales warehouse was established and has been continued therein since that date. The next year the Hughes, Ellis and Boyd Tobacco Warehouse bought three acres of land on the west side of 26th Street just opposite the Huntington Tobacco Warehouse and erected a warehouse thereon. Both companies made additions to their warehouses the next year. About this time the Warehouse Land Company sold several acres of land to the Liggett and Myers Tobacco Company who erected thereon a large brick and cement cigarette factory, storage sheds and railroad siding. This factory operated successfully during the war period but was discontinued at the close of the war. It is now used for dead storage. The Hughes, Ellis and Boyd Company ceased business about 1920 and leased their property to Grayson D. Thornton who operated the warehouse until 1925 when it was purchased by the Huntington Tobacco Warehouse Company. The number of pounds of tobacco sold with the average price is of interest but the lack of space precludes too much detail. Suffice to say that in 1910 there were eight million pounds of tobacco sold in Huntington at an average price of eight cents. The peak was reached in 1918 when 9,557,000 pounds were sold at 35.47 cents. In the season for 1934 only 3,547,000 pounds were sold at a price of 15.6 cents.

The warehouse people say that in excess of ten thousand farmers annually sell their tobacco through the Huntington warehouse, that the majority of these farmers grow less than two acres each.

At the time the Huntington warehouse was established there were few hard roads and about eighty per cent of the crop was brought into Huntington by river or rail and the balance by wagons. Since the advent of hard roads and motor trucks ninety-five per cent is brought in by trucks.

OIL AND GAS

We have seen that the Cabell County Petroleum Company drilled a dry hole on the Swann farm in 1865, but the Cabell County folks did not lose faith in the idea that oil and gas would be found eventually in the county. D. J. Jenkins and associates drilled a dry hole on the Jenkins farm at Greenbottom about 1895 and a few years afterwards Thomas H. Harvey and associates drilled a dry hole on the Hisey Fork at Four Pole. At the beginning of the century I. J. Harshbarger and some associates organized a company and drilled a dry hole on the Harshbarger farm but got two good gas wells on the W. W. Connor place. In 1903 a good oil well was brought in on the E. W. Beckett farm and there was a great deal of excitement about oil in Grant District. The development in the county has continued and good gas wells have been brought in in all the county districts except Union District. The oil production was confined to Grant District and there is little if any oil produced now.

VIII: GRAVEYARDS AND CEMETERIES

ON the corner of 5th Avenue and Guyan Street there is an old graveyard which is the oldest in the county. It is believed that on this lot stood the church which was erected through the efforts of William Steel, the Methodist missionary, in the year 1803 or 1804 and about which something is told elsewhere. This belief is strengthened by the fact that there is a deed of record made between the heirs at law of Thomas Buffington, dated March 10, 1855, which sets out the fact that Thomas Buffington in his lifetime gave his obligation to convey this lot, No. 16 Guyandotte, to certain trustees "for the use and purposes of a Methodist Church, school house and graveyard," and that the lot has not been used for a church or a school house for some years past but a part of it is occupied as a graveyard and they convey such interest as they have in that part of the lot which has not been occupied as a graveyard.

The Methodist Church moved from this lot to its present location about the middle of the nineteenth century and left the old church which was used for some years as a school house.

Gravestones in this old churchyard mark the graves of many persons who were born in the eighteenth century. One of these stones inscribed in both French and English marks the grave of Mrs. Eleanore La Tulle born May 3, 1763, died January, 1836. Another stone bearing the Masonic emblem marks the resting place of a Master Mason, Jacob Cooper, born in Washington County, Pennsylvania, and died September 1, 1829, age thirty-seven years and six months. This stone was restored in 1934 by the Western Star Lodge of Guyandotte and the probabilities are that this lodge gave Cooper a Masonic burial.

A few years ago the Sons of the American Revolution moved the remains of a number of soldiers of the Revolution to this lot.

In 1935 the Board of Park Commissioners enclosed the lot with a wall surmounted by an iron fence.

PAT'S BRANCH GRAVEYARD

There was a second graveyard in what was that part of Huntington which was Guyandotte on Pat's Branch. This graveyard was established about the middle of the last century. It has not been used for a good many years and as the land is low it is frequently under high water and it is in bad need of attention.

GRAVEYARDS AND CEMETERIES

BUFFINGTON GRAVEYARD

There was a graveyard on what is now Staunton Road at the southeast corner of the Cedar Grove lot. When the Cedar Grove property was divided into town lots, the bodies were disinterred and moved to Spring Hill. There were a number of old gravestones in this lot that marked the graves of numerous Buffingtons, Scales, Russells and other pioneers. Unfortunately these markers were not taken to Spring Hill but were destroyed. In the removal of these bodies the coffin containing the remains of William Buffington was broken open and his body was found to be in almost perfect state of preservation. Dr. E. S. Buffington, his grandson, saw the body and had no trouble in identifying it.

PRIVATE GRAVEYARDS

There are a number of private graveyards scattered throughout the county, but as time goes on and the persons interested in them pass on, these resting places are destroyed. However, there are some notable exceptions.

Thornburg Burial Plot: There is a Thornburg burial plot on the Guyandotte River not far from Barboursville that goes back for more than one hundred years which the Thornburg family has kept and is still keeping in good repair.

Yatesmont Burial Plot: This plot is on Mud River and what is now the Burdette farm and was established by William P. Yates as a family burial ground. Yates was a native of Culpeper County, Virginia. He served in the War of 1812. His wife was Elizabeth Lillard, a sister of Nancy Lillard, the wife of John Bryan and the grandmother of William Jennings Bryan. W. P. Yates, his wife, John Bryan and his wife, Nancy Lillard Bryan, are buried here. Here also lie Dr. Alexander M. MacCorkle and his wife Eleanor Summers Hanley MacCorkle. Dr. MacCorkle was a second cousin of governor William A. MacCorkle.

The private graveyards are now giving place to public cemeteries which provide perpetual care. There are four such cemeteries in Huntington: Spring Hill, established September 27, 1874; Highland, established June 10, 1892, both municipally owned, and Ridgelawn and Woodmere cemeteries, both privately owned.

IX: SOLDIERS OF THE REVOLUTION

NOTWITHSTANDING the statement which appears in the court record in the suit partitioning the Savage Grant to the effect that certain patentees in the Savage Grant took possession under the division of 1775 and had continued in possession, it cannot now be established that a single soldier who was named as a patentee in the Savage Grant settled in Cabell County, and just how many Revolutionary soldiers settled here is not known. There are two lists which contain the names, rank and other data of soldiers who served in the Revolutionary War, residing in Cabell County who were pensioned under the acts of March 18, 1818, and June 7, 1832, and there is a special report made in the United States Census for 1840 showing the names of these pensioners then living and the names of the heads of the family with whom they resided. From these lists it appears there were twenty-three of such pensioners, and F. L. Burdette has supplied us with the names of four other soldiers and some additional data relating to some of those who appear on the pension list. The first four names on this list are those furnished by Mr. Burdette:

John Morris, came from Kanawha near the mouth of Campbell Creek and settled near Bethesda Church. He served in George Rogers Clark's Illinois Expedition, 1778-1779. He was Captain of Kanawha Militia and served with Virginia Troops in the Whiskey Rebellion in Pennsylvania. He was the father of Bishop Thos. A. Morris and of Edmund Morris, first clerk of Cabell County. John Morris died in August, 1818.

Charles Love. Born 1753. Died 1824. He was placed on the pension roll in Kentucky before settling in Cabell County. He served from May 25, 1776 to March 5, 1778, private in Capt. Thomas Berry's Company, 8th Virginia Regiment.

Melchor Strupe lived near Barboursville on farm west of Horse Show Bend in Mud River, north side of river. Seems to have been related to the Merritt family. He applied for a pension in 1826 but died before his claim was approved.

James Cox. Born 1755. Died 1840. Of Buckingham County, Virginia. Served in the Illinois Expedition in 1778-1779 under Col. Joseph Crockett. Came to Cabell County about 1803 and settled on Mud River near the Great Falls (Blue Sulphur and Ona). Was the ancestor of various Cox, Herndon, DeFore and Hereford families of this section.

Allen Rece (Rice). Born in Bucks Valley, Pa. Oct. 7, 1759, Died Nov. 29, 1837. Married Mary Clymer in 1780. Came to Cabell County in 1803 and settled on Mud River on what was later the James Dundas and Edmund Frye farm a little north of Blue Sulphur. Served as a private with the Pennsylvania Militia. Pensioned in 1833.

SOLDIERS OF THE REVOLUTION

Daniel Davis. Born 1757. Died 1838. Served as private in garrison duty with Virginia Militia at Fort Randolph, King's Fort and Tott's Fort. Lived in Wayne County on Twelve Pole Creek. Placed on pension roll from Cabell County in 1833.

James Gillenwaters. Born 1756. Died 1856. Lived near Inez, and died at the home of Armstead B. Howell near Ousley's Gap. Enlisted in the service from Amherst County and served in the southern campaigns. Was wounded at Guilford Court House and rendered a permanent cripple. He received Land Bounty Warrant No. 6418 from the state of Virginia. Was pensioned under the Act of 1818.

James Turley. Born 1754 in Pennsylvania. Died 1838. Enlisted from Bedford County, Virginia. Served in the George Rogers Clark Illinois Expedition under Capt. John Chapman. Lived near the old State Road, later James River and Kanawha Turnpike, one mile east of Ona, later the Daniel Love farm. Served as private with Virginia State Troops and was pensioned in Cabell County in 1834.

Henry Peyton, (Payton). Born 1760 in Culpeper County, Virginia. Died 1836. Served first as a substitute at $20.00 a month, was on garrison duty at Point Pleasant, was at Guilford Court House and at Yorktown, later at Winchester guarding prisoners, a private in the Virginia Militia. Lived about one mile west of Tom's Creek beyond Martha where John Hash now lives. Was great-grandfather of Homer Peyton and Mrs. L. L. Wilson.

Thomas Laidley. Born in Ayrshire, Scotland Jan. 1, 1756 where he married Sarah Osborne. Died March 17, 1838. Served in Pennsylvania militia and Pennsylvania navy as private, captain and commander. Lived at Morgantown, West Virginia, for a time and came to Cabell County with his son John Laidley.

Nathaniel Scales. Born April 13, 1758. Died 1834. Served as private in North Carolina Militia during Revolution and against the Chickasaw Indians and against the Tories in North Carolina, also as guard over prisoners captured by Gen. Daniel Morgan. Marched from Staunton to Guilford Court House but the battle was over before he arrived. Was father-in-law of William Buffington, James Russell, Bishop Thomas A. Morris and Manoah Bostick of Cabell County.

Valentine Bloss. Born 1754. Died Sept. 4, 1850. Served as private in Virginia Militia. Lived in neighborhood of Beach Fork. Was an ancestor of Dr. James Bloss of Huntington, West Virginia.

Larose Merritt. Born 1738. Died July 30, 1831. Was a private in the Virginia line. Lived perhaps on Merritt's Creek of Guyan, west of Salt Rock. Came to Cabell County from Greenbrier County.

John Everett. Born Feb. 28, 1753. Died Feb. 13, 1845. Came from Albemarle County, Virginia in 1804 and settled on what is now the Cabell County farm for the aged and infirm at Ona. Married first, Sarah Tarlton, second, Sarah Deadman. Served in the Revolution in Capt. William Campbell's company, Col. Patrick Henry's regiment, guarded prisoners at Albemarle Barracks and was discharged at Winchester, Va. He was the father of Col. John Everett of Guyandotte, Nathan Everett of Ona, Mrs. John Morris of Teays Valley and Mrs. Abia Rece.

William Steele, Born 1734. Died Feb. 8, 1832. Was a corporal in the North Carolina Line.

John Adkins. Born in 1756.

Thomas Chandler. Born 1756. Was a private in the Virginia Line, and was in one engagement.

Adam Crom (Crum). Born in 1755. Lived on Nine Mile Creek.

John Leslie. Born in 1761. Lived with Milton Stratton.

William Meade. Born in 1762. Lived with Theophilus Goodwin.

Isaac Roberts. Born in 1760. Was a private in the Virginia Militia. Lived perhaps in what is now Lincoln County and was probably a brother of Thomas Roberts.

Thomas Roberts. Born in 1761, died March 13, 1848. Was a private in the Virginia Militia.

Robert Rutherford. Born in 1742. A private in the Virginia line. Was early a tailor in Barboursville, moved west.

John Stevenson. Born in 1762. Was a private in the Virginia Militia.

Peter Sullivan. Born in 1755.

Asher Crockett (alias James Anderson). Was a private in the Virginia Militia. Lived near Ona on the site now occupied by Onnie France's home. Later moved to Trout's Hill (Wayne C. H., Wayne) where he died.

John McComas, brother of Elisha McComas from Giles County, Virginia. Was a private in the Virginia Militia.

William Holderby the first of the name in the county is shown as a Revolutionary soldier in Eckenrode's *List of Virginia Soldiers,* but it does not indicate the branch or length of his service.

An examination of the court records of Cabell County shows the following persons, whose names are not included above, made claim before the court that they were soldiers of the Revolution:

Oeneaferus Damron made oath on September 23d, 1822, in the County Court, that he had served in the Revolutionary War and knew Asher Crockett and filed a schedule of his property, all of which was ordered certified to the Secretary of War to be considered on an application for a pension.

By an order made by the County Court on September 24, 1832, the court found that John Hutson and John Stephens, and four other soldiers who have been mentioned above, had served in the Revolutionary War and were entitled to a pension. The order did not show any regimental designation but Eckenrode's *List of Virginia Soldiers* shows John Hutson as a Revolutionary soldier and as an "express to Indian towns." This same list shows three John Stephens as Revolutionary soldiers.

Jeffrey Russell appeared in the Superior Court of Law on Wednesday, October 9, 1811, and made oath that about the last of 1776 in Mecklenburg County, Virginia, he enlisted for a term of three years and was placed as a private in the 14th Regiment, Virginia Line Continental Establishment and that he continued in service until December 28, 1779, when he was discharged in the city of Philadelphia, but that in making an application to the Auditor of Public Accounts for compensation allowed by the government to a soldier he had failed to retain a copy of his discharge and that he had not received the land warrant for his services. Mark Russell filed a supporting affidavit.

The County Court records show that Richard Lord Jones on June 26, 1827, and John Stephens, Henry Hampton—a captain or a lieutenant—Hugh Paul, and John Hudson* made application on September 24, 1832, for pensions as Revolutionary soldiers and that in each case the applicant had produced his declaration of oath that he had served as a soldier in the Revolutionary War but the record does not show the contents of the oath or the nature of the service but the court certified each of the foregoing men to the Secretary of War as eligible for pensions.

It will be recalled that the gravestone of Thomas Hannon, the first settler, records the fact that he was a soldier in the Revolutionary War but of this fact there is no record except that there is on file in the Bureau of Pensions in Washington, an application for a pension made in 1834 by Thomas Hannon, in which he states that he served one year in the Virginia Navy 1776-'7 and was drafted in the militia in August, 1781, and was near Yorktown at the time of the surrender. He stated that he had thrown away his discharge. The application was not allowed but was endorsed and held for further proof.

---

*Probably the same person as John Hutson.

X: THE WAR OF 1812

ON the 18th day of June, 1812, Congress passed an act declaring that war "be and the same is hereby declared to exist between the United Kingdom of Great Britain, etc., and the United States," and on the next day James Madison, then President, made proclamation thereof. In anticipation of this proclamation, on April 15, 1812, the Secretary of War by the President's direction made requisition on Governor Barbour of Virginia for 12,000 of the militia of Virginia, being Virginia's quota. On April 19, 1812, Governor Barbour issued general orders to the brigadier generals of the State militia establishment calling them into service. Included in this call was Captain John Simmons' Rifle Company attached to the 120th Regiment in Cabell County, estimated at fifty men.

By order of September 3, 1812, this company was ordered to repair to Point Pleasant as the place of general rendezvous and it became a part of the 2d Regiment of Virginia Militia under Lieutenant Colonel Dudley Evans, under the command of Brigadier General Joel Leftwich and had service in the northwest. This brigade crossed the Ohio River on October 20, 1812, and proceeded to Fort Meigs at the foot of Maumee Rapids in the northwestern portion of Ohio. It assisted in the erection and defense of Fort Meigs. Their enlistments expired in the April following and they returned home.

The regimental officers of the 120th Regiment militia from Cabell County appear as follows: Colonel Elisha McComas, date of commission July 5, 1813; Major Manoah Bostick, July 6, 1809; and Major Samuel Smiley, July 5, 1813. It does not appear they were ordered into Federal Service.

There was a cavalry company from Cabell County under the command of William Brumfield* which served at some period of the war as a part of the 3d Regiment of Virginia Cavalry at Norfolk and other places on the seaboard.

---

*A thorough search of the records in Richmond, Virginia, and of the Pension Bureau and Adjutant General's Office at Washington failed to disclose a muster roll of this company.

XI: THE WAR WITH MEXICO

HOSTILITIES between the United States and Mexico began on April 25, 1846, but war was not declared until by an act of Congress on May 13, 1847, it was declared that by "An act of the Republic of Mexico a state of war existed between that government and the United States." Prior to the declaration of war, on November 16, 1846, President Polk issued a call for troops and made a requisition on the Governor of Virginia for his quota. Two days later on November 18, 1846, Governor William Smith issued a proclamation calling for ten companies of volunteers to constitute a regiment and directed the rendezvous at Guyandotte in Cabell County. Later the place of rendezvous was changed to Richmond.

Virgil A. Lewis in his book entitled *Archives and History* gives the following account of conditions in Cabell County:

The Richmond *Enquirer* in its issue of January 16th, 1848, has the following under the caption "Volunteer Movements in Western Virginia:"

A letter from Cabell C. H., of the 6th of January, alludes to the formation of a volunteer company for Mexico. The Regiment was called together on the 4th instant, when fifty-three stepped forward and enrolled themselves as ready to march and fight in their country's cause. They were to start on the 7th for Wayne C. H. where the Regiment was to meet on the 9th, hoping to make up the requisite number. Though this company will be formed too late to be accepted by the State, it shows that there are some gallant spirits in Cabell County. The citizens of the Courthouse have subscribed $200 for their benefit, and Charles Conner (so public spirited a gentleman deserves to be named with praise) has made a donation of $100. Again, we say, well done old Cabell! She has set a patriotic example for her neighbors, which will not be lost upon them, should the country hereafter call upon Virginia for more of her sons to fight in a good cause.

CAPTAIN ELISHA W. MCCOMAS' COMPANY OF THE ELEVENTH UNITED STATES INFANTRY

The Virginia Regiment being full and already gone to Mexico, Elisha W. McComas and Joseph Samuels secured Commissions as Captain and First Lieutenant, and at Wheeling, and in Cabell and other counties bordering on the Ohio, raised a company which was attached as Company C of the Eleventh United States Infantry. The Rendezvous was Guyandotte, in Cabell County, from which the Company proceeded to Newport barracks, where it was mustered into service. "Yesterday," said the New Orleans *Delta*, in its issue of August 5, 1847, "Captain Elisha W. McComas and Lieutenant Joseph Samuels, with seventy-five privates of Company C of the Eleventh United States Infantry of the Regular Army, arrived on the steamer *Pontiac* from Newport barracks."

Captain McComas was discharged from the service in 1848 and returned to his home in Cabell and resumed the practice of law. He served in the Virginia Legislature and was lieutenant governor with Henry A. Wise. In the Douglas campaign he resigned as lieutenant governor and became the editor of the Chicago *Times*. Afterwards he moved to Fort Scott, Kansas, where he practiced law. He died March 11, 1890, at the age of seventy years.

Lieutenant Joseph Samuels was discharged at the same time and returned to his home at Barboursville but died a short time afterwards of fever contracted in Mexico.

XII: THE GREAT TRAGEDY

EARLY in 1861 Virginia seceded from the Union. As to the wisdom of this course men disagree but it seems certain that whatever course she pursued war was inevitable. If Virginia had remained in the Union it would have been her duty to furnish her quota of men to prosecute the war and if she seceded she would be called upon to protect her soil. Many persons cherished the illusion that the Federal government would not resort to war and if there were a war it would be short lived for the reason that a shortage of cotton in Europe would force European intervention, but as usual the forecasters were all wrong. The people west of the mountains were largely Union in their sympathies and we know that immediately after Virginia seceded, the restored State of Virginia was organized and later West Virginia was made a State. But these things are told of in another place. Cabell County was on the border. Its people were divided and this fact makes war—civil war—the more terrible.

Albert Gallatin Jenkins brought about the organization of the Border Rangers—which became Company E of the 8th Virginia Cavalry, C.S.A. This company was first organized at Guyandotte on December 10, 1860, for the purpose of protecting a Virginia flag which had been hoisted on a flagpole on the banks of the Ohio River. Ira J. McGinnis, later circuit judge, was elected captain. The company kept the flag up until the 20th of April, 1861, when Jenkins made a call on it and made a speech. The company then disbanded and went with Jenkins to his home at Green Bottom for dinner. Most of the men were armed with shotguns and after dinner each man provided himself with a piece of lead pipe. The group went to the old Green Bottom Church where they met a number of men from Mason County, organized themselves into a company, and elected Albert Gallatin Jenkins captain. (There were 101 men present.) They then went to St. Albans and were quartered in the Episcopal Parsonage and afterwards on the 20th day of May completed their organization by the election of H. C. Everett, first lieutenant, afterwards captain; A. H. Samuels, second lieutenant; G. W. Holderby, Junior, lieutenant, afterwards captain; W. R. Gunn, ordnance sergeant, afterwards captain of the Gunn Rangers, Company D, 8th Virginia Cavalry; Robert Stribling, first sergeant; James Smith, second sergeant; Isaac Ong, third sergeant; James Norman, fourth sergeant;

Albert Gallatin Jenkins, Brigadier General, C.S.A.

John Thompson, first corporal; Jesse Dodson, second corporal, James D. Sedinger, third corporal, and James M. Willington, fourth corporal. The company was sworn into the Confederate service on the 29th day of May, 1861. On July 14, 1861, it engaged in a skirmish with the 2d Kentucky at Barboursville. They took part in the battle at Scary. On July 1, 1861, the troop returned to Cabell and had the rare distinction of a troop of cavalry capturing a steamboat. It was accomplished in this manner: The steamer *Fanny McBrownie*, in charge of Captain Blagg and Pilot Holloway, was approaching Green Bottom. Captain Jenkins concealed his command near the river and then went out on the bank and hailed the boat. Captain Blagg thought Jenkins was a passenger and ran his boat up to the bank where it was captured.

There was a skirmish at Poore's Hill (Ona) in August, 1861, when the 5th West Virginia Infantry Volunteers fired on some Confederates and a man named Damron of the Confederate forces was killed.

On November 10, 1861, the company was again in Guyandotte and had a skirmish at the old suspension bridge which was recounted by one of the Rangers:

We arrived November 10th at nine o'clock at night to charge the town. The Border Rangers charged the suspension bridge and took it with orders to hold it. Upon arriving at the bridge the drummer boy was beating a long roll and never quit until some one shot a hole through his drum. The Yanks were forming in companies on each side of the bridge against the railing. We went through them and dismounted on the west side of the bridge and formed at the end of the pier. About five minutes after forming, the enemy concluded to cross and cut out. We waited until they were in fifty feet of us, when we opened fire on them. What became of them after that I never knew, but think they jumped over the rail into the river. . . . The company lost Al Long, killed, and Jo Collier and John McMahon wounded. Collier died from his wounds. We captured all we could find of the Yanks, their arms and Commissary stores, put out pickets and stayed all night and left town the next morning with one hundred and ten prisoners for Dixie. The picket about the center of the suspension bridge fired his gun and killed Al Long, some one of the company shot him. This happened as we charged the bridge. Why he did not throw down and surrender, was always a mystery to us. He was a small red-headed man, would weigh about one hundred and forty pounds.

After the skirmish was over Colonel John B. Clarkson was searching the Forest House, a hotel which stood on the corner of Guyan Street and the river front, and in a way not explained, but accidental,

Suspension bridge. Scene of the battle at Guyandotte, November, 1861

shot and killed Captain Huddleston of Kanawha County, an officer in Clarkson's Regiment.

The venerable H. C. Everett gives the following account of the affair at Guyandotte on the night of November 10, 1861:

We were living on a farm on the Guyandotte River where the Nickel Plant now is, and our house was near the road. One Sunday night about ten o'clock we heard the approach of horsemen. I went with my father, Talton Everett, out to the road to see the column pass. In a short time the column, which was a part of the 8th Va. Cavalry, C.S.A., passed going at a rapid rate. "Cooney" Ricketts was pretty near the head of the column, his saddle cloth was slipping from under his saddle and as he passed our fence he threw the saddle cloth over into our yard and hollered "How are you, Uncle Talt?" My father, Talton Everett, followed the column down the road towards Guyandotte, and just before he got to the town he saw a man crossing the road and hurrying down into a ditch. Father called out, "You need not run from me, I will not harm you." The man addressed was Captain William Turner who lived on a farm on the west side of the Guyandotte River opposite the Everett place but at that moment was a Captain in Colonel Whaley's (U.S.A.) recruiting party which consisted of some three hundred men and was stationed in the town of Guyandotte. Turner recognized my father and made no further effort to conceal himself.

After the fight the soldiers remained in Guyandotte until some time the next day when they left with a number of prisoners. Included among the prisoners were a number of civilians taken as hostages—Julius Freutel, John B. Alford, William Douthitt, and Dr. J. H. Rouse, T. J. Hapslip, afterwards county Recorder, and some others. The next day after the Confederates had gone, Colonel Ziegler of the Federal Army arrested a number of civilians among whom were Talton Everett, Elijah (Dad) Ricketts, who was the grandfather of "Cooney" Ricketts, Charles Everett, Saint Mark Russell, H. H. Miller and a number of the other southern sympathizers. These men were placed on a boat to be taken to Camp Chase, but just as the boat was leaving the wharf Captain William Turner appeared on the scene. When he saw Talton Everett among the prisoners he told the officer in charge that Talton Everett ought not to be taken. Immediately Everett was released. However, as the boat had already pushed off from the wharfboat, Mr. Everett had to jump over her side and wade ashore. Captain Turner told Mr. Everett, "You saved me last night, and I have saved you today." The other prisoners with the exception of Charles Everett were exchanged and after a time returned home. Charles Everett died at Camp Chase.

Mr. Everett said that the impression was current that it was H. C. Everett, lieutenant of the Border Rangers, who shot and killed the Federal guard.

Dr. J. H. Rouse, afterward an A.A. Surgeon, 9th Regiment, Virginia Volunteers (Federal) writes an account which he entitles "The Horrible Massacre at Guyandotte, Virginia." In this article the doctor says that Guyandotte had suffered from the "machinations" of the Rebels and it had become necessary to garrison the town with Federal soldiers, that Colonel K. V. Whaley was authorized to recruit the 9th Virginia Regiment and he began recruiting in September, 1861, and it was believed that he had restored peace and that there were no rebels in force within eighty miles of the place.

On Sunday night, November 10, 1861, Guyandotte was quiet; the church bells were pealing and most people were going to hear the Rev. J. C. Wheeler preach. Doctor Rouse concluded not to attend church but to visit a friend, so he left his office and made the visit. He was kindly received into the parlor in which there was a bright fire and was enjoying a social tete-a-tete with his friend, unconscious that "any foe was nigh." Suddenly in the peaceful Sunday night came the cry, "Corporal of the guard, post number five, Corporal of the guard, post number five, Corporal of the guard, post number five." The doctor rushed into the street and inquired of a friend the cause and was told that "we had been attacked." He hurried to his office where he had a minnie rifle and seven rounds of ammunition concealed and secured his rifle and ammunition and returned to the street where he found Captain Uriah Paine rallying his men. There had not been time enough for the drummer to beat the long roll. The Rebel cavalry came on at the charge and Captain Paine fired the first shot and Doctor Rouse the second shot and the firing became general. Colonel Whaley was in command and had one hundred and eighty men in camp. Of these, eighteen were in the hospital and some twenty men were cut off from their quarters and hence could not secure their arms. There were some eight hundred Rebels under the command of Colonel John Clarkson and A. G. Jenkins. The doctor soon fired his seven rounds of ammunition and then found himself between two detachments, so he concluded to retire and ran down to the Ohio River where there was a keel boat owned by Mr. Lawson of Gallipolis loaded with wheat. The doctor went on board and found Lawson and four men concealed among the grain sacks. The boat was unloosed from its mooring and pushed out in the stream but the eddy made by the junction of the Guyandotte and the Ohio forced the boat back to the bank. The crew succeeded in putting the boat off a second time but they were discovered by the Rebels who opened fire on them and yelled, "You d--n Yankees, land that boat or we will sink every devil of you." Dr. Rouse tried to handle the oars but he was an inexperienced boatman. He called on the men below to help

THE GREAT TRAGEDY

but because of the bullets from the Rebels' guns all of the men except Sheriff Johnson and one other man refused to help. In some way the oars were unslipped and the oarsmen, including Dr. Rouse were thrown in the river. Dr. Rouse swam ashore and hid himself in a cave on the bank where he remained for about four hours, but on account of his wet clothing and exposures he concluded to surrender and ask for quarter. He hailed Edward G. Veitegures whom he had known and whom he felt would be kind to him and surrendered. The doctor expected Veitegures to take him to his (Veitegures) home but Veitegures delivered him to the Rebels. In the Rebel camp Dr. Rouse found W. B. Moore, a former sheriff, who was elated at the doctor's capture. The doctor was taken to the house of A. J. Keenan, a Southern sympathizer, who treated him kindly and was kept there until the next morning. The doctor felt for a few minutes that he had been overlooked but there was no such good fortune. He was taken to the hospital, which had been converted into a guardhouse, where he met Dr. Morris, T. J. Hayslip, A. G. White, and many others. The sick and wounded lay in heaps upon the floor begging for water to quench their thirst and to have their wounds dressed but this was refused. Later the prisoners, ninety-eight in number, were tied with cords furnished by S. M. E. Russell, the wounded mounted on horses and the retreat started. Among the Rebels he recognized his acquaintances and fellow townsmen, Henry Everett, G. W. Holderby, G. D. Warren, and Alex Chapman. The march started at a full run, the prisoners being kept in the middle of the road in mud and mire from four to ten inches deep. To make matters worse, to his surprise and chagrin, Jennie Everett appeared "regaled in her secesh costume," adding insult to injury. He told in great detail of his suffering on the march and of meeting Douthitt, Hinchman, and Kyle, all of whom had held public office but were taken as civilian prisoners, and how on the second day Colonel K. V. Whaley, who had been taken prisoner, made his escape. He told how the civilian prisoners were designated as "Tories" and were required to march at the head of the column while the soldier prisoners were called "Damned Yankees," and of the bad condition of the prison in Richmond. He was finally released and Albert Laidley who was in Richmond furnished him with a small sum of money and he made his way back to Guyandotte.

In retaliation for this raid Colonel John L. Ziegler of the 5th West Virginia Infantry Volunteers burned the principal portions of Guyandotte.

J. K. (Doc) Suiter
The tall sycamore of the Guyandotte

THE GREAT TRAGEDY

This is told in an affidavit made by the late J. K. (Doc) Suiter, which follows:

State of West Virginia,

County of Cabell, SS:

Personally appeared this day before the undersigned authority, Joshua Suiter, who being first by me duly sworn, deposes and says that he was born in Lawrence County, Ohio, on October 20, 1845, and that during the rebellion was a resident of Bradrickville, in said Lawrence County; that in February, 1865, he enlisted in Company A of the 188th Ohio Infantry, in the service of the United States; that in the year 1861, at a time when General A. G. Jenkins, then a captain in the Confederate service made a raid upon the town of Guyandotte in said County Cabell, a large sidewheel steamboat carrying several companies of the Fifth Virginia Infantry, U.S.A., then stationed at Ceredo, West Virginia, landed at Proctorsville, on the Ohio River, and took aboard about as many as a company of what was then known to this affiant as members of the Ohio State militia; and that this affiant, along with other non-enlisted men and boys also went aboard said steamboat; that said steamboat went up the river to a point about one mile above the said town of Guyandotte, where all of said regular soldiers, said militia and non-enlisted men including this affiant, debarked, and forming into line of march went to said town of Guyandotte; that the said Confederate forces had left the said town of Guyandotte, when the said United States soldiers and the other militiamen and citizens of Ohio entered the same; that great confusion prevailed in said town and it was not known whether the said Confederate forces had abandoned their said raid or not, and the report was abroad that a number of soldiers and others had been killed; that the streets of said town in the business portion, were filled with goods and merchandise from store houses and that it was generally thought that the said Confederate forces would return and seize said goods and merchandise; that the said United States officers and soldiers were in command and direction, and that the greater portion of the dwellings and business houses in said town as well as said goods and merchandise were that day consumed by fire, which said fire was made as this affiant remembers and believes on the grounds of military necessity; that included in the buildings so burned were *all* of the buildings then situated on the east side of Guyandotte Street between Bridge Street and the Ohio River.

And further this deponent saith not.

JOSHUA SUITER.

TROOP MOVEMENT IN CABELL 1861-65

We know of the skirmishes which occurred in the county but there is no record which covers the troop movement therein or of the regiments or parts of regiments that were stationed in the county.

Before the Battle of Barboursville on July 14, 1861, a part of the 2d Kentucky under Colonel William E. Woodruff was camped on the field where the International Nickel Plant now is and another portion of this regiment under Lieutenant Colonel G. W. Neff was camped on the A. G. Jenkins place on Greenbottom. We have a picture that shows the 34th Regiment, Ohio Volunteer Infantry, marching east on Center Street in Barboursville in November, 1861.

Captain William Turner in command of an independent company which later became a part of the 9th Virginia (Federal) spent the winter of 1861-62 in and about the P. C. Buffington house, now the Chesapeake and Ohio hospital. During this same winter there was a Zouave regiment at Barboursville and H. C. Everett is the authority for the statement that it was men from this regiment who blew out the dam in the Guyandotte River at Roby Branch.

The War Department records show that there was an expedition to the Guyandotte Valley January 12-23, 1862, and that there was a skirmish on the Guyandotte November 15, 1862.

In 1862 and 1863 the 2d West Virginia Cavalry with Colonel John C. Paxton commanding spent almost a year in and around the mouth of the Guyandotte River. John L. Vance of Gallipolis was a captain in this regiment and was exceedingly popular.

There was an expedition through Cabell County from Camp Piatt, located in Kanawha County, just above Charleston, April 3-6, 1863, that had a skirmish at Mud River on April 5th.

There was another "scout" in Cabell County, March 16-18, 1864. The 7th West Virginia Cavalry under Colonel John H. Oley was stationed in the Kanawha Valley in the year 1864 and until August 1, 1865, the date of the muster out of the regiment, and Company F of this regiment under the command of Captain Edgar P. Blundon with First Lieutenant W. H. Newcomb—father of our W. H. Newcomb of the Anderson-Newcomb Company—was stationed at Guyandotte. During this period Blundon was promoted to major and Lieutenant Newcomb succeeded him in command but was not promoted to captain.

While there are no records of any organized Confederate groups in this county after A. G. Jenkins left in March, 1863, we do know that groups of Southern soldiers came into the county and carried on a guerrilla warfare of their own and there are still extant stories of these raiders hiding out in the woods during the day and operating during the night.

Records of the County Court disclose that in 1869 the county jail was overcrowded by reason of the number of soldiers confined therein, that the sanitary conditions of the jail by reason of this fact were exceedingly bad, that soldiers were guarding the jail but the records are silent as to who these men were or why they were confined or what troops were guarding them.

The Border Rangers in August, 1862, were with Jenkins on his raid to Ravenswood where they crossed over into Ohio and marched down to Racine, and after a skirmish recrossed to Virginia without loss. Jenkins went to his home at Greenbottom and a detachment sent to Mud River Bridge (Milton) went to Barboursville on a Sunday morning and drove out the Federal soldiers and then went on to Guyandotte and visited their friends until General Jenkins came along from Greenbottom and they rejoined their command. In March, 1863, after a skirmish at Point Pleasant they encamped a short time at Howell's Mill and this appears to be the last time the organization as a whole was in Cabell County. However, it had much service until the end of the war and many of its men made the supreme sacrifice. Captain Jenkins was in turn colonel of the 8th Virginia Cavalry, C.S.A., and brigadier general. He was wounded in the battle at Cloyde Mountain and died on May 9, 1864.

Included in the membership of this famous organization was Thomas Dunn English, author of *Ben Bolt*.

Other Cabell Countians were equally as ardent in the Southern cause. Among them were:

George McKendree was a young civil engineer working with the Chesapeake and Ohio Railway Company at Lewis Tunnel. He borrowed a contractor's team and drove to Covington, Virginia, to learn the news and heard that the State had seceded. He did not return to his work but entered the service and came out a major of artillery. He afterwards married Irene McComas and was sheriff of this county.

Lucien (Cooney) Ricketts and E. Stanard Buffington appropriated two horses belonging to Stanard Buffington's father and set out for Dixie. After some service they went to Virginia Military Institute and were with the V.M.I. Cadets on the glorious day at New Market. "Cooney" became a lawyer and was prosecuting attorney.

Dr. Buffington was one of the most beloved men in the county.

ON THE UNION SIDE

John S. Witcher became first lieutenant of the 3d Virginia Cavalry, December 13, 1862. He was successively captain, major, and on May 6, 1865, became lieutenant colonel and was brevet brigadier general of volunteers on March 13, 1865, for services in the Shenandoah Valley and in the final campaign. He was mustered out in 1865 and on June 30, 1880, he was made a paymaster in the regular army.

Henry J. Samuels who was later the circuit judge was adjutant general of the Restored State.

The adjutant general's report shows that Cabell County levied and paid $3,600.00 as local bounties for volunteers for the Federal service.

The 4th Regiment of Infantry Volunteers was organized in Mason County in the summer of 1861 and the 5th Regiment of Infantry Volunteers was organized at Ceredo the same summer and the rosters of these regiments carry the names of many of Cabell's sons. In February, 1862, the 9th Infantry Volunteers was organized at Guyandotte and it had its camp over near the hill near where the present Baltimore and Ohio station stands. The following made up its commissioned personnel:

Colonels: Leonard Skinner (resigned), and Isaac Harden Duval; Lieutenant Colonel William C. Starr; Major Benjamin M. Skinner; first lieutenants and adjutants: Joseph C. Wheeler, Henrie W. Brazie, and Cary B. Hayslipp; First Lieutenant Joseph C. Merrill; surgeons: William L. Grant and Jonathan Morris; assistant surgeons: William L. Grant and James H. Hysell; Chaplain Joseph M. Phelps; captains: Samuel Davis, John W. Spencer, Nathan M. McLaughlin, George W. Hicks, John S. P. Carroll, John M. Phelps, William Engelman, Oliver Phelps, Owen G. Chase, John W. Miller, Henry C. McWhorter, William B. Wetzel, Joseph C. Wheeler, William G. Smith, William Turner, Allen F. Bratton, William P. Pratt, Thomas Boggess, and Adonijah W. Rollins.

All of these regiments saw service and gave good accounts of themselves.

With the men who served with the colors there can be no quarrel. The Army with which they served is of no importance provided only the service was "honest and faithful," but there were groups of men who served in the so-called Home Guards that caused much needless suffering and distress and do not deserve to be called soldiers or to be classed as soldiers and we express the pious hope that "we shall not see their like again."

But to return to the soldiers of both Armies after the war ended. They returned to their respective homes and in a relatively short period the bitterness of the war was forgotten and they worked and lived together as part of a great people. Time has depleted their ranks—only a few survivors, like lone trees in a wood that has been burned over by fire, stand among their fellow citizens respected by all. Their comrades are gone—gone

"Where the sunset and the shadows dwell
And where the warrior winds
Chant an everlasting requiem
For the brave soldier dead."

With the beginning of Huntington many ex-service men from both armies cast their lots with the new city. They were splendid men and proved their worth in civil life as they had done on the battlefields. Many were the acknowledged leaders in commercial and industrial pursuits and it is safe to assert that they predominated in political life. Among these good men were:

General John H. Oley, who entered the service October 29, 1861 as major of the 7th West Virginia Cavalry and served successively as lieutenant colonel and then colonel and was made brevet brigadier general of volunteers March 13, 1865, and was easily the outstanding citizen in the community.

Captain H. Chester Parsons who was the local attorney for the Chesapeake and Ohio Railway Company.

Major E. A. Bennett, 6th Regiment, West Virginia Infantry Volunteers, one time auditor, member of the State Legislature and member of the city council.

Colonel Thomas Sikes, 33d Ohio Infantry Volunteers, many years city treasurer.

Sam Gideon, a successful merchant, member of the city council, board of education, and president of the County Court.

Frank L. Hersey, county assessor, and member of the Legislature.

George W. Hutchinson, George F. Ratcliff, and A. J. Miser each of whom served as justice of the peace.

From the men who wore the Gray came Captain Eustace Gibson who served two terms in Congress. On one occasion in the heat of a political campaign when his record as a soldier had been questioned, he appeared at a public meeting and exhibited an old pair of gray trousers the front of which along with a part of his belly had been shot away by a cannon ball, to prove that his war record was of the best.

"Cousin" George Cullen, one time mayor, who commanded the Montpelier Guards which was the advance unit of Jackson's command, and who was the first to come in contact with the enemy in the seven days' fight around Richmond.

Reverend W. J. Cocke for many years a minister, was an orderly sergeant in Company H of the 22d Virginia Infantry, C.S.A., at Chancellorsville when Jackson was shot and he furnished the litter bearers who carried the stricken general from the field.

Captain T. J. Burke was one of the early mayors of the city.

Thomas H. Harvey enlisted in the Kanawha Rifles C.S.A., when seventeen years of age. He was wounded in the shoulder in the second battle before Fort Donaldson and invalided home. He afterwards went to Washington College, studied law, became circuit judge and was one of the leading citizens in this community.

Thomas W. Taylor, when a boy in his teens, was wounded in the seven days fighting around Richmond. He was a successful lawyer, served as a justice of the peace and later as judge of the Common Pleas Court.

Judge J. N. Potts, lieutenant 18th Virginia Cavalry, C.S.A., served in many civil capacities and was a bulwark of the Baptist church.

Andy F. Southworth who in his teens, enlisted in Page's Battery, C.S.A., was at Gettysburg, and after the war served the Chesapeake and Ohio Railway Company in many capacities, as faithfully as he served the lost cause.

John Henry Cammack, private, 31st Virginia Infantry, was a successful business man and like Judge Potts, a bulwark in the Baptist church.

Cameron L. Thompson, private, 22d Virginia Infantry, was a prominent churchman and active in business and political life.

Many more could be named but this is not a roster and their omission must not be considered as any reflection on their sterling worth. In their generation they demonstrated again that it takes a strong people to fight a civil war. After its end the bugles were still for thirty-three years.

XIII: THE WAR WITH SPAIN

ON April 20, 1898, Congress passed a joint resolution demanding that Spain relinquish its authority over Cuba and withdraw its armed forces, and directed the President to use the land and naval forces of the United States to carry the resolution into effect. On the same day it passed an act increasing these forces and on the 23d of April the President called for 125,000 volunteers to be proportioned among the several states. On April 25th came the declaration of war.

The governor of West Virginia mobilized the brigade of West Virginia National Guard which consisted of two regiments of infantry at Camp Lee (now Kanawha City), West Virginia. On April 26, 1898, he accepted volunteers to form one regiment of infantry to be known as the First Regiment West Virginia Volunteer Infantry.

FIRST WEST VIRGINIA U. S. VOLUNTEER INFANTRY

The brigade commander, B. D. Spillman, the field officers, and certain captains of the two regiments volunteered and accepted commissions in the next lower grade as officers of the new regiment. Colonel W. H. Banks and Major W. H. Lyons of Huntington became major and captain respectively, and Captain I. H. Sabel of Huntington became a first lieutenant. Lyons and Sabel were restored to their former rank in the following May and served in these grades to the end of the war. There were three companies from Cabell County in the National Guard mobilized at Camp Lee, viz.: Company F of Milton, G and I of Huntington. The officers of Company F did not volunteer and most of the enlisted men returned home. Companies G and I were mustered into the United States service on May 11, 1898, as companies A and F, 1st West Virginia U. S. Volunteers, and continued in service until February 4, 1899, with the following officers from Huntington: Company A—Captain I. H. Sabel, Second Lieutenant Lester Ridenour; Company F—Captain J. E. Verlander, First Lieutenant Charles W. Cole, and Second Lieutenant Fred W. Lester.

Harry W. Jenkins was first lieutenant, Quartermaster Corps, and C. C. Hogg, first lieutenant, assistant surgeon.

Charles H. Ricketts, a member of an old Cabell County family, had joined the National Guard at its beginning and had attended the first National Guard camp at Gypsy Grove. Although considerably older than most soldiers, he volunteered and served as first duty sergeant,

Company A. Sergeant Ricketts was a younger brother of A. G. Ricketts of the Border Rangers, C.S.A., who was killed in eastern Tennessee and about whom a comrade wrote: "He was as brave a soldier as ever wore a spur." After the war Sergeant Ricketts re-enlisted in the guard and served until incapacitated by age.

Thomas B. Davis was an enlisted man in Company A. After the war he continued in the National Guard and served in the commission grades up to major. He was on duty in the coal strike on Cabin Creek in 1912 and 1913. In 1917 he was incapacitated for service on account of deafness but was named the acting adjutant general and served in that capacity until March, 1921. He was made chief of the fire department of the City of Huntington by Rufus Switzer, Mayor, and raised this organization to its highest efficiency.

SECOND WEST VIRGINIA U. S. VOLUNTEER INFANTRY

On April 25, 1898, the President made a call for 75,000 additional volunteers and an additional regiment of infantry was allocated to West Virginia.

Governor Atkinson ordered a provisional regiment to be formed at Camp Atkinson, which was located in the western part of the city of Charleston at the end of the new bridge across the Kanawha River, to be known as the 2d West Virginia U. S. Volunteer Infantry.

Robert L. Archer and George S. Wallace of Cabell County volunteered and were commissioned as first and second lieutenants respectively. This regiment was mustered in the United States service on June 23, 1898, and served until April 10, 1899.

W. H. Waldron of Huntington began his career as an enlisted man in Company E of this regiment. While a member of this company he was commissioned as a second lieutenant in the regular army and subsequently served through all of the grades up to and including colonel. During the World War he was Chief of Staff of the 80th Division, A.E.F. Colonel Waldron was awarded the D.S.C. for conduct at Tientsin, China, and the D.S.M. for distinguished service in the World War and is a member of the French Legion of Honor.

PHILIPPINE INSURRECTION

At the close of the Spanish-American War the United States organized some twenty regiments of volunteers for service in the Philippines. These regiments were recruited from the country at large. Quite a number of Cabell County men enlisted in this service and most of them had served in the State volunteers. Major W. H. Lyons was commissioned and served two years in the Philippines. Among the enlisted men were George T. Cullen, E. P. Cullen, Clay N. Keenan, John Boone, Clarence S. Barkla, and Leonard Neal, brother of Dr. W. E. Neal. The last two died in the service. Leonard Neal was a handsome man—a fine physical specimen, bright complexion, and beautiful teeth. His remains were shipped home and his old comrades of 1898 gave him a military funeral in the graveyard at Getaway, Ohio.

XIV: THE WORLD WAR

IN the early part of June, 1916, the National Guard of the several states was ordered into Federal service and sent to the Mexican Border ostensibly to be prepared for conditions that might arise in Mexico but more likely in anticipation of the United States entering the World War and to give the guard a period of preliminary training. Four companies from Huntington, viz.: G, H, and I of the 2d Infantry, and a machine gun company responded to the call on June 10, 1916, and served on the Mexican Border until early in the following spring when they returned home. After they had been home only a few weeks the governor called out the National Guard on April 2, 1917, and it continued in State service until its officers and men were drafted on the 5th day of August, 1917, into the Federal service in the same rank and grade that they held in the State service. The Huntington companies went to Camp Shelby, Mississippi, and became a part of the 150th Infantry, 75th Brigade, 38th Division, and sailed for overseas late in September, 1918, arriving in France in the early part of October. There it was broken up and its units sent to the 78th Division as replacements and its officers sent to various divisions.

Officers from Huntington with these units were:

Majors: Herbert C. McMillen and Heber H. Rice. The latter was discharged from service before going overseas.

Captains: Ira J. Barbour, Company I; Valkey W. Midkiff, Company G, and Austin M. Sikes, Company H.

First lieutenants: August C. Reinwald, C. Foster Templeton, Albert H. Peyton, and Delbert Fisher. Lieutenant Templeton did not go overseas.

Second lieutenants: R. Starr Thornburg, and John Eskew.

These men were in addition to Cabell County's quota to the National Army.

Just after the United States entered the World War, Governor John J. Cornwell summoned George S. Wallace of Huntington to Charleston and laid before him the confidential communication from Newton D. Baker, Secretary of War, in which the secretary stated that the proposed selective service act would probably pass Congress and outlined the plan to put selective service into effect. Governor Cornwell offered George S. Wallace the position of draft executive for the State which he accepted and agreed to. He reported at Charleston on the Monday following, April 25, 1917, to take up his duties.

When this appointment was communicated to Washington, General E. H. Crowder, provost marshal general, ordered Wallace on duty as a major, Judge Advocate General Department, and named him as United States Agent and Disbursing Officer for West Virginia. Major Wallace remained at Charleston until September 17th when he was ordered to the office of the Judge Advocate General in Washington. After a few months service in that office he was promoted to lieutenant colonel and was ordered to the headquarters of the A.E.F. in France, at which place he served as the senior assistant to the acting judge advocate general for France until the spring of 1919.

The first step in putting the selective service act into effect was the naming of registrars for the registration of all male persons between twenty-one and thirty years of age, both inclusive. Registration was accomplished by two registrars sitting in each of the several voting precincts on the 5th day of June, 1917, when the registrants presented themselves for registration.

Cabell County had 4,325 registrants.

The next step was the appointment of the draft boards for the several counties and two district appeal boards. In the least populous counties one republican and one democrat were named as members, and these two plus the county physician constituted the county draft board. Cabell County by reason of its larger population had three boards organized on a bi-partisan basis. These boards were charged with the duty of classifying registrants, passing on exemptions and the calling and inducting into the service the draftees from their respective counties.

The draft boards in Cabell County were composed of the following persons:

Territory outside of Guyandotte District: U. V. W. Darlington, Bishop of the M.E. Church, South, chairman, Barboursville; J. H. Harshbarger, Milton, and Dr. L. C. Morrison, Milton.

Huntington Division No. 1: John E. Norvell, chairman; E. E. Williams, and Dr. W. C. McGuire.

Huntington Division No. 2: Richard T. Everett, chairman; F. C. Leftwich, and Dr. C. T. Taylor.

In May, 1917, the first officers training camps were opened and approximately thirty young men from Cabell County volunteered and attended the training camp at Camp Benjamin Harrison. T. McK. Hays won the highest rank awarded to any West Virginian in this camp, namely, the rank of major of Infantry.

The first call was for September, 1917, and the men were sent to Camp Lee, Virginia, and became a part of the 80th Division. Cabell was one of three counties in the state whose volunteer enlistments in the National Guard exceeded her quota of the draft and did not furnish any men for the first draft. Cabell furnished for the war 1,796 men in addition to the volunteer enlistment in the National Guard. Of these, ninety were killed in action or died of wounds or disease.

The following officers and men from Cabell County were awarded decorations:

Colonel William H. Waldron, D.S.C., D.S.M. Citation for meritorious service, and the French Legion of Honor.

Second Lieutenant Walter V. Dial, D.S.C.

Captain Herman L. McNulty, D.S.C., Croix De Guerre.

First Lieutenant John C. Miller, Jr., D.S.C.

Private Herbert L. Howell, Citation in Orders.

First Lieutenant Charles E. Frampton, Croix De Guerre.

First Lieutenant James E. Moore, D.S.C.

Second Lieutenant Henry Winters Davis, D.S.C.

In addition to purely military activities in the county there were many civil activities and the government had the unstinted support of Cabell citizens. There was the organization of Four-Minute Men, of which H. A. Zeller was chairman, and Robert L. Archer and John B. Stevenson, associate chairmen; the local Council of Defense; Liberty Loan drives; War Savings Stamps; food and fuel administrations; Red Cross and numbers of other activities and, last but not least, the canteen service of which Mrs. D. A. Mossman was chairman and which operated a canteen at the railroad station. Men going and coming from the front have pleasant recollections of the help and hospitality of this canteen.

XV: THE MILITIA

VIRGINIA in the *Bill of Rights* of 1776 affirmed the proposition that "a well regulated militia composed of the body of people trained to arms is the proper, natural, and safe defense of a free state." In furtherance of this principle on December 22, 1792, the General Assembly passed an act regulating the militia of the Commonwealth. Under the provisions of this law Cabell County constituted a single regiment of a minimum strength of 300 men designated as the 120th Regiment of Militia of Cabell County. Later this county became a part of a brigade with the counties of Botetourt, Greenbrier, Bath, Kanawha, Nicholas, Mason, and Rockbridge. The officers of the militia were nominated by the County Court to the governor who made the appointments. The county was then subdivided into company districts and the commanding officers of companies were required to enroll every able-bodied white male citizen between the ages of eighteen and forty-five years with certain exceptions within their respective districts. The term of service when called into service was six months after the arrival at the rendezvous. Musters were held in the months of April and October annually and were great events. Musters were the time and place when the young cocks demonstrated their fistic abilities. The records of the County Court of Cabell County prior to May 3, 1814, are missing and we have no record of the nomination of militia officers prior to that date but the State Roster of Soldiers, War 1812-14 discloses that two majors and a colonel were commissioned in Cabell County in 1809 and 1813, respectively, and in the archive office in Richmond, Virginia, is a certified copy of an order made by the County Court, to-wit:

At a Court continued for Cabell County on Wednesday the 3d day of June, 1812, Present Thomas Ward, Elisha McComas, Mark Russell, Manoah Bostick, Daniel France, Henry Haynie, James Holanbey, and Noah Scales, Gentlemen Justices of the Peace in and .... the county aforesaid, being a majority of the Acting Magistrates of said County—

Ordered that William Spurlock be recommended as Ensign of the Militia of the 120th Regiment under Capt. Daniel France, William McComas, Jun Ensign under Captain Noah Scales, Stephen Wilson, Ensign under Captain William Buffington, Jesse Toney, Ensign under Capt. Peter Dingess & Thomas Morris, Ensign under Captain Cadwallader Chapman—To His Excellency the Governor and Council of this Commonwealth. A Copy.

Teste   EDWARD MORRIS, C.C.

The first nominations of militia officers of which there is a record in the clerk's office are those made by the County Court at the meeting of May 3, 1814, when the court nominated as officers of the 120th Regiment, Isaac Boult, captain; William Spurlock, lieutenant, and William Price, ensign. On August 2d following it nominated Daniel Morgan to fill the office of captain of a rifle company in the 120th Regiment in the room of Captain John Simons.

From these earlier records it is apparent that although Cabell County was the area for a regiment it apparently had one company of infantry and one of cavalry, and this conclusion is reached for the reason that the nominations of officers were for captain, lieutenant and ensign, an infantry company, and a captain, lieutenant and cornet, a cavalry company. The changes of the commissioned personnel were frequent and without the original regimental or company set-up it would be difficult to work up from these records a regimental roster. At a court held May 27, 1817, there is quite a list of nominations which follow:

John Smith, recommended as major in the room of Samuel Smiley, removed.

Thomas Morris, captain, in the room of Cadwallader Chapman, resigned.

Calvary Morris, lieutenant, in the room of Thomas Morris, promoted.

Andrew I. Chapman, first lieutenant, in the room of Nathaniel Everett, resigned.

Thomas McCallister, second lieutenant, in the room of George Chapman, resigned.

John Simple, cornet, in the room of Andrew I. Chapman, promoted.

Daniel Spurlock, captain, in the room of Achilles McGinnis, removed.

John McGinnis, ensign, in the room of Daniel Spurlock, promoted.

James Buffington, lieutenant in the place of Levi McCormick, who did not accept his commission.

Hansford Haney, ensign, in the room of James Buffington, promoted.

William Spurlock, captain, in the room of John Smith, promoted.

Samuel F. Clark, in the room of William Spurlock, promoted.

James Mays, ensign, in the room of Samuel F. Clark, promoted.

On May 26, 1818, William Buffington, who was a member of

THE MILITIA   99

the County Court was nominated to fill the office of colonel of the 120th Regiment, and Elisha McComas was made brigadier general, 22d Brigade, which was a part of the 5th Division.

Buffington resigned in 1825 and was succeeded by James Toney. How long Toney continued as colonel does not appear, but early in 1842 Joseph J. Mansfield was colonel and continued as such until sometime in the year 1846. Joseph Jefferson Mansfield, born in Bedford County, Virginia, was a lawyer but when Wayne County was cut off from Cabell his home was in Wayne County and this fact probably caused him to give up his commission as colonel. However, he immediately organized the Fairview Rifle Guards and at the outbreak of the Civil War he cast his lot with the Confederacy and was present at the skirmish at Barboursville, but before he was mustered into the service he reached Scary and took part in that battle where he was wounded and died before reaching home. The first intimation his wife had of his injury was when his body was brought home on a wagon. Colonel Mansfield married Amanda F. Smith and had two daughters—Columbia L. and America F., and three sons—William L., many years an editor, John Fletcher, and Joseph J., the congressman from Texas.

The militia act provided for both battalion and regimental Courts of Enquiry. These courts were primarily to impose fines incurred under the provisions of the act but they were given certain administrative powers and duties. By 1846 there were at least six companies in Cabell County and a musty record of the proceedings of the 1st and 2d battalion and regimental Courts of Enquiry of the 120th Regiment discloses the fact that the 120th Regiment consisted of two battalions with regimental, field, staff, and line officers as follows:

Colonel John B. McGinnis, October 16, 1846.
Lieutenant Colonel Henry W. Shelton.
Major Jerome Shelton.
Adjutant Aaron F. McKendree.
Sergeant Major H. J. Samuels.
Surgeon Henry B. Maupin.
Surgeon's Mate P. H. McCullough.
Paymaster Charles L. Roffe.
Quartermaster P. C. Buffington.
Provost Marshal Horatio H. Wood.
Clerk Thomas Thornburg.
The 1st Battalion consisted of the following companies: Captains

H. W. Shelton, James Wilson, James H. Brown, Sam W. Johnson, Thomas E. Hannon, R. N. B. Thompson, Samuel A. Childers.

Captains: Jerome Shelton, Allen I. Holstein, Ballard McComas, Jones Roberts, Allen Love.

A list of the places and time of musters were as follows:

No. 1—Sampson Johnson, General McComas', first Saturday, April, October.
No. 2—Jones Roberts, James Garrett's.
No. 3—Allen I. Holstein, James T. Carroll's, first Saturday, April, October.
No. 4—Everett Feazel, Isaac McComas', first Saturday, April, October.
No. 5—Thos. E. Hannon, John Hannon's, first Saturday, April, October.
No. 6—William Johnston, James Gallaher's, first Saturday, April, October.
No. 7—Thomas Turner, Guyandotte, third Saturday, April, October.
No. 8—Johnson Lusher, Barboursville, second Saturday, April, October.
No. 9—R. N. B. Thompson, John Morris', second Saturday, April, October.
No. 10—Edmund C. Rece, Adam Black's, third Saturday, April, October.
No. 11—Samuel Johnson, Barboursville, second Saturday, April, October.
No. 12—Sam A. Childers, Barboursville, second Saturday, April, October.

This record discloses that the court convened November 14, 1847, but adjourned on account of no quorum and met again on November 20, 1847. It was composed of the following officers:

Major Jerome Shelton, president; Captain Edmund C. Rece, Captain Sampson Johnson, Lieutenant John Forth, Captain William E. Feazell, and Captain Allen I. Holstein.

The record refers to both spring and fall petit musters and the regimental musters. Just what the petit musters mean is not clear. Entries made on the dates set out above are of interest.

Meeting of September 7, 1848:

Whereas, the adjutant general hath requested of the 120th Regiment in the County of Cabell that they report to him what number of militia fall in the county of Putnam and what would be the strength of the 120th Regiment if the militia of the County of Putnam should be formed into a new Regiment. Therefore, we a board of officers of the 120th Regt. of the Virginia Infantry of the line called for that purpose do certify that from the best information we can obtain that the number of persons within the limits of the County of Putnam subject to military duty taken from the county of Cabell to be fifty-two rank and file, and that that portion of the said 120th Regt. within the County of Cabell will exceed eight hundred rank and file, and it is ordered that the clerk of this board do immediately after the rising Thereof make out a true copy of this order and certify the same in due form to the adjutant General of Virginia.

Meeting of November 17, 1849:

Ordered that John Garrett be allowed $2.00 per day for his services as Drummer two days to-wit at the April and October muster of Capt. Becket's Company during the present year amounting to $4.00.

Ordered that Lieut. G. W. Summers be fined for failing to attend the Battallion Court of Enquiry $1.00.

Meeting of November 16, 1850:

Ordered that Lt. Col. Henry W. Shelton be fined for conduct unbecoming an officer and a gentleman on the day of the Regimental muster, the sum of $5.00.

At the last meeting November 19th, 1853, it was ordered that the court adjourn sine die. Why this adjournment without day does not appear but the fact is that about that time the powers of the Court of Enquiry were limited to disciplinary measures and perhaps that accounts for this entry. The earliest of the militia acts provided for volunteer companies, under certain restrictions, for drafts and for the hiring of substitutes. After West Virginia was created a State it adopted the militia system of Virginia and Cabell became a part of the 7th Brigade of the 2nd Division and the first act dealing with the subject limited musters to not more than three days in all in any calendar year. In 1889 the state adopted an act which made all male citizens between ages of eighteen and forty-five subject to military duty and provided for an active militia to be organized and designated as the West Virginia National Guard. The inactive militia was not enrolled but a provision was made for an enrollment to be made by the assessors when ordered by the governor. This act prohibited any independent or volunteer organization other than the National Guard. Immediately after the passage of this act a number of National Guard companies were organized. These continued in service as State organizations until the amendment of the National Defense Act two years ago which created the National Guard of the United States which is made up of the National Guard of the several states.

XVI: THE NATIONAL GUARD

IN 1886 the Huntington Light Infantry was organized with the following officers and non-commissioned officers: Captain W. H. Lyons, First Lieutenant H. E. Mathews, Second Lieutenant W. H. Banks, B. B. Harding, Edw. B. Enslow, C. H. Ricketts, B. L. Priddie, C. C. Hay, Ed. F. Lacock, Warren (Reddy) Wood, and Robt. L. Archer.

The ladies of the city presented the new company with a flag and the presentation took place in the Davis Opera House. The company had its armory and drill hall in the Poage Skating Rink on 12th Street and 4th Avenue. The company was disbanded in the year 1889 when private military organizations were prohibited by law.

The act establishing the National Guard and prohibiting all other military organizations was a tremendous advance over the old militia system. It provided an opportunity for young men to secure the rudiments of military training which was taken advantage of by a large number of patriotic men. The term of enlistment was five years and the State provided arms and equipment for the enlisted men and made the officers an allowance of $15.00 per year for a uniform. Organizations were required to drill a certain number of hours each year and to attend annual encampments for a period of ten days. Officers and men received no pay except for the time spent at the annual encampments. Company commanders were allowed $15.00 per quarter for clerical help. The first annual encampment was at Gypsy Grove near Clarksburg in 1891.

The first National Guard company organized in Huntington was in 1889 and designated as Company I, 2nd Infantry. It was mustered into service with the following commissioned and non-commissioned officers: Captain Thos. E. Hodges, First Lieutenant W. H. Banks, Second Lieutenant T. W. Peyton, First Sergeant George I. Neal, C. H. Ricketts, Robt. L. Archer, James E. Verlander, C. W. Cole, and D. W. (Pete) Frampton.

Hodges was succeeded by Banks as captain and Banks was followed by T. W. Peyton who in turn was succeeded by James E. Verlander. Hodges and Banks each served through the successive grades and in turn each was colonel of the 2nd Infantry.

In 1892 Company G, 2nd Infantry, was organized with Captain W. H. Lyons, First Lieutenant J. E. Middleton and Second Lieutenant

Strother S. Hay. Captain Lyons was promoted to major and was succeeded by I. H. Sabel.

On April 15, 1893, Company F located at Milton was mustered into service by Colonel Thomas E. Hodges. Milton at that time was only a village and this company was the first uniformed body of men in that community since the Civil War. The company officers were Captain M. L. Howes, First Lieutenant B. L. Nevill, and Second Lieutenant W. O. Wills. Captain Howes resigned in 1894 and was succeeded by D. L. Irwin who was promoted to major in 1895 when B. L. Perry was promoted to captain and continued in command until 1906 when the company was mustered out.

In 1895 the 2nd Regiment Band was organized with Edouard Lindemann as director. In the first band were Herbert McMillen, W. K. Cowden, Robert C. Ward, C. F. Wilcoxen, Robert Shore, Howard Gibson, R. A. Sang, George L. Shore, Robert T. Gladstone, and many other good fellows. Lindemann was discharged January 15, 1900, and was succeeded by Lewis S. Sievers who continued until May 19, 1901, when the band was mustered out. It was reorganized June 18, 1903, with Rhinehart A. Sang as the chief musician. Sang served continuously until September 23, 1908, when the band was mustered out.

At the time Coxey's Army marched on Washington, Kelly's Division took over a Chesapeake and Ohio Railroad train at Catlettsburg and intended to use it on to Washington. Companies I and G were called out and sent to Kenova at which point they captured Kelly's Division and escorted them out of the State.

Companies F, G, and I were called into service during the industrial disturbances in 1894 and 1895 in Kanawha and Fayette counties, and at Boggs' Run near Wheeling.

In 1896 and again in 1902 state encampments were held in Huntington.

At the outbreak of the Spanish-American War, Company I with Captain J. E. Verlander, First Lieutenant C. W. Cole, and Second Lieutenant F. W. Lester, and Company G with Captain I. H. Sabel, First Lieutenant R. M. Connor, and Second Lieutenant A. F. Van Fleet volunteered for service. Colonel Banks accepted a commission as major and Major Lyons and Captain Sabel accepted commissions in a lower grade.

It is not out of place to say that during this period the National Guard officer worked under many handicaps but was an earnest and enthusiastic citizen soldier. He gave much of his time and efforts to his organization and the country did not then and perhaps has not yet realized the debt it owes to them for unselfish service rendered. The enlisted personnel must not be overlooked, particularly when we keep in mind the fact that they were called upon to enforce law and order in industrial disturbances when the right or wrong of the quarrel was not always on the side of their sympathies. It can truly be said that it was the ambition of both the commissioned and enlisted personnel to prepare themselves for active service and this they did in spite of handicaps. The record made by the local companies when called out to aid civil authorities proved their worth to the State and the promptness with which they volunteered in 1898 demonstrated that they could be relied on in a national emergency.

At the conclusion of the Spanish-American War the National Guard officers who had volunteered for service therein were restored to the active list and set about promptly to reorganize their respective companies. Company I was reorganized with J. E. Verlander as captain, C. W. Cole as first lieutenant, and F. W. Lester as second lieutenant. Company G with I. H. Sabel as captain and Charles Gilmore as first lieutenant, and Thomas B. Davis as second lieutenant.

In the fall of 1899 a new company designated as Company H was organized with Fred W. Lester as captain, Herbert C. McMillen as first lieutenant, and B. R. Myers as second lieutenant.

In 1902 Companies G, H, and I were called out on account of industrial disturbances in Fayette County.

On January 21, 1903, in the Dick Bill, Congress for the first time made mention of the National Guard of the several states but treated it as the organized militia and designated all other male citizens of the several states between the ages of eighteen and forty-five as the reserve militia. The bill provided that the organization armament and discipline of the organized militia (National Guard) was in five years to be the same as those features of the regular army; that the guard was to be paid during its activities and was required to participate in practice marches or go into camps of instruction for five consecutive days and to assemble for drill at least twenty-four times during the year; and provided for the detail of regular officers at camps of instruction and as inspectors and instructors for the several states. Captain I. C. Jenks, a splendid soldier, was the first inspector and instructor in West Virginia under this act.

The bill was received with enthusiasm by the guard officers, and while it was a step in the right direction for the training and discipline of the guard, yet the guard as an organization was still militia and was subject to the constitutional limitations as to its use. The militia of the several States when called into service can only be used to uphold the law, to suppress insurrections and to repel invasions.

In 1904 the guard companies attended the first national maneuvers held under the auspices of the regular army at Manassas, Virginia, and every second year thereafter they attended such maneuvers as follows: Mt. Gretna in 1906, Benjamin Harrison in 1908, Gettysburg in 1910. In 1912 they were en route to maneuvers but were recalled on account of industrial disturbances.

In 1901 Captain Verlander of Company I was promoted to major and was succeeded by I. J. Davies who was followed by J. L. Graham who in turn was followed by George S. Wallace. Major Verlander was placed on the supernumerary list on December 31, 1911. I. H. Sabel was promoted to major on January 1, 1901, and was succeeded by T. B. Davis. Major I. H. Sabel resigned on December 27, 1909.

From 1908 to 1911 the State had a lease on the Thornburg farm between the Chesapeake and Ohio Railroad and the hill at 5th Street, West, and had thereon a 600 yard rifle range. In 1927 a rifle range for the several Huntington units was constructed on Route 52, six miles south of the city. The cost of the range as well as the rentals are paid by the Federal government.

In 1910 the three local companies were ordered out on account of an incipient riot at the courthouse occasioned by a demonstration of threatened violence against a man named Tom Wayne who had assaulted a woman in Fayette County. He had been saved from mob violence in Fayette and Summers counties by Captain S. L. Walker who, with Company F had brought the prisoner to the Cabell jail for safekeeping. In the early evening a mob began to form around the courthouse and the police and fire departments were called out to disperse them. The fire department attempted to turn the hose on the mob but the mob cut the hose. The situation began to look serious so Mayor Chapman and the sheriff called on the National Guard companies to support the civil authorities. The companies turned out promptly and Company I was the first on the scene. Major J. E. Verlander was in command and order was soon restored. However, the companies remained on duty in the courthouse yard for several days.

Captain Davis was promoted to major on the 27th day of June,

1910 and was succeeded by First Lieutenant C. F. Templeton who remained with the company only a few weeks when he resigned and accepted his old commission as first lieutenant and battalion adjutant. Captain F. W. Lester who had been placed on the supernumerary list on June 27, 1910 was restored to the active list and was placed in command of Company G. First Lieutenant Herbert C. McMillen was promoted to captain of Company H in June, 1910 and continued with this company until the 15th day of June, 1915, when he was promoted to major and was succeeded by Captain A. M. Sikes. Captain George S. Wallace was promoted to lieutenant colonel on the 1st day of October, 1910, and was succeeded by Ira J. Barbour.

In 1912 there were the three companies G, H and I located in Huntington and each occupied a separate armory and none of the armories were suitable to be designated by the name of armory. Lieutenant Colonel George S. Wallace brought about a contract with G. N. Biggs under the terms of which Mr. Biggs agreed to furnish a lot fronting one hundred and fifty feet on 5th Avenue between 1st and 2nd Streets and $18,000.00 in money to be used in the construction of an armory and to rent the premises to the State for $2,500.00 per year. At the end of a ten year period the State had the right to purchase the lot and the improvements thereon at the price of $25,000.00, plus a step-up in the value of the lot. Plans for the armory were drawn by R. F. Carson without charge and bids were taken. It was soon apparent that this building could not be completed for $18,000.00. To meet this situation Wallace extended an invitation to the two political parties to hold their nominating conventions in the city of Huntington in the new bulding which was not then under way. The advantages of having a permanent drill hall, 80 x 150 feet, was shown to the Chamber of Commerce and it went out and raised $5,000.00. This added to the $18,000.00 advanced by Mr. Biggs was sufficient to complete the drill hall and the exterior of the administration portion of the building. The two state conventions were held in the drill hall and the advantage of investing the $5,000.00 in a permanent hall rather than in a temporary wigwam was apparent to all. The guard companies moved into the new armory and by their own efforts raised funds to complete the interior of the administration building. In the flood of 1913 the armory was used to house refugees.

In 1921 the State of West Virginia exercised the option and took over the property for $33,000.00. A legislative committee visited the property before the appropriation was passed to make the purchase and the estimates this committee had as to the value of the property disclosed that the building alone could not be replaced for $75,000.00 at that time.

In midsummer 1912 the companies had started to Gettysburg for the national maneuvers when they were called back to Paint Creek because of industrial disturbances. Lieutenant Colonel George S. Wallace was made acting judge advocate general and Major Thomas B. Davis was named provost marshal. Martial law was proclaimed on three different occasions. While the companies returned home at intervals they were in almost continuous service for twelve months. During this period the officers demonstrated their efficiency and the discipline of the enlisted men was of the best.

In 1914 the guard was excused from national maneuvers on account of the field service rendered the State but it attended camp at Caddell.

Captain Lester was placed on the supernumerary list on February 13, 1913, and Valkey W. Midkiff succeeded him as captain of Company G. In 1914 a machine gun company was authorized in Huntington and C. F. Templeton was commissioned as captain. H. H. Rice who was a major in the J. A. G. department was designated by the adjutant general's office to and did take active charge of this organization. When the guard was ordered to the border in 1916 Templeton resigned his commission and accepted a commission as first lieutenant and continued in that grade. Rice was commissioned as major of infantry and the command of the machine gun company passed to an officer at Charleston.

In 1916 Congress passed the National Defense Act and again dealt with the National Guard, providing for its increase and pay for its personnel. This act gave the President express authority when authorized by Congress to use the land forces to draft the National Guard into the service of the United States. This was done in the World War. Before this act became effective the Huntington companies were called into Federal service on the Mexican Border.

When the National Guard was drafted into the Federal service on August 4, 1917, the commissioned personnel was transferred to the supernumerary list and the period of enlistment of the enlisted personnel continued to run while the enlisted man was in the United States service with the result that at the end of the war the term of enlistment of the enlisted men had expired and the guard officers who were restored to the active list were confronted with the problem of reorganization. The reaction following the war made it difficult to secure recruits and Huntington was no exception.

From 1919 to 1922 quite a number of persons interested themselves in an attempt to reorganize the guards but without success. On February 19, 1922, Captain Ira J. Barbour was restored to the active list and undertook the job and succeeded. He was assisted by Captain Lewis Simons, U. S. A., who was stationed at Charleston until 1923, when he was brought to Huntington, where he remained for two years. At the end of Captain Simons' detail the War Department reduced the regular personnel on duty with the guard to one officer with each regiment.

The new units at Huntington were to be a part of the 150th Infantry and the first organization authorized was the Headquarters Company on June 24, 1923, with Captain August C. Reinwald, commander. This company was federally recognized on June 24, 1924, but was mustered out in Huntington on June 15, 1927.

The Headquarters Company of the 3rd Battalion was authorized on May 28, 1923, and federally recognized on June 7, 1923, with First Lieutenant Henry A. Ackerman in command. Ackerman was succeeded by First Lieutenant George E. Pollard on February 8, 1924, who is still in command and has as his Second Lieutenant Edwin L. Murrill.

The 3rd Battalion Headquarters was organized on December 4, 1923, and Captain Barbour was promoted to major on that date.

The above named organizations were the first organizations to be paid under the provisions of the National Defense Act.

Company I was reorganized on March 4, 1924, with Captain Charles F. Burrill, First Lieutenant C. N. Rogers and Second Lieutenant W. B. Henderson. Its present officers are Captain Arthur S. Stuart, First Lieutenant C. N. Rogers, and Second Lieutenant Hubert Stuart.

Company K was organized October 10, 1924, with Captain C. N. Rogers, First Lieutenant Harley H. Thompson, and Second Lieutenant C. E. Copen. Its present officers are Captain Henry Clay Cox, First Lieutenant Paul L. Webb, and Second Lieutenant Chester Carter.

The Medical Detachment was organized and federally recognized June 14, 1927, with Captain Robert S. Van Metre who is still in command.

Huntington is represented on the National Guard staff by Major

THE NATIONAL GUARD

Harley H. Thompson, S. S. C. and D ordnance, and Major Fred O. Mitchell, S. S. C. and D., Q.M.

In 1924 the local companies went to Camp Knox for maneuvers with the 38th Division of which the 150th Infantry is a part. The next two years there was a State camp at Charleston. In 1927 a permanent camp was purchased in Mason County near Point Pleasant, and since then these companies have gone there for field training.

On June 4, 1920, the National Defense Act was amended and provided that the army of the United States was to consist of the Regular Army and the National Guard when called into service. This amendment still did not change the National Guard from a State to a Federal organization and there was an attempt to overcome this difficulty by commissioning guard officers in the Reserve Corps, but Congress in the exercise of the powers under the Constitution to raise and support armies, in 1933 passed an act creating the National Guard of the United States to be composed of the personnel of the National Guard of the several states. The result of this act is that every officer and enlisted man of the National Guard has a dual status, one as a State organization subject to the control of the governor as commander-in-chief; and a second and paramount status —a national organization subject to the control of the President as commander-in-chief.

In this act the faithful guardsmen have their reward—they are truly a part of the army of the United States.

In 1934 a radio station WLHB was built in the armory as a FERA project.

XVII: UNITED STATES ENGINEERS

THE U. S. Engineers, Huntington District, was established July 1, 1922. This district was formed by consolidating the former Wheeling District and the Cincinnati (Ohio), Second District. The new district was placed in charge of Major Malcolm Elliott, Corps of Engineers, who served from July 1, 1922, to August 12, 1922. The following is a list of succeeding officers with their terms of duty:

Major Milo P. Fox, Corps of Engineers, August 12, 1922, to April 19, 1923.

Major Wm. P. Stokey, Corps of Engineers, April 20, 1923, to June 30, 1923.

Major Harry M. Trippe, Corps of Engineers, June 30, 1923, to May 26, 1927.

Major E. D. Ardery, Corps of Engineers, May 27, 1927, to October 9, 1930.

Major Fred W. Herman, Corps of Engineers, October 10, 1930, to August 1, 1934.

Major John F. Conklin, Corps of Engineers, August 1, 1934, to date.

The district was originally under the supervision of the Upper Mississippi Valley Division (Ohio River Sector) with Colonel George R. Spalding, Corps of Engineers, in charge as division engineer. Effective December 1, 1933, the Ohio River Division was established with headquarters at Cincinnati, Ohio. The Huntington District was withdrawn from the Upper Mississippi Valley Division and transferred to the Ohio River Division on this date, with Lieutenant Colonel R. G. Powell, Corps of Engineers, as division engineer.

This district embraces those portions of the states of Ohio, Kentucky, West Virginia, North Carolina, and Pennsylvania, lying in the drainage basins of the Ohio River and tributaries from about mile 109 between Captina Island and Powhatan Point, Ohio, to about mile 317.5 just below the mouth of Big Sandy River, Kentucky, a distance of about 208.5 miles, including the following streams improved for slack-water navigation: Ohio River, West Virginia, with its locks and dams Nos. 14 to 28, inclusive; Little Kanawha River, West Virginia; Kanawha River, West Virginia; Big Sandy River, West Virginia, and Kentucky, including Tug and Levisa Forks.

The operating and care of the Muskingum River, Ohio, was under the jurisdiction of this district to June 30, 1934, at which time this river was transferred to the Zanesville, Ohio, District.

During the period 1922 to 1928, the activities of the district were confined entirely to maintenance and operating and care of completed locks and dams, and open channel dredging for the purpose of maintaining a nine-foot project depth. The office force during this period averaged about twenty-five employees annually.

In 1928-29 additional work was assigned to the district in the nature of examinations and surveys of the tributaries of the Ohio River with the view to flood control, power development, irrigation and navigation. These additional duties required an increase of about thirty-five employees in the technical forces of the district office.

From about 1931 to date a large amount of construction work has been under way on the Kanawha River, involving the replacement of ten old locks and dams with three new high-lift roller dams. This work has involved a large increase in both the technical and clerical forces of the district office, the average number of employees having grown to about 112 annually.

UNITED STATES RECRUITING OFFICERS

The country surrounding Huntington and the city itself has always been a recruiting point for the United States Army. The recruiting office was opened here just before the Spanish-American War with First Lieutenant W. H. Johnson as the recruiting officer. He was assigned to the 2d United States Infantry in the early part of 1898 but before he joined his regiment he sent a great number of recruits from this neighborhood to that regiment. Lieutenant Johnson afterwards became a general officer.

The next recruiting officer was Second Lieutenant W. E. Cole who is now a general officer. Among the men who have served in this capacity are Colonel Joseph Garred of the cavalry, Laurence Halstead, now a colonel on the general staff; E. H. Agnew, D.S.C., afterwards colonel of infantry and served with the 3d Division, A.E.F.; First Lieutenant Fred W. Bugbee, one time Rough Rider and later colonel in command of the 30th Infantry in the Siberian Expedition. The recruiting office is still here but there is no commissioned officer with it.

XVIII: THE ORGANIZED RESERVES

THE National Defense Act of 1916 provided for an Officers Reserve Corps but only a few men were commissioned therein before the World War. George S. Wallace was the first man in Cabell County commissioned in this corps, and perhaps the first man commissioned in the State. He was commissioned as a major in the J.A.G. Reserve Corps in November, 1916, along with five other lawyers which included Eugene Wambaugh of Harvard, and J. H. Wigmore of Northwestern University. After the close of the World War the government set about seriously to develop this organization and a great number of men who had held commissions in the World War were commissioned in the reserve corps. Just after the Armistice in 1918 the 100th Division* was organized at Camp Bowie, Texas, and this division was assigned to an area which included the State of West Virginia and was included in the Fifth Corps Area. In the beginning its headquarters were located at Charleston, with Lieutenant Colonel J. W. Leonard as the first chief of staff. On March 1, 1924, the headquarters were moved to Huntington with Lieutenant Colonel Allen Parker as chief of staff. On the first day of September, 1924, Colonel W. H. Waldron, one of Cabell's native sons, was chief of staff. Under Colonel Waldron's leadership this organization got away with a flying start. The training for reserve officers includes school one night each week conducted by the officers attached to the headquarters, a correspondence course and service with troops in the summer camps.

Commissions can be earned by men who complete the course at the C.M.T.C. and R.O.T.C. Specialists in various lines are commissioned in their particular fields without this training but are expected to take the fundamental training. Colonel Waldron at the completion of his detail had service with troops and a tour of duty in the War Department in Washington. During this time (from June 30, 1927, to October 1, 1933), Colonel Leon L. Roach was chief of staff with Colonel Pat Stevens as his assistant. Roach and Stevens were relieved on October 1, 1933, when Colonel Waldron came back as chief of staff with Major J. K. Cockrell as assistant.

There are approximately one hundred reserve officers located in and near Huntington and there is a local chapter of the Reserve Officers Association located here.

---

*The headquarters of the 100th Division were moved to Charleston at midnight, June 30, 1935.

XIX: UNITED STATES NAVAL COMMUNICATION RESERVES

ON July 5, 1932, the commandant, Fifth Naval District, Norfolk, Virginia, authorized the organization at Huntington, of Unit 2, United States Naval Commissioned Reserves to consist of four officers and twenty-seven enlisted men. Lieutenant (jg) W. G. McBride was designated as commanding officer. The primary purpose of the Naval Communication Reserves is to teach men to become radio operators. The enlisted personnel was soon secured and Marshall College, the Professional building on 4th Avenue, and the Cammack Junior High School were used in the order named for drill purposes. Then an arrangement was made and the unit used the National Guard armory but as the training required considerable class work this arrangement was not entirely satisfactory and the use of the Ohev Sholom Gymnasium was arranged.

This service made a popular appeal and two additional units, namely, Unit 4 and Unit 7, were authorized and were immediately recruited to full strength. The three units have a strength of twelve officers and eighty-one enlisted men.

In 1934 these organizations secured the use of the old elevator penthouse of the First Huntington National Bank Building for a radio station—receiving and transmitting—and were given a license by the Federal commission with the call N8MVF. In order to avail themselves of this license a code class has been organized which meets each Monday night for the training of radio operators.

In January, 1935, the FERA approved a project for the construction of a new transmitting and receiving station to cost $5,195.00.

The new postoffice building will include 1,835 square feet of space for these units and two fifty-foot radio towers which have been constructed as a part of the FERA project will be erected on the top of the building and put in use.

A number of the enlisted personnel of these units have been called into active duty and given additional training and graduated with the rate Radioman Third Class.

McBride continued as a commanding officer until the summer of 1934 when by reason of his taking employment at Charleston, he resigned his command.

By an order made on September 10, 1934, the personnel was reorganized with the following commissioned personnel:

Lieutenant (jg) R. E. Ramey, SC-V(S), USNR, commanding officer.

Lieutenant Paul H. Sanborn, E-V(S), USNR.

Lieutenant Daniel Wetzel, SC-V(S) USNR.

Lieutenant (jg) Kenneth Heyl, SC-V(S) USNR.

Lieutenant (jg) Lloyd A. Davis, E-V(S) USNR, executive officer and engineering officer.

Lieutenant (jg) James R. Brown, MC-V(G) USNR, medical officer.

Ensign Ray H. Honaker, C-V(S), USNR, communication officer.

Ensign Ernest C. Lawson, D-V(S) USNR, seamanship.

Ensign Hubert A. Hawes, SC-V(S), USNR, supply officer.

In addition to this personnel a number of the leading physicians in the community have accepted reserve commissions on the staff and have from time to time been called to active duty. This organization is full of enthusiasm and at the last two sessions of the Legislature has sponsored a bill to create a naval militia in the State but the bill failed of passage.

ROADS

The first problem in a new country is one of transportation and transportation primarily is roads. The first road from the east to what is now Cabell County and on to the west is now referred to as the State Road. Its location was generally the same as the road known as the James River and Kanawha Pike. It crossed the Guyandotte River at Barboursville and came down Pea Ridge to Russell Creek or below and swung around by what we know as the crossroads and came in by Spring Hill Cemetery, through the grounds of Marshall College and reached the Ohio River at a point later known as Brownsville—now about 5th Street, East—thence on to the Big Sandy and west. The genesis of the road is found in the act of 1780, which recites that the inhabitants of the county of Greenbrier "labor under great inconvenience for the want of a wagon road from their courthouse" to some place on the eastern waters from whence there was a wagon road to Richmond. The act authorized the justices of that county to open a wagon road from Greenbrier Courthouse, now Lewisburg, to the Warm Springs or to the wagon road at the mouth of the Cow Pasture. The taxpayer was given the right to pay this levy in money or hemp. A second act of October, 1782, was to the same effect.

In 1785 an act was passed appropriating certain arrears of taxes to opening a wagon road from Lewisburg to the Lower Falls of the Kanawha and accepting personal labor from the inhabitants in lieu of taxes and providing that the road was to be at least thirty feet wide. Finally in October, 1786, a road from the Falls of the Great Kanawha to Lexington in Kentucky was provided for and it is said this road reached the Ohio River before Cabell County was organized. Just how wide this road was we do not know but an order made by the County Court on April 26, 1830, required that all public roads be kept open twelve feet wide, with the exception of the road from the Big Sandy River to the Kanawha County line which was to be kept thirty feet wide from Guyandotte to the Kanawha line.

By 1831 over this road came a daily line of stages from Washington and Richmond to Guyandotte where there were steamboat connections on the river. Some time after this the citizens of Guyandotte built a road on the north side of the river to Barboursville. The State Road became the James River and Kanawha Road and later the James River and Kanawha Pike and is now Route 60, or the Midland Trail.

The Pike was four poles wide and was a first class road for the time. It had toll gates every four miles. Along this road streamed the emigrants going to the west, and to the east traveled drovers driving hogs, cattle and sometimes turkeys to the markets of the east. Hogs were half fattened when started from Kentucky and traveled about 8 miles per day and were fattened *en route*. The stage coaches drawn by four horses, carrying twelve or more passengers, thundering past the humbler vehicles and travelers were the aristocrats of the road.

With the completion of the Chesapeake and Ohio Railway the James River and Kanawha Pike fell into decay. Its right-of-way was encroached upon and in many places, particularly through West Huntington, it is occupied by the Chesapeake and Ohio Railway and apparently there is no map extant that shows its location.

In 1900-1908, the Chesapeake and Ohio Railway relocated its main line from Barboursville to the Putnam County line and in 1910 the County Court purchased this old right of way and used it as a part of this highway. After the State Highway Commission took over this road it relocated it in some places, widened the roadbed and hardsurfaced it so the old Pike, now Route 60, is again an east

The Adam Black House, built 1830. Long a tavern and a relay station on the James River

and west highway over which more people pass in a single day than did in a month in the halcyon days of old.

While the James River and Kanawha Pike was easily the most important road in the county, other roads meant equally as much to the folks who lived beside them and the County Court records abound with orders directing roads to be located from this point to that. By reason of the fact that such references are usually to a house or landmark that has long since disappeared no good idea can be formed now as to these roads. These early roads were primitive affairs, only trails, but Cabell County was abreast of the times at that early date and at the beginning of this century the question of good roads began to be urged and Cabell County promptly took the lead in this movement.

ROAD TO THE BIG SANDY

At an early date not fixed by the records there was a road from the mouth of the Guyandotte River to the west.

Across the mouth of the Guyandotte there was a ferry, as there was also across the Ohio, both owned by Thomas Buffington.

The county road from Guyandotte to Big Sandy was along the river banks, with large sycamore, elm, and other trees on the bank on both sides of the road. The early farmhouses were built near this road and the first below Guyandotte was that of the Buffingtons, then that of Robert Adams, then that of Jeffrey Russell, then James Buffington, who afterwards moved to Ohio, and John Russell took his place. Robert Adams' place went to Colonel William Buffington, afterwards to his daughter, Mrs. Judge Hagen. The Jeffrey Russell and John Russell farms went to Colonel William Buffington and afterwards to his son, Dr. John N. Buffington.

John Laidley, after the war in 1812, located in Cabell County, married Mary Scales Hite, and was the attorney for the commonwealth all his life. He bought the farm next below the Russell farm and moved there in February, 1828, and afterwards built thereon. This was known as the Neff place. Jacob Hite had purchased the farm next below and conveyed it to his brother, William Hite.

Dr. William Paine owned next below. Then came the property of Mrs. Lane, and then the farm of the Staley family.

In 1811-12 Henry Hampton sold to George and John Hollenback, two farms and (Dr. Henry) Hampton lived on the farm on which the academy was afterwards located, the James Holderby farm. Mark Russell purchased next below and lived the rest of his life thereon;

this passed to James Gallagher, afterwards to his son-in-law, James Harvey Poage.

The next farm below was that of Major Nathaniel Scales, which afterwards was the home of Frederick G. L. Beuhring.

Just below the Scales farm came that of Richard and Dr. Benjamin Brown. Richard sold out to the Doctor and moved to the forks of the Big Sandy, and Dr. Brown resided on his farm until his death in 1848, when this farm passed to Albert Laidley, who had married Vesta Brown. The farm next below was known as the Stribling farm.

Then came the farm of Captain Samuel Johnston, who purchased it of Henry Clark in 1849. Then came the farm of Isaac Johnston, and next was that of Alexander Pine, and then the farm of Mrs. Bellamy, and then Martin Hull, and then in order, William Poage, James Poage, James Negley, at the mouth of Four Pole, the McCormicks and Handleys, which took to the mouth of Twelve Pole Creek, and below are found Thomas L. Jordan and the Morgan Bottom to Big Sandy.

The river road was changed to the middle of the farms about 1833 or '34 and that accounts for some barns appearing in front of the houses.

GUYAN VALLEY ROAD

In 1808 a road was located along the Guyandotte River, from the mouth to the falls, and no doubt it was built piecemeal. While Sam Gideon was president of the County Court the southern portion of this road was located on its present route and it was hardsurfaced out of a bond issue of 1920.

LINCOLN COUNTY PIKE

The first mention of this road is an order made by the City of Huntington to build a road south from the Chesapeake and Ohio Railway through the Holderby and Shelton lands to the corporation line. The road was designated as the long route and a part of the Lincoln County Road. The County Court located the road south of the corporation line on February 17, 1888, and work was begun on July 2, 1888. For a long time it was a dirt road but its grade was regarded as very much better than the older roads and it was proudly referred to as the Pike. It was first paved in the city limits at the cost of the adjoining property owners, and was hardsurfaced beyond the city limits out of the proceeds of the 1920 million dollar bond issue.

MASON COUNTY ROAD

There was a road from Barboursville to the Mason County line by way of Merritt's Creek and Little Seven Mile, but it must have been a poor affair as the records are full of orders about its relocation and improvement. In 1841 William Jenkins was given permission to put gates across this road at one or more places at Hannon's Mills, and we also find the County Court trying to arrange for a bridge over Little Guyan as early as June 27, 1826. On June 23, 1845, John Hannon, William Jenkins, and Daniel Spurlock were named commissioners to contract for such a bridge but at a cost to this county not to exceed $100.00. Folks traveling from Guyandotte to Mason County used the river bank, water permitting, from a point about where the water works now are, then on the Stewart land, and came out on the Kyle place at Seven Mile and on the Barboursville-Mason County Road and from there north. There were many efforts made to build a road from Guyandotte to Little Seven Mile but these efforts did not go beyond the making of a report to the County Court until, on September 16, 1872, a road twelve feet wide was opened from Guyandotte to Files Branch.

In December, 1880, the County Court named Ed. Kyle, Dyke Bowen, and John W. Thornburg to locate a road from Guyandotte to the Mason County line. This was done and this road was let to contract the next year and completed in 1883. This road was hard-surfaced in 1912 but is now too narrow and is being widened by the State Road Commission.

MCCOY ROAD

At an early date there was a road known as the McCoy Road which went along what is now 14th Street, East, but at that time was on the east side of the Poage land. This road crossed Four Pole Creek and reached the top of the hill at a point about opposite the Shockey Knob, then on to Beach Fork and beyond. It was used extensively by the farmers from that section in traveling to the Holderby Landing at the foot of 16th Street. During this period there was a road which went through the 5th Street Gap which was then known as the Wayne Road. In 1884 a new road known as the Wayne Road was built by the city south on 8th Street and up the hill on its present location and intersected the old McCoy Road on top of the hill. The

McCoy Road was abandoned and the new road is sometimes referred to as the McCoy Road. This road was paved from Four Pole Creek to the corporation line with brick by the adjacent property owners. In 1920 it was included in the improvements being made by the State Road Commission and has been hardsurfaced its entire length and is now Route 8.

WATERWAYS

Surpassing in importance the roads, or perhaps more properly speaking trails, were the streams. Along the beds of the small streams that dried up in the summer the earlier settlers made their roads. When these small streams were full, they floated saw-logs and staves out to the main rivers. The smallest stream that would float logs was designated a floatable stream and so important were they to the welfare of the county that from an early date the State reserved from its grant the banks and beds of these streams for public use. The navigation of the smaller streams was improved by splash dams. The Ohio River is navigable in the truest sense and was the great highway to the west and the south. Steamboats came shortly after 1811 and this service was extended from Cincinnati to the mouth of the Big Sandy and the Guyandotte in 1831. There was the Hull landing at 14th Street, West, a landing at Brownsville (5th Street, East) and the Holderby Landing at 16th Street, and perhaps others between that point and the Guyandotte. Floods, or high waters as they are usually referred to, marked epochs in the lives of the people who lived along its banks. Floods that reached record breaking heights occurred in 1842, 1847, 1883, 1884, and 1913.

In 1848 the Board of Public Works of Virginia surveyed the Guyandotte River perhaps with a view of improving navigation thereon and in the following years the Guyandotte Navigation Company was chartered. The incorporators were J. W. Hite, P. S. Smith, H. H. Miller, N. S. Adams, A. M. Whitney, Jas. Emmons, W. C. Miller, John G. Miller, Irvin Lusher, J. L. Keller, Sampson Sanders, Solomon Thornburg, John Samuels, R. McKendree, and others. The capital for this company was furnished by outside people and the company built locks and dams in the Guyandotte River and there was navigation to Laurel Hill near Big Ugly in Logan County. The locks and dams in Cabell County were located at Everetts, now the Nickel Plant, at the mouth of Mud River, at Smith's Creek, Salt Rock, and the Falls of the Guyandotte. Captain Price who lived in Guyandotte had a steamboat named the *Major Adrian* which he used to bring out barges loaded with coal. This boat was sunk at Heath's Creek. He also owned and operated the *Louisa*, a two-deck boat. In 1855 the *R. H. Lindsey* began to run on a fixed schedule carrying freight and passengers. Sometime during this period Nick Longworth, who was the father of the man of the same name who was afterwards Speaker of the House, went up the river on his pleasure yacht as far as Laurel Hill. In 1862 United States troops were stationed at Barboursville and the Federal forces blew out the dam which was located at the Everett place so as to run flatboats to Barboursville for the purpose of transporting supplies. The blowing out of this dam put an end to slack water on the Guyandotte. However, the river continued to be used to some extent until the Guyan Valley Railroad was built. Pomp Wentz operated a small boat in the late 90's named the *J. T. Hutsler* and Captain George Godby had a boat built at Guyandotte which was named the *Guyandotte* and which he ran on that river as far up as Dusenberry Dam and when the water permitted he ran up to Big Ugly or Peck Shoals. This boat hauled supplies for the railroad contractors who were building the Guyan Valley branch and when the railroad was completed the *Guyandotte* was sold and went out on the big river. Millions of cubes of timber have been floated out of the Guyandotte River and in the early days the small landowners cut the timber off their own lands and rafted it down the river on timber tides. The arrival of these rafts at the mouth of the Guyandotte was the occasion of much business activity. The raftsmen were paid off and availed themselves of the pleasures of the city, and many stories are told of Doc Suiter—who was the town marshal of Guyandotte for many years—of his personal encounters with these raftsmen. In the later years the small landowners had cut off their timber and only the larger tracts of land remained to be cut. C. Crane and Company owned perhaps all of these larger tracts and was the big operator in the territory. At the beginning of the century it brought about the organization of the Guyan Boom Company which completed a boom about 1904 in the Guyandotte River near the mouth of Robey Branch. The practice was to brand the logs and roll them in the river and they would float down to the boom where they were caught and rafted and then taken in rafts down the Ohio River. C. Crane and Company ceased operations and H. C. Everett in 1917 blew out the boom and timbering ceased to be of importance. When the present bridge over the Guyandotte River at 3d Avenue was under construction there was a high water and a

Wharfboat, circa 1893

[122]

big run of logs on June 14, 1907, which took the bridge off its piers and set it on the bank at 31st Street. The boom company was required to pay $8,000.00 damages on this account.

The Guyandotte River now is not used but some of us foresee that with the locks and dams on the Ohio River today, in the future the Guyandotte River will be locked to make it navigable to Barboursville so that the land on either side of the river can be utilized for manufacturing sites with water transportation available.

THE OHIO RIVER

This river has always been the great thoroughfare of the several states which border thereon, and its history can not be included as a part of this work. But the river has had a part and will continue to have a part in the development of this community.

As we have seen there was a line of steamboats which made connection with the stage-coaches at Guyandotte as early as 1831 and river traffic, particularly passenger traffic, continued to grow until 1889 when the Chesapeake and Ohio Railway opened its new line along the Ohio River to Cincinnati. This event marked the end of passenger travel on the river except in a small way. The freight business continued in a modest way and then came the locks and dams with the nine foot stage. The passenger business has not come back as it was in the early days but many people are using the river for pleasure trips. The freight traffic is larger than ever before in the history of the river and is growing by leaps and bounds.

Between the date the Chesapeake and Ohio Railway reached Huntington and the time it extended its line to Cincinnati, it built two coal tipples and a grain elevator on the river. The first coal tipple was at the foot of 19th Street and the second one above the Ensign plant. The coal cars were run over to the river's edge and dumped into the barges. The grain elevator was used to transfer grain from the river boats to cars for train shipment east.

In 1905 James C. Beebe who was then connected with the United States Coal and Oil Company, which owned and operated the mines which are now owned by the Island Creek Coal Company, organized the Guyan Valley Fuel Company for the purpose of transporting coal by river from Huntington to points south. This company erected a coal tipple and ice-breaker at the foot of 14th Street, East, and began operations in 1906. At that time the towboats and barges were of wooden construction and the barges had a capacity of 450 tons. These barges could not be used for about three months in each year on account of the low water and during these years the volume of coal transported was less than 100,000 tons a year.

In 1915 the water stage in the river had been raised by the completion of a number of dams and this company whose name had then been changed to the Island Creek Fuel Company began to replace the wooden barges with steel barges of one thousand ton capacity and the towboats were replaced with boats of steel construction. By 1920 the Island Creek Coal Company which had taken over the Island Creek Fuel Company destroyed the last wooden barges.

In 1924 the Philadelphia and Cleveland Coal Company erected a coal terminal at the foot of 26th Street, East, and began transporting coal for anyone who cared to ship it to Huntington for transhipment by water. Some years later the West Virginia Coal and Coke Corporation who owned the properties at Omar which formerly belonged to the Main Island Creek Coal Company purchased this tipple and had it transferred to a subsidiary company named the Ohio River Company and this plant is now used exclusively by the parent company. At this writing there is in excess of two million tons of coal shipped annually from the Logan coal fields to Huntington and loaded over these tipples into barges for transportation to river points.

Some years ago there was a movement to secure a river and rail terminal at Huntington, but some opposition developed and the project has been dropped for the present.

XX: RAILROADS

THE Board of Public Works of Virginia planned the construction of a railroad from Covington, to the Ohio River, to be known as the Covington and Ohio Railroad. As early as September 24, 1853, it began to condemn land in this county for its rights-of-way. In 1861 some portions of its rights-of-way were graded and the piers for the bridge over the Guyandotte River were begun, but the work was stopped because of the Civil War. Up to that time the State had expended $3,000,000.00. At the close of the war the State of Virginia had been divided and the completion of the Covington and Ohio Railroad was a matter to be arranged by the States of Virginia and West Virginia. "Each state then passed an identical act to incorporate the Chesapeake and Ohio Railroad Company and the commissioners were appointed whose duty it was to offer the benefits of the charter to capitalists. . . . The acts passed by the States of Virginia and West Virginia authorized the Virginia Central Railroad Company to contract with the commissioners of the two states for the undertaking of the work which was to be done in the name of the Chesapeake and Ohio Railroad Company." The contract was duly made and executed on the 30th day of August, 1868, on behalf of the State of Virginia and by James Burley, Z. D. Ramsdell, Joel McPherson, and John S. Cunningham, commissioners of West Virginia and by E. Fontaine, president of the Virginia Central Railroad.

General Williams C. Wickham became the president of the new company and he interested Collis P. Huntington who served as its president from 1869 to 1888.

On April 4, 1868, the Board of Supervisors submitted a proposal to the voters that the county subscribe to $150,000.00 of the capital stock of the Chesapeake and Ohio Railroad Company. When the poll was taken the proposal was approved by the voters and the county did subscribe for this amount of stock. James H. Ferguson was named the agent of the county to subscribe for the stock.

The work was begun on both ends of the road and in August, 1871, an engine, a wood-burner named *Greenbrier*, was brought down the Ohio River by boat and unloaded at Huntington and was used in the construction of this end of the road. On January 29, 1873, C. R. Mason drove the last spike and the road was connected between Hawk's Nest and Kanawha Falls and was opened for through traffic.

Chesapeake and Ohio passenger station, 1873

A short time thereafter some water from the James River was brought to Huntington and mingled with that of the Ohio. On the first day of October, 1880, the Chesapeake and Ohio Railroad Company made a connection with the E. L. and B. S. Railway Company which gave it connection to Lexington and Louisville, Kentucky. Two years later a through passenger service known as the Louisville Express was put on between Richmond, Virginia, and Louisville, Kentucky. This was before the days of dining cars and trains stopped at Huntington for meals.

On the first day of January, 1889, the Chesapeake and Ohio Railway Company took over the Maysville and Big Sandy Railroad Company and thus had a direct line to Cincinnati. Upon the completion of the line to Cincinnati the Chesapeake and Ohio Railway Company put on a vestibuled train with its first dining car service. The new trains, Nos. 3 and 4, were named the F. F. V.—Fast Flying Virginian. These trains were painted orange and white. The orange was of a distinctive shade and the colors were mixed by James A. Gohen, boss painter at Huntington. This was the standard Chesapeake and Ohio color for many years.

The Guyan Valley branch was completed and put in operation from Barboursville to Big Creek on October 31, 1903.

In 1870 Henry Taylor Douglas, who had been a colonel of engineers, C. S. A., was transferred from construction on the Greenbrier portion of the road to Huntington and had charge of the construction of the shops at this point.

The Ohio River Railroad which is now a division of the Baltimore and Ohio Railroad completed its line to Guyandotte and at that point connected with the Chesapeake and Ohio line which it used between Guyandotte and Huntington. The old passenger station at Huntington was used by these lines jointly.

In 1890 the City of Huntington granted to the Huntington and Big Sandy Railroad Company and the Ohio River Railroad Company a franchise to construct and operate a railroad line over certain streets and avenues named, and in the end these two companies built a railroad from Guyandotte into the City of Huntington and thence on to Kenova. This road was completed in 1892 and from that date the Ohio River Railroad ceased to use the Chesapeake and Ohio Railroad tracks and depot. It used its own line and new depot which it had built at the foot of 11th Street and its train service was extended to Kenova. To accommodate local passenger service the Chesapeake

Baltimore and Ohio passenger station showing old horse car

[128]

and Ohio Railroad operated a local train between Huntington and Ashland which made a number of round trips daily and was known locally as "the shuttle train." The Ohio River Railroad had a train which consisted of an engine and one coach which it operated between Huntington and Kenova and this train was known as "the dummy train." There was a horse-car line which connected the Chesapeake and Ohio and the Baltimore and Ohio stations.

The train service in those days was not as impersonal as it now is. Mrs. L. Judson Williams, who then as now, lived at Kenova and was a frequent visitor to this city, tells the story of how on one occasion she came to Huntington on the "shuttle" to do some shopping, and on her trip up she told Bob Williamson, the conductor, that she was going to John Valentine's store to do some shopping but that she expected to go back with him on the return trip. Mrs. Williams took the horse-car to Valentine's store, which was then on 9th Street near 3d Avenue, and after she finished shopping she came out of the store, met the horse-car going toward Ohio River station. She knew the driver, Wm. Jordan, and told him that she was sorry he was not going to the Chesapeake and Ohio station as she wanted to return home on the "shuttle" and her time was getting short. Jordan, prompt to meet the situation, told her that it was all right as he would go back to the Chesapeake and Ohio station. Thereupon, he unhitched his team, hooked them to the back end of the car and headed toward the Chesapeake and Ohio station. Upon arrival there Mrs. Williams found Captain Williamson walking up and down the platform impatiently awaiting her arrival.

XXI: SCHOOLS

THE settlement of Cabell County does not date back far enough for us to be interested in the charity schools, the parish schools, or the private or select schools which were common in the eastern portion of Virginia. Our interest must begin with the period of about 1796 when the first settlers were known to be in this territory which we now know as Cabell County, but which was then a part of Kanawha County.

Virgil A. Lewis says that the common primary schools were established by frontiersmen who assembled in their respective neighborhoods and erected school houses at their own expense and then employed the teachers. These schools were open to all children whose parents were able and willing to pay the tuition. This type of school continued for a great many years and became known as the Old Field School.

The first Constitution of Virginia which was drawn by the great George Mason and Thomas Jefferson made no reference to a school system. The first legislation on the subject of schools passed by the new State of Virginia was the act of December 26, 1796, known as the Aldermanic School Law. This act provided that in each county of the state the people should annually elect three of the "most honest and able men to be called aldermen." These aldermen met annually on the second Monday in May at the courthouse and divided the county into sections based upon school population and named these several sections. After this division was made the householders in each section were required to meet on the first Monday of September following at a place designated by the aldermen and agree upon a site for a school house. If there was a tie vote on the location an alderman who lived outside of the section cast the deciding vote. After the site was selected it was the duty of the aldermen to erect a school house and to keep it in repair and to employ the teacher. At least one of the aldermen must visit the school at least once each half year to examine the pupils and to generally supervise. All free children were entitled to free tuition for a period of three years but if they continued in school thereafter tuition had to be paid.

The cost of the school buildings, and the salaries of the teachers were ascertained and the aldermen made a levy in an amount sufficient to pay these sums and this levy was collected by the sheriff as other public taxes and paid over to the aldermen for disbursement.

SCHOOLS

In 1809 the General Assembly passed an act which provided:

That all escheats, confiscations, forfeitures, and all personal property accruing to the Commonwealth as derelict and having no rightful owner, which have accrued since the second day of February one thousand eight hundred and ten, and which shall hereafter accrue to the Commonwealth, be, and the same are hereby *appropriated to the encouragement of learning;* and that all militia fines and the arrears thereof, due to the Commonwealth on the eleventh day of February one thousand eight hundred and eleven, and thenceforth accruing or to accrue, be also and the same are hereby appropriated to the *encouragement of learning*.

The act which thus created the "Literary Fund" declared that it should "be appropriated to the sole benefit of a school or schools to be kept within each and every county in the Commonwealth, subject to such orders and regulations as the General Assembly shall hereafter direct. . . . this present General Assembly solemnly protests against any other application of the said Fund by any succeeding General Assembly to any other object than *the education of the poor*."

In 1810 the Auditor of Public Accounts was directed by Act of the Assembly to open an account to be designated "The Literary Fund" and to place to its credit every payment made on account of any of the escheats, confiscations, forfeitures, fines and penalties appropriated to the encouragement of learning. In the same year the Governor, Lieutenant-Governor, Treasurer, Attorney-General, and President of the Court of Appeals, and their successors in office were constituted a body corporate under the name and style of the "President and Directors of the Literary Fund," of which the Governor was the presiding officer.

On the 9th of February, 1814, it was enacted that the titles to all lands and lots forfeited for the non-payment of taxes should vest in the President and Directors of the Literary Fund, and all tax thereon be extinguished, and all moneys afterward received from the redemption or sale of these lands and lots were absolutely deemed to be a part of the Literary Fund. . . .

To quote Virgil A. Lewis, the primary objective of the literary fund was the education of the children of indigent parents and for the purpose of carrying into effect the primary objective of its institution the Assembly of 1817 directed the president and directors to set aside annually the sum of $45,000.00 to be allocated to the several counties in the proportion as the free white population bore to that of the whole state, and at the same time the court of each county was required to appoint not less than five or more than fifteen discreet persons to be called school commissioners. The County Court of Cabell County on the 26th day of May, 1818, named the following persons as such commissioners: Elisha McComas, John Everett, Jr., Mark Russell, Jesse Spurlock, Edmund McGinnis, and John Samuels.

The act required that they meet annually in November at the courthouse to hold such special meetings as might be necessary. One of these commissioners was elected treasurer and was authorized to receive for his county its quota of the literary fund.

The commissioners were given power

To determine what number of poor children they would educate in their county; what sum should be paid for their education; to authorize each of themselves to select so many children as they may deem expedient; and to draw orders upon their treasurer for the payment of the expense of tuition and of furnishing such children with proper books and materials for writing and ciphering. The poor children thus selected were (with the assent of father, mother or guardian) sent to such school as was most convenient, therein to be taught, reading, writing, and arithmetic.

The said school commissioners were required to present annually a statement to the President and Directors of the Literary Fund, exhibiting the number of schools and indigent children in their county; the price paid for their tuition; the number of indigent children educated in such schools; and what further appropriation from the Literary Fund, would, in their opinion, be sufficient to furnish the means of education to all the indigent children in their county.

The literary fund increased rapidly and on September 30, 1833, it amounted to a sum in excess of one and one-half million dollars and the appropriation for the poor children had in the past thirteen years been largely increased.

In this year there was one common school at Barboursville and a primary school at Guyandotte. The statistics made by Mr. Lewis as of September of that year showed that Cabell County had seven school commissioners with seventeen primary common schools for poor children, and that there were two hundred poor children in the county of whom one hundred and seventeen had attended school with 6,399 aggregate days attendance, and with an average of fifty-five days attendance for each child at a cost of $287.76 to which the literary fund paid an average of $2.40 for each child. In 1837 Marshall Academy was established.

The next change in the school law was in 1846 when on the 5th of March of that year the General Assembly passed "an act amending the present primary school system." This act required the County Court at the ensuing October term to divide the county into districts having regard to the territorial extent and population and to appoint for each of the districts one school commissioner. The County Court of Cabell County divided the county as follows:

All that part of the county on the Ohio bottom from the Wayne County line to Three Mile Creek above the town of Guyandotte and the turnpike road below Russell Creek—District 1.

All that part of the county on the Ohio River from Three Mile Creek including Seven and Nine Mile Creek and the Little Guyan Creek—District 2.

All that part of the county west of the Guyandotte River above Russell Creek up to Smith's Creek—District 3.

All that part of the county on the east side of the Guyandotte River from opposite the mouth of Russell Creek to the mouth of Smith's Creek including Mud River to Rece's Bridge—District 4.

All that part of the county commonly known as Teay's Valley—District 5.

All that part of the county on Mud River and its branches above the bridge at Abia Rece's—District 6.

All that part of the county lying on the Guyandotte River above the mouth of Smith's Creek on both sides including its branches—District 7.

And named the following school commissioners:

John Laidley—1.
John Hannon—2.
Thos. Thornburg—3.
John Samuel—4.
John Morris—5.
Harvey Barrett—6.
James McComas—7.

The act required these commissioners to meet at the courthouse in the November following and to organize and to elect a superintendent of schools for the county who should perform the duties of the clerk and treasurer of the board. The first county superintendent of Cabell as shown by the record is Thomas Thornburg who gave bond as such on November 27, 1854.

The commissioner appointed for each district looked after the school property within his district, registered and reported to the county superintendent all the children in his district between the age of five and sixteen years and made a contract with the teachers of his district to teach a number of indigent children as many days as his district's portion of the county part of the literary fund would pay for and the teachers were required to keep an accurate account of the attendance of such children. There were other requirements as to keeping records and making reports.

There was a second act passed on March 5, 1846, entitled "An act for the establishment of a District Public School System." This act contained the provision that upon the petition of one-half of the qualified voters of any county to the court thereof that the court should submit to the vote of the county the question of "A district Public School System" and if two-thirds of the votes cast at such election favored this system it should be adopted. Cabell County does not seem to have availed itself of this act but Virgil Lewis is the authority for the statement that Cabell and Wayne counties voted to adopt the system prescribed for Patrick County but does not say what this system was, and that in 1860 there were three counties west of the Alleghanies which had free schools.

The Constitution of 1863 provided for a permanent school fund to be made up in the same manner as the literary fund and enjoined the Legislature to provide as soon as practical for the establishment of a thorough and efficient free school system, and to provide for the support of these schools, and to fix the amount to be contributed by each township for the purpose. This fund became known as the school fund and was limited by the Constitutional Amendment of 1902 to one million dollars and since that date has been referred to as the irreducible school fund.

On December 10, 1863, the Legislature of the new State of West Virginia passed an act providing for the establishment of a system of free schools. The counties were divided into townships and each township was a school district governed by a board of education which consisted of three school commissioners whose term of office was three years and the township was subdivided into sub-districts to contain not less than fifty youths of school age.

The school commissioners were made a public corporation, were given the authority to elect a clerk, and the school year was fixed at not less than six months. The board was given authority to establish a sufficient number of schools; to acquire lands and erect buildings; to appoint teachers and fix salaries; to prescribe the courses and to select the text books, and were required to visit each school at fixed periods and make a number of reports. They were given authority to provide for joint schools between townships but before a high school could be established a township meeting must be held and two-thirds of the qualified voters present approve the plan. If there were as many as thirty colored children in any township the board was required to provide them with a school. Township boards could not share in State funds unless and until they made the reports required by law. The county superintendent was elected by the people for a term of two years but the State superintendent was elected for the same period by the Legislature. The county superintendent examined the teachers and there were five different grades of certificates and the pay of the teachers was fixed upon the grade of the certificates. The free school fund fixed under the Constitution was required to be invested in United States or State bonds and the interest on this fund,

SCHOOLS

plus fines, a capitation tax and a state levy of not to exceed ten cents on $100.00 was distributed among the counties in the proportion that their enumerated scholars bore to the total state enumeration after deducting the pay of the state superintendent of schools.

To raise the difference between the amount received from the State and the cost of six months school a township meeting was held annually and the board submitted to them an estimate of the cost for the period of six months and the amount to be received from the State and the meeting fixed the assessment on township property at a rate not to exceed ten cents to provide the difference.

The governor, the auditor, the treasurer, the secretary of State, and superintendent of schools composed the board of school funds and had control of its investment.

The first school commissioners elected in Cabell County under the act of 1863 were John Scheneberg for three years, Isiah Ray for two years, J. Harvey Poage for one year. William F. Dusenberry was elected county superintendent of schools.

In April, 1865, conditions had apparently become more settled and we find that school commissioners were elected for three districts, namely: W. L. Clark, William O. Wright, and Samuel W. Johnston for the township of Guyandotte; John Knight, William Thompson, and George Grimes for the township of Barboursville; and Emil Telgener, Richard Bexfield, and John P. Jordan for the township of Union. William Algeo was elected county superintendent.

In 1867 Marshall College was made the State normal school. A State university was established and there were branch normal schools at Fairmont, West Liberty, Glenville and Shepherdstown, and the free school system of West Virginia was to continue to be developed on these general lines until 1933 when the county became the governmental unit for schools.

Both the Constitution and the law permitted independent schools to be established. In 1871 the City of Huntington was made an independent school district and will be told about in a separate chapter, and so much of the Guyandotte District as was outside of the city limits and the remaining districts each constituted a school district.

Under the new Constitution of 1872 the townships were changed into districts and the school government of the districts consisted of a president of the board of education with two commissioners but a trustee was elected in every subdivision of the district and this trustee was placed in charge of his district.

The election was in August, 1873, and the term of office was for two years. The power to make the levies instead of being voted on at a township meeting was submitted to the voters of the district. The board met in September annually to determine the school year, fix teachers' salaries according to their certificates and required them to make the same reports. The trustees who were under the control of the entire board appointed and made contracts with the teachers for their respective districts and had charge of the school houses therein. There was also a provision authorizing the establishment of high schools when authorized by vote of the people. The new act provided for a county board of examiners made up of a county superintendent and two experienced teachers, prohibited the employment of teachers without a certificate and contained provisions for a State and district levy for the schools. The state superintendent of schools became elective for a term of four years. The unfortunate feature of the new Constitution and new State law made under it was that the school fund might be invested in interest bearing securities of the United States or of this State *or otherwise.* The words in italics were to prove its undoing at a later time.

In 1902 a Constitutional Amendment was adopted limiting the accumulation of the school fund to $1,000,000.00 and directing all amounts in excess of that sum to be used for the support of the free schools. This fund usually referred to as the irreducible school fund has been from time to time invested but in 1933 it developed that much of it had been invested "otherwise" than in interest bearing securities of the United States or of the State and many of these investments were valueless. It was thought that a large part of the fund would be lost.

In 1897 the first compulsory attendance law was passed but was not effective for lack of enforcement, and in 1903 it was strengthened by a law providing for truant officers.

But to return to the schools. From the beginning of the State there was a four months school in this county and this term has been increased from time to time. The act of 1919 was up to that time the most comprehensive piece of legislation dealing with the school system. It provided for a minimum school term of one hundred and twenty school days in the school year of 1919-1920, and increased the term ten days on each succeeding two years until it reached the maximum of one hundred and sixty days for the school year of 1923-24 and each year thereafter. The district boards were given authority to extend these minimum terms. Junior high schools were authorized and school attendance was made compulsory but the district was still the school unit and school opportunities in the same county were unequal.

In 1933 the County Unit Bill was passed. The superintendent of the city schools and quite a number of the city teachers were opposed to the bill upon the theory that it would operate to the disadvantage of the city schools. When the act became effective it found Cabell County with two independent districts—the Huntington Independent District which is told about in another chapter and the Barboursville Independent District.

These units were abandoned and all of the schools in the county passed under the control of a single board which was to be elected at the general election in 1934 and to take office on July first following. The State superintendent of schools was given power to appoint an interim board and under this authority he appointed I. J. Kail, Walter M. Parker, Rolla D. Campbell, J. L. Blackwood, and P. A. Vallandingham. The county superintendent, Henry F. White, was continued in office for his unexpired term and H. A. Rice, the superintendent of city schools was made assistant superintendent and served until August, 1934, when he was succeeded by R. B. Marston. Olin C. Nutter served also as assistant superintendent in charge of the elementary schools of the county. There came under the control of the new board outside of the City of Huntington 104 elementary schools, one high school at Milton, one high school at Barboursville, and six junior high schools, but only one of which was carried on in its own building, and in the City of Huntington there were two high schools, i.e., the High School on 8th Street and the Douglas High School which was a combination high and junior high school in one building (for colored students); six Junior High Schools and nineteen graded schools, with a total school enrollment for the county of 19,308 pupils and 693 teachers, including principals. Of these totals 170 teachers and 4,784 pupils were in the schools outside of the city of Huntington. It will be remembered that in November, 1932, the Constitutional Amendment classifying property for taxation and limiting the respective levies on the several classes of property was adopted and the necessary effect of this limitation was to reduce the income of local levying bodies which included the school board, so the problem of how to meet the annual costs of the school was a burning one and there were many dire prophecies as to the effect of the new county unit law. All of these prophecies as to the effect of the law turned out to be false and the State, recognizing its obligation to support the free school system has, during the first two years of the county unit law contributed to Cabell County money approximating forty per cent of the annual budget or $402,000.00 to be used to pay what the State terms the basic wage for the necessary teachers. The number of teachers allowed to a county is worked out on a formula which takes into account the density of school children to the square mile as shown by the average daily attendance in the schools. The basic wage is based upon the qualifications of teachers as evidenced by their training and experience. The county furnishes the school buildings and pays the teachers certain amounts in excess of the basic wage allowed by the State. It is too much detail to recount just how these salaries are made up. There is a nine months school term throughout the county. Not only are grade schools located at points accessible to the scholars but school buses are provided to take the children to and from school. The fact that the primary and secondary roads are all hard surfaced the distance from the school is not of any great moment and during the two years of the county unit system twenty-five rural schools have been closed and the children transported to larger schools where they enjoy greater advantages.

At the end of the second year under this act it can be said that the city schools have not suffered but upon the contrary, inequalities between the sparsely settled and poorer magisterial districts and their more prosperous neighbors in the same county have been obliterated and the children of the same county are on an equal footing, so it can truly be said that we have traveled a long way from the days of the Old Field School.

XXII: HUNTINGTON SCHOOLS

THE legislation set out in the chapter about Cabell County schools is only the foundation of the free school system and there has been legislation from time to time in an attempt to improve the system. The act of 1919 was up to that time most comprehensive but the fundamental defect in the system was the school unit first, the township, and then the magisterial district. The law permitted independent school districts and Huntington was made such a district at the time of its incorporation.

An outline of the development of the Huntington school system is a striking example of how the children of the same county were given unequal opportunities for education. To be more explicit a portion of Guyandotte District was included in the independent school district of Huntington and the remainder of the district was a school district of its own. A child living on one side of an imaginary line and in that part of Guyandotte District not included in the city and which was sparsely populated had one opportunity and the child on the other side of this line in the more densely populated portion had every advantage of modern schools.

The new City of Huntington in its early years was fortunate in commanding the services of a number of its most representative and ablest men as members of its city council and at the first meeting a committee composed of Judge W. H. Hagen and D. W. Emmons were named to call on the sheriff to ascertain what school funds were available. At the next meeting a committee was named to select a school site in the west end and one in the east end. In March of 1872 the committee reported that they had selected three lots in Block 91 which were lots fronting on 4th Avenue between 7th and 8th Streets, and the east end committee reported a site on 1st Avenue between 25th and 26th Streets, a lot one hundred feet on 1st Avenue and in Block Number 251.

Both sites were adopted by the council. Plans were immediately prepared for the west end school and a contract was let to build a two-story brick building twenty-six by sixty feet. There was some difficulty about securing the east end site and the council made an order condemning this land but the order was rescinded. The west end school was ready for use and on November 12, 1872, councilmen A. J. Enslow, E. T. Mitchell, and J. O. Wall were authorized to engage the teachers and open the school. L. C. Chase was the first principal who appears to have been paid $75.00 a month. Miss Alice Maupin was on January 7, 1873, allowed $70.00 for two months' pay. For the immediate accommodation of the children in the eastern portions of the city the council made an arrangement with the State Board of Regents to pay the teachers in charge of the primary school at Marshall College on condition that tuition in the primary school should be free to the children living within the boundaries from the Guyandotte River at railroad along with railroad line to 26th Street, up 26th Street south to 9th Avenue, down 9th Avenue west to 16th Street, and down 16th Street north to the Ohio River and up Ohio and Guyandotte Rivers to starting point.

On October 1, 1872, councilmen W. H. Hagen and D. W. Emmons were named a committee to establish a public school at the Spring Hill school.

On November 22, 1872, bonds in the sum of $5,000.00 were sold and the proceeds placed to the credit of a contingent school fund.

In May, 1873, a committee was appointed to arrange a colored school and did arrange for such a school in the colored church at 12th Street.

In August, 1873, the committee on the east end school was authorized to buy the lot selected by the majority of the committee and to let a contract for a one-story brick building. A lot was secured at the corner of 3d Avenue and 22d Street and a contract was made with A. B. Palmer to erect the building for $1,700.00, the work to be completed in forty days. Mrs. A. J. Delaney was named to take charge of the east end school at a salary of $50.00 per month, and Miss Flora Scott, Miss Moorehead, and Miss Ella Kneff as assistant teachers at a salary of $40.00 each per month.

The allocation from the State fund for the year was $659.82 for white children and $57.36 for colored children.

In August, 1874, the salary of the superintendent was fixed at $750.00 per year and the pay of teachers who held certificates above Number 3, at $40.00 per month. A. D. Chesterman was superintendent that school year.

In October, 1874, Thomas J. Burke, mayor, and General John H. Oley, recorder were appointed a school committee to "take general charge of the public schools with power to act upon all ordinary expenditures." General Oley continued as Recorder until his death on March 11, 1888, and was practically in charge of the schools during that period.

In September, 1875, John Gibson was elected superintendent and served one year, being succeeded by Rev. A. Brown, who served for one year and was succeeded by Rev. James Madison who served two years.

In 1875 William James was elected to teach the colored school.

In 1876 the vote on the levy was taken for a seven months school but if Peabody funds were available the schools were to continue eight months.

In 1877 the school year was eight months, the salary of the superintendent was fixed at $60.00 per month, and teachers with a No. 1 and 2 certificate at $35.00 per month, and it was ordered that a diploma from Marshall College be treated as a No. 2 certificate pending an examination.

In September, 1878, a school was erected on the McCoy Road just south of the W. H. Newcomb home.

In 1880 it was agreed to employ no teachers who held No. 4 certificates. Two teachers were required to enumerate the scholars. James Liggins, colored, who had succeeded William James, enumerated the colored school children.

John Wigal was superintendent, 1879-1884.

A. D. Selby was superintendent, 1884-1886.

J. J. Allison was superintendent, 1886-1887.

By 1887 the school system included the four primary grades, three intermediate grades, two grammar grades and three high school grades. The first high school was established in this year. Its freshman and sophomore classes were housed in the prayer meeting room of the old Congregational Church at the southeast corner of 5th Avenue and 9th Street; later they were moved to the council chamber of the city hall which was then located on the east side of 9th Street and 4½ Alley. In this year James M. Lee was elected superintendent and served until 1896.

In 1888 in the face of considerable opposition a new school building which contained ten rooms, an office, and a finished basement was erected at the southeast corner of 5th Avenue and 13th Street and was named in honor of General John H. Oley who had died that year. The superintendent of schools established his office in this building.

On February 27, 1889, the Legislature passed an act effective from the date of its passage which provided for a school board of six members whose term of office was three years to administer the

Looking north on 13th Street from Oley school, circa 1888

school affairs of the Huntington Independent School District. Among the powers given the board was the power to make levies to support a public library. The first board elected under this law was Sam Gideon, B. H. Thackston, R. Enslow, H. M. Adams, W. O. Wiatt, and H. C. Simms. Sam Gideon was elected president and served as such with the exception of one year until 1899. James K. Oney was elected secretary and except for 1900-1903, when Robert L. Archer was secretary, served until September 10, 1928.

In 1890 the high school was given two rooms in the Oley school building. Mrs. Naomi Everett was made principal with a faculty of five: John Simpson, afterward Dean of the Medical School at West Virginia University; Miss Lizzie Smith, Misses Kate and Anna Ellis, and Miss Cora Trice. The graduating class of 1890 consisted of two members, Erna Wells and Chester Sanborn. Sam Gideon as president of the board presented the diplomas. The graduating class of 1935 is made up of 657 members. The high school continued in the Oley building until it was moved to its new home on 8th Street.

In 1891 the Holderby School with eight rooms was erected at 6th Avenue and 20th Street. One year later six additional rooms were added.

In 1893 the Douglass School, which is now known as the Barnett School, was built as a colored school at the corner of 16th Street and 8th Avenue. A north wing was added in 1910.

The Cabell School was built in 1896 and remodeled in 1914.

In 1896 W. D. Sterling succeeded J. M. Lee as superintendent and served two years; he was succeeded by W. H. Cole who remained until 1905 and was succeeded by Wilson M. Foulk.

In 1897 the Buffington School was built and the school on 4th Avenue was abandoned.

The Simms School was built in 1899. A new Simms School was erected in 1924.

In 1901 the old West End School on 4th Avenue between 7th and 8th Streets was conveyed to the City of Huntington upon the condition that within three years a hospital would be established therein and that the premises would be used for hospital purposes.

At a special session of the board held on January 6, 1902, the following minutes appear:

> Board accepted offer of Carnegie to give $25,000 for building *if city* would provide $2,500 per year for support and maintenance and provide site. Board of Education assumed obligation for support and maintenance under a law enacted February 22, 1901.

At a special session held on March 24, 1902, the following minutes appear:

Resolved, second that the thanks of this Board be and are hereby extended to Mr. Carnegie for his additional gift of $10,000, making $35,000 for a free Library building for the *City of Huntington.*

Resolved, third, that this Board of Education for itself and *its successors,* does hereby accept Mr. Carnegie's generous gift, and pledges itself to maintain the Library at an annual expenditure of not less than $3,500 for maintenance and increase of Library.

Resolved, fourth, that a certified copy of these resolutions be forwarded to Mr. Carnegie.

On February 18, 1902, the City of Huntington conveyed to the board of Education the lot 90x90 feet at the northeast corner of 9th Street and 5th Avenue with the condition that the board would commence the erection of a free library upon said lot within the period of twelve months from that date, and that the lot would be used for the purpose of a free library. On this lot was immediately erected the Carnegie Public Library which also houses the executive staff of the public school system.

In 1905 the Ensign School was erected and in the same year the Emmons School was built, but was rebuilt in 1923.

In 1908-09 the Jones building was erected on the lot just east of the Oley School, and in 1922 a north wing was added and these buildings were put under one roof. The west end of this building is still designated as Oley School but the remainder of the building is called the Central Junior High School.

In 1909 an amendment was made to the act of 1889 which increased the number of the board to eight members and provided that not more than four of these members could be of the same political party, and fixed their term of office for six years, one-half of the board to be elected every three years. The first members elected on the bi-partisan board were: John A. Jones, R. S. Prindle, U. S. Chadwick, and C. M. Hawes for the term of six years; J. L. Hawkins, Joseph R. Gallick, C. W. Kendle, and J. S. Shafer for three years.

By this time (1909) superintendent Foulk had added to the curricula modern languages, home economics, commercial subjects, and manual arts courses. This bi-partisan board was for a number of years made up of far-seeing business men who made every effort to and did build up a splendid school system. The bi-partisan plan was successful so long as the office sought the man, but unfortunately, in 1921 the board members were given a salary of $20.00 per month which in 1923 was raised to $50.00 per month with the result that a number of persons of small caliber made active canvasses for the office, were elected and under their government the board fell in disrepute.

To return to the workings of the new board. The board erected the Jefferson School in 1911, the Lincoln Elementary and Miller Schools in 1912, the Johnson School in 1915 and the Gallaher and Guyandotte Schools in 1916.

The new high school was completed on September 4, 1916 with a capacity to accommodate 1,100 students.

In 1917 Wilson M. Foulk accepted a position in Charleston and was succeeded by Clarence L. Wright as superintendent. Mr. Wright was a young man full of enthusiasm and soon became one of the outstanding educators of the nation, and with the active support of his board reorganized the school system and introduced the junior high school feature. The West Junior High, the Enslow Junior High and the Enslow Elementary Schools were built in the year 1917. Three of the five new buildings were changed from the 8-4 plan to the then comparatively new 6-3-3 plan, or the junior high school. The city school system immediately commanded statewide and national recognition. The purposes of the new organization included that of expanding the curriculum to satisfy the multiplying interests of the adolescent child, to provide him an opportunity to explore the major fields of learning, to afford through the development of the co-curricular program of the school, means of social development denied him in the traditional school, and in general through a richer school experience to encourage uninterrupted attendance throughout the remaining grades of the public school system.

Another innovation was the introduction in the elementary school of the so-called platoon system. This system was introduced into five of the twenty-two elementary schools, four for white children and one for colored children, namely: Guyandotte, Lincoln, Monroe, Simms and Barnett. It is asserted that this system has done for the elementary school what the junior high has done for the secondary school.

In 1921 the Kellogg School, now in Wayne County, and the Cammack Junior High School were built.

In 1923 the Monroe Elementary and the Lincoln Junior High Schools were erected and in the next year a colored high school was built and named the Douglas High School and the old Douglass School was named the Barnett School.

In 1925 the Huntington High School became a member of the North Central Association of High Schools and Colleges which means that credits earned at the high school will be accepted at the other high schools and colleges belonging to the association. To continue in this association the standards must be maintained and certain fixed requirements as to buildings, equipment, courses of study offered and the number of teachers employed must be met.

In March of 1925 the voters of Westmoreland approved the plan for that territory to become a part of the Huntington Independent School District and later the Vinson Junior High School was established there.

In October, 1927, an oral school for the deaf was opened in the Ensign building with an initial enrollment of seven, and five years later there were twenty of these pupils of various ages and degrees of deafness. The school was then housed on the first floor of the Oley School building with Miss Nida Saunders as principal assisted by Mrs. June Grandia, both trained teachers of the deaf. In the present school year there are ten children in this school which is now in charge of Miss Nettie Newall.

In 1930 an automobile mechanics' department was added to the high school but is housed in a separate building located on 8th Avenue between 6th and 7th Streets.

Beginning with the first enrollment the high school has increased by leaps and bounds and since the year 1928 it has been necessary to have two sessions during the day to take care of the students who at this time number 2,198.

It is said that Huntington has had more Rhodes scholars than any other city of its size in the United States. There have been six of these, namely: Rex Hersey, Roger Tyler, William Maier, John Wood, Walter L. Brown, and Julian W. Hagen, who were elected without examination on the basis of their records in high school and in college. These records include the qualities of manhood, truth, courage, moral force of character, and physical vigor as shown in outdoor sports and other ways.

In 1927 Dan Veron Smith, a senior in the arts department of the high school, in competition with forty-six States was awarded the Morgenthau Prize of $75.00 for the best poster in the Near East

Relief contest. The judges making the award were Howard Chandler Christy and Charles Dana Gibson.

In 1932 Miss Miriam Hyman, a graduate of the high school, had her short story "Waiting" selected for publication in the *American Short Story* magazine.

Except for 1922-1925, when John G. Graham served as superintendent, Wright continued until 1931 when he was succeeded by Harold A. Rice.

In 1933 Governor H. G. Kump realized that the school law which made the district the unit operated to the disadvantage of the sparsely settled and poorer districts and proposed a law which made the county the unit for school government. While this act was being considered by the Legislature there was considerable agitation over it. It was asserted by some of the city folks that if the act was passed the Huntington schools would pass under the control of a board elected by the people of the county, ignoring the fact that 83 plus per cent of the population of Cabell County is in the City of Huntington. However, the act passed and a new board of education of Cabell County was appointed by the State superintendent of free schools and all the schools in Cabell County passed under the control of this board.

The schools in that part of the City of Huntington which are located in Wayne County and formerly under the control of the city board passed to the control of the Wayne County board of education.

THE SCHOOLMASTER

The early schoolmasters have long since passed to their reward. Who they were and what manner of men they were is in most cases forgotten. Story tellers delight in picturing an uncouth stranger coming into a neighborhood soliciting a subscription school, then the teacher gathering "withes" to maintain discipline in the class room.

An old school teacher in describing the early days said that the school government was an absolute monarchy and continued:

> There was no janitor. It was generally understood that in the morning the teacher would assist the large boys in cutting a back log and rolling it on. A piece of rich pine was handy, some live coals were carried from home, and by the aid of dry or rotten wood, a fire was soon started. Perhaps some used "punk" and kindled a fire by striking sparks with a jack-knife from a piece of flint. The pupils soon began to arrive and the long session began, to end with the setting of the sun.
>
> Some were supplied with the New Testament, and some had the old "blue

back" reader, Pike's or Smiley's Arithmetic, and if any grammar at all was used, it was Murray's. Geography was seldom taught in the early days, but later some used Mitchell's.

We know that the school rooms were crude affairs with big open fireplaces, but we know too that out of these classrooms came men who took the first places in the professions and government. This fact justifies the conclusion that some of these early teachers were worth while.

The earliest teachers we have an account of follow:

William Paine, an Englishman who lived in the neighborhood of Guyandotte. He was a man of mature scholarship, a devout Methodist, and the first teacher of English grammar in the county. Thomas A. Morris was a pupil in his school and a member of the first grammar class taught in the neighborhood of Guyandotte. Charles Paine, a grandson of William Paine was county superintendent of Cabell County schools about forty years ago and his descendants still live in this county.

Thomas A. Morris, later Bishop of the Methodist Episcopal Church, taught part of one school term in a house near Spice Flat Cottage in the year 1814 or 1815. The school building burned after about three months of the contracted six months had been taught, and the remainder of the term was abandoned. The building is supposed to have stood on the east side of the Grand District Road on the Handley farm near Howell's Mill.

John B. McGinnis, who lived at or near Guyandotte was an early teacher in his own neighborhood and in the eastern section of the county at an early date. In 1838 he taught in Spice Flat Cottage, the former residence of Thomas A. Morris near Howell's Mill, the house at that time having been abandoned as a dwelling.

In the early 1840's Robert Stewart, formerly of Bath County, Virginia, taught one or more schools in the first community school building on the south side of the Midland Trail near Ona, in Grant District. He later moved to Guyandotte on the Ohio River just above the town, and perhaps taught in that neighborhood. He was the father of Mrs. Arthur Mitchell and Mrs. Harris of Huntington, and grandfather of Mrs. Timothy S. Scanlon.

Porter W. Wallace of Botetourt County, Virginia, a man of scholarly ability and great popularity, taught several terms in the same community building near Ona, where he had advanced classes in surveying, natural philosophy, grammar and Latin, in addition to

THE SCHOOLMASTER 149

the elementary branches. He found it necessary to have an assistant, and Miss Elizabeth Yates, later Mrs. James R. Burdette, was his assistant in 1851 and 1852. It was in this school that Samuel Everett Moore, son of Martin and Sarah Everett Moore, had his ankle severely bruised by its being caught in the crack of the puncheon floor, from which inflammation set in and caused his death in 1852. In the eastern part of the county at that time, many of the boys were named Porter Wallace in honor of this esteemed teacher.

In the 1840's a Mr. Cook, a Welshman of scholarly ability, taught school near Blue Sulphur in a building then owned by John Dundas.

Miss Ann Howard, who frequently contributed original productions written in verse, taught several private or pay schools in the county, chiefly in the eastern section.

Miss Lou Moore of Barboursville taught for a time in the new or second community school building at Howell's Mill.

James Nouning, a near relative of Mrs. Chapman W. Maupin and of Mrs. Robert Harvey, taught school at Barboursville and in the vicinity of Bethesda Church.

Jonathan Switzer, formerly of Botetourt County, Virginia, taught before the Civil War and during the first years of the war in the community building at Howell's Mill, at that time called Doolittle's Mill. He was a scholarly gentleman, a splendid teacher, a leader in the community, and had the power of making friends of all in his large circle of acquaintances. He was the father of Rufus Switzer, E. C. Switzer, and Mrs. Maine, of Huntington.

Prior to the Civil War and again after the war under the free school system, James A. Buckner, formerly of Meigs County, Ohio, taught in the county. After his return from service in the Confederate Army he married Miss Olga Handley and lived for a number of years in the Ona neighborhood, later moving to Carroll County, Missouri. He was the father of Mrs. Frank L. Burdette of Huntington.

B. H. Thackson, a scholarly man, graduate of the University of Virginia, and long a resident of Barboursville where he married Miss Eugenia Miller, was a member of the faculty of Marshall College, and for some years was the president or principal of the college. During the Civil War he taught school at Barboursville. He had great influence in the educational and social activities of the county and was for a time a member of the County Court.

William Algoe, a graduate of Jefferson College in Pennsylvania, a classmate of James G. Blaine, and a teacher in McComas District, was for many years an influence for the best type of scholarship in the public schools in the county.

During the Civil War there were no public or free schools open in the county and there were some subscription schools. Henry C. Dunkle was teaching at Davis Creek in 1864.

It is said the first free school in the county was taught at Barboursville in the fall of 1865 by C. H. Hall who came from Proctorville, Ohio.

MARSHALL COLLEGE

In the year 1837 on a knoll overlooking the Ohio River, about two miles below the mouth of the Guyandotte River, on the land of James Holderby, stood an old log house called Mt. Hebron. It was used for both a school and a church. Just how long it had been used as a school is open to enquiry.* However, the partition of the Savage Grant had been confirmed for these twenty years, and the owners of the river farms were secure in their titles. The bottom lands had been cleared, the land was good, and the farmers were getting on and building better homes for themselves, and a school was needed for their children. Just who launched the movement to establish an academy is lost in time, but at all events John Laidley was one of the leading spirits and brought about the incorporation of the academy and raised the necessary funds to buy the land. On March 13, 1838, the General Assembly of Virginia passed an act making Benjamin Brown, F. G. L. Beuhring, John Laidley, William Buffington, John Samuels, James Gallaher, Richard Brown, Benjamin H. Smith and George W. Summers a body politic as the "Trustees of Marshall Academy," to be located in Cabell County. Benjamin H. Smith and George W. Summers were prominent lawyers and lived at Charleston. John Samuels was the county clerk and lived at Barboursville, and the other gentlemen named lived in the neighborhood of the academy. The academy was named for the Chief Justice John Marshall. In June, following the incorporation, James Holderby and wife, in consideration of $40.00 conveyed to the trustees of Marshall Academy one and one-fourth acres of land on which stood the "academy" and put in the deed a provision that the land was to be used for school purposes and no other.

---

*The Brown family has a record that Ceres Brown, who was born April 10, 1821, attended school in this old building and continued on after the academy was organized.

John N. Peck was the first teacher and had an associate, Mr. Shepherd. The old building was too small to fill the needs and a new four-room building was erected, a well was dug, one room in the building set aside for public worship and designated as the chapel, and it was occupied on alternate Sundays by the Presbyterians and the Methodists who predominated in the immediate neighborhood. There were a few Episcopalians but they held no services of their own and these, like the entire community, attended services in the chapel regularly.*

After the completion of the new building, Mr. Peck and Mr. Shepherd continued as teachers, but Jacob Harris Patton came as principal in September, 1839, and continued until the autumn of the following year. He was followed by the Rev. Josiah B. Poage who was graduated from Princeton in 1843 and who served as principal 1843-1850. He built a large school, and had students from Kentucky, Ohio, and many of the counties in southern West Virginia. He was followed by Henry Clark and Joseph Foster, who served for brief periods, and in the fall of 1854 W. R. Boyer became principal with J. F. Stewart, Miss Hanna and Miss Scorill as assistants. He continued until 1858, when he was succeeded by Professor B. H. Thackston, 1858-1861.

At the organization meeting of the Western Virginia Conference of the Methodist Episcopal Church, South, held at Parkersburg, September 4, 1850, a proposal was made by the trustees of Marshall Academy (the terms of which the conference records do not disclose), the committee on education recommended its acceptance which was done, and Marshall Academy passed under the control of the Western Virginia Conference of the Methodist Episcopal Church, South. Seven years later the academy was in financial distress, and Bishop Pierce and twenty-nine other ministers donated $50.00 each toward paying the indebtedness.

The records of the County Court of Cabell County disclose that on February 14, 1857 (Deed Book 12, page 293), Marshall Academy by J. Laidley, president, conveyed to George W. Mason, trustee for Robert Holderby, the "lot of land in the County of Cabell owned by it on which is the Academy with all and singularly its appurtenances *except* the chapel and the free use of public preaching" to secure Robert Holderby the payment of a note of $650.00 which became due on February 16, 1858.

---
*W. S. Laidley's *Western End of West Virginia*.

In 1858 the General Assembly made the academy a college and changed its name to Marshall College, and the following gentlemen were its trustees: The Reverends Samuel Kelly, Staunton Field, S. K. Vaught, George B. Poage, C. M. Sullivan, William Bickers, J. F. Medley, R. A. Claughton, W. H. Fonerton, S. F. Mallory, and C. J. Warner, and the following laymen: F. G. L. Beuhring, Peter Cline Buffington, C. L. Roffe, J. H. Poage, Dr. G. C. Ricketts, John W. Wright, St. Mark Russell, Dr. P. H. McCullough, H. H. Miller, and T. W. Everett. They were Methodist, and while the college was under immediate control of the Methodist Episcopal Church, South, it was not a denominational school, and the act making it a college prohibited the establishment of a theological school in the institution. The school by this time was favorably known as evidenced by the following excerpt taken from the *Kanawha Valley Star* of November 11, 1856:

We would take occasion to call the attention of those who are interested in the subject of education to an excellent institution whose name heads this article. It is situated in a pleasant neighborhood, of easy access, on the Ohio River, two miles below the pleasant town of Guyandotte, Cabell County, Virginia.

It has been in operation some twenty years or more, and in that short period very many of its scholars have become prominent and leading men in the learned professions of law, physics, and divinity; and many of them have risen to high official stations, civil and military, not only in Virginia, but also in other states of the Union. Indeed, it is doubtful whether there is now an institution in the state, that in so short a time has sent forth so large a proportion of leading men.

So much for the part of its short history. Its future is still more promising. During the last session there were nearly a hundred students in attendance; and the high character won for the school by Mr. Boyers, the admirable and estimable teacher, at its head, is a harbinger of still greater success and usefulness.

The trustees, Messrs. John Laidley, F. G. L. Beuhring, P. C. Buffington, Dr. G. Ricketts and others are gentlemen whose names give character and currency to whatever they may be connected with. The Institution is further under the supervision and control of the Southern Methodist Conference of Western Virginia. This gives assurance that a moral and religious influence will breathe around it. Should any apprehend that sectarianism might therefore be inculcated, their fears will be quieted by the consideration of the fact that while the institution is under the control of the Methodist Conference, the principal of the Academy is a Presbyterian, thus showing a liberality of sentiment worthy of Christianity, and a prevalence and propriety on the part of those connected with the institution highly creditable to these different branches of the Church. Marshall Academy has many advantages, and it offers strong inducements to the public for its patronage.

The course of study, the rules and regulations, the privileges of the library and literary and debating societies, the price of food, the tuition, and such like, can be seen by reference to the printed catalogue for 1856, or by addressing the principal. The next session begins in November. . . .

The session will be divided into two terms of twenty weeks each. The expenses for tuition are very reasonable, the location is a beautiful one and the faculty unsurpassed in Western Virginia.

In 1861 the finances of the college had not improved and the unsettled conditions of the county occasioned by the war reduced the patronage of the school to such an extent that it was practically closed. It had not paid the note of Robert Holderby which was secured by the deed of trust. Some time before 1861, W. R. Boyer brought a chancery suit against Marshall College to subject its real estate to sale for the payment of its indebtedness. The Circuit Court made an order at the April term, 1861, rendering judgment in favor of Boyer and adjudged that upon failure to pay said judgment within thirty days after the rising of the court that Albert Laidley, who was appointed special commissioner for the purpose, should sell at public auction the lot of land with its appurtenances which had been conveyed by James Holderby and wife to the Trustees of Marshall Academy by deed dated June 30, 1838, subject to the lien of the deed of trust which had been given by Marshall College to Robert Holderby which was then owned by Staunton Field—who was probably the Reverend Staunton Field, one of the trustees. For some reason, possibly his absence in Richmond, for it will be remembered that Albert Laidley was elected to the Virginia Assembly in 1861, he did not carry out the decree and at the December, 1863, term of the Circuit Court, John Laidley, Jr., was substituted as commissioner in his stead.

John Laidley, Jr., made sale of the property as required by the terms of the decree to Mrs. Salina C. Mason for $1,500.00. The sale was confirmed and the purchase money paid but no deed was made to the buyer.

As we have said before because of unsettled conditions brought about by the war, work at the school was interrupted and there is no record extant of its activities but during the war period the local people, as well as the purchasers, knew of the provision in the James Holderby deed which required that the land be used for school purposes and for a time volunteers carried on the school and after the Masons purchased it they kept it open. There is a tradition that in the period from 1861 to 1865 the following persons served as principals: Reverend Brown, Professor Thrush, and the Reverend Staunton Field, but of this fact we find no official record.

Miss Mary Mason, an elderly lady, daughter of Salina C. Mason, gives the following account:

Marshall College was owned by the Methodist Church and was indebted to my grandfather, J. W. Hite. Some time in the 1860's grandfather took it over and moved in the college with his entire household, including a family of colored servants. The building at that time was brick; one part was three stories high and the other two stories high. The chapel was located in the three-story part. After we moved in my Aunt, Addie C. Hite, was married in the chapel. There was a double wedding* Oct. 22, 1865. Addie C. Hite married George Holderby and Mary Walton married George Laidley. Mr. J. D. McClintock officiated. It was his first wedding. We knew about the conditions in the Holderby deed requiring school to be kept and my mother and her two sisters, Kate Hite and Mrs. Addie C. Holderby all of whom were experienced teachers, taught in the college while we lived there. Grandfather Hite wanted to sell the place for $600.00, less than the price fixed by my mother, but my mother got her price. We lived in the college about two years but I can not fix the years.

In 1866 Marshall College was in private hands and the records of the Western Virginia Conference held on October 24, 1866, contain the following minutes:

Prior to the war our body had control of Marshall College near Guyandotte at which a number of young men were educated. During the war this college was sold by a decree of the court and passed out of our hands. Arrangements have been made by the Board of Trustees with the purchasers to reopen that institution under the control of this Conference: to effect which the board will be compelled to assume all its liabilities. About $2,750.00. Of this amount $1,500.00 are already pledged by the people of Cabell County in which the institution is located, and the committee in compliance with the request of the trustees ask that a member of this body be appointed to raise the remaining $1,250.00. The committee think that almost any one of your body can raise that sum without interfering with his regular pastoral work to any serious extent.

The Conference was unable to raise this small sum. However, the importance of the school to the community is shown by the fact that in the next year (1867) James H. Ferguson, one of the outstanding men of the county and who represented the county in the Legislature, brought about the passage of an act for the establishment of the State Normal School at Marshall College in Cabell County. The act provided for the appropriation of $30,000.00 to be expended under the

---

*The date of the above referred to double wedding would indicate that the Masons lived in the College 1865-66 and 1866-67.

direction of the regents in securing necessary grounds for said school over the period of three years in annual installments of $10,000.00 each and a further sum of $2,500.00 to be expended for furniture and necessary apparatus for the school. The act further provided that no part of this appropriation should be expended until the sum of $10,000.00 should be raised by those locally interested, but that the board of regents would accept the lands, buildings, and other property of Marshall College as the equivalent of $10,000.00. The act authorized the board of supervisors of Cabell County to levy a tax on the property in said county for an amount not to exceed $5,000.00, if after having submitted the question of this additional levy to a vote, a majority of the votes should be in favor of it. To avail themselves of the provisions of this act the board of supervisors of Cabell County, at a special meeting held on Tuesday, May 21, 1867, with John M. Blake, president, James H. Hysell and Rolland Bias, members, present, adopted a resolution reciting the various provisions of the act and submitted the question of an additional levy to be used for the purpose of purchasing Marshall College to be voted on at the next annual township election which was about to be held. At the meeting of the board held on May 23, 1867, a new board which had been elected in the interim appeared. John M. Blake was elected president and the record discloses that the returns of the election showed that a large majority of the votes cast on the proposal to make the levy was favorable. The board thereupon authorized the purchase of the property.

The board had apparently anticipated this result as its record shows that it had made a contract with Mrs. Salina C. Mason "the owner of Marshall College, its property and buildings, for the purchase thereof at the price of $3,600.00 in order that it might be conveyed to the regents of the State Normal School in pursuance of the act of February 27, 1867." The board then appropriated the sum of $3,600.00 and placed it at the disposal of the sheriff and directed him to make the purchase for the use of the State Normal School. Therefore, on the first day of August, 1867, a deed was made between John Laidley, Jr., Salina C. Mason, and the supervisors of the County of Cabell, of the first part, and the regents of the State Normal School, of the second part, conveying to the latter:

> The said lot of land with its premises and appurtenances including the buildings thereon known as Marshall College and all of the college appurtenances therein situate in said county of Cabell and a short distance below the town of Guyandotte and bounded as follows, to-wit:

Beginning at a stake standing S88 W 4 poles and 13 ft. from the College well, thence S 30 E 15 poles to a stake; thence N62½ E 12½ poles to a stake; thence N30 W 17 poles to a stake, thence to the beginning, containing 1¼ acres of land, be the same more or less.

The deed is a lengthy instrument and carries many "Whereases" containing a recital of the facts herein stated, and is of record in Deed Book 15, page 571.

The act of February 27, 1867, established the State Normal School at Marshall, the title to the land and its appurtenances was placed in the State and the college was free from debt. The regents expended the $30,000.00 for the purchase of twelve acres of the adjoining land and in making the addition of one story on the brick building which had been started under the Methodist administration, to make it a three-story building with an additional three-story wing on the west end.

To emphasize the fact that Marshall College had become a state institution the regents invited the Grand Lodge of Ancient, Free and Accepted Masons of the State of West Virginia to lay the corner stone of what was designated as the "State School at Marshall College." This was done on June 24, 1869, an account of which ceremony taken from the records of the Western Star Lodge, No. 11, Guyandotte, reads:

Proceedings of the M. W. Grand Lodge of Ancient, Free and Accepted Masons, of the State of West Virginia, November, 1869.

In Grand Lodge: A special communication of the M. W. Grand Lodge of Ancient, Free and Accepted Masons of the State of West Virginia was held at the hall of Western Star Lodge No. 11, in Guyandotte, Cabell County, on the Festival of St. John the Baptist, June 24th, A.L. 5869.

Present: M. W. H. J. Samuels as Grand Master; R. W. Alderson Workman, as Deputy Grand Master; R. W. H. R. Howard, as Senior Grand Warden; R. W. J. M. Ferguson, as Junior Grand Warden; R. W. John S. Everett, as Grand Treasurer; R. W. Thomas J. Hayslip, as Grand Secretary; R. W. Chas. W. Ferguson, as Senior Grand Deacon; R. W. George Martin, as Junior Grand Deacon; R. W. Thomas Thornburg, as Grand Marshal; R. W. Richard A. Claughton, as Grand Chaplain; R. W. D. N. Polsley, as Grand Tiler, and a large concourse of visiting brethren.

The Grand Lodge was opened in due form. The acting Grand Master announced that the present communication was held under a warrant from the Grand Master for the purpose of laying the corner stone of the state school at Marshall College, as requested by the authorities thereof.

The Grand Lodge then left the hall and repaired to the M. E. Church, where the lodges from Portsmouth, Ironton, Gallipolis, Point Pleasant, Buffalo, Barboursville, Wayne C. H., Ceredo, Catlettsburg and other places were assembled.

The preliminary arrangements being made, a procession was formed by the Grand Marshal, Thomas Thornburg, assisted by Deputy Grand Marshal, Thomas Dugan, of Portsmouth.

The procession being headed by the Portsmouth cornet band, and the officers of the Grand Lodge escorted by Sir Knights Wm. Boiles, J. H. Johnson, Francis Cleveland, G. W. Flanders, W. W. Reilly, Henry Pribble, Jas. Lodwick, Thos L. Jones, A. Dickinson, John K. Lodwick and A. C. L. White, templars of Portsmouth, after marching through the principal streets of Guyandotte, were conducted on board the steamer Fayette and proceeded down the Ohio River two miles to the Marshall College landing.

After disembarking from the steamer, the Grand Lodge was again formed in procession and conducted to the State Normal School building in process of erection at Marshall College, and the ceremony of laying the corner stone was performed in solemn form.

The procession, together with a large concourse of citizens was conducted to a grove nearby, where an address on education and the objects of the State Normal School was read by Prof. S. R. Thompson.

An elegant and appropriate oration was then delivered by Brother C. P. T. Moore of Minturn Lodge No. 19.

At the conclusion of which, dinner being announced and partaken of, the procession again repaired to the steamer and returned to the Masonic hall in Guyandotte.

The Grand Lodge was then closed.

H. P. SAMUELS,
Grand Master pro tem.
THOMAS J. HAYSLIP,
Grand Secretary pro tem.

The next year the Legislature passed an act which provided that when a student in the normal department of the school completed the course of study and discipline prescribed, he should be given a diploma which in itself was a certificate of qualification to teach common school. At the same time the Legislature made an appropriation of $5,000.00 a year for the next two years for the payment of teachers' salaries and necessary expenses.

After the City of Huntington was laid out in 1871 the college exchanged some of its land with the Central Land Company so that the college grounds would conform to the streets and avenues of the new city.

In the thirty years which followed the war the enrollment fluctuated but remained under 200 until the session of 1895-1896 when it went up to 222. During this same period the following gentlemen served as principals:

Samuel R. Thompson: 1868-1871.

J. B. Powell: 1871-1872.

Faculty at Marshall College, 1869. Samuel R. Thompson was principal. The lady on his right is Salina Hite Mason.

James E. Morrow: 1872-1873. (Mr. Morrow was the father of Dwight Morrow, who was born at Marshall College and who closed his career as United States Senator from New Jersey.)

James Beauchamp Clark: 1873-1874. (Who is the same person as "Champ" Clark and served for many years in Congress from Missouri; was for a time Speaker of the House and in 1912 a serious contender for the Democratic nomination against Woodrow Wilson for the Presidency.)

James D. Chesterman: 1874-1881.

Benjamin H. Thackston: 1881-1884.

W. J. Kenny: 1884-1886.

Thomas E. Hodges: 1886-1896. (Who resigned to accept a chair at the West Virginia University and was afterwards president of the University.)

Lawrence J. Corbly: 1896-1915.

Towards the end of Mr. Corbly's administration the title of principal was changed to that of president, and the following persons have filled that office:

Oscar I. Woodley: 1915-1919.

Frederic R. Hamilton: 1919-1923.

Morris P. Shawkey: 1923-1935.*

The first building of Marshall College was on the site of the east end of the present dormitory. In 1874 two new buildings were erected, one at a cost of $27,000.00, and a second one at $38,000.00. This building was remodeled in 1895 and is the western wing of the present dormitory; in 1897 the old east building and tower were torn down and a dormitory built on that end; in 1899 a building was erected in the space between the old east building and the building erected in 1895; in 1905-06 a fourth building was erected and additional buildings in the following order: in 1915, the science hall; in 1919, the physical education building; in 1930, the James E. Morrow Library, a beautiful building of colonial architecture at a cost of $225,000.00, and in 1933, the Shawkey Student Union Building.

There are other buildings on the campus, some of the more important ones being the training school building, the president's home, the music hall, Everett Hall, the home economics practice house, Champ Clark Hall, and the office of the college physician. But, suffice it to say, that from a modest beginning a wonderful school has been built.

---

*July 1, 1935. Dr. Shawkey was made President Emeritus and Dr. J. E. Allen was made President.

Marshall College in the 80's

Since 1919 additional grounds have been acquired and it is a part of the program of the college that additional adjoining lands be from time to time acquired.

The work of the college has kept pace with its plant. From 1867 to 1902 the work was wholly academic and in the latter year the department of education was organized and a training school opened. In March, 1902, the courses of study were extended to cover four years of secondary academic work and two advanced years of professional and academic work of such grade and quality as are necessary to have credits accepted in first-class colleges and universities. In February, 1920, Marshall College became a State Teachers' College and in June, 1921, conferred its first degree. In June, 1924, the college of arts and sciences was formally organized and now includes a two-year course in pre-engineering, pre-medical and pre-law courses.

During this period the attendance has more than kept pace with the increase in plant and faculty. It reached a total of 1,790 in the school year 1931-32, and in spite of the depression has not fallen below 1,500. The first and perhaps chief reason for this fact is that since 1920 the expansion of the school has been rapid.

When Marshall College attained its majority and was authorized to confer degrees its curriculum was enlarged and the college now includes the departments of political science, sociology, philosophy, commerce, psychology, library science, astronomy, geology, economics, biology, Bible, physical education, journalism, speech, dramatics, and mechanical drawing. Much improvement has been made in its library and laboratory facilities. Moreover, the quality and standards of the faculty have been improved. In its personnel it includes outstanding men and women who have come from the best schools in the country. Scholastic standards have been raised to meet the requirements of and have been recognized by the North Central Association of Colleges and Secondary Schools. A further reason is that the directing head of the college has seen to it that the comfort and recreational facilities for the student body have kept pace with the expansion of the college. Prior to 1897 the enrollment being small, the students lived in the dormitory and nearby homes and when in 1899 additional facilities were needed the boys began the organization of boarding clubs which since have become famous. Among these were the Jackson, Lincoln, and Jefferson Clubs. The method of operating these clubs was to appoint one boy as manager—he was allowed his board free for his services—who bought the food, looked after details and hired the cook. The cook was usually paid $.50 per week per boy. This amount added to the cost of the food and incidentals was divided among the members of the club and the average cost per student was from $1.50 to $2.00 per week for board. The girls, not to be outdone, organized the Martha Washington Club. These clubs have given way now to fraternities and sororities. Houses and ample restaurant and boarding-house facilities give the student body a wide choice of places to eat.

In those days there were many activities in which the students participated but for which they received no scholastic credit. One of these was for athletics. Nevertheless the boys had track meets, played tennis and croquet, and had football and baseball teams. For a short period, in 1896, there was a volunteer cadet corps. But one of the great features of student activity, and perhaps the most useful, was the debating societies—the Virginians whose membership came largely from the city and the Erosophian whose membership was recruited from the rural districts. Each of these societies had its own hall, and debates were held at stated intervals. Every student belonged to one or the other of these societies and was required to participate in a program at least once each quarter. After a time the boarding clubs organized their debating teams and entered these contests which were keen and profitable to the participants.

Athletics are no longer a volunteer activity but a required course. After a time the debating society ceased, and the student is now trained in speech by competent instructors. In the physical education department there are competent instructors for both sexes. The college has a gymnasium, two swimming pools, athletic fields, tennis courts, and the use of a football stadium with a seating capacity of 15,000.

The undergraduates participate in intramural contests which include tennis, touch football, speedball, volley and basketball, swimming, hockey, and bowling. Marshall College is a member of the Buckeye Conference for football, baseball and basketball with Tom Dandelet as the present head coach for football and basketball. Marshall teams are making a place for themselves in the athletic world. In addition to athletics there are many campus activities. The fraternities and sororities have much social life, and for the "Barbarians" there are student "mixes" at frequent intervals. So, no one need suffer for lack of companionship. And over and above and surrounding it all there is a hospitable people outside of the college who prize Marshall

College for its real worth in the community and who open their homes to the student body, making them welcome.

MORRIS HARVEY

In the same year that the courthouse was moved from Barboursville to Huntington some of the Barboursville people made an effort to have the County Court turn over the buildings and grounds for a school but they found that this could not be done legally.

In 1888, E. W. Blume, Henry Poteet, Henry Stowaser, Charles H. Miller, and Frederick Miller organized a company and each subscribed for $200.00 in stock and purchased at the price of $1,000.00 the buildings and grounds that had formerly been used as a courthouse and a deed was made to the corporation.

In 1888 the Barboursville Seminary was founded but it had difficulties in maintaining a school because of the lack of both money and equipment. The local people made overtures to the M. E. Church, South, to take over the property and operate it as a school. It was then agreed that if the stockholders of the old company would turn over the buildings and grounds to the M. E. Church, South, it would establish and operate a denominational college to be known as the Barboursville College. This was done and the property passed to the control of the West Virginia Annual Conference of the M. E. Church, South. T. S. Wade became the first president, and the Rev. G. W. Hampton the first vice president. In the first year of its life the Barboursville College had a total enrollment of 153 students and a faculty of seven, three of whom were women. It had three buildings, namely, Epworth Hall, the girls' dormitory, which was originally the Blume Hotel, the boys' dormitory, which had been the old county jail, and the main administration building which was formerly the courthouse.

In May, 1901, Morris Harvey of Fayette County made a large donation to the school and in recognition of this gift the board of trustees changed the name of the college to Morris Harvey College.

A short time afterwards the boys' hall was remodeled for a girls' hall and was named the Rosa Harvey Hall in honor of Morris Harvey's wife. At the completion of this work the Epworth Hall became the boys' dormitory. In 1906 Morris Harvey made another substantial contribution to the college and work was begun on a boys' dormitory in what is now the old section of Barboursville.

Morris Harvey died before this building was completed and Morris Billingsly furnished further funds for the completion, which was named in his honor Billingsly Hall, and Epworth Hall became the Music Hall.

From the time of its organization until the end of 1909 the school conferred degrees in education, literature, arts, and sciences. In that year the educational requirements fixed by the church were raised and Morris Harvey became a junior college and remained such until 1919 when it met the requirements of standard college rank.

In 1921 the new Methodist Episcopal Church, South, was built on the corner of Main and Water Streets and the building on the campus which had been used for a church became the college library. In the same year a new gymnasium was erected and the room in the administration building which had been used as a gymnasium was made the auditorium.

For a great many years high school classes were conducted in the college but upon the completion of the new boys' hall in 1927 Billingsly Hall on the south side became the high school. In 1928 two new dormitories were completed and the girls' dormitory was again named the Rosa Harvey Hall and the boys' hall was named the McDonald Hall.

Morris Harvey College now has an enrollment of four hundred students and a faculty of seventeen members.* Its courses include standard normal, provisional high school, B. A. and B. S. degrees. It has always had a number of extra-curricular organizations on the campus, excellent and active in athletic and forensic activities. At this time there are about ten such organizations including fraternities and sororities.

The following persons have served as president of the college:
D. Blain Shaw: 1905-1909.
R. H. Alderman: 1909-1914.
Paul H. Willis: 1914-1916.
U. V. W. Darlington: 1916-1921.
R. T. Webb: 1921-1922.
Charles S. Pettis: 1922-1923.
R. T. Brown: 1923-1926.
U. V. W. Darlington: 1926-1927.
R. H. Ruff: 1927-1929.
G. W. Diehl: 1929-1930.
David Kirby: 1930-1931.
Leonard Riggleman: 1931-

---

*At the beginning of the school year, September, 1935, this college was moved to Charleston.

THE PRICHARD SCHOOL

In the first decade of this century Fred C. Prichard, the son of Dr. Lewis Prichard, a very wealthy man of Charleston, came to Huntington. Business was booming. Backed by his father's fortune he soon took a prominent place in the business life of the community. He dealt largely in real estate, had some coal interests, organized and was the active executive of a bank, and finally built the Hotel Prichard. In the year 1926 he conceived the idea of organizing a school to bear his name. To this end he brought about the organization of the Prichard School and endowed it generously. The school bought a five-hundred-acre farm together with Howell's Mill and erected on the farm a wonderful building and outbuildings at a cost of $225,000.00. The farm was well equipped and a herd of thoroughbred cattle was acquired and a model dairy established. A corps of teachers was employed; twenty-five carefully selected orphans of both sexes were taken into the school to be educated and at the same time to be taught practical farming and dairying. The plan was working out most successfully. In the depression which began in the 1930's the income was so reduced that the school could not sustain itself. Although it is still struggling to maintain itself just what will be the outcome of this splendid project can not now be forecast.

EARLY DOCTORS

The early doctors, like the circuit riders, covered a large territory and their monetary reward was small. Unfortunately the names of most of these faithful men are lost. The first doctor in this county was Benjamin Brown who came in 1805 and lived at Brownsville where he died in 1848. Dr. Brown had an extensive practice which extended as far up as the forks of Sandy and on both sides of the Ohio River. In fact, the territory that he covered was larger than two or three of the present counties.

The next doctors in order of time were Henry Hampton who came from Fauquier County, Virginia, about the same time that Dr. Brown came, and lived on the farm which included the land on which Marshall College is now located, and William Paine, son of the school teacher, who in 1817 bought the farm just east of 24th Street. Dr. Patrick Talbott is mentioned as early as 1833 and Dr. John Seashols who lived in Barboursville was named jail physician in 1836. He afterwards married the widow Lucretia Creth Love.

Dr. Henry B. Maupin, uncle of our townsman, Albert B. Maupin, was a graduate from a medical school in Philadelphia in the early 1840's and in 1846 was a surgeon in the militia. He served in the General Assembly and had an apothecary shop at Barboursville during the Civil War. He met an accidental death in 1865 when he was caught between a steamboat and the wharfboat at Guyandotte.

Dr. P. H. McCullough, a graduate of Jefferson Medical College came to the county in 1840 and engaged in active practice. He moved to the present site of Huntington in 1862 and after the war served in the Legislature. He retired from active practice in 1888 and died in 1892.

Dr. Alexander M. MacCorkle, a second cousin of Governor W. A. MacCorkle, came from Rockbridge County, Virginia in the early 1840's. He practiced for many years in Guyandotte and owned the MacCorkle House in that village. This hotel was burned in 1861 and the doctor moved in the county and lived in the neighborhood of Barboursville. His second wife was the widow Hanley and they are both buried in the Yates Graveyard near Ona.

Dr. William A. Jenkins graduated in the early 1850's from Jefferson Medical College and practiced medicine in St. Louis in 1852-54, and then returned to Greenbottom. At the outbreak of the war he became a surgeon in the Confederate Army.

Dr. Girard C. Ricketts a graduate of Jefferson Medical College, who died in 1859, a comparatively young man, lived at Guyandotte and was for some twenty years an outstanding physician in the community.

Drs. Thomas J. and John N. Buffington lived in the neighborhood of Guyandotte and practiced medicine prior to the war but Dr. J. N. Buffington moved to Baton Rouge, Louisiana at an early date.

Dr. J. H. Rouse came to Guyandotte just before the Civil War and practiced medicine there until 1862 when he joined the Federal Army. For a time he was in the drug business under the firm name of Rouse and Ingham.

Dr. J. H. Hoof practiced medicine in the county during the period of the Civil War.

Dr. Bennett Clay Vinson, who was born in Tennessee but was educated in the Medical College at St. Louis, moved to this county and settled at Mud River Bridge, now Milton, and lived there more than a quarter of a century. He married Mary Simmons who still lives in the city of Huntington now past ninety years of age. Dr. Vinson was elected to the first Legislature under the Constitution of 1872.

It is interesting to note that four doctors were enlisted men in the Border Rangers, viz: James Hereford, William Jenkins, A. B. McGinnis, and Robert Timms.

Dr. David W. Dabney located in Guyandotte where he died in 1903. He practiced medicine in that community for a quarter of a century and was an outstanding and respectable citizen. In the last year of his life there was a smallpox epidemic and Dr. Dabney worked night and day in combating the dread disease. He made a long horseback trip to see a patient, contracted pneumonia and died.

Dr. John W. Brown came to Guyandotte in 1880 from North Carolina and was engaged in practice there some twenty years. He was a gentleman of the old school and had many friends.

At the close of the Civil War Dr. A. B. McGinnis who had been in the Confederate service began the practice of medicine in the county and Dr. Frank Murphy, father of James Murphy of Guyandotte, Drs. C. D. and Randolph Moss, and W. H. Bowles, who was a Confederate veteran, came to the county. They were followed a little later by Dr. A. J. Beardsley, a Union soldier who came in 1870.

After the city of Huntington was incorporated the business in the community began to center there and among the first doctors in the new city were J. O. Wall, George Rowland, Thomas Welsh, E. T. Saunders, M. L. Mayo, D. D. Wetzel, and E. S. Buffington and John D. Myers, the last two being Confederate veterans.

In the group which followed these gentlemen were Drs. C. R. Enslow, Thomas J. Prichard, W. D. Rowe, R. E. Vickers, C. C. Hogg, R. H. Pepper, J. L. Stump, Thos. F. Stuart, A. C. Burns, H. A. Brandebury, J. E. Rader and E. W. Grover, and following these came the men who are still active.

Among the later doctors who had a county practice were H. V. Sands who lived in Union District, J. W. Holstein who lived at Barboursville, A. Herrenkohl of Union Ridge, P. H. Swann of Barboursville, and more recently L. C. Morrison at Milton.

XXIII: STATE INSTITUTIONS

THERE are five State institutions in Cabell County. The Huntington State Hospital was created by an act of the Legislature in 1897 as the home for incurables. In 1901 this name was changed to the West Virginia Asylum and in 1916 it was changed to its present name. Mary Jackson Ruffner was instrumental in bringing about the organization of this institution and was its first general manager. Four years later Dr. L. V. Guthrie was appointed superintendent; he was succeeded by Dr. W. D. McClung, who was in turn succeeded by the present superintendent, Dr. C. T. Taylor. The institution is situated on a tract of land consisting of some thirty acres on the foothills in the eastern edge of Huntington, and fronts on Norway Avenue. The original home was a single building three stories high, but since that time a number of buildings have been added and the place is being constantly enlarged. In March, 1935 the state bought the old George McKendree farm of 450 acres near Barboursville, to be used in connection with this institution.

The West Virginia Colored Children's Home is located on a tract of 190 acres, located on Route 60, about six miles east of the courthouse. The building is a three story red brick building, modernly equipped and constructed. It was incorporated in January, 1900, in Bluefield, and was then called the West Virginia Normal Industrial School for Colored Orphans. It was first located in what was then Central City, now West Huntington, and later moved to its present site on the Guyan River. In 1911 it was purchased by the State and its name changed. Since that date it has been under the State Board of Control.

The West Virginia Home for Aged and Infirm Colored Men and Women: This institution was created by the acts of 1923, and as the name indicates, provides a home for colored men and women who because of extreme old age or infirmity, with no relatives, can be properly cared for. It was first located at Charleston, but in December, 1928, it was moved to its present site, 1635 8th Avenue. The property it occupies is not owned by the state.

The West Virginia Industrial Home: This institution was established by an act of the Legislature in 1921 but was not opened until March 11, 1926. It is located on Norway Avenue three miles east of the city limits. The farm contains fifteen acres on which there is a modern three-story brick, fireproof building and the necessary outhouses.

The Conley State Forest Nursery: This is located on the Ohio River Road six miles from Huntington. It was established in 1921, and covers twenty acres of ground. It produces four million trees each year, all forest trees and no ornamentals. It is hoped to increase this to seven million trees per year. These seedlings are sold to farmers and coal companies for about $5.00 a thousand for reforestation planting, but the demand can not be supplied at the present time.

XXIV: THE CITY OF HUNTINGTON

IN 1869-70, C. P. Huntington employed Albert Laidley to option the lands along the Ohio River from the mouth of the Guyandotte extending to a point about 1st Street, East. "The first farm below the mouth of the Guyandotte, was owned by James H. Buffington, containing 434 acres. This is the farm on which Colonel D. W. Emmons lived. The second farm was that of Dr. John N. Buffington, containing 258 acres. Dr. Buffington reserved for a daughter a portion of this farm afterwards laid out in what is later known as the Cedar Grove subdivision of this city. The third farm was that of Judge W. H. Hagen, and his wife, Mary Jane Hagen, who was formerly a Buffington. The reservation by them was afterwards sold and a Catholic school is now located on this reservation. The fourth farm was that of Dr. John Buffington; the fifth that of John Laidley, with a reservation thereon to L. H. Burks and wife, the daughter of John Laidley. The sixth farm was that of Henry Buffington. Seventh, Dr. Payne extending down to about 24th Street. The eighth was that of P. C. Buffington, extending down to Marshall College and 17th Street. Colonel Buffington reserved thirty-five acres from 5th Avenue south to the railroad on which now stands the Chesapeake and Ohio hospital. The ninth farm was that of W. P. Holderby, extending down to about 15th Street. Tenth, Harry Poage, down to about 11th Street. Eleventh, John Hanley on which stood a log cabin on the site of the B. W. Foster residence, extending down near 10th Street. The twelfth tract was that of Charles Everett. Thirteenth, Ephriam Frampton. Fourteenth, John M. Pennybaker. Fifteenth, Dr. P. H. McCullough. Sixteenth, a small tract sold by McCullough to E. T. Mitchell, where there was an old brick house known as the Brown House near the present incinerator. The seventeenth was that of G. A. and W. L. Johnson which extended from just below 3d Street to just below 1st Street.

"All of these tracts were conveyed to Albert Laidley and he conveyed them to C. P. Huntington in 1870. Mr. Huntington, after making reservation for the rights-of-way and shops for the Chesapeake and Ohio Railway Company conveyed the remainder on October 16, 1870, to the Central Land Company."

Rufus Cook, surveyor, of Boston, Massachusetts, made a map of the new city which was named Huntington. This map was filed in the recorder's office on December 6, 1871. The new city was to

Collis P. Huntington, founder of the city

occupy the plain lying between the river and the hills on the lands of the Central Land Company. Its avenues east and west are intersected at regular intervals by streets running north and south. The streets and avenues are wide and of uniform width but unfortunately the plan made no provision for parks or open spaces, and more unfortunate were the reservations in the several tracts of land above mentioned. A part of the P. C. Buffington reservation at 17th Street, East, was laid out in a subdivision and its streets and avenues did not conform to the Cook map. Later the same thing happened in the layout of a subdivision in the west end, and as a result there are some offsets in the avenues that might have been avoided. Anyway, Huntington is a tailor made city and has none of the disadvantages of a city which has grown out of a village that had not been planned and in which farm lanes had been the first streets and later had to be widened.

On the 27th day of February, 1871, the Legislature passed an act incorporating the new city with a mayor and councilmanic government, and provided for an election to be held under the supervision of J. C. Baker a justice of the peace at Marshall College Postoffice to elect the first city officials. This election was held on the 31st day of December, 1871, with E. M. Underwood and J. T. Hatfield, commissioners, and A. S. Emmons, clerk. P. C. Buffington was elected mayor, Dr. J. O. Wall, E. S. Holderby, D. W. Emmons, W. H. Hagen and E. T. Mitchell, councilmen. The charter made the territory included in the new city an independent school district and the governing body of the city the school board.

The first meeting of the council was held on the 6th day of January, 1872, and the following organization perfected: Isaac H. Mitchell was elected marshal, J. H. Poage, treasurer, L. H. Burks, assessor, and A. J. Enslow, street commissioner. General John H. Oley was elected recorder and he continued to fill this office until the date of his death on March 11, 1888.

The mayor's salary was fixed at $25.00, the recorder's at $35.00 and the marshal's salary at $30.00. The marshal was directed to act with a committee and instructed to prepare a safe and comfortable place to confine prisoners. This he did and reported the cost at $9.10.

The problems which confronted the new governing body were many. They were the heads of a new city which was in the making and they applied themselves to the problems with wonderful foresight. Their first act was the naming of a committee to examine and

Peter Cline Buffington, first Mayor of Huntington

report on the amount of work and the probable cost to improve the streets and sidewalks. At the following meeting this committee recommended that plank sidewalks be placed on 2nd Avenue from S. S. Coe's residence to 9th Street, on both sides of 7th and 8th Streets between 2nd and 3d Avenues, on the west side of 9th Street between 2nd and 3rd Avenues, on both sides of 3rd Avenue between 7th and 10th Streets, with the necessary number of street crossings. The report was adopted and the work was ordered done.

In October, 1873, the property owners on 3rd Avenue between 9th and 10th Streets were ordered to build a gutter of stone boulders in front of their property.

The first street lights were put on the street corners at 7th, 8th, and 9th Streets on 2nd Avenue and on the same streets on 3rd Avenue.

The city immediately bought lots 8, 9 and 10 in Block 95, which faced 4th Avenue just west of 9th Street and erected thereon a city hall 24x14 feet with a separate lock-up in the rear. At the same time it acquired lots 23, 24 and 25 in Block 91 which fronted on 4th Avenue between 7th and 8th Streets for the West End School.

The question of police was solved for the moment by the election of a marshal, but before the city was six months old the marshal was authorized to appoint special police needed to handle the crowd that attended a circus. Later, a night policeman was appointed, but by March, 1876, the council directed that the city was so peaceful that night police could be dispensed with. This was done but some months later, after much earnest debate, a night policeman was employed with a salary fixed at $1.25 per night and later it was agreed to raise his pay to $1.50 per night during the winter months. On June 6, 1876, the police were required to buy a uniform and a star. Among the early police was W. H. Bull who was later mayor. Kemp Hatfield served longest as a night policeman. The marshal was the head of the police department and he had many duties.

One of the first duties imposed upon the new marshal was the enumeration of school children. Then with the advice of Dr. J. O. Wall, councilman, he was "a Board of Health" and in order that his time might be fully taken up he was directed to examine every flue, grate, etc., in the new city for fire hazards.

Isaac H. Mitchell continued as marshal until June 27, 1876, when he was succeeded by S. C. Donella who served until 1886 when he was given an appointment in the Federal service and Colonel Thomas

Sikes was appointed marshal and served one year. He was succeeded by A. P. Mitchell who served until 1891.

One of the big problems was the question of opening streets and vacating public roads which did not coincide with the new streets and alleys. The very first change of the sort was the abandonment of that portion of the old pike which lay between 5th and 6th Avenues and 11th and 13th Streets, and using 13th Street and 5th Avenue in its stead.

In the fall of 1872 there was an epidemic of smallpox and Dr. George Rowland looked after it. The question of a health department and a city physician received the attention of the council. The councilmanic outlook was the same then as now. One member proposed that the poor of the city be permitted to select his or her physician and the city pay the bill. This proposal was promptly voted down and Dr. Thomas Welsh and Dr. George Rowland were placed in nomination for city physician. Dr. Welsh was elected.

The water supply for the city was provided by wells. The privilege of drilling the first well was on September 3, 1872, given to the Bank of Huntington, and L. D. Sanborn and some others who put a well down on the corner of 3d Avenue and 12th Street. This permission was conditioned that the parties would put in a pump and that the top of the well be built up in good condition. Other public wells were put down as follows: 10th Street and 3d Avenue; 8th Street and 3d Avenue; at the West End School, 4th Avenue and 9th Street, and later the city put caps and pumps on these wells.

On October 8, 1872, the voters in Huntington voted for a member of Congress but when the returns were submitted to the board of supervisors in October that body refused to receive them on the ground that the election day was on the fourth Thursday in October.

On May 27, 1873, the council named Dr. J. O. Wall, city physician, I. H. Mitchell, marshal, M. P. Lowther, street commissioner, W. H. Harper and T. J. Burke as the first board of health.

As early as 1873 an effort was made to raise funds by public subscription for fire equipment and on August 5th of that year the mayor reported he had been unsuccessful in his efforts. On February 13, 1874, A. C. Young and eighty others petitioned the city to buy a hook, ladder, and buckets for a fire company at a cost of $450.00. Young and eleven others of the signers agreed if this was done they would organize a hook and ladder company. The request was referred to a committee who without waiting to make a report to the

North side of 3rd Avenue, looking west from 10th Street, 1880

council placed an order with one M. A. Jones to build "a hook and ladder with carriage" for the sum of $450.00. This action was reported to the council and promptly confirmed. Mr. Young organized the company and was elected its first president. He was authorized to purchase four dozen wooden buckets for temporary use and was named on a committee with authority to have a building erected to house the equipment. In the August following an ordinance was passed creating a fire department to consist of the hook and ladder company already organized and such other fire engine and hose companies that might thereafter be organized, a chief engineer, fire wardens and fire police and the council limited the membership of the hook and ladder company to thirty-five members. S. Sexton was the first chief engineer.

On April 19, 1875, the council took action upon the death of P. C. Buffington who had been the first mayor, and then a member of the council.

In May, 1875, O. E. Young who was then fire warden informed the council that he had had a letter from the chief engineer of the fire department at Portsmouth saying that he had a second-hand fire engine which he would sell for $600.00. The matter was referred to the committee on fire and police protection who promptly reported a plan for supplying the city with water and apparatus for extinguishing fires. Acting upon the recommendation of this committee the council ordered five cisterns of a capacity of five hundred barrels each and to be not more than fifteen feet deep, and directed the committee to proceed to Portsmouth to negotiate the purchase of the hand fire engine. The committee purchased the engine and hose carriage and the apparatus accompanying them for $725.00 and their action was approved by the council. Arrangements were made with C. F. Parson for the use of his frame building as a temporary hose house. The mayor was directed to call a public meeting of citizens on August 5, 1875, for the purpose of organizing a fire company. This was done and the Excelsior Fire Company was organized. These two companies, the fire company and the hook and ladder company elected their officers and named a foreman and their lists of members together with the by-laws were from time to time submitted to the council for approval. They were further given the privilege of nominating fire police who were then appointed by the common council.

These volunteer fire companies were organized like regular cor-

South side of 4th Avenue, between 10th and 11th Streets, 1883

porations with a president, etc., but each had a foreman which corresponded to a captain, and the members were exempt from work on the road which had to be performed or in lieu thereof a payment of $1.50 per day.

Thomas Sikes, one time colonel in the Federal Army, was the foreman of the hook and ladder company and Eustace Gibson, one time captain in the Confederate Army, was foreman of the Excelsior Company.

The first list of fire police was submitted by the hook and ladder company. The fire police were W. P. Titus, W. Gibson, R. E. McIntosh, T. Palmer, and W. F. Wallace, and from this time on these fire police were made up of men that we now remember as outstanding business men and leaders, and included Sam Gideon, H. C. Simms, Frank B. Enslow, J. K. Oney, and many others.

In 1875 the Excelsior Fire Company was authorized to and did buy a fire bell for the city at the price of $101.00.

On February 7, 1876, a contract was given to Thomas Sikes for building four public cisterns, one at 2nd Avenue and 8th Street, one at 3d Avenue and 9th Street, one at 3d Avenue and 10th Street, and one at 3d Avenue and 12th Street, each to contain 500 barrels of water. Later a small cistern was put in at the corner of 7th Street and 3d Avenue, one at the West End School, and it cost $12.00 to fill one of these cisterns with water.

But to return to the activities of the council. In the beginning they took upon themselves the duty of advancing the interests of the city. On May 27, 1873, it requested the County Court to purchase the stock of private persons in the suspension bridge over the Guyandotte River and to make the bridge toll free. This was done a short time thereafter.

In May, 1874, Captain Gibson appeared before the council and protested the location of a soap factory in the center of the city on 3d Avenue between 12th and 13th Streets.

On July 1, 1874, the council allowed "Colonel" J. S. Kirk $200.00 to aid in bringing the Swift Iron Works from Newport, Kentucky, to Huntington.

On September 6, 1875, the council meeting lacked a quorum and the recorder gives as a reason that "some councilmen were absent pursuing the bank robbers." Councilman Henry C. Simms appeared in the meeting and referred to the exciting event of the Huntington bank robbery. On October 4, 1875, the council allowed Kenndry and Dixon, liverymen, $10.00 to cover the hire of horses used by citizens in the pursuit of the robbers.

THE JESSE JAMES ROBBERY

On the 6th day of September, 1875, a band of horsemen rode into the city and robbed the Huntington Bank which was located in the little brick building on the north side of 3d Avenue between 12th and 13th Streets. They left the city by way of the Wayne—then the McCoy Road—and at Hodge, just at the Wayne line they threw away a sack containing pennies which was picked up by people in that neighborhood. Who these robbers were no none knows but local folks have always called this robbery the Jesse James Robbery. At the time there was a Methodist Conference in session and some of the folks who saw the gang riding into town thought they were preachers but commented on what good horses they were riding. They stopped at the Catholic Church and talked with Father Quirk.

As soon as the robbery was reported, D. I. Smith, then sheriff, promptly organized a posse and started in pursuit but did not make a capture. Mr. Smith often laughed and told how, when his posse got close to the robbers, and he ordered a charge immediately some of his men had to tighten their saddle girths and before this was done the robbers were out of sight. One of the robbers named Thomas J. Webb was captured and returned here for trial. He was convicted on December 4, 1875, and sentenced to fourteen years in the penitentiary. When asked if he had anything to say he replied that he had not, that he was a young man and would serve his term and say nothing. He died in prison.

On October 4, 1875, Mayor T. J. Burke resigned. His resignation was not accepted and the council requested that he reconsider which he did. He served out his term and had a complimentary vote from the council.

On April 3, 1876, the council published the list of property owned in the city as follows:

Cemetery grounds	$ 3,000.00
City Hall, hook and ladder house, and lock up, 3 lots	3,000.00
4th Ave. School house and 3 lots	5,000.00
3d Ave. School house and 2 lots	3,500.00
Fire engine and hose carriage	747.00
Fire hose	655.00

THE CITY OF HUNTINGTON

Hook and ladder apparatus		450.00
School furniture		1,000.00
Total value of property		$17,352.00
Liabilities on above property		
School bonds No. 4 and 5	$2,000.00	
Amt. unpaid on cemetery	1,500.00	
Total liabilities	$3,500.00	3,500.00
Values of property above liabilities		$13,852.00

In this year Sam Gideon was a candidate for the first time for the office of councilman.

The council passed ordinances forbidding the playing of shinny on the streets, prohibiting a family from permitting more than two hogs to run at large and prohibiting at all hazard geese running at large.

Flora Wright fell off the footlog over Four Pole Creek and presented a bill to the city for damages. The council settled with her for $25.00 and discussed the erection of a bridge over Four Pole.

A Mrs. Scheff who was driving along the 31st Street Road drove into a hole of some sort and sustained an injury and brought suit against the city. She recovered the first judgment for damages against the city.

On June 6, 1876, an order was made requiring police officers to provide themselves with a uniform and a "star."

At 5:00 a.m., on June 26, 1876, Isaac H. Mitchell, town marshal, received a wire from Greenfield, Highland County, Ohio, asking the arrest of a man thirty-eight years of age and described as to height and clothing and who was said to be driving a fine horse and buggy. The man had evidently been through the city earlier in the day. Mitchell, accompanied by Tom C. Turner, a liveryman, started in pursuit of the stranger and overtook him about two o'clock the next morning on Route 60 just west of Hurricane Station. Mitchell jumped over the back of and into the buggy and called on the man to surrender. A rough and tumble fight took place and Mitchell was shot. The man then turned and shot Turner who, in his attempt to assist Mitchell, had snapped his pistol a number of times at the man in the buggy, but for some reason Turner's pistol did not discharge. The stranger abandoned the horse and buggy in which he was traveling

2nd Avenue, between 7th and 8th Streets, circa 1878

and stole a horse and buggy and set out in the direction of Gallipolis, Ohio. Some time later Mitchell was found one-half mile away from Turner, but still grimly holding to the horse. Turner was badly wounded and each thought the other was dead. Mitchell was taken to the home of Lewis Burdette where he died on the same day. Turner, seriously wounded, was brought to his home in Huntington but recoverd. The mayor offered a reward for the arrest of the murderer, and F. M. Ingersoll, who was marshal of Pomeroy, along with Henry Wyley and some others arrested a man who gave his name as Marshall Allen, but afterwards told the sheriff of Putnam County that it was not his right name. This man was brought to Huntington to give Turner, who was thought to be dying, an opportunity to identify him. Turner did identify him as the man who had done the shooting. Mitchell was a member of the Masonic Lodge and of the Christian Church and there was much excitement on account of his death. The sheriff of Putnam County, however, took charge of the prisoner and conveyed him to Winfield and lodged him in the Putnam County jail. A mob which is said to have been made up of some of the most representative men in the city and county went to Winfield and took the prisoner from the jail and lynched him. The question is still debated whether the man who was lynched knew at the time he fired the fatal shot that Mitchell and Turner were officers or whether he thought he was being held up.

On March 6, 1877 there was a petition from the hook and ladder company asking that the hook and ladder house be moved to a point on 3d Avenue so as to be more accessible in case of fire. About this time the Excelsior Fire Company asked that the council pay for the night watchman on duty at the engine house from March 1, 1877, for the reason that the members of the company had considerable expense in keeping up their organization. The council agreed to pay the man $3.00 a month from that day to take care of the fire company's apparatus and to give the alarm in case of fires but refused the request of the hook and ladder company to move their house.

The Legislature of 1877 amended the city charter and made the assessment with and payment of city taxes as a qualification of voting in the city election.

In 1878 an ordinance was passed forbidding driving faster than eight miles an hour. The marshal was directed to post notices of this ordinance on the roads leading into the city, and a cistern was built on 4th Avenue between 9th and 10th Streets.

In April, 1878, the council inaugurated a movement to move the courthouse from Barboursville to Huntington and made an offer to provide the land and to build the courthouse without cost to the county. On August 5th following it presented a petition to the County Court to take a vote on the removal of the courthouse but this the county court refused to do. On June 2, 1886, E. S. Doolittle and eight hundred other citizens and voters filed a similar petition and the County Court again refused to submit the question to the vote of the people but was compelled to do so by a mandamus. The vote was taken on November 2, 1886, and was favorable to the removal, but the result was challenged, the contestants alleging gross fraud and irregularities in the election in the City of Huntington but in the end did not prevail and the courthouse was moved into the city building.

In 1878 the city began negotiations to acquire a wharf site on the river near 9th Street. The railroad was unwilling to open 9th Street or to give up any land west of 9th Street. However, after continuous negotiations on June 7th, 1880, the wharf was acquired at the foot of 10th Street for the price of $2,500.00.

In January, 1879, the fire limits were established on 3d Avenue between 6th and 11th Streets and frame buildings were prohibited in this area. The question of issuing bonds to purchase a steam fire engine was submitted to the people and was defeated.

A municipal court was established and J. M. Layne was elected judge and Jas. T. Sample was elected clerk. Sample died in a few months and was succeeded by J. K. Oney who reported that for the year ending April, 1880, the court collections had netted the city $31.50. In this year Sam Gideon ran for mayor and was defeated by E. S. Buffington. A. F. Southworth was a candidate for councilman.

John W. Boone was put in charge of the pump at 3d Avenue and 8th Street, and Laidley and Johnson in charge of the one at 3d Avenue and 10th Street, to prevent a waste of water.

In April, 1883, a steam fire engine was purchased and a part of the fire department put on pay but the volunteer feature continued until 1897.

It might be pointed out that in the first twenty-five years in the city's life its council included the most representative men of the community. Among these names are found D. W. Emmons, Ely Ensign, T. S. Scanlon, A. F. Southworth, T. J. Bullock, E. S. Holderby, J. H. Poage, Dr. E. S. Buffington, A. J. Enslow, Henry C. Simms,

Laidley and Johnston's Grocery, southeast corner 10th Street and 3rd Avenue, circa 1874

E. T. Mitchell, D. E. Abbott, B. W. Foster, Sam Gideon, J. K. Oney, and many others.

The second ten years of the city's life was marked by substantial progress. The big fire on 2nd Avenue between 7th and 8th Streets helped to bring about the removal of the retail business from that avenue over to 3d Avenue. In this decade came the electric lights, street cars and city water, and the organization of the Barnum Club, a Democratic political organization named for W. H. Barnum, one of the officials of the Ensign Manufacturing Company. This club was for ten years a dominating factor in local politics and was more excoriated than Tammany Hall.

George I. Neal was admitted to the Bar on December 3, 1888. He was destined to be a dominant factor in city, county, and state politics.

In 1890 the city had its first artificial gas and the telephone came in the next year.

The first bond issue, the proceeds of which were used for the purpose of constructing sewers and the paving of streets, was authorized. Ninth Street was paved from the Chesapeake and Ohio Railroad station to 2nd Avenue, and 3d Avenue was paved from 7th Street to 20th Street. Second Avenue was paved between 8th and 10th Streets, and 8th Street was paved between 2nd and 4th Avenues.

In 1891 the charter was amended and an elective chief of police was substituted for town marshal. In the election which followed W. M. Staley defeated Arthur P. Mitchell for this office. Staley served as chief of police only a few months when he resigned and was succeeded on June 1, 1891, by Scott Turner, who continued as chief until the first day of January, 1897. In this year George I. Neal was a candidate for mayor and was defeated by Ham. Dickey.

Elliott Northcott, the present judge of the United States Circuit Court of Appeals, was admitted to the Bar on August 24, 1891.

On June 1, 1892, Huntington had its first free mail delivery and as a condition precedent to this service the city council required all houses to be numbered and the names of the streets and avenues to be put up at street intersections. J. C. LeSage, now living, was one of the four original mail carriers.

Allen Harrison was convicted of the murder of Betty Adams and sentenced to be hanged. After an appeal to the Supreme Court which confirmed the conviction and sentence, Harrison was hanged in what is now Ritter Park on November 22, 1892. This is the only legal execution which has taken place in the county.

In 1893 George I. Neal was elected mayor and served two terms.

During this period Huntington experienced the worst of the so-called Cleveland Panic. The Ensign shops shut down entirely and the Chesapeake and Ohio shops laid off a great number of their employees. As a consequence there was much distress and to alleviate this unemployment Mr. Ensign erected his handsome home on 3d Avenue between 13th and 14th Streets in order to give his shop employees work, and the city built the undergrade crossing at 16th Street and the first trunk sewer which was located in 16th Street. These two projects furnished employment as day laborers for many splendid mechanics who had been accustomed to earning top wages.

In 1894 the county went Republican for the first time in twenty-five years and elected the judge of the Criminal Court, the clerk of the Circuit Court and two members of the Legislature. In the next year the Legislature amended the city charter and repealed the provision which required a voter in a city election to be assessed with and pay a poll tax. In the spring election Dr. C. R. Enslow was a candidate for mayor against D. E. Mathews. The election was close and on the face of the returns Enslow and the Democratic council were elected. A notice of contest was given but before the contest was tried Judge Mathews withdrew and Dr. Enslow was mayor and the Democratic councilmen contestees held their offices.

In the spring of 1896 Ely Ensign was elected mayor but in the fall election the division in the Democratic party over the silver issue resulted in a sweeping Republican victory and there was much excitement in the city. On the day following the election the streets were filled with excited people discussing the result. Third Avenue between 9th and 10th Streets was at that time the business center of the town and well on into the day our good friend Levi Jones, who was much upset over the result of the election, came down 9th Street; turned east on the north side of 3d Avenue and for apparently no reason let out a yell of "Hurrah for Jeff Davis and the Southern Confederacy." This was the spark that set off the powder and a fight started in and around the entrance of the First National Bank. Just who hit whom or why, has not up to this time been explained, but quite a few of the most representative people in the city took part in the fight on one side or the other. Other people not so representative fell in for good measure, but anyway they all strove mightily. There were no fatalities and the instance was soon regarded as one of the colorful events in the city's life. The next year W. F. Hite, a young

South side 3rd Avenue, between 9th and 10th Streets, circa 1890. Present site of Anderson-

THE CITY OF HUNTINGTON   189

Republican, defeated A. F. Stewart, who was then the master mechanic of the Chesapeake and Ohio shops, for mayor and a Republican council was elected. The election was held the first of April and a special meeting of the new council was called and held on April 9th, and a clean sweep was made of the old appointees. Frank H. Tyree was named chief of police and, except for a period in 1899 when S. P. Wiley held that office continued as chief until 1901. Tyree was afterwards bodyguard for Theodore Roosevelt who made him United States Marshal for the Southern District of West Virginia, and he was afterwards twice elected sheriff of Cabell County.

In 1898 Hite had fallen out with some of the leaders of the party and a deal was made between the Democratic and Republican leaders under the terms of which it was agreed that the support of a certain element in the Republican party would be thrown to the heads of the Democratic ticket and that if the Democrats were successful they would name Tyree as chief of police. As some of the men who made this deal are still alive it is probably best not to give too many details. In all events the Democrats were successful and elected Charles A. Nash, mayor, C. A. Boxley, treasurer, and Dr. C. T. Taylor, city clerk. This was Dr. Taylor's first effort in politics. Tyree was named chief of police.

Shortly after the spring election the war with Spain was declared the fire bell sounded the military alarm and the two companies G and I assembled at their respective armories, in a few hours they marched to the Chesapeake and Ohio depot and entrained for Camp Lee located at Kanawha City just about opposite the present State Capital.

Dewey's victory at Manila was properly celebrated by the erection of a flagpole on the lot where the postoffice now stands and the raising of a flag thereon. Public speaking was had inside the Chesapeake and Ohio shop yards and at the Ensign Car Works. The war, of course, was soon over and aside from the passing excitement it had no effect on civic affairs.

At this period it was the custom for the outgoing council to fix the salaries of the incoming officers in advance of the city election, so in the closing days of this city administration the council passed an ordinance fixing the salary of the mayor at $10.00 per month, the chief of police at $50.00 per month, the treasurer at $25.00 per month, and the councilmen at $5.00 per month. Dr. H. A. Brandebury, a Republican, was elected mayor with a Republican council. He and

Northeast corner 9th Street and 4th Avenue, circa 1890

his associates served their respective terms on this meager pay. Just before the next city election the council passed an ordinance restoring the salaries. Dr. Brandebury was elected to succeed himself. At this time partisan feelings were high and there was a great deal of bitterness; elections were marked by illegal voting and violence, and the police began to take an active hand in them. At the November, 1899, grand jury, Hall Ross, a city employee in the street department, had two indictments returned against him for illegal voting. He was arraigned and pleaded guilty to one indictment and was fined $20.00; the second indictment was nollied. The case was much discussed, the prosecuting attorney came in for some criticism for indicting Ross for a misdemeanor when it was asserted that there was a statute covering this offense which made it a felony. Ross was proud of his notoriety and painted a sign on his pushcart boasting of his achievements. In the spring election of 1900 the Ross case was almost a campaign issue. Election day itself passed off quietly but on the day following the election there was some excitement on the streets as an aftermath. Ross came down 9th Street and looked into the *Advertiser* office which was then located on the west side of 9th Street between 4th and 5th Avenues, but seeing nobody in the front part of the building proceeded down 9th Street towards 3d Avenue. By the time he was a short distance north of 4th Avenue and traveling in the middle of the street. E. M. (Bub) MacCallister, Edmund Fry, and Seldon Sharitz were standing in a group on the west side of 9th Street in front of the Main Saloon. When Ross saw them, for reasons not clearly explained, and for no reason as contended by MacCallister and Fry, he opened fire on the group. The first shot struck Sharitz and was fatal. Sharitz put one arm around the telephone pole near which he had been standing and supporting himself emptied his pistol and then sank to the ground dead. While this was going on Fry and MacCallister were returning Ross's fire but for some unaccountable reason they all escaped injury. One of the shots, however, broke a window in a store on the east side of 9th Street and wounded a store clerk in the head. Almost before the shooting was over Doc Suitor, the constable, and Frank Tyree, chief of police, were on the scene and Suitor arrested Ross and Tyree arrested Fry and MacCallister. Ross was indicted for murder but obtained a change of venue to Kanawha County and got off with light punishment. The excitement following this event was considerable and the police ordered saloons closed for the remainder of the day.

North side 3rd Avenue looking east from 10th Street during 1884 flood

In the fall election John H. Holt was a candidate for governor and there was some excitement during that day. There were no registration laws and the question of who was, and who was not, entitled to vote was determined by the majority of the election commission. Enoch Baker, one of the Democratic workers, started into the precinct on 4th Avenue between 8th and 9th Streets to challenge a voter and was set upon by the police, given a severe beating, and without the knowledge of the election commissioner or any warrant was lodged in the county jail and retained until the next day. Baker brought suit against the sheriff on his bond for false imprisonment. When the suit was tried the circuit judge directed a verdict for the defendant and justified it on the grounds that no person had the right to come within sixty feet of the polls unless he came for the purpose of voting.

On February 4, 1901 the city charter was amended and the term of office for the mayor was fixed at two years and the number of councilmen was increased to twelve. The city election under the new charter was to be held on April 1, 1901, and the act provided that the council then in office who had been elected in 1900 were to continue in office until their successors were elected in 1903 and in the event of a vacancy in the elective office it required the vote of a majority of all members of the council elected to elect a successor.

On September 17, 1901, the first regular term of the United States District Court and the United States Circuit Court was held in Huntington with the Hon. B. F. Keller, judge, George W. Atkinson, district attorney, R. B. Bernheim, clerk, and John K. Thompson, marshal.

In 1905 the charter was again amended by two separate acts of the Legislature. The first was passed on February 16, 1905, and provided that the mayor, the city clerk, and the assessor might be removed from office at the pleasure of the council by a vote of three-fourths of all the members elected to the council. This act was effective from date of passage. The second amendment passed on February 2, 1905, became effective ninety days from its passage and contained the provision that the mayor might suspend a police officer, and that such officer could not be reinstated except by a majority vote of all members elected to the council.

C. M. Buck, Republican, was elected mayor in 1903 together with ten Republican councilmen. It was not very long until the Republican council and the mayor were in hopeless disagreement. Just before the city election of 1905 the council passed a resolution authorizing its police committee to appoint as many special policemen as it

The 1913 flood, 3rd Avenue, east from 10th Street

[194]

deemed necessary for duty on the coming election day but not to exceed twenty and that if any police officer was removed for any cause he might be reinstated by a majority of the police committee. With this setting the election of 1905 came and the police committee appointed the full quota of special police who were on hand at the down town precincts early in the morning. The election commissioners at the City Hall precinct on 9th Street called for deputy sheriff T. H. Nash and E. L. Baylous to take charge of an illegal voter. The special police interfered, Nash was beaten up and put in jail. There was a pistol battle between the special police on one side assisted by one of the election officers and the deputy sheriffs on the other side assisted by Jeremiah Adkins, a constable. A number of bystanders joined in on one side or the other. Adkins was wounded in the foot and Roy Hill, a policeman, was wounded in the body. Azel McCurdy, deputy sheriff, arrested Adkins and was going to the courthouse with his prisoner when the city police took the prisoner from him. Later warrants were issued for the city police who gave bond. They were released and in turn they released their prisoners. Indictments and trials followed with convictions and from this time hitherto there has been no police interference at elections.

The election, to the surprise of the knowing ones, resulted in the election of H. C. Gordon, mayor, by a majority of ten and of two Democratic councilmen from the second ward, viz: T. W. Taylor and C. W. Turner. This was brought about by the action of William Chaffin, the Republican clerk at precinct No. 6, at Huff's Shop in the second ward. There were quite a number of visiting brethren who voted for a price. Chaffin was following the customary practice of marking the ballots for this type of voter but for reasons not known he had fallen out with his own party and took this occasion to get even. The various tickets were printed in parallel columns on the ballot and if the voter desired to vote the straight ticket he drew lines from the top to the bottom of the tickets other than the one that he desired to vote. There were four tickets on the ballot, the Republican on the left, two independent tickets in the middle and the Democratic ticket on the right. When a voter came in who wanted to vote the straight Republican ticket Mr. Chaffin turned the ballot up-side-down and drew a line through the three columns on the right and the result was that the voter voted the straight Democratic ticket. This practice was not discovered and at the end of the day this precinct gave a substantial Democratic majority and brought about the election

The 1884 flood. South side 3rd Avenue, west of 10th Street

of two Democratic councilmen in the second ward. With a Republican mayor and a tie in the council things began to happen.

On June 19, 1905, G. L. Pickering, Republican member who had removed from the city, tendered his resignation as councilman. His resignation was accepted and Warren Wood, Democrat and I. R. Titus, Republican, were nominated to fill out his unexpired term. The vote was taken and Wood receiving 6 votes, Titus 4, the mayor declared Wood elected and the council adjourned. An application was made to the Circuit Court for a mandamus against the mayor directing him to change his ruling on the ground that a majority of all the council had not elected Wood. This litigation went to the Supreme Court and that court held that a majority of the council elected was necessary to elect Wood.

On July 17, 1905, the Democratic wing of the council passed a resolution dispensing with a number of police officers who held offices under an ordinance passed by council and were not protected by the charter provision and named an equal number of Democrats to fill these positions. The Republican police officers declined to give up their offices and the Republican mayor declined to recognize the Democratic police. The matter was taken into court, and while it was pending the city had two police forces. The Supreme Court on the same day it decided the Wood case decided that the council had acted within its right under the charter in the removal of the police and the appointment of the new ones. The council stood six to five Democrats and on the 7th day of August, 1905, J. M. Brown, a Republican member was appointed postmaster and resigned. In the early part of 1906 T. W. Taylor, a Democratic member and J. F. Holswade, a Republican member, both resigned.

On February 5, 1907, the charter was again amended and provided that any vacancies in the elective offices that were not filled by a majority of the elected council within fifteen days should be filled by appointments made by the mayor and that in the event that there was a vacancy in the office of the mayor which was not filled within the same time and in the same manner then the city clerk should succeed to the office of mayor.

The council consisted of five Democrats and three Republicans with no possible chance of a majority elected to agree on new members. Therefore, the mayor named four new members to the council, all Republicans, and they promptly adopted a resolution removing all of the Democratic appointees and substituted Republicans.

3rd Avenue just west of 10th Street during 1913 flood

At the city election of 1907, J. W. Ensign, Democrat, was elected mayor and the council was divided equally but with the vote of the mayor the Democrats had control. Mr. Ensign was conservative and his policies had the respect or perhaps the support of a large per cent of the people irrespective of party and his administration was free from turmoil. Mr. Ensign resigned on November 16, 1908, and John B. Stevenson was elected to fill out his unexpired term.

The turmoil in city government was believed by a considerable number of representative people to be harmful to the best interests of the city and a change in government was demanded. In response to this demand, in 1909 under the leadership of George I. Neal and Elliott Northcott, representative men of both of the political parties in Huntington made plans for the extension of its boundaries to include Guyandotte, the Neutral Strip and Central City and a bi-partisan commission form of government was agreed upon. This plan was provided for in an act of that year which gave Huntington a new charter; the city government to consist of four commissioners only two of whom might belong to the same political party. The commissioner who received the highest vote was to be mayor, and a bi-partisan board made up of members from each ward. Both parties were required to nominate four men for the office of commissioner only two of whom could be elected and in practice the party leaders agreed upon the two men they wanted from their respective sides for the office of commissioner and nominated these two men and two others as runners-up. When the election came there was no serious opposition to the four men agreed upon and it was soon apparent that those on the outside could not beat the machine as was demonstrated by several unsuccessful attempts. In all events this system gave the city Rufus Switzer and C. W. Campbell as mayors and while they have been equaled they will not be surpassed for either integrity or capacity. But change is inevitable and in 1921 the Legislature changed the city charter and abolished the bi-partisan commission. The new charter provided for a government consisting of a mayor and two commissioners with a citizens' board made up of two members from each ward. The board of commissioners named the appointive officers.

In 1923 the city limits were extended and Westmoreland in Wayne County was included.

In 1927 the charter was amended and provided for a member of the citizens' board to be elected at large and gave the mayor the power to appoint the chiefs of police and fire department, police judge, and jailer. Two years later the charter was again amended and the appointing power was taken from the mayor and given back to the board of commissioners.

In 1931 the charter was again amended and the mayor was given the sole right to name the police judge and other officers.

These amendments were, of course, made to offset as far as possible reversals which the party in power had sustained at the polls. By an act passed on February 16, 1934, and which became a law without the governor's signature, the charter was again amended and the government of the city was placed in a mayor and council. The mayor was given the appointing power. The term of office of the mayor and commissioners then in office was continued until the first day of June following when the citizens' board were on that date made the common council and were to elect a mayor and this government was to continue in office until December 31st following. The new city officers were to be elected in the general election in November but were not to take office until the first of the January following. This interim government, in a gesture for economy, created the office of director of public safety and the appointee to this office dominated the administration.

This last government is zero for comparison of all city governments that preceded it or that may follow it. There has been an effort to put the police and fire departments on civil service, but the administration of the civil service up to this time has not been very satisfactory.

XXV: CURRENT EVENTS 1871-1893

IT will be of interest to give some outline of the material development of the new city during its minority. Before the City of Huntington was organized, and even before the map was filed, there was great excitement about the purchase of the lots in the new city. D. W. Emmons who was the brother-in-law of C. P. Huntington was already on the ground to look after his affairs. General John H. Oley was sales agent and made a number of sales of lots even before the land company had obtained the deeds for the property. Lots sold rapidly and those along 2nd Avenue between 6th and 10th Streets were most in demand. Many lots were sold under a contract and the purchaser was given a "title bond." That is to say, the purchaser paid ten per cent on the purchase price and the land company gave him a contract in which it was agreed when its terms were complied with the purchaser would be given a deed, and many houses were started on lots before the purchaser had received his deed. The following shows the first purchasers who received deeds for their lots:

M. H. Brooks was given a deed April 28, 1871, for lot 11, Block 92, which fronted on 2nd Avenue and on which he erected a building and opened a drug store. He was the first postmaster and in this building was kept the first postoffice in the city. On May 1, 1871, B. W. Foster purchased the lot at the southwest corner of 3d Avenue and 9th Street, now occupied by the Huntington Dry Goods Company, the lot being still owned by the Foster Foundation. Dr. J. O. Wall had a deed on May 5, 1871, for the lot at the southeast corner of 3d Avenue and 8th Street on which he built a frame building that was used as the Wall and Buffington Drug Store. May 19, 1871, T. J. Burke was given a deed for a lot fronting on 7th Avenue between 7th and 8th Streets. General John G. Breslin bought two lots at the southeast corner of 3d Avenue and 9th Street. C. F. Parsons on June 7, 1871, purchased a lot at the northeast corner of this same intersection. O. G. Chase on June 24, 1871, purchased a lot on 2nd Avenue between 8th and 9th Streets and on this lot erected a building in which was located the *Independent*, the first newspaper in Huntington. George Scranage on June 22, 1871, bought two lots at the southwest corner of 9th Street and 2nd Avenue and erected thereon the Scranage Hotel, afterwards the Merchants Hotel. On June 19, 1871, A. J. Enslow and N. H. Pennybacker bought two lots on the corner of 2nd Avenue and 7th Street and erected two stores thereon. Felix H. Ware purchased three lots at the southeast corner of 8th Street and 2nd Avenue and erected thereon the Ware Hotel. General Thomas Ewing bought two lots at the northwest corner of 3d Avenue and 10th Street and two lots on the opposite corner, fronting the same avenue.

In the beginning of the city the retail stores, hotels and some residences were located on 2nd Avenue between 6th and 10th Streets, with residences on the avenues to the south. The Chesapeake and Ohio Railway Company built two rows of houses, one of brick and one of frame, fronting on 8th Avenue east of 21st Street, which were used by the engineers and others during the period of construction of the road. After the construction work was done these houses were converted into dwellings and were rented to Chesapeake and Ohio shop employees. Quite a number of people bought or leased small tracts of land on the south side of the Chesapeake and Ohio Railway near the entrance to the shops and erected homes thereon. This last neighborhood was called "The Patch."

There was a subdivision made of a part of the Buffington Reservation east of 17th Street which was called the Buffington Addition. It was soon built up and this group added to the residences and stores which had been built along 20th Street and 3d Avenue made another community.

In the western portion of the city around 1st Street and 3d Avenue was still another settlement.

All of the business of the new city was located along 2nd Avenue and the Chesapeake and Ohio passenger station was on the riverfront where connection was made with the steamboats. What was then called the new passenger station was built on the location of the present station some time in 1873 but this was not used for a time.

The hotels played a large part in the social life of the community and the people on Sunday afternoons would promenade along the river front to see the steamers land and would gather in the hotel parlors which they used as social clubs. The passenger steamers of that day were the *Bostonia* and *Fleetwood,* operated by the White Collar Line, and the *Andes, St. Lawrence, Ohio,* and others.

The first hotel was the Scranage, a two-story building at the southwest corner of 2nd Avenue and 9th Street which was erected in 1872 and operated by George Scranage who moved from Guyandotte. One square west of the southeast corner of 2nd Avenue and 8th Street

F. H. Ware built a three-story hotel which he called the Ware Hotel. This hotel was conducted by "Colonel' Ware for several years and then leased and the name changed to the Continental. Among the lessees who operated this hotel were Sam. A. Hawk and Eugene M. Campbell.

There was a three-story frame hotel on the north side of 3d Avenue between 9th and 10th Streets called the Breslin. R. A. Mathews came in 1873 and bought this property and renamed it the Third Avenue Hotel. In 1879 this hotel was burned and Mr. Mathews bought the Scranage Hotel and renamed it the Merchants Hotel. In 1887 Robert Shore built the Florentine Hotel which was located at the southeast corner of 9th Street and Robert A. Mathews bought this hotel, left the Merchants Hotel and moved to the Florentine.

The Continental did not continue very long as a hotel and was finally pulled down. The Merchants continued for a while under that name and was finally changed to the Elmwood Hotel and was operated as a cheap hotel until it was pulled down to make room for a business block a few years ago.

As the town grew, the business moved over on 3d Avenue and residential sections moved to 4th Avenue and the avenues south.

The activity in real estate in the new city was occasioned by the belief that Huntington was destined by reason of its location and its river and rail facilities to become a manufacturing center and that the industrial plants then in the making would be sufficient to support a considerable mercantile business. As an evidence of this faith, in 1872 *The Independent*, a newspaper which had formerly been published in the town of Guyandotte, moved to the new city. A number of churches were organized. The Masons organized Huntington Lodge No. 53 on November 13, 1872, with James E. Morrow, Anne Lindbergh's grandfather, as its first Master, and held its meetings in the Parson's Hall on 3d Avenue at 9th Street. Some time afterward they moved across the street into the Ward Building where they remained until 1913 when the Masonic Temple was completed. The Odd Fellows were meeting in Johnson's Hall at the southeast corner of 3d Avenue and 10th Street which property they afterwards acquired. The Bank of Huntington with a capital of $25,000.00 was organized with P. C. Buffington as president, John Hooe Russel, cashier, John N. Buffington, D. W. Emmons, J. H. Poage, P. C. Buffington, W. H. Hagen, and Robert T. Oney as directors, and was located in the two-story brick building which stands on the north

North side of 4th Avenue looking east from 8th Street during 1913 flood

[204]

side of 3d Avenue, east of 12th Street. The bank grew with the city and by change of name and merger is now a part of the First Huntington National Bank. The Chesapeake and Ohio Railway shops were the first major industrial enterprise and were completed by 1873. T. J. Hamer was the first master mechanic. The shops employed some 250 men. Many of these people lived in the downtown section and from the beginning the railroad company ran what was known as a shop train from the downtown section to the shops for their employees. This practice continues to the present.

In October, 1872, Ely Ensign, W. H. Barnum, and a number of others incorporated the Ensign Manufacturing Company and established a plant as a chilled tread car wheel factory. Senator W. H. Barnum of Connecticut was president and Ely Ensign was the secretary-treasurer and manager. It employed seventy people at the beginning. A few years later the Agrey Iron Foundry was added and in 1882 the plant expanded and built freight and mine cars and miscellaneous mine and mill supplies in certain lines. In 1899 this plant was merged with other car building plants and was taken over by the American Car and Foundry Company. Ely Ensign was made district manager and continued in this position until his death on January 2, 1902. L. M. Roe is now district manager, and this plant when operating on full time employs approximately 900 people. These two shops were the principal employers of labor but there were at this time and from time to time in the coming years, planing and saw mills which flourished for a time and then passed out. Among these were the Robert Shore, C. F. Millender, Thomas J. Sliger, Wilson Mill, at Wilson's Switch west of Guyandotte, and Sam Beswick. There was W. A. Lyons who had a stave mill at the foot of 16th Street, called the "bucker," all of which contributed something to the support of the growing city.

On the 6th day of August, 1877, the council records show the approval of a printing bill of the *Advertiser*—the first mention of that paper.

In the late 70's an effort was made to secure a steam fire engine but when the proposal to issue bonds for the purchase money was submitted to the vote of the people it was defeated. But two serious fires, one in 1879 on 3d Avenue between 9th and 10th Streets which destroyed the Harvey Building, the Third Avenue Hotel, a three-story building, and a number of other buildings, not only brought about a change of mind about the purchase of a steam fire engine but

Ely Ensign. Born 1840, died 1902. President, Ensign Manufacturing Company and Mayor of Huntington

also helped move the business and residential section away from 2nd Avenue.

The fire on 3d Avenue took place on a very cold night and the fire engine was the hand engine bought in Portsmouth. "Cousin" George Cullen who was afterwards mayor, came on the scene and found the Rev. W. P. Walker, the Baptist minister who was affectionately known as "Brother" Walker, and John Henry Cammack, also a pillar of the Baptist Church, working away on the hand pump. "Cousin" George said: "Brother Walker, what in the hell are you doing at that pump?" "Brother" Walker replied that he wanted to pump, had a right to pump and was going to pump. "Cousin" George said that he would not allow him to pump at that fire and put several idle negroes, who were standing around looking on, at work on the pump and kept them at it. At this fire Evan J. Davies, father of our own Oley Davies, who was one of the fire police, had his ears frosted.

J. W. Verlander was the chief engineer of the fire department but about this time the designation was changed to that of chief of the fire department. He was succeeded by J. W. Boone who served continuously until 1895 when he was succeeded by Sam Wright who served two years and was succeeded by W. C. Molter who served until 1905. Then came W. T. Welch, J. W. Church, and Thomas B. Davis in 1911 who reorganized the department and put it on a thoroughly efficient basis.

In April, 1883, a steam fire engine was purchased from the Aaron Engine Company of Cincinnati and J. W. Boone, fire chief, went to Cincinnati to bring it home. The engine was brought on a steamboat and unloaded at the wharf at the foot of 10th Street. Bill Taylor was the driver and the team was a pair of big dapple greys. Bill drove through the inquiring crowd with his eyes popping, more excited than his horses.

The ordinance provided for an engineer to run the new engine and a fireman to fire it. John Jarvis was the first engineer but was succeeded at the end of the year by George P. Ingram who had Thomas O'Neill as fireman and both served until 1897. Volumes might be written about George Ingram.

George was a man of many parts, an enthusiastic Democratic worker who stood high in the councils of the party. In 1895 he was the commander of the white squadron which some of the older people will remember as a group of shanty boats which certain party workers

The 1884 flood, 3rd Avenue, west from 10th Street, north side avenue

charged that the Democrats moved from the second to the third ward to get control of the council in the latter ward.

The new steam fire engine had not worn "the new off" when in May following its arrival John Kennett's livery stable, which was located on 2nd Avenue between 7th and 8th Streets, caught fire in the middle of the day and was totally destroyed along with most of the buildings in that block including B. T. Davis's drug store. A number of horses were burned and many more got loose and ran about the city for some hours before they were caught.

In 1886 Huntington experienced its first political upset in city government when the Republicans elected A. H. Woodworth, mayor, and D. E. Abbott, H. C. Bossinger, Evan J. Davies, H. M. Ensign, Sam Gideon, W. S. Gladstone, V. W. Mather, I. R. Titus and William Waldron, councilmen. General Oley, the recorder, was not opposed.

On July 28, 1886, the city bought the lots on the northeast corner of 9th Street and 5th Avenue and erected a city building and fire station. In the next year the fire station was moved from this place to Boone Hose House on 4th Avenue just west of 9th Street.

1888 was an eventful year. On January 10, George F. Miller, J. L. Caldwell, D. I. Smith, W. H. Hagen and others organized the First National Bank of Huntington, and on March 11, General J. H. Oley died. The new city was overwhelmed with grief at his passing and on the day of his funeral all stores were closed and business suspended for the day. General Oley was easily the first citizen. During this year the city installed four boxes of the Gamewell Fire Alarm Signal System and this system, greatly enlarged, is still in use here. Captain Eustace Gibson had some differences with the then Circuit Judge, Ira J. McGinnis, and expressed himself in no uncertain terms about the judge. The result was that he was cited for contempt of court and was fined and sentenced to jail. An appeal was taken and the finding was reversed on technical grounds. When the case came back, Judge McGinnis was no longer on the bench and the incident was closed.

Then, too, in this year the Supreme Court decided the first act of the celebrated Laidley case which grew out of the fact that on February 25, 1870, Sarah H. G. Pennybacher, the wife of John Pennybacher, was the owner of 240 acres of land situated in the city, between 5th and 7th Streets, East. She and her husband sold this land by deed dated February 25, 1870, to C. P. Huntington, who in turn conveyed it to the Central Land Company. John B. Laidley who was then a young lawyer, discovered that the acknowledgment of the wife to this deed did not conform to the West Virginia statute and after the death of her husband in 1882 he purchased from Mrs. Pennybacker this same tract of land and brought suit against the land company for possession. Laidley sold undivided interests in this tract to various other persons and the litigation over the title continued for a great many years. The case was contested with a great deal of bitterness and one branch of the case went to the Supreme Court of the United States. Before it was finally settled both Laidley and C. P. Huntington died and then a compromise was agreed to between the owners of the Laidley title and the receivers of the Central Land Company. A short time after this a local group organized the Huntington Land Company and bought the assets of the old Central Land Company. For the next twenty years there was great activity in Huntington real estate.

On September 2, 1889 the *Advertiser* became a daily paper.

At this time there was a German Club in the city which was given the name of the Gypsy Club in honor of the daughter of Governor A. B. Fleming. John Hooe Russell was its first president and included in its membership were the most representative people of the time. The club used the western side of the third floor of the Michael Block located on 3d Avenue between 11th and 12th Streets and it continued there until shortly after the Frederick Hotel was built. The Gypsy Germans were the social events of the year and remarkable to say the club still continues.

In 1890 the *Herald* was organized with E. E. Hood as editor.

On February 19, 1890 a charter was granted to the Board of Trade of Huntington, with the following stockholders and officers:

J. M. Layne, President, M. C. Dimick, secretary, Sam Gideon, W. H. H. Holswade, C. C. Dusenberry, Dan A. Mossman, C. F. Millender, C. E. Gwinn, D. E. Abbott, J. M. Layne, E. Ensign, H. M. Adams, Geo. F. Miller, Jr., Leon G. Brown, C. A. Boxley, T. S. Scanlon, R. A. Mathews, J. A. Emmons, J. K. Oney, James G. Sutphin, and James A. Gohen.

There are no minutes of this organization subsequent to April 7, 1891. On December 20, 1894, the Chamber of Commerce of Huntington, was organized and a charter was issued on January 3, 1895. The city records indicate, however, that the Chamber of Commerce was active before it was formally incorporated as the minutes of the

The New City Hall and Fire Station, 9th Street and 4½ Alley. Erected in 1887

council made on November 13, 1893 show that a communication from the Chamber of Commerce was read calling the council's attention to what the chamber considered a defect in the call for a proposed bond issue. On November 24, 1894, a committee was named from the council to meet the prospective investors in the city and included on this committee was H. C. Harvey, designated as the president of the Chamber of Commerce. After 1895 the records of the Chamber of Commerce are extant and disclose many things of interest in the business and industrial life of the community. Its first office was a room in the Foster Building for which Mr. Foster wanted $8.00 per month but after much discussion the chamber decided to offer Mr. Foster $6.25 per month rent. Early in 1895 the secretary was authorized to hire a man at a salary of $10.00 a month to act as assistant secretary, and it is a far cry from those early days to now with its highly organized staff and various bureaus. H. C. Harvey served as first president, 1895-1899. Dan A. Mossman and C. P. Snow each served six years as president, and other representative men have served in that capacity for shorter terms. T. S. Scanlon was the first secretary for two years with A. W. Werninger as assistant secretary, and then came H. E. Matthews who served from 1906 to 1928 and was succeeded by the present secretary, W. S. Rosenheim.

In 1890 the first trunk sewer was built along 9th Street from the Chesapeake and Ohio Railroad to the Ohio River. Two years later a second trunk sewer was built along 13th Street from the river to 4½ Alley, and in 1893 a trunk sewer was built along 16th Street from 8th Avenue to the Ohio River. In 1905 a trunk sewer was built along 20th Street from the Ohio River to Artisan Avenue, in 1907 on 4th and 7th Streets to 10½ Alley and in 1914 along 5th Avenue from the Guyandotte River to 24th Street, and in 1927 a storm sewer was built along the banks of Four Pole from 16th Street to its mouth.

On March 20, 1891, a proposal to issue paving and sewer bonds was approved by the voters and these bonds were sold in the June following. The paving was begun on 9th Street from 2nd Avenue to the Chesapeake and Ohio station, on 3d Avenue from 7th to 20th Streets, on 2nd Avenue from 8th to 10th Streets, on 4th Avenue from 8th to 10th Streets, on 8th Street from 2nd to 4th Avenues. This paving was not completed until the following year. Ninth Street was completed in August, 1892.

In 1891 C. P. Huntington made a proposal to the common council for the establishment of a city park which was rejected by a vote of 1 for and 6 against. There was no record made of the vote but much is told about the development of the parks in the city under a separate heading.

In 1891 the fire department consisted of a hook and ladder company, Victor Hose Company No. 1, Boone Engine Company No. 2, and the Canda Hose Company, organized that year and named for Mr. Canda one of the officials of the Ensign Manufacturing Company, the Ensign Hose Company No. 4, and the Steam Fire Engine. In the January following there was some trouble among the personnel who were threatening to quit but this was happily straightened out.

In the next year, 1892, the water company presented the city with two fountains which formerly stood at the corner of 5th Avenue and 9th Street and at 4th Avenue and 10th Street.

The question of a hospital was discussed and G. A. Flodding and others tried to interest the city council in the purchase of a poor farm. A city work house was discussed.

On the night of December 13, 1892, Burrell E. Forgey and Tom Collins boarded the F. F. V. Chesapeake and Ohio Train No. 4, which left Huntington a few minutes after midnight and while the train was still in the Huntington yards attempted a train robbery in the most approved wild west style. Both men wore masks and each was armed, and it is said they had carefully rehearsed the hold-up. They entered the day coach from the rear and Forgey walked to the front end of the coach and turned around with a pistol in each hand and covered the passengers. Collins was to do the collecting. One of the passengers, a German named Oscar Tueck, who was returning to his home in Saxony, jumped up and threw Forgey to the floor and one or more passengers went to his assistance. Both Collins and Forgey began to fire and Tueck was killed. Another passenger named Peter Drake was wounded. Zingerley, the Chesapeake and Ohio train collector came on the scene and promptly opened fire on the robbers. The train was stopped and the robbers got off but were arrested afterwards, tried and convicted of murder, and sentenced to life imprisonment. Some years later both were pardoned. Collins died a few years after his release but Forgey was arrested in Kentucky on another charge and committed suicide while in prison.

In the trial the witness Drake testified that the negro porter had gone through the coach just as the robbers entered the train and when asked if the porter was moving rapidly the witness answered: "He seemed to be making quite an effort."

Chamber of Commerce group, circa 1899

In 1892 the question of a city hospital was to the fore. On June 5, the mayor named a committee from the council to select a building for a hospital and at the meeting ten days later it reported that a temporary hospital had been established in the old mayor's office which was on 4th Avenue between 8th and 9th Streets, but it was full. On August 8, 1892, this committee was directed to confer with a committee of ladies and to coöperate with them in the maintenance of a hospital. In the next month a charter was issued for the Huntington Hospital with John Hooe Russel, Ely Ensign, John H. Holt, Gus Honshell, B. W. Foster, and F. L. Doolittle as incorporators but there is no record of any activity of this group. In August, 1893, the committee from the council reported that a hospital should be erected on the hills at 19th Street and should be located on a site of not less than two or more than five acres.

The next mention of a hospital is on May 1, 1901, when the board of education conveyed to the City of Huntington the old Buffington School House located on 4th Avenue between 7th and 8th Streets upon the condition that the city would establish a hospital therein within three years from that date. In April of this year the Huntington Hospital Association was incorporated by B. W. Foster, George F. Miller, E. Bierne, J. C. Christy, G. A. Northcott, James J. Brady, T. J. Prichard, R. E. Vickers, H. B. Hagen, D. E. Abbott, F. B. Enslow, and W. E. Drummond and the city turned this property over to them for hospital uses. The building was fitted up for a hospital and an adjoining building was secured for a nurses' home. On March 17, 1902, the council by a vote of 8 to 4 leased the building to the new company but the expense of operating the hospital was greater than the income and it got into financial difficulties. During this period the women had formed a hospital auxiliary and had from time to time raised money and paid for patients which they put in the hospital. Finally they formed a board of directors of twelve ladies consisting of Mrs. A. S. Emmons, Mrs. Haller, Mrs. Dornick, Mrs. Frank P. Swan, Mrs. C. R. Wyatt, Mrs. W. W. Dunn, Mrs. D. A. Mossman, Mrs. Dr. Haynes, Mrs. Gilmore, Mrs. L. A. Pollock, Mrs. John S. Marcum, and Mrs. G. J. Nicholson, and the men turned the hospital over to the ladies to operate.

This continued until May, 1910, when the Huntington General Hospital was incorporated by Drs. J. E. Rader, C. C. Hogg, K. C. Prichard, and C. T. Taylor, and they took over this hospital. In the same month the Mt. Hope Hospital was incorporated by Dr. R. E.

Hotel Adelphi, July 2, 1901

Vickers and associates who erected a hospital building on 4th Avenue just west of 5th Street and from that time on Huntington has had no lack of hospital facilities.

In June, 1893, a bond issue of $75,000.00 to be expended for sewers and streets had been authorized and these bonds were sold to Chaffin and Stanton Brothers of New York on installments but before the last portion was paid the purchasers and its sureties had become insolvent and the city lost $8,100.00. In the fall of this year George I. Neal as mayor suggested the matter of a plan to provide for work for the unemployed which was referred to a committee.

This year a new hotel called the Adelphi Hotel was built at the southeast corner of 9th Street and 6th Avenue. This was regarded as the up-to-date hotel and was extensively patronized until it was destroyed by fire on July 2, 1901.

On November 13, 1893, a communication from the Chamber of Commerce was read before the council and this was the first reference to the Chamber of Commerce in the public records.

Florentine Hotel

XXVI: THE CITY ATTAINS ITS MAJORITY

IN 1893 the city had passed its majority and we find the business and residential section had left 2d Avenue, and 3d Avenue between 8th and 11th Streets, was the principal business section. Residences had been built on all of the avenues south to the railroad. The Huntington National Bank was located at the northwest corner of 10th Street and 3d Avenue and the First National Bank had moved into the stone fronted building at 922-26 3d Avenue in the latter part of 1890. Ninth Street from 3d Avenue to the Chesapeake and Ohio Railroad was practically a business street. Broh Brothers had a store on the southeast corner of 9th Street and 3d Avenue and immediately on the rear of this lot was a residence occupied by Dr. Row. On the opposite side of the street the Foster Hardware store was located fronting on 3d Avenue with a residence in the rear. Both sides of 9th Street from 3½ Alley to 4th Avenue was occupied by business property. The postoffice was located at the northwest corner of 9th Street and 4th Avenue and the Florentine Hotel on the southwest corner. The city building and courthouse was at 4½ Alley and 9th Street; the Congregational Church at the southeast corner of 9th Street and 5th Avenue with residences on the west side of 9th Street between 5½ Alley and 6th Avenue. The new Adelphi Hotel was at the southeast corner of 9th Street and 6th Avenue and the Brick Row fronted on 9th Street from 6th Avenue to 6½ Alley. The Seventh Avenue Hotel was on the northwest corner of 9th Street and 7th Avenue, and the Carrolton Hotel, operated by J. F. Heffner, familiarly known as "Dad" was on the east side of 9th Street at about 7½ Alley. On the sign in front of the Bar, as you went toward the station were the words, "The last chance" and on the same sign as you came from the station north toward 3d Avenue were the words, "The first chance." There was no business on 4th Avenue. In the next year W. B. Prickett built the store just east of the Union Bank.

The Florentine Hotel was the social center for men. In the winter the town people filled the lobby and in the summer chairs were placed in the street, and friends and neighbors occupied these chairs and talked until late hours. The "Porch Climbers," a local organization, conceived by "Pres" Hays, held frequent initiations out in the middle of 9th Street. Politics were discussed with much heat and in the section of the street just inside of the curb was a fine elm tree under the shade of which weighty questions were decided until its

Dan Hill, the early cab driver

THE CITY ATTAINS ITS MAJORITY

destruction some years since. There was no vehicular traffic to disturb these meetings unless the horse-car came jingling along on one of its trips between the two railway depots. Or perhaps John Hider, or Dan Hill might come jolting along driving one of their ancient cabs.

Dan was a character. He began life as a train porter on the Chesapeake and Ohio Railway and in some way he lost an eye and then embarked in the cab business. Dan also had visions of wielding great political power. From time to time he would get out of step with his party and on more than one occasion announced that it was his purpose on a given evening to make a speech on 3d Avenue and 9th Street and expose its iniquities. As the time for the speech would draw near much excitement would develop on the "Bowery." When the day arrived Dan would put in his appearance well in advance of the hour set for speaking, clad in a Prince Albert coat and wearing a plug hat. In every instance but one Dan was placated and abandoned his purpose of speaking. However, on one occasion "they" failed to satisfy Dan and when the appointed hour arrived Dan, who had a wagon at the corner of 3d Avenue and 9th Street which he intended to use as a platform, mounted the wagon but someone gave it a push and its wheels came off. Dan did not speak and the Republican party was saved.

We now mention some of the men who cast their lot with the city at its birth and are still active in its affairs, and others who came later but in retrospect are old timers. Mention too must be made of that splendid group of men employed by the Chesapeake and Ohio Railway whose stay in the city was dependent upon the orders of their superiors and about these we will speak first. It is not possible to mention all, but among them were H. C. Vancleve who was the first division superintendent and was succeeded in 1873 by Captain Joseph E. Mallory who remained until 1883. Captain Mallory lived in the old Brown House on 2nd Avenue between 4th and 5th Streets. One of his daughters, Victoria B., married Major W. H. Lyons and the other Sarah, married Sam A. Hawk. Captain Mallory was succeeded by W. P. Harris who was here about a year and then the superintendent's office went to Hinton for a period of years. W. J. Harahan was here for a time as a division engineer; George H. Ingalls served a part of his apprenticeship here. Young Fitzhugh Lee thought he would make railroading his career and came for a brief moment but the Spanish-American War made things different and he joined the 7th Cavalry. J. M. Gill came in the early 90's and continued for ten

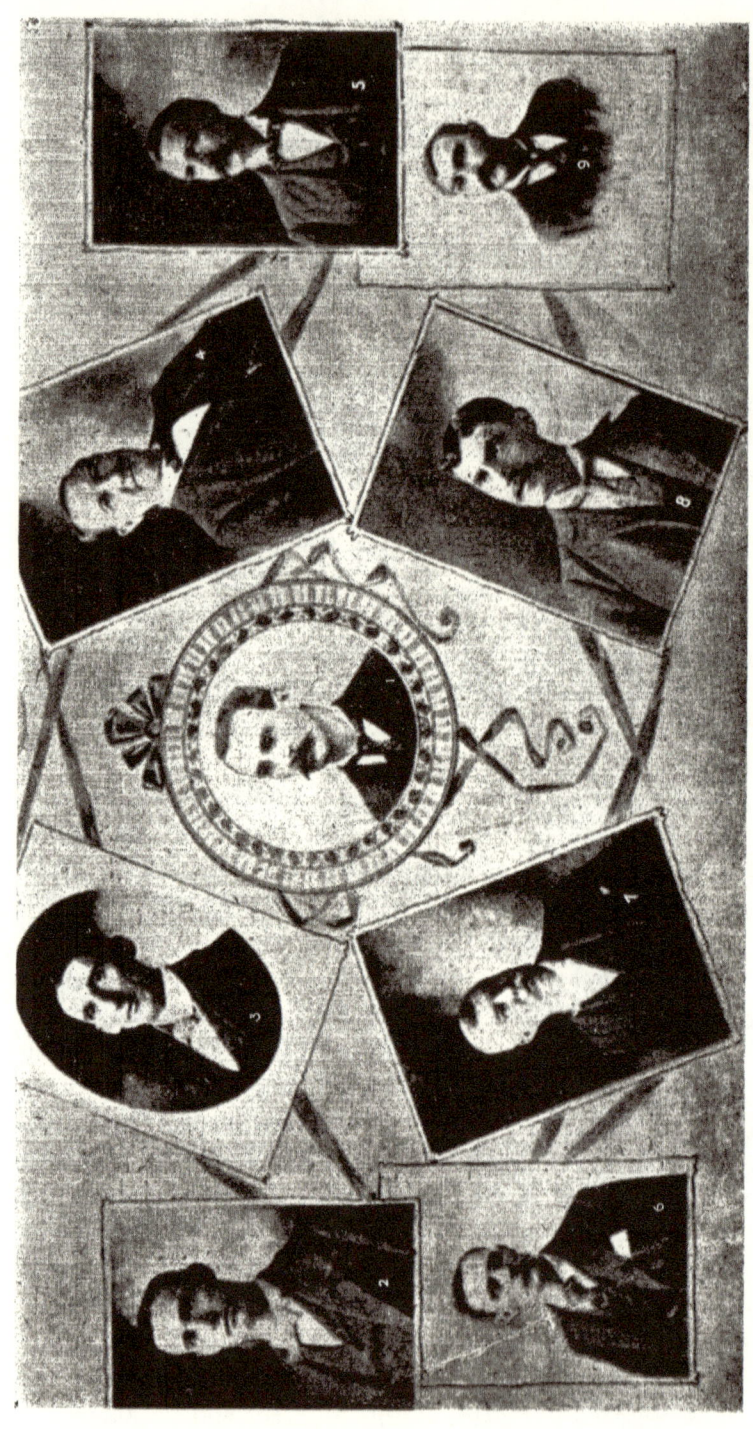

Officials of the Chesapeake and Ohio Railroad, circa 1894: 1—J. M. Gill, General Superintendent, Western Division; 2—Chas. Thackston, City Ticket Agent; 3—Mayor W. F. Hite, Traveling Freight Agent; 4—A. F. Stewart, Master Mechanic; 5—T. S. Garrigan, Traveling Passenger Agent; 6—R. B. Dickerson, Chief Train Dispatcher; 7—C. W. Hunter, City Freight Agent; 8—T. J. Gilmore, Chief Clerk under Mr. Gill; 9—E. L. Ryan, Train Master.

years and was one of the organizers of the Union Bank and Trust Company. When the shops were opened T. J. Hamer was the first master mechanic and was followed by T. L. Chapman and William Hassman in the order stated. Later came A. F. Stewart, then C. H. Terrell and now E. A. Murray. In the early days William Haller was clerk for the master mechanic and after him Austin Wigal who lived in Guyandotte. John Taylor was the general foreman in the machine shop, J. C. Tanner was the machinist foreman, R. W. Turney was gang foreman, and H. J. Derbyshire was brass foundry foreman. In the car department were H. C. Bossinger, master car builder, Schuyler Sexton, passenger car foreman, and Joe Webb, pattern shop foreman. In the shops today there are five men whose services began in the early 80's, C. R. Rolfe, J. R. Gould, Harry Chambers, J. W. Kinzer, and E. H. Freeland. In the train service George Sampson fired the first engine, the Greenbrier, for a short time after its arrival and was then promoted to engineman and served well into the present century. A. F. Southworth and T. J. Bullock came in the 70's and served continuously. They were both active in civic and political affairs. Then there was Bill Freutel who with two of his brothers lost their lives in the service, Dave Smith C. T. Pilcher and Billy Richardson the last two of whom were killed on their runs; H. R. McLaughlin who was first an engineer and afterwards trainmaster, and Thomas R. Bishop and C. C. Talley, who are still running after more than fifty years of service.

In the passenger service the first conductors were Nath Hubbard, P. A. Cason, J. D. Yarrington, who ran the local to Kanawha Falls and was afterward superintendent, and Nick Ragland. These men were followed by Charles W. Kilgore, now retired and W. T. Crawford who is still in harness. Captain B. P. Driggs came at an early date and was the first yardmaster. He was transferred to Hinton for a time. After some years he returned to Huntington where he was prominent in Masonic circles and represented the Knights and Ladies of Honor. J. M. Love was the first depot agent followed by ——— Engles, then C. M. Oakley, then Charles W. Hunter who served in that capacity a lifetime. "General" J. G. Breslin was the first ticket agent after the new station was opened on the present location. He was a man with a fine sense of humor and always insisted on being called "General." Among the more recent folks were James A. Garner who operated the lunch counters for a great many years, E. J. King, who after many years of service became the executive of the Huntington Gas and Development Company, Joe Newman, who was ticket agent for twenty years or longer, E. M. Green, who has been on the Huntington yards since the early 1890's, H. G. Webb, the present superintendent, and E. L. Bock, the present general superintendent.

Passing now to our townsmen who were not connected with the railroad, these men must be placed into two groups, the men who came in the very beginning and those who came later and are a link between the old timers and the present.

One of the first group is B. T. Davis, the venerable druggist. He came with the very first and had a drug store on 2nd Avenue but moved to his present location at the southeast corner of 3d Avenue and 8th Street in the year 1884. He took an active part in all movements which tended to the advancement of the growing city and built the Davis Opera House, about which something will be said in another chapter.

Delos W. Emmons was born at Oneonta, New York, December 17, 1828, and died April 19, 1905. He was a brother-in-law of C. P. Huntington. Emmons came to West Virginia in 1869 and was associated with the Chesapeake and Ohio Railroad Company in several capacities and was right-of-way agent for the western portion of the line. When the Central Land Company was organized Mr. Emmons was its general superintendent and continued as such until 1888.

He bought the old Thomas Buffington house on the Ohio River just below the mouth of the Guyandotte which he remodeled and named Pleasant View and for many years entertained all of the important personages who came to Huntington.

Delos W. Emmons served as a member of the city council, was a prominent Mason and a member of the First Presbyterian Church. He reared a family of four sons and one daughter. One of his sons, C. D. Emmons, is the head of the Emmons-Hawkins Hardware Company of Huntington.

W. H. H. Holswade began as a clerk in the first postoffice where he served two years, then he tried a bookstore for a short period and then went into the furniture business. He built up a fine business and he had a big store on the south side of 3d Avenue between 9th and 10th Streets where he continued until his death in the first decade of this century. The business was continued by his son, J. F. Holswade, until 1915 when he made an advantageous lease to Kresge and Company, closed the furniture business and engaged in other lines.

Delos W. Emmons, general manager of the Central Land Company, 1870-1888

Harry C. Harvey came from Putnam County to attend Marshall College. After he had completed his college course he took employment in the Wall and Buffington drug store. He next tried his fortune with the Harmison general store, which is said to be the first chain store in the city. Later he persuaded his father, Robert T. Harvey, to move to the city. The father and his two sons, Clayte and H. C., engaged in the dry goods business under the firm name of Robert T. Harvey and Sons. H. C. Harvey remained with his father until July, 1887, when he became a member of the firm of Harvey, Fuller and Hagen, the first wholesale grocery in the city. This partnership continued until 1893 when F. D. Fuller retired and H. C. Harvey and H. B. Hagen organized the corporation of Harvey, Hagen and Company and continued the business. In 1901 John F. Ratcliffe came to Huntington from Louisa, Kentucky. He and W. O. Wiatt purchased Mr. Harvey's interest in the corporation and the company name was changed to Hagen, Ratcliff and Company, and has continued one of the leading jobbing houses in this State.

T. S. Garland who served three terms as mayor was one of the men who came from Virginia in 1871 and cast his lot with the new city. He first engaged in the mercantile business with his brother-in-law, P. C. Buffington. This partnership continued until Mr. Buffington's death in 1875. At that time Garland bought the Buffington interest and continued the business until 1887 when, for three years, he was in partnership with John W. Valentine. He continued in the mercantile business on 3d Avenue until 1908 when the business was consolidated and became a part of the Valentine-Garland-Biggs Company and occupied a new building on 4th Avenue where the Keith-Albee Theatre now stands. This partnership continued only a short time when Garland's interest was sold and he retired from active business.

F. J. Harmison had a number of stores at points along the Ohio River including one in the town of Guyandotte. He moved the Guyandotte store to Huntington in 1871 and a short time thereafter R. A. Jack entered his employment as a clerk. Jack continued with him as a clerk until 1876 when he bought an interest in the business and became a partner. This partnership continued until 1885 when Mr. Jack bought out Harmison's interest and conducted the business in his own name until his death at the beginning of the century.

William F. Wallace who had served in the 74th Ohio Volunteer Infantry, U.S.A., came in December, 1871, and worked for a time

Valentine-Newcomb Store, north side 3rd Avenue, between 9th and 10th Streets, 1902. Man on extreme right is W. H. Newcomb. J. W. Valentine stands at the left of the door

on the *Huntington Independent*. In 1872 he commenced the publication of the *Huntington Argus* which he continued until his death at the close of the century. His son George E. Wallace succeeded his father and continued the paper until his death in 1906.

John T. Gibson was a North of Ireland man. He came from New York in 1872 and edited the *Commercial*, a Republican newspaper, for twenty years. Mr. Gibson was an ardent Republican and like all of his race decided in his views and undaunted by the fact that locally he was in the minority. He stood by his guns and even carried on an aggressive warfare. His daughter is the wife of C. D. Emmons.

Sam Gideon, one of the most public spirited citizens we ever had, came in 1872 and entered the clothing business on the first day of May of that year. He continued in this business until the time of his death on June 20, 1923. A few years before his death his son, Dave, was taken into the business and the store was conducted under the firm name of Sam and Dave Gideon but after "Uncle" Sam's death Dave sold the business.

John W. Valentine, one of the most popular merchants who ever lived in the city came at an early date and was a candidate for council soon after his arrival. After serving an apprenticeship in the store of Harmison and Jack he embarked in the mercantile business and continued therein until the time of his death. He was a partner in Garland and Valentine 1887-1890, and in September, 1895, he and W. H. Newcomb formed the partnership of Valentine and Newcomb which continued until 1902 when the firm purchased the lot fronting sixty feet on 3d Avenue between 9th and 10th Streets and erected thereon a three-story building. This business was incorporated under the name of Valentine, Newcomb and Carder, but in January, 1907, John W. Valentine sold his interest to E. G. Anderson of Portsmouth, Ohio. The corporate name became the Anderson-Newcomb Company, which continues to this time. In 1908 E. G. Anderson sold his interest to his brother, C. N. Anderson, who continued with the business until his death in 1926 when William B. Anderson, Jr., became president of the company and W. H. Newcomb chairman of the board. After Mr. Valentine sold his interest in the Valentine-Newcomb Company he leased a new building which had been erected by G. N. Biggs on 4th Avenue, between 9th and 10th Streets on the site now occupied by the Keith-Albee theatre and for a time conducted business there in his own name. It then became the Valentine, Garland, and Biggs Company, which firm continued in business only a short time. Mr. Valentine retired and again engaged in business in his own name and the business became Biggs, Wilson and Company and was continued as Zenner-Bradshaw Company until the building was destroyed by fire in December, 1925.

L. Doolittle, father of E. S. Doolittle, circuit judge and F. L. Doolittle, county clerk, came to Huntington from New York in 1872 and for many years was engaged in the grocery business.

W. H. Bull, R. B. Wolcott, J. W. Verlander, and Laidley and Johnson were among the principal grocers of early days. Laidley and Johnson occupied the southeast corner of 3d Avenue and 10th Street for many years.

H. O. Via came from "East" Virginia by rail to White Sulphur Springs and by stage-coach from that point to Charleston, and by rail from Charleston to Huntington. He reached Huntington in March, 1872, engaged in the restaurant business and served good meals. Now in a ripe and vigorous old age he is in charge of Camden Park.

George R. McIntosh, a native of Dundee, Scotland, came to Huntington at an early date. He took an active interest in civic affairs, was one of the early fire police and for many years was in the mail service. In 1887 he established the *Huntington Gazette*, a Republican newspaper. He is the father of our own George C. McIntosh, one of the most brilliant newspaper men our State has had.

John Hooe Russel came to Huntington in 1873 and formed a partnership with Erskine Miller of Staunton, Virginia, and engaged in the grocery business under the firm name of Miller and Russel. "General" Russel was a general on the governor's staff, was one of the organizers of the Huntington Bank and served as its cashier and president until the time of his death. "General" Russel was a successful business man and at the same time was the social leader of the city. His kinsman Russell Erskine, afterwards president of the Studebaker Company was employed by "General" Russel and lived in this city a number of years. Later Russell Erskine returned to Huntington and married Miss Anna Lyle Garland, daughter of T. S. Garland.

N. C. Petit was engaged in the coal and ice business from the beginning of the town and until well along in the present century. He also had time to take an active part in the political affairs of the city.

There are few old timers who do not recall John Kennett. John was an immense man, physically, weighing in excess of three hun-

Via's Restaurant, 1887

dred pounds. He conducted a livery stable from the beginning of the city until the time of his death in the first decade of this century. John moved all of the theatrical baggage and made the proud boast that he kept John Hooe Russel's buggy which cost $500.00. Kennett reached the height of fame when he was called upon to drive the victoria with a pair of white horses in which rode the Great Commoner, William Jennings Bryan, at the time he spoke in Huntington in the campaign of 1896.

William Keefe came to Huntington when he was sixteen years of age and began as a clerk in the drug store of M. H. Brooks. Four years later he embarked in the drug business for himself and continued in this business until the time of his death after the turn of the century. He took an active part in civic affairs and served more than one term in the city council.

C. F. Parsons came from Vermont to Huntington in the spring of 1871 before the town was incorporated. He embarked in the hardware business and built at the northeast corner of 9th Street and 3d Avenue one of the first stores in the city. He continued in the hardware business for twelve years when he formed a partnership with his son W. E. Parsons. In a short time C. F. Parsons retired from this business, and in 1884 the partnership became Parsons and (C. D.) Emmons. Mr. Parsons retired from the partnership and Mr. Emmons continued for a few months in his own name and then was joined by B. W. Marr. The partnership of Emmons and Marr continued until 1891 when Marr retired and J. L. Hawkins became the partner in the firm of Emmons and Hawkins. This business was incorporated in 1899 and some years ago moved to its present location on 3d Avenue between 10th and 11th Streets. It is one of the largest jobbing, retail hardware, and mine supply houses in this State.

B. W. Foster, whose wife was a local girl, came to Huntington in the beginning and purchased the lot at the southwest corner of 9th Street and 3d Avenue. He erected a small building thereon and opened a retail hardware business. This business flourished and in 1894 Mr. Foster incorporated the business. After a change of name it is now the Foster-Thornburg Hardware Company. The business was moved from 9th Street to the present location at 12th Street and 2d Avenue.

J. L. (Jake) Crider came in the early 70's, and had a drug store on 3d Avenue between 10th and 11th Streets. He was active in civic affairs, an enthusiastic Mason. He is now living and a hale and hearty man.

J. L. Crider's Drug Store, north side 3rd Avenue, between 10th and 11th Streets, circa 1876

THE CITY ATTAINS ITS MAJORITY 233

T. N. Boggess came a little later and continued in the drug business until his death. His name is still used by the people who succeeded to the business. Among the druggists of the next older men are, John Lowry and W. S. Vinson, and after them are Wild and Boette who came in 1902 from Parkersburg, and U. G. Wriston who carried on business for many years on 9th Street and was succeeded by J. Louis Hawkins.

A. J. Enslow, father of Frank B. Enslow and E. B. Enslow, came from Wheelersburg, Ohio. He was a contractor and did a great deal of work in grading the streets of the new city. He was a justice of the peace and after the city was incorporated he served as a member of the council.

Margaret Lallance, a widow from Meigs County, Ohio, brought with her four sons. She opened a millinery shop and later purchased a lot on the south side of 3d Avenue between 9th and 10th Streets which she still owns. One of her sons, John B. worked for a time for the Chesapeake and Ohio Railroad. He then had a planing mill at the foot of 13th Street and later was a building contractor. The other three sons, M. F., C. N., and R. S. Lallance were painters and paint contractors. C. N. Lallance built the three-story brick building on the northeast corner of 3d Avenue and 8th Street in the third story of which the Baptists held their first meetings. R. S. Lallance was active politically and served as police judge.

Adolph, Conrad, Lewis, and William Molter, fine German people, were among the early arrivals. Adolph had a bakery on 3d Avenue above 10th Street. Conrad bought a lot in 1873 on the north side of 3d Avenue between 8th and 9th Streets and established a bakery which he sold to Joe Flickenstein—twenty years afterwards.

Thomas Archer and his wife, Frances Mather Archer, came to Huntington in October, 1871. At the time of his death in 1877 Mr. Archer conducted a retail coal business at the corner of 2d Avenue and 10th Street. Mrs. Archer continued this business for several years after his death. At that time she was the first and only business woman in Huntington. Later she and her daughter,* Miss Richey, engaged in the mercantile business as E. M. Richey and Company. Mrs. Archer died in 1917 at the age of eighty-four.

George Cullen was in the jewelry business in the beginning except when he was occupied as mayor. His business was taken over by Frank Huff, who in turn was succeeded by Glen Hilton, and after

---
*See family account of Archer.

Hilton's death the business was taken over by C. M. Wallace who continued in the same place on 3d Avenue between 9th and 10th Streets for twenty-five years until his death.

On the last day of February, 1878, John Henry Cammack and his family arrived on the steamer, *Kate Stockdale*. They put up at the Continental Hotel but in a few days moved into a house on 4th Avenue between 7th and 8th Streets. Mr. Cammack brought with him a store of women's and men's wearing apparel and in a short time opened a store in the Lallance Building on the corner of 3d Avenue and 9th Street. Two years later the council records disclose that he was given permission to erect a frame building on 3d Avenue near 9th Street. A little later he moved to the Miller-Russell Building on 3d Avenue and 10th Street. Mr. Cammack continued in the mercantile business until 1890 when he joined J. N. Potts in the real estate and insurance business. These two stalwart Baptists continued together for a number of years and then Mr. Cammack joined his son, C. W. Cammack and continued with him until his death on May 6, 1920. John Henry Cammack was elected a deacon in the Baptist Church in 1870 and served until his death. He was always a positive force for good in the community. J. N. Potts was likewise a deacon in the Baptist Church. He came from Virginia at an early date and was for a time in the mercantile business but served at different times as city clerk, city judge, and held other public offices. However, his greatest contribution to the community was his long and faithful service to his church.

John H. and George Jarvis came in 1873 and were employed as machinists in the Chesapeake and Ohio shops. In 1879 they formed a partnership of Jarvis and Brother and operated a machine and repair shop which continued many years. They were followed by George P. Ingram and Tom O'Neil, who formed a partnership of Ingram and O'Neil and opened a machine shop on the southwest corner of 10th Street and 2d Avenue. The shop still carries on.

W. A. Ulmon came from Charleston a few years later and opened a shop which grew into the Huntington Stove and Foundry Company.

Edward F. Douthitt, a native of Guyandotte, established a harness making shop in 1880 and continued in this business until a few years ago. Ed was an enthusiastic sportsman and had many friends.

Emanuel Biern came in 1882 and with his brother-in-law, Jake Friedman, engaged in business. They were located for some years in the east room of the Ward Building on the northwest corner of

Ward Building, northwest corner of 3rd Avenue at 9th Street. Second floor, law offices; third floor, Masonic lodge hall.

3d Avenue and 9th Street. In 1890 an arrangement was made between Biern and Friedman, Jacob Ziegler, and Lewis Molter, each of whom owned a lot on 3d Avenue just west of the First National Bank to erect a single building thereon with three store rooms. This was done and Biern and Friedman owned the east part, Jacob Ziegler the middle, and Molter the west. Molter rented the west room to Henry Newman. This building is still standing, and is known as the Boston. Jacob Friedman a few years later moved to Charleston and Julius Friedman who came to this country in 1888 joined the partnership which continued until Mr. Biern's death in 1925. Mr. Biern served in the city council. Julius Friedman had been a commissioned officer in the Hungarian Army and in his vigorous old age his erect bearing was evidence of this fact.

T. S. (Tim) Scanlon came in 1883 and engaged in the retail shoe business for twenty years, but his love for politics kept him in public office. He served as city treasurer, councilman, member of the Legislature, city commissioner and a member of the State Road Commission. In his later years he was engaged in sewer and street contracting. He was a man of splendid qualities of heart and he and his good wife reared a large number of orphan children.

In 1884 C. A. Boxley came from Virginia and with W. R. Duerson bought out the grocery business of J. N. Potts located at the northwest corner of 8th Street and 3d Avenue. A little later Boxley bought out Duerson and during the next few years had one or more partners. His last partner was Peyton Dudley and the firm of Boxley and Dudley continued until Mr. Dudley's death. At the turn of the century Boxley quit the grocery business and went into the contracting business. He served two terms as councilman, was city treasurer and now as a retired business man is enjoying a vigorous old age.

In 1884, G. A. Northcott, who had been engaged in business with George F. Miller at Rupert, West Virginia, came to Huntington and formed a partnership with Heath Kelly. Mr. Kelly was the brother of Mrs. E. B. Enslow and had been a clerk in Clayte Harvey's store. This partnership was known as the Northcott and Kelly Company, and in February, 1885, started in the gents' furnishing business in a storeroom on the south side of 3d Avenue east of 9th Street. Later they moved in the middle room of the Ward Building on the north side of 3d Avenue. In 1888 Mr. Northcott sold his interest to T. S. Garland and joined P. C. Buffington in the firm of Northcott and Buffington, and opened a store in the McCrory Building. After

THE CITY ATTAINS ITS MAJORITY

three years Mr. Buffington retired and the business was continued as G. A. Northcott and Company, and some time afterwards moved into the Foster Building on the southwest corner of 9th Street and 3d Avenue. The business was incorporated as Northcott-Tate-Hagy Company and moved into the Frederick Building on 4th Avenue in 1906.

In 1887 Mike and Julius Broh, young men but a few years older than the town, arrived and opened a clothing store on 3d Avenue just west of the Ward Building. In the spring of 1889 their father bought the lot at the southeast corner of 3d Avenue and 9th Street and gave it to them. They erected thereon the three-story brick building which still stands. While the new building was in the course of construction the Broh Brothers occupied a small frame building which stood in the street. The partnership was dissolved in 1904. Mike continued in the clothing business until 1915 when he turned his attention to banking and continued therein until his death a few years ago. Julius engaged in the retail shoe business until 1920, when he embarked in other lines and continued until his retirement a few years ago. He is still active and enjoys the respect and esteem of the community. The only unsettled question in his life is his controversy with James A. Garner as to who really owned the first automobile in the city. The facts seem to be that Jim placed his order first for a four-cylinder Winton; Julius a few days later bought a one-cylinder Cadillac; there was some delay in delivery, and Julius's car arrived on May 5, 1905, and Jim's car arrived a few days later. Question: Who had the first car?

At that time the speed limit was eight miles per hour. These cars could not be operated at that speed so Julius took the mayor and chief of police out for a ride and explained the difficulty. These officers with the usual political acumen advised Julius to ignore the ordinance but to be cautious. Julius embarked on a trip to Ironton which he made in one hour and forty minutes and returned at the same speed.

In 1887 Peter Baer came from Meigs County, Ohio, and opened the first five and ten cent store on the north side of 3d Avenue just east of 10th Street. The next year he moved across the avenue and continued as a five and ten cent store but later changed it to a general store. In 1914 he moved to 20th Street where he continued in business until a few years ago when he retired.

In 1887 A. W. Werninger was a mail clerk running into Hunting-

Peter Baer and wife in front of Baer's first five-cent store, 1889

THE CITY ATTAINS ITS MAJORITY 239

ton. Several years later he transferred to the postoffice where he continued until a change in administrations. Gus then started in the insurance business. From the first he took a keen interest in civic affairs and has been helpful in everything that tended to advance the best interests of the community. Now in his old age he enjoys the respect and affection of his fellow citizens.

Paul Dober is a German-born citizen. He came to America when he was a small boy and was in early manhood engaged in business in Gallipolis, Ohio. One day in 1889 he loaded his stock of merchandise on the *Carrie Brown* and moved to Huntington and started business in what was the G. A. Flodding new building on the south side of 3d Avenue between 10th and 11th Streets. Now after forty-six years of continuous service he is in business in his own building on 4th Avenue just above 8th Street.

Joseph R. Damron came about this same time and opened a feed store on the Bowery and except for the years he was city treasurer he devoted his efforts to this business until his death two years ago. Joe's quaint humor and kind heart made him a host of friends.

James Johnston and J. Alden Emmons were in the furniture business on the north side of 3d Avenue between 9th and 10th Streets for some years. Mr. Emmons retired but Mr. Johnston continued the business adding undertaking. Twenty-five years ago he built on his lot on 4th Avenue east of 9th Street the building now occupied by M. D. Angel and Company. He occupied this building and carried on the undertaking business until his death.

Dan A. Mossman began as a coal and ice merchant but soon enlarged his business. He founded the business of Mossman and Brothers, and was active in many lines until his death.

Joseph R. Gallick was born in Italy and when a small boy was playing a harp on a river steamboat. He had some differences with the captain and Joe was put ashore at Guyandotte without money or friends. C. H. Hall took him, and Joe lived in that family a great many years. Joe had a bookstore on the north side of 3d Avenue in a room which he owned—that is, Joe bought the room outright from the owner of the building. He continued in this location for many years and then moved in the Frederick block. He was a great Mason and delighted in music and social affairs. He managed the Davis Theatre for some years and was identified with other amusements.

Frank Marchetti and Pete Biagi had a fruit store on 9th Street just south of the Broh Building. They were very successful. Pete's children are still in Huntington and Frank continues in business.

Jim Brackman started peddling "wieners" from a tin box but after a time acquired a wagon which used to stand in the street at the northwest corner of 3d Avenue and 9th Street. Jim saved his money and now in his old age is one of the substantial citizens.

For many years John A. Jones had a music store on 3d Avenue. There were signs advertising his merchandise scattered far and wide. He continued in business until his death and in his passing Huntington lost a man who had always stood for what was best in the community. He served several terms as member of the school board.

One of the most delightful men, Dr. Clarence Everett Haworth, son of a country physician of Jackson County came to Huntington in 1890 where he remained until his death in 1929. He was a capable composer of music and a talented pianist and organist, as well as a writer of excellent taste and style. Among his musical compositions were a Te Deum, Jubilate and Venite, still widely used in Episcopal church service. He was organist and director of the choir of Trinity Episcopal Church in Huntington for many years.

Dr. Haworth was a graduate of Colgate University with degrees of A.B., A.M., and Ph.D., and of the University of Louisville, with the degree of M.D. He came to Huntington to practice medicine but his attraction to letters led him to buy the *Huntington Herald,* of which he was editor and proprietor until 1907 when he sold his interest in the paper to become a professor of English and head of that department at Marshall College. He was vice president of the college for a number of years and for a short time its acting president.

Dr. Haworth contributed much to the development of the cultural life of Huntington. He was an excellent tennis player and golfer, as well as a scholar. He died of a heart attack while riding to Cincinnati by automobile to hear an opera there.

In 1890 Edmund Sehon who had been engaged in business at Point Pleasant along with G. N. Biggs, C. D. VanBibber, A. G. Blake, and J. M. Beale organized the firm of Sehon, Blake and Company and began business as wholesale grocers in a store room on the south side of 3d Avenue just east of the Davis Opera House. A year or two later they moved to a building on the east side of 10th Street south of the Baltimore and Ohio Railroad, now owned by the Gwinn Brothers Milling Company. The business was incorporated in 1897 as Sehon, Blake and Company but the name was changed for a brief period to Sehon, Blake and Stevenson. In 1901 the building was destroyed by fire and the company liquidated. Mr. Blake and Homer Bell engaged in business together and Mr. Sehon and John B. Stevenson formed a partnership and occupied a store on the south side of 3d Avenue between 10th and 11th Streets. The latter business was incorporated in 1908 as Sehon, Stevenson and Company and erected a new building on 11th Street south of 7th Avenue adjoining the Chesapeake and Ohio Railway. This company is one of the largest wholesale houses in southern West Virginia.

Early in 1890 W. D. Elder and C. S. Welch, his brother-in-law, secured some land from the Holderbys and established a shale brick plant on what is now the west side of 16th Street just north of the boulevard. The business was incorporated on August 11, 1891, as the Huntington Paving and Building Brick Company. In the next year the company secured a franchise and built a spur track from the Chesapeake and Ohio Railroad to its new plant. This company manufactured a superior paving brick but suffered in the panic of 1893-97 and ceased business.

In 1899 Bernhardt Tauber and associates organized the Ohio Valley Shingle Company whose name was later changed to the Huntington Roofing Tile Company and bought the plant of the Huntington Paving and Building Brick Company and manufactured roofing tile of a superior quality until its supply of shale was exhausted. In 1902 T. L. Evans of Clarksburg came to Huntington and organized the West Virginia Paving and Pressed Brick Company. This company purchased the spur track and twenty acres of land on the east side of 16th Street and has been manufacturing shale brick successfully since that date. T. L. Evans died a number of years ago but his sons, Dorsey and Tom, are active in the business.

C. W. Watts came from Gallia County, Ohio, in 1886 and was employed for a time with D. A. Mossman and then G. A. Northcott, but his energy and capacity destined him for bigger things. He assisted in the organization of the Barlow, Henderson Company in 1892 with B. F. Barlow, president, and C. W. Watts, secretary and treasurer. This name was changed in 1898 to Biggs, Watts and Company with G. N. Biggs, president. In 1906 it became Watts, Ritter and Company and in 1913 moved into its present location.

In what was then referred to as the East End or the Third Ward and centered around 3d Avenue and 20th Street was a small business section and among the merchants in that community were L. J. Ashworth who had come from Putnam County in 1888 and attained first rank as a citizen; James Biernbaum who began as a peddler and grew into a successful business man; L. V. Waugh, and a little later Hague and Plymale in the mercantile business, and C. A. Yates, the druggist.

The foregoing men who came to the city in the very beginning can properly be designated as the first settlers and they were followed by others, and in some cases, younger men who have carried on to our own day. In this second group we find:

D. E. Abbott who drove the Parsons' horses from Vermont to Huntington. After completing his education at Marshall College he began business as a photographer which he developed to the point that he began to enlarge pictures and then added thereto a framing department. He incorporated the business and located in what was then Central City, but is now West Huntington. Mr. Abbott has been identified with everything that has been good for the city and a detailed history of his life will be a history of Huntington covering the same period.

G. C. Ricketts was in the grocery business for a great many years and before he went out of business he owned and occupied the southwest corner of 10th Street and 3d Avenue which he sold at a handsome figure and retired.

S. V. Mathews followed George W. Kirk as a photographer and then went into business with D. E. Abbott.

In 1885 Hugh Bowen and his kinsman V. B. Davis, and Walter, his son, formed the partnership of Bowen, Davis and Company and embarked in the meat business on 3d Avenue. This business was later incorporated and continued successfully until 1933.

H. J. Homrich came to Huntington in September, 1892, and opened a jewelry store in the Burdick Building on 3d Avenue. His business grew and some year ago he built a handsome building on the east side of 9th Street, north of 3½ Alley and continued in this business until his retirement three years ago. This was the finest establishment in this valley.

While talking about people we must not overlook some of these who are not included in the business group yet added to the community life. The old timers will remember Jim Mooney of the Round House, sometimes of "The Patch," who was a strange Irishman of great physical strength. He had a horse and cart and hauled

THE CITY ATTAINS ITS MAJORITY 243

cinders from the Ensign shops, but his principal diversion was getting pretty well filled up with whiskey and fighting the police.

Another of these was "Uncle" Joe McCormick who came from Wayne and lived on 5th Avenue between 9th and 10th Streets. "Uncle" Joe's wife kept boarders. "Uncle" Joe wore jean breeches cut on the pattern of Turkish trousers with one breeches leg in his boot top and the other outside. He was full of humor and was almost an oracle. One morning "Uncle" Joe came down the street and reported that he had had a dream the night before and in this dream he had died and gone to the infernal regions. He told in much detail of the many prominent Huntingtonians whom he had seen and in every instance gave point to his story by emphasizing the weaknesses of these friends.

Then there was Cal Henley, the superannuated steamboat pilot who sometimes played a fiddle on the street. On one occasion when he felt a personal injury in the acquittal of a man who was charged with a criminal offense he gave utterance to the classic expression "with a billy goat judge and a Barboursville jury, of course, he was acquitted."

John Carter for many years janitor of the courthouse was a well known character. In the early days he was a train porter on the Chesapeake and Ohio Railway. One day a new superintendent made a trip over the line and saw how John worked. He instructed the conductor, S. C. Beach, to fire John upon arrival at Huntington. Captain Beach broke this news to John who at first refused to believe it. When he was finally convinced of the truth John said, "Well, Mr. Wood may be a good railroad man but he sure ain't no judge of a nigger." John was a very good man to forecast what a jury's verdict would be and he would frequently tell a lawyer, "You are going to win this case but it ain't going to do you no good 'cause they's going to repeal it on you." John's good friend and patron was A. F. Southworth, who was the treasurer of the Brotherhood of Locomotive Engineers, and John was janitor of its lodge room. On the morning "Andy" was in off his run he would go down to the lodge room and work on his books and deposit his collections. John would be right there and follow Andy like a shadow until the money was safely deposited and in most cases would get a small advance on his wages.

Enoch Baker came later after spending many years in the timber business on the Guyan River. He had a long white beard and looked like an old patriarch. He was a man of great physical strength, had the heart of a lion but was as kind as a child. At first he sold bath cabinets and fire extinguishers. When the fire alarm sounded he would rush to the fire and demonstrate his extinguishers and more than once he got into a fight with the firemen who claimed he was interfering with their work. "Uncle" Enoch although well past sixty years of age never picked a fight but he never avoided one. His most famous exploit was knocking out Jack Bingham who was a very young man and had some ambition to be a prize fighter.

John T. Wilson, Major E. A. Bennett and R. M. Parker, after they had passed their active years, were the high priests of the Democratic party. They met every day at the Florentine—in the summer under the elm tree and in the winter on the inside. They decided all great party questions and viewed with alarm the slightest disagreement of any party leader with any pronouncement of William Jennings Bryan.

XXVII: HUNTINGTON LAWYERS

THE opportunities of the new city attracted a great many lawyers. Among the first was Captain Eustace Gibson who came from Virginia by rail to the White Sulphur Springs, by coach to Charleston, and by rail from Charleston to Huntington. Captain Gibson at once took an active part in political and civic affairs. When the train which brought the railroad officials and distinguished guests from Richmond to Huntington for the ceremonies of mingling the waters of the James River with those of the Ohio River, Captain Gibson made the response on behalf of the new city. The speech making took place at the office of Captain Joseph E. Mallory which stood at Maple Grove Landing about 7th Street. Captain Gibson was the great jury lawyer of his day.

Thomas H. Harvey and his brother, William H. Harvey, afterwards famous as "Coin" Harvey in the Bryan campaign of 1896, were early arrivals and had a law partnership. "Coin" Harvey built the house on 3d Avenue next to the corner of 13th Street which still stands, but after a few years he left. Thomas H. Harvey continued in Huntington, served one term as circuit judge, was a successful lawyer and had his home on 4th Avenue near First Street which he devised to the city at the time of his death a few years ago.

A. W. Warner and William Martin who practiced as Warner and Martin were here for a few years and then left. Warner went to Cincinnati where he was afterwards made a judge.

C. W. Smith and T. B. Kline practiced as Smith and Kline and enjoyed a large practice.

Henry C. Simms came early and was associated with Eustace Gibson in the firm of Gibson and Simms but later formed the firm of Simms and Enslow which continued until December, 1906, at the death of Mr. Simms. This firm continued longer perhaps than any firm in the county. Mr. Simms had his law training at Harvard and Mr. Enslow was a self-educated man. The firm enjoyed a lucrative practice and among its clients was the Chesapeake and Ohio Railway Company. F. B. Enslow was a man of great energy and organizing ability; he was one of the organizers of the Triple State Gas Company and of the Columbia Gas and Electric Company.

Thomas W. Taylor came in 1874 and he had a long and successful career.

In the early 80's came T. W. Peyton, Thomas A. Wiatt, John B.

Laidley, T. J. Bryan, Rufus Switzer, E. S. Doolittle, T. L. Michie, and Z. T. Vinson. A few years later Wiatt formed a partnership with Rufus Switzer which continued until his death. Z. T. Vinson was in the firm of Harvey, Vinson and MacDonald. Judge Harvey went on the bench one year later. William R. Thompson came to Huntington in 1892 and the firm became Vinson, Thompson and MacDonald. Mr. MacDonald died in 1894 and the firm became Vinson and Thompson and this partnership continued until Mr. Vinson's death in 1929.

T. L. Michie became a partner in the firm of Gibson and Michie which continued until Mr. Michie moved to Cincinnati in the early 90's.

In 1882 J. J. Peterson came from Lewis County and was admitted to the Bar. He did not engage in practice but embarked in the newspaper business. During the Harrison administration he was named Minister to Honduras where he continued until Cleveland appointed a successor. Peterson returned to Huntington, and with C. E. Haworth bought the *Herald* from J. H. Long. They published it until after the Spanish-American War when Peterson was appointed sheriff of Manila and left Huntington.

C. W. Campbell came in 1883 and a few years later formed a partnership with John H. Holt who came from Wheeling. This partnership continued until 1904.

George J. McComas, L. D. Isbell, R. L. Blackwood, D. E. Mathews, George I. Neal, Thomas R. Shepherd, Gordon O'Brien, E. M. (Bub) McCallister, J. S. and Lace Marcum came in the late 80's.

E. E. Williams, Elliott Northcott, C. R. Wyatt, Paul W. Scott, and H. T. Lovett came in the early 1890's. Only a few of these men are still living and the young men who succeeded them are the older members of the Bar.

POLITICAL LEADERS

In the political world things had not stood still. On the Democratic side the elder statesmen, including Ira J. McGinnis, one time circuit judge, and who had lacked just one vote in the Democratic caucus of being nominated United States Senator, Thomas H. Harvey, circuit judge, and Captain Eustace Gibson, were giving place to younger men. In the younger group, but not the very much younger men, were George F. Miller, Jr., D. I. Smith, Bub McCallister, Ed. Kyle, W. T. Thompson, Cameron L. Thompson, Henry C. Simms, Frank B. Enslow, John S., J. H. and Lace Marcum, and Ely Ensign.

In the youthful class were C. W. Campbell, John H. Holt, the matchless lawyer, T. W. Peyton, T. S. Scanlon, George I. Neal, just elected mayor and destined to dominate Cabell politics for a generation, and Buck Harding, more practical than polished.

On the Republican side were Sam Gideon, F. L. and E. S. Doolittle, one to be county clerk and the other circuit judge, for two terms; Taylor Wellington, Frank L. Hersey, D. E. Abbott, Sam Hawk, and "Doc" Suitor, with a younger group which included Elliott Northcott, who was destined to hold high place in his party councils and in government, E. E. Williams, Paul W. Scott, W. H. Lyons, and Frank H. Tyree.

XXVIII: TO CONTINUE THE STORY

AT a council meeting in October, 1894, upon motion of T. J. Bullock and C. A. Boxley, Bailey Post G.A.R. was given four lots in Spring Hill Cemetery and on motion of B. W. Foster, Republican, Camp Garnett, the Confederate organization was given a refund of purchase money paid for cemetery lots.

On November 24, 1894, the council named a committee from its body to meet prospective investors in the city and included on this committee was H. C. Harvey, then president of the Chamber of Commerce.

In the period from 1890-97 (the so-called Cleveland panic years) there were only three banks in the city. The Commercial was taken over by the Huntington National Bank and the two remaining banks continued in business. There were a number of building and loan associations which did not fare so well and beginning with the receivership for the Ohio Valley Building and Loan Association in 1901 all went into liquidation. The borrowers and stockholders sustained great losses. To make the situation worse a number of outside building and loan associations had made a number of loans in the city and these associations went into liquidation and added to the trouble of the local borrowers.

In March, 1896, the city coöperated with the Chamber of Commerce and contributed to the expense of a committee to go to Washington to help bring about making Huntington one of the places in which to hold the new Federal court.

On the thirteenth day of September, 1899, the city council assumed the obligation of a contract made by the Chamber of Commerce with the West Virginia Home for Incurables under the terms of which the chamber had given 30.67 acres of land as a site for the home for incurables and had obligated itself to pay an amount not to exceed $5,000.00 on the cost of the building and to open certain streets and to build certain sewers.

On July 7, 1896, it was proposed to establish a city work house.

In 1897 the committee who made an audit of the books of the city treasurer discovered that a number of city orders which had been paid by the treasurer and turned over to the city clerk for safekeeping had not been sufficiently cancelled and had been taken from the office of the city clerk and cashed a second time. The extent of this theft was never accurately ascertained. The city clerk who had been in office at this time was indicted and a special prosecutor employed to prosecute, but the jury found him not guilty.

On October 8, 1898, a group of Huntington women met in the library of the late Henry C. Simms at 1137 3d Avenue, to discuss the organization of a Woman's Club. The leading spirits in this movement were Miss Amie Skelton, now Mrs. Kennedy of Brooklyn, New York, Mrs. Grace Smith Morris, Mrs. Sarah Sloan Wyatt, Mrs. Grace La Ferre Cammack, and Mrs. Morton Wortham Sloan. At this meeting fifteen of the thirty women present agreed to help in such an organization and a meeting was called for one week later at the home of Mrs. Ida Haning Brandebury. At this meeting an organization was effected and the following officers elected: Mrs. Morton Wortham Sloan, president; Mrs. Ida Haning Brandebury, vice president; Mrs. Harriet Vinton Haworth, secretary, and Mrs. Grace La Ferre Cammack, treasurer. The club grew from the beginning and almost at once it began to enlarge its activities to include an active and helpful interest in civic affairs. For a great many years the club held its meetings at Marshall College but in 1917 it purchased from Dr. T. W. Moore his residence on 11th Street and made it into a club house. Within three years it had paid for its new home and its membership had grown to such an extent that it had begun to make plans for a new home.

On November 11, 1922, the junior department of the Woman's Club was organized. This department has developed into an efficient organization of splendid workers.

In 1929 the club was incorporated and purchased the lot at the southeast corner of 12th Street and Charleston Avenue and a new club house was built thereon in which the first meeting was held on May 7, 1930. The membership of the club has grown to seven hundred and includes the most representative women of the city.

On April 17, 1899, Councilmen W. E. Drummond, W. H. Lyons, B. W. Marr, J. K. Oney, and Mayor C. A. Nash were named as a committee to arrange a celebration of the Triple State Gas Company bringing gas to the city.

On July 31, 1899, the city agreed to buy certain rights of way east of 16th Street to bring about the location of the Chesapeake and Ohio Hospital here, and in December the railway company purchased Forrest Hill, the old Buffington home, and converted it into a hospital which was opened in June of the next year with Dr. C. R. Enslow, chief surgeon, Dr. C. M. Hawes, resident surgeon and Miss Mary Gaule, superintendent of nurses.

V. M. Green, the city clerk, died September 27, 1900.

In 1901 the Florentine Hotel was remodeled and was then the most up-to-date hotel in this section. L. H. Cox who, with his brother, R. L. Cox, and his brother-in-law, "Uncle Bob" Jones, had come to Huntington about 1894, and rented the hotel, was the landlord. Dick O'Neil, his nephew, was the genial and popular clerk. Sunday dinners were unequaled. This continued until George F. Miller and his associates in 1906 built the Frederick Hotel and began the development of 4th Avenue. L. H. Cox and R. L. O'Neil organized an operating company and took charge of the Frederick which immediately became the popular hotel. The Florentine dropped into second place and continued as such until it was torn down two years ago. The erection of the Frederick Hotel on 4th Avenue was regarded as a tremendous experiment as there was no business on this avenue and the question was—would it come? The new hotel was larger than the immediate business would justify but the ground floor was taken by storerooms and all of the rooms above the ground floor along the 10th Street side were rented for offices. These were the best office rooms in the city and were soon filled. G. A. Northcott, leading men's furnishing store, moved into one of the 4th Avenue rooms. J. C. Carter, the furniture dealer took a second one, and John Rau, Jr., moved his barber shop to the new location. Not long after this G. N. Biggs built a beautiful white tile front store on the opposite side of the avenue and John W. Valentine moved in and things were beginning to look up. More startling still the First National Bank bought the M. E. Church property at the southwest corner of 10th Street and 4th Avenue and in 1913 erected its twelve-story building thereon and business was definitely on 4th Avenue.

The Guyandotte Valley Road was under construction. Z. T. Vinson made a sale of a large tract of coal land in Logan County to the United States Coal and Oil Company, now the Island Creek Coal Company.

George F. Miller and Thomas H. Harvey and associates bought the J. A. Neibert estate in Logan County and immediately sold the timber on a portion of the land for a sum sufficient to pay the price of the whole of the land.

Real estate became active and the city grew in all directions. People began to build south of the railroad and homes were started on the hill. C. L. Ritter and H. T. Lovett erected the first two homes on the hill and they were followed by John A. Sheppard and B. B. Burns.

In September, 1902, the Chesapeake and Ohio Railway made a proposal to make Huntington the terminal of certain of its divisions as a consideration for putting an undergrade crossing at 8th and at 20th Streets, and to close 10th Street, one-half of the cost of the undergrades to be borne by the city and the other one-half by the railroad company. After a great deal of negotiating this contract was accepted. The work began in March, 1903 and these undergrades were completed in 1906. The 10th Street undergrade crossing was completed and opened in 1918 and the undergrade crossing at 14th Street, West, in 1925.

In 1903 the Guyandotte Club was incorporated, followed in 1906 by the Cabell County Country Club, which was the first country club in the county to be organized and which had its golf course on the premises now occupied by St. Cloud Commons. In 1911 this club was moved to Westmoreland and the name changed to the Westmoreland Country Club. This club was abandoned in 1920 when the New Guyan Country Club was organized. The Spring Valley Country Club was organized in 1922.

The Guyandotte Club was the legitimate successor of the Irving Club which was organized in the 80's by Ely Ensign, John Hooe Russel, Henry C. Simms, J. K. Oney, and others as a men's club. Its club rooms were on the second floor of the eastern portion of the old Huntington National Bank Building.

On July 18, 1904, the city council gave R. E. Vickers the exclusive right to operate a wharf within the corporate limits of the city but the franchise contained a recapture clause. On February 25, 1929, the city made a new contract with the Greene Terminal Company which had acquired the Vickers franchise. One of the terms of this contract was that the Greene Terminal Company release the monopolistic provisions of the original franchise.

In 1905 there was a bond election to provide for paving 16th Street from 3d Avenue to the undergrade, 20th Street from 3d Avenue to the undergrade, 4th Avenue from 8th Street to the Central City line, and 8th Avenue from 16th to 20th Streets. This was the beginning of paving activity in the city which continued for a number of years. Other streets and avenues were paved at the cost of the abutting property owners.

In 1907 the council recommended sale of the city property on 9th Street and 4th Avenue and the erection of a new city hall.

The Huntington spirit brought about the organization of the Huntington Tin and Planish Plate Company early in 1902 but the venture was not successful. The plant was bought by Al. Baumgardner who operated the Huntington Rail Company until 1907 when the West Virginia Rail Company was organized with E. N. Higgins, president, A. W. Werninger, vice president, L. A. Pollock, secretary and H. A. Zeller, treasurer and general manager. The new company bought the old plant which consisted of a wood building 60x120 feet on a three acre tract with facilities to roll four sizes of light rail and employed forty people. In 1909 Joseph Schonthal of Columbus, Ohio, became president and the plant continued to develop. The plant is now located on twenty acres and the buildings cover four to five acres. It produces 300 shapes and sizes of products with a capacity of 125,000 tons per year. Mr. Schonthal is dead and his son, Dez. C. Schonthal, is the vice president and active executive of the company. H. A. Zeller continues as treasurer and general manager.

About this time a postoffice was authorized and its location was an issue. The first postoffice in Huntington was located in the Brooks Drug Store on 2nd Avenue. It was then moved to the John T. Gibson Building at 933 3d Avenue, and from there to the building next to the northeast corner of 3d Avenue and 10th Street, thence to the Harvey Building on the northwest corner of 3d Avenue and 10th Street, then back to the Burdick Building on the south side of 3d Avenue between 9th and 10th Streets, then to the Caldwell Building on the northwest corner of 4th Avenue and 9th Street, back to the Harvey Building, and finally on July 8, 1908, it was located in the present and permanent Federal building. The location on 5th Avenue and 9th Street was somewhat away from the business center but it was above any high water mark so this site was selected to the surprise and chagrin of the people who owned property on 4th Avenue. Before this location was determined upon a number of sites were offered to the government and a hearing was held to decide upon the desirability of the several locations. The 4th Avenue group contended that 5th Avenue and 9th Street was too far out and was outside of the center of business as well as population but they overlooked the fact that there was an election precinct which included the territory between the river and the Chesapeake and Ohio Railroad and 8th and 9th Streets with a voting place at the 4th Avenue Fire Engine House which was then known as the "Black Maria," and in which the votes cast were very much greater in number than the population in the same territory seemed to justify. Dan A. Mossman, one of the property owners interested in the 9th Street and 5th Avenue location, secured a certificate of an election return from this precinct and based upon this return he convinced the investigators that this location was in a very populous section of the city so the postoffice was located and built on 9th Street and 5th Avenue. In the year 1909 Huntington's first skyscraper, the Robson and Prichard Building was erected on 9th Street just south of the postoffice.

By the time Greater Huntington was incorporated, the retail business was over on 4th Avenue, the vacant spaces between sections had been built up and the city covered the plain between the river, and the hill between the Guyandotte River and Four Pole Creek.

On October 14, 1910, George Lenz, the special agent of the Chesapeake and Ohio Railway arrested a negro who was identified as George, alias Red Johnson, alias Charles Kitchen, near the entrance to the shops in the east end of the Huntington yards and started with his prisoner towards the city. Lenz apparently did not search his prisoner because the negro shot Lenz through his body and left him seriously wounded on the railroad right of way and made his escape to the reservoir hill. Almost immediately the police were notified. Captain C. C. Clingenpeel, who was then on the night shift, was called and he together with a number of police officers went in pursuit of the fugitive. Charles Hale, who owned a pair of bloodhounds, was called and with his dogs joined in the pursuit. It wasn't long before the police officers and the fugitive were engaged in a gun battle. The police were reinforced by a number of citizens and a desultory battle was kept up until about four o'clock in the afternoon when the negro was killed. Charles Hale was wounded and afterwards died in the hospital. George Bias, Chesapeake and Ohio brakeman was killed. Willis Lowe, a policeman, was shot with a shotgun. William Hutchinson was shot in the arm. J. D. Thomason was wounded and George Stewart was shot through his mouth. L. O. Riley had a bullet hole through his coat.

In this year the Huntington Hotel was erected on the site of the first Adelphi Hotel. A. E. Kelly, the genial Irishman, operated the new hostelry and the shamrock was featured in its decoration.

In February, 1911, an order to buy the site for the new city hall

D. W. Emmons and wife, on their porch; overlooking the Ohio and Guyan rivers

was made and in the month following a site was purchased for the city market. The city hall was completed late in 1914 and occupied early in 1915 and the new market house completed and established in 1915.

In the closing days of March, 1913, the flood in the Ohio River was the highest on record and the greater part of the city was under water—all lights, water and gas were cut off. The people organized and for more than a week maintained feeding stations on the high land between Guyandotte and West Huntington where food was distributed in an orderly way and there was no suffering. When the flood subsided these committees saw that proper sanitary precautions were taken and all relief work was coördinated. There was no overlapping and the people who suffered losses by the flood were assisted according to their needs.

Early in 1914 the First National Bank Building was completed and the bank moved in.

In 1917 our country entered the World War and for the next two years Huntington people supported whole-heartedly all of the measures proposed for the support of the government in the great emergency.

In the next year Leon S. Wiles was elected mayor and the Farr Hotel was completed and opened in November. In the fall of this year Huntington suffered from an epidemic of the flu. The number of persons who were stricken was appalling but the people formed a volunteer association, established headquarters in the city hall and with the coöperation of the doctors and professional nurses worked night and day until the worst was over. There were many deaths and one of these was Mayor Wiles who had worked faithfully but was stricken and died on October 19, 1918, after a brief illness.

In 1920 the Huntington National Bank took over the Day and Night Bank, and in the same year A. S. Shoffstall and W. L. Witherspoon came to Huntington and made a survey to determine its suitability for a plant of the International Nickel Company. Their report was favorable and the company purchased eighty-seven and one-half acres of land on the Guyandotte River and began the erection of a plant thereon in January, 1921. The plant was completed and the first monel metal was poured in May, 1922, and sheets were rolled in June. The ore for this plant is mined at Sudbury in the province of Ontario, Canada. This ore is shipped to Huntington in a partially reduced form where the refining, rolling and shipping is completed.

The finished products are sold all over the world. A. S. Shoffstall was the first, and is still the general manager of this plant. It employs twelve hundred men.

In 1921 Glenn E. Chase was the owner of WSAZ a 100 watt radio broadcasting station which was located at Pomeroy, Ohio. In February, 1926, a local group acquired control of this station and moved it to Huntington at a cost of approximately $1,000.00. After the formation of the Federal Radio Commission the Huntington station was assigned a "frequency of 580 and operated with 250 watts until 1931 when the power was raised to 500 and on May 1, 1935, the Huntington station was assigned to a frequency of 1190 and has been operating on 1000 watts since." The station now represents an investment of $165,000.00 and is regarded as the greatest advertising medium for the city.

In 1924 the Huntington National Bank and the First National Bank were merged, and formed the First Huntington National Bank. In the same year work was begun on the Union Bank Building and Coal Exchange Building, both modern office buildings, and upon the new Prichard Hotel. These new buildings were ready for occupancy early in 1925 and the First Huntington National Bank in that year built an addition on the rear of its building. "Mine Host" Kelly gave up the Huntington Hotel and leased the Prichard Hotel but the new hotel was not a success financially and a few years later it was taken over by the stockholders and leased to L. M. Gibson.

In 1925 the business boom which the city had enjoyed for so many years appeared definitely at its end. The local banks were beginning to experience withdrawals. On April 15, 1927, the American Banking and Trust Company closed its doors. The Huntington people would not admit a failure and promptly set about and organized the Coal Exchange Bank in an effort to save the depositors of the American Bank but the new bank was unsuccessful and closed its doors on October 26, 1928. The next year the banking business had not improved; deposits continued to go off and collections could not be made. January 10, 1931, the Cabell County Bank closed its doors and on the 28th of the same month the Union Bank and Trust Company, the second largest bank in the city, went into a receivership. In June, 1931, the Ohio Valley Bank went into liquidation but its deposits were assumed by the Huntington Banking and Trust Company which also failed on April 8, 1933. The 20th Street Bank, after the bank holiday in 1933, went on a restricted basis on April 10th of that year. During this period the First Huntington National Bank for no reason at all experienced a number of "runs" but was strong enough to stand them.

In 1930 the Chesapeake and Ohio Railway Company leased two floors in the Robson-Prichard Building for certain operating departments which it was moving to the city. In the spring of 1935 it purchased the Coal Exchange Building and changed its name to The Chesapeake and Ohio Building.

Beginning in 1931 the unemployment situation in Huntington was most acute and conditions were made worse by the banking situation. To relieve the situation there was first, the RFC, which became the FERA and was supplemented for a time in 1933-34 by the CWA. A great amount of money has been distributed for this work from State and Federal funds.

XXIX: MANUFACTURERS AND WHOLESALERS

HUNTINGTON is fully alive to its obligation to the larger plants for its commercial advancement but it has not overlooked the part that the jobbing houses and smaller but diversified manufacturers have played in its commercial development, and some account will be given of the jobbing houses and these industries.

The first mine and mill supply jobber in the city, and for a good many years, the only one serving this section outside of Cincinnati, was the Smith-Hobson-Brandt Company which was organized in 1894 and had its place of business in the Kelly Building at 2½ Alley and 9th Street. This company failed in 1897 and was succeeded by the Miller Supply Company, organized by J. G. Tinsley of Richmond, and his son-in-law, J. C. Miller, who was president. This company enjoyed the business incident to the development of Southern West Virginia and in 1924 was combined with the Banks-Miller Supply Company which had been organized ten years earlier by Major W. H. Banks. The name changed to the Banks-Miller Supply Company.

The Newberry-Clay Shoe Company, wholesale shoe merchants, was organized in 1900 with Jeff Newberry, president, and George B. Clay, vice president. After a time it established a shoe factory at the corner of 2nd Avenue and 10th Street, diagonally across the alley from the entrance to the jobbing house. In 1910 Mr. Newberry retired and the company became the Norvell-Chambers Shoe Company. The factory was divorced from the jobbing house and was operated by the Mountain State Shoe Company, a subsidiary corporation. Mr. Newberry organized the Jeff Newberry Shoe Company, located at the corner of 3d Avenue and 11th Street. In 1913 the Mountain State Shoe Company was taken over by Walter E. Perry of Cincinnati and George W. Norvell who changed the name to the Perry-Norvell Shoe Company. In 1920 the G. R. Kinney Company acquired the stock in this company and two years later moved to the location at 25th Street and Guyan Avenue in a modern fireproof structure. Its output is sold through the medium of 330 retail stores of G. R. Kinney Company, Incorporated, of New York City. The plant employs 350 people, sixty per cent of whom are women, and does a gross annual business in excess of one and one-half millions of dollars. In 1928 the Norvell-Chambers Shoe Company changed its name to the Kipling Shoe Company under which name the business is still carried on.

The glass industry has played an important part in the industrial life of the city. It had its beginning in 1890 with Addison Thompson and associates who built a plant between 14th and 15th Streets, Washington and Virginia Avenues and for some years manufactured blown and pressed tableware and novelties in crystal and colors. The plant employed about 150 people and occupied the building now owned by D. E. Abbott.

In 1891 L. H. Cox and associates organized two plants. The first was the West Virginia Window Glass Company with a plant between 15th and 16th Streets and Madison and Jefferson Avenues. This plant manufactured window glass and in the beginning employed some seventy-five men. It operated about three years, was idle for a time and was taken over by Forbes Holton who organized the Union Glass Works which continued in business until 1904. Several years later the plant was dismantled. The second plant organized by Cox and associates was the West Virginia Flint Bottle Company which had its factory facing 15th Street between Jefferson and Madison Avenues and manufactured bottles, fruit jars, etc. It operated about two years and was sold to Forbes Holton who operated it a short time then sold it to A. Zihlman who organized the Huntington Tumbler Company which operated successfully until some time in 1932. It employed some 150 persons in the manufacture of high grade tableware.

In 1913 the Camp Glass Company of Mount Vernon, Ohio, moved its plant to 26th Street. T. W. Camp was president and John G. Todd general manager. This company manufactured handblown window glass and continued in business until 1924 when it was taken over by the Interstate Window Glass Company. They operated only a few months and the plant was then run as a coöperative business for a short period by the Window Glass Workers' Union. They made a high grade window glass and employed three hundred skilled workers. The plant is now dismantled.

In 1913 Mr. Charles Boldt of Cincinnati, Ohio, was attracted to Huntington by the prospects of securing five cent gas. He purchased the site on the south side of the Chesapeake and Ohio Railway at 5th Street, West, and built a plant with three furnaces. T. H. Morris was in charge. The plant used the Owens type machines and confined its production to manufacturing bottles exclusively. Later a wood box shop was placed on the property. This plant by change of name has now become the Owens-Illinois Glass Company and is under the charge of Dave Denelsbeck. It employs fifteen hundred people and has a capacity of 1,000,000 bottles daily, as well as a complete carrying box department in which they manufacture all containers. In addition they have a complete decorating shop. Traffic amounts to 5,500 outbound cars finished goods and 3,100 inbound cars of raw materials annually.

In 1915 J. W. Lawton organized the Glass Brick Company and built the plant on Virginia Avenue between 15th and 17th Streets, West, and began the manufacture of glass bricks for store fronts, bath rooms, etc. It was not successful and quit business in 1919. The plant remained idle until 1928 when the St. Clair Glass Company, under the management of J. A. Morehead, took over the plant and has been operating it in the production of a line of specialties in various colors as well as lenses for use in signal colors and automobile lights. The plant employs sixty-five persons and finds a market for its wares all over the country.

In 1919 the Schramm Glass Company of St. Louis, Missouri, built a plant on the west side of Four Pole Creek for the manufacture of fruit jars. It produced machine made fruit jars until 1925 when the plant was sold to Ball Brothers of Muncie, Indiana, who produced a similar line. The plant is not now in operation but has been kept in good condition.

In 1920 the Superior Glass Products Company of Columbus, Ohio, leased a tract of land from the Baltimore and Ohio Railway Company at 19th Street, West, and built a factory thereon and employed 150 men. The plant was destroyed by fire after operating only seven months and has not been rebuilt.

In 1925 the Bonita Glass Company of Wheeling built a plant at 15th Street, West, and Adams Avenue which was managed by Otto Jaeger. This company bought high grade glass and china and decorated it. It went out of business in 1929.

In 1932 A. H. Kerr of Sand Springs, Oklahoma, built a plant just outside of the eastern city limits as a branch of the Oklahoma plant and began the manufacture of Kerr Patented Fruit Jars in various sizes for domestic use. The plant operates for seven months yearly and employs seventy-three persons. Its production is five hundred gross tons jars daily.

The most recent addition in this line is the Polan Glass Company plant, now under construction at 30th Street between the two railroads. This plant has a small furnace and proposes to manufacture optical and spectacle glass. In the beginning it will employ twenty-five persons. It is said that very little of this product is made in this country and will find market in North and South America.

The Huntington Stove and Foundry Company was organized in 1901 by a group of men which included B. W. Foster, Dan A. Mossman, T. N. Boggess, A. W. Werninger, and W. A. Ullman. They established a plant at the foot of 20th Street. It manufactures coal and cooking stoves and does a general commercial foundry business. Its plant has more than doubled in size and it is one of the successful manufacturing plants in the city.

The West Virginia Stove and Foundry Company was established by Frank C. Boggess in 1907. Its specialty is the Burnside and Wesco Heaters and Torch Light Cooking Stoves. It manufactures all of the coal stoves used by the Baltimore and Ohio Railway Company which are of a special design and used in its stations and cabooses.

The Standard Stamping Machine Company came in 1917 from Maysville, Ohio, and in 1922 it became the Armstrong Manufacturing Company under the direction of C. C. Armstrong. It manufactured electric stoves. In 1928 it merged with the New Era Electric Range Company, a new Jersey corporation, and became the Armstrong Electric and Manufacturing Corporation with T. E. Spence of New Jersey as president and Mr. Armstrong as director and chief engineer. It operated successfully until three years ago.

The A. F. Thompson Manufacturing Company began in a small way in 1920 and owed its beginning to Gus Thompson who had patented the Bunsen Burner Cooking stove and used this company to manufacture and market it. Since that time Mr. Thompson has obtained ten other patents. The plant is now located at Vernon Street and the Chesapeake and Ohio Railway Company and employs more than one hundred people. It manufactures more than 30,000 gas stoves annually. This is a family organization for the reason that A. F. Thompson is president, his wife is vice president, and his sons occupy the other offices of the company.

In 1901 George J. Nicholson came to Huntington from Manchester, Ohio, and organized the Nicholson Furniture Company which built a small plant near the foot of 20th Street and began the manufacture of furniture. A little later C. W. Kendle became interested and the corporation name was changed to the Nicholson-Kendle Furniture Company. Its business prospered until it employed 160 people. The business was devoted entirely to the manufacture of bedroom furniture and by reason of its growth it required a considerable amount of

Log cabin of John Q. and Eliza Adams, southwest corner 5th Avenue and 11th Street

mirrors. To meet this requirement it organized the Huntington Mirror Plate Company as a subsidiary which in addition to manufacturing mirrors, added glass as a jobbing line.

In 1917 C. W. Kendle retired from the furniture company and took active charge of the Huntington Mirror Plate Company which was merged into the Central Glass Company and had plants in a number of cities. In 1922 Mr. Nicholson disposed of his holdings and retired and the management of the plant passed to M. J. Whalen and Charles R. Vose.

In 1906 the Penn Table Company, with F. D. Sebaugh as president, was organized and was followed in the next year by the Empire Furniture Company with C. L. Ritter, president, and C. W. Watts, vice president. The plants are located close to the Nicholson-Kendle Furniture Company. The Penn Table Company manufactures tables and chairs and the Empire Furniture Company buffets and servers. These companies worked in close relation and for many years were successful. On June 1, 1933, the Empire Furniture Company and the Nicholson-Kendle Company merged, but in the next year by reason of the general business depression they became involved in financial difficulties and have been liquidated through the Huntington Furniture Lines Liquidating Company. The Penn Table Company remains under its original management.

In 1902 J. M. McCoach organized the J. M. McCoach Company and began business in the building on the west side of 11th Street at 2½ Alley. A year earlier C. M. Davidson of Ohio organized the Huntington Cold Storage and Commission Company and bought the tract of land between 13th and 14th Streets on the south side of 7th Avenue and erected thereon a modern ice and cold storage plant. After the completion of the building the company lacked funds to pay the labor and material men and the plant was sold to satisfy these liens. J. M. McCoach and Company bought the plant and moved to the new location.

The Standard Printing and Publishing Company was organized in 1903 with C. L. Ritter, president, and W. W. McCue, superintendent. At first it employed seven persons and by increase of business this number has been increased to fifty-three. The company was recently reorganized with Herman P. Dean as president and W. W. McCue as secretary. It is the only plant in the state of West Virginia using all three basic printing processes, relief or letter press, offset lithography, and steel and copper plate engraving.

In 1904 W. J. Harvey and George Fowler came to Huntington and brought about the organization of the Huntington China Company. To finance the enterprise they got a price from the Huntington Land Company on a tract of land which they subdivided into the Ceramic Subdivision and reserved a site for the pottery. The lots were sold locally by a group of citizens for $300.00 each on the theory that a new industry would help the city and the amount realized from this sale was sufficient to pay the purchase price of the land and a substantial amount on the construction and equipment of the building. The plant was then bonded for an amount sufficient to equip it and perhaps something above. It was operated for only a short time when it got into difficulties and was sold to satisfy creditors. At this sale H. R. Wyllie of Lancaster, Ohio, purchased the plant and organized the H. R. Wyllie China Company. Mr. Wyllie was a practical potter and the plant was successfully operated during his lifetime and enjoyed considerable prosperity during the period of the war. Since Mr. Wyllie's death Daniel Churton has been in charge of the plant.

The Huntington Sash Door and Trim Company came from Alderson in 1909 and was located for some years at 19th Street and 2nd Avenue. Several years ago it moved to larger quarters on Camden Road. F. N. Mann is the principal owner and manager of the company which, as its name indicates, manufactures interior finish, doors, sash and cabinet work to architects' specifications. The plant employs sixty persons.

The Huntington Seating Company had its beginning in 1910 and its plant was in Guyandotte and was operated and controlled by W. M. Brooke. It maufactured church furniture.

The Blue Jay Manufacturing Company is a subsidiary or affiliate of the Watts-Ritter Company. It was organized in 1911 for the purpose of manufacturing working clothes. It employs 350 persons, principally female, with an annual payroll of $240,000.00 based on a thirty-six hour per week schedule.

The Minter Homes Corporation was organized as the Huntington Lumber and Supply Company in 1912. It specializes in the manufacture of ready-cut houses. It employs 200 people in its plant and from two to six hundred people in the field and does an annual business of something like three million dollars.

An internationally known plant in the city is the Standard Ultramarine Company. Omar T. Frick and associates were operating an ultramarine plant at Tiffin, Ohio, and in 1912 they were attracted to

Huntington by the prospects of cheap gas. They established a plant on a half acre of ground on 5th Avenue just east of the Baltimore and Ohio Railway. Omar T. Frick is president of the company and Major Henry Dourif is treasurer. Major Dourif is an outstanding chemist and under his technical direction, with Mr. Frick's business acumen, this plant has grown from twenty employees to some two hundred. Its products are ultramarine blues, and it manufactures colors that are not matched. In 1925 an aniline dye plant was installed and in 1931 a barium products plant. This plant is the leader in this line of specialties and finds its market in the United States and a great many foreign countries.

In 1913 James J. Weiler came to Huntington as sales agent for the steel fabricators. In 1919 he and his sons purchased some property and established an iron yard at Elm Street and Commerce Avenue and in 1924 they began business as James J. Weiler and Sons, as fabricators for structural steel and ornamental iron. James J. Weiler was president of the company and his sons filled the other official positions. James J. Weiler died on March 6, 1933, and was succeeded by Frank Weiler. The plant now employs thirty people.

The Washington Manufacturing Company was established in 1917 and manufactures men's and boys' pants. Its products are sold mainly to mail order houses, chain stores and jobbers. It employs three hundred people.

The Imperial Ice Cream Company was established in 1922. It manufactures ice cream and purchases a large amount of dairy products locally. Its products are marketed in southern Ohio, eastern Kentucky and southern West Virginia.

The Huntington Forge and Machinery Company was organized in 1921. A. P. Martin is president and G. T. Smith is secretary. It is engaged in pipe fitting and general machinery work, boiler and sheet metal work, and electrical welding.

In 1924 the Star Car and Foundry Company was organized by local people. A plant was built in Westmoreland for the purpose of manufacturing mine cars. The venture was not successful and the property was sold and purchased by the Enterprise Wheel and Car Corporation whose principal office is in Bristol, Tennessee. It is now operating this plant and has twenty-four employees.

The Bradshaw-Diehl-Romer Company had its beginning in 1915 with J. R. McMahon and H. T. Diehl operating a dry goods store on 3d Avenue between 10th and 11th Streets under the name of

McMahon-Diehl Company. It was incorporated in 1917 and expanded and took over a number of pieces of property including the Odd Fellows Building on the corner of 3d Avenue and 10th Street and the business became a department store. After the death of J. R. McMahon, George D. Bradshaw became interested in the business. In 1926 the corporate name was changed to Bradshaw-Diehl Company. Mr. Bradshaw was elected mayor of the city in 1932 and served until June, 1934. In his absence from the business I. B. Romer was taken in and the name changed to the Bradshaw-Diehl-Romer Company. The organization now is I. Ben Romer, president, George D. Bradshaw, vice president, and H. T. Diehl, secretary-treasurer.

In 1923 Meyer Mittenthal came to Huntington and arranged for a long time lease on the Foster Building at the southwest corner of 3d Avenue and 9th Street, at a rental that astounded the local people. He organized the Huntington Dry Goods Company and along with M. J. Federman owned its capital stock. The company took over the lease, made some alterations in the building and opened a department store with Mr. Mittenthal in charge. Mr. Federman was connected with a buying organization in New York city and gave the new company the benefit of this connection with the result that it was able to buy merchandise about as cheap as the average jobber. The benefit of this purchasing power was transferred to the customer and the new company enjoyed a good business from the start. In 1926 Mr. Mittenthal took an executive position out of the city and in 1929 the stock of the Huntington Dry Goods Company was taken over by a chain organization which still owns and operates it. In 1933 Mr. Mittenthal returned to Huntington and is again in charge of the business. He has identified himself with the local interests and is a helpful and useful citizen.

The first of the chain stores to come to Huntington was the McCrory 5 and 10 cent store which located here at the beginning of the century. As the city grew it was followed by many others.

Huntington has become headquarters for a number of coal companies and other companies whose businesses are with the coal operators in adjacent fields. These organizations have brought a fine type of citizen to the community but any account of the companies is out of place in a local history.

XXX: PARKS AND PLAYGROUNDS

THE first reference to parks found in the city records appears in the council records of July, 1891. On the 16th day of that month the council adopted a resolution directing the city attorney to prepare an ordinance to bond the city for $7,500.00 to be used to buy a city park. At this meeting B. W. Foster, agent for the Central Land Company appeared and offered to sell the city for park purposes three city blocks and a portion of a fourth block for the price of $7,500.00, but his proposal was rejected by a vote of seven to one. The council then adopted an ordinance proposing a bond issue of $15,000.00 to be used to buy a city park, a market house and an infirmary, this proposal to be submitted to a vote of the people.

At the next meeting of the council on July 13, 1891, a proposal from C. P. Huntington, special receiver of the Central Land Company, for the establishment of a park was submitted. Just what this proposal was is not disclosed, but in any event it was rejected by a vote of six to one.

Nothing was done with the bond issue and on February 19, 1896, a committee from the Chamber of Commerce, of which Sam Gideon was chairman, H. C. Simms, H. C. Harvey and F. L. Doolittle were members, appeared before the council relative to the purchase of Holderby Grove, located between 7th Avenue and the Chesapeake and Ohio Railroad, 14th and 16th Streets, and some ground in the foothills south of Four Pole Creek, for park purposes, as proposed by C. P. Huntington. After some discussion, the mayor appointed a committee consisting of John W. Shively, H. B. Hagen and Don Russell, to act with the Chamber of Commerce committee, and directed the city engineer to make a survey and plat of all land suitable for park purposes and report at the next meeting.

On March 17, 1896, Sam Gideon, with J. L. Hawkins, C. E. Gwinn and T. S. Scanlon, appeared before the council and reported their findings but no action was taken on the report. The city clerk was instructed to write a letter to C. P. Huntington and thank him for donating twenty-five acres of land for park purposes, but this donation for a park was never made.

On May 11, 1896, a committee from the council recommended that the city purchase the tract known as College Grove, on the north side of 4th Avenue, opposite Marshall College, at the price of $7,000.00 and the Holderby Grove at the price of $8,000.00. This report was received and the clerk directed to make a proposal to Mr. Huntington, special receiver, to purchase these tracts and request that he give the council an answer on his offer to donate twenty-five acres of land, along with the Council's request for fifteen acres of additional hill land.

At the next meeting the Council received a reply from Mr. Huntington in which he declined to sell the two tracts for $15,000.00, but offered to sell them for $20,000.00. Nothing further was done until July 27, 1897, when Sam Gideon again appeared and requested the mayor to name a special committee consisting of a member from each ward to consider the purchase of land opposite Marshall College. Nothing came of this request but on August 21, 1899, the committee from the Chamber of Commerce again appeared before the council and attempted to interest them in the purchase of a park to be located in the vicinity of Four Pole Creek, east of 8th Street, and after much discussion by the council and other persons, it was asserted that former councils had been guilty of almost criminal negligence of the welfare of the city in failing to provide for parks. A special committee consisting of John W. Valentine, W. E. Drummond, and John B. Stevenson were named to act with the Chamber of Commerce committee and they were directed to try to secure from C. P. Huntington, special receiver, twenty-five acres which they understood that he had before agreed to give, and see if he would sell an additional fifteen acres in the hills adjoining the city at $100.00 per acre. These efforts came to naught.

In 1908 there was a discussion in the council about the purchase of a site for an infirmary. Two sites were offered, one south of 13th Avenue between 8th and 12th Streets and the second the Enslow farm on Four Pole Creek, just west of 16th Street. After considerable debate, on March 2, 1908, there was a motion made by Rufus Switzer and seconded by Councilman Black, that the city buy fifty-five acres adjacent to and south of 13th Avenue, between the McCoy Road and 12th Street, for an incinerator at the price of $18,000.00. This motion was carried and the land company by deed dated June 30, 1908, conveyed to the city two tracts of land, one for 50.35 acres and the second of 4.38 acres for this purpose.

There were a number of parliamentary battles as to the point the incinerator should be located on this tract and it was finally established near 8th Street. The property owners adjacent thereto applied for and obtained a temporary injunction. While these matters were

PARKS AND PLAYGROUNDS

pending, Rufus Switzer was elected mayor and he took the "bull by the horns" and established a city park on this land. About this time they made an agreement with C. L. Ritter, under the terms of which C. L. Ritter donated to the city seventeen acres of land adjoining these two tracts to be used in conjunction with, and as a part of, the new city park. As consideration for this conveyance, the city agreed to and did build a road extending from 8th Street and into what is now Enslow Park. The new park was named Ritter Park and was the beginning of the Huntington park system.

In 1913 plans and specifications were prepared for a boulevard on both sides of Four Pole Creek from 8th Street, East, to 5th Street, West, and soon afterwards dirt roads were opened on these routes but no effort was made to extend the park system or to develop Ritter Park south of Four Pole Creek.

In 1920 there was a revival of civic interest and under the leadership of the Rotary Club an attempt was made to form a civic committee composed of representatives of the several civic clubs for the purpose of developing a general city plan and especially parks and playgrounds. There was one meeting of this group but jealousy developed and nothing was accomplished. In 1921 the Rotary Club named a park and playground committee and the Kiwanis Club at the same time named a similar committee. These two committees had a joint meeting and elected a common chairman and invited the coöperation of other civic clubs. There was coöperation from time to time of other civic clubs. The committee then agreed upon a plan which visualized not only the present Huntington but what it conceived to be the Huntington of the future. The plan provided for parks along the foothills from the east to the west end of the city connected by hard roads or boulevards with playgrounds and play fields at points in the plain between the river and the hills and a river front driveway. The ultimate aim was to have recreation centers so located that any person in the city could reach one of these centers by traveling less than one mile. In furtherance of this project the committee caused a map be made and locations were fixed for park areas. In furtherance of this project, property was acquired lying along Four Pole Creek west of 5th Street, West. There was some land donated but a purchase was made of sixteen acres at the price of $14,000.00 and the purchase money was immediately raised by public subscription. Among those who subscribed were C. W. Campbell, then mayor, who gave $12,500.00, and Julius Broh who gave $5,000.00.

The city authorities named the park in the west end after the Kiwanis Club and the park in the east end after the Rotary Club. There were no roads west of 5th Street, West, and there was no road connecting Rotary Park to any city street. Another feature of the committee's program was a Memorial Boulevard for the World War soldiers to extend along the north bank of Four Pole Creek from a point at 7th Street, West, to about 12th Street, West, this boulevard to have memorial trees planted on each side and a proper memorial at the entrance to the driveway. This plan appealed to the ex-service men and at once an independent organization was created, known as the Cabell County War Memorial Association, of which Robert L. Archer was president, and which included in its executive group H. A. Zeller, C. D. Emmons, T. McK. Hays, and a number of others. This group erected the Memorial Arch at the head of Memorial Boulevard, and then to the Boulevard to Ritter Park. Washington vember 11, 1929. The park committee continued its activities and in 1925 brought about the enactment of an act of the Legislature which created the Board of Park Commissioners of the City of Huntington. This board is bi-partisan and an independent municipal corporation with power to levy taxes within the limits. It has been fortunate in its membership in that it has had representative men who were thoroughly interested in the progress of the parks. Its first major development was bringing about the erection of Fairfield Stadium which was built by funds furnished jointly by the Board of Education, the Board of Park Commissioners and Marshall College. The park board has continued on a progressive development of the park system. Rotary Park now consisting of 200 acres has been graded and improved and is connected by a hard road to Washington Boulevard, and thence on the Boulevard to Ritter Park. Washington Boulevard has been paved with asphalt to 5th Street, West, and its extension to the western corporation limits has been macadamized with limestone macadam. Kiwanis Park is being developed and has been added to and now consists of 100 acres. Ritter Park has been developed south of the creek and contains an open air theatre, a handsome rose garden, a number of pools and a greenhouse in charge of a trained horticulturist. At 17th Street, West, and Van Buren Avenue, the city had a tract of six or eight acres of land on which was formerly located the pest house and incinerator. In 1932 this property was turned over to the Board of Park Commissioners, the old pest house was demolished, the incinerator taken down, and certain additional lands acquired. There has been erected thereon a handsome community house which is available for public purposes, a baseball and football field, wading pool, band stand, tennis courts and an outdoor bowling green. This is called the St. Cloud Commons.

Ovens and dining tables that can be used for picnic purposes have been put in all three of the parks.

In the rear of the Holderby School the park board has over two acres of land which is used for a baseball field. This field is called the Holderby Commons.

XXXI: THEATRES

IN the early 70's Robert T. Harvey built an opera house in the third floor of the Harvey Building at the northwest corner of 3d Avenue and 10th Street. Measured by present standards this was a very crude affair. The lighting was with oil lamps and the floor was all on one level with some seats raised in the rear which were designated as the "peanut" gallery. This building was destroyed by the fire of 1879 and Huntington was without an opera house until 1884 when B. T. Davis began the erection of the Davis Opera House on the southeast corner of 8th Street and 3d Avenue, which was completed in the early part of 1885. The new building cost $35,000.00, and seated 800 people. The theatre was located in the front of the building on the second floor with the stage on the 3d Avenue side and the main entrance on 8th Street, then up a long flight of stairs to the main floor. On the ground floor were a number of store rooms, the corner one of which was at that time, and has been at all times since, occupied by the Davis Drug store. In 1892 the building was remodeled and the name changed to the Huntington Theatre. The remodeled theatre was 60x160 feet with a stage 40x60 feet and seated 1,400 people. E. B. Enslow was one of the first managers. He was followed by Joseph R. Gallick who served for fourteen years and in 1904 C. C. Beeber purchased the building. A few years later he sold it to the Fred Nixon-Nirdlinger interests and it was managed by various persons for this concern until it was purchased in 1915 by Abe and Sol Hyman. After the advent of the movies this theatre fell into disuse and a few years ago was sold and the building converted into a market house.

The first moving picture house was known as the Dreamland and opened in 1905 in the building on the present site of the Farr Hotel. About the same time a second house known as the Wonderland on 3d Avenue was opened and these were followed in 1906 by small houses, the White City on 9th Street, Fairyland on 3d Avenue, below 9th Street, the Gem in 1908 on 3d Avenue between 9th and 10th Streets. In 1910 the old skating rink on 4th Avenue between 8th and 9th Streets was taken over by Floyd S. Chapman and converted into a movie house and named the Lyric. It was proposed that a Mr. Parker would run the movie house but he was accidentally killed by the falling of a sign. Mr. Chapman sold his interests to Sol and Abe Hyman and they made this an up-to-date moving picture house and continued at this location until some time in the year 1927 when Mr. Hyman interested some outside interests. A long time lease was entered into for 120 feet fronting on 4th Avenue between 9th and 10th Street from the Biggs-Long Realty Company and there was erected thereon the Keith-Albee Theatre, operated by the Keith-Albee Theatre Corporation of which A. B. Hyman is president. This building was opened in May, 1928. It then and now is the last word in a modern theatre and surpasses theatres located in most of the larger cities. It is air cooled and has a seating capacity of 3,000, divided 1,800 on the lower floor, 1,000 in the balcony and 200 loge seats.

On November 15, 1926 the Palace Amusement Company, under the guidance of L. Roy Smith, president, opened with a combination stage and screen show. In the next year talking pictures were introduced in this house with *Don Juan* for the first picture. In 1928 vaudeville was offered and in the following year photophone equipment was installed and put on the Fox Movietone Follies. This management has carried on a consistent policy of improvement, and in 1934 installed the latest sound equipment which is identical with that used in Radio City Music Hall in New York City.

XXXII: PUBLIC UTILITIES

STREET RAILWAYS

ON June 13, 1888, the Huntington Electric Light and Street Railway Company was chartered. It built and operated an electric street car line on 3d Avenue from the Guyandotte Bridge to 7th Street, East. This is said to have been the second electric car line in the world. The company also furnished the city with electric lights. On November 20, 1890, the City of Huntington granted a franchise to the Huntington Belt Line for a street railway along 4th Avenue, 10th Street, 6th Avenue, 16th Street and 8th Avenue, and in 1892 a franchise on 4th Avenue to Central City.

On July 14, 1892 the Consolidated Light and Railway Company acquired all of these properties.

In 1899 the street railway in the City of Huntington was apparently making little, if any, profit and the same was true of the lines in Ashland and Catlettsburg, Kentucky, but notwithstanding this fact Z. T. Vinson conceived the idea of acquiring these properties, putting them in first class condition and building a connecting line and establishing interurban service between Huntington and Ashland. Mr. Vinson secured an option on the street railroads and organized the Ohio Valley Electric Company on August 2, 1899. He interested Johnson N. Camden who purchased bonds of the new company in a sufficient amount to pay for these properties, build the necessary lines and bring the old lines up to standard. The new company on December 13, 1899, purchased the Consolidated Light and Railway Company and the street railways in Catlettsburg and Ashland and built a connecting line between them. The work was soon completed and the interstate service begun. Just as the completion of the Chesapeake and Ohio Railroad had put an end to the stage lines the extension of this road to Cincinnati in 1889 had put an end to the passenger business by river. The extension of the Huntington Street Railway to Ashland put an end to the "shuttle train" business on the Chesapeake and Ohio and the "dummy train" on the Ohio River roads.

On December 13, 1900, the Ohio Valley Electric Railway Company changed its name to the Camden Interstate Railway Company. On February 24, 1904, the Huntington and Charleston Railroad Company was granted a franchise along certain streets and avenues south of the Chesapeake and Ohio Railroad and this property was taken over by the Camden Interstate Railway Company, first by a lease for

The first street car. Note the Huntington-Ensign-Guyandotte

a period of fifty years and purchased outright on October 20, 1916. The Camden Interstate Railway Company changed its name to the Ohio Valley Electric Company on October 20, 1916, and on November 1, 1916, it sold all of its power stations and distributions to the Consolidated Light, Heat and Power Company.

In 1912 some local people were led to believe that electric current could be sold very much cheaper than it was being done and the seller still make a profit. They organized the Consumer's Light and Power Company and made a very low price to the city to furnish it street lighting. The city accepted its bid and at the same time gave the new company a franchise for ten years. The new company installed a plant on 7th Avenue about 7th Street and began to furnish current. It soon developed that its prices were entirely too low and so J. E. Thompson, who was one of its largest stockholders, brought about a sale of its assets other than its power plant to the Consolidated Light, Heat and Power Company. The effect of these transfers was to put the railroad property in one company and the light property in another. The light property was transfered to the Appalachian Electric Power Company, its present owner, on April 23, 1926.

About 1908 the Ohio Valley Electric Company by stock ownership became the property of the American Gas and Electric Company which held it until 1927 when the stock was sold to the Central Public Utility Corporation and six years later it was taken over by F. W. Samworth and some local people. Mr. Samworth is now its president and active operating manager.

D. W. B. McCown, town marshal of Guyandotte, went out of office in the spring of 1909 and with admirable foresight, but perhaps poor judgment, bought a truck and for a brief period operated a bus line for passengers between Huntington and Guyandotte in competition with the electric railway company. The venture was not successful financially but it has the distinction of being the first motor bus line in the county.

When the hard roads were completed, and before a certificate of convenience was required to operate a passenger bus many persons bought motor vehicles and operated taxi lines. Among the first of these was Joe Henderson. The hard road was completed to Barboursville on November 6, 1917, and Joe started the Huntington-Barboursville line on January 1st following. On February 1st of the same year R. M. Cackley put on a competing taxi. In 1920 after the law requiring a certificate of convenience went into effect, Cackley was given the permit and is still operating a bus on this route with the distinction of being the first bus line west of Charleston.

In the spring of 1918 J. R. Saul with a one-ton Ford truck operated a trucking line between Glenwood and Huntington. At first he hauled only milk and farm products but found a demand for passenger service. In the fall of the same year he had a one-ton truck with an end trailer and made two round trips daily and hauled passengers as well as products. Saul is now with the Atlantic Greyhound lines, but in the same year Jack Jordan started a line between Point Pleasant and Huntington which he still operates.

About this same time the Union Transfer Company operated taxis in the City of Huntington and established passenger service between Huntington, Barboursville and Milton. In the spring of 1919 it purchased eight passenger bus bodies and mounted them on Ford chassis for this service.

In 1919 J. R. Saul, Leo Stevens, and Zack Bunch formed a partnership and operated as the White Transportation Company between Huntington and Milton. The equipment of this partnership was steadily improved and in 1923 the company extended its lines into St. Albans where it made connections with the interurban line for Charleston. This business was highly competitive for the reason that two other companies, the Huntington-Charleston Motor Bus Company and the Ferguson Bus Company and a number of individuals were operating over certain parts of this route. By 1922 there were thirty-two pieces of equipment on portions of the highway between Huntington and Hurricane.

In 1920 R. E. Jimison started a line from Huntington to Griffithsville which he afterwards sold to Dr. N. E. Steele who still operates it as an independent line and also owns and operates the Logan and Williamson lines.

In 1920 James Grubb, doing business as the Cannonball Transportation Company, established service between Huntington, Ironton, and Portsmouth with seven passenger cars. This business was sold in 1926 to Williams Brothers of Portsmouth who put into service twenty-one passenger Yellow coaches called the Interstate Motor Transit Company, and had its terminal in the Lewis Arcade Building.

In June, 1924, Arthur M. Hill purchased the Huntington-Charleston Motor Bus Company and consolidated it with the White Transportation Company and formed the Midland Trail Transit Company which has since become the Blue and Grey Transit Company, which in 1931 was succeeded by the Atlantic Greyhound Lines. This line had its terminal on 9th Street between 2d and 3d Avenues, then moved to the Hines Building on the south side of 5th Avenue between 9th and 10th Streets, and now is in the Union Terminal Building.

The line to Gallipolis was started in 1929 by Zack Bunch, who still owns and operates it.

In 1929 the old Lyric Theatre Building was leased for a bus terminal and after it was remodeled in February, 1930, all bus lines entering the city began using it as a union terminal.

About the time the law requiring a certificate of convenience to be issued by the State Road Commission was put into effect an agitation was begun to have the city regulate motor transportation routes within the city limits. On March 16, 1925, the City of Huntington granted a franchise to operate bus lines to the Westova Bus Company, which had been organized by John B. Stevenson and others, to operate passenger buses over three routes within the city limits. This franchise was sold to the Ohio Valley Bus Company, an affiliate of the Ohio Valley Electric Railway, on June 1, 1926. At the time of the sale the selling company was only operating over one route. The new purchaser in that year started a line from Ironton to Huntington and one from Kenova to Huntington and in 1929 established the 11th Avenue line, in 1930 the Monroe Avenue line, and in 1933 the line to the Veterans' Hospital.

The terminal for the buses was established where it still is on 4th Avenue between 8th and 9th Streets. The line from Ironton to Huntington has been sold to the Atlantic Greyhound Company, which still operates it.

ARTIFICIAL GAS

At a very early date several applications were made to the city council for a franchise to furnish the city with artificial gas but none of these franchises were granted until John Hooe Russel and associates were given a franchise on October 7, 1890. This franchise passed into the hands of the Consolidated Light and Railway Company, a small plant was erected near Johnson's Lane and artificial gas was supplied for domestic uses, but its cost for fuel as compared with coal prevented its use to any great extent.

WATER COMPANY

The earliest city water supply was that of public wells equipped with pumps located at street corners in the more populous parts of the city. Fire protection was provided by public cisterns. This system continued until November 22, 1886, when the city granted W. S. Kuhn and associates a franchise to build and maintain a waterworks to supply the city and its people with water for fire protection and for domestic uses upon the condition that the plant should be in successful operation before the last day of December, 1887. The franchise imposed an obligation on the grantee to constantly keep all fire hydrants supplied with water for fire service and gave the city the right to purchase the plant upon the terms therein set out. This franchise was transferred to the Huntington Water Company and the plant was in operation within the time limit. Since that date it has supplied the city with a sufficient supply of wholesome water with the exception that, on one occasion, July 2, 1901, the Hotel Adelphi, then located on 6th Avenue and 9th Street, was discovered on fire and when the city firemen arrived it was found that there was no water in the fire hydrant.

The first local manager was W. W. Adams who served the company a quarter of a century and he was succeeded by H. E. Watt who is still in charge.

In 1917 a Delaware corporation of the same name was incorporated and this company purchased the Guyandotte Water Works and the Huntington Water Company and in 1924 it purchased the plant of the Suburban Water Company which supplied water in Westmoreland, which was then outside the city limits of Huntington. This company is now controlled by the American Water Works and Electric Company.

TELEPHONES

In 1882 George S. Page and H. C. Everett entered into a contract with the Southern Bell Telephone and Telegraph Company of Richmond, the terms of which were that Page and Everett were permitted to build and operate a telephone line in Cabell County until such time as the Southern Bell Telephone Company might build an exchange therein, then the Page and Everett line was to be turned over to the telephone company. Under this contract a telephone line was built from Page's Store in Guyandotte to the new store of Herman Jenkins on 3d Avenue between 9th and 10th Streets. Page and Everett's first plan was to put the Huntington end of the line at the Albert Mills, which were then being operated by Mr. Everett, located on 4th Avenue between 9th and 10th Streets, on the site of the Keith-Albee Theatre. They concluded that the mills were too

Bicycle Club. Taken at the west side of the Bank of Huntington Building at the northeast corner of 3rd Avenue and 10th Street. On the left is Ed. Douthit, R. Mather Archer, Mr. and Mrs. Lon Hutchinson, and others.

far from the business section and used the other location. After the line was established Mr. Jenkins gave a dinner and invited a number of guests, including John Hooe Russel, president of the Huntington Bank; T. L. Chapman, master mechanic of the Chesapeake and Ohio Railway Company shops; A. J. Rosebury, of the Guyandotte Woolen Mills; George S. Page, H. C. Everett, and others to witness a demonstration of the new telephone. The plan was to charge ten cents for each call and the telephone operator at the receiving end to be the messenger to find the persons wanted. Mr. Jenkins was paid a commission on his gross receipts. A short time afterwards, a company was formed which included J. E. Johnston, F. L. Hersey, J. W. Hagen, and Frank B. Enslow, and the line was extended to Barboursville.

Some time in 1883 the Southern Bell Telephone Company entered into an arrangement with Lon H. Hutchison who was then the manager of the Western Union Telegraph Company to put in telephone service in Huntington. On January 7, 1884, Mr. Hutchison secured a franchise from the City of Huntington to put in telephones in the city and a short time after the company began to do business it took over the Page and Everett lines and had twenty or thirty subscribers. The venture was not successful and after a year or two the enterprise was abandoned.

Several years later the Bell Company concluded the time was ripe to try again in Huntington. It secured a new franchise from the city on January 5, 1891, which was supplemented on July 13th of the same year, and began business again with Lon Hutchison as its manager. The first central office was located in the Harvey Building at the northwest corner of 3d Avenue and 10th Streets but later it was moved into a small room in the rear of the Huntington National Bank on the east side of 10th Street. At this time Mr. Hutchison was manager of the telephone company, manager and operator for the Western Union Telegraph Company which had its office in the same room, was the agent for and sold Remington typewriters and bicycles. He was also weather agent for the government, and with all of his duties he had time to take part in the Arian Quartet, composed of John A. Jones, J. R. Gallick, M. C. Dimmick, and Lon H. Hutchison, with Dr. C. E. Haworth, accompanist. In the course of time Mr. Hutchison gave up various duties except the duties of weather agent which place he filled until his death.

In 1901 Huntington was provided with long distance service. The "central" remained on the east side of 10th Street until 1902 when it was moved to the Advertiser Building on 4th Avenue between 9th and 10th Streets where it remained until 1906 when the company erected a new building on 10th Street at 4½ Alley.

In 1895 the Huntington Mutual Telephone Company was organized by local people as an independent telephone company. H. E. Mathew was for many years secretary of this company. The central operator in both companies knew all of their respective subscribers, their ways and manners. It was not necessary to give the operator a telephone number it was only necessary to inform her that you desired to speak to such and such a person or to such and such a residence and the operator would promptly give you the number or perhaps tell you the party was absent at that particular time. In 1906 the Bell Company began the installation of the underground system and greatly improved all of its facilities. A year or two later it purchased the Huntington Mutual Telephone Company and in 1910 took over its business. At the conclusion of this merger there were 2,272 telephones in service. The survey made by the telephone company estimated that in 1942 there will be 33,200 telephones in service and in anticipation of this development it erected in 1925 a beautiful office building on 6th Avenue near 12th Street.

NATURAL GAS

Just before the outbreak of the Civil War, John B. Floyd, one time governor of Virginia and Secretary of War, together with certain associates began a development at Warfield, Kentucky, to mine coal and salt and transport them by river. The company did produce some coal, but was not successful in transporting a single barge of coal or salt below the forks of the Big Sandy. This company some time in the 1860's in drilling a salt well struck gas but did not plug the well, with the result that the gas flowed therefrom some twenty odd years and during part of the time the well was on fire.

In 1898 E. G. Germer and associates organized the Triple State Natural Gas and Oil Company. This company took over a franchise that had been granted to Germer and associates by the City of Huntington to furnish natural gas. This new company acquired the gas property at Warfield including the well which had been flowing all of these years and built a pipe line from Warfield to Huntington and began to supply gas for light and heat purposes in July, 1899. In the beginning it had four hundred customers. E. G. Germer was the first president, H. C. Reaser was secretary and treasurer, and John A. Landing was general manager. The Triple State Company continued in business until February, 1905, when it was taken over by the United States Natural Gas Company which latter company was taken over in 1909 by the United Fuel Gas Company, a subsidiary of the Columbia Gas and Electric Company.

In 1912 the Huntington Chamber of Commerce sponsored a community project to supply the citizens and industries of Huntington with cheaper gas and to this end brought about the organization of the Huntington Development and Gas Company. All of the capital stock was subscribed by local people and to safeguard the community's interest the control of the corporation was placed in the hands of a board of directors of the Chamber of Commerce as trustees for the purposes as stated in the trust arrangement to prevent the control of the company from passing to competitors or to interests not devoted primarily to the public welfare. It had a limited acreage but reduced the gas rate from twenty to fifteen cents per thousand. In the next year the company leased a large boundary of additional acreage under an arrangement with E. W. Clark and Company of Philadelphia, which involved the increase in its capital from $200,000.00 to $800,000.00, divided $200,000.00 preferred and $600,000.00 common and a bond issue of $225,000.00. Clark and Company took the bond issue but at a discount and was given a bonus of $390,000.00 of stock and the reorganized company laid a twelve-inch line to Ashland and made a contract to supply the Ashland Steel Company with industrial gas for five years at six and one-half cents per thousand. On April 5, 1916, there was a reorganization of the Huntington Development and Gas Company and it took over the properties of the Guyandotte Land Association. Its new capital structure was $3,000,000.00 six per cent first mortgage bonds, $1,500,000.00 six per cent cumulative preferred stock, and $4,000,000.00 common stock. Out of the sale of the mortgage bonds $600,000.00 was to be used for extensions and improvements. The company continued as an independent one until 1924 when a man named Pierce, who was supposed to be representing an independent group, made a contract to take over the outstanding stock and agreed that he would make certain improvements. After the contract was executed it developed that the stock purchase had been made on behalf of some of the Columbia Gas and Electric Company interests and a few months later the management of the property passed under the control of H. A. Wallace who was then and is now the executive head of the United Fuel Gas Company. He is one of the best practical gas men in the United States.

At this time the United Fuel Gas Company had 12,373 customers and the Huntington Development and Gas Company 6,023 customers, making a total of 18,356 customers as contrasted with 400 customers in 1899. Huntington is almost in the center of the systems controlled by the Columbia Gas and Electric Company and the certainty of the service and supply of gas cannot be surpassed.

ELECTRIC LIGHTS

On August 4, 1886, the council agreed to adopt electric lights for street lighting with certain limitations as to cost "for additions to the plant of the company." Just what this means we cannot say, but in all events the first lights came in the middle of November, 1886. The account of this event is chronicled in the *Advertiser* of November 20, 1886:

> The last of the electric lamps was put in position and connections made on Friday of last week, and the lights were turned on Friday night. The evening was dark and wet and the pedestrians who were picking their way over crossings and relieving their overcharged feelings by choice profanity, hailed with joy the sudden flash of 15 globes of electric fire, having a light equal in power to the light of 30,000 candles.
>
> Owing to the imperfect connections and newness of machinery the lights burned fitfully and irregularly, many of them after burning a short time going out entirely. On each succeeding evening the lights have grown steadier and brighter and in a short time a degree of perfection will be attained in the operation of the machinery that will give a light eminently satisfactory to the citizens of this enlightened city.
>
> The people were almost unanimous in their commendations of the light and in their desire to have the system extended throughout the city. With electric lights, water works assured, and the finest opera house in the state, all we need to rival New York in dignity and importance is an elevated railway and boodle aldermen.

The location of this plant was on 4th Avenue between 9th and 10th Streets. The generator was operated by power furnished from the Shore Planing Mill located on an adjoining lot. This service continued until some time after January 25, 1889, on which date the city made a contract with the Huntington Electric Light and Street Railway Company to furnish city lights and in this contract it is stated that:

> The present system of lighting the streets of the said city is inefficient and unsatisfactory because the instrumentalities of the plant belonging to the city are so defective in construction and so incapable of repair that it is

PUBLIC UTILITIES

deemed desirable to procure some better and more efficient system for lighting the city; and said company of the first part having proposed to furnish a new plant at its own cost, and to provide the city with 45 first class electric arc lamps of at least 1,200 candle power each and to keep the same lighted at nights to the full satisfaction of the council.

There are two volumes of council records missing but from the foregoing quotations it is fair to assume that the city ventured into the field of municipal ownership and that the first electric lights came from this plant.

The Huntington Electric Light and Street Railway acquired the city plant. It was moved to Johnson's Lane and the railway company continued to furnish city lighting until this end of the business passed to a separate organization.

XXXIII: CHURCHES
BAPTIST

IN 1807 the Rev. John Alderson from the Greenbrier Valley organized the Mud River Baptist Church at Blue Sulphur Springs, the first Baptist church within the limits of Cabell County. At that time its membership was scattered from the falls of the Guyandotte River near Branchland to the town of Guyandotte, thence up the Ohio River as far as Greenbottom and then east as far as Poplar Fork in what is now Putnam County. (At this time [1935] there are some twenty-two Baptist churches within this same territory, not including those in the City of Huntington.) The new church was a log structure with a stone chimney and occupied the site of the present church which was built in 1841 but has been remodeled and enlarged.

The first congregation failed to secure a deed for the land on which the church was built but afterwards, in 1821, Henry and Thomas Dundas who had acquired the land, deeded one acre to the congregation described as the Mud River Baptist Society. The first preacher was the Rev. John Lee who continued until 1821.

The church records do not show who the first members were but it is assumed that they are recorded in the order of their membership. The names of Allen Rece and Mary, his wife; John Morris and Margaret, his wife; Edward Morris; John Everett and Sarah, his wife; James Cox and Elizabeth, his wife; Joel Estes and wife; Hezekiah Adkins and wife; James Serey and wife; —— Burton and wife; Benjamin Swan and wife; and Jeremiah Ward and Margaret, his wife are the earliest names on the roll. These are followed by Valentine Herndon and Elizabeth, his wife; Nathan Everett and Sarah, his wife; Abia Rece and Elizabeth, his wife; John Bryant and Nancy, his wife; William P. Yates and Elizabeth, his wife; Charles Love and Elizabeth, his wife; William Love and Susan, his wife; Daniel Love and Cynthia, his wife; and William A. Love and Eliza, his wife, were enrolled as members prior to 1830.

The first clerk is said to have been Edmund Morris, who was also county clerk.

After the Rev. John Lee, among the preachers were Thomas Harmon, Hezekiah Chilton, great uncle of ex-Senator William E. Chilton, John Calvin Rece, Thomas Hawkins, Columbus Roberts, A. M. Simms, and J. D. McClung, brother-in-law of the Rev. W. P. Walker.

CHURCHES

Among the early clerks were James Cox, William A. Love, and Daniel Love, and among the early Deacons were William Love, Allen Rece, Valentine Herndon, Daniel Love, John D. Holroyd, William P. Yates, Robert Stewart, Joseph Newman, Asa L. Wilson, James T. Herndon, Elijah Cyrus, and William H. Douglass.

Out of the membership of this church twelve have become ministers of the gospel, namely: Benjamin Swan, Thomas Swan, Elias Humphrey, James Gray, —— Burton, Hezekiah Adkins, Morris Rece, J. C. Rece, Melchor Merritt, George W. Carter, John D. Carter, and William J. Weaver.

The Baptist organization kept abreast of the developments which began following the Civil War and in 1870 had a temporary organization at Barboursville and conducted services in the courthouse. In the early 70's, at a date not fixed, H. M. Thornburg, who was afterwards a deacon in the 5th Avenue Baptist Church, established and conducted for a number of years a Sunday School at St. Cloud.

The first church in the City of Huntington was in 1872 and had the Rev. A. M. Simms, a young minister from Richmond, as the first preacher. He divided his time between Huntington and Guyandotte. Services were held in Burdick's Hall on 3d Avenue between 9th and 10th Streets. In something less than a year Mr. Simms accepted another call and this organization went to pieces.

After Mr. Simms' departure the Rev. Joel Hardwick, pastor of the Guyandotte church gave a portion of his time to the Huntington field and this continued until the end of 1874. In 1875-76 the Baptists in Huntington had neither preacher nor meeting place. On April 22, 1877, at a chance meeting on the northwest corner of 4th Avenue and 8th Street, Elisha J. Eastman, Judge J. N. Potts, H. D. Stewart, and Major W. S. Downer—then the owner of the *Huntington Independent*—discussed the organization of a Baptist church. Judge Potts informed the group that the Rev. W. P. Walker, then pastor of the Baptist church at Williamstown, might be induced to come to Huntington and take the charge. The group agreed to attempt the organization and Major Downer wired the West Virginia Baptist Association then in session at Parkersburg: "Give Walker two hundred dollars and send him to Huntington. The life of the cause seems to depend on it. Signed—W. S. Downer." A favorable reply was received to this wire and the group set about to find a meeting place but the only available room was the Lallance Hall on the third floor of a building on the northwest corner of 8th Street and 3d Avenue,

Churches of Huntington, 1900: 1—Central Christian; 2—Northern Methodist; 3—Episcopal; 4—Catholic; 5—Southern Methodist; 6—First Presbyterian, 5th Avenue; 7—Congregational; 8—Jewish Synagogue; 9—Twentieth Street Baptist; 10—Baptist, 5th Avenue and 10th Street.

the ground floor of which was occupied by Jack Cogbill's saloon. W. P. Walker, later made a D.D. and always affectionately and familiarly known as "Dr. Walker" arrived the first week of May, 1877, and on May 13th conducted his first services. The charter members of his flock on that day were exactly thirteen. In April, 1878, the church moved to the Laidley and Johnson Hall at the southeast corner of 3d Avenue and 10th Street and held services there until April, 1881, when they were unable to renew the lease and for the next year they used the Congregational Church at such times as it was not in use by others. However, the membership had grown and the church was on a sound basis and it set about getting a home of its own. On July 27, 1881, the building committee was directed to buy a lot from the land company and to proceed with the building of the church. The land company offered the lot fronting sixty feet on the north side of 5th Avenue at the northwest corner of 10th Street for the price of $3,000.00. After the church made a payment of $270.00 on this amount the land company donated the remainder. A church and parsonage were erected thereon and the church was dedicated May 7, 1882. There was some question about naming the new church the First Baptist Church but it developed that a colored Baptist group had priority on that name so the new organization was named the 5th Avenue Baptist Church. Huntington, then as now, was spread over great distances, but the means of transportation were few and in order to take care of this situation, in the next year Deacon A. M. Thornburg established a Sunday School in the west end.

At a business meeting held on April 8, 1891, a committee was appointed to provide a building on Washington Avenue at 10th Street, West, to be used as a chapel for Baptist residents in that part of the city. This building was completed in the following year and in May the Rev. W. G. Hoover, then a missionary, was called and took up this work in July. He remained a few months and then went to Logan. He was followed by the Rev. W. A. Lust, a student from the Southern Baptist Theological Seminary, who divided his time between this charge and Ceredo. He remained but a short time and was succeeded by the Rev. T. H. Fitzgerald on March 1, 1894, who served a good many years. This is now a strong and flourishing church. In 1888 the 5th Avenue Baptist Church turned its attention to the east end of the town and a committee composed of F. D. Boyer, Gordon Lunsford, J. H. Cammack, G. H. Hall, and Phillip Rogers, with Dr. Walker added, was named to investigate this situation. On

March 18, 1888, it recommended that a lot be purchased at the northwest corner of 20th Street and 5th Avenue and that a chapel be built thereon. This recommendation was approved and carried into effect and the building was completed within the year. Sunday School was organized at this point in October, 1889, with J. H. Cammack as superintendent and Gordon Lunsford as his assistant. Mr. Lunsford succeeded Mr. Cammack and continued in this office until his death in 1922. A separate church organization at 20th Street was contemplated and recognized on March 9, 1892. A. G. Lovins, a graduate of Richmond College, was the first pastor. This church has grown and now has a splendid brick building on this location.

The 20th Street Baptists inherited the evangelistic spirit of the mother church and in 1910 established a mission in Highlawn which on February 14, 1914, was organized as the Highlawn Baptist Church. In the next year a part of the 20th Street Baptist congregation which lived on the south side of the Chesapeake and Ohio Railway, organized the Temple Baptist Church which now has its own church at 9th Avenue and 21st Street and boasts of the second largest Sunday School in the city. The Rev. J. J. Cook is its pastor.

The 5th Avenue Baptist Church was remodeled in 1893. Dr. Walker, its pastor, died on May 17, 1905, respected and beloved by the entire community. The church which started under his leadership was then one of the largest in the city. After Dr. Walker's death Dr. M. L. Wood was his worthy successor and under his leadership the old church was sold for $93,800.00 and a lot at the southwest corner of 5th Avenue and 12th Street was purchased and a handsome edifice was erected thereon at a cost of $182,000.00. The new building was dedicated on March 2, 1919. Dr. Wood continued until his death on the 12th of June, 1932, and was succeeded by Dr. Norman W. Cox. From a small and humble beginning the church has grown to a membership of 1,766 with a Sunday School enrollment of 1,500.

Included in this congregation were men, and are still men, who have made history in Huntington. No mention of this church can be made without bringing to mind such stalwarts as John Henry Cammack, Judge J. N. Potts, A. F. Southworth, J. L. Hawkins, F. D. Boyer, T. J. Bullock, Robert Odell, D. B. Smith, C. C. Dusenberry, R. L. Hutchinson, and Judge Thomas R. Shepherd, and in later years E. L. Hogsett, S. E. Langfitt, Dennis McNeil, W. L. Rece, and George I. Neal.

DR. WILLIAM PARKINSON WALKER

Born on Little Mill Creek, Jackson County, Virginia, on May 14, 1834, when the country was wild and settlers scarce, roads few and communications slow, this small farmer's son knew much of hardship during his boyhood. The schools were few and difficult to reach, consequently he grew up with a meagre education. Equipped with a rugged and physically strong body, and an equally strong mentality he went out into the world at a very tender age to make his own way. Accepting the first work which offered he took berth in a towboat on the Ohio River.

In 1855 he married Mary Jane McClung, young, attractive, and a sincere christian and her great endeavor was to have him become a christian. In October, 1857, she saw this hope realized. It seemed from this time he felt the call to the ministry. They both soon realized he must have more education, so in 1858 off they started across the mountains for Allegheny College in Greenbrier County. The next year the Civil War broke out, the college was abandoned and during those four war years the young preacher served churches in and around Fayette County. In June, 1866, he accepted a call to Williamstown in Wood County, where he remained until he left for Huntington in 1877.

The first sermon preached in Huntington was from the text "In The Name of Our God Will We Set Up Our Banner," and never for a moment did he let that banner trail. The early years were filled with struggle, hardships and many discouragements, but the indomitable will, intrepid spirit and fine consecration of this man of God overcame all obstacles and rode on to victory.

Beginning his ministry as he did with thirteen members he saw additions to the church at practically every meeting, and in 1881 the little group bravely and proudly erected their first church at a cost of $5,000.00. Later, in 1894, a new church was erected over the old one, on the site now occupied by the Huntington Publishing Company. The new church cost $20,000.00 and was a very handsome building, being occupied until the congregation moved to the present site at 5th Avenue and 12th Street.

In May, 1905, the summons came to him to cease his labors here and join the heavenly host who sing praises about the throne of Jehovah forever. An editorial of the *Advertiser* of that date says: "Peace be to this servant who living worked for the Master and who dying left a legacy of faith to many thousands of his followers. Peace to this man beloved of men for his own sake. Remember how good and upright he was, how gentle and patient and unselfish; how he suffered without murmur and died without reproach." And in the *Herald* of the same date we find: "The current of his life was too deep for disturbance, whether under calm, storm, sunshine, stress or strain he found safe refuge in a broad conservative judgment that never failed him. The ripened fruits of his life will abide forever."

The funeral services were set for 2:30 o'clock but more than an hour before that time the church was filled to capacity, while the sidewalks and streets were filled with a sorrowing throng. All places of business including the saloons were closed during the service as a mark of respect and of appreciation of the good this man had done the community, and this in spite of the fact that he was an uncompromising enemy of the liquor traffic.

When this strong foundation had been laid by one with so powerful and sure a hand, and the superstructure begun with so noble and chaste a design, what hand had God prepared to "carry on" in a way acceptable to Him and the people the task from which he had taken the Head Builder?

In less than six months God had lead to a man after His own heart who carried the work forward for another twenty-seven years. Dr. M. L. Wood, then pastor of the Baptist Church at Staunton, Virginia, was unanimously called and accepted the pastorate of the 5th Avenue Church, beginning his ministry October 15, 1905.

When Dr. Wood assumed the pastorate there was a membership of about 580. At his passing June 12, 1932, the membership approximated 2,000. The following appreciation was written by one of the members of his church upon request of the Baptist State Convention of West Virginia, and was published in the Convention Annual Report for 1932.

DR. MATTHEW L. WOOD

On Sunday, October 19, 1930, the congregation of the 5th Avenue Baptist Church celebrated the twenty-fifth anniversary of the pastorate of Dr. Matthew L. Wood. Responding then to the loving tributes which had been accorded him, Dr. Wood concluded his remarks in these words:

"As we lean for a moment against this mile-stone by the way, we look with eager eye toward, but not into the future. We know not what tomorrow holds for any of us. But the same wise and loving Father who has graciously led us all this way that we have come, who was with us at the beginning of this pastorate, is with us still to direct and determine our course.

> "And so beside the silent sea
> I wait the muffled oar,
> No harm from Him can come to me
> On ocean or on shore.
> I know not where His islands lift
> Their fronded palms in air,
> I only know I cannot drift
> Beyond his love and care."

On the night of June 12, 1932, the final call came for Dr. Wood and he slipped out of life serenely to enter upon the reward that awaits the good—the righteous—the just.

When the news of his death came to his congregation worshipping as usual on Sunday evening, the throng burst into tears. And next morning when the tidings burst upon the city thousands more wept. His congregation loved him. The city loved him. In the hour of death his saintliness seemed more important than his career. But it was a notable career, one of service and achievement, stamped by courage as well as forbearance; by unyielding adherence to the right as he saw it as well as by a wise and gentle tolerance. What shall we say of him, now that he rests from his labors, save, "Servant of God, well done"?

"Earth holds up to her master no fruit like the finished man." In conversation with one of another denomination some years ago, the writer was struck by the emphasis with which she said, "Dr. Wood is a gentleman."

Many times since there has been added in my mind, "Not only a gentleman but a man." "A man is one whose body has been trained to be the ready servant of his mind, whose passions are trained to be the servants of his will; who enjoys the beautiful, loves truth, hates wrong, loves to do good, and respects others as himself."

As he stood before us nearly twenty-seven years ago we who were used to the rugged features and emphatic utterance of his predecessor wondered a little about this mild mannered, gentle man. And again when he came into our homes with a modesty which amounted to diffidence and which rendered conversation difficult we wondered if we would ever be at ease with him.

We had only to wait a while until the strangeness wore off to see the true nobility and kindness of his soul. The untold numbers to whom he has ministered in time of sorrow and bereavement, those with whom he has rejoiced in time of happiness, the great host whom he has joined in holy wedlock, the hundreds he has led into the Kingdom of God, all form a mighty host on whom his blessed ministry has been expended and who will ever hold him in loving memory and rise up to call him blessed.

It was, however, as an adviser and friend to those in perplexity and uncertainty that perhaps his greatest ministry was given. All those in trouble felt free to come to him for help and advice and all went away helped and comforted, "For the wisdom that is from above is first pure, then peaceable, gentle, and easy to be intreated, full of mercy and good fruits, without partiality, and without hypocrisy."

In emphasizing his kindness, gentleness and love of peace, let no one think he was not all the leader. Once convinced of the course to pursue no human interference could divert him. One of his latest utterances in the pulpit was, "There come times in the life of a man when he cannot afford to confer with human agencies—it is a matter between him and his God." This sums up in a few words the great underlying principle of his life—God first.

The personal ministrations mentioned and the spiritual messages given from the pulpit will ever keep his memory green locally, the wisdom which characterized his habit of mind and speech will be written into the Baptist history of the State, but his most far reaching ministry was in the fidelity with which he kept his church tied up to the Denominational program, and his own participation in the affairs of the Northern Baptist Convention so reaching out to the uttermost parts of the world. In all of these places he will be sorely missed and our hearts are sad and lonely as we thank God for the life and ministry of Matthew Lawrence Wood. Truly, "a great Prince in Israel is fallen this day."

Mrs. R. L. Hutchinson.

CATHOLIC

Thomas Carroll who was born in Ireland came from Baltimore to Guyandotte, November 2, 1852, and was the only known Catholic in this county. It was through his efforts that a number of priests visited the parish and mass was said in the northwest room of his home. Mr. Carroll had nine children and all of them were baptized in the church. Among the early Catholics to participate in these services were Michael Hines and family, who came from White Sulphur Springs, John B. Scheneberg and wife, and Victor LaTulle, a naturalized Frenchman. Among the visiting priests came Bishop Gilmore, then a priest in Columbus, Ohio, Bishop Wheelan, and Fathers McKernan, R. P. O'Neal, Philip McDonoghan, J. W. Stenger, and David Walsh.

On September 12, 1872, Father Thomas A. Quirk came to Guyandotte and organized a parish. He lived with the Carrolls for exactly twelve years to the day. L. T. Moore donated an acre of land near the Chesapeake and Ohio depot to the Catholic Church by deed dated October 4, 1872, which contained the provision that a church or school edifice for the use of the Roman Catholics should be erected thereon within the year. This provision was met and a brick church was completed in 1872 which was called St. Peter's. Among the members of this church were Andrew Kennedy and family, Timothy Mulcahy and family, Captain Joseph Anderson, Thomas Layne, Hugh Mullen, and Chris Witzgall.

In the same year Father Quirk built a frame building on 8th Avenue and 20th Street and used it for a school and church. In 1884 he laid the foundation for the present St. Joseph's Church.

Father Quirk was succeeded by Father John W. Werninger on September 12, 1884, who remained at the Carroll home two weeks and then found a residence in the larger and growing city of Huntington.

Under Father Werninger's charge St. Joseph's Church was completed and its early congregation consisted of about thirty families. He prepared a schoolroom in the rear of the building which was separated from the church auditorium and conducted a school therein, assisted by his sister, Gertrude Werninger. In 1899 Father Werninger was transferred to Benwood, and was succeeded by Father Henry B. Altmeyer, afterwards Monsignor, who served continuously until his death on August 22, 1930.

Father Altmeyer remodelled and enlarged the present St. Joseph's Church, a building of brick, stone and stucco, several times, bringing it to its existing seating capacity of 600. Just north of the church on 13th Street, Father Altmeyer built a school for the grades, containing eight class-rooms. The building is of brick, its housing capacity being 300 pupils. In 1927 Father Altmeyer purchased a house and commercial garage on the corner lot, 6th Avenue and 13th Street, remodeled the house to be used as a three-room high school, the garage as gymnasium and cafeteria. The faculty of the grade school is composed of Sisters of St. Joseph; that of the high school, of these Sisters, helped by lay teachers and priests.

On Monsignor Altmeyer's death in August, 1930, Monsignor James F. Newcomb, superintendent of Diocesan schools of West Virginia, and director of church music in the Diocese of Wheeling, was appointed parish priest of St. Joseph's. Monsignor Newcomb at once arranged for the demolition of the remodelled house and garage used as high school and the building of the present brick and stone St. Joseph's High School.

The Catholic Church in Huntington, until 1925, grew consistently but very slowly. In the last ten years, it has evidenced new life. In ten years, the Catholic population has more than doubled. In 1925 there were less than 300 children in the parish schools, and only a few Catholic children in the public schools. Today's enrollment at St. Joseph's graded and high schools is 515. Another 200 Catholic children attend the various public schools of their own neighborhoods. At the request of Monsignor Newcomb, a new parish was erected in Huntington, December 23, 1934, under the title of the "Sacred Heart of Jesus," with Reverend Wilbert M. Burke, formerly of Bluefield, as pastor.

The Sacred Heart Parish takes care of the 150 Catholic families in the western end of the city. The parish priest is also chaplain of the Veterans' Hospital in Spring Valley. The mother parish, St. Joseph's, retains 800 families (about 2,500 people, the largest parish in West Virginia) and shows such marked signs of increase in number of families that a further division in the near future is foreshadowed.

Before 1936, work among the colored will have been started by the Catholic Church in Huntington. The Most Reverend John J. Swint, Bishop of Wheeling, has entrusted this work to the Fathers of the Precious Blood, who will send a missioner or two for this work beginning in November, 1935.

Among the early members of St. Joseph's congregation were Tim Dwyer, father of our late sheriff, T. P. Dwyer, Andrew Eisenmann, father of Dr. Andrew Eisenmann, J. W. Verlander, Thomas Downey, T. S. Scanlon, Daniel Ahern, James Brady, and W. M. Seiber, all of whom have left many descendants in the community.

Outside the congregations, namely, the original, St. Joseph's, the new one for the west end, Sacred Heart, and the prospective church for the colored, there have been two other major Catholic works in action in Huntington, the defunct St. Edward's College, and the prospering St. Mary's Hospital. On March 1, 1905, Bishop Donahue of Wheeling acquired a tract of three acres on which he erected St. Edward's College-Preparatory, putting in charge a faculty of priests and laymen, under the presidency of Rev. John Werninger, who came from the immediate pastorate of Benwood. After ten years, Father Werninger was succeeded in the presidency of this preparatory school, whose average yearly enrollment was in excess of 100, by Father Scheuermann, now pastor of St. Margaret Mary's, Parkersburg, and later by Rev. William Lee, now pastor of Corpus Christi, Warwood. The year before the college was closed Xaverian Brothers took charge.

The Pallottine Sisters bought college grounds and buildings from Bishop Swint, after the college's closing, remodelled the old building for hospital accommodation and for convent use, and built a splendid new unit. Recently the Sisters have purchased the three-acre tract opposite the hospital, the Harrison estate, on which they intend to erect a nurses' home and new hospital units, reserving the part of the tract bordering Collis Avenue for parish church, house and school for the east end of town. Recently St. Mary's Convent, on the hospital grounds, has been made the Motherhouse for the American Province of Pallottines. About fifty Sisters are in residence. The hospital, St. Mary's, has the approval of the American Medical Association.

CONGREGATIONAL

Among the associates of C. P. Huntington in the Chesapeake and Ohio Railway enterprise was A. S. Hatch of the firm of Fisk and Hatch of New York City. Mr. Hatch was a New Englander, a Congregationalist, and interested in his church. Among the people who had moved to the new City of Huntington were a number of splendid folk from New England who were of this persuasion. In 1872 the Rev. Joseph E. Roy, who was a missionary of the Congregational Church with headquarters in Chicago and covered the states of Illinois, Ohio, Indiana, Eastern Kentucky, and West Virginia, was in New York in an attempt to interest people in this work. W. A. Hatch, his wife, and his sister, Miss Storrs, prevailed upon Rev. Roy to make an investigation of the situation in Huntington and report to them what the outlook was for the establishment of a Congregational Church in this city. Mr. Roy made this investigation and reported the field as a very favorable one. Mr. Hatch immediately proposed that he would contribute $4,000.00 towards the erection of a Congregational Church in the new city if the local people would raise an equal amount. His offer was subsequently modified in that Mr. Hatch and his associates Harvey Fisk, A. A. Lowe, C. P. Huntington, William H. Aspinwall, William Withington and Jas. H. Storrs and some others agreed to donate $6,000.00 to build a $10,000.00 church. As soon as this offer was made E. E. Randall, who had a furniture store on the north side of 3rd Avenue just west of 9th Street, called a meeting to be held in his home over the storeroom June 1, 1872. At this meeting the Rev. Jos. E. Roy was present and was elected as chairman, and Merton H. Brook, the druggist and first postmaster, who had come from Swanton, Vermont, was secretary. There were exactly thirteen persons present who became charter members as follows:

E. E. Randall, Sarah E. Randall, Aaron Walker, H. S. Clark, Rhoda M. Clark, Rev. Jos. E. Roy, Lydia M. Proctor, Merton H. Brooks, C. F. Parsons, H. Chester Parsons, Nellie C. Parsons, T. B. Campbell, and Elizabeth J. Campbell.

A board of trustees was elected, made up of E. B. Randall, T. B. Campbell, and H. Chester Parsons, who was also made treasurer of the organization. The trustees were instructed to secure at once a site and to proceed with the construction of a church and it was ordered that a council meeting be held two weeks later in the Burdick Hall. Letters were sent calling a council composed of pastors and delegates from the Congregational Churches and in response to these invitations the council assembled in Burdick's Hall on Saturday night, June 15, 1872. There were present representatives from a number of out of town churches. The council approved the plans and on the next day a service of recognition was held in the same hall. Randall was made deacon of the newly organized church and a call was extended to Charles Swan Walker, former pastor of a Cincinnati church, to come to Huntington and take over the work. Mr. Walker accepted the call and came to Huntington in July, 1872, and preached every other Sunday morning in Burdick's Hall. The other Sunday mornings were taken up by the Baptists who used the same hall.

In 1873 came the panic and it was becoming difficult to raise the money to pay for the church. Mr. Walker was sent on a trip to the east to attempt to raise $3,000.00. While on this trip he accepted another call and did not return. He was succeeded in July, 1873, by Albert S. Bowers. On April 6, 1873, this church was admitted to the Miami Congregational Conference. Mr. Bowers was employed as a supply pastor for the first twelve months and then became the regular pastor in August, 1874. During this period the congregation worshipped at Burdick's Hall, then in a vacant storeroom on the north side of 3rd Avenue between 10th and 11th Streets, and in Ingham's Hall on the second floor of the building on the north side of 3rd Avenue between 8th and 9th Streets.

The Central Land Company proposed to the trustees that if they would erect a church to cost not less than $11,000.00 it would donate a lot. This offer was accepted and the land company gave the new organization the sixty foot lot at the southeast corner of 9th Street and 5th Avenue and the new church was erected thereon and was dedicated November 8, 1874, with an impressive ceremony, attended by all of the local and many out of town ministers.

Up to this time the Sunday School had been conducted under the direction of Captain H. C. Parsons as superintendent and was a union Sunday School. When the new church was completed it was determined to have a Congregational Sunday School and Captain Parsons declined to serve in anything except a union Sunday School. He was succeeded by O. W. Hale. During that time the church had a number of pastors, the best remembered one being John McCarty who came in 1897 and continued until 1910. The church continued at this location until about 1910 when the Rev. John Lewis Hoyt arrived to take charge and found that the property had been sold for $55,000.00 and a new lot purchased at the southwest corner of 7th Street and 5th Avenue for $9,000.00 on which was being erected a beautiful edifice of colonial architecture 50x150 feet, built of brick laid in flemish bond, finished in old English oak, with all modern conveniences. The new church was dedicated with appropriate ceremonies and Rev. Hoyt continued as pastor until October 1, 1920, when he accepted the position as executive secretary of the Stark County Sunday School Association at Canton, Ohio, and was followed by Fred W. Hagen who served until June, 1926, being followed by F. H. Jacobs until November, 1926, when J. A. Symington came and continued until May, 1934. He was succeeded by Jesse Pindell Peirce, the present pastor, who came on November 15, 1934.

CHURCHES
METHODISTS

In a book entitled *Methodism in Ohio and West Virginia* and quoted by Virgil A. Lewis in his *History of West Virginia* it is said an old man by the name of Miller, who lived at Greenbottom and who came from Washington County, Pennsylvania, was the first member of that church who interested himself in the establishment of a Methodist Church within the present limits of this county. By reason of a petition signed by Miller and a number of other persons, the Baltimore Conference in 1803 sent William Steele, a traveling preacher under its jurisdiction to explore this country. The result of his exploration and efforts was the establishment in that year, or a short time afterwards, of a Methodist Church in the town of "Guiandot."

In 1804 the Western Conference created a circuit which included Guyandotte and embraced the settlements along the Ohio River up the Guyandotte Valley and the Great Kanawha Valley. A pastor was appointed to this vast circuit and the romance of these early circuit riders fills volumes. The first of these pastors who had charge of the church in Guyandotte was Asa Shinn who is referred to as the founder of the Methodist Protestant Church, and he was followed each year by a new preacher.

The church in Guyandotte was located on Lot 16 which at this time fronts on 5th Avenue just east of Guyan Street. This lot was given to the church by Thomas Buffington "for the use and purposes of a Methodist Church, school yard and graveyard" and was continued there until the division of the church in 1844. After that time the building was used for a number of years for school purposes.

In 1811 a revival was held in the Ona neighborhood under the leadership of the Rev. Samuel West, and as a result of this revival a Methodist Church was established on Mud River. Two years later a camp meeting was held in the same neighborhood under the leadership of the Rev. David Young, presiding elder in this district. Then came the Rev. Samuel Brown, followed by the Rev. John Cord who became minister in this circuit and who appointed Thomas A. Morris as class leader. In the same year Thomas A. Morris married Abigail Scales, daughter of Nathaniel Scales an early resident of what is now the city of Huntington, and established a home which he called "Spice Flat Cottage" near Howell's Mill. Thomas A. Morris became a minister and was made a bishop in 1836. He was one of the most distinguished citizens in this county. In 1814 the Rev. Henry B. Bascum succeeded the Rev. Mr. Cord in this circuit. He frequently held services and classes of instruction in the Spice Flat Cottage and later was made a bishop of the Methodist Church.

In 1814 the first Methodist Church in that community was organized and it was thought to have been organized at Spice Flat Cottage.

After the Rev. Mr. Bascum came John Dew and he named Thomas Morris as assistant circuit rider in this field.

For many years it was the practice of the Methodists to hold revival services at the homes of members where it was convenient for neighborhood gatherings.

In 1844 this county was included in the Guyandotte District of the Kentucky Conference and after the division of the church the Southern Church included this county in the Western Virginia Conference. The result of this division was the abandonment of the chapel on the lot which had been donated by Thomas Buffington and the construction by each branch of the Methodists of their own church in the village.

One branch retained the name of the Methodist Episcopal Church, and the other adopted the name of the Methodist Episcopal Church, South.

We will tell of these in their order:

METHODIST EPISCOPAL CHURCH

After the division, the Southern Methodists were in the majority in this section, but the Methodist Episcopal Church held together and had for that year and the next William F. Hard as pastor. He was followed by David Smith, 1845-46. A small church was erected on Main Street near where the George Burk house stands.

In 1852 James Follansby whose wife was an aunt of Mrs. James Murphy was the minister.

In 1858 the present building on Bridge Street was erected. The stalwarts of that time were Dudley D. Smith, father of D. I. Smith, his two brothers, Ed and Percival S., Noah Wellington and his family, the Clarks, Freutels and the Hites. Many of their descendants are still members of this church.

In 1915 the church was remodeled and W. F. Hite made a substantial contribution. This church is still a growing organization which includes in its membership many splendid men and women of that old community.

METHODIST EPISCOPAL CHURCH, HUNTINGTON

The Methodist Episcopal Church in Huntington found its beginning participating in the union Sunday School that had been established by E. E. Randall of the Congregationalist Church. Mrs. J. L. Crider relates how on a cold, snowy Sunday in February, 1872, she accompanied her father, Dr. O. G. Chase, to the union Sunday School which met in the carpenter shop of A. B. Palmer. The shop had been cleaned for the purpose and various things were used for seats. There were two Bible classes with thirty-five members with Dr. Chase and Dr. Campbell teachers; a testament class with fifteen members, and an infant's class with four members. This organization continued as a union Sunday School until the Burdick Building was completed when the Methodist Episcopal Sunday School was organized and moved to this building. The first sermon was preached by Robert D. Callahan, of Kentucky. The Rev. J. A. Kibbie, stationed at Guyandotte, preached an occasional sermon until the spring of 1873 when he became the regular and the first minister.

The congregation purchased the lot at the southwest corner of 4th Avenue and 10th Street and erected a small chapel which was dedicated on January 24, 1875, by the Rev. W. M. Mullinix of Charleston. The Rev. Wesley Prettyman was the pastor. The first marriage celebrated in the chapel was in October, 1875, when Mr. and Mrs. J. L. Crider were married.

In the fall of 1880 the first conference was held in this city with Bishop Peck presiding.

In 1888 the Rev. W. W. King came as pastor for this church. He was young and full of enthusiasm and soon had his congregation aroused to the need of a larger edifice. To that end a building committee composed of A. B. Palmer, H. C. Bossinger, J. L. Crider, H. C. Gordon, M. N. Hambilton, and T. C. Palmer was appointed, and on April 19, 1891, a splendid new building was dedicated. It was the largest church in the city.

The building was dedicated by Bishop Joyce, assisted by Dr. (afterwards Bishop) Moore. The first sermon was preached in it by the Rev. W. W. King who referred to the fact that there were in attendance a number of women whose presence was an inspiration and named as "The Mothers of the Church," Mesdames Crider, Louderback, Fox, Sampson, and Hawkins.

In October, 1891, the Seventh Avenue Methodist Episcopal Church was dedicated and the one at the cross-roads was dedicated in the next year.

The Methodist Episcopal Chapel at the southwest corner of 10th Street and 4th Avenue, 1882

In 1912 the church sold its property to the First National Bank for $55,000.00 and bought the lot 130x200 feet on 5th Avenue between 11th and 12th Strets. The pastor Dr. A. J. Hiatt named W. H. Newcomb, C. H. Terrell, D. E. Hewitt, H. C. Bossinger, and G. R. Heffley a building committee under whose direction a new church with a stone front, costing $100,000.00 was started in the fall of this year. It was completed in June, 1914, and dedicated by Bishop Earl Cranston. At this time there was an indebtedness of about $50,000.00 on the church but by Easter Sunday, 1930, this debt had been paid in full, and on this occasion there was a jubilee service at which the mortgage was burned.

METHODIST EPISCOPAL CHURCH, SOUTH

In 1848 this church purchased a lot from Robert and Susan Holderby on Main Street, the site of the present location, and erected a brick church thereon. The trustees of this congregation were John Laidley, William Buffington, J. W. Hite, John Everett, the Revolutionary soldier, Burgess Stewart, Jacob Miller, and William Paine. Prior to the Civil War this was the only church of this denomination in this section. Among its members were "Father" Ong, S. W. Scott, Dr. A. B. McGinnis, Mrs. Eliza McGinnis, Mrs. J. W. Hite, William Hite, St. Mark Russell, Burgess Stewart, and John W. McGinnis. St. Mark Russell was easily the most colorful figure in the congregation. He was a preacher, a justice of the peace, mayor of the town, and a church worker whose energy, zeal and enthusiasm knew no bounds. He lived to the ripe old age of eighty-eight years, but a few years before his death he became blind.

During the Civil War the church was used by Federal soldiers for storing hay. The church had a gallery across the front which was reserved for the use of colored folks. One day Noah Wellington's cow got into the gallery and was eating hay. A soldier attempted to drive the cow off and she jumped over the railing into the auditorium below.

At the end of the war the church was practically destroyed and unfit for use and the local congregation built a platform on the foundation. Services were held thereon when the weather permitted and at other times the congregation met in private homes. This continued until 1869 when J. F. Medley, presiding elder, who was a good carpenter and builder took charge of this district, and with the assistance of volunteer labor actually erected a new church which was completed in 1870. This building has been remodeled and improved and has in addition a modern Sunday School building. The Western Virginia Conference was held in this church, in 1856 Bishop John Early, in 1875 William M. Wightman, and in 1890 Bishop W. W. Duncan presiding. It has grown from a membership of 150 twenty years ago to over 400 at the present time.

In 1905 the United States Government provided a payment of $2,000.00 to compensate the church for the damage done to its building by the soldiers.

HUNTINGTON CHURCHES

After the outbreak of the Civil War the Southern Methodists who lived west of the Guyandotte River established a branch of the Guyandotte Church in the chapel at Marshall College and some time afterwards the Southern Presbyterians did the same. These two congregations used the chapel on alternate Sundays. In 1867 Marshall College became a state institution and its chapel was no longer available for these two congregations. They jointly built a chapel in Holderby Grove at about the corner of 7th Avenue and 16th Street. This chapel was under the jurisdiction of the Guyandotte Church and the preacher in the Guyandotte church supplied this chapel. The Methodists continued there until about 1878, in which year L. B. Madison was in charge of the Guyandotte Church. He foresaw the possibilities in the growing city and the needs of establishing a new church therein and in the fall of that year he called on H. C. Harvey and suggested to him that he and his wife transfer from the Guyandotte Church to the church in Holderby Grove, and gave as a reason for the change that their services were needed in the latter church. On a Sunday in October following, with the permission of the Rev. Mr. Madison, the congregation resolved itself into a conference and at this conference P. H. McCullough, L. H. Burks, and H. C. Harvey made the proposal that the church move into the new city. The proposal met with some opposition but after considerable discussion and agreement on the part of the proponents to pay the rent for the first year and to pay the cost of chairs and other equipment it was agreed to, and they did move, to Crider's Hall which was over a store building at 1005 3d Avenue on a site now occupied and included in the Bradshaw-Diehl-Romer Company Building, next to the Laidley and Johnson Hall.

Rev. Mr. Madison was succeeded by J. T. Follansbee who served as supply pastor for several months and in 1878 the Huntington congregation was organized as a separate church.

In 1881 the congregation acquired a lot 60 feet fronting on 4th Avenue between 10th and 11th Streets at the price of $1,500.00 and on this lot they erected a church thirty-five feet wide and sixty feet deep with a parsonage in the rear at a cost of $5,500.00. This church was dedicated in the fall of 1881 and was the most pretentious home the Southern Methodists had had in Huntington since the beginning. The church prospered in its new location and in 1887 J. L. Thornburg, who had been in charge of the Sunday School of the Holderby Grove church, and who was an energetic worker in the church, established a mission and Sunday School in the east end. This was located in a store room on 20th Street and was attended by citizens of many denominations. The movement finally resulted in an East End Church which was built on the southwest corner of 6th Avenue and 20th Street. Later this property was sold and the church we now know as the Emanuel M. E. Church, South, on the corner of 6th Avenue and 17th Street was built.

In 1889 the downtown church had for its pastor the Rev. J. W. Johnson who thought that the congregation had outgrown their accommodations and should have a new home. To that end L. H. Burks was named to close a deal for a site on the southwest corner of 10th Street and 5th Avenue which was acquired at the price of $3,500.00. Before the new church was built Rev. Mr. Johnson died and the Rev. W. W. Royal came to Huntington and named a committee composed of George F. Miller, L. H. Burks, T. S. Garland, and H. C. Harvey to continue the work. The new building was completed in 1892 and was named the Johnson Memorial Church in honor of the Rev. Mr. Johnson whose death was due to an accident which he sustained in an initiation ceremony in a fraternal society. The new church cost $25,000.00. In 1909 the Rev. U. V. W. Darlington, who has since become a bishop, was assigned to Huntington and a year later began a movement to build a new church on this site. A building committee was named consisting of G. D. Miller, H. B. Hagen, C. W. Thompson, I. H. Harshbarger, V. B. Davis, Lee A. D. Tate, S. M. Croft, J. A. Chambers, and W. W. Whieldon. A new church was built at a cost of approximately $100,000.00 and was formally dedicated on June 22, 1913, by Bishop Eugene Russell Hendricks of Kansas City, Missouri. From this time the Johnson Memorial Church has enjoyed a continued and consistent growth.

Among its preachers have been T. S. Hamilton, J. W. Pierson and many others, all of whom have been outstanding men in the community.

The membership has included men and women of the highest type. Among the earliest of these were Mrs. Lou Garland Buffington, Mrs. Virginia Ricketts, and the Thornburgs. Among the men are those we have already named together with C. W. Thornburg, Lee A. D. Tate, and Jeff Newberry.

The membership at this time (1935) is 1,907 with a Sunday School enrollment of 1,051. For many years it was said that its Bible class was the largest organization of its kind in the world.

OHEV SHOLOM

Sam Gideon and his family were the first members of this congregation to reach Huntington. The Gideons lived for many years in a house that stood about the center of the site of the Frederick Hotel and fronted on 4th Avenue. Several years elapsed before there were enough people of this faith to organize a congregation, but in August, 1887, there were a sufficient number and an organization was accomplished. Sam Gideon was elected president, Joe Levy, vice president, Ed Meyerson, secretary, and Leon Sternberger, treasurer. The first services were held on the third floor of the store building on 3rd Avenue just east of the First National Bank Building owned by William Biggs. Included in the membership at that time were L. Leftwitch, Lee Kahn, Lester Kelner, Jacob Ziegler, E. Biern, Jake Friedman, Benjamin Wolf, Mose Borheim, Mike and Julius Broh. The first Rabbi was the Rabbi Strauss. Sam Gideon was a real leader and it was not long before the young congregation had visions of a permanent home. A lot was purchased in 1891 at the corner of 5th Avenue and 10th Street and in the next year a new synagogue was completed thereon.

In this group were many persons whose civic activities are mentioned elsewhere but there is one whom the congregation itself delights to remember as the mother of the Jewish people but a better appraisal would be one of the mothers of Israel, for her charity knew no bounds of creed or race. We write now of Bettie Wolf, born Bettie Newman and the wife of Benjamin Wolf. All those in distress were her children. At that period there were no hospitals or professional nurses and sick people depended upon the help of friends. "Mother" Wolf could be counted on as the first to help. Her work in this field was greater than her strength and hastened her end. She died in August, 1895, beloved, respected, and mourned by the whole community. On the day of her funeral all stores were closed and business suspended in the city. This is the only time this honor has been paid to a woman.

But to return to the congregation. It grew with the city and included in its membership were many outstanding men of the city. In 1919 the congregation purchased the lot at the southwest corner of 10th Avenue and 10th Street and not long afterwards began the erection of the synagogue. The structure was completed in 1926 and dedicated with an impressive ceremony on the evening of June 11, 1926. Rabbi David Phillipson of Cincinnati preached the dedicatory sermon and Rabbi Abba Hillil Silver of Cleveland delivered an address. The auditorium was filled to capacity. The service began with a recital on the new pipe organ, then came a procession headed by Julius Friedman and Samuel Oppenheim, the two oldest members who bore the scrolls of the Torah. Following these came the officers of the congregation and visiting Rabbis. Rabbi Abraham Feinstein of the local congregation received the scrolls from the bearers and repeated the ritual and placed the scrolls in the Ark. Then followed the lighting of the perpetual light as a memorial to Mr. and Mrs. Sam Gideon which was done by Dave Gideon, their eldest son. The keys of the synagogue were presented by Sam Biern, chairman of the building committee, to Dez. C. Schonthal, president of the congregation, who in accepting them paid a tribute to Sam Gideon and E. Biern. In these services too, Bettie Wolf was not forgotten. The climax came when the venerable Joseph Schonthal of Columbus, Ohio, blessed his son in the final address of the dedication —"May the Lord bless thee; may the Lord let his countenance to shine upon thee and be gracious to thee, and may the Lord lift up His countenance upon thee and give thee peace."

PRESBYTERIANS

There was a church at Burlington on the Ohio side at a very early date and the earlier settlers in this county of the Presbyterian faith belonged to this church.

In 1838 before the new building at Marshall Academy was completed the local Presbyterians held a service therein. This service was the beginning of a series of meetings conducted by the Rev. J. N. Brown of Charleston, and on July 28, 1838, the first Presbyterian church in Cabell County was organized in the chapel of the academy. It was named the Western Church of the Greenbrier Presbytery. The charter members were Dr. Benjamin Brown who built the first brick residence in the county at what was known as Brownsville and now on 2nd Avenue between 4th and 5th Streets; Matilda, his wife; Mrs. Elizabeth Gardner; James Johnston and Martha, his wife; Mrs. Jane Merritt; John McCormick; Joseph Naglee and Hannah, his wife; James Poage and Jemima, his wife; William Poage and Ann, his wife; Miss Elizabeth Staley; Mrs. Mary Thom; Mrs. Catherine Wright; Mary Handley, and Robert Handley. Of these eighteen charter members, fifteen brought letters from the Burlington Church. The records disclose that Susie, a colored slave girl who belonged to the Rev. A. E. Thom became a member of this church in 1841. The first board of Elders were William and James Poage, Joseph Naglee, and James Johnston. They extended a call to the Rev. Alfred E. Thom a recent graduate from the Theological School and Seminary who was the pastor of the Presbyterian Church in Burlington. Under the arrangement Mr. Thom was to give one-half of his time to the new church and the other half to the Ohio congregation and his salary was fixed at $500.00 a year to be divided between them. It is said that Mr. Thom maintained his residence in West Virginia for the reason that he owned the colored slave girl, Susie, and slavery was prohibited in the Northwest Territory of which Ohio was a part. Thom continued until 1842 when he resigned and was succeeded by the Rev. Josiah B. Poage of Pocahontas County, who was a teacher at Marshall College, and who was employed on half time but with an increase of salary to $400.00. J. B. Poage left in 1849 and the church was without a pastor until 1857. Then came the Rev. Dr. John C. Bayless who agreed to give one-fourth of his time to the work at a stipend of $200.00 per year, the remainder of his time to be spent in Kentucky. A year later Bayless found his health impaired on account of overwork and he was succeeded by the Rev. A. J. McMillen of the Burlington church who gave one-half of his time to the work. McMillen remained until 1861 when services were abandoned on account of the war. Dr. Bayless returned in March, 1862, and served on a half time basis until the coming of the Rev. John D. McClintock in 1863, who gave half of his time to the work at Catlettsburg and the other half to Cabell County. This arrangement continued until 1873. In 1867 Marshall Academy was taken over by the State and as the Presbyterians could no longer use this chapel for services, they were held at irregular intervals in the homes of various persons. In 1870 the Presbyterians and the Southern Methodists entered into an arrangement under the terms of which they secured a half acre of ground in the old Holderby Grove for the price of $50.00 and these two congregations erected thereon a frame chapel which was used jointly by them. For a time in 1870 when James E. Morrow was the head of Marshall College the Presbyterians were invited to and did hold their services in the chapel in that institution. In 1872 the church appointed a committee to secure a lot in the downtown portion of the new city and this committee reported that the land company would sell a lot for church purposes at a price named and would donate ninety per cent of the purchase price. The contract was made; the Presbyterians secured the plot of ground on the south side of 5th Avenue between 10th and 11th Streets on which they erected a chapel which was ready for use in 1872. This chapel was built on the rear of the lot and the name of the church was changed from the Western Church to the Huntington Presbyterian Church. Two years later in 1873 the name was changed to the First Presbyterian Church of Huntington.

Rev. McClintock continued in charge of the work on a half time basis until 1873 when he was installed as pastor on a full time basis. He continued as such until 1876 when he resigned. The same Dr. J. N. Brown who had helped establish the church in 1838 followed Mr. McClintock for a few months. He was followed by Dr. J. C. Barr, and then came the Rev. Goodrich A. Wilson who served for two years and was followed by J. M. Shearer who served three years. Then came Rev. J. C. Brown who gave one-fourth of his time during 1883 and was followed by C. A. Monroe who served until May 1, 1885. Then came the Rev. J. M. Sloan who served for eight years. During this time the church had grown and its buildings had to be enlarged. Mr. Sloan was succeeded by Rev. Newton N. Donaldson who was employed on June 11, 1893, and served until 1916. Under his direction the present church was built in 1895. Dr. Donaldson was succeeded in 1917 by Dr. J. Layton Mauze who served until September 15, 1928, and was succeeded by Dr. J. Blanton Belk who served until October, 1933, and was succeeded by Dr. A. L. Currie who is now in charge.

PROTESTANT EPISCOPAL CHURCH

Beginning in 1825, the Rev. Mr. Page, rector of the St. Johns Protestant Episcopal Church at Charleston held regular services for

5th Avenue looking west from a point just west of 11th Street, showing the Episcopal Church at the left, then the spire of the First Presbyterian Church, then the First Congregational Church with the Fifth Avenue Baptist Church on the right, with the city hall and jail beyond

several years at Barboursville and Guyandotte, but as quaintly expressed by the late Cameron L. Thompson, "the seed sown by our reverend brother must have fallen on very hard and stony ground for the harvest was scant indeed; however, some seed must have caught in good ground for in the year 1843 . . . John Laidley rode horseback from his farm on the Ohio River just below Guyandotte to Staten's Run on the Kanawha River, a distance of forty miles, to attend a service of the church held at that place by Bishop Meade." These services were held in an old still house which had been set up for church services and on that occasion Bishop Meade confirmed a class, one of whom was John Laidley.

Between this time and the Civil War at long intervals services were held by ministers of the Episcopal Church in the chapel at Marshall College but during the war no services were held in this region by any Episcopal clergyman. On October 22, 1869, Rev. Horace E. Hayden, rector of the Christ Church at Pt. Pleasant held services at Barboursville. After the services a meeting was held and it was determined that a parish to be called Cabell be established and its bounds to include the county, and that a church to be called Trinity be organized. The following vestry was elected: Dr. Charles Burnett, Judge H. J. Samuels, Thomas B. Kline, Abraham Suydam, and R. M. McLeod, secretary.

From that time on services were held regularly once each month by the Rev. C. B. Mee, rector of the church at Coal's Mouth, now St. Albans, and in the next year the County Court gave the new congregation permission to use the courthouse.

In 1872 General John H. Oley had moved to Huntington and on April 1st of that year a vestry consisting of Dr. C. J. Burnett, Dr. John N. Buffington, J. M. Love, J. D. Moncure, Gouvernor Morris, L. C. Ricketts, and General John H. Oley was elected. Dr. Burnett was elected senior warden, J. M. Love, junior warden, Gouvernor Morris, registrar, and General Oley, treasurer. After this was done the vestry meetings were held in Huntington. In June of this year Bishop Johns of Virginia, accompanied by the Rev. Mr. Highland of Parkersburg visited the parish and held services in the chapel of Marshall College and confirmed a class of four, one of whom was Miss Hattie Stoddard, afterwards Mrs. Willis E. Parsons. General Oley was an enthusiastic churchman and a man of tremendous driving force. By October he made a contract for the use of Crider's Hall (which was located in the second story of a frame building on the south side of 3rd Avenue near the corner of 10th Street and now included in the Bradshaw-Diehl Company building) as a place of worship and had drafted Champ Clark, then principal at Marshall College, as chief chorister. At this time Cabell Parish was a part of a diocese of Virginia and Bishop Johns sent the Rev. E. Valentine Jones, a deacon of the church, to take charge of the missions at Barboursville and Huntington. Mr. Jones arrived on September 7, 1872. In the next month the Rev. Dr. Minnegerode and the Rev. Mr. Lindsay were sent by Bishop Johns to inspect the parish and report their needs. These ministers held two services in this parish, both in Crider's Hall. On October 25, 1872, A. J. Enslow, J. H. Oley, and John Hooe Russel were named as trustees to hold the church property and the vestry adopted a resolution designating the church as Trinity Church of Huntington, West Virginia, Cabell Parish. In November, 1872, the new church purchased the two lots at the southwest corner of 5th Avenue and 10th Streets on which is now located the Johnson Memorial Church. A short time afterwards A. A. Lowe of New York was in Huntington and learned of the effort to build an Episcopal Church and he suggested that a change be made to the southeast corner of 11th Street and 5th Avenue, and agreed to make a liberal contribution towards the cost of a new church. His suggestion was acted upon and Mr. Lowe made a large contribution. In April, 1873, Dr. J. N. Buffington, J. D. Moncure, J. H. Oley, G. F. Herndon, Ely Ensign, James Nelson, and J. M. Lowe were vestrymen and in the same year the Rev. E. V. Jones resigned and the church was without a rector until October 28, 1877, when the Rev. Mr. Dashiel was sent by Bishop Whittle to look over the field and report on the prospects. What his report was is not known but in the following year George W. Peterkin was elected Bishop of the new Diocese of West Virginia and in August, he together with R. A. Cobbs and the Rev. Hugo Lacey were in Huntington in conference with the vestry with reference to securing a rector for the parish. As a result of this meeting the Rev. John W. Lea who was in charge of St. Mark's in St Albans, was placed in charge and regular services were held twice a month. The first class for confirmation after the separation of this diocese from Virginia was presented by him. The building committee which consisted of General J. H. Oley, Ely Ensign, W. S. Gladstone, and F. B. Enslow was appointed and $7,500.00 in cash and pledges was raised. Plans were secured and on March 15, 1883, a contract was made with Hoback and Cochran for the erection of the present church. While

Trinity Episcopal Church, 11th Street and 5th Avenue, circa 1884

the building was under construction services were held for a time in a room in the Central Land Company building at the southwest corner of 12th Street and 4th Avenue. Mr. Lea died on May 15, 1884, and was succeeded by the Rev. J. B. Fitzpatrick as missionary in charge from October, 1884, until September 20, 1886. During this period the church was completed and the first services held in the Guild Room in November, 1884.

On November 29, 1886, a call was extended to the Rev. Carl E. Grammar which was declined and in May, 1887, Norman F. Marshall was called and served for five years when he resigned on account of ill health. In March, 1888, General J. H. Oley died, which was a great blow to his church. It was his driving force that accounted for much of its progress. He organized the first choir with Mrs. B. W. Foster as organist and director. In this year the council of the Diocese of West Virginia met in the Trinity Church. In March, 1892, Rev. Mr. Marshall resigned and in September following the Rev. John S. Gibson, from St. George's Church in Virginia, took over the work. The church had been without a rector for six months, its membership was small and the debt on the property was large. The cost of the rectory and church was about $13,000.00, a greater part of which had been borrowed. The buildings were scantily furnished and poorly equipped and to make matters worse the panic of 1893-96 came on. However, he went into the work with enthusiasm and not only attended the needs of this congregation but held services at Kenova and Williamson.

On January 27, 1902, the church lost two of its most faithful officers. H. J. Derbyshire was taken in the early morning and in the evening of the same day Ely Ensign, senior warden was stricken and died.

In 1903, twenty years after the beginning of the church, the debt was paid in full and on March 17, 1903, it was consecrated by the Rev. John S. Gibson, assisted by the Rev. W. H. Hampton of Ironton, Ohio, and the Rev. A. M. Lewis, of Powellton, West Virginia. Bishop George W. Peterkin preached the sermon. The instruments of donation were read by the senior warden, Cameron L. Thompson, and Bishop Peterkin's sentence of consecration was read by the rector. In September, 1911, the Rev. John S. Gibson resigned and accepted a call in Virginia. In the December following, the Rev. John S. Douglass of Martinsburg became the rector and continued until October 15, 1916, when he accepted a call to St. Andrew's Church at Louisville, Kentucky, and was succeeded by the Rev. Roger S. Tyler who assumed charge on Thanksgiving Day, 1916. In this year the church purchased the Garner property just east of the church for a rectory and used the old rectory as a Sunday School until 1924 when the new parish house was built.

The men who served longest on the vestry include G. A. Northcott, C. D. Emmons, R. L. Archer, F. D. Fuller and Harry Chambers, all of whom are still alive, and Henry J. Derbyshire, Ely Ensign, F. B. Enslow, C. L. Thompson, Edmund Sehon, and John W. Ensign, deceased.

This church has grown both in membership and influence and its baptized membership now is 1,000. In addition to its original church it established in 1920 a mission and Sunday School in the western end of the city and services were first held in the Jefferson School at 19th Street, West. The present site of St. Peter's Church was acquired in May, 1921, and the church building erected in 1922 to which a parish house was added in 1933. This church is now in charge of Elden B. Mowers.

XXXIV: THE TOWN OF BARBOURSVILLE

BARBOURSVILLE is a village of 1,500 inhabitants located on the Guyandotte River and the Chesapeake and Ohio Railway at the point of junction with the Guyan Valley Division. It is the home of Morris Harvey College, has a high school, a graded school, a number of churches and nice residences. It has the following industries: A flour mill, a brick plant and the Chesapeake and Ohio reclamation plant. Barboursville has city water, a bank and a number of mercantile establishments. It is the second oldest village in the county and much history has been made there. It lays claim as the home town of many of the most distinguished men that this county has produced.

Barboursville was established by an act of the General Assembly passed January 14, 1813, which named the following persons as trustees: Elisha McComas, Manoah Bostick, Edmund Morris, Sampson Sanders and Thomas Hatfield.

The courthouse was moved there in 1814 and Barboursville continued the county seat except for a short period during the Civil War until the 26th day of December, 1887, when the courthouse was moved to Huntington.

That the new village at an early date was not lacking in social life is shown by the following invitation:

"The pleasure of Miss Elizabeth Hereford's company is solicited to a BALL at Mr. Joseph Gardner's in Barboursville, on the 4th day of July next.

Signed: JOHN LAIDLEY,
F. G. L. BEUHRING,
JOHN SAMUELS,
Managers."

June, 1823.

A plat of the new village showed a layout of thirty-four lots with two streets paralleling the Guyandotte River, the first called Water Street and the other Center Street. These streets were intersected by Main Street which is the present east and west thoroughfare through the village.

On December 28, 1824, the General Assembly authorized the sale of town lots in the public square and the County Court under the authority of this act made an order in September, 1828, naming John Samuels as a commissioner to superintend the sale of these lots

BARBOURSVILLE
Nov. 1861. 34th Reg't O.V.I.

and the deeds of record indicate that two lots, one on the southwest corner of the public square, and the other on the southeast corner of the public square, were sold to F. G. L. Beuhring, and there is no record of any further sales.

One of the common schools reported in the county in 1832 was located here and five years afterwards the County Court gave the town people the right to use the courthouse for a school.

In 1846 Elisha McComas recruited a company for the Mexican War and for a time a portion of this company was in camp in Barboursville on the site of what was until recently known as the Mike Saunders house, but later this company went on to Guyandotte.

On December 16, 1853, the Grand Lodge of Virginia issued charter No. 56 to the Minerva Lodge, A. F. & A. M., and a second charter was issued to this lodge by the Grand Lodge of West Virginia on January 24, 1867.

The first Masters were William W. McComas, Joseph Foster, H. J. Samuels, Thomas Thornburg, and P. H. McCullough. The first petitions for members received were from George W. Summers, Thomas Thornburg, and Abner W. Wing.

From 1855 to the beginning of the Civil War Barboursville was a port of call for steamboats running on the Guyan River and the *R. H. Lindsey,* a steamboat which ran on a fixed schedule, carried both passengers and freight. It is claimed that this boat had both a clerk and a colored porter to assist the ladies on and off the boat.

During this period Barboursville was quite an industrial center and boasted of a furniture factory, a hat factory, wagon and buggy factory, some harness shops, a tanner, and a sawmill which specialized in manufacturing bottoms for boats.

At the outbreak of the Civil War there were only two bridges in the county, both of them being the old-fashioned covered style. One still stands near Milton. The other was over Mud River at Barboursville and was burned during the war.

During the Civil War it was the scene of two skirmishes, the first of which took place July 14, 1861, between a unit of the 16th Virginia Cavalry, C.S.A., commanded by Colonel Milton Jamison Ferguson and the Militia from Wayne and Cabell counties commanded by Colonel J. J. Mansfield, supported by the Border Rangers under Albert Gallatin Jenkins on the Confederate side, and the 2d Kentucky commanded by Colonel William E. Woodruff and Lieutenant Colonel G. W. Neff. One of the members of the Border Rangers in his diary gives the following account of this action and has something to say about Lieutenant Colonel Neff who with a part of the 2d Kentucky camped at Greenbottom:

On the morning of the 14th, the Second Kentucky advanced to Barboursville and charged the militia that was posted on the hill in front of the town. The militia, after delivering one fire, broke and left the field. The Company marched off the hill in order, without firing a gun and marched back to Coalsmouth without the loss of a man or horse. We took the fire of the regiment but no one was hurt of the company. A Mr. Reynolds was killed by the fire and three others slightly wounded of the Militia. The loss to the 2nd Kentucky was four killed and twenty wounded.*

After the battle of Scary, Colonels Woodruff, De Villius and Lieutenant Colonel Neff and Captains Hurd and Austin were made prisoners, and the Border Ranger tells about the capture as follows:

While sitting there in line Col. Woodruff, Col. Devillius and their staff rode up to Captain Jenkins and said to him, "Well, you have given the Rebels a good sound thrashing today," when he ordered them to surrender which they did with considerable grumbling. It was twilight and they could not distinguish our uniforms from theirs. . . . When we found Col. Neff after the fight he was wounded and left on the field. The Captain asked him who he was and he told him he was Colonel Neff. The Captain dismounted took him by the hand and told him Mrs. Jenkins words should be made good, that he should be treated gentlemanly and if we remember correctly he was paroled after having his wound dressed. It was in reply to what Colonel Neff had told the Captain's (Albert Gallatin Jenkins) wife that if he ever caught her husband, he intended to hang him, but the tables were turned on the gallant Colonel in this his first fight.

The second action took place on September 8, 1862, between some of the 2d West Virginia Volunteer Cavalry, commanded by Colonel William H. Powell, and a portion of the 8th Virginia Cavalry, C.S.A., under Albert Gallatin Jenkins. In this action one Union soldier was killed. The Border Ranger gives an account of this engagement as follows:

Ten men in charge of an officer were sent from Buffalo to Mud River Bridge, now Milton, with orders, if anything was wrong in Cabell to report to the General at Green Bottom. The ten men that went to Milton continued down the turnpike to within half a mile of Barboursville. There they met two citizens in a buggy whom they knew, who told them to go back for God's sake, as the town was full of Yanks. After inquiring from the citizens, we found that all they knew was that they saw an officer and eight or ten men turn the corner and they supposed they were merely the advance of some regiment coming to take possession of the town. We concluded to ride into

---

*The Confederate casualties were one killed, James Reynolds of Milton, and Absolom Ballinger, wounded.

Thomas Thornburg, then his son George E. Thornburg's store house at Barboursville

the town and take a look at them. We rode in as far as Thornburg's store on top of the hill where the officers ordered a charge, having seen a blue coat. We found them at Hatfield's Hotel. About half of them went over the River Bank and the rest ran in all directions, the boys firing at them as they ran. We caught two of them before they could get out of the Hotel. Lieut. Brown, the officer in command of the Yanks, hid in a bake oven in the back yard of Oscar Mather's house. This was the Sabbath Day and Church was going on at the time in Southern Methodist church. Three or four bullets struck the building and the preacher did not have to dismiss the congregation. The congregation was found getting toward home as fast as they could possibly go, without waiting for the benediction. The boys felt good even over the result of their charge. We went on to Guyandotte—charged the town, found no one but citizens; told them to stay at home and they should not be disturbed. We went around town, shook hands with everyone and felt as if we were at home once more. We waited for the command to come down the Ohio from Green Bottom, rejoined the Company and went to Barboursville, where a scout from Hurricane came down and reported to the General that Lightburn and all the forces in the Kanawha Valley were retreating by the way of the Barboursville road. We left one of the Company of the Cavalry to watch them and fell back up the Guyan River and made forced march through Wayne County up Twelve Pole into Logan County.

At the close of the war the courthouse was returned to Barboursville and the village took up the even tenor of its ways until the activities attending the construction of the new railway brought a great many people there. In 1869 it boasted of a brass band which was given permission to use the courthouse for practice. The next year there were enough Baptists and Episcopalians in the village to organize and each group was given permission to organize and hold services in the courthouse.

Upon the completion of the railroad Huntington soon became the center of business activity in the county and Barboursville began to feel the effects of this growth which immediately manifested itself in a movement to remove the courthouse to Huntington and this was accomplished in 1887.

Immediately after the removal of the courthouse the Barboursville people organized the Barboursville Seminary and attempted to maintain a school in the old courthouse but they failed in their efforts and the school was turned over to the Methodist Church and has since become the Morris Harvey College.

Barboursville now is enjoying a steady and prosperous growth and is a community made up of some of the most representative people in the county.

XXXV: CENTRAL CITY

IN 1891 a number of local people organized the Huntington and Kenova Land Development Company, acquired some land adjoining Huntington on the west and laid out a new city called Central City. The plan included in its boundaries the old Saint Cloud Subdivision. Major George McKendree made the map of Central City which was filed in the clerk's office on the 6th day of October, 1891. A short time after this the land company had a successful lot sale. On the 31st day of July, 1893, upon the petition of John S. Farr and others, the Circuit Court incorporated the new city and from this order C. S. Elder, who was opposed to the incorporation, took an appeal to the Supreme Court but this court on March 27, 1895, affirmed the Circuit Court. The contest was characteristic for it was but one of the many that arose during the life of this municipality for the reason that her sons—daughters had no vote in those days—were fully alive to their civic duties. Notwithstanding the contest pending, the incorporators organized on September 11, 1893, with M. V. Chapman (grandfather of the present mayor of Huntington) as mayor, Thomas Sikes, John S. Farr, Hunter Evans, and D. H. Brinker, councilmen; George M. McDermitt was elected recorder and A. G. Plymale, sergeant.

The land company located a number of industries in the new city. Among them were several glass plants, a handle factory managed by Enos Hartzell, a bung factory in charge of Al. Hickman. These last two operated successfully for a number of years but are now closed. There was a successful brick plant located on Four Pole Creek at about 10th Street, West, which had its beginning with George and Morris Arthur. In 1891 A. J. Crawford and Company, composed of A. J. Crawford, A. H. Evans, A. C. Howell, and Lizzie Crawford, took over this plant and operated as a partnership until 1905 when it became the Central City Brick Company and later the Huntington Red Brick Company. This company manufactured brick successfully until 1917 when most of its men were called to war and it concluded to close.

In 1894 William Seiber established the Central Veneer Company in Central City and began the manufacture of veneer. In 1917 this business was sold to the Wood Mosaic Poplar Veneer Company which has enlarged its plant and now employs sixty people.

The American Brewing Company came early and built a large

plant on 14th Street and Madison Avenue. In April, 1899, the West Virginia Brewing Company was organized by James Clark, John Keating, William Buckholtz, John J., Micheal, and Andrew J. Fesenmeier, and John J. Kearney. The new company took over the American Brewing Company and was engaged in the brewing and ice business successfully until the state adopted prohibition in 1914. The ice business was continued and in the following year a packing business was started under the name of the Fesenmeier Packing Company. The packing business continued until 1922 when the company engaged in cold storage along with the ice business and when the prohibition amendment was repealed in the State in 1934, the plant was equipped with modern machinery and resumed as a brewery. In 1934 it changed its name to the Fesenmeier Brewing Company with J. F. Fesenmeier, president; John P. Kearney, vice president; M. W. Fesenmeier, secretary, and C. M. Gohen, treasurer. During the summer months this company employs in excess of one hundred men.

In 1898 D. E. Abbott took over the building at 14th Street and Washington Avenue which had been built by one of the glass factories, and moved his business from Huntington to that point. D. E. Abbott and Company manufactured picture frames and had a corps of artists who enlarged pictures and made portraits. The company has enjoyed a successful and profitable business. A few years ago it sold the picture framing business to Cravens-Green Company which has continued in that line. D. E. Abbott and Company are still in the business of enlarging pictures and painting portraits.

Returning to the political life of Central City it can be said that William Seiber served more frequently as mayor than any other person and a number of representative men served in its council. Among these were R. D. Wylie, M. M. Spitler, D. W. Frampton, and J. S. Ball, who was sergeant for a number of years. At this time there was a large Indian mound standing at the intersection of 13th Street and Monroe Avenue, but the city authorities later leveled this mound and used the dirt to fill a sewer.

In 1908 a movement was started for a greater Huntington to include Central City and Guyandotte and on the 7th day of December, 1908, the common council adopted a resolution to become a part of Huntington and appointed a committee to help to bring this about.

The last meeting of the city council was held on June 3, 1909, with these men present: William Seiber, mayor; J. W. Huffman, clerk; T. A. B. Kincaid, Fred Meshel, and Fred Toney, councilmen, and J. S. Ball, sergeant and treasurer. The council settled the accounts with the treasurer and voted to come into Huntington and adjourned *sine die*.

NEUTRAL STRIP

After the incorporation of Central City there was a strip of land of irregular shape between the western limits of Huntington and the eastern limits of Central City, known locally as the Neutral Strip. Some portions of it had been subdivided into small tracts and in some instances town lots and quite a number of houses had been built on it. In the enlargement of the boundaries of Huntington in 1909 the Neutral Strip became a part of the City of Huntington.

XXXVI: CULLODEN

THIS is an unincorporated village on Route 60, the Midland Trail, near the Putnam County line. It finds an early mention when in 1818 a tavern license was granted at that point and the tavern continued there until the Civil War.* At the outbreak of the war, John Morris, an elderly man of Southern sympathies, owned and operated the tavern and had been operating it a good many years. The Federal soldiers burned the building and Morris refugeed to Wytheville, Virginia. After the war the Chesapeake and Ohio Railroad was built along the present Midland Trail and there was a freight and passenger station in the village. The village then as now was unincorporated. In the early 90's Captain B. H. Justice wanted a saloon license but the County Court would not grant a liquor license in the county of Cabell so Justice brought about the incorporation of the village by an order of the Circuit Court made on July 16, 1894, under the provisions of Chapter 47 of the Code. It is said that in arranging the corporation line it was done entirely with reference to the view that a prospective citizen might have on the wet and dry question. That is to say, the land of one man living a considerable distance from the Chesapeake and Ohio station, which was the center of the city, would be included in the corporate limits, but the land of another man who happened to be opposed to the license was left outside the corporation, even though he lived closer to the station. After the town was incorporated it granted saloon licenses but after a time the lack of police protection made conditions in the village unbearable and the council refused to license saloons. As a result of this refusal interest in the corporation lagged and in a short time the corporation died from non-use. Culloden is now a pleasant community with good schools, a number of stores, and many pleasant and comfortable homes.

---

*This tavern was at the T. J. Berkeley place on the old Pike about a mile west of the present village.

XXXVII: THE TOWN OF GUYANDOTTE

THERE must have been a settlement at the mouth of the Guyandotte River before the county was organized for the record shows that in 1802 William Huff was appointed a constable for "the neighborhood of the mouth of the Guyandotte" and in the next year, 1803, Thomas Buffington had established a ferry across the mouth of the Guyandotte and one across the Ohio River and a few months later he was indicted for not keeping better boats. It is also reported that in the years 1805, 1806, and 1807 there were 8,000 bear skins shipped from the mouth of the Big Sandy and the Guyandotte. At the time the county was organized Guyandotte must have been the largest community in the new county or it would not have been selected as the county seat, and in the following year, 1810, the town of Guyandotte was established by an Act of the General Assembly which stated that twenty acres of land owned by Thomas Buffington was made a town by the name of Guyandotte. The following persons were named trustees: Noah Scales, Henry Brown, Richard Crump, Thomas Kilgore, Edmund Morris, and Elisha McComas. Three years later the General Assembly passed an act authorizing the sale of town lots and it is believed that these lots were sold at auction by the trustees. Thomas Buffington executed the deeds for the lots and collected the purchase money.

The map of the new city showed six streets, three running east and west and intersected at right angles with the same number of streets running north and south. The streets paralleling the Ohio River were Ohio (sometimes called Water or Front Street and which is almost washed away), Middle and Court Streets. The cross streets beginning at the Guyandotte River were Guyan, Center (now Main) and Eastern (now Richmond) Streets.

"The first deed recorded was to Sanders Witcher for $67 then deeds to Daniel Witcher, John Rogers, Abram Witcher, Edmund McGinnis, William Merritt, Edmund Morris, Richard Crump, John Simmons, James Gallaher, and others.

"Whether they all became residents, or whether they were speculators at a boom sale of town lots, we did not learn, but James Gallaher, who lived at Gallipolis, floated his home down to Guyandotte and set it up and went into business. After living there until about 1833 he purchased the Mark Russell farm and built his brick house thereon."

THE TOWN OF GUYANDOTTE

Apparently the building on the lots was slow and we find that two years later the General Assembly passed an act giving the purchasers further time in which to build.

In 1814 the courthouse was moved from Guyandotte to Barboursville where it remained until January 5, 1863, when on account of the troubles incident to the war it was moved to Guyandotte and continued there until September 2, 1865, when it was returned to Barboursville.

In 1831 there was a daily stage from Washington and Richmond which made connections with steamboats on the Ohio River and Guyandotte was the most important shipping point in Western Virginia except Wheeling.

By 1835 the village contained "forty dwellings, five store houses, one house of public worship free to all denominations, one primary school, a steam grist and sawmill and a carding machine propelled by the same power, one saddler, two cabinet makers and a number of other mechanics." But complaint was made at that early date of the want of enterprise in its citizens. The house of public worship mentioned was on a lot which adjoins the old graveyard on Guyan and 3d Streets (now 5th Avenue). This building was used as a schoolhouse until some time in the 1850's when it was destroyed.

On November 16, 1846, Guyandotte was designated by the Secretary of War as the place of rendezvous for the infantry regiment of volunteers called for service in Mexico but this rendezvous was at the request of the governor of Virginia changed to Richmond.

Captain Elisha W. McComas rendezvoused his company in Guyandotte and embarked there for New Orleans en route to Mexico.

Sam D. Hayslip relates that at the time of the Mexican War he was attending school in the old building which stood on the lot which adjoined the old graveyard and that his father who was the teacher let out the school so that the children might see Captain McComas's company march past on the way to the wharf en route to Mexico.

In 1849 Guyandotte was incorporated and the trustees were: Peter Clarke, J. B. Hite, August S. Wolcott, Robert Holderby, A. M. Whitney, James Emmons, H. H. Miller, William Buffington, N. S. Adams, Jacob Miller, John W. Hite, and P. S. Smith. Its corporation limits were enlarged in 1852-53 and again in 1857-58. As an answer to the criticism that Guyandotte had not made the most of its opportunities it can be said that in 1830 the Guyandotte folks brought about the organization of the Guyandotte Turnpike Company and built the road on the north side of the Guyandotte River to Barboursville and the stage line used this road in place of the original State road or pike.

Three additions were added to the town, viz: the Southern in 1820, the Eastern in 1850, and the William Buffington in 1853.

In 1848 the Guyandotte Bridge Company was incorporated by J. W. Hite, John Laidley, F. G. L. Beuhring, J. B. Hite, Peter Clark, P. S. Smith, and P. C. Buffington. This company built the suspension bridge over the Guyandotte River which was not completed until about 1852. A portion of its capital stock was owned by the State of Virginia and afterwards came into the hands of the County Court who purchased the stock held by individuals and made the bridge free in the early 70's. This bridge was replaced by the present bridge in 1908.

In 1849 the Guyandotte Navigation Company was chartered and this company built the locks and dams in the Guyan River.

March 2, 1854, an act was passed incorporating the Bank of Guyandotte. This act was amended on February 5, 1863, and the latter act fixed the authorized capital stock at not less than $100,000.00 and not more than $300,000.00, shares to be $100.00 each, the subscription books to be opened on March 2, 1863, under the supervision of John Laidley, Sr., Thomas J. Hayslip, and James H. Poage, and permission was given to use either name—the Bank of Guyandotte or the Bank of West Virginia. The subscriptions apparently did not materialize because there is no record of this bank ever being organized.

In 1858 the Guyandotte Railway was incorporated but did not get beyond the paper stage. However, it was almost fifty years before such a railroad was built.

In the early part of 1861 the Cabell County Petroleum Company was organized by H. J. Samuels, Granville Parker, H. H. Miller, A. N. Hill, W. E. Freezell, H. C. Everett, L. M. Wolcott, W. C. Rogers, W. I. Gray, and Thomas Thornburg. This company was apparently inactive until 1865 when its minutes show that it held a meeting at Barboursville on December 4th of that year and began activities. It drilled an oil well near Salt Rock which some of the local people think was on the P. H. Swann farm. In the same year it drilled a well at Fall Creek on the Guyandotte River which is in Lincoln County. From this record it would indicate that Guyandotte people were pioneers in the oil development in this section.

While the village was progressing in a commercial way the fact that it had a place of public worship free to all denominations indicates that the community had a spiritual life at a very early date.

The Western Star Masonic Lodge which is still in existence points with pride to the fact that its charter bears the date 1818 and no longer ago than in 1934 this lodge restored the gravestone of a Mason who had been buried in the old graveyard in 1828, perhaps by this lodge. So we cheerfully find that the complaint of want of enterprise in Guyandotte citizens is not supported.

In 1858 the County Court for the first time constituted patrols under the statute to visit all "negro quarters and other places suspected of having therein unlawful assemblies or such slaves as may stroll from one plantation to another without permission." Guyandotte had such a patrol with Charles W. Summerson as captain, and H. H. Miller, William L. Peters, and Aaron Moore as privates.

In November, 1860, to demonstrate its Southern sympathies the citizens of Guyandotte erected a flagpole, hoisted a Southern flag thereon and organized a company to protect it and, as is told elsewhere, this flag stayed up until April, 1861, when the company disbanded. In the early part of 1861, probably soon after the local company left, a Federal recruiting office was established at Guyandotte in charge of Colonel Whaley.

On November 10, 1861, Colonel John Clarkson's regiment, the 8th Virginia Cavalry, C.S.A., which included Albert Gallatin Jenkins and the Border Rangers, made a raid on the town and had a skirmish with the Federal forces and took some prisoners. On the next day, November 11, 1861, Colonel Zeigler of the U. S. Army burned the larger portion of the town. As a result of this fire the close of the Civil War found all of the business portion and quite a large part of the residential section of the town burned and this included the Buffington Mill and the principal hotels. There were three hotels which operated after the war. Both the Bukey House, kept by Rodolphus Bukey, and the Jacob Hiltbruner Hotel—which became the Crawley House and was operated by Crawley Smith, have long since disappeared. The Merchant's Hotel on the north side of Bridge Street continued until ten or fifteen years ago. Its last proprietor was Vint Stephenson.

W. S. Laidley tells an intimate story of the beginning of Guyandotte and its older people:

We might say that the town of Guyandotte was occasioned by the hunters and surveyors going to Kentucky, by the settlers on the Savage grant, who desired to form a camp for protection against the Indians, in the first place, and afterwards by more substantial improvements made for protection, then for business and association.

We must now ask, why was the place named Guyandotte? Most probably because it had so long been known as the "Mouth of the Guyandotte," it has naturally assumed this name for short. But where did the river get the name of Guyandotte? This question has never been satisfactorily answered. Some give one and some another explanation.

When it was visited by the surveyors in 1771-2, they called this stream "Little Sandy" and so marked it on their map or plat of their survey.

The first time the name was ever heard of is found in a book called *Dunmore's War* which is a history of the year 1774 and the battle of Point Pleasant, in which book is found "Hanson's Journal," which gives an account of the travels and work of a company of surveyors that went from Fincastle County, Virginia, in April, 1774, to Kentucky. They reached the mouth of Elk April 16, the mouth of Coal on the 18th, and passed the mouth of Pocatalico on that day, and on the 20th they reached the mouth of the Kanawha, where they met some traders and learned that the Indians were numerous and unfriendly on the Ohio river.

On the 22nd of April, this company with eighteen men and four canoes started down the Ohio and on the 24th they went to the Little Gui-an-dot, where they found a battoe loaded with corn and they took about three bushels, and on the 26th, while in camp, other men came to them, and on the 27th they went to the Great Guiandot, 20 miles, where they saw some Delaware Indians, who told them there were fifty other Indians below them, and they proceeded on the 29th to Big Sandy Creek, 13 miles, where they stopped and "cooked their kettle"—See *Dunmore's War,* 116.

There was no mention of a house or a residence, and yet they name the streams and the distances apart. Here we see for the first time the name of Gui-an-dot. The first surveyor that ever came in 1771-2, with William Crawford, called the same stream, Little Sandy, but Crawford lived in Nederick or Berkeley County, Virginia, and Hanson did not get the name from him.

We suppose Thos. Buffington called it "Gui-an-dot" in his attempt to pronounce it as the Delaware Indians called it, Wyandot tribe, which tribe was said to have been driven therefrom by the Mohawks long ago, but where did Hanson get it, as he had never seen Buffington nor anyone that was ever supposed to have seen the stream?

We have imagined that it was intended to pronounce Wyandot, and by some manner or means, had become twisted into Guiandotte. Some say that there was a Frenchman by the name of Guion that was an Indian trader that had located there and given it the name. If the trader could be established at the mouth of the river, the story would be plausible. There was a tribe known as the Wyandots and by way of Indian pronunciation, there is but the slightest difference between Wyandot and Guiandot, and we have no evidence of the trader, so we have adopted the name of the tribe with an Indian twang thereto. The surveyors of 1775 adopted the name of Guyandotte, and it has stuck to the stream ever since.

It has been brought down by tradition that the William Holderby that occupied the field, kept the hotel on the corner of the streets on the Ohio and Guyandotte banks, that he was an Englishman from Yorktown, Virginia.

Dr. Henry Hampton owned considerable land in farms below Guyandotte and lived near where the Academy was afterward built. There is a history to this man, about his killing Mr. Shortridge, and was tried and the trial destroyed his fortune, and one of his farms was sold to James Holderby.

Henry Brown was one of the first justices, and he was appointed the sheriff after the first year, and while sheriff he was supposed to have been killed, his horse and his hat were found, but his body never was.

There was the same Holderby Hotel kept afterwards by Gen'l John Smith, and afterwards the famous John G. Wright kept the same for years, and after others had kept it, it was kept by A. M. Whitney, and it was always well kept.

The passengers by stage from the east and by boat from Cincinnati and Pittsburgh were all entertained at this noted hotel.

The timber business from the Guyandotte, and the sawing into lumber, and many other profitable undertakings, all assumed extensive proportions and the town continued to grow.

Many will remember the hotel of Jacob Bumgardner and some the hotel of Tom Carroll, the Irishman, the saw mill of Peter Clarke, and others.

Here we would state that from our earliest recollection there was a man who lived on the lower side of the river and kept the ferry across the mouth of Guyandotte. He was Sam'l Mark Russell and was, besides being the good ferryman, mail carrier to Big Sandy, an auctioneer, a temperance lecturer, and a minister of the gospel. He did them all and did them well, and he lived to see the bridge take the place of his ferry and continued to live in Guyandotte for a good long life and died honored and beloved by all men.

This brings us down to within the memory of many who do not admit they are old.

We remember some men that we then regarded as the old men of the place. There was old Mr. Ricketts, who was the constable, and the father of G. C. Ricketts, the physician. There was old man John Ong, the elder, and Colonel Isaac Ong, the tailor, and the prominent democratic politician of the place. There was old Mr. Sanford Scott and his two boys; old Mr. Wellington, the carpenter; Victor LeTuttle, the grocer; Mr. Hiltbruner, the tinner, P. H. Keenan, that made saddles and harness; Mr. Sedinger, the shoemaker; Jos. Wheeler, the editor of the *Herald;* Mr. Wolcott, the wharfmaster; Mr. Hayslip, who was always postmaster, and was a born mathematician. There were others in many other businesses but these have remained in my memory and with whom we had business as a boy and we learned to know their worth.

It would be gratifying to tell of the peculiarities of many residents of this old town that I, as a boy, once knew so well; but this gratification would be too personal and only interesting to a few.

We also have a desire to record the names of the scholars that attended the school at the old Academy; the many boys that made up many classes, in whole or in part; that made up a large part of the games played on the ball ground; that made the road lively going to and from the said school, but this too, perhaps should not be done.

But there was an incident that we shall relate, though perhaps it would be best to omit. We, as country boys, went into the old town where we were wont to get the mail, and after attending to our duties, we strolled down towards the hotel on the bank of the Ohio river, and we met a young lady wearing an apron which to us was unusual and which we did not comprehend, yet we felt sure it was indication of some sentiments and we dared not ask her to explain.

We reached the hotel and in front of it on the river bank there had been erected a flag staff and thereon there had been hoisted a flag or banner, the like of which we had never seen before, and we noticed the resemblance of the flag to the apron. We were struck with the new emblems, but were slow to take in the significance of the same. Just then a large side wheeled steamboat came down the river, whose name was Ohio No. 3. She seemed to be covered with passengers and flags and all of those flags were the old stars and stripes, the only kind we had ever seen before. The boat landed almost under the strange flag on the bank.

There was nothing said about the stars and bars, but everyone seemed to comprehend the matter better than we did. The intensity of the excitement seemed to create a silence. Soon the boat rounded out and was gone and the people on the shore all repaired to their work and those few that were visible on the street yet we were under the same excitement and could but ask, what does it all mean? and the only answer that came was, that it meant the border of two governments, and no more the United States. Taking a seat on the sidewalk in front of the hotel, on the side next to the river and still considering the two flags, and endeavoring to take in the effect of all of it, we heard something strike the brick wall of the hotel just over my head. We soon took it in that it was from a gun from the opposite corner of the hotel. We became satisfied that the flag meant more than a sentiment, and the bullet more than a man's joke, and once in our lives, perhaps, we were near right.

In giving the history of the place, we have to admit that we have not always been able to harmonize tradition with record evidence, nor to determine which is the nearest to the facts. We have been compelled to guess at much that has transpired and we never claimed to be a good guesser.

What is here given can be taken for what it is worth. We have not, of ourselves, made up much of it, but have endeavored to state it as we found it.

From the time of which Mr. Laidley speaks until Guyandotte became a part of the City of Huntington it continued to be one of the most interesting communities in the county. A greater part of its people were conservative and law-abiding and the men who followed those of whom Mr. Laidley tells include many who were known to the folks now living. Ed. Smith who lived in the brick house at the corner of Bridge and Guyan Streets was mayor and fined C. P. Huntington for riding his horse on the sidewalk. It is said that C. P. Huntington in retaliation located the Chesapeake and Ohio depot

J. L. Caldwell. Born 1846, died October 18, 1893. President, First National Bank

on the west side of the Guyandotte River until the Legislature enacted a law requiring railway stations to be located closer to the towns. J. L. Caldwell, with his father-in-law, Nicholas Smith, had a store on Guyan Street near the bridge. Mr. Caldwell was also in the timber business and the story is still told how, on one occasion, when there was a timber run in the Guyandotte River he became alarmed and excited about his rafts getting out into the Ohio River and ran down on the bank urging his men on the rafts to "ride 'em." Old Bill Porter from Mud River, who was on a raft, came ashore and said, "You ride 'em, Mr. Caldwell, we need some good men on the bank." L. H. Burks was in the timber business. Sam D. Hayslip, many times assessor, was a colorful figure. D. I. Smith was mayor more than once, and J. K. (Doc) Suiter was town marshal, and a better-hearted or more kindly man than "Doc" never lived. He was a Republican but had many Democratic friends and in addition to his duties, or perhaps between times, "Doc" operated a ladies' hack between Huntington and Guyandotte. After he ceased to be town marshal "Doc" was elected constable but on one or more occasions when he failed to be elected to the office his Democratic friends had him appointed constable so he was always a constable and his boast was "Give me a paper and I will serve it."

J. H. Page had the drug store now operated by Murphy and Son. Charles H. Summerson drove a stage over the old pike and married Miss Emma McMahon, and in his later years was a constable. George S. Page and H. C. Everett were in the grocery business. Frank L. Hersey, Taylor Wellington, John B. Hite, Sam Hennon, and others were names synonymous with "first citizens."

In a little younger group than these mentioned was John M. Beale, who was a merchant for many years; Bernhardt Tauber, who came to Guyandotte about 1880 and engaged in the saw and planing mill business until 1899, when he entered the roofing and tile business, and continued therein until he died.

Mary C. Lyons, a daughter of Julius Freutel, for many years successfully carried on business as a general store.

And last but not least were Captain Joe Anderson and Jim Sedinger, the great Democrats of their generation. Many a hot political battle they helped plan in James Murphy's drug store. James Murphy, who took over Page's drug store, and Dr. D. W. Dabney represented the best there was in the medical world. All of this group except H. C. Everett, John M. Beale, and James Murphy have died.

But while these men were going into their middle age a younger set was coming on which included men who have since made their own place in the community, some of whom are still carrying on. We have early recollections of C. W. Thornburg, W. F. Kahler, John Hennon, Frank Clarke, W. C. Dusenberry, and Okey Hayslip, all of whom were enthusiastic Masons and who could be relied upon to travel to Huntington from Guyandotte for any Masonic event. At that time the 3d Avenue Street car line had its eastern terminus on the west side of the Guyandotte Bridge. The story is that W. F. Kahler and some others of the group just mentioned were waiting at the west end of the bridge to take the street car to Huntington where they proposed to take a train for Cincinnati. While they were waiting on the car they saw in Colonel Emmons' lot what they thought was a white rabbit and "Bill" Kahler went over the fence to catch the rabbit. He caught the rabbit all right, but it turned out not to be a rabbit but a skunk and "Bill" abandoned his trip.

The political mantle of these old warriors fell upon a group of younger men all of whom are now past middle age which included Mat W. Dugan, Chal and Carl Poindexter, Stoney and Jim Sedinger, Herb Wells, Ira O. Harrold, Marion Walker, Rich T. Everett, and Wiatt Smith. They were always active politically and as the city elections came every year they had plenty of opportunity to display their talents and they never missed an opportunity.

Guyandotte also had some picturesque characters who were not rated as conservatives. Probably the most outstanding of these were Charley Fry, his wife Ida, and his daughter, Emma. Charley was somewhat turbulent and at the time that Coxey's Army marched on Washington in 1893, the Kelly Division came this way. Charley was anxious to welcome Kelly and his Army into Guyandotte but the town authorities thought otherwise, and Bob Owens, then town marshal, was ordered not to extend to Kelly the freedom of the city. Bob Owens made good on all of his orders and in the argument which followed he shot Charley. On another occasion Charley and his household engaged in a battle with Humpy Sloan which terminated on Bridge Street, in the rear of the Edward Smith house. Charley was on one side of the street and Humpy on the other, exchanging pistol shots which failed to take effect. Emma appeared on the scene armed with a shotgun and Humpy fled around the well house in the Smith yard. Just before he reached shelter Emma fired her trusty piece and peppered Humpy's hump with bird shot. All were indicted and tried. In the trial of Humpy he testified in his own defense that he was on one side of the street behind a tree and that Charley Fry was on the other side behind a telephone pole and that he had fired only in self defense. The prosecutor asked him: "Humpy, what were you doing between the time you drew your pistol and the time you fired?" Humpy promptly answered: "Waiting for Charley Fry to pull his pistol so I could shoot him in self defense." The punishments meted out to the miscreants were light and they soon returned to their haunts on Guyan Street.

In 1909 Guyandotte was given the opportunity to become part of Greater Huntington but her citizens indignantly spurned the opportunity and to emphasize this refusal in the next year 1910, the one hundredth anniversary of its founding, it decided to have a Centennial homecoming. An organization was perfected with John M. Beale, president; H. O. Thornburg, vice president; Wiatt Smith, secretary, and M. W. Dugan, treasurer. An elaborate program was arranged and carried out successfully. The program, of course, included a monster parade. James Murphy had charge of a cavalcade of ladies who were dressed in white, wore red sashes, and rode horseback. They rode from Guyandotte and joined the parade at 3d Avenue and 14th Street, but they were caught in a shower and were thoroughly drenched with the result that the red of the sashes ran and stained the white dresses. The shower was soon over and the celebration proceeded as scheduled. There was a barbecue, a sham battle and the biggest crowd that had ever assembled in the county.

The Centennial celebration being over Guyandotte again resumed the even tenor of its ways. In the spring election, 1911, the question of Guyandotte becoming a part of the City of Huntington was submitted to the vote of the people. On April 11, 1911, at a meeting of the council with O. H. Wells, mayor; C. W. Poindexter, recorder; James Murphy, John M. Beale, F. A. Knight, R. H. Miller, and Wirt Brown, councilmen, present, the vote was canvassed and it appeared that there had been 260 votes for and 70 against the proposal, whereupon the council declared Guyandotte to be a part of the City of Huntington and adjourned *sine die*.

XXXVIII: HARVEYTOWN

FORTY years ago the late Thomas H. Harvey subdivided a tract of land lying along the county road south of Four Pole Creek and along the banks of the Hisey Fork of Four Pole. The lots were cheap and the community grew rapidly. The road in those days crossed Four Pole Creek at a ford at what is now 14th Street, West, and for many years the building of a bridge at or near this point was agitated. This was the issue in more than one political campaign and about thirty years ago the present bridge across Four Pole Creek was built.

A short time after that the road from the south end of the bridge for a short distance was paved and later the hardsurfacing was continued to the Wayne County line. The result of this improvement is that many good homes have been built along this road and the community supports churches, stores, schools, and many substantial homes. Recently it was included within the corporate limits of the City of Huntington. Its citizens are active participants in political affairs and it manfully asserts its right to be called Harveytown.

To emphasize its individuality Harveytown has the unique distinction of having a small glass plant which manufactures only communion glasses and these glasses are sold all over the United States. The plant is owned and operated by Shelby Earls, a glass blower who was thrown out of work four years ago and built a small plant on his premises. The first plant was of the crudest type but has been added to from time to time. Earls, assisted by his son and brother-in-law, and five or six hired helpers, operates the plant.

XXXIX: THE LOST CITY

IT has been mentioned that the State Road first reached the Ohio River at a point about three miles below the mouth of the Guyandotte River. This was on Lot 37 of the Savage Grant which was owned by the Brown family and in 1812 was owned by Richard and Benjamin Brown. There was a good river landing at this point for the reason that the water in the river is of sufficient depth at all seasons of the year for steam and other boats to land. The point was first named South Landing. It was incorporated by the General Assembly at a session of 1831-1832 under the name of Brownsville. The town was then laid off by Claude Crozet, the great French engineer who had served under Napoleon and was State engineer for Virginia. The promoters of the town predicted that it would be the point where the daily stages from Fredericksburg and other places in the east would meet the steamboats on the Ohio and where the "great western Virginia landing will be eventually permanently fixed." The lots, however, do not seem to have been put on the market, and in 1835 it is recorded that there were five or six dwelling houses and two mercantile stores established. The records of the County Court do not disclose that a single lot was ever sold in this village and the entire tract of land owned by the Brown family is now included in the City of Huntington. Brownsville was probably located about 5th or 6th Street, East.

Top—Slave quarters, built about 1830 at the Yates home.
Bottom—Old Mud River bridge near Milton, circa 1835

XL: MILTON

THIS village had its beginning as a way station on the Chesapeake and Ohio Railway. It was named for Milton Rece, a large landowner in that neighborhood. It was chartered on September 16, 1876. At that time the main line of the Chesapeake and Ohio Railway passed through the village but thirty years ago it relocated its line and built its main line about one mile south of Milton. This line is connected with the town by a spur track. The change of the main line railroad has not hurt the town which is also located on Highway 60. It is a prosperous town of 1300 inhabitants, has paved streets, its own water works, nice residences, a bank, flour mill, churches, and a number of good stores. It is the home of the Blenko Glass Company, manufacturers of stained and leaded glass windows. This company was organized by William Blenko, an Englishman. Mr. Blenko had operated a glass plant in England and made two unsuccessful attempts, one in 1893 and a second in 1909, to establish this industry in America. He attributed these failures to the fact that at that time the prevailing opinion was that stained glass could not be made in America and the orders for the finer glass of this character went to England or Germany.

In 1923 Mr. Blenko returned to America and established his plant at Milton—attracted there by the abundance of natural gas as a cheap fuel—although materials that go into the making of the glass are shipped in. This time his venture was a success and this plant produces over four hundred shades and colors of stained glass, some of which have been pronounced by experts to be superior to the Lost Art Colors now seen in the twelfth and thirteenth century examples in Europe. Products of this plant are shipped to every state in the Union and abroad.

William Blenko died in 1934 at the age of seventy-nine, and has been succeeded by his son, W. H. Blenko, who has inherited his father's pride of craftsmanship and is striving to continue the product of a distinctive and colorful line rather than to produce in quantities.

When the depression came and there was small demand for stained glass windows this company utilized its experience in color by beginning the manufacture of vases and tableware manufactured entirely by hand. In this it has been more than successful and is creating a distinctive and colorful product that compares with the best craftsmanship of European or American glass workers.

Not far from Milton is the Old Union Church which Federal soldiers camped around during the Civil War and where portions of the earthworks built by these soldiers can still be seen.

Milton is the birthplace of George I. Neal, one of the greatest political leaders West Virginia has ever produced.

XLI: ONA*

ONA is an unincorporated hamlet at the point of intersection of the Fudge Creek Road with Route 60. Before the Chesapeake and Ohio Railway relocated its main line Ona was a depot. On the north side of Route 60 at this point is Poore Hill on which is located Cabell County's home for aged and infirm white people. From the knoll just above the sign which carries the name of the home it is said the Federal forces placed a small cannon which was fired in the skirmish of August, 1861. C. M. Love, who lives at the Maples a short distance east of this point, has a round shot which was fired on that occasion and is one of two such shots that struck in the yard at the Maples.

Ona has a chain store and a number of substantial dwellings.

---

*Not to be confused with the present Chesapeake and Ohio Railway station of this name.

XLII: SALT ROCK

SALT ROCK is a hamlet on the west side of the Guyandotte River at the point where the bridge on the Lincoln Pike crosses the river. There was a settlement here at a very early date and it is said that the place got its name from the practice of farmers living in this neighborhood, during the summer months when the small streams were dried up, of putting salt on the big rocks near the waters' edge to induce the cattle to come in for salt and water. However, salt was produced from the salt rock which underlies this territory at a very early date and it is possible that the name was derived from this fact.

Thomas Ward, the first sheriff, is said to have produced salt in this neighborhood as early as 1817. There is a deed of record dated June 30, 1830 (Deed Book 4, Page 589), which conveyed a tract of land on Swamp Creek and one of the calls in the deed refers to the creek as emptying into the Guyandotte River near "Wards' Salt Gum."

For the uninitiated we understand that in the early days it was the practice to cut a section of a hollow tree and fix it at a point where it was proposed to dig a salt well then put a man on the inside of the log and let him dig out the well. In this manner the log or gum would sink until the salt rock was reached and the gum served the purpose of a casing.

XLIII: SAINT CLOUD

SAINT CLOUD was an unincorporated village which adjoined the original City of Huntington on the west. It had its beginning when its map was filed on October 31, 1874, and its territory was roughly between 5th Street, West, and 11th Street, West. The present 9th Street, West, was known as Park Street of Saint Cloud. The village lost its identity when it was included in the boundary lines of the new city, Central City, which afterwards became a part of the City of Huntington.

On the east side of 9th Street (west)—once Park Street—is a white two-story frame dwelling standing in a large yard surrounded by splendid trees. This home was built in 1870 by Captain H. Chester Parsons of Vermont before Huntington was incorporated or the Saint Cloud subdivision made. Captain Parsons was an officer in the Union Army. He sustained a serious wound and returned to a farm in Vermont to recuperate. One of his close neighbors was the Abbott family and he talked to them of his purpose to go to the new State of West Virginia. Captain Parsons came to Huntington and was the local attorney for the Chesapeake and Ohio Railway Company, and was on its board of directors. He was a man of affairs and had much to do with the beginning of the city. In 1872 Captain Parsons had a pair of horses in Vermont which he wanted in his new home and his neighbor's son, D. E. Abbott, then a boy in his teens, agreed to and did drive them down. He was on the road three weeks but came through without mishap and spent his first night in Huntington in Captain Parsons' house. Captain Parsons moved to Virginia at an early date and his brother, Warren J. Parsons bought the property and lived there a great many years. Some years ago D. E. Abbott, who had become one of Huntington's outstanding citizens and business men, purchased this property and now makes his home therein.

H. Chester Parson's House, St. Cloud, circa 1870. (Now the residence of D. E. Abbott.)

XLIV: FAMILIES

ABBOTT

FOR almost half a century the name Darwin E. Abbott has been a synonym of all that is best in citizenship because he has been identified with every movement for the advancement of this community.

D. E. Abbott, the son of Mason D. and Angeline M. Abbott, was born April 29, 1856, in the family settlement known as Abbott's Corner, Province of Quebec, about one-half mile from the Vermont line. His father was a native of Abbott's Corner. His mother was born in Orwell, Vermont. The family moved to Vermont when Darwin was a small child and he remained there until 1873, when he drove the horses of H. Chester Parsons from Vermont to Huntington. After he reached the city he attended Marshall College. His first employment after leaving school was making photographs of various places in West Virginia for *Harper's Magazine.* When he completed this work he embarked in the business of a photographer but his ability as an organizer soon asserted itself and he enlarged his business to include the making of large portraits, picture frames, etc. It was not long before he acquired the lot at the northeast corner of 4th Avenue and 9th Street and erected thereon a three-story building, the upper stories of which he used in his business. The business prospered and in 1900 he incorporated the D. E. Abbott and Company and moved its plant to 14th Street, Central City, now West Huntington, where he has established one of the largest businesses of its kind in this section of the United States. Some years ago he sold the manufacturing and plant equipment to Cravens-Green Company but continued his own business in a smaller way to give employment to his faithful employees.

D. E. Abbott has not sought public office but has served as a member of the city council, president of the first citizen's board, and has been director of the Chamber of Commerce and served as its president a number of times. Governor A. B. White named him a colonel on his staff.

He is president of the Foster Foundation, a charitable institution endowed by the late B. W. Foster which maintains a home for aged ladies and assists worthy young men and women in securing an education.

D. E. Abbott married in 1884 Elizabeth B. Driggs of Huntington, daughter of Captain B. P. Driggs. She died in 1924. They had no children. Mr. Abbott lives in the old Parsons' home at 9th Street, West, in which he spent the first night upon his arrival in Huntington in 1873.

D. E. Abbott had four sisters: Mary, married John B. Stevenson; Mae, married Henry M. Ensign; Leonore, married A. Higgins; and Harriet, married J. W. Forsinger of Chicago, Illinois.

MONSIGNOR HENRY B. ALTMEYER, LL.D.

Monsignor Altmeyer was born in Wheeling, January 5, 1870, the fourth of the nine children of Jacob and Martha (Quinn) Altmeyer. His paternal grandfather, John Altmeyer, came from Alsace-Lorraine, his maternal grandfather from County Tyrone, Ireland.

Father Altmeyer attended the parochial school at Benwood, the public school at Bellaire, Ohio, Duquesne University, St. Vincent's, and St. Mary's On his ordination to the priesthood in Wheeling in 1897, he was assigned as assistant at the cathedral, acting, at the same time, as Bishop Donahoe's secretary. He was promoted to Huntington, in succession to Father Werninger, in 1899, and remained parish priest of Huntington until his death on August 22, 1930.

When Father Altmeyer came to Huntington as pastor of St. Joseph's, he found a promising parish of sixty-five good families. In the thirty years of his pastorate, Father Altmeyer saw his parish become one of nearly 500 families, with a membership of 1,800 souls; erected the present grade school; enlarged and completed the church; moved the former parish house a lot east and remodelled it into the present convent; built the present parish house; purchased the present high school lot, upon which he erected a temporary high school and gymnasium that preceded the existing St. Joseph's High School. During his pastorate, St. Edward's College Preparatory School was closed, the buildings and grounds becoming the property of the Pallottine Missionary Sisters, who were introduced into this diocese by Most Reverend J. J. Swint, Bishop of Wheeling. These Sisters now manage the splendid St. Mary's Hospital, which has proved a boon to the entire community.

In 1923, Father Altmeyer was made a Domestic Prelate to His Holiness, Pope Pius XI, with title of Monsignor. Monsignor Altmeyer was widely known as a lecturer and writer, his works comprising several books of sermons, a dissertation on "Christianity," and two valuable pamphlets, one devotional, the "Way of the Cross," the other educational, "Practical Essentials of Canon Law."

During the World War, Father Altmeyer was a four-minute speaker, and a patriotic laborer, always at the beck and call of his country. He was a 4th degree Knight of Columbus, a member of the order for a quarter of a century. He was, furthermore, a member of International Rotary. A patient, wise, and good man, Father Altmeyer was ideally fitted for life in the priesthood anywhere, but seemed especially fitted for his work in Huntington, where, at his death, he was universally mourned.

ARCHER

The career of Robert L. Archer has been intimately interwoven with that of Huntington. He is outstanding as a civic leader, a man of broad culture, a churchman and a patriot.

Mr. Archer is of direct English descent, from a family that dates back to the days of William the Norman. His father, Thomas Archer came to the United States from England in 1849, and settled at Cleves, Hamilton County, Ohio. Thomas Archer's first wife died there. In 1868 he married Francis Louise Mather, a descendant of a long line of illustrious New England ancestors, amongst whom was the Rev. Richard Mather, who came to Massachusetts in 1635, and the Rev. Increase Mather, who was president of Harvard University from 1688 to 1701, as well as the famous Cotton Mather, New England divine and author.

To Thomas Archer and Frances (Mather) Archer were born three sons, Richard Mather Archer, who died in Wheeling in 1930; Robert Lamley Archer; and Frank Mather Archer, now a resident of Bluefield. Frances (Mather) Archer was also the mother of a daughter, Emily Mather Richey, by a former marriage.

Mr. and Mrs. Thomas Archer settled in Huntington in 1871. Until the time of his death in 1877, Mr. Archer conducted a retail coal business at the corner of 2d Avenue and 10th Street. After his death, Mrs. Archer continued the business several years, thus becoming the first and only business woman here at that time. Later she and her daughter, Miss Richey engaged in the mercantile business as E. M. Richey and Company. Mrs. Archer, mother of Robert L. Archer, died in 1917 at the age of eighty-four.

Robert L. Archer began his career as a collection clerk in the old First National Bank in 1890, and was successively bookkeeper, teller, assistant cashier, and cashier, until his election as vice president in 1920. He continued with the First National Bank until shortly before his election as president of the Union Bank and Trust Company, which he served as president from 1923 to 1931. Since then Mr. Archer has been engaged in the investment and insurance business.

Robert L. Archer was married on September 20, 1893, at West Columbia, to Irma Louise Knight, daughter of Dr. A. L. Knight, who served as a surgeon in the 8th Virginia Cavalry, C.S.A.

Mr. Archer was secretary and treasurer of the West Virginia Bankers' Association from 1901 to 1903: president of the same association from 1903 to 1904; member of the executive council of the American Bankers' Association from 1908 to 1911; director of the Huntington Chamber of Commerce from 1920 to 1924, and 1927 to 1933; and president of the Huntington Association of Credit Men from 1916 to 1918.

His record as a patriot and civic leader includes such services as captain and adjutant of the West Virginia National Guard, from 1890 to 1893; first lieutenant and adjutant second regiment, West Virginia Volunteer Infantry, Spanish-American War; chairman of the first and second Liberty Loan campaigns, World War; State director of War Savings for West Virginia 1917-1918; director, Rotary Club, 1918-1920, 1922-1924, 1927-1929; president, Rotary Club, 1923-1924; member of board of education, 1910-1918; member, Sons of American Revolution; member, Founders and Patriots of America; member of the vestry, Trinity Episcopal Church; deputy to general convention Episcopal Church, 1922, 1925, 1928, and 1931.

As a writer Mr. Archer has made several notable contributions to various magazines. His articles include "Early American Financing (1774-1850)"; "Financing the Civil War"; "Financing the Confederacy"; "What are Greenbacks?"; "Cleveland and the Gold Standard"; "Free Silver Campaign of 1896"; "Currency Inflation in France (1789-1797)"; "The Contest for the Ohio Valley"; "The Ohio Valley Before the Revolution"; "The Ohio Valley During the Revolution"; "The Ohio Valley After the Revolution," and "Organization of the Federal Reserve System."

BEUHRING

Frederick George Louis Beuhring was born March 31, 1792, in Scharmbuk, a suburb of Bremen, Germany, and died in Cabell County, June 27, 1859. His father held a government position but

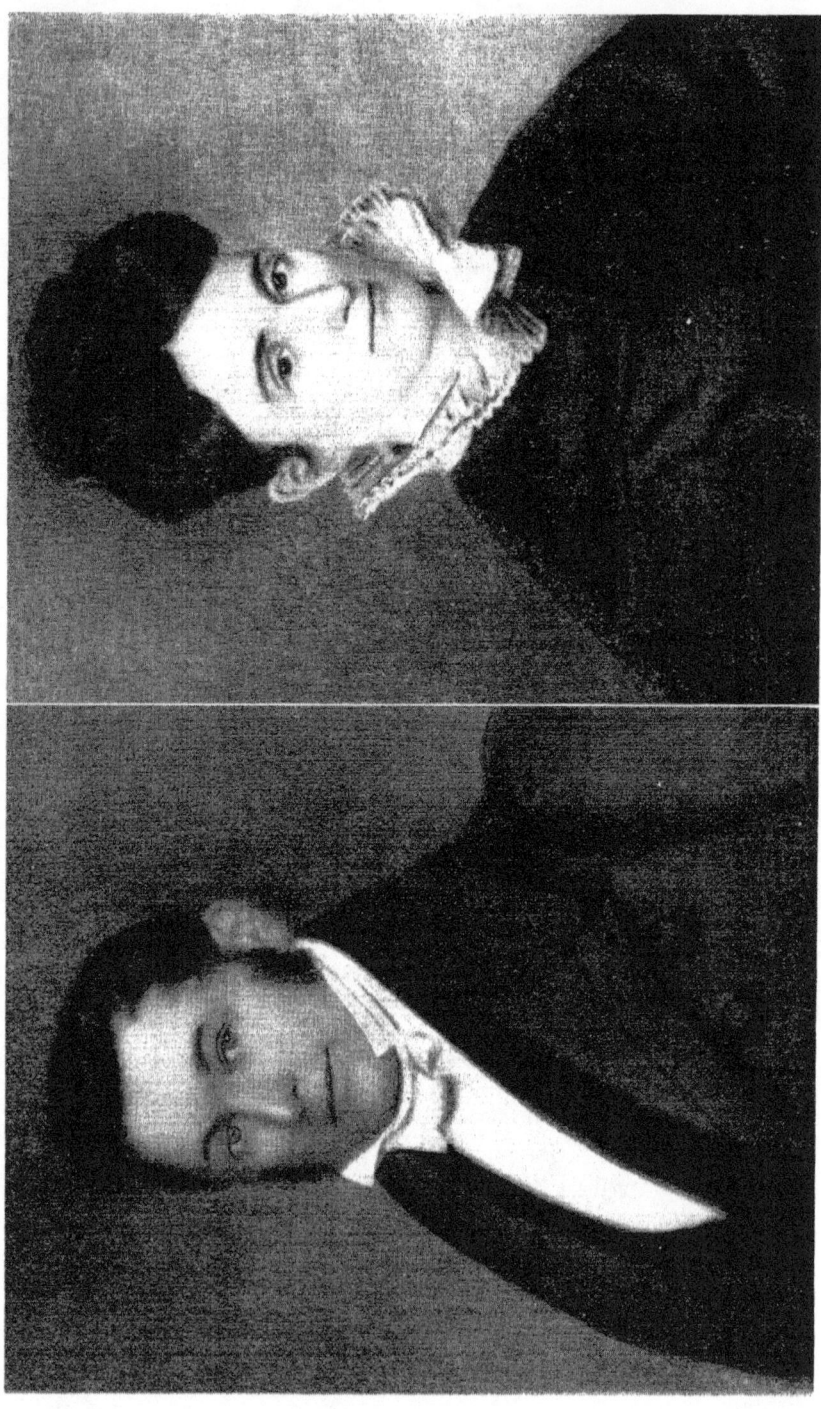

Frederick G. L. Beuhring, born 1792, died 1859, an early sheriff and member of the Legislature. Frances Dannenberg Beuhring, born 1797, died 1841

[350]

died when Mr. Beuhring was quite young. Frederick Beuhring came to America and located in Baltimore early in the nineteenth century. He was connected with the firm Konig and Company, the biggest wholesale shipping and importing house in the city of Baltimore. This business took him to the West Indies, Yucatan and many states of the Union. He spoke several languages and was a man of great activity and energy. At the time of the British invasion in the War of 1812 he joined a volunteer force in the defense of Baltimore. He moved to Cabell County at a date not known, but the court records show that he served as a juryman on May 3, 1819. He took an immediate interest in public affairs and was known for his open and fearless advocacy of the side he espoused.

In the year 1820 Mr. Beuhring married Frances Eleanora Dannenberg (June 1, 1797-June 16, 1841) at Château Blanch the country home of her uncle, Frederick Konig. She was the daughter of Frederick Dannenberg of New York, who had come to this country, shortly after the Revolutionary War, from Coerland, a part of Russia that had belonged to Germany, and Dorothea Louisa Konig (married April 16, 1795) who had come from Hamburg, Germany with her parents and brother, Frederick Konig, and her sister, Eliza Konig, who after Louisa's death in 1803 married Dannenberg as his second wife.

Shortly after their marriage, Mr. and Mrs. Beuhring came to Barboursville and remained there till about 1836 when they bought the beautiful place on the Ohio River called Maple Grove. This had been the home of Major Nathaniel Scales and was situated at the place in the present city of Huntington just above 7th Street, and extended up on the hill. The headquarters of the Daughters of the American Revolution is the spot where the keeper of the Beuhring vineyard lived.

The Beuhrings lived at Maple Grove with their four children, Anna Maria, born June 1, 1821; Louisa Mayer, born May 27, 1825; Frederick Konig Dannenberg, born July 17, 1828; and Emma Adelaide, born January 12, 1832, until the oldest daughter married in 1840 and moved to Charleston. Mrs. Beuhring died in 1841.

Mr. Beuhring married again and died June 27, 1859. He and his first wife now lie in Spring Hill Cemetery at Huntington.

I.

Mary (Anna Maria) Beuhring married James Madison Laidley,

nephew of John O. Laidley of Lamartine, April 14, 1840, and died November, 1904.

Their ten children were:

A. Frederick Alexander, married Julia Rooke and had four children: Rooke,[1] Elsie,[2] Margaret,[3] and Mary Beuhring.[4]
B. Frances Amelia, single.
C. Harriet Corinne, married Dunbar Baines, and had one daughter: Alys,[1] single.
D. Mary Rowena, single.
E. John James, married Josephine Wilson, and had seven children:
   1. Florence, married Frank Field and had two children:
      a. Frank Field, married Virginia Chenoweth; two children: Frank[1] and Virginia[2].
      b. Virginia, married Edward Hutchinson.
   2. Lillian, married Fred Johnstone, has one child:
      a. Anne Frederick.
   3. Virginia Beuhring, married Robert Keck.
   4. Anna, married Edwin E. Raine and has one child:
      a. Anne Laidley.
   5. Josephine, deceased.
   6. Dick, married Gladys Lanham and has one child:
      a. Frances.
   7. Clarence, deceased.
F. Emma Louisa, married Henry Whitteker and had two children:
   1. May, deceased.
   2. Robert, married Grace Williams and had one child:
      a. Keith, married Eugene Smith.
G. George Summers, well-known educator, married Cora Bradford (first wife) and Mary Byrd Fontaine (second wife). He had four children by his first wife:
   1. George, single.
   2. Lillian, married William Buck.
   3. William Dannenberg, married Hannah Tamplin; had four children:
      a. Lillian Bradford, married William Hughey.
      b. Mary Elizabeth.
      c. Bradford Dannenberg, Junior.
      d. Amelia Jo.
   4. Bradford, married Mary Rogers.

FAMILIES 353

H. Annie, married Fred Johnstone and had three children:
  1. Lynn, married Grace Pugh and had one child:
    a. Florence Mildred.
  2. Mildred, deceased.
  3. Fred, married Lillian Laidley and had one daughter:
    a. Ann Frederick.
I. Madison Monroe, married Fannie Smith and had three daughters.
J. Juliette Shrewsbury, married J. G. Eskew; had four children:
  1. Juliette Shrewsbury married Paul G. Edmunds; two children:
    a. John Venable.
    b. Polly Gray.
  2. Garnet Laidlaw, married Nancy Beatty.
  3. Roderick Koenig, married Agnes Brown, had one child:
    a. Juliette.
  4. Mary Lovell, married Arthur Loring Pitman, has one child:
    a. James Eskew.

II.

Louisa Mayer Beuhring, graduated from Steubenville Female Academy in April, 1841, married James Henry Brown who lived on the adjoining farm (just below 7th Street, in the present city of Huntington) on September 12, 1844, and lived first at Maple Grove, then at Beechgrove on Four Pole Creek where their first child, Virginia, was born September 23, 1847. In 1848 or 1849 Mr. and Mrs. Brown moved to Charleston, and shortly after bought the Elms. This place, though now in the heart of the city, is still occupied by their grandchildren and great-grandchildren, the property coming down through their son, James Frederick Brown. (More about this family under head of Brown).

III.

Frederick Beuhring (born March 12, 1838, died October 12, 1882) married first, Fannie Miller, in 1857, at Guyandotte.
A. Emma, married Ira J. McGinnis; one son:
  1. Ira J. on December 10, 1911, married Mabel E. Chapman; has three children:
    a. Eloise.
    b. Lyle.
    c. Betty.

B. Virginia Elenor, married John Lee Hawkins; five children:
  1. Nannie Lee, married Harvey Carter Taylor; six children:
     a. Harvey Carter, Junior, married Dorothy Aleen Frantz.
     b. Nancy Beuhring.
     c. John Wallace.
     d. Charles Henry Kennon.
     e. Marjery Trueheart.
     f. Elinore.
  2. Fred Marshall, married Anna White; four children:
     a. Virginia White.
     b. Betty Hanbury.
     c. John.
     d. Fred.
  3. Louise Beuhring, married Adrian Bastianelli; four children:
     a. Adrian.
     b. Harry.
     c. Barbara.
     d. Raphael.
  4. John Howell, married Irene Kelly; two children:
     a. Mary Howell.
     b. Irene.
  5. Elinore, married J. Calvin Sheets.
C. Lee Davis, married Mame Hovey; three children:
  1. Lucille, unmarried.
  2. Raymond, a graduate of Washington and Lee University, a lawyer and served in A.E.F., married Dorothea Sandman.
  3. Frances, married W. E. Brinker.
D. Mary Louisa, married John Davis; three children:
  1. Frances Miller, married Edward Prichard; one daughter:
     a. Louise Beuhring.
  2. Henry Winter (Bill) unmarried, killed in action in the A.E.F., on October 14, 1918.
  3. Paul Dannenberg (Jack), married Nan Temple; no children.
E. Henry, married Ora Peyton (died ten days after marriage).
F. Frederick, unmarried, died of typhoid at age of eighteen.
G. Edgar Francis, married Nancy Lee Slater.
H. Nora Belle (Bird), married Marshall Hawkins; two children:
  1. Edward Donald.

FAMILIES

2. Howard Burk, married Mary McGregor; one child:
   a. James Marshall.
I. Walter Dannenberg, married Lilian Huff and had one son:
   1. Robert Beuhring.
Frederick Beuhring married a second time and had two sons, Victor and Harold Earl.

IV.

Emma Beuhring, married August 26, 1856, Howell Lovell; six children:
A. Betty Lewis, died in infancy.
B. Frederick Beuhring, died in infancy.
C. Mary Louisa, married J. William Sayre and died 1935; two children:
   1. Howell Lovell, died single.
   2. Wilhelma, married Dudley Short; had one son:
      a. Marion.
D. Howell Lewis, Junior, married May Rogers, no children.
E. Frances Beuhring, single, deceased.
F. Virginia Lee, married John Hodge, no children.

BILLUPS

The first of this name in Virginia was George Billups who came in 1653 and had a grant from Richard Bennett, Esquire, Knight Governor, etc., for 750 acres of land located in what is now Matthews County, Virginia, on which some of his descendants still live, although many of them have followed the course of the empire to the west.

Samuel Billups migrated from Virginia at an early date to that part of Cabell County now included in Wayne County and lived at Billups' Gap on Tabor Creek about two and a half miles from Fort Gay. He had a family of six boys and three girls. One of his sons, John L., born 1842, died February 19, 1928, served in the same regiment C.S.A. with Judge Thomas H. Harvey and was high sheriff of Wayne County, 1905-08. He lived one mile out of Fort Gay, married Mary Frances Wellman, born 1844 and who is still living. To this union were born:

1. Sarah, married Lat Bowe, half brother of J. F. Ratcliff.
2. Ida, married Hope Wellman of Catlettsburg.
3. Bunia, married Mat Rowe.
4. Dora, married Dr. J. F. York.

5. Virginia, married a Riggins and lives in Illinois.
6. Ella, married J. L. Stewart.
7. Mary Frances, married Oliver Ritz and lives in Edwards, Illinois.
8. Fred, married Clara Frazier.
9. Burt, married Bessie Ratcliff.
10. John S., born September 8, 1880, married December 22, 1903, Emma Sipple of Fort Gay. Their children were Margaret Frances, who died in infancy, and Harold E.

John L. Billups engaged in the mercantile business, and as a partner with John Y. York was engaged in the timber business in a big way for more than thirty years. He was a man whose yea was yea and whose nay was nay and known as a man whose word was as good as his bond, and one of the most successful men of his county. His son, John S., was educated in the common schools at Fort Gay and at Louisa, Kentucky, and studied telegraphy at Shelbyville, Kentucky, but never took employment in that capacity.

John S. Billups worked in a clerical position until his father was elected sheriff in 1904, when he was made a deputy and served in that position during his father's term of office and then four years more as deputy to Sam J. Crum. In 1920 he was elected sheriff and served a full term of four years. After leaving the sheriff's office he went into the road contracting business in which he is still engaged.

He moved to Huntington in 1922, and in 1931 became a candidate on the Democratic ticket for city commissioner, won the nomination and in the general election which followed he was the only Democrat elected. His tenure of office was marked by the practical common sense which he applied to all matters arising before him. When he was urged by a local committee of road enthusiasts to approve a levy of $15,000 a year for six years to be used to extend Route 60 on the north side of the Chesapeake and Ohio Railway west of Camden Crossing he declined to do so, but upon the contrary brought about the change of the western limits of the city of Huntington, leaving this portion of the road in Wayne County, and it was later built by the State Road Commission. After the fill west of Camden Park had been completed another committee of road enthusiasts appeared before the commission and urged that gravel costing $5,000.00 be put on top of the road before it had settled. John Billups again applied his road experience and declined to do it, giving as a reason that it would be clear loss. Time has vindicated his judgment.

Radio cars were needed for the police department and the city was

FAMILIES 357

without funds to buy them. John Billups appealed to the merchants and $1,000 was donated and radio cars were installed.

The jobs that he did on the undergrade crossings with FERA and CWA labor speak for themselves.

BOSTICK

One of the first gentlemen justices and delegates to the General Assembly was Manoah Bostick. Who he was or from whence he came is not known. He was named as one of the defendants in the chancery suit to partition the Savage Grant, and the records show that he purchased 100 acres of this grant in 1814.

He was an active trader in land and owned at one time some 1,200 acres, and at different times had as many as thirty-six trust deeds on other tracts. In 1833 he sold 150 acres of land on Four Pole to William Buffington, which disposed of his last interest in the county. This deed was acknowledged before a notary in Montgomery County, Tennessee. Apparently he had removed there.

Manoah Bostick married Jency Scales, who died in 1819, and nothing is known of his descendants.

BRADSHAW

George D. Bradshaw, one of the leading merchants of the city and president of the Huntington Chamber of Commerce, is the son of Dr. J. E. Bradshaw and Jenny Linn Jewell. He was born in Wayne County, New York, July 29, 1872, attended the public schools of that county, and Leavenworth Institute at Wolcott, New York. He first planned to study medicine but abandoned the idea and embarked upon what has been a successful business career.

Mr. Bradshaw in 1895 went to Syracuse, New York, and spent five years with Dey Brothers and Company. He left Dey Brothers and spent another five years in the D. McCarthy Department Store. He was then given two years leave of absence and went to Newark, Ohio, to assist in the formulation of a plan to organize a department store in that city and became president of the Powers Miller Company. He held this position five years, leaving to take a position as merchandise manager of the David C. Biggs Company, Columbus, Ohio, the largest department store in that city. It occupied a nine-story building and had forty-four departments.

In 1911 he joined Henry Zenner in the purchase of the Biggs Wilson Dry Goods Company which occupied the beautiful white front building on 4th Avenue on the present site of the Keith Albee Theater, and organized the Zenner Bradshaw Company. This company continued in business until December, 1925, when the building and the entire stock of merchandise was destroyed by fire. Mr. Bradshaw spent the next twelve months adjusting insurance claims and liquidating the company. He was then invited to join the McMahon Diehl Company, which he did and became its president and the name was changed to the Bradshaw Diehl Company. In 1932 Mayor Floyd S. Chapman died and the common council elected Mr. Bradshaw mayor to fill out the unexpired term which ended June, 1934. Mayor Bradshaw's administration was marked by his conservative good sense, and his application of business principles to city government, and he was a fine example of a business man in politics.

George D. Bradshaw married on September 15, 1909, Grace Devine of Newark, Ohio. They have no children.

Mr. Bradshaw takes a keen interest in civic affairs and has given much time and attention to the Chamber of Commerce. He is a member of the Methodist Episcopal Church, the Masonic bodies, including the Shrine, and the Elks.

He comes from old American lineage. His father, Dr. J. E. Bradshaw, was born August 26, 1849, in Sodus, now Wayne County, New York, and died at Clifton Springs, New York, March 7, 1933. He was educated at the Chili Seminary and the Buffalo University, graduating from the latter institution in medicine in 1876. Dr. Bradshaw married on June 1, 1871, Jennie Linn Jewell, who was born in Ithaca, New York, 1852, and died in 1881. She was of English descent on the paternal side and Holland Dutch on the maternal side. To this union were born two children. The second child was Franklin, born February, 1881, and died in infancy.

Dr. J. E. Bradshaw was the son of Edmund D. Bradshaw, born March 17, 1823, died March 27, 1892, and married June, 1848, Elizabeth Goewey, born in Warren County, New York, 1826, and died 1913. She was one of twelve children of Solomon and Polly Goewey. Elizabeth Goewey was a descendant on the maternal side from Elder Brewer, who came over on the *Mayflower*. Edmund D. Bradshaw, grandfather of George D. Bradshaw, was the second son and one of the seven children of James Bradshaw, born in Sodus, now Wayne County, New York, 1787, and the son of John Bradshaw, an Englishman who had migrated to Massachusetts, and his wife, Ennis Wood, born September 23, 1800, died October 29, 1875, who was a member of an old central New York family of English origin.

BROH

The man who has solved the age-old problem how to grow old gracefully is Julius Broh. For many years one of Huntington's successful business men he acquired a competency and several years ago began to drop his business cares and now with only the burdens incident to the presidency of the Huntington Coca-Cola Company he is enjoying his retirement. He is active mentally and physically and is doing now what he always did—helping in any movement that is for the betterment of the community.

Julius Broh is the son of Adolph Broh who was born in Germany and migrated to America when seventeen years of age and settled in Memphis, Tennessee. Adolph Broh moved to Cincinnati, Ohio, where he married in 1862, Jettie, daughter of Solomon Rose who was born in Germany. Jettie was born in New Orleans. To this union was born: Mike, Dan, Julius, Eph, Sidney, Harry L., Belle, Lillian, Mayme, and Rose. The family moved to Cynthiana, Kentucky, and then to Mt. Sterling, Kentucky. The father was a Confederate soldier, a successful business man, and was able in 1887 to establish his two sons, Mike and Julius in the clothing business in the city of Huntington under the firm name of Broh Brothers, and two years later he bought and later sold them the lot at the southeast corner of 9th Street and 3d Avenue, on which they built a brick building, still known as the Broh Corner. Julius and Mike Broh were successful from the start and were charter members of the Ohev Sholom Congregation. Julius has served as president and secretary of this congregation. They assisted in the organization of the Chamber of Commerce, The Guyandot Club, the first Country Club, the Automobile Club and the Business Men's Club. Mike Broh served as president of the Chamber of Commerce, the Huntington Business Men's Association and was up to the time of his death an active director and a member of the executive committee of the First Huntington National Bank.

After Julius and Mike Broh had become well established in business and began to succeed they brought their parents to Huntington where they spent their last years. They also brought their brothers Eph, Harry, Sidney, and their sister, Mrs. Ed. Meyerson and her husband, to the new city where they have all made a place for themselves. Harry was particularly active in the Masonic Order.

Julius Broh married first, Fannie Moses of Charleston, West Virginia, and had a daughter, Evelyn, who married Harry Polan of Charleston. Fannie Moses Broh died in 1920 and in the same year Harry L. Broh died and left a widow and son, Harry L., Jr. Three years later, Julius Broh married Ruth Broh, the widow of Harry L. Broh.

Mike Broh married Ida Gideon, and had a son Herman L. who died while a student at the University of Virginia, and a daughter, Dorothy, who married Ben Frank, an architect in Baltimore, Maryland. Mike Broh died in 1931.

Julius Broh has given generously to his church and to other worthy charities and he has been particularly generous in his gifts to the fund to buy park lands for the city.

DOUGLAS WALTER BROWN

Douglas Walter Brown was born at Hillsville, the county seat of Carroll County, Virginia, on August 11, 1877, the son of Douglas Baker Brown and Mary Lindsey, his wife. His grandfather, the Rev. Lee C. Brown, who founded and for several years conducted the Studium, a small classical school in Southwestern Virginia, came to Hillsville as the pastor of its Presbyterian church and a member of the faculty of Ben Thompson Academy, a boys' school. His father, Douglas Baker Brown, the youngest of four sons, received a thorough academic training under his parents and had commenced the study of law at the outbreak of the Civil War. Enlisting with his three brothers in the first company of volunteers from Carroll County, he served throughout the war in Pickett's famous division and, upon returning home, abandoned his legal studies to marry and commence teaching in the schools of Carroll County.

Douglas Walter was the youngest of six children. During his early years his father was superintendent of schools of Carroll County and the publisher of a newspaper in Hillsville. When he was still quite young his family moved to Washington where his father took a position with the United States Department of Public Printing; but after a few years they returned to Virginia and his father became the head of Wytheville Male Academy at Wytheville. Mr. Brown's formal education was received in the public schools of Washington and under his father at Wytheville Male Academy. At the age of sixteen he entered the office of Frank S. Blair, a former attorney general of Virginia, at Wytheville, and read law while working as a stenographer.

At the age of twenty-one Mr. Brown came to Williamson, then a rising young town in the rapidly developing Mingo County coal fields. There he commenced the practice of law and, in 1902, married Mary Glidden Williams, the daughter of John E. Williams, a coal operator in the Mingo territory, and Flora Glidden Williams.

Mr. Brown made Cabell County his home in 1919 when he moved to Huntington and formed a partnership with the late Judge C. W. Campbell and Cary N. Davis. Ten years later the firm became Fitzpatrick, Campbell, Brown and Davis upon association with Herbert Fitzpatrick, the surviving member of the older firm of Enslow, Fitzpatrick and Baker, and a few years later the name was changed to Fitzpatrick, Brown and Davis when Judge Campbell retired.

Universally considered one of the leading lawyers of the State, Mr. Brown has brought recognition to Cabell County through his outstanding professional ability. He was president of the Cabell County Bar Association about 1915, president of the West Virginia Bar Association in 1922, and has been a member of the general council of the American Bar Association since 1927. His wife, a graduate of Chicago Conservatory of Music, where she studied violin and piano, in addition to prominence in musical, club and civic activities in Huntington, is well known in politics. She was delegate-at-large to the Democratic National Convention in 1932 and State chairman of the woman's division of NRA in 1934. Among other positions in the local and State organizations of her party, Mrs. Brown organized and was the first president of the Young Women's Democratic Clubs of the State and has been associate chairman of the Cabell County Democratic Committee since 1924.

Mr. and Mrs. Brown have six living children and three grandchildren. The eldest, Walter Lindsey, a graduate of the University of Virginia and Oxford University, England, married Dorothy Ann Rardin of Huntington. John E. Williams, educated at Augusta Military Academy, Virginia, and the University of Virginia, married Lynda Jeanne Potter of Memphis, Tennessee, and has a son, Douglas W. Brown, III. Both of the elder sons are associated with their father in the practice of law. Charlotte Helen, educated at Sweet Briar College, Virginia, and Marshall College, Huntington, married Philip Bradley Harder, of Philmont, New York, and resides there with her husband and two children, Judith Glidden Harder and Charlotte Van

Dr. Henry Brown House, 2nd Avenue, between 4th and 5th Streets. Built by Richard Brown about 1810 and said to have been the first brick house in Cabell County.

Slyke Harder. Of the remaining children, all unmarried, Flo Glidden, educated at Marshall College, The Castle, Tarrytown-on-the-Hudson, New York, and Sweet Briar College, resides with her parents, while Douglas W., Junior, and William Campbell are students at the University of Virginia.

JAMES HENRY BROWN

Sir William Brown of England was one of the adventurers named in the Virginia Charter of May 23, 1609, granted by James I to Robert, Earl of Salisbury, and others. He had a son (1) Colonel Henry Brown, member of the Virginia Council of 1642, who was the father of (2) William Brown of Rappahannock County, Virginia, and a member of the House of Burgesses 1659-1660, from Surry County. This William Brown had a son (3) Maxfield of Richmond County, born 1675, died 1745, who married Elizabeth Newman and had a son (4) George Brown of King George County, who was the father of (5) George Newman Brown of Prince William County, Virginia, who was a soldier in the Revolutionary War and present at the battle of Yorktown. His wife was Sarah Hampton of Bloomsbury, a near relative of General Wade Hampton of South Carolina.

George Newman Brown and his two sons, Richard and Benjamin, acquired an interest in the Savage Grant.

Dr. Benjamin Brown, together with his two brothers, Henry and Richard, came from Prince William County, Virginia, in 1805 to what was then Kanawha County (now Cabell) and settled in the wilderness between Guyandotte and the Great Tatteroi (now Big Sandy). They built and lived in a hewn log house which has been framed over and which still stands at the corner of 6th Street and 13th Avenue, lately occupied by Dr. H. E. Summers.

Henry Brown, son of George Newman Brown, was the second Sheriff of Cabell County and was killed during the discharge of his official duty in 1810.

George Newman Brown (5) by deed dated January 17, 1812, conveyed his undivided interest in the Savage Grant to his sons Richard and Benjamin Brown. Afterwards, John Laidley, named as special commissioner in the chancery suit of Coleman et al vs. Morgan, in which the Savage Grant was partitioned, conveyed to Benjamin Brown and Richard Brown, by deed dated February 1, 1821, two hundred acres of Lot 37, of the Savage Grant lying now between 4th and 7th Streets, fronting on the Ohio River and extending back to the hills, Richard Brown to have one hundred acres along the Ohio River, and Benjamin Brown to have one hundred acres on the back part of the tract along Four Pole Creek.

Richard Brown built, sometime later, the brick residence, a part of which still stands on 2d Avenue just west of 5th Street and which was afterwards owned in turn by Albert Laidley and Dr. P. H. Mc-Cullough. This house is said to have been the first brick residence in this county. At or near this residence was a store and boat landing and the place in early days was first known as South Landing and later as Brownsville.

Richard Brown married Sarah Haney of Bourbon County, Kentucky, and later sold his farm to his brother Benjamin and moved to the forks of Sandy. He had a number of children, one of whom was Judge George Newman Brown, father of the late Thomas R. Brown of Catlettsburg, Kentucky, and grandfather of George B. Martin, distinguished lawyer and one-time United States Senator from Kentucky.

Dr. Benjamin Brown was born in 1786 and died in 1848. He married Matilda Scales, youngest daughter of Nathaniel Scales, a Revolutionary soldier, and was one of the most successful physicians in Cabell County, practicing on both sides of the Ohio River, up the Guyandotte, Big Sandy and in Four Pole Valley. He had four children:

I. James Henry, married Louisa M. Beuhring, daughter of Frederick George Lewis Beuhring.

II. Vesta, married Albert Laidley; their children were Alberta and John.

III. Ceres, born April 10, 1821, in Cabell County, Virginia. She attended school in the old log schoolhouse near the Ohio River on the James Holderby farm before Marshall Academy was erected, then attended school at the academy, and also at Marietta, Ohio. She possessed a mind of extraordinary quickness and vigor, well-stored with knowledge, the accumulated treasures of books, travel and observation. Her wit and humor were mingled with sympathy with human suffering which made her whole life a labor of love and charity to others, especially the poor, the sick, and the unfortunate. She was beloved by all who knew her. She early united with the Presbyterian church and through life showed her religion more in works than in words. She left a vacancy in the family circle which could not be filled nor forgotten, as was shown by having a great niece

Matilda Scales, born in North Carolina, 1797, died October 28, 1878. Wife of Dr. Benjamin Brown

named for her. She died at the home of James H. Brown in Charleston, July 20, 1866.

IV. Josephine, born February 5, 1826, died April 25, 1885. She married on February 5, 1846, the Rev. Robert Osborne, born August 27, 1813, died July, 1878, a Presbyterian minister, and to this union were born nine children: Ethan Brown and Anna Matilda who died in childhood; Maria Mitchell, born January 28, 1852; Benjamin Brown, born February 17, 1854, married Alice Waugh Stevens and had three children, Robert, Sydney who married Josephine Miller, and Josephine; Mary Elizabeth, born February 13, 1856, who became an influential woman physician; James Robert, born October 15, 1858, died in July, 1882, who was a lawyer; Virginia Alberta, born September 4, 1860, a very successful teacher of deaf mutes; Sara Josephine, born March 28, 1863, who devoted many years to nursing the sick; and John, born August 22, 1865, who married Virginia E. Wolgamuth and died in Philadelphia.

James Henry Brown, born in Cabell County, December 25, 1818, died October 28, 1900, attended Marietta College, graduated from Augusta College, Kentucky, read law with the late John Laidley, Senior, of Cabell County and was admitted to the bar in 1842. He practiced a circuit in Cabell, Wayne, Logan, Mason, Jackson, and Kanawha, and in Federal and appellate courts.

He moved in 1848 to Kanawha County and ever after made Charleston his home.

"As Circuit Judge under the Commonwealth of Virginia, he was one of those strong, determined men, who, amid the perils of Civil war, inaugurated and successfully conducted the movement to erect a new and sovereign State from the counties of the Old Dominion lying west of the Alleghenies, and was one of the judges of the first Supreme Court of Appeals of the new State and later president of that court. He was a finished lawyer and speaker, and of wide reputation for ability and scholarly attainments, for his force of character and loyalty to his convictions; and more, he was a man of decision and action. He early took interest in matters of public concern and an active part in political contests, State and National, which preceded the war."

When the clouds of war began to gather he did not hesitate but took position for the maintenance of the Union, and threw himself into the struggle with all the earnestness of his character. He took the stump in opposition to the Ordinance of Secession. The Union

J. H. Brown, Judge of the Circuit Court of Cabell County and one of the first judges of the Supreme Court of Appeals of West Virginia

The Elms, home of Judge James Henry Brown. Now 127 Alderson Street, Charleston

sentiment was strengthened. Those who so earnestly opposed the action of the Virginia Convention acted promptly and at once met, organized a State government loyal to the Union, elected a Legislature, assembled a convention to consider the formation of a new State; framed for it a constitution, secured its adoption by the people, and made application to Congress for recognition, which after a struggle was accorded, and West Virginia became one of the States of the Union, a thing long desired, and made necessary by unjust treatment, but which would never have been accomplished but for this opportunity, and the unrelenting efforts of the determined men who braved the slings and arrows of many of their contemporaries in the old State, and regardless of personal risk, carried the dream of statehood to realization. Judge Brown was one of the foremost of these men and one of the first to act.

Upon the seceding of Virginia he was elected to represent the County of Kanawha in the Legislature of reorganization; and while serving in that capacity was also elected a member of the convention called to formulate the Constitution for the proposed new state.

While still member of both bodies, he was elected judge of the Eighteenth Judicial Circuit and later was, without consultation, re-elected by his people, to the Constitutional Convention to fill the vacancy occasioned by his own resignation. No appeal was ever taken from any decision rendered by him while circuit judge.

He was a prominent figure in both legislature and convention, as chairman of the judiciary committee of the latter, and had much to do with the most important provisions of the first Constitution, framed for, and adopted by the people of West Virginia.

His service to the Union and to West Virginia cannot be measured. He had already distingushed himself at the bar and on the bench. As judge of the Supreme Court of Appeals, the highest court of the State, he fully sustained his reputation, and stamped his impression upon the State.

"There never was a man of more striking instance of unswerving moral courage. In the evening of his life he stood among us as stands the giant tree of the forest—the growth of former generations."

The children of James H. Brown and Louisa M. Beuhring were:
I. Virginia, married William Sydney Laidley; their children were:
   1. Mary Louisa, married Bradford Clarkson.

2. Virginia Amacetta, married Byrne Givin; their child was Nelle Brown.
3. Theodora Beuhring, deceased.
4. Lucy, married Jo Lane Stern; their children are: Louise Beuhring, Josephine Lane, Cornelia Anne, Virginia Laidley, Elizabeth Jane, and Lewis Henry, who married Margaret Carper.
5. Madelon Dannenburg, unmarried.
6. Dorothy Osborn, married Mumford August.
7. William Sydney, unmarried, who enlisted in the World War.
8. Twins: Douglas Scales, deceased, and Janet Scales, who married Earl B. Snider; their children are John Andrew and William Sydney Laidley.

II. James Frederick, son of Judge James H. Brown, born March 7, 1852, and died December 5, 1921. Graduating from West Virginia University in 1873 with degree of A.B., there was later conferred upon him that of M.A. and LL.D. He was admitted to the bar in 1875 and devoted his life to his profession. He was outstanding in his generation, attaining an eminence not surpassed by any lawyer in the State. His kindliness of nature, unfailing geniality, devotion and loyalty were the personal charms which cannot be estimated.

He was senior member of the well known firm of Brown, Jackson, and Knight. His practice in the legal profession extended to most of the important cases of his district and into the adjoining States, both in State and Federal courts, including both the Supreme Court of Appeals of the State and the Supreme Court of the United States.

His thorough acquaintance with the intricate land laws of Virginia and West Virginia and his detailed knowledge of old land grants covering the latter state and of questions affecting them had made his service in this branch especially sought. He was a Democrat of the old type, and by nature of fixed purpose and aggressive in any cause he espoused. He was nominated from Kanawha County to the Legislature while his father, then law-partner, was also nominated for the same office by the opposing party; the son received the highest number of votes cast and the father the next highest. Both were elected upon opposing tickets and served as two out of three members to which the county was entitled.

He served under successive governors of different politics on the board of regents of West Virginia University.

He showed excellent judgment and safe conduct as a legislator and leader. He attained distinction as a lawyer, but also stood high because of his sound judgment in matters of business.

He was long identified with banking, industrial and mining interests and for years was vice president of the Kanawha Valley Bank, one of the leading institutions of the State.

And as the late John H. Holt, in speaking of him, said:

"He was never intolerant of the views of others but listened with patience and charming courtesy. He was indulgent and helpful to the young, kindly to the old, and just to him with whom he fought.

"Indeed, he went through life an able lawyer, useful citizen, and charming man. As found in *Rob Roy,* 'Happy is he whose good intentions have borne fruit in deeds, and whose evil thoughts have perished in the blossom.'"

James Frederick Brown married on September 13, 1877, Jennie M. Woodbridge of Marietta, Ohio, and had the following children:

1. Louise Beuhring, married Oscar Penn Fitzgerald; their children are Jean Banks, Gwendolen, and Oscar Penn, Junior.
2. Jean Morgan, unmarried.
3. Elizabeth Woodbridge, married Angus W. MacDonald.
4. Ceres, unmarried.
5. Ruth Dannenburg, married Briscoe W. Peyton. Their children are Briscoe W., James Frederick Brown, Katherine Woodbridge, and Angus Eugene.

III. Lucy, married Dr. Timothy Lawrence Barber; their children are:

1. James Brown, born August 13, 1886, died October 27, 1901.
2. Timothy Lawrence, who married Elizabeth Brown. Their child, Timothy Lawrence, went overseas July 5, 1918, was engaged in the battle of Montfaucon which lasted several days, and lost his life in connection with it, October 10, 1918. He was buried at Roumagne Cemetery, southwest of Verdun.
3. Sarah Couch, unmarried.
4. Lucy, unmarried.
5. Thomas Maxfield, married Florence Crowell, was given the Distinguished Service Cross at the Battle of Cantigny. Their children are: Thomas Maxfield, Curtis Crowell, Florence, and Lawrence Graham.

6. Beuhring Hulverson, born September 27, 1895, died October 3, 1911.
7. Daniel Newman, married Edith Naismith. He worked with the Red Cross Ambulance Company overseas. Their children are: Daniel Brown, James David, and Timothy Naismith.

IV. Emma Matilda Scales, married John Franklin Bickmore. Their children are:
1. Thankful, unmarried.
2. John Franklin, II, married Norine King and later married Judith ———. Their children are John Franklin, III, and Judith.

V. Eleanora Dannenburg, who was born August 30, 1868. She was genial, artistic, travelled a good deal, and was devoted to her family. She grew up in Charleston where she spent most of her time, but the last days of her life were lived in Denver, Colorado, where she died July 24, 1924. She was unmarried.

VI. Benjamin Beuhring, born ———————, attended the University of West Virginia and took his law course at the University of Virginia. He married Annie Dickinson and afterwards went to Denver where he was connected with a number of business enterprises. He travelled extensively, later went to France for his health, and died in Nice, France, on December 30, 1906. To this union was born:
1. Mary Dickinson, married Charles Lowell, and had one son, Benjamin Franklin.
2. James Frederick, married Lucille Ravencroft. Their children are: Mary Dickinson, Lucille Ravencroft, Margaret, and Benjamin Beuhring.
3. Sallie Lewis, married Edward A. Whitaker, II. Their children are: Edward A., III, Annie Dickinson, Benjamin Brown, deceased, and Brown.

Benjamin B. Brown was born March 14, 1893, and continues to reside in the old homestead in Charleston where he and his father were born, and where five generations of the family have lived, surrounded by a grove of ancient elms preserved in the heart of the city.

He is a graduate of Princeton, 1914, and of Harvard Law School, 1917, with degrees of A.B. and LL.B. He served in France with the Marines of the Second Division in the World War and on his return to this country became associated with his father in the law firm of

Brown, Jackson and Knight, of which he is now an active member, maintaining the same high ideals and respect for the law as his father and grandfather. He married Hester M. Newhall of Lynn, Massachusetts, and their children are Gertrude Woodbridge, James Frederick, Benjamin Beuhring, and Elizabeth Newhall.

BUFFINGTON

William Buffington of Hampshire County purchased from John Savage his interest in the Savage Grant and by his will dated in 1784 devised this interest to his sons, Thomas and William, Junior, to be held in trust for his children, Joel, Thomas, William, David, Richard, Jonathan, Susanna, Ruth, and Mary.

Thomas, his son, was born in 1751, died in 1836. He married Ann Cline in 1775 and they had twelve children only four of whom lived to be grown. He built on the point overlooking the Ohio River just below the mouth of the Guyandotte. His son William, born in 1787, died in 1858, married Nancy Scales, born in 1795, died in 1882. William built the brick house called Cedar Grove just below the residence of his father, Thomas Buffington. William Buffington was the first surveyor of lands for the county, colonel of the militia and held many county offices. His oldest son was Peter Cline Buffington, born in 1814, and died in 1875, who was in turn an assistant county surveyor, member of the Legislature and the first mayor of Huntington. Peter Cline Buffington married first, Eliza Jane Stanard, and second, Lou Garland. He owned the farm known as Forest Hill and his residence is now a part of the Chesapeake and Ohio Hospital. He was the father of Dr. E. Stanard Buffington, one of the most beloved men in the county, and of Peter Cline Buffington, late sheriff of Cabell County. Thomas Buffington, Junior, the second son of Thomas Buffington and Ann Cline died unmarried; Susan married Martin Hull; Rebecca married John Russell, and James married a Miss Lane and moved to Ohio.

Other children of William Buffington and Nancy Scales were Amanda, born 1816, died 1873, who married Michael Tiernan and lived in Ohio; William Henry, born 1818, died 1899; Dr. Thomas J., born 1821, moved to Baton Rouge, Louisiana; Mary Jane, born 1824, died 1886, married William H. Hagen and lived here where the Saint Mary's Hospital now stands; James H., born 1829, attended Marshall College and owned the house on the point which he sold to D. W. Emmons, and removed to Kentucky; and Dr. John N., born 1832,

Left: Nancy Scales Buffington. *Right:* William Buffington, the first county surveyor. He also

died 1878, who married a Miss Thompson of Culpeper County, Virginia, and practiced medicine until the Civil War. After the war he married a second time, Julia L. Garland, and a daughter of this union, Florence, married E. W. Staunton of Charleston.

BURDETTE

The Burdette family, members of which emigrated to England shortly after the Norman Conquest, is of French origin. In America, representatives bearing the family name settled in New York, Maryland, Virginia, and other Colonies. Sir Richard Burdette is known to have been in Maryland prior to and after 1700. Thomas Burdette was one of the Tobacco Reviewers in Accomac County, Virginia, in 1629, and one of the Episcopal vestrymen in 1633. Colonial records, in referring to other members of the family, spell the name variously, as Burdette, Burdett, Burdet, and Burdit.

Earliest of the name in the region which is now West Virginia were John Burdette of Greenbrier County and William, Giles, and Archibald of Monroe County. The latter three, supposedly brothers, were residents of Monroe County when it was organized in 1799. According to tradition, these brothers were the sons of James Burdette of Culpeper County by his first wife. The second wife of James Burdette was Mary Hill, daughter of Richard Hill of Culpeper, and they were the parents of Frederick and Samuel Burdette of Taylor County. Robert J. Burdette, noted Baptist clergyman and humorist, was a grandson of Frederick.

William Burdette of Monroe County (who was born in 1755 and died May 21, 1839), first married Sarah Cornwell, who died February 17, 1817. Sarah Cornwell was the granddaughter of Edmund Cornwell, Revolutionary soldier and patriot. William Burdette in 1818 married Jane Scott, daughter of James and Catherine Sullivan Scott of Monroe County. Both of William's wives were of Scotch families. To William and his first wife were born thirteen children, eight sons and five daughters; and by the second marriage three sons were born. Of these sixteen children, fifteen lived to maturity, married, and had families. Descendants of at least six of the children of William Burdette live in Cabell County, most of them in Huntington. These descendants now bear various family names, and many of them are prominent in the community.

Alexander, tenth child of William and Sarah Cornwell Burdette, who was born April 24, 1802, in 1823 married Mary Lively Hill, daughter of James Hill, Junior, and Elizabeth Lively Hill. Alexander later moved to Putnam County, where he died January 21, 1863. He was the father of twelve children, five sons and seven daughters.

James Roberson Burdette, third child of Alexander and Mary L. Hill Burdette, was born in Monroe County, March 16, 1828. He first married, November 1, 1859, Elizabeth, daughter of William P. and Elizabeth Lillard Yates of Cabell County. The Yates family had been early inhabitants of Maryland, where George Yates was colonial surveyor in 1682. His grandson, also George Yates, married a Calvert, said to have been a sister of Lord Baltimore, and settled in Caroline County, Virginia. Michael, one of the sons of the latter George Yates, married Martha Marshall, aunt of Chief Justice John Marshall. They are the ancestors of the members of the Yates family long prominent in Illinois. Elizabeth Lillard, wife of William P. Yates and mother of Mrs. James R. Burdette, was a sister of Nancy Lillard Bryan, grandmother of William Jennings Bryan. William P. Yates and John Bryan, his brother-in-law, settled in Cabell County near Ona in November, 1826. The Bryan family remained three years and then moved to Mason County. After the death of John and Nancy Lillard Bryan, several of their children moved West. Among them was Silas L. Bryan, father of William Jennings.

James R. Burdette, after living in Putnam County, where all of his children were born, moved in 1870 to Cabell County and lived until his death, March 9, 1909, at Yatesmont, near Ona. His first wife died August 17, 1890, and on May 3, 1892, he married Willie Ann Hardwick, widow of James Woomeldorff. By his first marriage James R. Burdette had four children, two sons and two daughters, three of whom lived to maturity.

Frank L. Burdette, the youngest child of James R. and Elizabeth Yates Burdette, was born January 20, 1867. On July 6, 1910, he married Laura Buckner, daughter of Joseph A. and Olga Handley Buckner of Cabell County. He lives in Huntington, was educated in Cabell County, at Marshall College, at George Peabody College in Nashville, and at the University of Chicago. He is an educator and has filled positions in Cabell County, at Clarksville, Tennessee (principal, high school), at Weston, West Virginia (superintendent four years), at Clarksburg (superintendent nineteen years), at Romney (superintendent school for deaf and blind, three years), and was a member of the State Board of Education, 1914-'17.

Franklin L. Burdette, only child of Frank L. and Laura B. Burdette, was born in Huntington, December 7, 1911; educated at Romney and in Huntington; received his A.B., *summa cum laude,* from Marshall College in 1934; M.A., University of Nebraska, 1935; assistant in political science and student for the Ph.D., at the University of North Carolina, 1935-'36.

In the direct line of ancestry of Frank L. Burdette, Thomas Lillard, John Lillard, John Garrett, Richard Yates, James Hill, Joseph Richeson, and Edmund Cornwell served in the Revolution; and William Burdette, James Hill, Junior, and William P. Yates served in the War of 1812.

CAMPBELL

Charles William Campbell was born near Red Sulphur Springs, Monroe County, September 29, 1856, and died in Huntington, on the 22d day of March, 1935. He was the son of Robert D. and Mary Catherine (Johnson) Campbell. He attended the county schools, the State Normal School at Athens for a short time and afterwards taught school in Monroe County and read law during the latter period. In 1880 he moved to Hamlin and after an examination before Judges Evermont Ward, Ira J. McGinnis, and David E. Johnston he was admitted to the Bar in April, 1881. Early in 1888 he located in Huntington and on August 28th of that year married Jennie Ratliff, the daughter of George F. and Nancy Frazier Ratliff. She died in 1919. To this union was born Rolla D., a graduate of Harvard, married Ruth Cammack; Charles W., married Lillian Bronson; Nan, married Coleman A. Statts; Ruth, married A. M. Hewitt, and Jennie Eloise, married P. Walker Long.

C. W. Campbell continued in active practice until 1924 and his first and longest association was with the late John H. Holt which began shortly after they came to Huntington and continued until the end of 1904. His last association was with his son, Rolla D. Campbell. He was the leading counsel in the litigation known as the Kings suit which involved the title to a vast tract of land in Logan, Mingo, Wyoming, Boone and other southern counties in West Virginia and was in court from 1892 until about 1913. He was counsel for C. Crane and Company, J. L. Caldwell, J. Q. Dickerson and supervised the acquisition of many thousand acres of coal land in the southern counties. He was active in bringing about the construction of the Guyan Valley branch of the Chesapeake and Ohio Railway and much coal development in southern West Virginia particularly Logan County.

Politically he was a Democrat and was the nominee for circuit judge in 1904, served a number of times in the common council of the City of Huntington and during one period was the only Democrat in the council; was a member of the Legislature in 1911 and was the chairman of the judiciary committee and a member of the finance committee; was mayor of the City of Huntington 1919-22 and a delegate to several national conventions. He went as a matter of course as a delegate to all state and local conventions. He was for many years an elder in the First Presbyterian Church of Huntington and was charitable to the highest degree. He contributed generously to his own church, the Salvation Army, the Community Chest, the Crippled Children's Hospital and any worthy cause. He was particularly interested in the development of the parks of Huntington and contributed $12,500.00 at one time to the purchase of park lands which were turned over to the city.

In 1924 he retired and went to Monroe County and occupied himself farming. He took an active interest in the church and community affairs. He was blessed with splendid health until a few months before his death.

C. W. Campbell was one of the most quiet and gentle of men but possessed both moral and physical courage and when his mind was once made up that a thing was right there was no swerving him from that position.

COX

There is a railway station on the Baltimore and Ohio seven miles east of Huntington named Cox's Landing. It is a mute reminder of the fact that prior to the coming of the railroad there was a steamboat landing at this point of the same name. This landing was established by William Cox who was born in Buckingham County, Virginia, and moved to Mason County in the early 1790's. In 1811 he married Sarah White and moved to the Baker farm in Cabell County where he remained until 1835 and in that year bought the farm at Cox's Landing from Adam Woodyard. He had a store which stood under the river bank for a great many years and was replaced by the present building forty or fifty years ago.

William Cox had eleven sons and one daughter. These children and his grandchildren were active in that community and in this county.

One of his sons, John Cox had three children, two girls, Maude and Pearl, both of whom married and moved away; a son, John, who married a Miss Miller of Guyandotte. They were the parents of Albert E. Cox who was a merchant in Huntington; H. McP. Cox, and William T. Cox who was one time a member of the County Court and is said to have been the first man in the county to come out for prohibition. He joined the Temperance Union in 1876.

DARLINGTON

Urban Valentine Williams Darlington, Bishop of the M. E. Church, South, in the year 1934 completed a service of eight years as Bishop of the European District of the church which includes the three conferences of Poland, Belgium, and Czechoslovakia. He is now assigned to the district which includes the conferences of Kentucky, Tennessee, Louisville, and Illinois, but maintains his home in Huntington, where he has lived since 1909.

Bishop Darlington, the son of James Henderson and Kitty (Pemberton) Darlington, was born in Shelby County, Kentucky, August 3, 1870. He was educated in the public schools of Shelby County and was a student at Kentucky Wesleyan College, Winchester, 1889-1895, where he prepared for the ministry. He has the degree of D.D. from that institution. He was admitted as a minister of the Kentucky Conference in 1896 and his first pastorate was Washington, Kentucky, where he remained four years. The next year he was at Millersburg, Kentucky, at which place he married on October 29, 1901, Lyda Clark, who died in 1911. To this union was born Lyda Clark and Urban V. W., Junior. He married again on February 12, 1913, Virginia Bourne, of Stanford, Kentucky, and to this union has been born Kitty Scott and Julian Trueheart.

In 1900 he went to the Scott Street Church in Covington, Kentucky, and remained there until 1905 when he was assigned to St. Paul's Church, Parkersburg. After four years there he came to the Johnson Memorial Church in Huntington (1905-1913). Under his leadership the congregation of this church built the handsome brownstone edifice on the corner of 10th Street and 5th Avenue. At the end of his pastorate in Huntington he was secretary of education of the Western Virginia Conference, 1914-1916; Presiding Elder, 1915; president of Morris Harvey College, 1917-1918; member of Ecumenical Methodist Conference, 1911-1921; and in May of 1918 was elected Bishop.

Bishop Darlington is a man's man—an unusual personality. His sympathies are easily enlisted and anyone in trouble finds him not only a sympathetic friend but one who will do all that is humanly possible to lighten the burden. As an evidence of his many-sidedness he served as a member of the Draft Board for Cabell County, 1917-1918, perhaps the only Bishop in the world who did such service.

He is now a member of the board of missions of the M. E. Church, South, president of the board of trustees, Paine College, Augusta, Georgia, and a trustee of Emory University, Atlanta, Georgia. He is in the full vigor of his mature manhood and has the promise of many years of usefulness.

DAUGHTERS OF THE AMERICAN REVOLUTION

Buford Chapter, Daughters of the American Revolution, named for Captain William E. Buford, of the 15th Virginia Regiment, was organized June 1, 1910, with twenty-two charter members. The chapter has grown steadily until it has a present membership of 127.

The outstanding work of the chapter in Cabell County has been to permanently mark a corner of the Savage Grant, a tract of land patented December 15, 1772, by the Earl of Dunmore, last Royal Governor of Virginia, to John Savage and sixty other soldiers for services in the French and Indian War. Six Revolutionary soldiers' graves have been marked, also the wives' graves of five of the soldiers. During the World War the chapter was actively engaged in the Red Cross work and established a War Savings Society. Educational work is carried on in the junior and senior high schools by the awarding twice yearly of Good Citizenship medals in compliance with the Good Citizenship plan of the D.A.R. Over three thousand dollars has been loaned to students in Marshall College to further their education.

In 1920 an old log cabin, said to have been built in 1787, was torn down and a log chapter house was erected in its place on Savage Grant lot number 37. This chapter house was dedicated in 1922 and now represents an expenditure of $11,500.00.

Complete Revolutionary ancestral lines are on file in Memorial Continental Hall, Washington, of the following, who are members of Buford Chapter:

MESDAMES

Andrews, Lucy J.
Armstrong, Eunice Boggess
Armstrong, Nellie Alexander

Bannister, Katherine Morgan
Biern, Marion Moses
Biggs, Sallie J. Hedges

FAMILIES

Bragonier, Dorothy Berry
Bristol, Ellen Gallup
Burgess, Adelia (Miss)
Burgess, Frances (Miss)
Burns, Ethel Bronson
Cain, Virginia Stutler
Caldwell, Irene Bowles
Calley, Eunice Woodruff
Cowherd, Mary Meyers
Cox, Evelyn Bearden
Crenshaw, Katherine Park
Cubbedge, Annie Perkins
Davis, Margaret Battaile
Deardorff, Samantha Miller
Dickinson, Helen Hutchinson
Diehl, Pollye Richards
Dimick, Josephine D.
Dingess, Jane Adams
Donaldson, Anna M. Walker
Ducker, Frances Talbot
Dugan, Davy (Miss)
Duling, Orva McMillan
Dunn, Mary Henderson
Emmons, Jennie Petrie
Emmons, Margarita Champion
Faulkner, Zona McIntire
Foster, Maud Conley
Francis, Permele Elliott
Geiger, Minnie Walker
Geiger, Frances Ann
Gillespie, Margaret (Miss)
Gohen, Bessie Emmons
Greear, Winifred Sugg
Hagen, Emma Rece
Harer, Hazel (Miss)
Harer, Sadie Barner
Hawkins, Willie Reed Carpenter
Hereford, Sarah Handley
Heron, Beatrice Huntington
Hirshman, Margaret Ostrander
Hodges, Amine Adams
Hogg, Lillie Lee (Miss)
Holswade, Daisy Staats
Holton, Myrtilla Davis
Homrich, Bertha Edwards
Honaker, Celeste Homrich
Jones, Maud Noel
Kappes, Frances Kenney
Kyle, Marion C. Ewing
Lauhon, Helen Tufts
Lawrence, Virginia Davidson
Long, Cora Thompson
Long, Hilda Sheets
Long, Jennie Eloise Campbell
Lowry, Bess Mann
Marshall, Mahrea Goucher
Maupin, Leah Drown
Miller, Grace Conger
Mitchell, Rose Morgan
Moore, Miriam Leckie
Nash, Josephine Thornburg
Neal, Eunice Earp
Neale, Lessie Sheets
Northcott, Mary S. Wilson
Norvell, Mary Whelan
Oney, Xinia Womack
Perry, Anna Johnson
Peyton, Pearl Maupin
Quay, Virginia Talbott
Reeser, Alice J. Seltzer
Richmond, Lelia Snyder
Ritter, Mabel McClintock
Roberts, Catherine Donnally
 (Miss)
Roberts, Maud A. Allen
Sanders, Emilie McCarthy
Sebaugh, Celia Palmer
Smith, Lois Keeler

The Daughters of the American Revolution cabin

Snyder, Bessie McCormick
Starcher, Clara Armstrong
Stevenson, Mary Abbott
Summers, Nellie Reeser
Templeton, Marjorie K. (Miss)
Thornburg, Gertrude Casto
Toney, Mary G. Keister
Tufts, Marie (Miss)
Tyree, Clara Burdick
Van Bibber, Lucy E.
Vaughan, Jewel Asbury
Vickers, Victoria Thornburg
Waddell, Ethel Wheeler
Watts, Ouida Caldwell
White, Iva E.
Whitzel, Henrietta Stafford
Whitzel, Lucy Adele (Miss)
Wilcoxen, Harriet J. (Miss)
Wilkinson, Katherine Wells
Williams, Harriet Peck
Willis, Tevan Bowman
Wilson, Inez Healy
Wiswell, Tensie Ash
Wright, Myra A. Snyder
Wylie, Harriette McAdoo

NON-RESIDENT MEMBERS

Anderson, Lou Warwick
Burdick, Melissa Butt
Chaney, Genevieve L.
Ford, Stella Eastman
Goodykoontz, Irene Hooker
Jenkins, Ada Grace (Miss)
Miler, Anna Mann
Powell, Minnie Lyon
Ritter, Laurie W. Stewart
Staats, Juliette Wiles
Stewart, Susan Senoretta
Taylor, Josephine Curtis
Templeton, Decima Burns
Tracy, Sarah J. Stewart
Williams, Edith E. Stone
Wilcoxen, Lucille Hays

DOUTHAT

Rudenz Sharp Douthat was born at Rolla, Phelps County, Missouri, December 27, 1873, the second son and fourth child of Dr. Robert William Douthat, of Christiansburg, Mongomery County, Virginia, the first child of David Greiner Douthat, the third son of Robert Douthat, of Staunton, Augusta County, Virginia, and Mary Eleanor Polly (Yost) Douthat, daughter of Henry Yost and Mary (Waggoner) Yost, and Mary Ann (Adams) Douthat, daughter of William Adams and Sarah (Stratton) Adams, daughter of John Hampton Stratton and Mary Ann (Turner) Stratton, a son of Edward Stratton, III, son of Edward Stratton, II, son of Edward Stratton, I, on the father's side of the family, and Mary Jane (Wells) Douthat, wife of Robert W. Douthat, youngest daughter of Captain Job Sidwell Wells of Floyd County, Virginia, a son of Abner Wells and Debora (Sidwell?) Wells, of Frederick County, Virginia, and Elizabeth (Shelor) Wells, daughter of William Shelor, a son of Daniel

Shelor, a son of Lawrence Shelor, who came across the Atlantic with a brother, from Germany, the brother dying on the way over, Lawrence marrying "an American lady."

Mr. Douthat attended the public schools of Rolla, until 1884, removing to Raton, New Mexico, where he attended Marcey and McChesney Institute, removed to Kansas City, Missouri, in 1886, where he was employed as a Western Union messenger boy; removed to Booneville, Arkansas, where he attended Quitman Institute; removed to Farmdale, Kentucky, where he attended the Kentucky Military Institute, removed to Barboursville, where he attended Barboursville College (now Morris Harvey College), removed to Huntington, where he was employed in the office of W. W. Point, roundhouse foreman, then for a short time as a stenographer in the First National Bank, then with the Barlow-Henderson Company, then with Simms and Enslow, attorneys, then as the official stenographic reporter of the Criminal Court of Cabell County, and in 1914 elected as County Clerk of Cabell County, serving until December 31, 1932.

Mr. Douthat married Roxie Orelia Salmon, daughter of Joel Kellogg Salmon and Martha Blake, of Barboursville, at Ironton, Ohio, on December 27, 1894, and has five children, three sons and two daughters.

EVERETT

John Everett, a Revolutionary soldier, is buried on the south knoll of the old Everett farm at Old Ona. A gravestone marks his resting place. He is the first of the name in the county and came in 1807 from Albemarle County, Virginia, and it is said that he and his wife made the journey on horseback. Near his residence in Albemarle County, "Colonel" Everett, as he was called, in about 1800 laid out a town which he called Travelers Grove but he sold only three or four lots, then changed the name to Pleasant Grove, and kept a tavern there for some years. His first wife was Sarah, daughter of Tarleton Woodson, and his second wife was Sarah, daughter of Samuel Dedman. Tarleton Woodson lived in Goochland County, Virginia, where the name Tarleton was fairly common. It is said that at the time of Tarleton's raid through Virginia he was in Goochland County and in one of the homes saw a picture of the Tarleton coat of arms on the wall which enraged him so that he cut it down with his sabre. But to return to John Everett, he had a son, John Everett, Junior, who served in the General Assembly and was Sheriff, and had a son, Tarleton Woodson, whose name has been corrupted

Bradley Waters Foster, born 1834, died 1922

to Talton, born in 1821, who married Elizabeth Moore, born the same year. To this couple were born nine children: John F., Virginia, William, George S., Chattie, Fannie, Laban T., Carrie, and Henry Clay. Henry Clay Everett married Nettie, daughter of Charles H. Summerson and in early life was a miller, later engaged in the grocery business with George S. Page in Guyandotte, and they also owned the wharfboat. He has two children, Richard T., who married Stella, daughter of T. W. Wilson, and Hallie Call, who married Hugh L. Russell, of Ashland, Kentucky, and has two sons Hugh Everett and Henry Clay Russell.

B. W. FOSTER

The name B. W. Foster was long a magic name in Huntington. It stood for stability. It stood for high character. It stood for financial acumen of the highest order. It stood above all for a supreme faith in the future of Huntington.

Many was the time when others faltered and lost their faith in the future of Huntington, either from personal vicissitudes or adversities of the world of commerce, that the sure touch, the ready sympathy, and the keen vision of Bradley Waters Foster restored equilibrium, brought order out of chaos, and proved the inspiration for a resumption of the forward march to greater achievements.

Mr. Foster was a gentle man. He was the antithesis of the stormy, blustering type. He got his way by suasion rather than force. He was a financial power in the community, a man who invested in the land on which the city stood. As the city grew his lands grew more and more valuable. But he was ever at the elbow of the man who needed a home, and saw the larger gain of a community of happy homes.

When he died on March 22, 1922, he was full of years, and it well could have been written as his epitaph that he was one of the makers of Huntington. Certainly the city would not be what it is but for his unflagging, quiet zeal.

He was kin, by marriage, of the family from which the city took its name of Huntington. While there were those, possibly, who thought his thrift and providence for the future an exaggerated trait—for there was no premonition in 1922 of the world-wide depression of 1929-1935—those who now look back upon his rugged career can only surmise what a tower of strength he would have proven to be in the present depression, as he was in the depression of 1873-1879, which like the present one lasted for six years, while the city was in its infancy.

Mr. Foster was born December 2, 1834, of New England stock. His paternal grandfather was Joseph Foster, who died in Dixfield, Maine. Joseph S. Foster, son of the aforenamed Joseph, was born in Kennebec County, Maine, and lived to be eighty-six years old. The latter married Sarah K. Holman, and to their marriage were born four children, of which Bradley Waters Foster was the second.

B. W. Foster toiled until about twenty-one on his father's farmstead. Then he went into business in Lewisburg, Maine, and thence to Cohoes, New York. He came to Huntington in 1871—the year the city was chartered—and thus was one of the founders. He was one of the organizers of the First National Bank, now the First Huntington National Bank.

The various early enterprises with which he was associated form almost the entire roster of the commercial activity of the young city. He became president of the Huntington Land Company. He served as a member of the city council. He was a devout member of the Presbyterian church.

At Oneonta, New York, in 1868, Mr. Foster married Mary Lenora Huntington, a niece of the great railroad man, Collis P. Huntington, whose name the city bears. She was the daughter of Harriet S. Huntington. Mrs. Foster was born in 1841, and died in 1920, two years before her husband.

Dying, Mr. Foster willed his wealth to the city that he had helped to build. He created the Foster Foundation, a home for widows and unmarried women over sixty-five. It is a model institution of its kind, and doubtless Mr. Foster, who was of the old school of rugged individualism, had no thought that so soon, such institutional care for the aged and needy would be taken over by the State and Federal governments on a pension basis for men and women alike.

His own old age was unclouded by any financial worry. But he never varied from the simple economies, and quiet, inexpensive mode of living that had characterized his life. He was the type of capitalist who felt that the custodianship of large wealth carried with it a social responsibility to the community whence it had been derived.

The many thousands of people who now dwell in the beautiful city of Huntington with its wide, well-shaded streets, its churches, schools, theaters, and factories that in ordinary times give steady employment, undoubtedly owe a great debt to Mr. Foster. There were critical times, when the city was growing, wherein he, gentle and retiring though he was, proved a veritable rock of Gibraltar, and prevented the city from becoming a mere mushroom growth. His private charities were countless throughout his life and his acts of kindness were known and appreciated by more than one struggling young business man to whom he flung out, often unsolicited, the financial life line.

No one would have imagined on entering his unpretentious office in the old Huntington Land Company building—now occupied by the Huntington Dry Goods Company—that there sat one of the keenest intellects in the city and one who had an unfaltering faith in its ultimate destiny.

FRAMPTON

The Framptons are English and trace their descent from William Frampton who was Regent General, Province of Pennsylvania, 1686, and are immediately descended from John Frampton and Anna Barbara Martin, his wife. John was a Revolutionary soldier. He had a number of children. Martin, born near Lewistown, Pennsylvania, June 13, 1788, moved to Lawrence County, Ohio, opposite Huntington, and died in 1850, married Sarah Mann in 1818 and had eleven children. One son, James Robert, bought 244 acres of land on the Ohio River in Cabell in 1882. The second son, Isaac, born near Lewistown, Pennsylvania, 1790, married Jane Mann in 1862, and lived on a farm just above Burlington, Ohio. He later bought a large farm on the Ohio River in Wayne County and moved on it and in 1848 bought 269 acres of land on the river above Four Pole in this county. Afterwards he acquired other lands and became one of the large landowners in this section. He had five children:

(1) Ephriam, married Nancy Mann Woods and had two children, Rebecca and Horace. In 1863 he got 242 acres on the Ohio River out of his father's estate.

(2) David acquired 303 acres of land on the Ohio River in 1863 out of his father's estate, married Clara Beams and they had three sons: James, Albert C., and David W. David W. Frampton, Junior, whom we know as "Pete" and who served as constable, deputy U. S. Marshal and justice of the peace, married Ruth H. Delebar and had the following children: Peyton G., Charles E., D. W., Junior, and John M.

(3) Hiram, married Clarissa Beams and had one daughter Ora, who married ——— Bailey and had a son George.

(4) Isaac, died unmarried.

(5) Rebecca Jane, who married C. F. Everett and had two children.

FRANCIS

James Draper Francis was born February 28, 1884, in Pike County, Kentucky, the only son of David Livingston Francis and Kate Dean Francis, his wife. He was educated at Pikeville College, from which he graduated in 1903; Centre College, Danville, Kentucky; University of Virginia, LL.B., 1908, and is a member of the Delta Chi Fraternity.

He began the practice of law at Pikeville with the firm of Auxier, Harman and Francis in 1908. In 1918 he was made counsel and vice president of the Island Creek Coal Company, and moved his family to Huntington. Mr. Francis has devoted his time to the coal business in its largest aspects and was one of the principal leaders in the formation of Appalachian Coals, Incorporated, which was a movement sponsored by a number of southern coal producers to stabilize marketing conditions, and which plan was approved by the Supreme Court of the United States.

James D. Francis is president of the Mallory Coal Company, the Pond Creek Pocahontas Coal Company and the Island Creek Coal Company. He is an elder in the First Presbyterian Church of Huntington, a Mason, a member of the National Society, Sons of the American Revolution, the Guyandot Club and the Guyan Country Club of Huntington, and of the Racquet Club in Washington.

In 1910 he married Permele Crawford Elliott of Charlottesville, Virginia, daughter of John Francis Elliott of Albemarle County, Virginia, and Ellie Crawford Elliott of Augusta County, Virginia. To this union was born:

John Elliott Francis, born 1911; died 1934. Graduate of Hill School, Pottstown, Pennsylvania, 1929; Yale University, 1933; entered junior year of Yale Law School, 1934. Beta Theta Pi, Yale.

David Livingston Francis, born 1914, Hill School, class of 1933; Yale University, class of 1937; Chi Psi, Yale.

Permele Crawford Francis, born 1925.

Mrs. Permele Elliott Francis is a graduate of Mary Baldwin Seminary at Staunton, Virginia. She served as first general chairman and organizer of the Pike County Red Cross Society during the World

War and since she moved to Huntington in 1918 has been active in church, club, and social life, as well as in various patriotic organizations. She holds membership in the following: Life member Huntington Woman's Club; charter member, Huntington Garden Club; Cabell County Committee of Colonial Dames; Daughters of the American Revolution, Regent, 1930-1931; Sons and Daughters of the Pilgrims; Colonial Descendants of America; Daughters of 1812; United Daughters of the Confederacy; Order of The Crown in America; Daughters of the Barons of Runnymede; Descendants of Knights of the Garter; Huguenot Society of Washington; Order of the Knights of the Golden Horseshoe; First Families of Virginia, 1607-1620.

FREEMAN

Freeman is an old name in Virginia. The earliest one is Captain Bridges Freeman who was a Burgess from Pasbehaighs in 1629-30 and later Bridges Freeman, justice in James City County in 1680. Eckenrode's list of Revolutionary soldiers from that state carries the names of just twenty-seven Freemans so it is fair to assume that the name is not only an old one but a numerous one, and those readers who know Virginians and know how far they claim kin can imagine how many of this tribe count themselves cousins and what a problem it would be to work out their kinship.

In the unsettled conditions which followed the Civil War the one great opportunity for the young man of that date was the Chesapeake and Ohio Railroad. They came first with the construction forces and after the railroad was completed they entered the transportation service. In this group who came to West Virginia was Richard Valery Freeman who was born in Richmond, Virginia, in 1857, and was killed in a wreck on the Chesapeake and Ohio two miles east of Huntington, November 27, 1889. Valery Freeman's parents were both natives of Richmond. He married Maria Hagan whose parents also came from Richmond and to this union was born: Blanche, who married James A. Pack, and Charles Wilkerson.

Charles Wilkerson Freeman was born in Huntington, October 1, 1887, and graduated from Huntington High School in 1905. He then attended West Virginia University and was graduated from its law department in 1909 and admitted to the Bar in the same year. He specialized in land titles and is regarded as an authority in this branch of the law. "Wilkie," as he is universally known, is a prominent Elk and a keen sportsman who takes great interest in athletic contests. He was helpful in bringing about the construction of the Fairfield Stadium and has served on its governing board for several years. He is active in Democratic politics. He has served several times as chairman of the Democratic County Executive Committee and has a host of friends. He married on April 6, 1914, Fae Preston, who died May 3, 1931, and to this union was born a daughter Allene. He married second, Irene Ansell Bishop, on September 20, 1933, who is a member of the Ansell family who came to Cabell County in 1809, settling at what is now known as Green Bottom.

GALLAHER

James Gallaher was born at Brownsville, Pennsylvania, in 1784 of Irish parents. As a young man he was engaged in the river trade between Pittsburgh and New Orleans. In 1810 he was one of the first purchasers of lots in the new town of Guyandotte, and floated a house from Gallipolis, Ohio, to Guyandotte, and put it on his lot. He lived in Guyandotte sixteen years, was a successful business man, being interested in a store, a tannery, a shoe and saddle shop, saw and grist mill, a distillery and a carding mill. He was a Whig and a Presbyterian. In 1836 he bought the Mark Russell farm which lay between 11th and 14th Streets and built a brick house which fronted on the old pike at a point now in the alley between 5th and 6th Avenues and 12th and 13th Streets, but at that time was the forks of the road and a favorite stopping place for drovers en route east from Kentucky with cattle and hogs.

His family were Ann, born 1819, married R. C. Poage of Ashland, Kentucky; Eliza, born 1820, died 1856, married T. L. Jordan in 1855; George, born 1822, died 1900, moved to Benton County, Missouri; William, born 1824, died 1893, moved to Benton County, Missouri; James, born February 22, 1827, died January 18, 1895, married Mary Elizabeth, daughter of Samuel W. Johnston, and to this union were born: Willie, who married J. K. Oney, and Georgella, who married W. H. H. Holswade; Sarah, born 1829, died 1895, married J. Harvey Poage and inherited the home place from her father and resided there during their lives; (the old house which was pulled down a few years ago was then known as the Poage house). Thomas, born 1832, died 1864, lived in Ashland, Kentucky; John, born 1837, married Drusilla, a daughter of Edward Wright and lived in the town of Gallahersville, now a part of the city of Huntington.

GIBSON

John Shackelford Gibson, D.D., was a great friend of Bishop George W. Peterkin and it was this friendship that caused Dr. Gibson to give up his work at Trinity Church, Fredericksburg, Virginia, and accept the call to Trinity Church at Huntington in September, 1892. On his arrival he found the parish had been without a rector for some months and the church somewhat disorganized. The membership was small and the church in debt. The buildings were poorly furnished and to make conditions worse the next year saw the beginning of the so-called Cleveland Panic. Dr. Gibson was a man of much decision, an ardent churchman and made no compromise when a principle was at stake. He entered upon his work with enthusiasm and not only attended to the needs of his own church but at stated intervals had services at Kenova, Williamson, and later in Logan. His wife was an able assistant and for many years published the *Parish Messenger*, a booklet which served to keep up the interest of the congregation, the revenue from the sale of which was of material help to the church. Just ten years after the arrival of Dr. and Mrs. Gibson they saw the church entirely freed of debt.

Dr. Gibson continued in Huntington until September, 1911, when he accepted a call to Virginia, and continued there until December 4, 1912, when he died from a sudden heart attack.

John Shackelford Gibson was born at Port Tobacco, Maryland, December 22, 1853. He was the son of Isaac Gibson, an Episcopal clergyman and his wife, Ann Sophia Wingerd. He was educated at the Hanover Academy, Hanover County, Virginia, the Central University at Lexington, Kentucky, the University of Cincinnati, and the Virginia Theological Seminary at Alexandria, Virginia. For many years he was an outstanding member of the church and participated in its general conventions. He married on January 12, 1881, Ilicia Wheeler Davis of Trenton, New Jersey, and to this union were born:

Frances Gibson, married George S. Wallace.

James Davis, who like his father was a clergyman and married Mary Leadbetter. He died in Covington, Kentucky, March 5, 1932; at which place he was rector of the church of which his grandfather had been rector.

Anna, married Lieutenant Colonel J. M. Willis, Medical Corps, U. S. Army.

John Shackelford, Junior, a Major, Medical Corps, U.S.A., married Patty Braxton.

Philip Pendleton, a prominent lawyer in Huntington, married Morrell Sanford Gibson.

Isaac Gibson, father of Dr. John Shackelford Gibson, was born at Bowling Green, Flint Hill, Rappahannock County, Virginia, January 30, 1828, and died June 12, 1906, at Norristown, Pennsylvania. He was the son of Minor Winn Gibson and Elizabeth Pendleton Shackelford, daughter of John Shackelford of Culpeper County, Virginia, and a grandniece of Edmund Pendleton. Isaac Gibson for a time was rector of the Old Fork Church in Hanover County, Virginia, and during this period his children attended a school kept by a Miss Nelson, and they were friends and schoolmates of the late Thomas Nelson Page.

EUSTACE GIBSON

One of the early arrivals in Huntington was Eustace Gibson. He was an unusual character, a lawyer—not well trained on the technical side, but a wonderful judge of the human elements of a case and a great jury lawyer. He was a man of great personal courage, a dominating man who assumed leadership at once. It has been told in another chapter of his being captain of the fire company and the older people still remember and tell of the cold day when the Huntington Hotel burned and how Eustace Gibson worked at the fire when he was covered with ice. Then, too, he had many political battles that are historical—one with the Jacksons of Wood County and more than one with Sam Vinson, but he was accustomed to battles, political and otherwise.

He was the son of Colonel Jonathan Catlett Gibson and Mary W. Shackelford Gibson, his wife, of Culpeper County, Virginia, and was born in that county October 4, 1842. He died in Clifton Forge, Virginia, December 10, 1900.

He had a common school education in the ordinary Virginia schools of that day and studied law and in the spring of 1861 had commenced the practice of his profession. He enlisted in the Confederate Army in June, 1861, and was made a first lieutenant. He was promoted to captain in 1863 but was retired on account of wounds received in action.

In 1867 he was elected from Giles County as a member of the Constitutional Convention of Virginia of 1867-8 known as the Black and Tan Convention. His brother, Catlett Gibson, was a member of this convention from Rappahannock County, Virginia.

Eustace Gibson, leader of the Conservative Democrats, was in constant turmoil, and had more than one physical encounter. On one occasion after he had been unusually obstreperous and a motion to expel him from the convention was being debated a colored delegate from Tidewater section of Virginia took the floor in defense of Captain Gibson and at the close of his remarks said, "that Captain Gibson is as good as we are, although he is a white man."

Captain Gibson came to Huntington in 1871 and practiced law until 1900. He was a senior member of the firm of Gibson, Simms, and Enslow for a short time, but his longest association was with Thomas L. Michie and the firm of Gibson and Michie was a leading one, Michie possessing all the qualities that his partner lacked and the two together made a formidable team. Captain Gibson was elected to the House of Delegates from Cabell County in 1876 and by that House was elected Speaker. He was a Hancock elector in 1880 and in 1882 was elected to the 48th Congress as a Democrat, receiving 11,157 votes against 9,836 for Loomis the Republican candidate. He was reëlected in 1884.

Captain Gibson married Mattie Lackland and they had three children: E. St. Pierre, who like his father was a lawyer; Howard, and Lee.

Captain Gibson and his wife are buried in Spring Hill Cemetery.

GIDEON

Sam Gideon was born in Wurtemburg, Germany, October 19, 1836, and died in Huntington, June 20, 1923. His wife, Dora Eppinger was born in Germany, March 14, 1846, and died in Huntington, February 20, 1923.

Sam Gideon came to America in 1856 and located at Rock Island, Illinois, and soon learned to speak English and began to take interest in political questions. He heard the debate between Abraham Lincoln and Stephen A. Douglas in 1861. He enlisted in the Federal Army and served until the end of the war at which time he was a first lieutenant and was made a brevet captain. After he left the army he located in Cincinnati, Ohio, and on August 15, 1865, married Dora Eppinger. They remained a short time in Cincinnati and then located in Manchester, Ohio, where he remained until 1872, then moved his family to Huntington, and spent the remainder of his life in the new city.

Sam Gideon was a man of splendid qualities and from the first took a leading part in the civil and political affairs of this community. It has been told elsewhere of his political and business activities and of his effort to establish a city park but these by no means cover the field of his activities. He was a member of the city council, served a great many years on the school board, was a pioneer in the movement for good roads and as a member of the County Court, completed the new courthouse and built the first iron bridge in the county. He was an active member of the I.O.O.F., and served as commander of the Bailey Post, 9th G.A.R. and his kindness of heart and human sympathy endeared him to the people of the community who in 1915, when he celebrated his golden wedding anniversary made it almost a community event.

Mrs. Gideon came of splendid German stock and while she took no active part in public affairs she was endeared to her friends and neighbors by her kindness of heart and charity. She was active in her church work and was one of the original sponsors of the *Herald Dispatch* milk and ice fund which for years supplied milk and ice to the poor babies and children of Huntington. She served as president of the Ladies Hebrew Society.

To this union were born: Dave, who is the publisher of the Huntington *Herald Dispatch,* and has been an active political figure in the county and state for a number of years; William H., a prominent banker in Baltimore, Maryland, married Lillian Gottschalk, and they have a son, William, who is a student at St. John's, Annapolis, Maryland; Ray, married M. Lehman of Portsmouth, Ohio, and has four children; Carolyn, Simon, Sylvan, and Doris; Ida, married Mike Broh, and had a son, Herman L., who died while a student at the University of Virginia, and a daughter, Dorothy, married Ben Frank, an architect in Baltimore, Maryland; Daisy, married Sol Birke, and Blanche. The daughters, except Mrs. Lehman, live in Huntington.

HALL

William Hadder Hall migrated from Bedford County, Virginia, to Lawrence County, Ohio, early in the nineteenth century and located on a farm between Proctorsville and Rome. As his three sons William Dixon, Robert, and Henry grew up he located them on adjoining farms. William Dixon Hall married Elizabeth Radford and to this union were born: Charles H., who came to Cabell about the close of the Civil War, and was the first teacher in the public schools of this county; Sarah Ann; and Henry.

William Dixon Hall married second, Mary Ann Matthews, daughter of Sam Matthews and a sister of Joe and Sam Matthews who were at one time engaged in business as photographers in Huntington, and later Sam was the State Banking Commissioner. To this union was born Samuel B. and Matthew S. Samuel B. married Eliza E. Neff, daughter of Henry Clay Neff and Jane M. Ellis Neff. Henry Clay Neff was a first lieutenant in the U. S. Army 1861-65, was a son of Jacob Neff whose father, Henry, migrated to Cabell County from New York State in the early part of the nineteenth century and owned a farm of 342 acres on the Ohio River below the mouth of the Guyandotte which was known in later years as the Burks farm. Jane M. Ellis Neff was the daughter of Hiram Ellis who migrated from New York State and settled on Quaker Bottom in Lawrence County. To this union were born: Ruel W., who served in the 1st West Virginia, U. S. Volunteers, 1898-99; Luna Bernice; Charles Henry; Essie, married R. E. Guinn; Vivian H., married C. D. Lewis, and D. A.

Samuel B. Hall remained on the farm in Lawrence County until 1895 and then moved to Huntington and rented a farm which lay between 16th and 20th Streets, south of Artisan Avenue and included that part of the city now in Rickett's Place. In 1904 he formed a contracting firm composed of himself, his brother, M. S., and his sons, R. W., and D. A. Hall, which under the firm name of Hall Brothers and Company built a great number of houses in Huntington.

D. A. Hall, the son, married in 1910, Lillian Moore from Buckhannon, who is a descendant of Charles Wirtenbaker, one-time president of Washington and Lee University, and to this union was born Mildred Louise, September 7, 1918.

D. A. Hall was for many years a banker in Huntington, but is now active in the insurance business.

HAMPTON

William Hampton, born in England in 1586, died in Gloucester County, Virginia, in 1652. He was a member of the ancient family of the Hamptons of Middlesex and Stafford counties, England, and came to Virginia in 1620 on the ship *Bono Novo* and was followed the next year by his wife, Joan, and their three children who came over on the ship *Abagail*.

William Hampton (1) had a son, Thomas (2) born April 16,

1623, in Virginia, and died in James City County, October 12, 1690, who was an Episcopal minister, and whose eldest son, John (3) lived at Hampfield in Gloucester County, and moved to King William County where he died in 1718. His son, John, Junior (4), born June 3, 1683, is the ancestor of General Wade Hampton of South Carolina.

John Hampton (4) had a son, Henry (5), born October 5, 1721, in King William County, died at his home at Buckland, Prince William County, March 27, 1778, who was a half-brother of Sarah, the wife of George Newman Brown. (See account of the Brown family.)

Henry (5) acquired by purchase an interest in the Savage Grant. In his will he refers to "800 acres of soldiers' land which I purchased" already lotted, being upon the Sandy Creek below the mouth of the Great Kanawha. This interest was devised to a son, Dr. Cary Henry Hampton who was born November 16, 1754, died in August, 1840, and who came out to these lands about 1802. This Dr. Henry Hampton (who dropped the name Cary after his father's death) was an assistant surgeon or surgeon-mate in the Revolutionary War. In the partition of the Savage Grant by a decree of December, 1818, he was given lots 37 and 38 of that grant as assignee of James Samuels and Hugh Paul. In a deed from James Samuels to the Hamptons he described his interest as lot "5th ticket drawn" of Colonel Washington land for service at the Meadows. He (Henry Hampton) began to dispose of this land very early and the last portion of tract 38 was sold to James Holderby in 1821.

Dr. Hampton had his home on the Ohio River east of 16th Street on the high ground on which Marshall College is now located, and his grandson, Oliver Hampton, who attended Marshall College in 1850, said that at that time some remains of the old house were still noticeable, as well as some of the snags of cedar trees that had stood in front of it.

Dr. Henry Hampton had a son, William, who married Malinda Shortridge, daughter of Colonel George Shortridge who had been a Revolutionary soldier, but after this couple had lived together a while some disagreement arose and the wife went to the home of her father who lived over on Sandy. After a time busybodies got to work and Colonel Shortridge heard that some evil-disposed person had told Dr. Henry Hampton that he, Colonel Shortridge, had proposed to do him some physical violence. The colonel concluded that the easiest and best way to settle the matter was to go over and talk it out, and suiting his action to the thought he saddled his horse and took his rifle and rode through the wilderness to Hampton's. When he reached the fence which enclosed the house he dismounted and took his rifle and started towards the house. Dr. Hampton saw him coming and concluded that his mission was hostile so he took his own rifle and shot the colonel, killing him. This tragic event was probably the cause of his disposing of his holdings here and moving to what was then White's Creek, but now called Doc's Creek after Doctor Hampton. This creek empties into the Sandy River not very far from Neal's Station.

William and Malinda made up their differences and lived out their lives together.

Dr. Henry Hampton had a son, Anthony, also a physician, who likewise lived on Doc's Creek and it was with this Dr. Anthony Hampton that Dr. Henry Hampton spent the last years of his life.

Dr. Anthony Hampton had a daughter who married Colonel John L. Zeigler. Colonel Zeigler was living on Doc's Creek taking care of his aged in-laws when the Civil War started. The Hampton family has been a distinguished one and includes therein many professional men. The Rev. William Hampton who was a grandson of the first Dr. Henry Hampton, was a distinguished preacher and is the man who laid out Hampton City, now included in Catlettsburg, and not the least of these descendants was the Rev. John W. Hampton, a Confederate veteran, who was pastor of the Johnson Memorial Church, 1894-97.

HANNAN

Tradition and written history record the fact that when Thomas Buffington came to the Savage Grant in the latter part of the eighteenth century—some fix the date at 1786 and others at 1796—found Thomas Hannan settled on Greenbottom, and that Hannan was the first settler in what is now Cabell County. The claim that he was the first settler has been challenged. Thomas Hannan was born in Frederick County, Virginia, in 1757 and died in Mason County, April 18, 1835. He made application for a pension as a Revolutionary soldier in 1834, and in the application said that he had moved to Mason County in 1791. The land records show that Hannan had patents for 5,000 acres in Mason County and the first deed on record in Cabell County to a Hannan is dated October 26, 1810, from Thomas Hannon to John Hannan, conveying 200 acres on Little Guyan which was part of a 1,000-acre patent and in 1825 this John

Hannan got forty-three acres out of the north end of the Green Bottom tract. It is possible that the larger part of the Hannan land was north of the Little Guyan, although he had that part which is in Cabell under cultivation when Buffington came, and this fact was the reason for saying he was the first settler in the county.

Hannan was an active fellow and lived for a time in the Block house at Point Pleasant, and it is said that his son, Esom Hannan, was born in the Block house. It has been said that Thomas Hannan was a soldier at the battle of Point Pleasant but the list of soldiers who took part in this battle, compiled by Virgil A. Lewis, does not contain his name. However, he was a friend of Daniel Boone and was an active woodsman as he located a trace (a road) from St. Albans to the Ohio River which crossed the Ohio River near the mouth of Little Guyan and thence on to Chillicothe. Mason County named a magisterial district for him and a number of his descendants are worthy citizens of Cabell County and others live on the Ohio side at Swann Creek.

But to return to the question—who was the first settler in Cabell? There was a partial division of the Savage Grant in 1775 and it is interesting to note that in this division there were only fifteen portions assigned and these were numbered beginning with one at the Sandy and extending up the river and in the partition suit decided in 1818 the court, in the course of its opinion said that some of the patentees or their assignees had taken possession at the division of 1775 and had continued in possession since it did not say who they were or on what part they had settled and it is possible that these settlements, if there were any, might have been in what is now Wayne County. In all events there is no authentic tradition or record of any settler on the Savage Grant in Cabell County at that early date.

HARRISON

The Harrison family was founded in Virginia by Benjamin Harrison, born in London in 1673, father of Benjamin Harrison who was one of the Signers of the *Declaration of Independence* and ancestor of William Henry and Benjamin Harrison who were Presidents of the United States.

William Henry Harrison (a namesake and cousin of the William Henry Harrison who was president) came with his son, Otis, to Cabell County from Franklin County, Virginia, about 1843. Otis Harrison, born 1827, died 1910, married Ruth Frances Taylor, born

1832, died 1918, a teacher in the schools of Cabell and Kanawha County and a daughter of John Taylor, a silversmith, and his wife, Miranda Stokes Taylor. Miranda Stokes (Taylor) was brought to this country, following her parents' death, when a small girl, by her uncle, Sir Francis G. Barrington, and reared on a large plantation near Wilmington, North Carolina, where she was educated by tutors from England. John Taylor and his wife, Miranda, came to Gallipolis, Ohio, and settled there because of his strong opposition to slavery which prevailed in the South. In addition to Ruth Frances this couple had two other children, a daughter Anne, who was educated in the public schools in Marietta, Ohio, and was a school teacher, and a son who died when a small boy.

Otis Harrison and Ruth Frances Taylor were married at Gallipolis, Ohio, but lived in Cabell County. Some forty years ago Otis Harrison built the house we now know as the old Harrison homestead on 1st Avenue just opposite St. Mary's Hospital. He and his wife spent the remainder of their lives there. One daughter, Eugenia, who married a Massey and lived a number of years near Springfield, Ohio, when she felt death approaching came back to the old homestead and died.

To Otis Harrison and Frances Taylor Harrison were born the following children:

1. Orin, who died in 1900, at Dayton, Ohio.
2. Flora, who married a LeSage.
3. Mary, who married a Brown.
4. Ella, who married a Ferguson.
5. L. E. (Rev.).
6. Charles O.

Rev. L. E. Harrison married Nannie B. Trent, a teacher in the Nicholas County schools and who is now teaching in the Cabell County schools. She is a sister of W. W. Trent, the present State Superintendent of Schools.

Charles O. Harrison married Nancy Adkins, a teacher in the schools of Huntington and in Wayne County.

The Rev. L. E. Harrison and his brother, Charles O. Harrison, have contributed much to the cultural and material progress of Cabell County. For more than a third of a century these two brothers have been active in their communities, Charles O. confining his activities to Cabell County, in the capacity of farmer, merchant, banker and contractor. He entered the contracting business in the 90's and in 1905 organized the firm of Harrison and Dean with F. E. Dean of

Niagara Falls, New York. This business was very successful and continues to this time. Although not active since 1929, it has to its credit many completed paving contracts in Huntington, the excellent construction on which is a continuing testimonial to the thoroughness and efficiency of the builders.

In addition to his business activities, C. O. Harrison has found time to take a leading part in the civic affairs of his community. He served a number of times on the city council, for many years on the board of education, and is a member of the board of stewards of the Johnson Memorial M. E. Church, South.

The Rev. L. E. Harrison began his career as a school teacher. His later activities were bounded by the Western Virginia Conference of the Methodist Episcopal Church, South, in which organization he has filled many pulpits for thirty-eight years, and has been instrumental in building a number of churches.

HARSHBARGER

One of the substantial and outstanding men of Cabell County is Ira J. Harshbarger. Three times elected sheriff by the vote of the people is a testimonial few men have received. This, added to the fact that his father, David Harshbarger, was a candidate for sheriff and that his half-brother, Captain John Harshbarger, was elected and served as sheriff, speaks volumes as to the standing of the family.

Ira J. Harshbarger's life has been an eventful one. He was born at Barboursville, November 30, 1858, and when he was four years old his father moved on a farm near Ona and continued there ten years. The family then moved to Milton. Ira J. joined the Methodist Church, South, at sixteen years of age and is still an active member and a trustee of the Johnson M. E. Church. He worked on the farm, attended the common schools, and after he grew up his father gave him an interest in the farm. He farmed and raised cattle until he was thirty years old when he and his half-brother, John, embarked in the milling business at Milton. When Ira J. went into the mill in 1888 he remodeled it and made it up-to-date. Later John sold his interest to George W. Harshbarger, who was a full brother to Ira, and the business became Harshbarger Brothers Milling Company and was later incorporated. It continues to this date as one of the splendid milling companies in this end of the state. Ira J. Harshbarger is still the president.

In 1903 Ira J. Harshbarger organized the Bank of Milton and for a long time was president and its largest stockholder. But it is in the field of oil and gas development that he was the real pioneer notwithstanding the fact that the late I. C. White, the State Geologist had expressed the view that there was neither oil or gas south of the Little Kanawha River. Men were skeptical of that judgment and Ira J. Harshbarger was one of the skeptics. In 1898 he organized the Milton Oil and Gas Company and leased 6,500 acres of land and drilled three wells. He has the distinction of having drilled the first oil well south of the Kanawha River. He then organized the Cabell Oil and Gas Company and this company with the Milton Oil and Gas Company became the Harshbarger Oil and Gas Company which has drilled more than thirty wells and has a number of producing oil wells and gas wells. Mr. Harshbarger was for many years its president and general manager. He was president of the Milton Drilling Company and for a time was president and sole owner of the Fought Oil and Gas Company, as well as president of the Montgomery Gas Company, Montgomery, for ten years. In addition to these interests he has been interested in the First Huntington National Bank, the Gwinn Brothers Milling Company, and the Jackson Milling Company of Ohio.

Ira J. Harshbarger married in 1881 Clara M. Crooks, daughter of Dr. James M. Crooks of Bridgeton, Indiana, and they have three children: Hattie L., Maude, and Harrison M.

The Harshbarger family came to Cabell at an early date. William, the paternal grandfather of Ira J., was a German by birth, a farmer and blacksmith and came to his death by drowning in Mud River. His wife was a Garrett, whose father James Garrett lived in Lincoln County.

William Harshbarger had a son, William, who moved to Aldney, Illinois, where his descendants are still living and had another son, David, who was a farmer and was born in Botetourt County, Virginia, October 11, 1811, and died in Cabell County on March 4, 1898. The records disclose that David was an overseer of the roads in his district as early as 1828. He was married twice and the mother of Ira J. Harshbarger was a Virginia woman. David by another wife had two sons; Peter, who went to Aldney, Illinois, after the Civil War where he died, and John who was a captain in the Third Regiment of the West Virginia Cavalry Volunteers, and after the Civil War was elected sheriff. During this period there was much difficulty with the sheriff's office but John Harshbarger annually settled his accounts and this account is spread on the court records. He closed his office in balance and has the distinction of being the first sheriff whose accounts are thus shown. John is the father of J. H. Harshbarger of Milton.

HENRY DRURY HATFIELD

Henry Drury Hatfield is one of the great surgeons of the State. He was graduated from Franklin College, New Athens, Ohio, in 1890, and then attended the University of Louisville and graduated with an M.D. in 1894, and ten years later was graduated from the New York University with an M.D. Since that date he has taken five post-graduate courses which included graduate courses at Polyclinic Medical School and Hospital, New York Post Graduate School and Hospital, and Cornell University.

Immediately upon his graduation from the University of Louisville he entered into active practice and has continued in the practice except for the periods he was taking other courses and the time he was governor of the State. He located at Eckman, W. Va., in 1894, and in the next year was made surgeon for the Norfolk and Western Railway Company which position he held until 1913. He served as commissioner of health in Mingo County from 1895 to 1900. He was surgeon-in-chief and president of the board of directors of the West Virginia Miners Hospital No. 1, at Welch from 1899 to 1913. During the World War Dr. Hatfield served as a major in the Medical Corps and had charge of Base Hospital No. 36. He is now a lieutenant colonel in the Medical Reserve. At the end of his term as governor, Dr. Hatfield moved to Huntington and has identified himself with the Huntington General Hospital, now the Huntington Memorial Hospital. He brought about the organization of the Hatfield-Lawson Hospital at Logan, and became consulting surgeon for the Norfolk and Western Railway which connection continued until 1929.

Dr. Hatfield is a man of great physical strength and the amount of work he does is enormous. He practices his profession for the love of the work and the hold he has on the people he treats professionally is unusually strong.

Henry Drury Hatfield was born in Logan County, West Virginia, the son of Elias and Elizabeth Hatfield. He married on March 27, 1895, S. C. Bronson, and to them has been born a daughter, Hazel, who is the wife of J. R. Sproul.

While Dr. Hatfield's profession has been his first interest he has always taken an active interest in public affairs. He served as secretary of the Republican county committee, McDowell County for eight years, chairman of the Republican county committee of Cabell County for four years, a member of the Republican state committee, 1920-24, member of the County Court of McDowell County, 1906-1912, State senator, 1909-1912, and president of the Senate in 1911, delegate to the Republican National Convention, 1912, governor, 1913-1916, and United States Senator, 1929-1934.

Dr. Hatfield is a liberal Republican who at an early date advocated many things which were then in advance of contemporary thought—one of the most important of which was the public service commission of the State—yet he has stood firmly for orderly government under the Constitution and in the closing years of his term as Senator he opposed many of President Roosevelt's policies on the ground that they were in conflict with the Constitution.

Dr. Hatfield received the degree of LL.D. from Bethany College, from Franklin College, and the West Virginia University in 1915. He is a Fellow of the American College of Surgeons and the Southern Medical Association; a member of the American, West Virginia, and Cabell County Medical Societies; Southern States Association of Railway Surgeons; Association Military Surgeons of the United States, and an honorary member of the McDowell County Medical Society; the American Legion; U. S. Reserve Officers Association; Elk; Masonic, and Odd Fellow lodges.

ADAM HATFIELD

Adam Hatfield came from eastern Virginia and settled in Cabell County on a farm at Ousley's Gap at what is now Inez early in the nineteenth century, and on October 30, 1810, secured a deed from Alonzo Hatfield for 128 acres of land on the Guyan River on which he lived and on which his descendants reside. He had four sons, Moses, Henry, George, Lou, and several daughters. The son, Moses, married Penina Beckett of Inez and had the following children: Martha, married Adam Hinchman, Lucinda, Hannah, Joe, Bert, Adam, and J. G.

J. G. Hatfield was born April 26, 1857, and as a young man taught school and later engaged in the contracting business. On January 20, 1886, he married Mary M. Seamonds, also a school teacher, daughter of William H. Seamonds of Blue Sulphur, and had the following children:

(1) William Moses, born April 8, 1887, served with Company F, 350th Engineers, A.E.F., and died in October, 1932.

(2) Mary Inez, born November 3, 1889. Married Robert Swann of Inez, and has ten children: William, Louise, Ralph, Fred, Freda, Robert, Rosalie, Jane, Patty Lou, and Jimmy.

(3) Robert Pearl, born May 11, 1892. Served in the Motor Transport Corps, A.E.F. Married Nell Floyd, and has two children: Mary Lou and Robert, Junior.

(4) Lulu Susan, born February 3, 1895. Married O. F. Keyser and has six children: Lois who married Graham Stark; Lucile, Homer Lee, Mona, Peggy Ruth, and Davy Neal.

(5) James Benjamin, born August 10, 1897.

(6) Homer Whitesel, born May 4, 1900. Married Emily Burgess and has a daughter, Dorothy.

(7) Ola Alberta, born August 3, 1903, died December 12, 1906.

(8) Mona Pauline, born December 4, 1905. Married John Quillan and has a son, Johnnie.

J. G. Hatfield was a Mason, a member of the First Methodist Episcopal Church, and served six years as a member of the County Court. In 1914 he moved to Huntington and organized the Hatfield Construction Company which consisted of himself and his two eldest sons, Moses and Robert, and they were successful contractors until the death of J. G. Hatfield on January 28, 1919. At this time the two sons, Moses and Robert were in France with the A.E.F. They got their discharge a short time afterwards and returned home and continued the business under the same firm name. Since the death of Moses, the brothers Benjamin and Homer have been taken into the firm, and it continues to be very successful.

Robert P. Hatfield recently purchased the Patterson home on Staunton Road overlooking the Ohio River, one of the most attractive homes in Huntington.

HAWORTH-CAMMACK-MATHEWS

When Captain Morgan and his Confederate raiders came to grips with the Ohio Home Guard near Portland, Ohio, much of the ensuing fighting occurred on the farm of Dr. Samuel Milton Haworth. Soon after the Civil War, Dr. Haworth and his family moved across the river to Ravenswood, West Virginia, where he died February 14, 1886. His widow, born Hannah Amsden, his son and his four daughters survived him. All but the oldest daughter subsequently lived in Cabell County.

The Haworth family originated in England. George Haworth the founder of the family in America, emigrated from the village of Bacup, Lancastershire, to Philadelphia in 1699 with a party of followers of William Penn. Many of the same family now live at and near Manchester, England.

Dr. Samuel Milton Haworth was born near Philadelphia, and came with his father, John Haworth, to Ohio while a small boy. He spent his life as a country doctor.

His son, Clarence Everett Haworth, born at Portland, Ohio, May 10, 1860, followed his father in the study of medicine. He won the degree of M.D. at Starling Medical College, now a part of the University of Louisville, Kentucky, and did post-graduate work at the Cincinnati College of Medicine. Degrees of A.B., A.M., and Ph.D., followed at Colgate College. In 1884 he went to Ravenswood to practice medicine.

The profession, however, had little attraction for him. He was a scholar by instinct, a musician, composer and writer by natural inclination. Nevertheless he practiced medicine for several years, and seeking a larger field than that afforded in Jackson County, he came to Huntington in 1889 and opened an office.

In 1893 he had opportunity to purchase the Huntington Herald, and was its owner and editor until 1907. In the following year he sold the paper, and became a member of the faculty of Marshall College, as professor of English literature. Meanwhile he had been very active as a leader in the struggling cultural life of the young town of Huntington.

His wife, born Harriet Vinton, died July 1, 1901. He married Miss Louise Fay, of Chicopee Falls, Massachusetts, in 1904, while she was a teacher of voice at Marshall College.

On July 19, 1929, while travelling by automobile to Cincinnati to hear an opera at the Zoölogical Garden, he died of a heart attack, leaving his widow and two sons, Samuel Vinton Haworth and James Rodgers Haworth, surviving.

Dr. Haworth was a man of gentle and courteous character and companiable manner, who had many devoted friends.

Before Dr. Haworth moved to Huntington, his sister, Alice, had come from Ravenswood to teach music. She was followed by her mother and two of her sisters, Bertha Luella and Essie M. Haworth.

They resided first on 6th Avenue near 11th Street, and later on 10th Street near 7th Avenue. Alma Haworth remained in Ravenswood, where she married Alonzo T. Keeney, who died in 1933. In 1935 she was still living in the old Haworth home in Ravenswood.

In the Haworth home in Huntington a delightful and exemplary family life developed. The home was constantly open to visitors who were attracted by the friendly and open cordiality of those who lived there. Mrs. Haworth, her daughters and her sons-in-law lived together in the home for many years, and it was a subject of general remark that so many should occupy the same house so long in harmony.

Bertha Luella Haworth married Charles W. Cammack. He was a son of John Henry Cammack, who was born December 12, 1843, at Dayton, Rockingham County, Virginia, a veteran of the Confederate Army. John Henry Cammack's life in Huntington, aside from his business, was devoted principally to the work of the Baptist church, of which he was long a deacon, and in maintaining a spirit of comradeship among the Confederate Army veterans who lived in Cabell County. Until his death he was commander of the Huntington post of Confederate veterans.

A part of the war career of Mr. Cammack is contained in a printed book of his reminiscences, published by his sons, Lucius H. Cammack and Charles W. Cammack, under the title, *Personal Recollections of Private John Henry Cammack*.

Mr. Cammack, with his resources greatly reduced by the war, came to Huntington with his family in February, 1878. He opened a store, which he operated successfully for some years, and subsequently engaged in the fire insurance business with J. N. Potts, another well remembered early resident of Huntington. The insurance business thrived, and when Mr. Cammack's son, Charles W. Cammack, joined him, the firm engaged extensively in real estate development also. Three large insurance firms at present operating in Huntington were started by former employes of the Cammack agency, who had bought out portions of the firm's business.

John Henry Cammack died May 6, 1920, one of Huntington's most beloved citizens, whose memory is greatly revered.

Charles Walker Cammack was born at Williamstown, Wood County, October 6, 1870. He married Luella Haworth June 12, 1893, in Huntington. She died January 25, 1926. On February 21, 1928, he married her sister, Essie, then the widow of Egede C. McMillen, thus continuing the felicitous family life of the Haworths and their connections together.

Mr. Cammack has been an active and influential figure in the business and civic life of Huntington. His energetic capacities in the field of insurance and real estate strongly influenced the growth and development of Huntington. As a young man he was employed by the First National Bank, working in various capacities until 1895. He was vice president of the Union Bank and Trust Company for twenty years. As a member of the Huntington Chamber of Commerce and other organizations he was active in promoting the commercial development of the city, and he has been interested in various other phases of civic life, striking among which is the Huntington Union Mission Settlement for orphan children, of which he has been president since its foundation.

Since January 23, 1892, he has been state agent for the John Hancock Mutual Life Insurance Company. His son, Howard Haworth Cammack, is state agent for Missouri of the same company, with offices in St. Louis, and another son, Charles W. Cammack, Junior, is associated with his father in the agency in Huntington. His daughter, Ruth, is married to Rolla D. Campbell, attorney, of Huntington.

Egede C. McMillen, the first husband of Essie M. Haworth, was the son of Archibald James McMillen, chaplain of the 14th Kentucky Regiment of the Union Army in the Civil War. He was born at Deerfield, Muskingum County, Ohio, November 18, 1865, and came with his father, who had accepted a call to the Presbyterian church, to Ravenswood. There he met his future wife, whom he married in a double wedding with her sister, Alice, and David E. Mathews, in Huntington, in 1892. He had been employed in the store of Coleman Staats, in Ravenswood, and in Huntington was employed as traveling salesman for the John A. Jones Company, dealers in musical instruments. He was of genial and witty nature, and widely popular. He died in Huntington on March 21, 1904. Mrs. Hannah Amsden Haworth died two weeks later, April 4, 1904.

Judge David E. Mathews, who married Alice Elizabeth Haworth, was one of Huntington's most remarkable men in various capacities. Born in the home of an immigrant from Wales, at Syracuse, Ohio, he overcame many handicaps to become a prominent figure in law and in politics. He was born September 30, 1858. As a boy he worked in the coal mines at Syracuse, gleaning what education he could from his own reading. He had little schooling, but secured a broad, cultural education through his reading and personal study. In 1886 he went to Ravenswood to undertake to sell insurance, and met his future wife there. After a brief course in law at Washington and Lee University, he came to Huntington in 1888, passed the State Bar examinations, and engaged in the practice of law.

He was active in politics in Huntington in the early history of the town, running unsuccessfully as the Republican candidate for mayor on two occasions, on one of which he was shown to have been elected on the face of unofficial returns, but failing on a contest to hold the advantage. In 1899 he was elected judge of the Criminal Court of Cabell County. At the expiration of his term he was appointed assistant attorney general of West Virginia under Clark W. May, then attorney general. In 1918, he was elected judge of the Common Pleas Court of Cabell County, serving a term of six years. In 1935 he is engaged in the practice of law in Huntington.

Mrs. Mathews died January 25, 1933.

HITE

Jost Hite—spelled Heydt or Heidt—was born in Germany and died in Virginia in 1761; married in 1709 Anna Maria Dubois. He migrated to America in 1731 and purchased a large boundary of land in what is now Frederick County, Virginia, where he settled in 1732. Two of his grandsons came to Cabell County in the beginning of the nineteenth century. Jacob came first and in 1810 bought from Jeremiah Ward 100 acres of land on the Ohio River which was a part of tract 41 of the Savage Grant. He married Sally—or Sarah—Scales. The brother, William, born 1771, died 1855, married Elizabeth Brown, followed and in 1817 bought from Manoah Bostick parts of tracts 45 and 61 of the Savage Grant, which lay on the south side of the Guyandotte River just above the mouth of Russell's Creek.

Jacob Hite had a daughter, Mary Scales Hite, who married John Laidley, and one son, John W., who was a prominent merchant and business man in Guyandotte, who had a number of daughters. Salina C. married George W. Mason, Addie C. married George W. Holderby, and Isabella, born June 30, 1821, died June 3, 1908, married W. T. Moore, in January, 1884.

William Hite spent his last years in Guyandotte and was the father of John B. Hite, William Hite, and Frank W. Hite.

John B. Hite had a tanyard, the building of which was still standing a few years ago. He lived on Main Street in Guyandotte up to the time of his death several years ago. He married Elizabeth A. Johnson, and had a son, John B. Hite, Junior, born in 1855, who spent his life in Guyandotte and who served in the town council, and a daughter Mrs. Alfred A. Fisher.

Frank W. Hite, born 1818, died 1891, married Mary Brammer, and had eight children among whom were Fannie, Gertie, Kate, Charley who died in infancy, Edward who was a Methodist minister and had one of the larger churches in New York City, H. C. Hite who spent his life in the service of the Chesapeake and Ohio Railroad and has recently been retired, and William F. who began life as a telegraph operator for the Chesapeake and Ohio Railroad and retired as a division freight agent. William F. Hite served one term as mayor of Huntington and married Anna Ensign, daughter of Ely Ensign.

HOLDERBY

The Holderbys are English. There is a village in North Hampshire, England, named Holderby, and it is said that this name is a contraction of Holderboro.

William Holderby who died October 10, 1812, came to what is now Cabell County at the beginning of the nineteenth century and is said to have been born on York River in Eastern Virginia. He served as a private in the Revolutionary War and it was in his field in the town of Guyandotte on which the first courthouse was erected. His wife was Priscilla Pendleton of Richmond, Virginia, and his children were James, Robert, Absolom, William, Nancy, Fanny, and Eliza. Nancy married a man named Helverson. Fanny married Philemon Chapman, and Eliza married Allen McGinnis. James Holderby, born 1782, and died 1855, purchased in 1821 from George Hollenback and Henry Hampton part of tracts 38 and 39 of the Savage Grant which lay between 14th and 17th Streets, fronting on the river and extending back taking in some of the hill lands and included in its boundary the land on which Marshall College now stands. He built a home which still stands at the foot of 16th Street and at that point was a river landing known as Holderby Landing. The McCoy Road, which is now Route 8 to Wayne, came to the river at this point. At his death this farm was divided between his two sons and W. P. had that part which lies north of the Chesapeake and Ohio Railroad. James Holderby married first, Areanna Lane and by this marriage had a daughter, Areanna, who married Elisha W. McComas. His

James Holderby

Robert Holderby Home

Robert Holderby, Sr.

Susan Ann Chapman, wife of Robert Holderby

second wife was Lucy Wright, an English woman who came with her parents to Richmond, Virginia, and later moved with her brother, Edward, to Charleston. To this union was born a daughter, Emma, who married Dr. James H. Rogers of Charleston; a son, William P., who married Hallie Valentine, had a daughter, Willie Mae. James Holderby's second son, Edward S., was born February 1, 1844, and died June 4, 1890. He had that part of his father's farm that lay south of the Chesapeake and Ohio Railroad, and built a home on the knoll on 16th Street where the present brick house stands. He married on August 23, 1870, Columbia A. Stewart and had three daughters, Lucy, wife of Alex C. Nelson; Sadie, wife of Dr. H. C. Solter; Emma, wife of Harry H. Darnall.

Robert Holderby married Susan Ann Chapman, daughter of George and Elizabeth Parker Chapman, and lived in the brick house which we now know as the Altizer house, later called Lawson Hall, which burned a few years ago. Their children were: Susan L., who married Thomas J. Jenkins; Dudley Drake, C.S.A., killed January 10, 1862; Robert S., first lieutenant, C.S.A., died July 9, 1864; Mary Phenton, who married Thomas C. Buffington, July 14, 1856; Eliza Priscilla, died without issue; George William, first lieutenant, Border Rangers, born 1838, died 1903, married Addie C. Hite (daughter of John W. Hite), October 22, 1865; Elizabeth Parker, married in 1859 Samuel Coale.

Absolom, third son of William Holderby married America Gardner, and had two daughters. One married an Allen, and the other married H. B. Maupin and died without issue.

William Holderby, II, born circa 1765, died circa 1870, married Rebecca Hoskinson and had twelve children which included Abner, Absolom, William, James, Robert, Rebecca, and Mahaley. Absolom had a son, William Robert Holderby, who was the father of T. E. Holderby, former member of the school board.

HOLLENBECK

W. S. Laidley, writing about the farms fronting on the Ohio River, after locating the Staley farm, said, "The farms next below were held by the Hollenbeck families," but these families are no longer represented in this county. Martin Hollenbeck was one of the defendants in the suit to partition the Savage Grant, but why, does not appear from the records in the clerk's office. The decree does not confirm him in any holding, and there are no deeds of record giving him any interest therein. Notwithstanding this fact, in 1820 he conveyed 100 acres on the Ohio River to John Hollenbeck, and in the next year conveyed 100 acres to Martin, Jr., and 100 acres to George. The tracts conveyed to George and Martin afterwards went to James Holderby. In 1811 Henry Hampton conveyed two tracts of 100 acres each on the Ohio River to John and George Hollenbeck, respectively, and two years later conveyed a second 100 acres on the Ohio River to George.

In 1851 Henry Hollenbeck made a deed to Edmund McGinnis for a tract of land on Four Pole which disposed of all the land owned by Hollenbecks in the county. The family held no public office and no mention is made of it in the public records. When it originated is not known, but the last of them moved further West about the middle of the nineteenth century.

HULL*

Martin Hull, who married Susan Buffington and lived in the log house shown in the picture at 14th Street, West, is said to have come to the county as early as 1800. This couple had a son, James, who married a Miss Smith and moved on the Sandy. After the death of Susan Buffington, Martin Hull married again, and raised a large family, all of whom are said to have moved to the West.

JENKINS

William Jenkins lived in Tidewater, Virginia, and operated a line of ships from the James River to South America. He lived for a time in Rockbridge County, Virginia, where in 1824 he married Jeannette G. McNutt, daughter of Alexander and Rachael Grigsby McNutt. In 1825 he moved, with his wife and infant daughter, to Greenbottom. Here he erected a temporary home and here his three sons were born, all of whom were graduated in the same year, 1848, from Jefferson College, then located at Canonsburg, Pennsylvania. In 1835 Captain Jenkins built the brick house which stands near Clover Station on the Baltimore and Ohio Railroad, now known as the General Jenkins house. The house has a stone foundation and the bricks were made on the place. The timbers are hand-hewn, and put together with wooden pegs and are in a good state of preservation to this date. The house fronts on the river and in the rear there was a

---

*Written from information secured from the article, "The Western End of Virginia," by W. S. Laidley.

brick kitchen and an office built apart from the house but these buildings have been taken down in the past twenty years.

Mrs. Jenkins died in 1843 and Captain Jenkins in 1859 and the Greenbottom estate was devised to his three sons. To this union were born:

1. A daughter, Eustatia A., who married Pembroke Waugh of Lynchburg, Virginia.

2. Thomas Jefferson Jenkins, born November 22, 1826, died August 1, 1872. He was a private 1861-63, and a major 1863-65, C.S.A. He married on November 18, 1856, Susan L. Holderby, who was born in 1836 and died in 1927. To them were born:
   1. Julia, born 1857, died 1903.
   2. Laura P., born 1859, died 1879.
   3. D. J., who was sheriff of Cabell County, 1893-1896. Married Elizabeth Leete of Ironton, Ohio.
   4. Grace.
   5. George Robert, now a dentist in New York City.
   6. Albert Gallatin.

3. William Alexander Jenkins, born November 21, 1828, died April 8, 1877. He was a student at Jefferson Medical College and practiced medicine in St. Louis, Missouri, 1852-54. He served as a surgeon in the C.S.A. Married on December 22, 1853, Julia M. Reed of St. Louis. She was born January 13, 1829, and died November 19, 1894. They had the following children:
   1. Jeannette A.
   2. William G.
   3. Henrick A.
   4. Charles McNutt.
   5. Julia M.
   6. Susan M., who married C. E. Gwinn of Huntington.

4. Albert Gallatin Jenkins, born November 10, 1830, prepared for college at Marshall Academy, then went to Jefferson College. He was prominent in literary activities and was one of the founders of the Phi Gamma Delta Fraternity, and graduated in 1848 with honors. Perhaps through the influence of a fraternity brother, John Temple McCarty, who stopped at Greenbottom on his way to Indiana, Albert Gallatin Jenkins attended Harvard Law School, and was graduated in 1850. He practiced law for a short time in Charleston but soon took up his residence at Greenbottom. In 1856 he was a delegate to the National Democratic Convention which nominated James Buch-

Samuel W. Johnston House, circa 1850

anan. In the same year he defeated John S. Carlile for Congress and served two terms. He was a delegate to the Provisional Confederate Congress in 1861. His connection with the Border Rangers has been told of in another chapter. On August 1, 1862, he was commissioned brigadier general, joined his command and led his brigade through Buchanan across into Ohio. In March of the next year he again reached the Ohio River and in June was near Harrisburg, Pennsylvania. He was wounded the second day of the Battle at Gettysburg. In the next year he was wounded at Cloyds' Mountain and died on May 21, 1864, at Dublin Depot, Virginia. His remains now rest in Spring Hill Cemetery in Huntington.

General Jenkins was regarded as one of the greatest cavalry leaders of the Civil War and his reputation was international. He married on July 15, 1858, Virginia Southard Bowlin of St. Louis, Missouri. They had four children: James Bowlin, Alberta Gallatin, Margaret Virginia, and George.

JAMES JOHNSTON

The early Presbyterian families were Scotch-Irish. Among these was the Johnston family. In 1817 James Johnston married Martha Logan in the County Antrim, Ireland. In 1818 accompanied by his wife and his brothers he migrated to America. They landed at Quebec and spent some time in Canada and in Pittsburgh and in the year 1820 came down the Ohio River in a flatboat to Burlington. The brothers, Benjamin and John settled on the Ohio side near South Point. In 1821 James bought a farm between 5th and 9th Streets, West. He built perhaps two houses on this land before he built the two-story frame house which stands at the intersection of Jefferson Avenue and 7th Street, West. James Johnston had the respect of his neighbors and when he died he was buried at Burlington and had one of the largest and most impressive funerals of that period. On the trip down the Ohio, Martha Johnston, wife of James Johnston, gave birth to a son who was named William. Among the other children was a daughter, Elizabeth, who married John B. Hite of Guyandotte, a daughter, Sara, and a son, John L., who was ordained as an elder on February 8, 1859, and served until November 22, 1906. He married a Miss Kincaid of Ashland, Kentucky, and built the house at the southeast corner of 6th Avenue and 2d Street, where John H. Meek now lives.

SAMUEL WOODROW JOHNSTON

Samuel Woodrow Johnston traces his lineage direct to Captain Archibald Johnston, a Revolutionary soldier, who came from Scotland to Dutchess County, New York, and migrated to Salisbury Township, Connecticut, early in the eighteenth century. He married Sarah Damron and was the father of five children by that union. He died in 1789.

Archibald Johnston's fifth son, Samuel Berry, born 1768, died 1815, was the father of Samuel Woodrow Johnston, born 1812 and died 1883. He married Mary McCormick. The family lived in Connecticut and Pennsylvania. The boy, Samuel, came to Cabell County from Harrisburg, Pennsylvania, about 1836. By profession a millwright, he located at Dusenberry Dam, and shortly thereafter married Rebecca Martin, who became the mother of his three children, Mary, who married James Gallaher, and was the mother of Mrs. J. K. Oney, Mrs. W. H. H. Holswade, Effie and Leslie Gallaher; a daughter Ann, who died in childhood, and Napoleon Bonaparte, who married Sarah Dundas.

S. W. Johnston's first wife died in 1846. He married Eliza Kilgore, a niece of Sampson Sanders, who died in 1913. In 1849 he bought 211 acres of land, part of tract 36 of the Savage Grant, which lay between 1st and 5th Streets, West, the Ohio River on the north, and Four Pole on the south. The old home is still standing on 7th Avenue and 3d Street, West, and is now the residence of a son, Benjamin Franklin Johnston.

Samuel and Eliza Johnston had the following issue: Fannie, married John Pollard; Martha, married John Kincade of Ashland, Kentucky; Emily, the wife of George C. Wood; Albert, married Mary Jane Kennett; Abner, married Melinda Kennett, of Delaware; Benjamin, married Pattie Taylor; Samuel, Junior, married Edwina McCormick; Daniel (single); Thomas, married Minnie Gaefe; Bell, and two other smaller children who died in infancy.

Samuel Woodrow Johnston died in 1883 and he and his wife are buried in Spring Hill Cemetery.

KAIL

Irish J. Kail, one of the leading dentists of the State, is the second son of Samuel Palmer Kail and his wife, Jane Conrad Hollandshead. He was born in Wyandotte County, Ohio, August 6, 1882, and was educated at the Ohio Northern College and the Ohio State University and awarded a degree of DD.S. by the last named institution in 1908. Dr. Kail was immediately appointed resident dental surgeon in the Ohio Hospital for Epileptics at Gallipolis and remained there until 1911 when he located at Huntington, and from the first has enjoyed a high reputation as a dental surgeon. At the outbreak of the war Dr. Kail volunteered and was commissioned a lieutenant in the Dental Corps in July, 1917, and was mustered out as major in December, 1918. Since the war he has continued to hold a commission in the Reserve Corps and now has the rank of colonel.

In 1933 he was named as a member of the school board under the new county unit plan, took office July 1, 1933, and was elected President. At the election of 1934 he was reëlected to the board and was again elected its president. He is an active member of the American Legion and past Post Commander, a member of the Rotary Club (past president), the Guyandotte Club, the Guyan Country Club, and has for many years been an enthusiastic supporter of the Boy Scouts.

Dr. Kail is the second son of Samuel Palmer Kail who was born in Carroll County, Ohio, on July 30, 1853, died July 9, 1916, and of Matilda Jane Hollandshead who was born in Wyandotte County, Ohio, on October 14, 1855. They were married on October 21, 1879. Matilda was the daughter of Jacob Hollandshead who came from Frederick County, Virginia, to Ohio in 1824 and married Jane Conrad. Samuel Palmer Kail was a son of Andrew Jackson Kail and Julia Lindsay, and a grandson of Adam Kail who died in October, 1852, and whose forbears came from Heidelberg, Germany, and his wife Anna Copper.

In 1912 Irish J. Kail married Marilla Bovie of Gallipolis, Ohio, and to this union has been born Samuel Goodhue, now a cadet at the United States Military Academy at West Point; Joe, and Mary.

The Bovies are of French descent. Frederick Bovie was born in 1799 at Troy, New York, and married Mercy Marie Clark who was born in Connecticut, but who had moved to Ohio shortly after 1812 and settled in Kinsman Center, Warren County. Mercy Marie Clark was the daughter of Abraham Clark, one of the Signers of the *Declaration of Independence*. To this union was born in 1848 Frederick Morgan Bovie, who served in the Union Army during the Civil War, and in 1870 married Lucy Vernon Alexander (born 1850 in Summerfield, Butler County, Ohio). To this union was born Marilla, the wife of Dr. Irish J. Kail. Frederick Morgan Bovie was for many years a partner of the firm of Henking, Bovie and Company, one of the most successful wholesale grocery houses in the Ohio Valley.

KILGORE

In 1801 Thomas Kilgore, a Scotch-Irishman, born in Pennsylvania in 1766, bought a tract of land in the lower Teay's Valley, now the southeastern part of Cabell County, and through which runs a creek that bears his name; and another tract west of Milton on Mud River. The first tract included the site of the Morris Memorial Farm. His home was on the Walker Johnson farm which adjoins the Morris Memorial Farm. The Kilgore graveyard is at the rear of the hospital.

Thomas Kilgore was one of the gentlemen justices who composed the County Court and was Sheriff 1832-33. He married Hettie Sanders,* sister of Sampson Sanders about whom we have written, who married Anne Guinn (now spelled Gwinn) and died without issue, and his estate except the slaves went to his sister's children.

Thomas and Hettie Kilgore had the following children:
1. George, who married twice and had a large family.
2. Martha, who married Charles K. Morris, a farmer, and lived in Teay's Valley. (See account of Morris Family.)
3. Melinda, who married Thomas Lee Jordan, a farmer. They lived in Kentucky and had the following children:
   a. Emma, married.
   b. Robert.
4. Linie, married a Ball.
5. Polly, married William Simmons and is the mother of Mrs. Fannie Vinson and the grandmother of John, Ed, and C. A. Love of Barboursville.
6. Jeremiah, married Nancy Fullerton. Their children were:
   a. Eliza, married Captain Samuel Johnston. (See account of Samuel W. Johnston Family.)
   b. Julia, married James McKeand. Their family lives in Wayne County.
   c. Mary, married James Duncan and moved to Illinois.
   d. Hettie, married John Gwinn.
   e. Thomas W., married Mary McCormick, a granddaughter of

---

*Hettie and Sampson Sanders were the children of William Sanders, born near Dixon Springs, Smith County, Tennessee, and died in Kanawha County. See Eunice Proctor Perkins account.

FAMILIES

James McCormick who came to Cabell County in 1795. (See McCormick Family.) Their children were:
a. J. C., married Betty Everett.
b. J. E., married Miss Plymale.
c. C. W. (now retired Chesapeake and Ohio passenger conductor), married Clara Belle Gillock of Staunton, Virginia.
d. B. V., married Miss McCormick of Kansas.
e. Robert, married Miss Burns.
f. Nettie, married Mr. Barker of Kentucky.

KYLE

The legendary history of the Kyle family begins in the first part of the sixteenth century when one known as "William the Tory" came with his brothers from Scotland to Ireland. The recorded history of the family begins with Robert Kyle who was born in 1775 in the town of Derry in the County of Tyrone. He died in Lawrence County, Ohio, in 1869. In 1800 he maried Sophia Thompson, born 1780 on the Island of St. Helena, and died 1870. Robert Kyle was a farmer and operated a grindstone quarry on the Manor of Hastings. While he lived in Tyrone there was much religious bitterness and an incident occurred which is reported in the biography of the late Bishop McCloskey of Pittsburgh, Pennsylvania, as follows:

"On the evening of a cold wet day in the last of the seventeenth century, there came a knock at the door of my grandfather's home on his estate in County Tyrone, Ireland. Someone went to the door and found a man, cold, wet, and hungry. It was reported to my grandfather.

"The man said: 'There are some men after me to kill me. Will you give me protection?'

"My grandfather said: 'I will, come in.' The wayfarer was given dry clothes and a warm supper. About this time there was a second knock at the door. Grandfather and the bishop were in a front room in which there was an old high bedstead and a stand.

"Grandfather went to the door. He was met by a man who said, 'Is the Bishop McCloskey here?' 'He is.' 'I will give you twenty-five pounds for the sight of him.' 'All right; put your money on the stand.' The money was counted and laid on the stand. Grandfather went to the bed and lifting the cover up, said, 'There he is.' The man started for the bishop. 'Stop,' said grandfather, 'You can't touch him—you said you would give twenty-five pounds for the sight of him.'

"Now, grandfather had an estate and besides was running a millstone quarry. He had quite a lot of men or members belonging to his clan. This man who tried to get at McCloskey had some men with him but he knew that he could do nothing so he went away, saying he would be back and see about it.

"Grandfather ordered his men to get three horses ready immediately. He soon had the bishop on his way with two guards, for the coast. Soon after the man who was searching for the priest came back with stronger help. He knocked at the door. 'I want the Bishop.' 'Well, take him.' 'Where is he?' 'I don't know.' 'Well, I will find him.' 'All right, go ahead.' Grandfather hinted that he might be here and there, holding them back all he could. Meantime the Bishop got down to the coast among his friends, and on a ship bound for America.

"Some years later grandfather came to America and located at Pittsburgh, Pa. He was walking along the street and came face to face with the bishop. They recognized each other instantly.

"Many an evening the bishop could be found at the home of my grandfather, always wanting to help him get started in America."

Robert Kyle and his wife had thirteen children, all of whom were born in Ireland, and when he migrated to America in 1833 two of his children had died in infancy and his daughter, Mary Ann, the oldest child, had married and remained in Ireland. The rest of the family accompanied him to America and lived in Pittsburgh. The families, of course, have drifted to many parts of the United States and many of them have obtained positions of prominence. Included in this group is Senator Kyle, late United States Senator from North Dakota.

Edmund Kyle, the ninth child of Robert Kyle, was born in 1816, in Derry, County Tyrone, and died in Cabell County in 1900. He located in Wetzel County and served as auditor of the restored State of Virginia, 1861 to June 20, 1863, and when the new State of West Virginia was formed he opened the first set of books in the auditor's office and was employed there for several years. He was sergeant-at-arms of the Senate in 1863, and a member of the House of Delegates from Wetzel County, 1863-64-65. Just after the close of the Civil War he purchased a farm at the upper end of Quaker Bottom in Lawrence County, Ohio, and lived there a few years, then bought a tract of 800 acres on the Ohio River at Little Seven Mile in this county, which formerly belonged to the children of Robert Holderby, and lived there until his death.

Edmund Kyle was an excellent farmer and one year raised 18,000 bushels of wheat which is said to have been the largest wheat crop ever raised in the county. He served two terms as sheriff, was a member of the County Court and was active in politics his entire lifetime. He gave the land for the first free school in his neighborhood, and gave the land for the site of the Olive Baptist Church and then paid for the furnishings in the church.

Edmund Kyle married in 1853, Sarah West, and to this union was born four boys and three girls: Robert Thompson, married Molly Baumgardner, and had two sons, Stanard and Cecil; William Galbraith, married Tate Russell; Jemima Belle, married William Nurnberger; Mary Sophia, married H. C. Watters; Martha, married H. McP. Cox, had two daughters Pauline and Maxine; Edmund Kelly, married Nancy Shy, had the following children: Ona, died without issue; B. E.; Nellie, married C. C. Dickey; William, married Hazel Byrd; Frank, married Stella Bumgardner; Marie, married Sherl Edler; Roy, married Ilda Montgomery; Earl, married Violet Thompson.

Henry McDowell, nicknamed "John" married Rachael Tompkins of Kanawha County on February 14, 1901, and had the following children: John McDowell, born September 7, 1902; Bennette B., born April 20, 1904, married Pauline Damron; Valentine, born August 24, 1908, married Marie Watts.

LAIDLEY

Thomas Laidley was born Laidlaw, January 1, 1756, in Ayrshire, Scotland, died March 17, 1838, in Cabell County. He was the fourth child of James L., an Episcopal minister, and his wife, Jane Stewart Laidlaw. Thomas came to America in 1774, landed in New York and moved to Lancaster, Pennsylvania. On June 18, 1778, he married Sarah Osborne in Philadelphia. She was born October 12, 1762, and died March 25, 1844, in Cabell County. He served in the Revolutionary War, and it is said he changed his name to Laidley to distinguish himself from his own kin who were Loyalist. He served under Washington at Trenton and commanded a boat on the Delaware when Philadelphia was occupied. He came with Albert Gallatin to Monongalia County and bought a large tract of land. He lived in Morgantown until late in life when he and his wife came to Cabell,

John Laidley, Prosecuting Attorney, 1817-1860, and one of the founders of Marshall Academy, and his wife, Mary Scales Hite.

and lived with their son, John. Thomas Laidley and Sarah, his wife, had two sons:

James Grant, who practiced law in Parkersburg, and was the grandfather of George S. Laidley, who for many years was superintendent of schools in Charleston.

John Osborne Laidley, born in Morgantown, April 28, 1791, and died in Cabell County, April, 1863. He had a limited education, and in 1810 was the editor of the *Monongahela Gazette*.

At the January, 1813 term the clerk of the Wood County Court certified that John Osborne Laidley was twenty-one years of age, a man of good character, and had resided in that county for ten months last past, and on June 14th following Judges Daniel Smith, Dabney Carr, and James Allen certified that they had examined the said Laidley and found him qualified to practice law. He came to Cabell County with John Samuels and located at Barboursville. He served for a short period in Captain Kennedy's artillery company which was near Norfolk, but whether this was in 1812 or in 1813 is not entirely clear. After coming to Cabell County, John Laidley dropped his middle name "Osborne" and he appears in the records of this county simply as John Laidley. He represented the county in the General Assembly, was prosecuting attorney from 1817 to 1860, was a member of the Virginia Convention of 1829-30, and was the outstanding lawyer of his day. He was a Democrat, but a Union man.

In 1821 he purchased from the heirs of Mark Russell, 175 acres of land which adjoined the Peter Scales farm and which the Russells had bought from Henry Hampton in 1811. This place he named Lamartine. It is located just west of 26th Street, and is now known as the Burk's place. In 1816 he married Mary Scales Hite, and to them were born: (1) Amacetta, married George William Summers of Kanawha County; (2) Louise, married W. H. Buffington; (3) Theodore, graduated from West Point in 1842, served in the Mexican War, and retired as a colonel of ordnance; (4) Albert, married Vesta Brown, and had two children, Alberta who died without issue, and John B., who was a lawyer and died in 1898; (5) Thomas M., a physician, who moved to Texas; (6) Ulysses; (7) Sallie; (8) John, who was admitted to the Bar at the beginning of the Civil War; (9) Eliza; (10) James; (11) Helen M., married Lou H. Burks, born May 26, 1840, and lived in the home place. He served in Company D, 8th Virginia Cavalry, C.S.A.; and (12) William Sydney, born June 27, 1839, at Lamartine, Cabell County, and died in Kanawha County, July 9, 1917. He attended Marshall College, then went to North Carolina to assist his brother, Colonel Theodore Laidley, commander of the Arsenal at Fayetteville. In 1863 he went to Charleston, read law in the office of his brother-in-law, Judge George William Summers, was admitted to the Bar in 1865, and was a member of the firm of Summers and Laidley. After Judge Summers' death he formed a partnership with Colonel William Henry Hogeman, which lasted until Colonel Hogeman's death. He served a term in the Legislature in 1872, was chairman of the Democratic Executive Committee for years, and was elected judge of the County Court in 1900. He was a charter member of the Historical Society and editor of the magazine, doing much of the writing himself.

He was a member of St. John's Episcopal Church, having been sent as a delegate many times, not only to Diocesan councils, but to the General Conventions.

He had a keen sense of humor, the Scotch love of justice and honesty, a passion for books and pictures, and a keen appreciation of music. His greatest joy, however, was in historical things and the discovery of events of the past. He wrote a *History of Kanawha County*, published in 1911.

In September, 1869, he married Virginia Brown, oldest daughter of Judge James H. Brown and Louisa Mayer Beuhring, at Charleston. She was born in Cabell County, September 23, 1847. She was a graduate of Steubenville Female Seminary, a woman of rare charm and culture, whose presence was felt everywhere she went. She was an influence in the church, for years being head of the Woman's Auxiliary of St. John's. She died December 14th, 1928. They had nine children:

I. Mary Louise, married Henry Bradford Clarkson (deceased).

II. Virginia Amacetta, married (1) H. W. Goodwin, who died, and (2) William Byrne Givin. They had one daughter:
    a. Nelle Brown Givin.

III. Theodora Beuhring, deceased.

IV. Lucie Brown, married General Jo Lane Stern of Richmond, Virginia; six children:
    a. Louise Beuhring.
    b. Josephine Lane.
    c. Cornelia Anne.
    d. Lewis Henry, married Margaret Carper.

e. Virginia Laidley.

f. Elizabeth Jane.

V. Madelon Dannenberg, unmarried.

VI. Dorothy Osborn, married Robert Mumford August of Richmond, Virginia.

VII. William Sydney, Junior, unmarried.

VIII. Douglas Scales, died in infancy.

IX. Janet Scales, married Earl Bailey Snider of Uniontown, Pennsylvania; two sons:

a. John Andrew.

b. William Sydney Laidley.

LANE*

The Lane family, which came from Virginia, consisted of a widow and a number of children. They lived for a short time on the farm now occupied by the American Car and Foundry Company plant. One of the daughters, Areanna, married James Holderby, and another daughter, Eleanor, married on August 8, 1822, James Buffington. The other children are said to have moved to South America.

LAYNE

(1) Carney M. Layne is the son of William M. Layne and Nancy Ellen Truesdell-Layne. He was born in Crown City, Gallia County, Ohio, on March 2, 1878. He was educated in the public schools, and afterwards taught school in Gallia County, Ohio, and Cabell County. He graduated from Eastman National Business College, Poughkeepsie, New York, in 1899, and for some years was engaged as bookkeeper, serving four years in the office of the Treasurer of the United States at Washington. He attended the law school of George Washington University, Washington, and graduated with the degree of LL.B. in 1904. He came to Huntington in 1905 and shortly thereafter engaged in the practice of law, which he has made his life work. In politics he is a Democrat, having been chairman as well as secretary of the Democratic Executive Committee. In 1915 he represented his county in the Legislature. He was married on November 21, 1916, to Alice Mary Lanahan of Washington. They have two children, Nancy Ellen Layne, born May 1, 1919, and Carney Milton Layne, born June 18, 1921. He has always been active in civic, professional and fraternal

---

*Written from information secured from the article, "The Western End of Virginia," by W. S. Laidley.

affairs, having served as president of the Cabell County Bar Association. He has been active in the Masonic lodge, having served as Master and High Priest of the local lodges and was Grand High Priest of the Grand Chapter of Royal Arch Masons of West Virginia in 1930-31. He is also a member of the Delta Tau Delta Fraternity. Mrs. Layne is a member of the Catholic church, a graduate of Notre Dame College and takes an active part in the Catholic Daughters of America. He has the following brothers and sisters:

Garrett A. Layne, born June 6, 1870.

Ora O. Layne-Drummond, born February 6, 1876.

Ernest Layne, born November 30, 1882.

Stanley A. Layne, born June 9, 1887.

Eric L. Layne, born at Crown City, Ohio.

(2) William M. Layne, the son of Nelson Layne and Elizabeth Jane White-Layne. Born May 9, 1849, near Crown City, Gallia County, Ohio. He is a staunch Democrat and has been engaged in the live-stock business and farming at Crown City, Ohio. He has one living brother, Elmore Layne, who was born near Crown City, Ohio, on June 8, 1868, and who now lives on a farm below Chesapeake, Ohio.

(3) Nancy Ellen Truesdell-Layne, the daughter of Columbus Truesdell and Sarah Williams Truesdell. Born in Lawrence County, Ohio, May 5, 1853, and died September 7, 1889. She has one living brother, Christopher Columbus Truesdell, who resides at Chesapeake, Ohio.

(4) Nelson Layne, the son of Woodson Layne and Sarah Fowler Layne. Born in Bedford County, Virginia, in 1808; died in Lawrence County, Ohio, January 7, 1882. His occupation was farming.

(5) Elizabeth Jane White-Layne, the daughter of David White and Winnie Garlic White. Born near Crown City, Ohio, on December 10, 1823; died on March 25, 1909.

(6) Columbus Truesdell, the son of James Truesdell. Born in Lawrence County, Ohio, in 1820, and died in 1875. His occupation was farming.

(7) Sarah Williams Truesdell, the daughter of John Williams and Lucy Sartin Williams. Born in Gallia County, Ohio, in 1821, and died in 1870.

(8) Woodson Layne, the son of Robert Layne. Born in Bedford County, Virginia, in 1785, of English parentage. He removed to Guyan Township, Gallia County, Ohio, about 1810, and settled

on a section of land on a branch which bears his name. He was one of the early pioneers in this section.

(9) Sarah Jane Fowler-Layne, the wife of Woodson Layne. Born in Bedford County, Virginia, in 1789. She was likewise of English parentage.

(10) David White, the father of Elizabeth Jane White-Layne. Born in the Dominion of Canada on March 2, 1796. He was the youngest of six children, and of English birth. When quite a small child his father moved the family to Canandaigua County, New York, where they resided until 1817; in that year he and his father removed to and settled at the mouth of Shoal Creek on the north bank of the Ohio River in Lawrence County, Ohio, where he married Winnie Garlic and reared a large family. He was one of the most refined and cultured men to be found among the early pioneers. He was well read, particularly in the common law of England, but never made it a profession.

(11) Winnie Garlic White, wife of David White, and mother of Elizabeth Jane White-Layne. Born September 11, 1802, in South Carolina. She was said to be of French extraction. She removed with her father's family about 1818 to the mouth of Swann Creek, Gallia County, Ohio. She came from a well-bred family. Her mother's maiden name was Cooke.

(12) James Truesdell, father of Columbus Truesdell. Born in what is now the State of Indiana about the year 1800. He was of Dutch descent. He removed to Lawrence County, Ohio, about 1820.

(13) John Williams, father of Sarah Williams Truesdell. Born in Greenbrier County, Virginia. He was of English lineage; removed to Guyan Township, Gallia County, Ohio, about 1815, being one of the early pioneers. He spent his life in that neighborhood.

(14) Lucy Sartin Williams, wife of John Williams, and mother of Sarah Williams-Truesdell. Born in Giles County, Virginia. She was of English descent and was one of the first of those early settlers to migrate to the north bank of the Ohio River, where she spent her life and died at a ripe old age.

(15) Robert Layne, the father of Woodson Layne, was said to have been born in the State of Carolina, and afterwards removed to Bedford County, Virginia. Little is known about him.

LE SAGE

Dr. Isaac Richard Le Sage, of Huntington, who, for a number

of years, has been recognized as one of the leading physicians of West Virginia, is descended, as his name denotes, from ancestors whose nationality was that of one whose heroic life is closely interwoven with the most momentous period of our history, General de Lafayette.

(I) Michael Le Sage, great-grandfather of Dr. Isaac Richard Le Sage, was born in Paris, France, and married Sophia Duval, a native of the same city, where both passed their entire lives.

(II) Jules F. M., son of Michael and Sophia (Duval) Le Sage, was born in 1811, in Paris, France, and in his early manhood served in the French campaign in Algiers. Soon after, he emigrated to the United States, and lived for a time in Philadelphia, later removing to New York, where he engaged in business as a hat and bandbox manufacturer. In 1851 he came to Cabell County, and there passed the remainder of his life. In politics he was a Whig, and during the Civil War served in the Union Army, afterwards identifying himself with the Republican party. He was one of the promoters of the Icarian Society that settled in Nauvoo, Illinois, in the early forties. In religion he was a Catholic. He married, in 1834, in Philadelphia, Mary M. Bellemere, and they became the parents of two sons: Francis J., and Joseph A., mentioned below. The town of Le Sage is understood to have been named in honor of Jules F. M. Le Sage.

(III) Joseph A., son of Jules F. M. and Mary M. (Bellemere) Le Sage, was born in August, 1838, in Philadelphia, and spent his early manhood on a farm at Le Sage. At the outbreak of the Civil War he enlisted in the Union Army, and after the expiration of his term of service, moved to Ironton, Ohio, where he engaged in business as a contractor and builder. He married Mary C. E. Dovel, born October, 1839, in Page County, Virginia, daughter of Isaac C. and Esther (Keyser) Dovel, both natives of that county. Mrs. Dovel was a daughter of Andrew Keyser who accompanied General Braddock on his ill-fated expedition to Fort Duquesne. Mr. and Mrs. Le Sage had two sons: Isaac Richard, mentioned below; and Joseph C., born February 2, 1871, at Ironton, Ohio.

(IV) Dr. Isaac Richard Le Sage, elder son of Joseph A. and Mary C. E. (Dovel) Le Sage, was born April 12, 1866, at Le Sage, and received his earlier education in the public schools of Ironton, Ohio, later becoming a student at Marshall College, Huntington, from which he graduated in 1884. His professional training was obtained at the Ohio Medical College, Cincinnati, that institution conferring

Le Sage House, Le Sage

upon him, in 1888, the degree of Doctor of Medicine. After graduating, Dr. Le Sage spent six months in Illinois, and in the autumn of 1889 returned to Huntington, where he has since continuously practiced, acquiring large and lucrative connections and building up a most enviable reputation. In the year 1897 he became president of the board of health, and also city physician, serving ten years in both of these very responsible offices.

When the United States entered the World War, he was one of the first in the county to offer his services. He received a commission as lieutenant, Medical Corps, and was sent to Fort Harrison for a time; later being transferred to Columbus, Ohio, to take charge of the Students Army Training Corps unit of the Ohio State University. He carried this contingent through the fearful "flu" epidemic of the fall of 1918 with the lowest mortality of any training camp in the country. After finishing his services there he was transferred to Colgate University, from which he was discharged with honorable mention.

Dr. Le Sage married, December 22, 1897, at Gap Mills, Monroe County, West Virginia, Mary E. Humphreys, born March 12, 1870, at Sweet Chalybeate, Virginia, daughter of Andrew J. and Eliza Humphreys, who were parents of three other children: William J., Leonidas W., and Rose I. Humphreys. Mr. Humphreys was a millwright, and during the War Between the States served in the Confederate Army. There was born to Dr. and Mrs. Le Sage, a son, William Dovel, whose biographical sketch follows:

(V) William Dovel Le Sage, only son of Dr. Isaac Richard Le Sage and Mary E. (Humphreys) Le Sage was born March 31, 1899, at Huntington. He received his early education in the Huntington public schools, and after graduating from high school, attended the University of Virginia and the Ohio State University. He later studied law at West Virginia University, and accounting at the Pace Institute.

Mr. Le Sage is employed as statistician with the Appalachian Electric Power Company.

Mr. Le Sage has won much recognition in the field of pictorial photography, his chosen hobby, having his photographs hung in salons all over the world. In 1934 the Royal Photographic Society of Great Britain conferred the honor of associateship upon him, carrying the privilege of using the letters A.R.P.S. after his name.

In 1920 Mr. Le Sage married Mary Lucile, only daughter of Owen M. and Kathleen (Hartigan) Brown, born at Rogersville, Tennessee, and to them was born one son, William Dovel, Junior, on October 28, 1920.

LONG

Joseph Harvey Long traces the line of his forbears through the Pennsylvania family of Lang to Christian Lang, who emigrated from the German Palatinate to Philadelphia in 1683-4, and some years later established his home at Hickorytown, now Lancaster, Pennsylvania. Christian Lang was born in about the year 1664, and was first of his family to come to America.

At about the time of the Civil War the Lang family Anglacized, the name, altering it to Long.

Joseph Harvey Long was the son of Edward Christian Long and grandson of Joseph Long. He was born May 21, 1863, near Jonestown, Pennsylvania. His father was not physically fitted for farming, and after clerical employment in a store near Ashland, Pennsylvania, moved to Pittsburgh in 1874 as bookkeeper for a glass manufacturing firm.

The young Joseph Harvey Long acquired a small hand printing press and a few fonts of type, and the acquisition determined his future career.

A disastrous venture in glass manufacturing, terminated by a receiver for the plant at LaGrange, Ohio, interrupted his career as a printer briefly. He worked successively for the *Ohio Press*, at Stubenville, Ohio, with Dana Hubbard on the *Wheeling Sunday Leader* at Wheeling, and followed Hubbard to Erie when he became editor of the *Morning Dispatch* there. Other jobs were held on the *Oswego Palladium*, at Oswego, New York, and the most important of all in its effect upon his subsequent career, on the *Wheeling Register*, at Wheeling.

Herschel C. Ogden, after graduation from West Virginia University, came to work in the news department of *The Register*. The two joined forces and bought an almost defunct labor paper called the *Sunday News Letter* in 1890. The name was changed to *The News*, and, backed by vigorous ambition, the youthful publishers started a program of improvement both in editorial policy and mechanical equipment.

The News bought the first Linotype in West Virginia. Mr. Long went to Brooklyn to learn to operate it in the Mergenthaler Linotype Company plant there. Improvements in news gathering facilities, both telegraph and local, and enterprise shown by the publishers of the paper which provided their readers with service superior to that supplied by any competing newspaper, bore excellent fruit. The paper succeeded.

Hearing that a newspaper was for sale in Huntington, Mr. Long investigated, with the result that he bought the *Huntington Herald* in 1893 and sold his interest in the *Wheeling News* to Mr. Ogden. *The Herald* was sold to James J. Peterson in 1895, and in the same year Mr. Long purchased *The Advertiser* from J. G. Downtain and Son.

Under his energetic and businesslike management, *The Advertiser* succeeded, developing in equipment and facilities to meet changing conditions, increased circulation, and influence. In 1923 he started building a model plant at 5th Avenue and 10th Street, and in the following year the paper moved into the new building. Three years later the Huntington Publishing Company was organized to complete a merger of the *Huntington Herald-Dispatch* and *The Advertiser.*

Mr. Long acquired the title of colonel by appointment on the staff of Governor William E. Glasscock in 1911.

As a newspaper publisher and a citizen interested in political and civic affairs, Colonel Long has taken a spirited part in activities of the Democratic party in West Virginia as well as in civic organization work.

Since 1924 he has been chairman of the good roads committee of the Huntington Chamber of Commerce, and chairman of a similar committee of the Huntington Rotary Club. In that capacity he informed himself extensively on road engineering and construction problems. He was postmaster of Huntington from June 5, 1916, to July 1, 1921. He is president of the Huntington Publishing Company, and publisher of *The Advertiser.*

In 1932, as chairman of the Victory Drive for West Virginia he personally organized the fifty-five counties of the State and was able to raise nearly $10,000 for the Democratic campaign fund of that year without expense to the national committee. In the same year he was elected a delegate-at-large to the Democratic National Convention. In March, 1932, he was one of the organizers of the Roosevelt-for-President Club, sponsoring the organization meeting in Huntington. In the following year he was appointed by Governor Kump a member of the State's Century of Progress committee, but was unable to accept the appointment because of the press of other business.

He was made a member of the Cabell County Welfare board in 1932 when the board was organized, and continued a member through its various successive changes.

In 1933 he was drafted by President Roosevelt to be a member of the Public Works Administration advisory board for West Virginia.

A work in which he took much pride was done by a committee appointed by Governor Gore of West Virginia in 1926 to make a survey of the State's difficult tax problems, and to report recommendations for tax reforms.

He derived almost as much satisfaction from his election to the presidency of the Long Family Association of Pennsylvania, during which time he was publisher of the history and genealogy of the family. In 1935 he was honorary president of the association and his son, Luther T. Long, was its president. At the annual reunion he arranged for United States Senator Huey P. Long of Louisiana, whose personal friend he was, to deliver the principal address. A few days afterwards Senator Long was assassinated at Baton Rouge. Colonel Long attended the funeral services, and was greatly affected by the senator's death.

In 1934 he was manager of the successful campaign of Rush Dew Holt, of Weston, for United States Senator on the Democratic ticket.

Because of his active support of the Democratic party, and his successful participation in its affairs, Colonel Long has for years wielded substantial influence in the party. When the campaign year of 1934 was young, he was discussed throughout the State as a probable candidate for the Democratic nomination for the senatorship, but concluded not to make the race.

Colonel Long was married to Miss Cora Hildreth Thompson, daughter of Henry Arnold Thompson and Hannah Niblack Thompson of Steubenville, Ohio, June 12, 1884. She was born at Steubenville, November 25, 1862, the daughter of an old American family, of which the founder was Arnold Henry Dohrman, born at Hamburg in 1749. Dohrman commanded a privateer during the War of the Revolution, in behalf of the Colonies, and rendered many other valuable services which were recognized by President Washington and the Congress later.

Colonel and Mrs. Long have three sons, Luther Thompson Long, Paul Walker Long, and Edward H. Long, all executives of the Huntington Publishing Company.

L. T. Long is business manager of the company. In 1935, he was appointed a member of the Cabell County Court to fill a vacancy. He is president of the Huntington Campfire Girls, and active in other civic affairs, particularly with respect to Marshall College, where he has been an interested supporter of the athletics program, as has his father.

Luther T. Long was born in Huntington November 16, 1885. He married Ann Louise Ratcliff, daughter of John Ratcliff, of Huntington, who died January 12, 1934. They had five children. Luther Thompson Long, Junior, was born October 14, 1916; John Ratcliff Long, born May 16, 1918, was fatally injured in an automobile accident near Allentown, Pennsylvania, while returning home from school on June 2, 1935, and died June 12, in a hospital in Allentown; Mary Rebecca Long was born October 30, 1920; Jo-Harvey Long was born August 29, 1924; Ann Louise Long was born September 24, 1931.

Luther T. Long's energy and ambition are marked characteristics which have contributed substantially to the success of the publishing company of which he is manager. He is familiar with every department of the business, and in an emergency can fill competently any position in the plant. He started work in the business while a schoolboy and worked through from the ranks to the top position in the company.

In 1935 Mr. Long married Mrs. Carolyn Westcott Whittington, a widow with two children, Westcott and Emma Jean. They reside in Campbell Park, Huntington.

Paul Walker Long was born October 20, 1896. He was married to Jennie Eloise Campbell, daughter of Judge C. W. Campbell, of Huntington, and has six children: Eloise Campbell Long, born September 4, 1922; Suzanne Hamilton Long, born July 21, 1924; Phoebe Frazier Long, born May 11, 1928; Paul Walker Long, Junior, born July 23, 1929; Robert Dunbar Campbell Long, born January 26, 1931; and Margot Maxwell Long, born December 5, 1933.

Paul Walker Long is secretary of the Huntington Publishing Company and managing editor of *The Advertiser*. During the World War he served in the aviation section of the Navy. He is a graduate of Cornell University in the class of 1918. In 1927 he was elected a member of the State Legislature for one term and refused to run again for that office or any other public position for which his friends undertook to draft him. He is president of the Huntington Y.M.C.A., and active and influential in business, civic, and political enterprises.

Edward Harvey Long, treasurer of the Huntington Publishing Company was born November 14, 1898. He is married to Hilda Sheets, and resides in Huntington. He entered the Huntington Publishing Company organization in 1920 after graduation from Washington and Lee University. They have no children.

LOVE

Charles Love, a son of William Love, Senior, and a brother of William Love, Junior, both of whom served in the Continental Line, Revolutionary War, was the progenitor of the Love family in Cabell County. He was born in Westmoreland County, Pennsylvania, in 1753, and died in Cabell County, March, 1824. In 1774 he married Susanna Childs (born 1756, died 1821) in Philadelphia, and migrated to Mecklenburg County, Virginia. After a time he moved to Catlettsburg, Kentucky, and then to Cabell County. The Cabell County records show that on December 14, 1816, he bought from Manoah Bostick 353 acres of land on Mud River on which he lived, and on January 28, 1817, he resigned his office as justice of the peace.

Charles Love served in the Pennsylvania Militia, 1775, and was a private in Captain Thomas Berry's Company, 8th Virginia Regiment, 1776-1778. He afterwards went in the Infantry, Virginia Line, Continental Establishment. He participated in the battles of Brandywine and Germantown.

Charles Love and Susanna Childs had the following children:

I. Allen Love.

II. William Love, born 1781, married Susanna Brame, and later married Elizabeth Hampton, a widow. His son William A., was the father of Peter E. Love, born January 13, 1833, died November 28, 1912, and the grandfather of H. E. Love, late sheriff of Cabell County.

III. Agnes Love, married Ingram Rolfe.

IV. Mary Love, married a Rucker.

V. Susanna Love, married Dr. Anthony Hampton.

VI. Elizabeth Ann Love, married a Shortridge.

VII. Daniel Love, born December 19, 1797, died December, 1876, married on January 4, 1818, Cynthia Chadwick (born December 22, 1800, died 1890). Their children were:

    a. Leah Margaret, married S. M. Scott of Selma, Alabama.

    b. John Allen, died in infancy.

c. Charles Henson, married Elizabeth A. Ekin, and lived in Pittsburgh. They had three children: a son, Llewellyn; a daughter, Jennie, and another daughter.
d. Thomas Jefferson, married and lived in Wisconsin, and raised a family.
e. Sallie Virginia, married a Cater in Anniston, Alabama, and had four children:
  1. Daniel.
  2. George.
  3. Henson.
  4. Mima.
f. Francis Marion, married Elizabeth Wardrop, and lived in Pittsburgh, Pennsylvania. They had three children:
  1. Richard.
  2. Annie, married George Clapp.
  3. Elizabeth, married Dr. Hutchinson, Superintendent of the Pennsylvania State Asylum for the Insane at Dixmont, Pennsylvania.
g. Washington Lafayette, died in infancy.
h. Elizabeth Susan Frances, married Charles W. Handley of Ona. They had four children:
  1. Marion L., who went to Pittsburgh, married, and had one son and two daughters.
  2. Frank, now dead, who lived at Eaton, Ohio, where he married and had a number of children.
  3. Leonidas B., who went to Eaton, married, and has several children.
  4. Ona, for whom the village of Ona was named. She married a Switzer and lives on a farm near Eaton.
i. William Liggon, who died while young.
j. Shelby Jackson, who married Katherine McCleary, and lived at the old Love place above old Ona. They had eight children:
  1. F. Henson (now dead), married Myrtle Steele; one son:
    a. F. Henson, Junior, now living in California, married to Katherine Bond. They have one daughter: Katherine.
  2. Harry, a country doctor who died unmarried in young manhood.
  3. Edward S., married Ella Skeens, and lives in Huntington. They have four children:
    a. Edward S., Junior.

FAMILIES 441

  b. Helen Frances.
  c. Marian.
  d. Betty Jane.
 4. Sallie, who married D. O. Hinerman, and had four children:
  a. Mary Love, married Albert Lee Johnson.
  b. Harry H., married Margaret Ann Miller; one child: Joyce Helene.
  c. Muriel Helen.
  d. Margie Ann.
 5. Mary, who married W. C. Pew, lives at Ona. One daughter:
  a. Shelba Glenn.
 6. Anna Virginia, unmarried, teaches in the public schools.
 7. John, died in infancy.
 8. Ella, died in infancy.
k. John Erwin, married Irene Kimbrough, and lives in St. Louis. They have seven children:
 1. Edward K.
 2. John, Junior.
 3. Roland (killed in a football game at Harvard).
 4. Lacy.
 5. Erwin.
 6. Eula.
 7. Irene.
l. Leonidas Louis, who was killed at Jonesville, Virginia, while serving in the Confederate Army. He is buried in the Confederate Soldiers plot at Spring Hill Cemetery.
m. Theodotius Alphonso (April 22, 1846-April 1, 1924), married in 1866, Mary Hester Sweetland (June 30, 1846-February 15, 1918). They had three children:
 1. Cynthia Anne, married Dr. L. L. Love. One son:
  a. Lewis A., went to Seattle, where he married, and raised a family.
 2. Mary Sweetland, married A. S. J. Southworth. They have two children:
  a. A. S. J., Junior, married Aileen Davis.
  b. Louis Sweetland.
 3. Charles Marion Love, born October 16, 1869, married on December 30, 1896, Minnie Elizabeth Moore. Seven children:
  a. Samuel A., married Virginia Stuart, lives in New York

City, where he is a well-known writer and columnist. One son: Stuart Moore.

b. Charles Marion, Junior, married Naomi Nale. He is a prominent attorney of Charleston, with the firm of Blue, Dayton, and Campbell. Two children: Naomi and Lucy Temple.

c. Anne, married Harry Keeler; two children: David and Jane.

d. Jennie, married Robert Starcher; two children: Elizabeth and Clare.

e. Mary Moore, married Robert Daley of Chatham, New York. They have one son: Robert H. Daley, Junior.

f. Minnie, married C. M. Hawes, Junior, and is living in Chicago.

g. Daniel, still in school.

GEORGE MARSHALL LYON

George Marshall Lyon, the son of Marshall Allen Lyon and Harriet Bell Law Lyon, was born at Union City, Pennsylvania, on February 8, 1895. His father, who was a member of the same branch of the Lyon family as Mary Lyon, founder of Mount Holyoke College, died in 1900, and the support and rearing of the family devolved upon his mother, who carried on in a manner most remarkable, and with her characteristic courage and never failing, sweet personality. In that same year she moved to West Virginia with her family, and actively engaged in public school work and continued therein until 1909 in which year she took charge of the teachers' training school at Marshall College, where she continues to this time.

George Marshall Lyon attended the public schools in Sistersville, and was graduated from Marshall College in 1912. He was associate professor, Physics, Franklin College, Franklin, Indiana, 1915-1916, and was given a degree of B.S. at Denison University in 1916. During the war he was (1) M. E. R. C., 1917-18; (2) Research in war gases, senior toxicologist, Bureau of Mines and U. S. Chemical Warfare service, summer, 1918; determined minimal lethal dose of mustard gas (June, 1918), and Lewisite (August, 1918); perfected method of biological determination of toxicity mustard gas and Lewisite.

At the conclusion of the war he became resident house officer in pediatrics, Johns Hopkins Hospital, 1919-21, under preceptorship of Drs. Howland, Blackfan, Powers, and Park, and at the same time took a course in the Johns Hopkins University, and was graduated therefrom in 1920 with the degree of M.D. He is a member of the Phi Gamma Delta Fraternity, of Nu Sigma Nu, and of the medical fraternity at Johns Hopkins.

On September 1, 1921, Dr. Lyon located in Huntington, where he has been engaged in private practice in pediatrics since. During this time he has been made a member of the following: Fellow, American College of Physicians (1928), Fellow, American Academy of Pediatrics (1932), member, American Pediatric Society (1932), and member, Society for Research in Child Development (1934). In 1933 he served as chairman, West Virginia White House Conference on Child Health and Protection (was appointed by Governor Conley, and served under Governor Kump); chairman, Advisory Health Council to Cabell County Board of Education, 1933-36, official delegate of the United States, Seventh Pan-American Congress on the Child, Mexico City, October, 1935; consultant in Child Health, Children's Bureaus, U. S. Department of Labor; special clinician in pediatrics, committee on Clinical Education, Medical Society of Virginia, and Medical College of Virginia, 1934 and 1935.

Dr. Lyon is the author of the following research publications: (1) Infections on central nervous system, particularly meningococcus meningitis, acute poliomyelitis and encephalitis; (2) Allergy; (3) Infant mortality studies in West Virginia; (4) Bacillary dysentery; (5) Health careers of normal children; (6) Medical participation in school health programs, and other scientific publications, and in addition to this has developed a new technic for administering serum in meningococcus meningitis, and for removal of obstruction of aqueduct of Sylvius, a most delicate operation.

He is a lieutenant commander, M. C. (V) S, U. S. Naval Reserve, 1935, a member of the West Virginia State Advisory Council, FERA nursing program, 1933-36, a member of the Guyan Country Club, of the Presbyterian Church, and in politics is a Republican.

On May 24, 1922, George Marshall Lyon married Virginia Berkeley Sutherland, daughter of United States Senator Howard Sutherland, and to this union were born: Virginia Berkeley, May 2, 1923; Natalie Sutherland, September 5, 1924; and Elizabeth Harriet, June 13, 1926. Virginia Sutherland Lyon died on June 20, 1926.

George Marshall Lyon, married, second, Theeta Carrington Searcy of Columbia, Missouri, a professor of home economics at Marshall College, on July 29, 1927.

MARCUM

John St. Clair Marcum was born July 14, 1851, on a farm near Cassville, now Fort Gay, Wayne County, Virginia. His father was Stephen M. Marcum, and his mother was Jane Dameron Marcum. He was the fifth of the six sons of his parents, there being also four daughters in the family.

His formal education was limited to that of the country schools, then noted rather for the soundness of their teaching of the "three R's" than for their equipment or their leadership. But if by education is meant the discovery and development of latent powers, then other early experiences contributed largely to his training.

John Marcum was in turn a "hand" on the home farm; a helper in his father's shop, where were made the smooth-bore, muzzle-loading rifles bearing the familiar "S M" burned into their walnut stocks; a clerk in the general store of his brother, Thomas D. Marcum's store at Louisa, across the Big Sandy River in Kentucky; a blacksmith in logging camps; a rafter on timber fleets which were assembled at Cassville and floated down the Big Sandy and the Ohio Rivers to Cincinnati and Louisville; and a teacher in the country schools.

His father and his grandfather had been gentlemen justices under appointment by the governor of Virginia. Early experiences in observing the operations of the frontier courts conducted by his forbears developed in young John Marcum the ambition for a career at the Bar. Hence, while teaching school for a livelihood, he read Blackstone's *Commentaries,* and Chitty's *Pleading* and Greenleaf's *Evidence.* Also, for three evenings each week for nearly three years, he and two of his contemporaries recited to their sponsor and good friend, Judge Milton J. Ferguson, of Louisa.

Having completed these studies to the satisfaction of his mentor, Marcum applied to Judge Evermont Ward for a certificate of qualification to practice law, as was provided by the statutes then in effect relating to admission to the Bar. Judge Ward asked the young applicant but one question, to which he gave an incorrect answer. But after several hours of exposition of the question and its correct answer, Judge Ward signed the certificate. The other two judges to whom the applicant then went for signatures accepted judgment of Judge Ward and signed without further examination.

Marcum presented his certificate at the Bar of the Wayne Circuit Court in 1878 and was admitted and established his office at Cassville. In March, 1879, he was admitted to the Cabell County Bar.

In the general elections of 1880, he was made prosecuting attorney of Wayne County. On December 21 of that year, at Ceredo, he was married to Emma Wellman, daughter of John D. and Martha Adkins Wellman, and immediately established his home at Wayne, then known as Trout's Hill. He was reëlected prosecuting attorney in 1884, and at the expiration of that term, he removed his office and his home to Huntington.

On August 20, 1890, Lucien Ricketts having resigned as prosecuting attorney of Cabell County, John S. Marcum was appointed by Judge Thomas H. Harvey to the unexpired term, which he served with apparent satisfaction to the court and to the public.

Early in his Huntington practice, Mr. Marcum formed a partnership with Captain Thomas West Peyton, who had recently completed a term as circuit clerk, under the firm name of Marcum and Peyton. When his brother Lace Marcum (who had succeeded him as prosecutor in Wayne) later moved to Huntington, he became a member of the firm, the name being changed to Marcum, Peyton and Marcum.

Thomas R. Shepherd, present judge of the Circuit Court of Cabell County, had been associated with John S. Marcum since 1889, and when Captain Peyton retired from the practice and removed to Barboursville, Judge Shepherd became a member of the firm, the name being changed to Marcum, Marcum and Shepherd. This arrangement continued until 1905, when John S. Marcum withdrew from the firm to form a partnership with his son, J. R. Marcum, who had been admitted to the Bar in July of that year. This association continued until the retirement of John S. Marcum in 1930.

One of his achievements in which Mr. Marcum took great pride was his having organized a Baptist church at Wayne and having led the small congregation in the courageous task of erecting a house of worship. He was for many years a teacher in and superintendent of the 5th Avenue Baptist Sunday School in Huntington and was still a teacher in that Sunday School at the time of his death.

As a lawyer, he was recognized as preëminent in trial work, more particularly in criminal trial work. He had participated in more than five hundred murder trials and was leading counsel in many of the "causes celebres" which grew out of the border feuds of the pioneer days. His spirit of loyalty to his client led a famous jurist to say of him, "John Marcum never defended a guilty man nor prosecuted an innocent man." His logical development of his own case, his great skill as a cross-examiner, his accurate and comprehensive knowledge of criminal law, his persuasive and convincing arguments before juries and courts and his untiring labor in the preparation and presentation of his cause combined to make him a great trial lawyer.

John S. Marcum died at his home in Huntington, on March 12, 1933, "full of years and of honors," and was buried March 14, 1933, in the family plot in Spring Hill Cemetery. His wife died December 27, 1927. They were survived by a son J. Roy Marcum, and a daughter, Martha, wife of L. W. Wells of Ben's Run, who has two children, Lew, Junior, and May.

MARTIN

William Marshall Martin, the present assessor of Cabell County, is one of the younger men who is recognized as a leader in the political affairs of the county and one of the most efficient assessors in the State. In recognition of this fact he was elected president of the State Association of County Assessors in West Virginia in 1933, re-elected in 1934, and again in 1935.

Will Martin was born near Belva, Nicholas County, May 13, 1889, the son of Joseph A. and Annie E. Martin. He attended the public schools in Nicholas, then took an academic course at Fayetteville and was graduated from Huntington Business College and from Sikes Commercial College in Huntington. After his graduation he was employed as errand boy and handyman in the County Court clerk's office by the late F. F. McCullough. When he attained his majority he was made a deputy clerk, and in a short time was made chief deputy clerk, which position he continued to fill under R. S. Douthat.

In 1924 Mr. Martin was eleected assessor but was defeated four years later in the Republican landslide although he ran some 5,200 ahead of his ticket. In 1932 he was again nominated, and was elected by the largest majority given any candidate on the ticket.

Mr. Martin is an active member of the 5th Avenue Baptist Church, a member of the board of deacons of the church, clerk and superintendent of the Sunday School which has the distinction of having the largest membership and attendance of any Protestant church in the State, and is president of the Guyandotte Baptist Association.

He married on December 21, 1910, Effie Ewing Hawes, daughter of William J. and Sarah Jane Hawes of Huntington, and to this union were born: William Marshall, Junior, born March, 1912, and Dorothy Maxine, born March 7, 1923.

MAUPIN

In early 1790 Thomas Maupin of Albemarle County, Virginia,

settled on Coal River near St. Albans. He had two wives and two sets of children. By his second wife, Margaret, he had Beverly W., Chapman W., Henry B., William L., and Mildred.

In 1819 Thomas Maupin moved to a farm in Cabell County about three miles west of Milton, close to the Love Place. This farm is still referred to as the Old Maupin place. One son, Beverly W. Maupin, moved to Jackson County. William L. was a physician and moved to Wayne County. Mildred married a Becker and moved to Minnesota. Chapman W. Maupin married Matilda Hope and had eight children, seven of whom grew to maturity.

(1) William R., was a Chesapeake and Ohio locomotive engineer.
(2) Alice, married George Sampson.
(3) Lucy, married J. T. Doyle.
(4) Fannie, married C. C. Crawford.
(5) Thomas, a farmer.
(6) Shelby, moved to the West.
(7) A. B., taught school and later became a civil engineer, and is affectionately known as "Uncle Albert."

Henry B. Maupin was a physician, and held a number of offices. He was killed in 1865 by being crushed between a steamboat and the wharfboat at Guyandotte. He married first on June 22, 1847, Martha E. Holderby, a daughter of Absolom Holderby, and had a daughter, who died in infancy. He married second Lucinda Smith, and had three children: S. A. (Soc), lived in Huntington; Henry B., who moved to Portsmouth, Ohio, and Betty, who married John Hager of Ashland, Kentucky.

McCOMAS

The McComas family is Scotch-Irish and its immigrant ancestor was David McComas who settled in Harford, County, Maryland, at the beginning of the eighteenth century. John McComas, the progenitor of the Cabell County family, migrated from Western Maryland in about 1778, and settled near Pearisburg, Giles County, Virginia. Five of his sons came by way of New River to the Guyan Valley in 1779 and settled in what is now Lincoln County. Another son, Elisha, came later and settled at Salt Rock. Elisha McComas was for many years a member of the County Court, was trustee of both the towns of Guyandotte and Barboursville, a member of the General Assembly, and was major, colonel, and brigadier general of militia, but he was not called into Federal service in the war of 1812-14. His home still stands just south of Barboursville. He had a number of sons—William, who was a lawyer and a Methodist minister, served in Congress, and was a member of the Secession Convention in Richmond; David, who was a lawyer, was judge of the Circuit Superior Court, and a member of the General Court; and James.

William McComas, the lawyer-preacher, married Mildred Ward, daughter of Thos. Ward, the first sheriff. They had six sons who grew to manhood—Mathew, who served in the Mexican War, and died young; Elisha W., who was a captain in the Mexican War, later lieutenant governor of Virginia, and about whom something was said under the chapter on the Mexican War; W. W., a doctor, who commanded a company of artillery in the Confederate Army, and was killed in the battle of South Mills, North Carolina; A. C., a lawyer, who was a colonel in the Union Army, afterwards practiced law in the West, and he together with his family were killed by Comanche Indians at Silver City, New Mexico; Rufus F., banker and manufacturer of Lincoln, Nebraska; Benjamin J., a lawyer and a captain of Infantry in the Confederate Army; and one daughter, Irene O., who married Major George McKendree, and had three daughters, one of whom, Mary, married George W. Johnson of Parkersburg.

George J., son of Benjamin J., was one of the leaders of the Cabell County Bar, and served one term as prosecuting attorney. He married Betty Martin Curtis of Richmond, Kentucky, and had two children, Margaret, who married Charles W. Purcell; and a son, B. Curtis McComas, now a captain of artillery in the United States Army.

McCORMICK

In the 1775 partition of the Savage Grant, James McCormack was given what are now lots 33 and 34 which included the mouth of Twelve Pole and Four Pole Creeks. Who this James McCormack was is not known except the tradition is that he came from Virginia. There is a deed of record in the clerk's office dated October 28, 1817, from James McCormick and Jemima, his wife, to Eli McCormick, which recites that the grantor is the son of the James McCormack who in 1775 was allotted 1,200 acres of land which included the mouth of Twelve Pole and Four Pole Creeks, and that this James had reserved to the grantor a life interest in 300 acres of that land which the grantor by that deed conveyed to Eli McCormick.

James McCormick, the grantor in this deed, made a will in 1841 which was probated in 1865, and named the following children:
1. John.
2. Moses.
3. Levi.
4. David.
5. George.
6. Charles (then in Indiana).
7. Isaac.
8. Eli.
9. Jane.
10. Sarah.
11. Hester.
12. Jemima, married James Poage, December 6, 1821.

Levi McCormick was one of the gentlemen justices of the County Court and was Sheriff of the county 1834-36. His children were:
1. John.
2. James.
3. Walstein.
4. Armistead.
5. Joe.
6. Eliza, married on February 21, 1839, Isaac Hanley, lived on the farm at Kellogg, and was the mother of Calvert and Lee Hanley.
7. Patsy.
8. Eleanor.
9. Margaret, married T. W. Kilgore.

All of the sons except Joe moved to Kansas in the latter part of 1850, and Joe, familiarly known as Uncle Joe, lived during his last years on 5th Avenue in Huntington.

McGINNIS

This family is Scotch-Irish and their immigrant ancestor was Edmund McGinnis, who settled first near Philadelphia, then moved to Frederick County, Virginia, and later to Little Levels in Greenbrier County. There is a break between this Edmund McGinnis and those McGinnises who settled in Cabell. Some of the descendants assert that the first Edmund in Cabell was the immigrant, but the age of Edmund McGinnis of Cabell is against this supposition, and if he was a brother to James and Phyrus the records show that in 1809 Edmund made a deed to James and described him as James, Junior.

This fact would seem to show that their father was named James. In all events the three McGinnises were here as early as 1802, and tradition says they were brothers.

Edmund McGinnis was one of the large landowners in the county. In 1809 he purchased from the Larue heirs for the sum of $200.00 their interest in lots 47, 48, 58, 59, and 60 of the Savage Grant which aggregated 2,100 acres, and which their ancestor had bought from the original patentees. Edmund McGinnis, who was one of the first gentlemen justices, had a home just across the road from the entrance to the Guyan Country Club, and owned the ferry across the Ohio River above the mouth of the Guyandotte River. He held a number of county offices, and represented the county in the General Assembly of Virginia. He reared a large family all of whom except a son, Allen A., moved to the West.

Allen A. was, like his father, a prominent man, and was a magistrate, sheriff, and represented the county in the General Assembly. He married Eliza Holderby, and they had nine children, three of whom remained in Cabell, namely, Dr. A. B., Judge Ira J., and a daughter, Sarah P., who married J. W. Thornburg.

Ira J. was prosecuting attorney in 1861, but gave up his office and went with the Confederacy, and served in the army to the end of the war. In 1872 he was elected to the State Senate from this Senatorial district. He was a member of the board of directors of the hospital for the insane at Weston, and in 1880 was elected judge of the 8th Judicial Circuit for the term of eight years. In 1881 he married Kate Hite, daughter of John W. Hite, and after her death married Frances E. Beuhring. (See account of the F. G. L. Beuhring Family.) They had one son, Ira J. Judge McGinnis died March 27, 1900.

James McGinnis, on May 16, 1810, purchased from Edmund eighty acres of land on the Ohio River which was part of the Savage Grant, and in this deed he is described as James, Junior. On February 16, 1816, James McGinnis was one of the gentlemen justices composing the County Court.

Phyrus was not a landowner and the first mention of him in the county records is as a member of the grand jury in 1815.

MEEK

John Henry Meek, attorney, the son of Edward and Amy (Kirk) Meek, was born in Louisa, Kentucky, on September 8, 1877, He was educated in the common schools and at the Oak View Academy, Wayne, West Virginia, and taught school a short time. He attended

George F. Miller, Jr.

the law school at West Virginia University, and was graduated in 1897 with the degree of LL.B. The same year he was admitted to the Bar at Wayne, and was associated with P. H. Napier in the firm of Napier and Meek.

On November 14, 1901, he married Charlie Burgess (daughter of Clara Ferguson Burgess and Dr. George Roberts Burgess). They have three children:

John Burgess Meek, born in Wayne, attended New York Military Academy and the University of Virginia, from which he has degrees of A.B. and LL.B. He practices law in Huntington.

Amy Kirk Meek, born in Wayne, attended Low-Heywood School at Stamford, Connecticut, and Holton Arms, Washington. She married Jack Carlos Dew, of St. Petersburg, Florida, where they reside. They have one son, John Carlos Dew.

Howard Ferguson Meek attended Kiskiminetas Springs, a preparatory school at Saltsburg, Pennsylvania, received his A.B. degree from Amherst College, and his LL.B. from the University of Virginia. He practices law in Huntington.

In 1902 and 1903 John Henry Meek served as prosecuting attorney of Wayne County. In 1909 he moved to Huntington to practice law. Some time later he formed the partnership of Meek and Renshaw, which continued until 1920 when it combined with the firm of Vinson and Thompson, which became the firm of Vinson, Thompson, Meek and Renshaw. Some years later Mr. Renshaw retired, and Harry Scherr joined the firm and it became Vinson, Thompson, Meek and Scherr, which is one of the leading law firms of the State, numbering among its clients some of the largest interests in the State.

Mr. Meek is a member of the Cabell County Bar Association (president, 1924-1925); the State and American Bar Association; he is a Mason; a member of the Guyandotte Club, the Guyan Country Club, and the M.E. Church, South.

He is identified with a number of business interests which include a directorship in the First Huntington National Bank. His tact and fund of good stories make him a valuable addition to any gathering.

GEORGE F. MILLER

Frederick Miller, a German emigrant, arrived in America at New Orleans. He went by flatboat from that point to the mouth of the Guyandotte and overland to Logan but later returned to Barboursville where he located. One son, George F. Miller, Senior, was born in Germany, in 1816, learned the tanner trade and then became a merchant. In 1843 he married Mary M. Shelton, daughter of Anthony Shelton, and to this union were born: Christian S.; Hannah C., who married D. I. Smith; George F., Junior; William C., who married Mary Eugene Samuels; Mary, who married J. B. Poage.

In the 1860's George F. Miller became surety on the bond of Sheriff Underwood, who became involved in his accounts and Miller took charge of his office. In 1876 he was elected sheriff and served four years. George F. Miller, Junior, was educated in a select school taught by B. H. Thackston, and began his business career as a clerk in a store. When D. I. Smith was elected sheriff, George F. Miller, Junior, was made a deputy, and he served under Smith for six years, and then served four years more under his father. After he left the sheriff's office, George F. Miller, Junior, engaged in various business enterprises, assisted in the organization of the First Huntington National Bank, and became its cashier. He continued in that position until his death on September 6, 1910.

George F. Miller, Junior, was easily the most constructive business man of his generation, and to enumerate his many business interests would mean to list all or most of the successful enterprises in the community. He married first, Lucy B. McConnell of Catlettsburg, Kentucky, and had four children: James I.; Charles F.; Belle H., and G. D. His first wife died January 8, 1889, and he married on November 12, 1890, Florence G. Miller, daughter of William Clendenin Miller.

JOSEPH S. MILLER

Christian Miller, who was born in Germany, came to America and served in the Revolutionary War, and died at Woodstock, Virginia, April 28, 1836. He married Catherine Wiseman and their third son, John, migrated to the Kanawha Valley and married, January 26, 1806, Sophia Clendenin, daughter of William Clendenin and a niece of Colonel George Clendenin. This couple moved to Cabell County, and a daughter, Margaret, married Thomas Thornburg; and a son, William Clendenin Miller (died July 27, 1886), married on March 6, 1836, Eliza Gardner, the daughter of Joseph Gardner, who had graduated from Harvard Law School, but who loved the sea, and following his graduation bought a ship and went to San Domingo, where he married a French girl, Marie Therese Clothilde Raison de la Geneste. When the Black Insurrection started Joseph Gardner and his family went to Boston, then to Kentucky, and later to Barboursville. The court records disclose that on June 30, 1841, an order was made to enable them to obtain some property in France to which the wife was entitled. Two of the Gardner children married in Cabell County, one the Eliza above, and Emily, who married John Samuels.

William Clendenin Miller and his wife Eliza had the following children:

(1) Eugenia, married Professor B. H. Thackston, and had seven children.

(2) Florence, married George F. Miller.

(3) Joseph S., born in Barboursville, August 17, 1848, and died in Huntington, February 22, 1922. He was appointed circuit clerk August 1, 1869, and served in that office for four years, then was elected county clerk. Four years later, he was elected auditor and moved to Wheeling during his term of office. He was a most attractive personality and a close friend of Grover Cleveland, who appointed him Commissioner of Internal Revenue in both of his administrations. "Joe" Miller interested Cleveland and some of his friends in coal lands in Wayne County and this fact was helpful in bringing about the construction of the Norfolk and Western Railway. Mr. Miller became interested in Kenova and at the time of his death was president of the First National Bank of Kenova. He married Florence Tice of Maryland and their children are: Lavalette, married George L. Shelley of Orange, New Jersey, and Lee, who lives in Detroit, Michigan.

(4) John W., married Annie Curtis of Kentucky, and had a daughter, Dollie, who married Earl Spencer; Bessie; and Thomas E.

MOORE

Thomas Waterman Moore, M.D., was born at Catlettsburg, Kentucky, October 4, 1866, the oldest child of Vincent Morgan Moore and Addie Marion (Moore). He was graduated from the Medico Chirurgical College (now University of Pennsylvania), Philadelphia, Pennsylvania, in 1893, and began the practice of medicine at Everett, Pennsylvania. He removed to Huntington in 1897, specializing in diseases of the eye, ear, nose, and throat. After coming to Huntington he studied at the Herman Knapp Memorial Eye Hospital, New York, and in 1900, 1911, 1928, and 1929, attended the clinics in Vienna, Austria, and in 1914 studied in London and Paris.

Dr. Moore is a Fellow of the American College of Surgeons, member of American Medical Association, Southern Medical Association (president, 1929), West Virginia State Medical Association (president, 1910), Central Tri-State Medical Association (president, 1925), the American Academy of Ophthalmology and Oto-Laryngology, American Laryngological and Rhinological Society, and honorary member of the American Bronchoscopic Society, and is registered by both the American Board of Ophthalmology and the Board of Oto-Laryngology.

Dr. Moore has contributed medical articles to numerous societies and since entering the profession has been an ardent supporter of medical organizations.

He is a director of the First Huntington National Bank, a Mason and Knight Templar, a member of the Guyandotte Club, and of Trinity Episcopal Church.

The Moore family has been prominent in West Virginia for many years. Dr. Moore is a nephew of the late Judge C. P. T. Moore, who was twice elected as a Judge of the Supreme Court of Appeals of West Virginia, and who, in his college days, founded the Phi Kappa Psi Fraternity.

On June 28th, 1899, Dr. Moore married Harriet Prentice Hallock, elder daughter of Joseph Hallock and Susan Prentice (Ensign). She was born at Catskill, New York, October 11, 1872, and educated at the Burnham School, Northampton, Massachusetts, later graduating from Smith College, A.B., 1897.

Mrs. Moore is a director of the Woman's Club, member of the American Association of University Women (president, Huntington Branch, 1920-1922), vice chairman of the Huntington Chapter, American Red Cross, member of the Grey Ladies Corps, member of Trinity Episcopal Church.

To these were born:

Joseph Hallock Moore, July 7, 1902. Graduate of Sewanee Military Academy, 1920, Lafayette College, B.S., 1924, University of Iowa, M.D., 1929. After three and one-half years at Bellevue Hospital, New York City, he entered the practice of ear, nose, and throat, and is associated with his father. He is a first lieutenant in the Medical Reserve Corps, U.S.A.

Dr. Joseph Hallock Moore is certificated by the American Board of Oto-Laryngology, a diplomat of the National Boards, member American Medical Association and the State and county medical societies. He is also a member of the Phi Kappa Psi, Nu Sigma Nu, and Pi Delta Epsilon Fraternities, and a member of the Guyan Country Club.

Dr. Hallock Moore married Priscilla Alden Belknap of Marblehead, Massachusetts, June 14, 1934.

Thomas Waterman Moore, Junior, born December 20, 1906. Graduated from Sewanee Military Academy, 1924; University of the South, A.B., 1928, and the University of Virginia, LL.B., 1934.

BISHOP THOMAS ASBURY MORRIS

William Morris who was born, in 1722, in London, England, and died in Kanawha County in 1799, came to Philadelphia when he was about twelve years of age. He married Elizabeth Stipes of Orange County, Virginia, and lived in Culpeper County for a time, and reared most of his family there. About 1773 he migrated to the western portion of Greenbrier County and located on the Kanawha. He had ten children, one of whom was John Morris, a Revolutionary soldier, who was born in 1741, and died in August, 1818.

John Morris owned considerable land on Mud River and Hurricane Creek. He was early identified in the public affairs of Kanawha County; was an active participant in the organization of that county and is said to have been at the battle of Point Pleasant.

He married Margaret Droddy and moved to what is now Cabell County at an early date and owned the farm now called Yatesmont which his heirs in 1818 sold to Esom Hannan.

John Morris had three daughters: Miriam (called Polly), married Esom Hannan; Calvary, married her cousin, Charles Hensford; and a third daughter, Elizabeth, married Joseph Hilyard; and five sons: John, Junior; Edmund, Levi, William, and Thomas Asbury.

John, Junior, and William lived in Cabell County, and some of their descendants are still here. We have no account of Levi. Edmund was the first county clerk.

Thomas Asbury was born on April 29, 1794. His place of birth is given by Virgil A. Lewis as in Cabell County some seven miles east of Barboursville, and this statement is repeated in Hardesty's *Encyclopedia*. But other persons, including Franklin L. Burdette, Senior, who is an authority on Cabell County history, says that he was born in Kanawha County near Campbell's Creek. In all events his parents bought a farm near Bethesda Church about 1804, and the boy came with them to the new home. He died in Springfield, Ohio, September 2, 1874.

Thomas Asbury attended the grammar school of William Paine, taught school for a few months and served for a time as a deputy to his brother, Edmund Morris, who was clerk of the county and circuit courts. In 1813 a camp meeting was held in the neighborhood of Bethesda Church and it is probable that at this meeting Morris united with the church. In any event in August, 1813, although his parents were members of the Baptist Church he joined the Methodist Episcopal Church. In 1814 he married Abigail Scales, and it is supposed that the marriage took place in the Beuhring home which was located near the Ohio on 7th Street, East, in Huntington. This supposition is based on the fact that in an account of Bishop Morris' life which was published in the last quarter of the nineteenth century it is stated that he was married in a house in the city of Huntington which was then standing and was being used as a telegraph and express office. Residents of Huntington still living remember that at that time there was only one telegraph and express office in the city, and it was located in what had been the Beuhring residence on 7th Street, East, near 2d Avenue, so it is fair to assume that this was the house referred to.

After his marriage Thomas A. Morris established a home on the MacCorkle farm near Howell's Mill which he called the Spice Flat Cottage, and it was thought that the first Methodist church or society in the community was organized in this house. Thomas A. Morris preached his first sermon on Christmas Day, 1814, and the account of this event is set out in Virgil A. Lewis' *History of West Virginia,* as follows:

"We will let the Bishop tell of this, his first sermon, himself, as he told it to a company of friends who gathered at his residence on the occasion of his 79th birthday. Said he: 'I had a long hard struggle to find peace. On Christmas Day, 1814, there being no minister present, Thomas Buffington, a licensed exhorter, and I held a meeting for exhortation and prayer. He exhorted and I prayed. When about to dismiss, he suggested a meeting for the evening. I said, 'Just as you like.' Said he, 'If we do have meeting, will you exhort?' With some hesitation I replied, 'Yes, if you judge it best.' Whereupon he announced, 'There will be a meeting tonight at father's, and Brother Morris will exhort.' This meeting was on the lower junction of the Ohio and Guyandotte rivers. As it was my first effort at public speaking, I began with fear and trembling though I had often felt before that I should make an effort in that direction. I spoke some forty minutes with a freedom and unction that surprised myself. I was filled with a strange peace of mind, and concluded, 'This is what I have prayed for so long . . . that is, I am converted.' "

In 1816 he joined the Ohio Conference and for several years he traveled the circuit, then served as elder. In 1836 he was ordained Bishop of the Methodist Episcopal Church, and was the last of the Methodist Bishops to make his rounds of the circuit on horseback.

Bishop Morris has been described as "one of the most eminent men whose name appears upon the pages of the church history of the United States."

MORRIS

In the article on Bishop Thomas Asbury Morris, an account is given of William Morris, the elder, and of his son, John. In view of the fact that a large number of this family, descended from another son of William Morris, Senior, are still in Cabell County, a more detailed account of its beginning in Kanawha County is not out of place.

W. S. Laidley in his *History of Charleston and the Kanawha Valley* said that the upper settlement in the Kanawha Valley was made by the Morris family, which was the first white family to become permanent settlers in the Kanawha Valley. Fourteen years later the lower settlement at the mouth of the Elk River was made by the Clendenin family. There had been an attempt made by Walter Kelly, who came with his family from Greenbrier County, to make a settlement on the Kanawha River at the mouth of Kelly's Creek, but he sent his family back. A short time afterwards, at a date not fixed, but believed to have been in 1773, when Colonel Fields, a black man, and Kelly were in the Kelly home, an attack was made by the Indians, and Kelly and the black man were killed. Colonel Fields escaped and went back to Culpeper County, and afterwards was present at the battle of Point Pleasant in command of soldiers from Culpeper County. The next year the Morrises came and took possession of the place left by Kelly.* It is said that William Morris was on the ground in the fall of 1774, and was followed later by his family at a date not definitely known.

William Morris, Senior, had ten children, to wit: William, Junior; Henry, Leonard, Joshua, John, Carroll, Levi, Benjamin, Elizabeth, married a See; and Frances, the wife of John Jones, who was said to be "much of a man." William Morris, Senior, at this time was getting old and was a quiet, peaceful man whose chief business in life was to protect his family. His eldest son was William, Junior, a

---

*The home of William Morris at Kelly's Creek was a "fort" or outpost during the period of the Revolutionary War, and is referred to as Fort Morris or Kelly's Post in Great Kanawha Valley.

strong, hardy man of much decision of character, and he was the leader of the family. Henry was a giant physically. When the Indians killed one of his daughters he swore vengeance and never let an opportunity pass to kill an Indian. Leonard was a strong character, and the best known member of the family. He took an interest in affairs generally, and was thought to be the first of the family to settle on the south side of the Kanawha in what was then Montgomery County. Joshua and John were both strong men, of good judgment, but the three sons, Carroll, Levi, and Benjamin were quiet men. See died early and is thought to have been killed by the Indians. In all events these eleven men were amply able to, and did take care of themselves and their families. There is no record of any successful Indian attack on their homes. The Morrises lived on the road used by travelers to Kentucky, and when Andrew Lewis and his army passed their home on his way to Point Pleasant, John Jones and his brother-in-law, John Morris, went with him. For a more detailed account of this family in Kanawha, persons interested can consult Mr. Laidley's history.

An account has been given of John Morris, the son of William Morris, Senior. The other son identified with Cabell County is Joshua who was born in Virginia in 1752, settled in Teay's Valley, and died there in 1825. He married Frances Simms of Virginia (born 1759, died 1795), and to this union were born:

1. William, married Sarah Hansford, and lived at Gauley Bridge and later moved to Missouri. Their children were Fenton, Joshua, and John.
2. Edmund.
3. Henry.
4. Elizabeth.
5. Lucy, married a Chapman.
6. Nancy, married John Harriman.
7. Thomas.
8. Mary.
9. John, who was born in Culpeper County, Virginia, in 1794, and died in Wytheville, Virginia, in 1862. He can properly be called John Morris of Teay's Valley, Cabell County.

This John Morris had his house and tavern on the old pike just west of the present location of Culloden. He was an extensive stock raiser, represented the county in the Legislature and was a man of wealth. He was a strong Southern sympathizer, and at the beginning of the war went with his slaves to Wytheville where he died in 1862. During his absence his home was burned and a great deal of his property confiscated by Federal troops. A new house was built on the site of the old by T. J. Berkeley, who had married Ida Morris, a daughter of Charles K. Morris.

John Morris married first, Mary Everett and had a daughter Eliza, who married William A. Love. Mary Everett died in 1819, and John Morris then married Mary Kinard, born 1800, died 1876. Their children were:

1. Charles K., married Martha Kilgore and had the following children:
   a. Mary, married Dr. Randolph.
   b. John, married Em Gwinn.
   c. Ellen, married Arthur Williams.
   d. Edna, married T. Heber Rece, who was with Company D, 8th Virginia Cavalry, C.S.A.
   e. Ida, married T. J. Berkeley.
   f. Charlie R., married Myrtle Ayres.
2. Arthur A., died without issue.
3. Joseph W., a Captain in the 16th Virginia Cavalry, C.S.A., who was killed on the Monocacy River near Frederick, Maryland, July 9, 1864; married Sarah A. Russell, and had the following children:
   a. John O., born July 12, 1845, died July 4, 1913, one-time sheriff of Putnam County, married March 14, 1867, Eliza Love, daughter of William A. Love and had:
      1. Russell Love, born November 14, 1868, was for many years professor of Engineering at West Virginia University at Morgantown. He married Olive Hite, and had one son, John.
      2. Guy Leland, born August 29, 1872, and located in Pasadena, California, married Letha Richardson, and had three daughters, Letha, Mildred, and Fannie.
      3. Anna.
      4. Lena.
   b. Mary Rebecca, married Fred G. Handley, and lived at Scott Depot. Their children were:
      1. Claude E., married Laura McMasters.
      2. Gordon, married Kate Wahrheit.
      3. Stella, died without issue.

FAMILIES 461

  4. Ida Josephine, married R. R. MacGregor.
  5. Fred G., married Marian Blaney.
  6. Frank A., married Grace Johnson.
  7. Charles, died without issue.
  8. Sallie, married Dr. W. D. Hereford of Huntington.
  9. Mary, married L. W. Baker.
  10. Clifton, married Gladys ——— of Gloucester, Ohio.
 c. Josephine, married William MacCallister, and lived at Hurricane.
 d. James, a physician, who located in Stanford, Kentucky.
 e. Joseph, married Lucy Chinn, and lives in Ashland, Kentucky.
4. Edna E., married Addison T. Buffington, who was a steamboat man, and lived in Parkersburg, where his descendants still live.
5. James R., born 1830, died 1910, was a second lieutenant, 16th Virginia Cavalry, C.S.A., and in the troop of which his brother Joseph W., was captain. He married Helen M. Russell, born 1829, died 1895, a sister of Sarah A. Russell. Their children were:
 a. Joseph W., married Fannie McKendree, and lived at Milton. They had the following children:
   1. Albert, who lives in Virginia.
   2. Charles, died without issue.
   3. Edward.
   4. Eva, married Frank S. Rockwell.
   5. Thomas L.
   6. George.
   7. Harry.
   8. Sidney.
 b. Albert A., married Carrie King and lives in Oklahoma.
 c. Walter T., died without issue. He gave the old Morris homestead near Milton for the Morris Memorial Hospital.
 d. Sallie, who was the second wife of James H. Blackwood.
 e. Fannie, who was the first wife of James H. Blackwood. Their children were:
   1. Owen.
   2. Helen.
 f. Eugene, married in Texas.
 g. Beauregard, married in Texas.
 h. Addison Ferd, born 1866, married June 5, 1901, Emma Barrett, born 1875. He graduated in law from West Virginia

University in 1888, and became a very successful lawyer. Their children are:
1. Russell, graduated from West Virginia University in 1927.
2. James E., graduated from Marshall College.
3. Mary Jane, graduated from Marshall College.
4. Florence, graduated from the University of Kentucky.

i. Gertrude, married Dr. James J. Reynolds.
6. Mary S., married first, Ira T. McConihay, and had two children:
   a. Dr. John McConihay of Charleston.
   b. A daughter, married Dr. Stuart of Huntington.

Mary S. Morris McConihay then married John P. Sebrell, and lived on the Kanawha River near Arbuckle.

NAGLEE

Joseph Naglee and his wife, Hannah, moved here from Philadelphia in 1836 and brought with them their three children, Ellen, Benjamin, and Frank. Joseph Naglee purchased from Jessie Toney a farm consisting of 668 acres of land at the mouth of Four Pole Creek. The Wayne-Cabell line runs through the middle of the tract. Twelve years later Naglee sold this land to William Williams and returned to Philadelphia. A portion of this farm passed to Arthur Williams, a son of William, and then to his daughter, Fanny, who married James H. Marcum. It was recently subdivided into the Marcum Subdivision.

NASH

The family is Scotch and just when it came to America is not known, but James J. Nash migrated from Tennessee to Ohio. He was married twice, and by his first wife had a son, John, a millwright, who put in the old Merritt mill, the Howell, and the Dusenberry mills. By his second wife, Frances Gillette, James J. Nash had ten children. A son, named Thomas Jefferson, who married America Payne, and located near Laurel Hill, then Cabell County, now Lincoln County, was engaged in the timber business on a large scale. One of the dams across the Guyandotte River was located at this point, and in 1863 a Federal raiding party blew out the dam and destroyed Thomas Jefferson Nash's lumber camp. Although a semi-invalid, he got up out of his sick bed and refugeed to Logan Courthouse. He made the trip in a severe storm and never entirely recovered from the exposure. His wife, America, secured two horses that the soldiers had abandoned and took her three children to Lawrence County, Ohio, where she was later joined by her husband, and the family made their home on Big Paddy Creek. In 1877 Ohio passed a compulsory school law, and at the same time permitted mixed schools, and T. J. Nash was unwilling to permit his children to attend school with colored children so he bought a farm on Davis Creek in Cabell County and moved thereon. His son, Gus Nash, still lives on this farm.

Thomas J. and America Nash had nine children, seven girls and two boys. He died when T. H. (Henry) the eldest son was fifteen years old and the support of the family devolved upon Henry. This responsibility made it necessary for him to give up school and go to work, which he did, and supported his mother and the children for ten years.

In 1865 T. H. Nash married Nancy Morrison, daughter of P. H. Morrison, Junior and Malinda Hensley, his wife. The Hensleys came from Illinois. Nancy Morrison is a granddaughter of P. H. Morrison, Senior and Ann Ward,* his wife, who came from Virginia in the early part of the nineteenth century.

To this union were born: Ethel, now a teacher in the Barboursville High School; and Clifton, who married Ann Herndon, and has a son, James.

In 1896 T. H. Nash was elected to the Barboursville district school board, and served continuously for twelve years. In 1905-1908 he served as a deputy sheriff under W. S. Spencer. In 1922 he was elected a member of the County Court, and has been reëlected from time to time, serving continuously from that date. He is now president of this court.

Henry Nash is one of the most faithful and efficient public servants the county ever had. He has good business judgment and gave special attention to roads. It was he who conceived the idea of buying the farm at Ona, and establishing thereon a home for the aged and infirm. He has not only made this a model institution of its kind, but has made a profit on the operation of the farm which has materially reduced the cost of maintenance.

NEAL

In many places in the text the name George I. Neal has been mentioned, but no history of Cabell County for the past forty-five years,

---

*A daughter of Thomas Ward, the first sheriff.

or of the State covering the same period, can be written without a mention of his name for the reason that he has helped make history. He was born near Milton, March 23, 1868, attended the Milton schools, taught school for a brief period, and then attended West Virginia University, and was graduated from the college of law in 1888, and admitted to the Bar December 3, 1888. At once his bent for politics, and his ability as a manager of men began to show itself. He was the unsuccessful candidate for mayor of Huntington in 1892, but was elected in 1893 and again in 1894. His efforts to find employment to relieve the unemployment situation which arose at that time smack some of the Public Works program of the present emergency. He won after a hard fight the Democratic nomination for Congress in 1898, and in the campaign which followed he earned the sobriquet of the "penniless wonder." He was one of the early presidents of the Chamber of Commerce and has helped shape all the important programs in the city's development. He was particularly active in 1909 in bringing about the commission form of government for Huntington. He was the unsuccessful Democratic candidate for Congress in 1914, has served many years on the Democratic State Committee, and has been a factor in State politics. He is now the United States Attorney for the Southern District of West Virginia.

George Ira Neal is of Irish extraction. The first of his family name in West Virginia was Captain James Neal of Green County, Pennsylvania, a Revolutionary soldier who had a grant for land for military services and settled in Wood County about 1785.

His grandfather, James Neal, lived in Fayette County, and married a Miss Layne. One of his children was Andrew Dickinson Neal, born April 25, 1837, died June 7, 1900, who located in Cabell at an early date, and was for many years a justice of the peace. He married, on January 13, 1857, Malinda Newman, born in 1839, died in 1917, the daughter of Russell and Sarah Harbour Newman, and reared a remarkable family:

Charles Henry, for twenty-five years was a judge in the State of Washington.

Albert Gallatin, a lawyer, who moved to Washington State, and met his death by drowning.

John M., who lived and is buried at Milton.

Alice E., who moved to Washington, and there married A. E. Stookey. Now a widow, she lives at Olympia.

Margaret Ann, married Dr. B. L. Neville, and moved to Oklahoma. George Ira.

George I. Neal married December 5, 1912, Eunice Virginia Earp of Winchester, Kentucky, whose mother was Ann Wayne Summerson, the daughter of Charles Henry Summerson of Guyandotte. Mrs. Neal is a descendant of Major William McMahon who served first in Dunmore's War, 1772-74, and later in the 3d and 4th Virginia Continental Regiments, and was killed in action under Mad Anthony Wayne, June 30, 1794, at Fort Recovery.

To George I. Neal and Eunice Earp Neal have been born three children: Virginia, deceased; Irene; and George I. Neal, Junior.

Both Mr. and Mrs. Neal are active members of the 5th Avenue Baptist Church, and Mr. Neal is one of the deacons and a teacher in the Sunday School. He is prominent in lay movements of the State, and in the Northern Baptist conventions. He gives much time to civic organizations and their work in and about Huntington.

Dr. W. E. NEAL

Dr. William Elmer Neal, born in Lawrence County, Ohio, October 14, 1875, is a splendid type of the fast disappearing general practitioner. He was educated in the public schools of Lawrence County and graduated from the Proctorsville High School in 1894, and then taught school for a number of years. In 1900 he graduated from the National Normal University, Labanon, Ohio, and then entered upon the study of medicine at the Medical College of Ohio, now a part of the University of Cincinnati. He graduated in 1906 and spent the next year as an interne in the Good Samaritan Hospital in Cincinnati, Ohio. In 1907 he moved to Huntington and entered upon a successful career.

He is a member of the Cabell County (a past president), the West Virginia, and the American Medical Societies. His fraternity is Nu Sigma Nu. He is a Kiwanian, a Mason, an Odd Fellow, a member of the Chamber of Commerce, and of the M. E. Church.

Dr. Neal, a Republican, was elected and served as mayor, 1925-1928. His colleagues, the commissioners, were Democrats, but notwithstanding this fact, his tact and good judgment secured the cooperation of his associates and his administration was marked by good common sense and the absence of bickering and petty politics. He is now a member of the board of park commissioners.

Dr. Neal married on September 11, 1912, Susan Witten, and to this union were born: William Leonard, Thomas Witten, Bernard Gale, and Joseph Guthrie.

Dr. Neal is the son of Thomas J. Neal, born 1852, died 1904, who had a general store in Braderick, Ohio, and his wife, Alice Langdon, born 1855, died 1892, the daughter of Elijah Langdon, a Lawrence County farmer. Thomas J. Neal had another son, Leonard B., who served in the first West Virginia U. S. Infantry and then enlisted in the second U. S. Infantry. He was a corporal in Company I when he died in the Philippines.

Thomas J. Neal was the son of Elliott Neal, born about 1830 in Lawrence County, died 1892, and his wife, Mary Brammer, both of whom spent their lives on a farm in Lawrence County. Elliott Neal was a son of Thomas O'Neal, born 1795, died 1870, and Sophia Corbin Neal, born 1799, died 1877. The O'Neal family migrated from Ireland, and Tom ran away from home, dropped the prefix "O" from his name and settled for a time at the Kanawha Salines. He later moved to Ohio and reared a family.

Mrs. W. E. Neal was born Susan Witten, on January 28, 1888. She was educated at Marshall and Marietta Colleges. Her great-great-grandfather, Philip Witten, made the first settlement in Monroe County, Ohio, in 1790. He married Ruth Dickerson, a sister of H. Vaich and Noah Dickerson, famous Indian fighters.

Mrs. Neal is active in the Woman's Club and a teacher in the Methodist Episcopal Sunday School.

JOHN HUNT OLEY

General Oley as he was known to the people of Huntington was born in Utica, New York, September 24, 1830, and was the son of Simon Van Antwerp Oley and Rachael Hunt Oley. He was a member of the 7th Regiment of New York National Guard at the beginning of the Civil War, and was sent to West Virginia. In the fall of 1861 he organized the 8th Regiment, Virginia Infantry, in the Kanawha Valley, with headquarters at Charleston, and it was mustered into the Federal service at Wheeling, October 29, 1861, with John Hunt Oley as a major. The regiment afterwards became the 7th West Virginia Cavalry. It had a good deal of service, and Oley was promoted to lieutenant colonel, October 2, 1862, and to colonel, March 1, 1863. The regiment was stationed in the Kanawha Valley for the year preceding the surrender at Appomattox, and was mustered out at Charleston, August 1, 1865. In June, 1865, Colonel Oley

John Hunt Oley, Brevet Brigadier General, U.S.A.

was made a brevet brigadier general to rank from March 13, 1865, for gallant and meritorious services in West Virginia and the Shenandoah Valley. He was appointed Commissioner of Internal Revenue in 1871. He moved to Huntington at its beginning, and as we have told elsewhere served as city recorder from the time of the organization of the new city until the date of his death, March 11, 1888. He was a man of much personal attraction and this fact is proved when we consider that during his life Huntington was dominated by men of Southern sympathies, many of whom had served in the Confederate Army, but notwithstanding this fact John Hunt Oley was easily the most commanding figure in the city. He was agent for the land company; served as a member of the school board, and was in truth and in fact the school board. He helped organize the Episcopal church, and with his own purse hired an organist. He was an intimate friend of D. W. Emmons, and always took Sunday dinner at the Emmons home and spent the afternoon and night there. In fact he had his own room in their home, and it was there that General Oley died. He had just partaken of a good dinner and retired to his room when the family heard a fall and went to investigate and found that General Oley had passed away.

On the day of his funeral all business in the city was suspended, and it can be truthfully said he was the most genuinely mourned man who up to this time has been a citizen of this community. He was buried in Spring Hill Cemetery, and his grave is marked by a handsome red granite monument which was paid for by public subscription, the first subscriber to which was C. P. Huntington. General Oley never married.

PAGE

Robert Page, a great grandson of Mann Page of Virginia, migrated in 1804 from Loudoun County to Wood County. He reared a family of five sons and one daughter. A son, George, was the father of George Selden Page who was born in Wood County, October 23, 1843, and moved to Guyandotte in 1872, where he lived until his death, December 31, 1912. George S. Page was a born merchant, and was first in business with Joseph Anderson, and then opened a store on Bridge Street with his brother-in-law, A. E. Smith. In 1883 H. C. Everett bought E. A. Smith's interest, and the firm became Page and Everett, one of the leading wholesale and retail firms in this end of the State. They owned the wharfboat and sold groceries and timber supplies. This firm had a large trade in the counties along the Guyandotte River which trade was supplied by pushboats. The trade thrived until the Norfolk and Western Railroad was built in 1892, when it was much reduced, and finally destroyed when the Guyan Valley road was built.

During these days Page and Everett's store was the meeting place for the active men from Logan and Lincoln counties. Vinson, Goble, and Prichard, and afterwards L. H. Burks, as agent for the Cole, Crane Company, had an office in the store. To facilitate their business this firm built the first telephone line in the county as told of in another chapter. After the Norfolk and Western was built Mr. Everett sold out to Mr. Page who continued the business in his own name until his death. Mr. Page never sought public office, but was a student of contemporary affairs, and a staunch Democrat. He was a man of few words, but of sound business judgment, and practiced in his daily life the Golden Rule. He had the respect of the entire community. When the First National Bank was organized, he was elected a director, and served as one until his death. Mr. Page married Emily Cordelia Smith, daughter of William Crawley Smith, and they had three daughters and one son: Garnett, married Wm. F. Kahler; Pearl, died in infancy; Ruby Louise, married F. Emerson Magee, and had a daughter, Eloise, who married Joel W. Adams; and Nighbert Smith, married Florence Bristol.

PAINE

William Paine, the first of the name in Cabell County, was an Englishman, and it has been told in the text that he taught the first grammar school in the county. His descendants do not have any information about his sojournings before he came to this county, other than that he lived for a time in Bath County, and his wife was a Miss Davidson. This couple had a son, Dr. William Paine, born 1785, in Bath County, died August 22, 1865, in Cabell County, who was a surgeon in the War of 1812.

Dr. William Paine married Elizabeth Russell, and built, and lived in the old brick house that stood on the east side of 24th Street at Collis Avenue, and in the early years of Huntington was known as the Dr. Cheeseman house. He was one of the earliest doctors in the county, and is buried in the old Stephenson Graveyard on the 16th Street Road, just outside the city limits. Dr. William Paine and his wife, Elizabeth, had the following children:

William, born 1815, died 1855, a physician, who lived in Proctorsville; two sons, Thomas and John who moved to the West; Mary, married Calvary Stephenson, lived on Four Pole, and died in June, 1912; Henry B., born 1823, married first a McGinnis and then a McCormick; Elizabeth, born 1826, died 1852, married Sylvester Fuller; Sarah, born 1828, died 1868, married Albert Russell; Charles Wesley, a school teacher, who was superintendent of schools of Cabell County, and the father of Sid Paine, who worked many years in the postoffice; Fannie; Ann, married Alfred Seamonds, and lived in Milton; Ella, married J. P. Davis; Geoffrey, and John.

PANCAKE

Isaac Pancake and his three brothers migrated from Germany in 1790. One of these brothers died shortly after his arrival in America, one settled near Staunton, Virginia, one went to the far West, and Isaac located in the Scioto Valley in Ohio. One of his descendants, Daniel Jefferson Pancake, was born in 1862 in Deering, Ohio, and died in Huntington, in 1928. He was for many years general agent for the Singer Sewing Machine Company in the tri-state region, and made his home at different times at Catlettsburg, Kentucky, Charleston, Clarksburg, Moundsville, and Ronceverte. He married first, in 1885, and had a daughter, Madge, now Mrs. F. H. Hall, and a son Kenna. In 1894 he married a second wife, Ella Hatcher Teays, who was a daughter of James Stephens Teays and a granddaughter of Thomas Teays, who came from Bedford County about 1774, and settled in Teays Valley, and for whom the valley was named.

In the early part of the nineteenth century James Stephens Teays owned the farm on which the International Nickel Company plant is now located, and lived in a log house which was not torn down until the company began the erection of its plant. He sold this farm in 1821 for $172, and moved to Cole's Mouth, now St. Albans.

To the union of Daniel Jefferson Pancake and Ella Teays Pancake were born: Stella, married J. Bert Schroeder; John Teays; and Paul Clinton, who served in the navy 1918-1919, and in 1934 married Mary Martha Taylor of Portsmouth, Ohio.

In 1913 Daniel Jefferson Pancake moved from Ronceverte to Huntington, and engaged in the real estate business. He continued in this business until 1919, when his son, Paul, returned from his war service, and D. J. Pancake, and his three sons, organized the D. J. Pancake and Sons Real Estate Company, which did a successful business until

John Teays Pancake took a position with the Internal Revenue Department. Then Paul C. Pancake organized the Pancake Realty Company, which is one of the outstanding real estate agencies in the city.

PINE*

Alexander Pine was a Virginian, and lived on the farm next below the Johnstons. He had a small saw and grist mill on Four Pole which was afterwards owned by J. L. Thornburg. Uncle Alex, as he was known, moved to Texas in 1850.

POAGE*

J. Harvey Poage came to Cabell County in the 1850's from Ashland, Kentucky, and married Sarah A., the daughter of James Gallaher. His wife inherited from her father the farm which lay between 11th and 14th Street, East, and the river and the hills. They made their home in the old house which fronted on the pike which ran along what is now known as 5½ Alley between 12th and 13th Streets.

To this couple were born Edgar; J. Baylous, married Mayme Miller; George; Robert; Anna, married Joseph R. Shelton, and Sarah, died unmarried.

The Poages, who acquired an interest in the Savage Grant, came from the Scotch-Irish settlement in Rockbridge County, Virginia, to Greenup County, Kentucky, and came direct from there to Cabell County. James Poage married Jemima McCormick, and William Poage married Ann. They each had farms below the Hull farm, on which they built brick houses, but sold out early, and moved to the west.

THE RT. REV. MSGR. THOMAS A. QUIRK

On May 22, 1935, there gathered in Camden, a small farming center in the vicinity of Weston, many dignitaries of the Catholic Church to honor an old man who had spent his life in serving others. The occasion was the investing by Most Reverend John J. Swint, Bishop of Wheeling, once Father Quirk's altar boy, of the veteran priest with the robes of Domestic Prelacy to His Holiness, Pope Pius XI, an honorary office which carries with it the ancient ecclesiastical title of Monsignor. This occasion proved once more that what counts in life is not where a man lives, but how he lives. This old man was Huntington's first resident Catholic parish priest.

---

*Written from information secured from the article, "The Western End of Virginia," by W. S. Laidley.

Thomas A. Quirk was born in Clonmel, Ireland, March 7, 1845. His father was a captain in the English Army. The tradition is that Father Quirk might have had an English title, but preferred to consecrate himself to His Master's work and to serve mankind. These years of service have been crowned, in Monsignor Quirk's ninety-second year, with recognition from Rome, the head and center of Catholicism. Monsignor Quirk has thousands of friends and acquaintances, all sincere admirers. who know that he was not much impressed with his new honors and would wager that, if he lives another near-century of years, he would continue to be the same simple and kindly God-fearing man the cycle of years he has lived has shown him to be.

Shortly after Father Quirk came to America, he entered service in the Federal Army. When the war was over, he began his preparation for the priesthood into which he was ordained in 1870. On September 12, 1872, he came to Huntington, or rather Guyandotte, where he took up his residence with the Carroll family, the first of this district. With this family he lived twelve years to the day. When he first came to Huntington, he found only two other Catholic families besides the Carroll family, one in Ceredo, the other the Floyds in Logan County, and, naturally, no organization of the Catholic Church as such. Father Quirk, however, was not dismayed. He was in the full strength of manhood, and he bent all his energy and strength towards the building up of a parish, the mainspring of life in a Catholic community.

The people of Guyandotte were anxious that the church's activities should at least start in that section. Laban T. Moore and wife donated an acre of land for church and graveyard. On this land, a small and rather beautiful chapel was built, but services were held in this church only a few times. Catholics were coming into the section below Guyandotte on the Ohio River, and Father Quirk had the foresight that Huntington was to be the city, and in Huntington he determined to build.

At first, mass was said in a shanty at the Chesapeake and Ohio roundhouse. Later a lot was secured at 20th Street and 7th Avenue, on Father Quirk's personal credit. On this same credit, lumber and hardware were bought, and a church erected. Father Quirk always called this early structure a "sneer" at architecture, for, as a building, it violated all architectural rules; nevertheless, it was the Catholics' own, and was built on their land. This little structure opened its door for the first Catholic service on the third Sunday of October, 1872. Almost immediately, a school was started by Father Quirk, who for years remained its sole teacher, walking daily from and to Guyandotte in his journeys between church-and-school, and his home with the Carrolls. After twelve years, Father Quirk was transferred to his present field.

Father Quirk's love for good horses brought him into contact with the bank robbers who visited and robbed the Bank of Huntington on September 6, 1875. Standing near his chapel, his eye was attracted by a group of men mounted on fine horses. He approached them and started to converse with them about horses in general, theirs in particular. In the course of the conversation, he directed them to the bank. He had not, of course, the slightest idea of their intention, remembering them as pleasant, well-mannered men. Only later in the day did he learn the purpose of their visit to Huntington.

Father Quirk went from Huntington to a mountain parish of great extent, where three churches had to be attended, near Weston. These churches are at Sand Fork, Goosepeb Run, and Orlando. Here he has been for fifty-one years. Until recently, he covered his field on the back of a faithful old horse that seemed to know the roads as well as did his rider. In the last few years, Father Quirk has "succumbed to the blandishments," as he would put it, of the automobile. The people of the mountain-farm districts of Lewis and Braxton counties will be slow in forgetting the figure of a bent old man in clerical garb riding over the rough trails to administer to the spiritual and temporal needs of his flock.

RICHMOND

J. L. Richmond of the Union Sand and Gravel Company, who has lived in Huntington more or less continuously since 1905, is the son of W. A. and Alice N. Richmond. He was born March 23, 1882, at Rural Retreat, Wytheville County, Virginia. He was educated in the country schools and later took an engineering course at Virginia Polytechnic Institute. After leaving school he was engaged with the Norfolk and Western Railway in its engineering department for seven years, then went with the United Thacker Coal Company, and remained eighteen months, then went back to the Norfolk and Western for two years. In 1908 he went with the United States Government, Engineer Corps, and was engaged on lock and dam construction for eighteen months.

In 1909 he married Lelia Burgess Snyder, daughter of Augustus Snyder of Louisa, Kentucky, They have one son, George, a student at Woodberry Forest School.

From 1909 to 1922 Mr. Richmond was a successful contractor, but he gave up this business to join the Union Sand and Gravel Company, which is one of the large producing companies of the Tri-State region.

RICKETTS

Dr. Girard C. Ricketts, born February 11, 1823, died March 6, 1859, a graduate of Jefferson Medical College, came to Guyandotte from Fauquier County, Virginia, about 1840. After he was established, his father, Elijah Ricketts, born December 31, 1793, died March 16, 1865, came out and brought his wife, Eleanor Compton, born 1800, died June 16, 1863, and family. In the family was a foster daughter, Ann Cole. Elijah Ricketts was a big, upstanding fellow, and was elected constable on November 23, 1847. When the Civil War came he was a strong Southern man, and was one of the men arrested by Colonel Zeigler, and taken to Camp Chase. On his return from Camp Chase he was taken sick, and his foster daughter, Ann Cole, who had married Leander Varnum, and lived at Millersport, Ohio, came down, and took him to her home where he died and was buried. Dr. Girard C. Ricketts had a cousin, Dr. G. R. Ricketts, who lived in Proctorsville, and was the father of Doctors Ed. Merrill and Joe Ricketts.

Dr. Girard C. Ricketts married on February 15, 1844, Virginia Everett, born April 23, 1826, and to this union were born: Albert Gallatin, January 1, 1845, killed in action, December 22, 1863; L. C. (Cooney), born November 6, 1846, married Fannie Miller, and had three children, John G., Ella, and Cora; George Henry, born July 3, 1849, died without issue; Dr. John E., born September 5, 1851, graduated in medicine, and located at Logan Courthouse; Girard C., born June 26, 1855, for many years one of the leading grocerymen in the city; Charles H., born October 19, 1856, married Jennie Peyton; Sarah Eleanor, married first, William Holloway, and second, Rankin Wiley.

Mrs. Virginia Ricketts, the mother of these children, lived to the age of ninety-seven, and was for many years an active member of the Methodist Church, South. In her old age she retained her interest in many things, and was one of the remarkable women of her time.

ROLFE-McLAUGHLIN

Peter Ruffner, the son of a Hanoverian Baron, who emigrated to Switzerland from Germany, was born in Switzerland in 1713, and came to this country when a very young man. Peter married Mary Steinman in Pennsylvania, and settled in Virginia. His son, Joseph, born in 1740, moved with his wife to Kanawha County in 1795, where he became interested in the town of Charleston. He owned all the salt property that was then known, and with the beginning of a new country, and a new town, in a new business, he invested heavily and wisely.

Daniel Ruffner, the son of Peter and Mary, was born in 1779, and came as a lad with his parents, in 1795, to Kanawha. Charles, their son, born in 1801, married Ann Hedrick.

Mary E., daughter of Charles, born 1832, was unusual in point of education, talent, and courage. In 1855 she married Charles L. Rolfe, whose extensive land holdings extended from Barboursville along the Guyan River to what was then called Ashland,* Virginia. He was born in Mecklenburg County, Virginia, in 1808. During the Civil War he was too old for service in the army of the Confederacy, but was active in behalf of the Confederate forces to whom he supplied provisions constantly, until he was taken prisoner by the Federal forces. He was held prisoner in Guyandotte until near the close of the war.

During the time of Charles Rolfe's imprisonment, Mary was informed that her husband and his fellow prisoners were ill from lack of food. Filling a basket with provisions she started on horseback to their relief. When she reached the Holderby homestead, known in recent years as the Altizer place, she was turned back by the Union outposts. Nothing daunted, she forced her horse to swim the Guyan River and came down on the western side until she was opposite the town. She did not attempt to cross the suspension bridge, but again started to swim the river. In this she was discovered by the Union soldiers who fired on her as she reached the eastern shore. Her horse was struck by a bullet, but the animal plunged on into the night, and ran for half a mile before dropping beneath her. She finished her journey on foot, and was permitted, when the Union officers discovered the purpose of her visit, to deliver the food to the prisoners.

---

*Ashland was a postoffice on the Guyandotte River about two miles above Barboursville.

Charles and Mary moved to Huntington with their family soon after the close of the Civil War, where he died in 1883. Mary died in 1912. The children of Mary and Charles are as follows: Ida; Ann; Augusta; Sue; Katherine, born in 1865; and Charles R.

Katherine Rolfe married Hernando Ridgeway McLaughlin in 1890. Ridgeway, born in 1860, at the old McLaughlin homestead, Springfield, in Caroline County, Virginia, was the son of Emma and James A. McLaughlin. In 1875 he came to Huntington to work for the Chesapeake and Ohio Railroad. While but a youth he fired the locomotives which pulled the trains across the mountains.

He rose from the cab to assistant superintendent of the Coal River Division. He was a man of outstanding ability, and well versed in the science of railroading. He had a deep interest in the worker, and the success of the road. On the morning of September 16, 1924, he was fatally wounded by a former employee of the railroad.

The children of Katherine and Ridgeway McLaughlin are: 1, George Minor, born in 1892, educated in law at Washington and Lee University, served in France in the 21st Field Artillery of the Fifth Division during the World War. He was retained in the Army of Occupation until August, 1919, and since receiving his discharge has practiced law in Huntington. In 1928 he married Lulu M. Humphries. 2, Mary Sue, married Ira Morton Nickell in 1926. Their children are: James Minor, born 1930, and Morton Carol, born 1931.

JOHN HOOE RUSSEL

On John Hooe Russel's desk, in the old Bank of Huntington building, there used to repose a brace of pistols of the kind that were used in the War Between the States. In those days bank deposits were not insured. Such armament, as well as huge iron vaults, was considered essential to the protection of the funds of banks. Bandits of the old blood and thunder type, who galloped across countryside as they now do in the motion pictures, were no rarity.

Mr. Russel was utterly fearless, but the day the Jesse James gang of highwaymen visited the bank September 6, 1876—the pistols were not in reach, and the robbers, after appropriating a considerable part of the bank's cash, also helped themselves to the brace of pistols. When one of the gang later was captured, the bandit had these pistols in his possession, and was identified by them. John Hooe Russel's son, Albert Lacy Russel, has one of them at the present day. The other is in possession of the First Huntington National Bank.

John Hooe Russel, president, Bank of Huntington, and of the Huntington National Bank

The above incident was only one of the many stirring events that marked the infancy of Huntington. Another in which Mr. Russel figured was that of the burning of the Kennet livery stable in May, 1883. Mr. Russel was a fancier of high-bred horses, and kept a beautiful pair in the Kennet livery stable. It was about noon when the fire broke out. All of the stable hands were at the wharfboat to meet a packet which was coming in with some horses. The blaze spread with rapidity. Soon the entire block was ablaze. Though Will Hamlin, the stable boss, risked his life by plunging into the roaring furnace, he was unable to save Mr. Russel's horses.

John Hooe Russel, born in Huntsville, Alabama, June 15. 1842, brought to this city the social refinements of the aristocratic Old South, and as organizer and president of the Gypsy Club, set the very highest standards for membership, and rigorously insisted upon their observance. He died in Huntington in 1903.

He was a grandson of Colonel Albert Russel, of Loudoun County, Virginia, and Anna Frances (Hooe) Russel. He was the son of Dr. Albert Russel and Martha Jane (Lacy) Russel. Colonel Russel was a charter member of the Virginia Society of the Cincinnati.

John Hooe Russel was one of the founders of the Bank of Huntington, and was its first cashier. He later became president, and at the time was the youngest bank president in the United States. His first wife was Nettie M. Phelps, of Richmond, Kentucky. She died soon after the birth of John Hooe Russel, Junior, who lived only a little more than a year.

Mr. Russel's second wife was Minerva Parke Phelps, a cousin of his first wife. To that union was born, in 1902, Albert Lacy Russel, now of 3816 Broadview Drive, Cincinnati, Ohio, who was graduated from Yale with the degree of Bachelor of Arts, in June, 1923, just one hundred years after his grandfather, Dr. Albert Russel graduated from Yale, in 1823. Albert Lacy Russel, in the fall of 1923, entered the law office of Taft, Stettinius and Hollister in Cincinnati, and five years later was made a member of the firm. He married, in 1926, Caroline H. Collier, of Cincinnati, and they have one daughter, Mary Ellen Russel, born February 14, 1935.

Mr. Russel was one of the potent forces for the upbuilding of Huntington. He labored continuously for the advancement of the community, was a recognized social leader, and an arbiter of both society and finance. He was a close friend and associate of Ely

Ensign, who was connected with the Ensign foundry, one of the city's major industries.

It was undoubtedly the presence of such men as he that was responsible, in a large degree for the city's phenomenal growth. He had a high degree of civic pride, a keen business judgment, and through his social graces contributed much to the morale of the growing community.

JEFFREY RUSSELL

Jeffrey Russell made an affidavit before the Circuit Superior Court of Law, October 9, 1811, making application for a pension as a Revolutionary soldier, and in this affidavit he set out that he had enlisted in Mecklenburg County, Virginia, and it is fair to assume that this was his native county. He died in 1813. The records show that his wife at the time of his death was Elizabeth Brown, and that they had the following children: Patty, married a Wilson; Thomas; Lewis; Daniel; Nancy, married Samuel Parker; Henry; Mark, Junior; Elizabeth or Betsy, married William Paine; and John.

John Russell was born September 18, 1798, died January 7, 1847, and was a soldier in the War of 1812. His grave in Spring Hill Cemetery, Huntington, has been marked by the Daughters of 1812. He married first, March 12, 1820, Rebecca Buffington, daughter of Thomas Buffington, born March 24, 1801, died January 10, 1837, and to this union were born:

1. Frank or Francis, moved to Missouri, and became a lawyer.

2. Thomas A., moved to Missouri, attended the University of Missouri, and became a judge in St. Louis. He married M. L. Lenoir, and had two daughters.

3. Sarah A., married Joseph W. Morris, who became a captain in the C.S.A. (See account of Morris family.)

4. Helen M., married James R. Morris, a lieutenant, C.S.A.

5. Marian, born July 28, 1831, died November 23, 1920, married in 1851, Dr. J. P. Harriman.

6. Eliza, married Ferd Overstall, and lived in St. Louis, Missouri.

John Russell married second, Sarah Maxon, and to this union were born William, who died without issue; Romaine; and John, who was a physician, and lived some years in the West, but returned to Red House, where he died.

MARK RUSSELL

Mark Russell, one of the first gentlemen justices of the County Court, and who was sheriff, died in 1821, survived by his wife, who was born Esther Dean, and who died several months later. By this wife he had three children: Benjamin Henry Harrison, Sarah Dean, and Henry Louis. Other children mentioned in the will were Jeffrey, Charles, William Junior, Wesley, Phillip, Polly Dean, Tabithia, Edmund, and St. Mark.

This first Mark Russell owned and lived on a three-hundred-acre tract of land on the Ohio River, two hundred acres of which was confirmed to him as assignee of Henry Hampton in the chancery suit partitioning the Savage Grant, and one hundred acres of which he purchased from Henry Hampton in 1811. This farm was located west of 15th Street, and was afterwards known as the Gallaher-Poage place. He had a son, St. Mark Russell, who lived on the lower side of the Guyandotte. He was a ferryman, mail carrier, auctioneer, preacher, and temperance lecturer. He married Dolly McMillan, and to this union were born: Albert, married Sarah Paine, and lived in Guyandotte; Henry, married a Handley, and lived in Huntington; Theodore, died without issue; Elizabeth; Alice; and St. Mark, who was a merchant in Guyandotte.

RUTHERFORD

Robert Rutherford acquired eleven shares of the Savage Grant, nine of them were in Cabell County and lay above the Guyandotte River. He never lived in the county, and in the final decree in the chancery suit to partition the grant, his shares were confirmed to John Morrow, who had shown himself entitled to them as devisee and executor of Rutherford.

The acknowledgement on several deeds wherein Morrow was grantor was before a notary in Berkeley County, and this fact supports the tradition that Robert Rutherford was one and the same Robert Rutherford who was the first member of Congress from beyond the Blue Ridge, serving 1793-1797, and who had his home in Berkeley County.

SAMUELS

John Samuels came to Cabell County with John Laidley about 1812, and a short time afterwards these two went to Norfolk, Virginia, and served a few months in the army. John Samuels was clerk of the County from February, 1816, until 1858. He married Emily Gardner whose antecedents are told about under the account of William Clendenin Miller, and had the following children: Mary, married

Moses Thornburg; America, married Rev. A. J. McMillan; John, married Mary Gardner of Kentucky; Lafayette, married Fannie Lusher, and was the father of Mary Eugenia, who married William C. Miller; Alex H., lieutenant Border Rangers, C.S.A., and was killed in action, and Henry Jefferson, who attended Marshall Academy about 1839, served a few months as the first adjutant general of the Restored State of Virginia, and was the first judge of this circuit under the new State. It is said he suggested the motto *Montani Semper Liberi* for the State Seal. He married Rebecca Bartram of Pennsylvania, and had the following children: Nettie, married Bailey Thornburg; Ceres, married David Peters, and had one daughter, who is now Ethel Peters Simon.

SAMWORTH

Fred Samworth, who was born in Birmingham, England, migrated to the United States in 1884 and settled in Wilmington, Delaware, where he was engaged as a building contractor. In 1887 he married Elizabeth Hall of Wilmington, and to this union was born on February 23, 1892, Fred W. Samworth.

Young Samworth attended the common schools in Wilmington, and then the Mount Herman School in Massachusetts. In 1910 he took employment with the Wilmington Street Railway Company, and two years later, on February 5, 1912, he married Alice Virginia Blackwell. Their children are Leonard, Robert, and Henry.

F. W. Samworth continued with the Wilmington City Railway until 1925, when he came to Huntington as operating manager of the Ohio Valley Electric Railway. In 1933 he acquired all of the stock of the Ohio Valley Electric Railway Company, and is now the president of the company. This property is a most valuable one, well equipped and well managed. The company's relations with its employees are unusual, in that at an early date the company began to provide recreational facilities for them.

Mr. Samworth not only operates the street railway but he keeps abreast of the times in transportation, and has taken over a number of bus lines operating in the city, and has recently been given franchises for additional routes. He is a Mason, a member of the Guyandotte Club, and the Guyan Country Club.

SCALES

Nathaniel Scales, whose wife's name was Mary Frances and died in 1826, came from North Carolina by way of Patrick County, Virginia. His services as a Revolutionary soldier have been shown elsewhere. He stopped for a time at the Salines on the Kanawha, but in 1805 purchased a part of the Savage Grant which lay roughly between 7th and 11th Streets, fronting on the Ohio River. He had the following children: Elizabeth, married Robert Adams; Sally, married Jacob Hite; Mary, married James Scales, and remained in North Carolina; Jensy, married Manoah Bostick; Peter, born in 1790, and died in 1863, married Ann Minor of Woodlawn, Orange County, Virginia, who spent only a short part of his life in this county, and was engaged in an engineering corps under Claude Crozet. Upon the death of his wife's parents he went to Orange County; Abigail, born 1793, died 1842, married Bishop Thomas A. Morris; Nancy, born 1795, died 1882, married Colonel William Buffington; and Matilda, born 1797, married Dr. Benjamin Brown.

SCHERR

Harry Scherr, lawyer, the son of Arnold C. and Katherine Nickel Scherr, was born at Maysville, Grant County, W. Va., on June 6, 1881. He was educated in the public schools, at Allegany County Military Academy (Cumberland, Maryland), and at the West Virginia University, from which latter institution he was graduated in June, 1905.

Having been admitted to the Bar, he located for the practice of his profession at Williamson. He associated himself with the law firm of Sheppard and Goodykoontz, the firm later becoming Sheppard, Goodykoontz and Scherr, and still later Goodykoontz and Scherr. From 1905 to 1909 he served as assistant prosecuting attorney of Mingo County.

On January 1, 1925, he accepted an invitation to come to Huntington as a member of the law firm of Vinson, Thompson, Meek, and Renshaw, later reorganized as Vinson, Thompson, Meek, and Scherr. While Mr. Scherr has devoted himself consistently to the practice of law, he is interested in business, being a director, among others, of the National Bank of Commerce of Williamson, Green Bag Cement Company of West Virginia, and Inter-Ocean Casualty Company.

On June 24, 1913, he married Miss Rosa L. Wall, at Summerfield, North Carolina. They have three children: Harry, now a student at Yale; Barbara, and Betty.

Mr. Scherr is a member of the Kappa Alpha and Delta Chi Fraternities; American Academy of Political and Social Science; American, West Virginia, and Cabell County Bar Associations; director, Chamber of Commerce of the United States, Huntington Chamber of Commerce, Huntington Community Chest, and Huntington Civic Music Association. He is an Episcopalian, and a vestryman of .Trinity Church.

Arnold C. Scherr, the father, was the son of Joseph and Gertrude Arnold Scherr, and was born in Zurich, Switzerland, on August 21, 1847. He came to America with his parents at an early age, and resided in Preston County. In early manhood he located in Grant County, at Maysville, and later at Keyser, in Mineral County, where he engaged in woolen manufacturing, having a plant at each place, and the mercantile business. He took an active part in politics, was elected sheriff of Grant County in 1868, again in 1872, and a third time in 1880. He was elected to the House of Delegates in 1878, served many years on the Republican State Committee, and served two terms as State Auditor (1901-1909). He was a candidate for the Republican nomination for governor in 1908. As a result of a bitter contest Mr. Scherr and his opponent, C. W. Swisher, claimed the nomination, but both later withdrew in the interest of party harmony. He died at Charleston in 1917.

Joseph Scherr, the father of Arnold C. Scherr, also born in Switzerland, was educated as a soldier, and at an early age entered the military service of his country, rising to the rank of Colonel. At the outbreak of the Crimean War he went to England and tendered his services to the British government. They were accepted and later he and other Swiss officers organized the British-Swiss Legion which occupied an important place in the British military forces during that war. Among other services assigned to him Colonel Scherr was Provost Marshal of Southampton, England. During the War Between the States he was offered a commission, first as a captain of infantry, and later as a colonel on the staff of General Segel, but physical disabilities prevented his acceptance of either assignment. He died in 1883.

SCOTT

Paul W. Scott is the senior member in the law firm of Scott, Graham and Wiswell, with offices in the First Huntington National Bank building. He was admitted to the Bar in 1893, was associated for many years with E. E. Williams and H. T. Lovett as partners, and since their deaths, with the members of the present firm.

He was born August 25, 1869, at Middleport, Ohio, and is the son of Hugh Bartlett Scott, a Presbyterian minister, and Anna Whitten Scott. His father served for many years as superintendent of schools, first at Middleport, Ohio, and later at Ashland, Kentucky. His mother was prominent in educational work in Ohio, as institute lecturer and instructor. Both were of pioneer American stock, and their forbears from Pennsylvania and Maine joined the trek across the Alleghenies after the Revolutionary War.

Mr. Scott graduated from the high school in his home town, taught school in Ohio and Minnesota, and graduated from Marietta College in 1890. In the same year he became principal of Buffington School in Huntington. After three years of service there, he began the practice of law, securing admission to the Bar as a result of private study.

On December 5, 1908, he married Dolores Pearl McNeill of Sutton, a daughter of Asa McNeill and Nancy Buckley McNeill, members of pioneer families whose founders settled in Pocahontas County between 1768 and 1770. Mr. and Mrs. Scott have a daughter, Anna Pauline, born January 18, 1910. She is a graduate of Huntington High School and Ohio State University, and married Thomas Dale Wilson.

Mr. Scott is a Presbyterian, a Republican, a member of Phi Beta Kappa and Alpha Sigma Phi Fraternities. He was city attorney of Huntington for eight years, a former president of the Cabell County Bar Association, a member of the State and American Bar Associations, and is a trustee of the Foster Foundation. In May, 1934, he was chosen by the governor of West Virginia to serve for the four-year term as one of the nine members of the State Judicial Council, created by the Legislature.

SEAMONDS

Elijah Seamonds, who was born in Albemarle County, Virginia, came to Cabell County at an early date. He was the son of Ephriam Seamonds, who served in the Albemarle Militia during the Revolutionary War and died in 1801.

Elijah Seamonds married a Keeton, sister to Mrs. Justine Keeton Sandridge, wife of Reubens Sandridge, who were early settlers in Cabell County, and it has been said that the two families came to the county at the same time, as they both lived near Barboursville, one on Mud River, and the other on Merritts Creek, a tributary of Mud River.

Elijah Seamonds was one of the early school teachers, and was a man of influence in his day. He had a number of children; among them being William R., and Elijah G., Junior, who lived near Davis' Creek.

William R. was born in Cabell County in 1812, and died in 1889. He was a United States Deputy Marshal, and had arduous service. He married Nancy Harshbarger, daughter of David Harshbarger, Senior, and to this union was born: P. H., who served in the C.S.A., and was long employed by the Chesapeake and Ohio Railway, and was the father of "Gal," John, Charles, and Jim, railroad men who moved to Texas in the '80's; Charles, killed in the service, C.S.A.; Alf; Mary, married Ben Shy; Lucy, married a Coffman; Elizabeth, married a McCain; Susan, married George Crump; Nannie, married V. B. Davis; and William H.

William H. Seamonds, born June 21, 1840, died February 22, 1919, married Sarah J. Lusher, and to this union were born: Mary M., married J. G. Hatfield, and is the mother of Robert P. Hatfield; Randolph M.; Susie L.; William; George R., born February 17, 1873, has been three times elected clerk of the Circuit Court; Maggie; Andrew J.; and Kate.

SHEPHERD

Thomas Rogers Shepherd was born at Charlestown, a son of the Rev. Thos. B. Shepherd, a Baptist minister, and his wife, who was born Ella Rogers, of Loudoun County, Virginia. As a boy he attended the Charlestown Academy, and was afterward graduated from West Virginia University in 1886. He later returned to that institution, and was graduated from the law college in 1888. Upon his graduation he located in Huntington, and was admitted to the Bar on December 10, 1888.

His first association was with Captain Eustace Gibson and Thomas Michie, which lasted eight months, but his friendship for Captain Gibson was life long, and when the Captain was in his last years, and fortune no longer smiled on him, it was Tom Shepherd who looked after him in his sickness, and on many occasions nursed him. After leaving Gibson and Michie, Shepherd went with the firm of Marcum and Peyton, afterwards Marcum, Peyton, and Marcum. He lived in the home of the late John S. Marcum for many years, and was regarded as a member of the family. Shortly after his admission to the Bar he was named by Judge Thomas H. Harvey as a Commissioner in Chancery, which position he held until he was elected prosecuting attorney in 1920, and was Referee in Bankruptcy, 1913-20. After T. W. Peyton retired from the firm of Marcum, Peyton, and Marcum, Thomas R. Shepherd became a partner, and the firm was Marcum, Marcum, and Shepherd. When J. R. Marcum was admitted to the Bar, Lace Marcum and John Marcum separated and Thomas R. Shepherd became a partner of Lace Marcum under the firm name of Marcum and Shepherd. In March, 1923, he was named as interim judge to fill the vacancy as judge of the 6th Judicial Circuit occasioned by the resignation of Judge John T. Graham, in the following year was elected for the unexpired term, and in 1928 was elected for the full term of eight years.

Judge Shepherd is an active outdoors man, a keen sportsman and delights in fishing and hunting. He is an earnest and consistent member of the 5th Avenue Baptist Church, and has had a Sunday School class in that institution for more than thirty years.

SHOFFSTALL

In 1920 Arthur Scott Shoffstall and W. L. Wotherspoon were sent to Huntington to look over conditions with a view to selecting a site to build a rolling mill for the International Nickel Company. The report of their investigation was favorable and the result was that the International Nickel Company purchased a site and erected a modern mill for the production of malleable nickel, monel metal, and other copper nickel alloys.

Arthur Scott Shoffstall was in 1921 appointed general manager of the Huntington works, the construction work began in that year, the plant was completed, and production began in 1922. Mr. Shoffstall not only performs his duties as an executive of one of the large plants in the city, but he has identified himself with the community life. He is a member of the Presbyterian Church, and of the several Masonic bodies, including the Shrine, a Rotarian, an active member of the Chamber of Commerce, and has supported every movement that had for its purpose the advancement of his new home. He is reserved, and a man of few words, but his feet are always on the ground.

Arthur Scott Shoffstall was born near Coolspring, Jefferson County, Pennsylvania, February 20, 1876. He is the son of Josiah Shoffstall, born 1847, died 1915, and his wife, Elizabeth Jane Harmon Shoffstall, born 1856, died 1933. He attended the various township public schools until he was thirteen years of age when he secured employment as a chore boy in the home of Mrs. Kate D. Marlin at Brookville, Pennsylvania. He then enrolled in and attended the graded public school at that place until 1895, when his employer sent him to the Pennsylvania State College. The cryptic sentence, "His employer sent him to the Pennsylvania State College," by no means tells the whole story of the interest of the employer, and the affection and appreciation of the boy.

The employer, Mrs. Kate D. Marlin, was the daughter of John Dougherty, an Irishman, who migrated to America early in the nineteenth century, and stopped first at the Stone Inn, near New Bethlehem, Pennsylvania, which still stands. He made a fortune in the new world. The daughter, Kate, married Captain Silas J. Marlin, who served in the volunteer forces of the United States Army, 1861-65, and had two sons, John, who died when the mother was on a visit to her husband in the field, and Silas J., Junior, a man now sixty-eight years of age, and a bachelor. Mrs. Marlin had the generous impulses of her race, and with it the decided likes and dislikes. If she liked it was strong, but if she disliked it required no lie detector to acquaint the object of her dislike of that fact.

Arthur Scott Shoffstall was a faithful chore boy, but an ambitious one, and his whole ambition was to equip himself so he might enter the Pierce Business College in Philadelphia. He planned to defray the cost of this course by working as a motorman or conductor on the Philadelphia street railway. One night his employer found him studying late, and she inquired what he was doing. He told of his ambition to go to college. She was interested, but suggested that Arthur's carriage was bad and why not go to West Point. The boy was not interested. She then suggested that he go to Lehigh and become an engineer or go to the University of Pennsylvania and become a physician, but the boy answered no, that he would like to go to the Pennsylvania State College and study chemistry and metallurgy. Mrs. Marlin was not sure about this plan so she consulted George A. Jenks, a prominent lawyer who had been in President Cleveland's official family, and he at once put his stamp of approval on the boy's ambition. The good woman not only approved but financed the plan.

Arthur Scott Shoffstall is one of the big men in his line in America, but he still holds in grateful memory and esteem the woman who aided him in his youth, and if she in the great beyond, could know the innermost workings of his heart she would be amply repaid for her kindness to him.

But to return to Arthur Scott Shoffstall. After one year in the preparatory department of the Pennsylvania State College he matriculated in its school of natural science from which he graduated in 1900 with a degree of B.Sc. That year he was appointed assistant in the laboratories of the department of chemistry, at the Pennsylvania State College, from which position he resigned in 1901. From 1902 to 1905 he was an instructor in this department and obtained a degree of M.S. in the latter year.

In the fall of 1905 he joined the E. I. DuPont de Nemours Company as superintendent of its sulphuric acid plants, Repanno Works, Gibbstown, New Jersey, which position he resigned in 1907 to accept that of superintendent of acid plants, U. S. Bureau of Ordnance, Naval Proving Ground, Indian Head, Maryland. On November 20, 1908, he became associated with the International Nickel Company in various operating capacities of its Orford Works, Bayonne, New Jersey, where he remained until 1920 when he came to Huntington.

Arthur Scott Shoffstall married first, Jennie Pearsall of Grove City, Pennsylvania, who died without issue. He married second, on February 20, 1908, Lillian Middleton, and to this union has been born three children: Arthur Marlin, Mary Jane, and Lillian Isobel. They live in a pleasant home overlooking Ritter Park.

SIKES

Thomas Sikes was born at Portsmouth, Ohio, in 1836 and came to Huntington in 1872. He was for many years a brick and building contractor. He was the son of Levi Sikes, born in Massachusetts in 1796, a Baptist minister and grandson of John J. Sikes of Massachusetts, who was a soldier in the Revolutionary War.

Thomas Sikes entered the Federal service in the Civil War in Company G, 1st Ohio Regiment, Volunteer Infantry, and served three months. He was then commissioned captain, Company E, 33d Regiment Ohio Volunteers Infantry, and served through the several grades, and was commissioned a colonel. He had four years and ten months of service, and participated in some thirty engagements including the first Bull Run, Stone River, Chickamauga, Missionary Ridge, and Lookout Mountain. His organization was a part of the 14th Army Corps under General George H. Thomas for whom Colonel Sikes had so much affection that he named a son for him. Colonel Sikes was a Royal Arch Mason, an active member of the G.A.R., served as town marshal in 1886-7, was a member of the city council of Central City, and served as city treasurer of Huntington five years. He married Minerva J. Williams, and they had the following children: Ida M., married Sam Johnston; Maude, assistant librarian; Mamie K.; George H., a brick contractor; Austin M.; Herbert A.; and Robert, who died without issue.

His son, Austin M. Sikes, is the veteran circuit court reporter, which position he has filled for more than thirty years. He served as a captain in the 2d Infantry, West Virginia National Guard, during the civil disorders in 1912-13, on Cabin Creek, and went with this organization to the Mexican Border in 1916. In 1917 he went into the Federal service with his regiment, was a captain in the 150th Infantry, and went overseas in 1918, as regimental adjutant.

Captain Sikes married first, in 1903, Clara Frazier, who died January 30, 1905, and to this union was born a son, Thomas. He married second, in September, 1909, Lillie Byus, and had a son, Glenn Austin, who is a first classman at West Point; Helen Louise, and Janet N.

SIMMONS

In the article on W. O. Walton an account was given of William Simmons, the cabinetmaker who came from Baltimore, and is the ancestor of Mr. Walton's wife. But there was a John Simmons who was no relative of this William, and who was the captain of the Rifle Company that served in the campaign at Fort Meigs, 1812-1813. Where he came from is not known. In 1809 Thomas Clap conveyed to this John Simmons a tract of land on the east side of the Guyandotte River, the beginning point of which was a large buffalo lick about two and one-half miles above the mouth of Mud River. There is no deed from John Simmons for this land. He died in the latter part of May, 1814, and left no will, and the county records do not disclose anything that will throw any light on his heirs.

SPURLOCK

Jesse Spurlock, the progenitor of the family of this name in Cabell and adjoining counties, was a Virginian, and with his wife Sarah or Sallie Harber settled on a site now occupied by Wilbur Smith's Business College in Lexington, Kentucky, about the last of the eighteenth century, moving from there to what was then Kanawha County to locate on Greenbottom, Cabell County,* and moved from there to a farm about two miles north of Wayne Courthouse, where he is buried. Sarah was the sister of Charlie Harber, a great circuit rider and pioneer preacher. Just where Jesse Spurlock originated or just where he stopped or how long he stayed at any place on his trek is not known, but he was one of the gentlemen justices of Cabell County in 1814. He was the third sheriff of the county, and represented the county in the General Assembly.

The children born to this couple were:

1. Stephen, born March 19, 1786, died December 31, 1870, married on May 1, 1806, Nancy Amos (born February 8, 1784, died May 1, 1872). He was a pioneer Methodist preacher and was performing marriages in Cabell County as early as January, 1813. His deacon's orders, signed by Bishop Francis Asbury in 1815 at the last conference held by him at Lebanon, Kentucky, and his elder's orders, which were signed by William McKendree at Lexington, Kentucky, in 1821, are still in the possession of a descendant, the Rev. Arden P. Keyser of Catlettsburg.

Stephen Spurlock was assigned to the Guyandotte Circuit, and preached in Guyandotte in 1816 and 1817, but his activities were confined largely to the territory now included in Cabell, Lincoln, and Wayne counties. He settled on the west side of Twelve Pole, just above the old bridge at Dickson and later moved to near the mouth of Long Branch on Beech Fork. He built a stone chapel not far from Dickson, and a second chapel, now known as the Bowen Chapel, on Beech Fork near which he was buried. At the outbreak of the Civil War his sympathies were strongly Southern. When Captain M. J. Ferguson's company (C.S.A.) assembled at Wayne preparatory to leaving for Dixie, he was too old to go either as a soldier or as Chaplain, but he knew most, if not all of the men personally, so when the company left Wayne he went with it for a day's march. The next morning before he left, at the request of the men, he assembled the company, and offered up a prayer for their safe return. Captain Ferguson and others who heard the prayer bear witness to the fact that in their respective judgments it was the most wonderful prayer that ever fell

---

*It will be remembered that in the deed made by Joshua Fry to Peyton Short for the lower half of Greenbottom he reserves to ———— Spurlock the right to remain in the tenement on which he has settled for seven years from March 1, 1805. This was probably Jesse, and it can be accounted for by the fact that Joshua Fry lived in Woodford County, Kentucky, and Jesse had just left there and maybe there was a contract before he left.

from the old man's lips. The burden of the prayer was that the Great Master and God of battles might take, and keep the men in care, and return them home. The company saw much hard service. Many members were wounded, some captured, and many replacements sent to the company were killed, but not a single man who was present at the prayer was killed in action, and they attribute this fact to the efficacy of the prayer. Stephen Spurlock was the father of the following:
   a. Cassia, born July 24, 1809, died October 8, 1843, married on January 12, 1826, Reuben Booten, a pioneer preacher.
   b. Jesse, born January 30, 1811, married on September 17, 1829, Cynthia Booker.
   c. Wesley, born January 15, 1813.
   d. Abigail, born March 12, 1815.
   e. William, died in infancy.
   f. Milton, born April 9, 1820, died June 20, 1865, married August 3, 1846, Rebecca A. E. Davis.
   g. Francis A., born September 28, 1822, died October 7, 1855, married January 9, 1846, Rebecca Booten.
   h. Stephen Marshall, died in infancy.
   i. Hester Ann, born March 24, 1831, died February 27, 1906, married February 14, 1847, James P. Keyser.
   2. Burwell,* born 1790 in Montgomery County, Virginia, and died August 5, 1879, on the farm on which his father had lived in Wayne County. There is a chapel on Wilson Creek erected in his memory. He married Sallie Morrison, and had the following children:
   a. Cassandra.
   b. Levi.
   c. Roxanna.
   d. Mero.
His second wife was Nancy Garrett, and to this union were born:
   e. Leander.
   f. Hurston, a captain in the C.S.A., whose daughter, Arma, married Charley Hoard of Ceredo.
   g. Sanders, a lieutenant in the C.S.A., and later sheriff of Wayne County.
   h. Burwell, Junior.
   i. Electra, married Levi Morris.
   j. Leatha, married Chapman Adkins.

---

*Burwell Spurlock was commissioned a Captain of Militia on December 5, 1810, and was on active duty February 24th to March 7, 1815.

k. Mary, married first, Calvin Harrison, and second, Sylvester Crockett.

l. America.

Burwell Spurlock, Senior, was a self-educated man. He was admitted to a traveling connection in the Ohio Conference in 1819, and appointed to the Guyandotte Circuit. On November 23, 1819, he gave bond before the County Court of Cabell, and was authorized to celebrate marriages. The church records show that he supplied the Guyandotte Church, 1818-1821, inclusive, and 1823 and 1824. His activities extend to Eastern Kentucky, and Cabell, Wayne, and Logan counties. After the division of the church he was readmitted in the Western Virginia Conference M. E. Church, South, at its organization in 1850, and the next year he was assigned to the Wayne Circuit as a supernumerary. In 1860 he was opposed to Secession, and when he was elected to the Secession Convention in Richmond, he with another Methodist minister, William McComas of Cabell, voted against the Ordinance of Secession; but of this let W. L. Mansfield speak:

"In the election of a delegate to represent the county at Richmond the several elements, except the avowed Unionists and the 'Peace-at-any-price' contingent, pooled their issues and interests.

"They supported Rev. Burwell Spurlock, a man noted for his conservatism, trusted for a high order of personal integrity, and honored for his great native intellectuality. Rev. Spurlock was near 70 years of age, and because of his advanced years, had retired from the laborious duties of a mountain Methodist circuit rider. In the ministry he had acquired a fame reaching far beyond the confines of his conference for soul-stirring eloquence, profound thought and deep spirituality. Reared in the backwoods without the advantage of schools or technical education, he had attained an intimate knowledge of the best books; could quote Homer and other classics by the hour; could pluck a blade of grass and hold tirelessly the interest of his listener while he disclosed the delicate processes of the development of vegetation or simplified some abstruse principle of natural science. When too old to leave his home and too infirm to even stand on his feet, men sought him to pay homage to his unostentatious abilities or sit at his feet and learn wisdom. So distinguished an authority as the late Judge James H. Ferguson, declared that Rev. Burwell Spurlock was naturally the greatest character he had ever known and with the advantages of a technical education he would have been forced out from the

Burwell Spurlock. Born 1790, died 1879. The great preacher.

solitude of the forests and the obscurity of his native hills into the foremost ranks of the bishops.

"This picture may seem to be overdrawn and while the admiration and reverence of the writer for this great man may have led him unto the verge of fulsomeness, the delineation does not approach hyperbole.

"The Union candidate was William Ratcliff, also an aged citizen of recognized probity of mind and character, a man of strong native abilities and sterling integrity. While the greater number of the prominent families with which he was connected by ties of consanguinity or affinity, were identified with the other side, Mr. Ratcliff, who was noted as a man of original thought and independent action, remained a staunch adherent of the Union.

"Seldom have two such strong and vigorous native characters been pitted against each other as in this memorable contest. Both were able, both were sincere, and each had the respect of all parties and the full confidence of his adherents. The issue, however, was not one of men, and Rev. Spurlock was elected. As a proof that the public faith in Mr. Ratcliff was not diminished by the attitude he assumed in 1861, some years after the war, and when the influences which defeated him for the Virginia convention came back into the ascendency, he was elected president of the county court. For six years he administered the police and fiscal affairs of the county with judicious judgment, and punctilious fidelity to the interests of the people.

"Because of the remoteness of his county and the lack of any facilities for travel, except horseback riding, Mr. Spurlock was delayed and did not reach Richmond until after the convention had organized. He arrived and took his seat, however, in time to vote against the Ordinance of Secession as it was expected that he would do to avert war, if possible. After the convention voted for Secession he accepted the situation as a loyal Virginian and participated in its deliberations until its close. A large majority of the members from west of the mountains withdrew from the convention even before the final vote was taken on the Ordinance. Realizing that his course had been such that even a man of his age could not hope to reside on the border undisturbed, he remained in Virginia during the war. When peace was restored he returned in time to be made party defendant, with numerous other Wayne citizens of Southern predilections, in suits seeking to recover large damages for property alleged to have been lost during the war and for personal indignities and restraints imposed by Confederate soldiers."

At the Clarksburg Conference held on September 8, 1879, the resolutions committee had this to say about him:

"In 1851 we find him on the Wayne Circuit as a Supernumerary, which relation he sustained, with perhaps a brief space of a few years, until the end of life, laboring as his strength would permit until on August 5, 1879, in the 90th year of his age and the 60th year of his ministry he exchanged the sword for the palm, the cross for the crown, and earth for heaven.

"Father Spurlock was a feeble man physically, but endowed with much more than ordinary intellectual powers. He read extensively, studied deeply, and scrutinized closely what he read. In thought and diction he was pure, in conception grand, in method systematic, and in delivery rapid and powerful. The gospel of Christ as preached by him was indeed the 'power of God unto salvation to them that believed it.'

"We believe he held deep and close communion with God and enjoyed in a good degree those blessings which result from a genuine faith and a well-founded hope. He had few superiors as a pulpit orator."

3. William was the captain of militia in Cabell. He married Frances Morris, daughter of William Morris who lived at Hawks Nest, and moved to Kentucky. One of his daughters, Martha Ann, married George Roberts Burgess of Giles County, Virginia, and to this union were born:

a. Judge G. G.
b. Dr. G. R.
c. Rev. Strother, a Presbyterian minister.
d. John B.
e. William.
f. Octavia.
g. Sarah.
h. Susan Margaret.
i. Amelia.
j. Virginia.
k. Charity.
l. Alice.
m. Catherine.
n. Leonora, who died in infancy.

4. Daniel is said to have lived on the Ohio River, perhaps at or near Greenbottom. In 1814 he was recommended for one of the gentlemen justices. His daughter, Nancy, married Nimrod Bryan, Senior, and was the mother of the late T. J. Bryan. This couple lived on Bryan's Creek in Union District, and Nimrod, Senior, was a mighty hunter—fleet of foot, keen-eyed. It is said that he killed thirty to fifty deer each season and he dressed in a hunter's garb that made one think he was a companion of Daniel Boone. Another story about Nimrod told by his son, Jeff, is that when Nimrod moved from near Ona to Bryan's Creek the streams in the new neighborhood were full of fish, and that he had a trick of catching fish with his hands. This land at that date was covered with walnut timber which was cut off, and some of it used for fence rails, and the remainder burned. As late as 1904 there were a few good walnut fence rails still in and around the T. J. Bryan place.

5. Charles.
6. John S.
7. Sallie, married William Morris.

One of Jesse's sons lived on the Ohio River. The older folks say he was an odd turned fellow who asserted that he lived in a house that God had made for him, meaning that he was living in a rock house.

There was a George Spurlock who was one of the gentlemen justices in 1814. Who he was cannot now be determined but Charles E. Walker of Wayne who knows about the family says he was a member of it.

STALEY*

Stephen Staley acquired a farm on the Ohio River at an early date which he conveyed to Mike and Joseph Staley in 1825. Who Stephen Staley was and where he came from is not now known, but his sons were Jack, Michael, Daniel, Joseph, and Stephen. Joseph married Miss Hiezey, a German, whose family lived on Four Pole. The records show that John and Philip Hiezey in 1828 bought 112 acres of land on Four Pole Creek and the Hisey Fork of Four Pole gets its name from this family. Joseph Staley and his family moved to Urbana, Illinois, and one of his sons, Calvin, became a judge. Jacob Staley married Alice Burks and moved from the county. She was a

---

*Written from information secured from the article, "The Western End of Virginia," by W. S. Laidley.

daughter of James Burks who had come from Virginia, and had a number of sons who followed the river, and another son, Lewis H. Burks, who was a timber man, and married Helen M. Laidley.

SWITZER

Rufus Switzer, former Mayor of Huntington, and now one of the city's most distinguished citizens, comes from the very earliest American stock. Even before this nation declared its Independence on July 4, 1776, there are records of the Switzers as active and substantial people in the Colony of Virginia.

Henry Switzer, great-great-grandfather of the Hon. Rufus Switzer, was among those who responded to the call made by Benjamin Franklin to carry supplies to General Braddock's Army in the latter's disastrous attempt to capture Fort Duquesne (now Pittsburgh), in the English war against the French and Indians. Nathan Switzer, great-grandfather of the present Mr. Switzer, rode a pack horse with supplies for Braddock's Army, in which at the time was the young George Washington. The Switzer family settled in Botetourt County prior to 1755.

Jonathan Switzer, father of Rufus Switzer was born and reared in Botetourt County, Virginia, and came to Cabell County in 1854. On December 27, 1854, he married Ellen Doolittle. He lived in Cabell until his death in 1865. During the eleven years he was a resident of Cabell County, Jonathan Switzer displayed a high civic spirit. He was the prime mover in establishing a school in his neighborhood, and the building by subscription of a school building. It was finally donated to the free school system.

There were four children of Jonathan Switzer and Ellen Doolittle Switzer, and all but one, a daughter, Virginia, are now living. These are Rufus, Clymer and Vera Switzer. Ellen Doolittle, mother of Rufus Switzer, was a daughter of Ambrose L. Doolittle, who was born in 1800, and came to Cabell County from Lawrence County, Ohio, previous to 1821. Ambrose Doolittle married Sarah Brown, of Augusta County, Virginia. The career of Ambrose Doolittle shows him to have been a man of force and enterprise. He began as a cabinetmaker, but in 1829 bought a tract of land embracing a mill site, and proceeded to build a flour mill, which at one time was the largest in this section. He also added a carding machine, for the carding of wool into rolls, a sawmill, and as well a shop and lathes for the making of furniture. This combination flour, wool, lumber, and furniture factory was for a long time known as the Doolittle Mills on Mud River. It was about a mile from what is now Ona. The court records show that this elder Doolittle, grandfather of the present Mr. Switzer, was once sued for backing the water a mile up the river in the year 1830. He carried the case to the Supreme Court at Richmond, rather than submit to what he regarded as an unjust claim. Whilst Mr. Doolittle was a Whig and anti-slavery man, Mr. Switzer's paternal grandfather was a Democrat and a slave-owner.

There was quite a settlement in the neighborhood of "Doolittle's Mills." There were two general stores near by, as well as a blacksmith shop, a shoe shop, and a wagon shop. Part of these mills still stand and are now owned by the Prichard School.

Rufus Switzer was born in Cabell County, October 25, 1855. He was educated in the common schools, attended Marshall College, and after he completed his course, taught school for three years. He then entered the University of Virginia, took a law course in 1880-81, and was admitted to the Bar in 1881. He located at Winfield, Putnam County, where he formed a partnership with Thomas H. Harvey which continued until Judge Harvey went on the bench in 1889.

In 1884 Mr. Switzer was elected State Senator from this district. In July, 1887, he married Emma E. Merrill of Catlettsburg, Kentucky. In 1891 he located at Huntington, and a short time thereafter formed a partnership with Thomas A. Wiatt which partnership continued until he was elected mayor in 1909, and since that time Mr. Switzer has not been actively engaged in the practice of law.

In 1908 Mr. Switzer was elected a member of the common council of Huntington. When the form of government was changed from councilmanic to the commission form Mr. Switzer was the first mayor and served from 1909 to 1912. In 1918 he was appointed mayor after the death of Leon S. Wiles.

Rufus Switzer is one of the builders of Huntington. He has a lively sense of humor, has demonstrated his ability as a lawyer, banker, real estate developer, and a private citizen, and in his conduct of public affairs he has been noted for economy and common sense. Probably the achievement for which Mr. Switzer will longest be remembered by the people of Huntington is the fight which he made for the establishment of Ritter Park. It has been told elsewhere how the site of Ritter Park was bought for an incinerator and incredible though it may seem when Mr. Switzer proposed to turn the site into a park there was tremendous opposition to the plan. He silenced all opposition when he announced that if the people did not want it as a park he would take the land off the city's hands at the price which it paid for it. Ritter Park was established, and it is now one of the most beautiful parks in the United States. Rufus Switzer is the man who established it, and whatever other persons may have done towards the park and boulevard system in the city, Rufus Switzer is entitled as a matter of right to be called the father of the system.

TAYLOR

Thomas Wallace Taylor was born in Mecklenburg County, North Carolina, September 23, 1842. He attended the Academy at Oxford, Granville County, North Carolina, and then had five years at J. H. Horner's Academy. He was a student at the University of North Carolina when the Civil War broke out and he enlisted in Company B of the 12th North Carolina Infantry, C.S.A., but sustained severe wounds at the Battle of Gaines Mill, on June 27, 1862, and was rendered unfit for field service. After the close of the war he entered the law school of the University of Virginia, and was graduated in June, 1867. While in the University he became a member of the Delta Psi Fraternity. On May 30, 1911, the University of North Carolina gave him his degree of Bachelor of Arts. Thomas W. Taylor practiced law for a few years in North Carolina, and in 1872 married, at Staunton, Virginia, Maria L. Trueheart, daughter of Charles Scott and Virginia Crump Trueheart, who was born in Powhatan County, Virginia, in 1842, and whose grandfather was Dr. William Crump, Minister to Chile in the administration of President Tyler.

The Taylor family trace their lineage to Baron Tailliefer, who came with William the Conqueror to England, and whose descendents became the Earls of Pennington. Colonel James Taylor of this family in 1635 migrated from Carlisle, England, to Virginia, and is the progenitor of the American branch. His son, of the same name, was a member of the House of Burgesses, and a Knight of the Golden Horseshoe.

Charles Henry Kennon Taylor was born in 1818, in Oxford County, North Carolina, and died in Huntington in 1901. He married Martha Archer Field, daughter of Thomas and Susan Green Field, and was the father of Thomas Wallace Taylor.

Thomas Wallace Taylor came to Huntington in the spring of 1874, and for a time practiced law alone. Later he was a member of the firm of Hoge, Harvey and Taylor, but in 1884 he was elected magistrate, and served in that office for twelve years. He then served as a member of the council, and was afterwards elected judge of the Criminal Court of Cabell County, which later became the Common Pleas Court. He served in that capacity for twelve years. He was a Democrat, and an elder in the Presbyterian Church. He had six children: a son, William, who died in infancy; Powhatan and Wallace, who died in early manhood; Charles Trueheart, born in Townsville, Granville County, North Carolina, on August 8, 1872, and educated in the Huntington public schools, Marshall College, Central University at Richmond, Kentucky, and was graduated from the Hospital College of Medicine in Louisville, Kentucky, and did graduate work in 1899, and again in 1905. Trueheart, as he is generally known, was a great athlete in college days, and has continued to be interested in out-of-door sports. He has been active in the practice of his profession, but has always been interested in politics, and was elected clerk of Huntington in 1898-9, and has been a member of the city, county, and state executive committees. He is now superintendent of the Huntington State Hospital. In his college days he was a member of Phi Delta Theta, and is Past Exalted Ruler of the Huntington Lodge of Elks, is a Shriner, and has served as head physician for the Modern Woodmen of America in West Virginia. He is a member of the Sons of American Revolution, and of the county, State, Tri-State, and American Medical Societies, and during the World War was a member of one of the draft boards in this county. He married, December 11, 1901, Bernice Stevenson, born 1878, and died January 27, 1911, daughter of James and Jerusha Stevenson (James Stevenson was born in the County of Tyrone in 1832, came to America in 1844, and died in 1907), and to this union were born a daughter Bernice, January 15, 1903, who married John W. Long, and a son, Charles Trueheart, Junior, born August 11, 1905. Dr. Taylor married, second, Stella Moore of Newark, New Jersey, the daughter of William and Mary T. Moore, and they have one daughter, Jane, born December 11, 1913.

Harvey C. Taylor, the youngest son of Thomas Wallace Taylor was born in Huntington, November 2, 1884. He married on May 23, 1908, Nannie Lee Hawkins, daughter of John L. and Virginia E. Hawkins, who was born September 24, 1885, and to this union has been born: Carter, born August 25, 1911, married Dorothy Frantz, born November 28, 1912, on June 23, 1930; Nancy, born April 30,

1915; John, born July 24, 1916; Kennon, born October 14, 1918; Margery, born October 24, 1922; Elenore, born November 26, 1929.

Harvey C. Taylor has been an active and successful real estate man, and at the same time has taken an active part in politics. He has served as chairman of the Democratic County Executive Committee, was named by the governor to fill out an unexpired term in the Legislature and was elected and served a full term as State Senator.

Lady Taylor, the daughter of Thomas Wallace Taylor married R. M. Baker, who practiced law a number of years in Huntington, and they have a son, Thomas Taylor Baker, who graduated from the West Virginia University, and was admitted to the Bar in 1935, and a daughter, Virginia, who married John Stuart, and has twin sons.

THORNBURG

Thornburg was originally German and spelled Thornborough, but the family came to Britain many years ago, and its name is found both in England and Scotland. It has been in Virginia since Colonial days. Those in Cabell County are descendants from two brothers— Thomas and Hezekiah, who lived in that part of Berkeley County which is now Jefferson County.

Thomas Thornburg was married twice. By his first wife he had a son, Ephriam, who married Rachael Simmons, and lived in Ohio County. Ephriam and Rachael Thornburg had ten children. A daughter, Rachael, married Dr. P. H. McCullough, and was the mother of F. F. McCullough and Emma F. Harvey, wife of Judge Thomas H. Harvey; another son, Moses Thornburg, was at one time clerk of the County Court of this county, and a son, John William Thornburg, married Sarah P. McGinnis, is the father of H. O. Thornburg of Huntington.

Thomas Thornburg by his second wife, Prudence Bently Collins, a widow, had a son, Solomon, born 1791, died December 30, 1854, who moved from Jefferson County at an early date to Cabell, and came by way of Wheeling, and down the Ohio River by boat. He bought a farm not far from Barboursville, which is still owned by his descendants, Howard and Robert Thornburg. The court records show that Solomon Thornburg in 1814 served as a juror; in August, 1822, he was one of the gentlemen justices of the court; he served a number of times as a member of the General Assembly, and was sheriff of the county in 1842-1843.

Solomon Thornburg married in 1812, Mary Staley, and to this

union were born five children: Elizabeth, married John Griffin; Thomas; John W.; James L., and Mary. Thomas married Margaret Miller, and lived to the age of eighty years. He was engaged in the mercantile business at Barboursville, and was one of the first school commissioners of the county named under the law of 1846. He was the county superintendent of schools, and perhaps the first of these. Although the records do not show the original appointment, he served in this capacity from 1849 to 1860. He was a member of the General Assembly of Virginia, a member of the Constitutional Convention of 1872, and was named as proxy to vote the stock owned by the county in the Chesapeake and Ohio Railway Company. He was a charter member of Minerva Lodge, 13, A. F. & A. M. of Barboursville, and a strong union man.

Thomas Thornburg and his wife, Margaret Miller Thornburg, had five children: Thomas Bailey; Elizabeth, married Dr. A. B. McGinnis; Ellen E., married Captain W. M. Hovey, and was the grandmother of Captain T. W. Peyton; John, a lieutenant in the C.S.A., married Mary Long of Mason County, and died without issue; and George E., born June 28, 1846, married Nancy Wilson, succeeded to his father's mercantile business in Barboursville at the close of the war, and continued therein until the time of his death. He was an active Mason, and at one time Grand Master of the State. He died without issue.

Thomas Bailey Thornburg married Nettie Samuels, and had two children.

John W. Thornburg, son of Solomon Thornburg, married Emily Handley, and had a number of children. A son, Claude, married Emma Fox, and is the father of Robert E. and Howard Thornburg. Robert E. Thornburg was for many years deputy county clerk, and is now a part of the Thornburg-Watts Insurance Agency. He is an active Methodist, conservative in all of the relations of life. He married, in 1905, Gertrude Casto of Jackson County, had one daughter, Roberta, who graduated from Radcliffe College, and married Charles Terwillinger, and lives in New York City.

James L., born October 28, 1835, died August 24, 1904, son of Solomon Thornburg, married Virginia F. Handley, daughter of Alex Handley of Putnam County, April 16, 1858. He was educated at Marshall College, was a surveyor, and was for many years county surveyor of Cabell County. He assisted Rufus Cook in the survey of the city of Huntington. To this union were born: Charles; McCullough, who died in infancy; Addie; John D., who died in infancy; Victoria; James Harvey, and Ruth.

Thomas Thornburg (1) had a son, Thomas, who had three wives, and by his third wife had a son, Collins T., who married Leonore Miller, daughter of H. H. Miller of Guyandotte, and were the parents of E. H. Thornburg, who married Bertha McGlathery, and had a son Paul L., who married Mary Stringer, and has two children, one a daughter Catherine, who graduated from Mount Holyoke, and married Dr. Charles P. Staats, of Charleston.

E. H. Thornburg was born in Berkeley County, but came to Huntington at the age of ten years, and lived on a farm in Guyandotte district. He is self-educated, and is the president and directing head of the Foster-Thornburg Hardware Company, and one of the trustees of the Foster Foundation. Like most of the Thornburgs he is a strong Democrat, and an earnest Methodist. He has been married twice, his present wife was Norma Mildred Wright of Keyser, an educated woman of superior attainments, who was a teacher at Marshall College, one of the West Virginia appointees of the General Federation of Women's Clubs Overseas Unit working with soldiers during the World War in France, past-president of the Huntington Woman's Club, and a leader in women's affairs.

Hezekiah Thornburg, brother of Thomas Thornburg (1) settled at Wheeling, and in 1785 married Rachael Crawford. They had five sons and one daughter. One of their sons, Moses Shepherd Thornburg, while a resident of Ohio County, married on June 8, 1852, Caroline Handley, a granddaughter of John Handley, who served in the Revolutionary War, in Captain John Bartresse's Company of Jefferson County. This couple lived in Ohio County until about the close of the Civil War, when they moved to Cabell. They had a number of children, one of whom is Charles William Thornburg, who on September 5, 1893, married Josephine Harris of Culpeper County, Virginia, and has two children, Charles Irvin, was a lieutenant in the A.E.F., married Marie Arnold, and has one son, and Josephine, who married Herbert G. Nash, and has three children. She is the Regent of the Buford Chapter, D.A.R.

Charles William Thornburg is one of the substantial business men of the county. He was educated in the common schools, and taught school when a young man. He has not lost interest in the profession, but for many years has been a member of the board of trustees of Morris Harvey College, and has contributed much energy and time

union were born five children: Elizabeth, married John Griffin; Thomas; John W.; James L., and Mary. Thomas married Margaret Miller, and lived to the age of eighty years. He was engaged in the mercantile business at Barboursville, and was one of the first school commissioners of the county named under the law of 1846. He was the county superintendent of schools, and perhaps the first of these. Although the records do not show the original appointment, he served in this capacity from 1849 to 1860. He was a member of the General Assembly of Virginia, a member of the Constitutional Convention of 1872, and was named as proxy to vote the stock owned by the county in the Chesapeake and Ohio Railway Company. He was a charter member of Minerva Lodge, 13, A. F. & A. M. of Barboursville, and a strong union man.

Thomas Thornburg and his wife, Margaret Miller Thornburg, had five children: Thomas Bailey; Elizabeth, married Dr. A. B. McGinnis; Ellen E., married Captain W. M. Hovey, and was the grandmother of Captain T. W. Peyton; John, a lieutenant in the C.S.A., married Mary Long of Mason County, and died without issue; and George E., born June 28, 1846, married Nancy Wilson, succeeded to his father's mercantile business in Barboursville at the close of the war, and continued therein until the time of his death. He was an active Mason, and at one time Grand Master of the State. He died without issue.

Thomas Bailey Thornburg married Nettie Samuels, and had two children.

John W. Thornburg, son of Solomon Thornburg, married Emily Handley, and had a number of children. A son, Claude, married Emma Fox, and is the father of Robert E. and Howard Thornburg. Robert E. Thornburg was for many years deputy county clerk, and is now a part of the Thornburg-Watts Insurance Agency. He is an active Methodist, conservative in all of the relations of life. He married, in 1905, Gertrude Casto of Jackson County, had one daughter, Roberta, who graduated from Radcliffe College, and married Charles Terwillinger, and lives in New York City.

James L., born October 28, 1835, died August 24, 1904, son of Solomon Thornburg, married Virginia F. Handley, daughter of Alex Handley of Putnam County, April 16, 1858. He was educated at Marshall College, was a surveyor, and was for many years county surveyor of Cabell County. He assisted Rufus Cook in the survey of the city of Huntington. To this union were born: Charles; McCul-

of Guyandotte. He exemplifies in the highest degree the qualities of the old Virginian, and combines with them a fine professional and business acumen, which has attracted to him a clientele of large business interests who are glad to have his services as a lawyer, but recognize his independence of thought and liberal views which reflect the Southern background. Among Mr. Tynes' clients are a number of New York interests who have large land holdings in the State of Kentucky, and this necessitated his maintaining, for a number of years, law offices in eastern Kentucky. His experience with these clients has made him an authority on the questions affecting real estate, oil, gas, timber, and coal matters.

Mr. Tynes has served as chairman of the Democratic Executive Committee of Huntington. He is a member of the American Bar Association, the Cabell County Bar Association, the Guyandotte Club, and the Guyan Country Club, and of the Presbyterian Church.

VINSON

One of the most picturesque of all the pioneers of this region was the late Samuel Sperry Vinson, whose wife, "Aunt Polly," was known, as he was, far and wide in Southern West Virginia and Eastern Kentucky. Sam Vinson was a man of reckless courage, a dominant man, generous to a fault, and so widespread were his interests, and such were the claims on his hospitality, that it was a saying that "at times Aunt Polly Vinson fed more people than they fed at the Florentine Hotel," which was the leading hostelry of its day. No one was ever turned away hungry from the door of their homestead.

When the Civil War broke out, Sam Vinson cast his lot with the Confederate States. He had a grey uniform made with yellow stripes up and down the seams of his pants, and having donned the same, proceeded to have himself ferried across the Big Sandy River from the Kentucky to the Virginia side of the river.

Slapping the seams of his trousers with his broad palm, he remarked to the ferryman, who was his kinsman, but a man of pronounced Northern sympathies:

"The next time you see these, you can shoot at them!"

He had enlisted in June, 1861, in the Confederate Army, 8th Virginia Cavalry, where he commanded a company, with the rank of first lieutenant. He served until March, 1865, when he was captured by guerrillas, and taken to Lexington, Kentucky. Having given his oath not to take up arms, he reached home just before the surrender of Lee at Appomattox. He suffered two wounds during the four years he served with the Stars and Bars, and one of the most interesting events in his career as a soldier occurred in what is now Fayette County. The Federal forces had their headquarters at Gauley Bridge, and there was a scout named Lamb who operated in Fayette, and adjoining counties. He was a fine looking man, and a very efficient scout. He rode with his carbine in his right hand—cocked—with its butt resting on his thigh. The country people called him the Pet Lamb, and, of course, he was hated by the Southern folks. One gloomy winter afternoon Sam Vinson came along accompanied by a single companion, and learned that the Pet Lamb was in the neighborhood, and Vinson started after him. Vinson learned that the Pet Lamb had gone to the home of Fenton Morris not far from Boomer Creek, and he went straight there. Mr. Morris tried to dissuade Vinson from attacking Lamb, for fear that the Federal forces might burn his home, but Vinson was not to be dissuaded, and went into the house and found that Lamb and another soldier had retired to the upstairs. He asked that he be shown the room, but this was refused. A boy in the family indicated with his hand which room they were in. Vinson's companion did not want to go further. Thereupon Vinson took a candle in one hand, and his pistol in the other, and ascended the stairs, and knocked on the door of Lamb's room, and demanded admittance which was refused. Vinson then kicked the door down, and both of the men on the inside attempted to shoot him, but for some reason their guns failed to fire, and he shot, and killed them both.

Sam Vinson was born in Lawrence County, Kentucky, on April 14, 1833, on the Tug Fork of Big Sandy, but moved to Wayne County when he was two years old, and except for a period of eight or nine years spent in Lawrence County, Kentucky, he lived in Wayne County until his death, June 19, 1904.

At the peak of his affairs, Sam Vinson owned over 10,000 acres of land on or near the Ohio and Big Sandy rivers in West Virginia and Kentucky. He was intense in his friendships and his hates, though withal a devoutly religious man, and generous to a fault. He was one of the founders of the Christian Church in Wayne County in 1882.

The Vinson family is necessarily identified with the history of Huntington and Cabell County. Their old home place, near Kellogg, just across the Cabell-Wayne line, was long one of the show places of the Valley. His sons, Taylor and Lindsay Vinson, played a prominent part in the affairs of Huntington, as did his daughter, Mrs. Belle Vinson Hughes.

It is no exaggeration to say that Sam Vinson was typical of the early American pioneer stock such as has made this a great nation. Robust, handsome in appearance, dashing in manner, utterly unafraid, he exercised a great influence in the history of this locality throughout his unusually active life.

He was the son of James and Rhoda (Sperry) Vinson. He married Mary Damron, a daughter of Samuel and Vashti (Jarrell) Damron. The children of Mr. and Mrs. Samuel Vinson were as follows:

Tennessee, June 4, 1853; Zachary Taylor, December 22, 1857, died January 30, 1929; Josephine, February 10, 1862; William, January 1, 1866; Ida Belle, July 30, 1868 (who married Congressman James A. Hughes); Lynn Boyd, September 25, 1871; Lindsay T., August 28, 1874 (long a prominent physician in Huntington); and Mary, February 16, 1878 (who married Donald Clark).

Taylor Vinson, one of the sons of Sam Vinson, was long a prominent attorney in West Virginia, and as well a powerful figure in finance, politics, and civic affairs. He had many of the qualities of his father, and after he began the practice of law he represented his father in a number of law suits, but said that his father was the most difficult client that he ever had for the reason that he insisted on managing his own cases. Taylor Vinson was educated in the common schools of Wayne County, was graduated from Bethany College in 1878, attended the law school at the University of Virginia, and the Boston University Law School. He was admitted to practice in 1886, and a short time afterwards located in Huntington, where he became a partner with the late Judge Thomas H. Harvey in the firm of Harvey, Vinson and McDonald. Judge Harvey went on the bench, and in 1892 the firm became Vinson, Thompson and McDonald, and a year later Mr. McDonald died. Taylor Vinson, as he was called, had a part in, and made a substantial sum of money in the building of the Huntington and Big Sandy Railroad, now a part of the Baltimore and Ohio system. He was a loyal and devoted son, and when business reverses overtook his father in the panic of 1893-94, Taylor put his entire fortune at his father's disposal with the result that it was wiped out. Then came the campaign of 1896, and Sam Vinson, his father, remained regular and supported the Bryan ticket. Taylor was a Gold Democrat. He and his father had several joint debates to the amusement and delight of their friends and relatives. A short time after this Taylor was stricken with an illness and remained in bed for several years. His fortune was gone, and he was unable to practice law. He was not one bit discouraged, but laid on his bed, read, and enjoyed his friends. His health returned at the turn of the century, and he immediately brought about the sale of a boundary of coal land in Logan County to the Island Creek group, and out of the commission he was able to pay off his old debts. He shared these commissions with some associate, who had assisted him in the deal, and from that time he dealt in coal land and became comfortably well off. He was a good lawyer, a most plausible advocate, and was a powerful figure in State affairs. He married on June 19, 1901, at Richmond, Virginia, Mary Chafin, daughter of Richard and Sarah Harvie Chafin, and who is a descendant from Colonel John Harvie, member of the Virginia Convention, 1775, and who served as a colonel during the Revolutionary War. To this union was born on February 7, 1904, a son, Taylor Vinson, Junior, who after being educated at Bethany College and the University of Virginia, was admitted to the Bar in 1930, and is now associated with the law firm of Vinson, Thompson, Meek, and Scherr. Taylor Vinson, Junior, married Betty Jane Nelson, daughter of C. P. Nelson, and to them has been born a son, who is named for his grandfather, Z. Taylor Vinson.

WALTON

W. O. Walton, president of the Huntington Land Company, is a successful business man who came to Huntington just after he completed his college course, and engaged in the timber business with the Lyons Lumber Company. Later he took employment with Lawrence Johnson and Company, timber operators, remained with them eighteen years, then engaged in business for himself and succeeded. He has real estate holdings, and oil and gas interests.

Mr. Walton was elected sheriff of Cabell County in 1896, and served successfully four years, and he has the distinction of being the first Republican to be elected to this office in this county. He is a 32d degree Mason, a Knight Templar, a Shriner, and a member of the Blue Lodge, 390 McCandleless of Pittsburgh, Pennsylvania. He is the son of William Walton, born 1832, and his wife, Martha Allen Walton, both of whom were born in England, and emigrated to America in 1865 with their four older children, and settled in Pittsburgh, Pennsylvania. William Walton was a jeweler and diamond setter, and for a time followed this trade, then engaged in business on his own account. He was a successful business man, and attained a position of prominence and influence in Pittsburgh, was a fire commissioner, and active in the fire department of that city. He acquired a competency and retired ten years before his death in September, 1898, while on a visit to his son, W. O. Walton in Huntington. William Walton and Martha, his wife, had six children: Francis Henry, married Josephine McMaster, and had four children, Thomas, Frances Richmond, David, and Elsie; Mary, married Luther L. Smith of Chicago, and has four children, Benjamin, Richard, Mark, and Elizabeth; William O.; Nellie, married Marshall L. Jenkins, and had three children, Marguerite, Edith, and Walter; Martha, married George K. Anderson, and had two children, Marguerite and Helen; John, who served as deputy sheriff under his brother, and who died without issue.

William O. Walton, the third child, married on May 22, 1883, Clara Grace Vinson, daughter of Dr. Bennett Clay Vinson, who was born in Benton County, Missouri, and had eight children: Mary Martha; Grace Maud, married J. Coleman Alderson; William Bennett; Ethel Vinson, married Tunis Dills of Charleston, and has a child, Grace Walton Dills; Lawrence Johnson; Daniel Porter; Vinson Oliver, and William O., Junior. All of these children were born in Cabell County.

Dr. Bennett Clay Vinson, father of Mrs. Walton, was a son of William Vinson, and was born in Gallatin, Tennessee. He studied medicine in St. Louis, and after practicing a few years in that city during the period of the Civil War, moved to Mud River Bridge, now Milton, and made that his home for the remainder of his life. He immediately became one of the leading physicians of the county, took an active part in local politics, and was elected to the Legislature on the Democratic ticket. He married Mary Frances, daughter of William Simmons, who came, as a boy, from Baltimore to Guyandotte and was a leading cabinetmaker and bridge builder in the county. William Simmons had a son Colonel Simmons. Dr. Bennett Clay Vinson and his wife, Mary Frances, had the following children: Clara Grace; William Sampson; Frances V., wife of W. T. Cooley; B. C., Junior; Charles C.; Lulu Maud, and James A. Dr. Bennett Clay Vinson died August 2, 1888, and his widow, now past ninety years, is still living.

WALLACE

There was a John Wallace who served on a grand jury in March, 1816, and a Peter Wallace on a jury in March, 1847. In 1852 Thomas Wallace was living on the ridge between Mill Creek and the Little Guyan. Porter Wallace, the school teacher, was here in the 1850's, and Taliaferro Wallace came in the same decade. These two and George S., told about herein, are related.

Hugh, Washington, and Jesse Wallace came from Lunenburg County, Virginia, about the beginning of the Civil War, and are the progenitors of the numerous Wallaces in Grant District.

GEORGE SELDEN WALLACE

George Selden Wallace, the son of Charles Irving and Maria Sclater Wallace, was born September 6, 1871, on the Wallace place near Greenwood, in Albemarle County, Virginia. He came to Huntington early in March, 1893, as a train dispatcher in the employ of the Chesapeake and Ohio Railway. He was educated in the public schools in Richmond, Virginia. He entered the employ of the Chesapeake and Ohio when a boy as a telegraph messenger, and served successively as telegraph operator, manager of division telegraph office, and train dispatcher.

He supplemented his education by self-education, and attended the West Virginia University, where he was graduated in law in 1897. He was at once admitted to the Bar, and has continued in active practice except during the time he has been in the military service.

He married on October 4, 1905, Frances Bodine Gibson (see account of Gibson family), and has the following children:

Frances, a graduate of Vassar College.

Champe C., a graduate of Barnard College.

Elizabeth, a graduate of National Cathedral School, and Marshall College.

Margaret, a graduate of Marshall College.

William, in school.

George, in school.

WELLMAN

Clyde Anderson Wellman, editor of the *Advertiser*, was born in Central City, now a part of Huntington, on September 29, 1890, the son of Robert Lee and Martha Ann (Walker) Wellman.

He was educated in the public schools, Marshall College, and West

Virginia University. He studied law, but entered upon newspaper work in May, 1913, shortly after his scholastic preparation.

He began as a reporter for the *Advertiser,* but at the end of two years removed to Cleveland where he served on the editorial staffs of the *Cleveland News* and the *Cleveland Sunday Leader.*

Mr. Wellman returned to the Huntington newspaper field in the fall of 1917 to become city editor of the *Advertiser.* He was made editor of that paper in October, 1920, a position he has filled ever since.

He was married on December 25, 1915, to Mary Virginia Werth of Ceredo, the daughter of John McRae and Cora Cornelia (Minter) Werth. To this union two children have been born, Betty Gene Wellman on November 2, 1919, and Mary Eleanor Wellman on July 11, 1928.

Mr. Wellman was elected president of the Citizens Board of Huntington in the election of 1925 for a three-year term. He was a candidate for presidential elector on the Democratic ticket of Franklin D. Roosevelt, and John Nance Garner, in 1932.

He was elected president of the Marshall College Alumni Association in 1935. He is a Democrat in politics, and a member of the Baptist Church.

Mr. Wellman's genealogical background is spread over the counties of Wayne, Logan, and Mingo. He is descended from Bennett Wellman, who with his wife, May Mulligan, whom he married in Baltimore, in 1777, settled at the Forks of Sandy, now Fort Gay, in October, 1802. Bennett Wellman and his wife continued in Baltimore to the end of the Revolutionary War, migrating some time in the 1780's to the Clinch Valley country in what was then Washington, later Russell County, Virginia.

His ancestral line comes through John, one of seven sons of Bennett, who was born August 2, 1779, in Baltimore, married Nancy Webb, the daughter of Robert and Susannah Webb, also pioneers in the Big Sandy Valley, and in the Clinch Valley country, in 1800, and died near Fort Gay on December 25, 1865.

The Wellmans settled in the Big Sandy country when it was a part of Kanawha County, and seven years before Cabell County was formed. John Wellman was a justice of Cabell for more than thirty years, and served as sheriff, for one term, by appointment from Governor Pleasants. He was active in the movement for partitioning Wayne County in 1842. He was designated by the act of the Legislature creating Wayne to serve as a commissioner, with Burwell Spurlock and Joseph Naglee, to fix the bounds of the county.

Mr. Wellman's great-grandfather, Robert Wellman, born at the Forks of Sandy in 1806, was the third son of John. His grandfather, Laban T. Wellman, a son of Robert and Mahala (Short) Wellman, served in the Confederate Army during the Civil War as a lieutenant in Colonel Jimerson Ferguson's Sixteenth Virginia Cavalry. His maternal grandfather, Matthew Walker, born in Lexington, Rockbridge County, Virginia, in 1838, also was a soldier of the Confederacy, serving in the Eighth Virginia Cavalry under Captain William Gunn. Mr. Wellman's paternal grandmother was Sarah Ann Dingess, daughter of William Anderson Dingess, the first white child born in Logan County. Through this connection, Mr. Wellman is related to a number of the pioneer families of the Guyandotte Valley and Mercer County, such as the Dingesses, Frenches, Smiths, Strattons, and Lawsons. Through both paternal grandparents he is connected with the Frashers, Bromleys, Damrons, Vinsons, Marcums, Napiers, and Blosses, all numerous families in Wayne County.

REVEREND JOHN W. WERNINGER

Father John Walter Werninger was the son of William and Rebecca Werninger, and grandson of Augustus, a highly educated German who was one of the incorporators of Monongalia Academy, and in the War of 1812, a soldier in Captain William N. Jarrett's Company, recruited from Monongalia County. John W. Werninger was born near West Milford, Harrison County, April 22, 1850, and died November 28, 1919. His body is buried in Calvary Cemetery, Wheeling.

Father Werninger was a convert to the Church, becoming a Catholic when he was nineteen years of age. After his conversion, he taught school for several years, then began his study for the priesthood, at St. Mary's Seminary, Baltimore, where he was ordained priest, December 22, 1883. He served as an assistant in Charleston until he came to Huntington, as Father Quirk's successor, on September 12, 1884.

When Father Werninger came to Huntington, he found the little chapel at 20th Street outmoded and overcrowded. The foundations for the first third of the present St. Joseph's Church were already laid. Father Werninger abandoned the 20th Street Chapel, erected a superstructure over the church foundations on 13th Street, and used the building for both school and church purposes. For a number of years,

Father Werninger and his sister taught the pupils of the parish school. They were succeeded in this teaching by Sisters of Charity, and then by the present teaching force, the Sisters of St. Joseph of Wheeling.

After fifteen years as parish priest (during which time he built the church at Hinton, being allowed a few months leave for this purpose by Bishop Kain), Father Werninger was transferred to Benwood, to take charge of St. John's Parish. He left behind him in Huntington a well-established and growing parish.

After ten years as parish priest of St. John's, Benwood, Bishop Donahoe made Father Werninger president of the newly-founded St. Edward's Preparatory School. Father Werninger remained in charge of this school for nine years, when Bishop Donahoe appointed him parish priest of a recently organized parish in Parkersburg, St. Margaret Mary's. The zealous man was stricken with pneumonia, and died before he could assume charge of his new parish.

John Walter Werninger, a reserved and gentle man, was an earnest Christian whose life, consecrated to the service of God and man, was useful and exemplary.

WIATT

The Wiatt family finds its beginning in Boxley Parish, Kent County, England, and one of the names which stand out in its history is Sir Henry Wiatt, who, on account of his loyalty to Henry VII, was imprisoned by Richard III, and was saved from starvation by a cat which brought him food. There is a monumental inscription in the Boxley Church to the Wiatt family recording this fact, and a manuscript lately in the possession of a representative of the Wiatt family in England contains an account as follows:

"He was imprisoned often; once in a cold and narrow tower where he had neither bed to lie on . . . nor meat for his mouth. He would have starved there had not God . . . sent . . . a cat both for to feed and warm him. . . . A cat came one day down to the dungeon unto him, and as it were offered herself to him. . . . He laid her in his bosom to warm him . . . and after this she would come every day to him divers times and when she could get one bring him a pigeon . . . and the keeper dressed for him from time to time such pigeons as the cat provided."

When Sir Francis Wiatt was governor of Jamestown Colony a younger brother, the Rev. Hawte Wiatt, came over with him and was rector of the old Church at Jamestown during the period that his brother was governor. The father of this Rev. Hawte Wiatt was George, the son of Sir Thomas Wiatt, the younger, who was beheaded for political activities, and his mother was Jane, the daughter of Sir William Hawte. Rev. Hawte Wiatt returned to England and died there but two of his sons came back to Virginia and settled there, and from one of these sons the Wiatt family in Cabell County is descended.

Just what year the first of the family crossed the mountains cannot be definitely fixed but in all events a Thomas Wiatt—spelled with an "e"—was a member of Captain Hugh Caperton's company of Rangers on duty on the frontier of Greenbrier and Kanawha counties, May 6, 1792, and we have told in the text of a later Tom Wiatt doing duty service in Cabell County in March, 1829.

John Wiatt of Virginia, in 1832, bought a farm in what is now Putnam County which was a part of a grant made to George Washington. His son, John William Wiatt, married Flora Ann Roseberry whose grandfathers William Owens and John Roseberry served in the Revolutionary War, and were at Valley Forge. This couple continued on the farm until the death of the husband in 1869, when the widow and her children settled in Guyandotte.

John William Wiatt and Flora Ann Roseberry Wiatt had the following children:

Thomas Andrew, born August 11, 1857, died December 22, 1915, who on account of the conditions following the Civil War was deprived of educational advantages other than the common school, but who was by nature a student, and in the end became in the fullest sense a self-educated man. He read law in the office of Judge Evermont Ward, and was admitted to the Bar on March 8, 1881. For a time he practiced alone, and then formed a partnership with L. D. Isbell, which continued for a few years. He then joined the firm of Switzer and Wiatt which continued until his death. Tom was a big man physically and mentally. He was a sound lawyer and a good counsellor. He delighted in people, and his friends were found in every walk of life, and the quaintness of his character would furnish material for numberless stories. He was an active Democrat, but could not be induced to hold office. His death was the cause of sorrow to a great number of people.

John Robert was a merchant, and was in partnership with his brother-in-law, S. E. McCoy, engaged in the retail shoe business under the firm name of McCoy and Wiatt. He died in 1912.

William Owen, born November 26, 1861, died December 11, 1931, was educated at the Buffalo Academy in Putnam County, then learned the printer's trade in the office of the *Putnam Democrat,* and at Gallipolis, Ohio. He joined his mother in Guyandotte in the early 70's, and worked on a local newspaper. In 1883-87 he was secretary to Eustace Gibson, who was then in Congress and spent most of his time in Washington. In 1889 he became a partner with C. L. Thompson, bought the *Advertiser,* which was immediately made a daily newspaper, and later sold his interest to Mr. Thompson, but continued with the paper, contributing to its editorial column. He was an accomplished writer, and like his brother, Tom, took a keen interest in politics, but could not be induced to run for or accept public office. In 1893 he married Fannie Holt, a sister of John H. Holt, but she lived only a few years and there were no children born to this union. Owen Wiatt left the newspaper in 1890, and for a time had a clerical position with the Ensign Manufacturing Company, and from there went to Harvey-Hagen and Company, where he soon became a partner. After the business was incorporated, and its name changed to Hagen-Ratcliff and Company, he became its vice-president, and continued as such to the date of his death, although he retired from active business several years earlier on account of ill health. He had many social interests, and was one of the organizers of the Gypsy Club, the Guyandot Club, and of the several country clubs.

Susan Turner, died unmarried.

Anna Maria, married S. E. McCoy, and died without issue.

Sallie, married A. E. Smith, who, for many years, was a merchant in Guyandotte. To this union were born: Emmet, who died in 1908; Louise, married a Ballard, and died in 1931; Wiatt, the newspaperman whose column "Your Friends and Mine" is read by hundreds of people; Tom P. of Newark, New Jersey; Robert, who died, in 1892, in infancy; Warren C. of the First Huntington National Bank; Flora, married a Johnson; and Winifred, who died in 1932.

WILSON

David Wilson came from Edinburgh, Scotland, and settled in that part of Augusta County, now included in Rockbridge County, Virginia, not very far from Lexington and Staunton. He had a son, or perhaps a grandson named David, who served in the Revolutionary War. In McCallister's *Virginia Militia* he is shown as an Ensign in 1780. This David Wilson afterwards moved to Fayette County, now

West Virginia, where he owned a large tract of land. His home was near Beckwith, and he was a large slave owner. Some of his descendants still own portions of this land.

Anderson Wilson, son of David Wilson (II) was a Southern sympathizer, and had a son in the Confederate Army. This fact caused the Federal forces to occupy his farm, and most of his personal property thereon was taken by them for their use. On one occasion a detail of Federal soldiers arrested Anderson Wilson and took him to their headquarters at Kanawha Falls. On the trip one of the soldiers in the guard fell down three times, and each time discharged his piece. The third shot wounded Anderson Wilson seriously. He was detained as a prisoner for six months, and after his return home died of this wound.

James Hiram Wilson, son of Anderson Wilson, was born in Beckwith, Fayette County, March 31, 1844, and at the outbreak of the war, at the age of seventeen years, enlisted in Company K, 22d Virginia Regiment of Infantry, C.S.A. He participated in the Battle of Scary, served in the Shenandoah Valley, was wounded at Cold Harbor, and surrendered at Appomattox. At the time of the surrender he was a second lieutenant, and was in command of Company K, 22d Virginia Regiment. After the surrender he walked from Appomattox Courthouse to his home in Fayette County. Like many returned soldiers he became dissatisfied and moved to Kansas, where he met Ella Ohlinger, daughter of Henry Ohlinger, whose family had emigrated from Tennessee. They were married and lived in Kansas a few years, but returned to Fayette County about 1870, where he engaged in the merchandise and timber business. In 1884 James Hiram Wilson moved to Milton, where he lived until his death in August, 1917. His wife, Ella, died August 20, 1928, and both are buried at Milton. To this union were born the following children:

Walter Wilson (now deceased), married Lola Gwinn, daughter of John Gwinn of Cabell County.

Henry Anderson Wilson, married Hattie Rust of Kansas, is engaged in banking, merchandise, and farming business at Allen, Kansas.

M. J. (Jack) Wilson, married Lelia Boyd of Milton, resides in Huntington, and is engaged in the farm machinery business.

L. L. Wilson, married Kate Blackwood, daughter of J. Harvey Blackwood of Cabell County, and now resides in Huntington, and is engaged in the practice of law. They have a son, Neal, who is also a lawyer.

Etta Wilson, unmarried, resides in Huntington, and is governess for her two nieces, Jo and Margery Nowery.

Fred Wilson, married Anna Conner of Cabell County, and is engaged in the gas business.

J. H. Wilson, married Ethel Swann, daughter of T. A. Swann of Cabell County, resides in Huntington, and is engaged in the oil and gas business.

Annie Wilson, married C. H. Nowery of Parkersburg, both of whom are now deceased. They left two children, Jo and Margery Nowery, who reside in Huntington.

XLV: THE SAVAGE GRANT*

GEORGE THE THIRD, by the Grace of God of Great Britain, France and Ireland, King defender of the faith &., TO ALL to Whom these presents shall come greeting, KNOW YE that for divers good causes and considerations, but more especially for the consideration mentioned in a Proclamation of Robert Dinwiddie, Esquire, late Lieutenant Governor and Commander in Chief of our Colony and Dominion of Virginia, bearing date the 19th day of February, 1754, for encouraging men to enlist in the service of our Late Royal Grandfather for the defence and security of the said Colony, We have given, granted and confirmed, and by these presents for us our heirs and successors do give grant and confirm unto John Savage, Robert Longdon, Robert Tunstall, Edmund Wagener, Richard Trotter, Wire Johnson, Hugh McKoy, Richard Smith, John Smith, Charles Smith, Angus McDonald, Nathan Chapman, Joseph Gatewood, James Samuel, Michael Scully, Edward Goodwin, William Bailey, Henry Bailey, William Cofland, Mathew Doran, John Ramsey, Charles James, Mathew Cox, Marshett Pratt, John Wilson, William Johnson, John Wilson, Nathaniel Barrett, David Gorman, Patrick Galloway, Timothy Conway, Christian Bomgardner, John Houston, John Maid, James Ford, William Boroughton, William Carnes, Edward Evans, Thomas Moss, Mathew Jones, Phillip Gatewood, Hugh Paul, Daniel Maples, William Sowry, James Ludlow, James Latrot, James Guinn, Joshua Jordan, William Jenkins, James Commack, Richard Morris, John Gholston, Robert Jones, William Hogan, John Franklin, John Bishop, George Matcomb, William Coleman, Richard Bolton, John Kincaid, and George Hurst, one certain tract or parcel of land containing 28,627 acres, lying and being in the County of Fincastle and bounded as followeth, towit: (Description by metes and bounds omitted.)

WITH ALL woods, underwoods, marshes, swamps, lowgrounds meadows feedings and their due share of all veins mines and quarries as well discovered as not discovered within the bounds aforesaid, being a part of the said quantity of 28,627 acres of land and the rivers waters and water courses therein contained together with all the privileges of hunting hawking, fishing, fowling, and all other profits and hereditaments to the same or any part thereof belonging,

---

*John Savage was a lieutenant in the regiment under Lt. Col. George Washington and served at Fort Necessity, Great Meadows.

THE SAVAGE GRANT

or in any wise appertaining, TO HAVE HOLD possess and enjoy the said tract or parcel of land and all other the before mentioned premises and every part thereof, with their and every of their appurtenances unto the said John Savage, Robert Langdon, Robert Tunstall, Edmund Wagener, Richard Trotter, Wire Johnson, Hugh McKoy, Richard Smith, John Smith, Charles Smith, Angus McDonald, Nathan Chapman, Joseph Gatewood, James Samuel, Michael Scully, Edward Goodwin, William Bailey, William Copeland, Mathew Doran, John Ramsey, Charles James, Mathew Cox, Marshall Pratt, John Wilson, William Johnson, John Wilson, Nathaniel Barrett, David Goreman, Patrick Galloway, Timothy Conway, Christian Bomgardner, John Houston, John Maid, James Ford, William Broughton, William Carnes, Edward Evans, Thomas Moss, Mathew Jones, Phillipp Gatewood, Hugh Paul, Daniel Staples, William Sowry, James Ludlow, James Latrot, James Guinn, Joshua Jordan, William Jenkins, James Commack, Richard Worrit, John Gholston, Robert Janes, William Hogan, John Franklin, John Bishop, George Malcomb, William Coleman, Richard Belton, John Kinkaid, and George Merrit and their heirs and assigns forever to the only use and behoof to them the said, John Savage, Robert Longton, Robert Tunstall, Edmund Wagener, Richard Trotter, Wire Johnson, Hugh McKoy, Richard Smith, John Smith, Charles Smith, Angus McDonald, Nathan Chapman, Joseph Gatewood, James Samuel, Michael Scully, Edward Goodwin, William Bailley, Henry Bailey, William Cofland, Mathew Doran, John Ramsey, Charles James, Mathew Cox, Marshall Pratt, John Wilson, William Johnson, John Wilson, Nathaniel Barrett, David Goreman, Patrick Galloway, Timothy Conway, Christian Bomgardener, John Houston, John Maid, James Ford, William Broughton, William Carnes, Edward Evans, Thomas Moss, Mathew Jones, Philip Gatewood, Hugh Paul, Daniel Staples, William Lowry, James Ludlow, James Latrot, James Guinn, Joshua Jordan, William Jenkins, James Carmack, Richard Morris, John Gholston, Robert Jones, William Hogan, John Franklin, John Bishop, George Malcomb, William Coleman, Richard Bolton, John Kikaid, and George Hurst, and their heirs and assigns forever, TO BE HELD to us our heirs and successors as of our manor of Estate Greenwich in the County of Kent, in free and common soccage and not in Capite or by Knights service, YIELDING AND PAYING unto us our heirs and successors forever fifty acres of land and so proportionately for a lesser or greater quantity than fifty acres the fee rent of one shilling yearly to be paid upon the feast day of Saint Michael the Arch Angel next after 15 years from this date of these presents, and also cultivating and improving three acres part of every fifty of the tract above mentioned within three years after the date of these presents, PROVIDED always that if three years of the said fee rent from and after the expiration of the 15 years aforesaid shall at any time be in arrear and unpaid or if the said John Savage, Robert Longdon, Robert Tunstall, Edmund Wagener, Rochard Trotter, Wire Johnson, Hugh McKoy, Richard Smith, John Smith, Charles Smith, Angus McDonald, Nathan Chapman, Joseph Gatewood, James Samuel, Michael Scully, Edward Goodwin, William Bailey, Henry Bailey, William Cofland, Mathew Doran, John Ramsey, Charles James, Mathew Cox, Marshall Pratt, John Wilson, William Johnson, John Wilson, Nathaniel Barrett, David Goreman, Patrick Galloway, Timothy Conway, Christian Bomgardener, John Houston, John Maid, James Ford, William Broughton, William Carnes, Edward Evans, Thomas Moss, Mathew Jones, Philip Gatewood, Hugh Paul, Daniel Staples, William Lowry, James Ludlow, James Latrot, James Guinn, Joshua Jordan, William Jenkins, James Carmack, Richard Morris, John Gholston, Robert Jones, William Hogan, John Franklin, John Bishop, George Malcomb, William Coleman, Richard Bolton, John Kinkaid and George Hurst and their heirs do not within the space of three years next coming after the date of these presents cultivate and improve three acres part of every fifth of the tract above mentioned, then the estate hereby granted shall cease and be utterly determined and thereafter it shall and may be lawful to and for us our heirs and successors to grant the same lands and premises with the appurtenances unto such other persons or person as we our heirs and successors shall think fit; IN WITNESS whereof we have caused these our letters Pattent to be made; WITNESS our trusty and welbeloved JOHN EARL OF DUNMORE our Lieutenant and Governor General of our said Colony and Dominion at Williamsburg under the seal of our said Colony the 15th day of December, 1772, in the 13th year of our Reign.

DUNMORE.

SEAL. Land Office Richmond Virginia.
I hereby certify that the foregoing is a true copy from the records of this Office. Witness my hand and seal of Office this 6th day of October, 1913.

Signed: JOHN W. RICHARDSON,
Register Land Office.

THE SAVAGE GRANT

OWNERS OF THE SAVAGE GRANT

(When partition was confirmed, 1818)

The Savage Grant was divided into sixty-one separate parcels. Lot 33 lies partly in Wayne County and partly in Cabell County. Lots 34 to 61 inclusive (numbered up stream) are in Cabell County. These parcels were confirmed to the several owners as follows:

Lot No.	Owner.	Assignee of:
33	James McCormack	James Ford
34	James McCormack	Timothy Conway
35	John Wilson	
36	Magnus Tate	John Wilson
37	Henry Hampton	James Samuels
38	Henry Hampton	Hugh Paul
39	Edward Swiggers	William Lowry
40	Van Swearengen	John Bishop
41	Angus McDonald	
42	William Buffington	John Savage
43	Edmund Taylor	William Broughton
44	Edmund Taylor	Edmund Wagoner
45	Edmund Taylor	Mathew Jones
46	Wise Johnston	
47	Isaac Larue	David Gorman
48	Isaac Larue	Nathaniel Barrett
49	Robert Rutherford	Robert Turnstall
50	Robert Rutherford	Robert Langdon
51	Robert Rutherford	Joshua Jourdan
52	Robert Rutherford	Edward Evans
53	Robert Rutherford	John Ramsey
54	Robert Rutherford	Michael Sulley
55	Robert Rutherford	Marshall Pratt
56	Robert Rutherford	James Gwin
57	Robert Rutherford	William Hogan
58	Isaac Larue	James Cammack
59	Isaac Larue	Patrick Galloway
60	Isaac Larue	Hugh McCoy
61	Gabriel Throgmartin	Joseph Gatewood

XLVI: COUNTY, STATE, AND FEDERAL OFFICIALS
CABELL COUNTY MEN IN THE FEDERAL GOVERNMENT

In the Diplomatic Service:

Elliott Northcott, Envoy Extraordinary and Minister Plenipotentiary Colombia, 1909-11; Nicaragua, February-December, 1911; Venezuela, 1911-13.

Chris Payne, Consul General to the Danish West Indies, 1903 to the date of his death in 1925.

In the Senate of the United States:

Henry D. Hatfield, Republican, 1929—1934.

In the lower House of Congress:

William McComas, Whig, 1833—1837.
Albert Gallatin Jenkins, Democrat, 1857—1861.
John S. Witcher, Republican, 1869—1871.
Eustace Gibson, Democrat, 1883—1887.
James A. Hughes, Republican, 1900—1914, and 1919—1930.

In the Judiciary:

Elliott Northcott, United States Circuit Judge since April 6, 1927.

United States District Attorney:

Elliott Northcott, 1905—1909, February 15, 1926—April 6, 1927.
George I. Neal, November 23, 1933—

United States Marshal:

Frank H. Tyree, 1910—1914.

And last, but not least:

Joseph S. Miller, Commissioner of Internal Revenue, two terms under Grover Cleveland.

CIRCUIT COURT JUDGES

John Coalter: 1809-1810
James Allen: 1811-1818
Lewis Summers: 1819-1843
David McComas: 1843-1852
George W. Summers: 1853-1858
David McComas: 1858-1862
James H. Brown: 1862-1863
Henry J. Samuels: 1863-1866
William Lockhart Hindman: 1866-1868
Henry L. Gillaspie: 1868-1869
James H. Ferguson: 1869-1870
Charles W. Smith: 1870-1872
Evermont Ward: 1873-1880
Ira J. McGinnis: 1881-1889
Thomas H. Harvey: 1889-1896
E. S. Doolittle: 1897-1912
John T. Graham: 1913-1923
Thomas R. Shepherd: 1923-

SHERIFFS

Thomas Ward: February, 1809—July, 1810.
Henry Brown: July, 1810—March, 1811.

Jesse Spurlock: March, 1811—July, 1812.
Samuel Short: July, 1812—June, 1814.
Mark Russell: June, 1814—July, 1816.
Elisha McComas: 1816.
John Hannon: 1817—1818.
James Holderby: 1819—July, 1821.
William Toney: July, 1821—July, 1823.
John Wellman: July, 1823—December, 1825.
Edmund McGinnis: 1826—1827.
William Fullerton: 1828—1829.
William Buffington: 1830—1831.
Thomas Kilgore: 1832—1833.
Levi McCormick: 1834—1835.
John Everett, Jr.: 1836—1837.
Abia Rece: 1838—1840.
Elisha W. McComas: 1840—1841.
Solomon Thornburg: 1842—1843.
John Hannon: 1844—1845.
Benjamin Drown: 1846—1847.
Benjamin Drown: 1848.
F. G. L. Beuhring: 1848—1850.
Allen McGinnis: 1851—1852.
Enock M. Underwood: 1853—1856.
Wm. B. Moore: 1857—1860.
John S. Wilkinson: January 1, 1861—
D. P. Ferguson: December 26, 1861—
John B. Alford: 1863—1866.
John Harshbarger: 1867—1870.
D. I. Smith: 1871—1876.
Geo. F. Miller, Sr.: 1877—1880.
E. Kyle: 1881—1884.
Geo. McKendree: 1885—1888.
E. Kyle: 1889—1892.
D. J. Jenkins: 1893—1896.
W. O. Walton: 1897—1900.
I. J. Harshbarger: 1901—1904.
W. S. Spencer: 1905—1908.
I. J. Harshbarger: 1909—1912.
P. C. Buffington: 1913—1916.
H. E. Love: 1917—1920.
W. A. Williams: 1921—1924.
Harry Herndon: 1925—Died October 14, 1925.
Harvey C. Taylor: October 21, 1925—November 11, 1926.
F. H. Tyree: November 11, 1926—December 31, 1932.
T. P. Dwyer: January 1, 1933—July 21, 1934.
Effie M. Dwyer: July 21, 1934—November 22, 1934.
Ira J. Harshbarger: November 22, 1934 —

CIRCUIT CLERKS

From 1809 to June 20, 1863, the circuit clerks were the same as the county clerks. Between June 20, 1863, and December 31, 1872, county recorders were substituted for county clerks and Thomas J. Hayslip was county recorder during this period.

Thomas J. Merritt: Elected May 28, 1863, for four year term but died in May, 1864.

William Merritt: Appointed clerk pro tem and in October, 1864, was elected for the unexpired term. He resigned August 11, 1869.

Joseph Miller: Appointed August 11, 1869, to serve out the unexpired term of William Merritt, and was elected October 11, 1870. Served until December 31, 1872.

Moses S. Thornburg: January 1, 1873—December 31, 1884.

T. W. Peyton: January 1, 1885—December 31, 1890.

B. C. Wilson: January 1, 1891—April, 1894.

Joel K. Salmons: 1894—November 26, 1894.

Frank Diehl: November 26, 1894—December 31, 1896.

R. W. McWilliams: January 1, 1897—March 19, 1913, when he died.

W. B. McWilliams: Appointed March 21, 1913—November, 1914.

George R. Seamonds: 1914—1932.

M. C. Blake: January 1, 1933—

COUNTY CLERKS

Edmund Morris: 1809—1815

John Samuels: January, 1816—Middle 1858.

H. H. Wood: August, 1858—May 6, 1861.

John S. Witcher: June 2, 1862—June 1, 1863.

The Constitution of 1863, which became effective June 20, 1863, abolished the office of the county clerk and substituted a county recorder. The record shows no county clerk after the entry made June 1, 1863, by J. S. Witcher, signed by T. J. Merritt as deputy, until an entry made by Thomas J. Hayslip as recorder on January 12, 1865.

The first record by the board of commissioners is a meeting held on July 30, 1864, and at that meeting Thomas J. Hayslip appears as clerk of the board of supervisors and perforce county recorder.

There were two clerks of the board of supervisors, namely: J. W. Church and Joel K. Salmons, but these men had nothing to do with the county records other than to keep the records of the board of supervisors. Under the Constitution of 1872 the county clerks were provided for to take office January 1, 1873.

Thomas J. Hayslip (recorder): July 30, 1864—December 31, 1872.

Joseph S. Miller: January 1, 1873—October 6, 1876.

Moses S. Thornburg: October, 1876—December 31, 1884.

F. F. McCullough (First and second terms): January 1, 1885—July 18, 1897.

Frank L. Doolittle: July, 1897—December 31, 1902.

COUNTY, STATE, AND FEDEDAL OFFICIALS 525

F. F. McCullough (Third and fourth terms): January 1, 1903—December 31, 1914.
R. S. Douthat: January 1, 1915—December 31, 1932.
F. A. Ware: January 1, 1933—

PROSECUTING ATTORNEYS

James Wilson: 1809—1817.
John Laidley: 1817—1860.
Ira J. McGinnis: 1860—May 2, 1862.
John Laidley: May 2, 1862—March 2, 1863.
B. D. McGinnis: March 2, 1863—May 28, 1863.
E. M. Fitzgerald: May 28, 1863—1865.
B. D. McGinnis: May 1, 1865—February 1, 1869.
T. B. Kline: 1869—1870.
W. H. Tomlinson: January 1, 1871—1872.
L. C. Ricketts: January 1, 1873—1876.
Wm. T. Thompson: January 1, 1877—Dec. 31. 1884.
George F. Donella: January 1, 1885—December 31, 1888.
L. C. Ricketts: January 1, 1889—August 6, 1889.
John S. Marcum: August 6, 1889—November 1, 1890.
R. L. Blackwood: November, 1890—December 31, 1892.
George J. McComas: 1893—1896.
E. E. Williams: 1897—1904.
George S. Wallace: 1905—1908.
Jean F. Smith: 1909—1912.
Henry Simms: 1913—1916:
R. L. Blackwood: 1917—1920.
Thos. R. Shepherd: 1921—1923.
Lace Marcum: 1923—1924.
L. R. Via: 1925—1928.
Lucian W. Blankenship: 1929—1932.
E. E. Winters, Jr.: 1933—

MEMBERS OF THE GENERAL ASSEMBLY OF VIRGINIA
(As shown by a list made up by Virgil A. Lewis)

December, 1809—February, 1810: Elisha W. McComas and Manoah Bostick.
December, 1810—February, 1811: Elisha W. McComas and Jesse Spurlock.
December, 1811—February, 1812: Elisha W. McComas and Thomas Ward.
November, 1812—February, 1813: Elisha W. McComas and Manoah Bostick.
May, 1813—May, 1814: John Morris and Edmund McGinnis.
December, 1813—February, 1814: John Morris and Edmund McGinnis.
October, 1814—January, 1815: Elisha W. McComas and Manoah Bostick.
December, 1815—February, 1816: Elisha W. McComas and John Morris.
November, 1816—February, 1817: John Smith and Andrew Burnett.
December, 1817—February, 1818: Elisha W. McComas and Edward McGinnis.

December, 1818—March, 1819: Elisha W. McComas and Edward McGinnis.
December, 1819—February, 1820: John Laidley and Edward McGinnis.
December, 1820—March, 1821: Elisha W. McComas and Edward McGinnis.
December, 1821—March, 1822: Alexander Catlett and Edward McGinnis.
December, 1822—February, 1823: John Everett, Jr., and F. G. L. Beuhring.
December, 1823—March, 1824: John Everett, Jr., and John Laidley.
November, 1824—February, 1825: John Everett and John Laidley.
December, 1825—March, 1826: Elisha W. McComas and John Everett, Jr.
December, 1826—March, 1827: Elisha W. McComas and John Everett, Jr.
December, 1827—March, 1828: Solomon Thornburg and John Everett, Jr.
December, 1828—February, 1829: Solomon Thornburg and John Everett, Jr.
December, 1829—February, 1830: William Spurlock and F. G. L. Beuhring.
December, 1830—April, 1831: (Representation reduced): William Spurlock.
December, 1831—March, 1832: William Spurlock.
December, 1832—March, 1833: Elisha W. McComas.
December, 1833—March, 1834: Allen McGinnis.
December, 1834—March, 1835: Wade Hampton.
December, 1835—March, 1836: F. G. L. Beuhring.
December, 1836—March, 1837: Thomas McAllister.
December, 1837—March, 1838: Solomon Thornburg.
January to April, 1838: Solomon Thornburg.
January to April, 1839: Solomon Thornburg.
December, 1839—March, 1840: Solomon Thornburg.
December, 1840—March, 1841: P. C. Buffington.
December, 1841—March, 1842: Frederick Moore.
December, 1842—March, 1843: Frederick Moore. (Cabell and Wayne joined).
December, 1843—February, 1844: Henry W. Shelton.
December, 1844—March, 1845: F. G. L. Beuhring.
December, 1845—March, 1846: Elijah Adkins.
December, 1846—March, 1847: John Morris.
December, 1847—April, 1848: Allen McGinnis.
December, 1848—August, 1849: Frederick Moore (Cabell, Wayne and Putnam).
December, 1849—March, 1850: John Morris.
December, 1850—March, 1851: Jeremiah Wellman.
January to June, 1852: Jeremiah Wellman.
November, 1852—April, 1853: Henry B. Maupin (Dr.), Cabell in single district.
December, 1853—March, 1854: Andrew McComas.
December, 1857—April, 1858: Thomas Thornburg.
December, 1859—April, 1860: Henry B. Maupin.

COUNTY, STATE, AND FEDEDAL OFFICIALS 527

December, 1861—March, 1862: Albert Laidley.
December, 1863—March, 1864: P. C. Buffington.
In the first Legislature of the new State of West Virginia, William H. Copley of Guyandotte was Senator, and Edward D. Wright of Guyandotte was a delegate.

MAYORS OF HUNTINGTON

1872-1874: Peter Cline Buffington.
1874-1876: Thomas J. Burke.
1876-1877: M. G. Nichols.
1877-1878: Thomas J. Burke.
1878-1879: J. M. Layne.
1879-1880: E. S. Buffington.
1880-1882: George Cullen.
1882-1883: J. M. Layne.
1883-1884: Hamilton Dickey.
1884-1885: A. L. Crider.
1885-1886: E. A. Bennett.
1886-1887: A. H. Woodworth.
1887-1889: T. S. Garland.
1889-1890: R. E. Hagan.
1890-1891: T. S. Garland.
1891-1892: Hamilton Dickey.
1892-1893: W. H. Bull.
1893-1895: George I. Neal.
1895-1896: C. R. Enslow.
1896-1897: Ely Ensign.
1897-1898: W. F. Hite.
1898-1899: Charles Nash.
1899-1900: H. A. Brandebury.
1900-1901: H. A. Brandebury.
1901-1903: H. C. Gordon.
1903-1905: C. M. Buck.
1905-1906: H. C. Gordon.
1906-1908: John W. Ensign.
1908-1909: J. B. Stevenson.
1909-1912: Rufus Switzer.
1912-1915: Floyd S. Chapman.
1915-1918: Edmond Sehon.
1918-1918: L. S. Wiles.
1918-1918: Ira J. Harshbarger.
1918-1919: Rufus Switzer.
1919-1922: C. W. Campbell.
1922-1925: Floyd S. Chapman.
1925-1928: W. E. Neal.
1928-1931: J. Boyce Taylor.
1931-1932: Floyd S. Chapman.
1932-1934: George D. Bradshaw.
1934———: Martin V. Chapman.

XLVII: MUSTER ROLLS

ROLL OF JOHN SIMMONS' COMPANY

MUSTER roll of a company of riflemen of the requisition from Virginia then in the United States service under the command of Brigadier General Joel Leftwich, commanded by Captain John Simmons from Cabell County. This company became a part of the 2d Regiment Virginia Militia commanded by Lieutenant Colonel Dudley Evans. The first muster rolls show that the service began September 27, 1812, and the last muster roll was March 29, 1813:

NAME	PAY PER MO.	RANK	REMARKS
John Simmons	$40.	Captain	
Holley Crump	30.	Lieutenant	
Richard Brown	20.	Ensign	
James Ray	8.	1 Sergeant	
Phillip Russell	8.	2 Sergeant	
George Hollenback	8.	3 Sergeant	On Extra Duty
Thomas Ewen	8.	4 Sergeant	
Peter Barnhart	6.66	1 Corporal	Employed driving an ox team
Abraham Archer	6.66	2 Corporal	Employed driving a wagon
(b) Abraham Pratt	7.33	3 Corporal	Discharged Feb. 9, 1813
Sylvester Woodard	7.33	4 Corporal	
Alexander Boyd	6.66	Private	
(b) Byrd Brumfield	6.66	Private	Deserted prior to Oct. 31, 1812
(b) Jonathan Casey	6.66	Private	Sick left at Delaware
(b) Henry Casebolt	6.66	Private	Sick left at Delaware
(b) Peter Darton	6.66	Private	Deserted prior to Oct. 31, 1812
Edmund Daniel	6.66	Private	
Daniel Douthit	6.66	Private	
(a) Aaron Drowdy	6.66	Private	Substitute for Daniel Neal November 4, 1812
(b) Cyremons Emmons	6.66	Private	Discharged Oct. 14, 1812
Henry France	6.66	Private	On command at Norton
George Fulcher	6.66	Private	
James Ford	6.66	Private	
(b) James Gray	6.66	Private	Discharged Oct., 1812
(b) Isarale Heath	6.66	Private	Discharged Oct., 1812
Marton Hollenback	6.66	Private	
Jacob Hite	6.66	Private	On command Artillery B. House

(a) Indicates soldiers who joined subsequent to the first pay day.
(b) Indicates that the soldiers did not continue in service for reason set opposite the name.

MUSTER ROLLS 529

NAME	PAY PER MO.	RANK	REMARKS
(b) Joseph Hilyard	6.66	Private	Discharged Oct. 14th
James Hoskinson	6.66	Private	
(a) Henry Helphinstine	6.66	Private	Substitute for Sanders Witchers
James Morman	6.66	Private	
John Merritt	7.33	Private	Promoted Nov. 1812 to Corp.
(b) Edmund McGinnis	6.66	Private	Discharged Oct., 1812
(b) Samuel McGinnis	6.66	Private	Discharged Oct., 1812
(a) Valentine McCormick	6.66	Private	Substituted for Sam McGinnis
(a) Asa H. Munsel	6.66	Private	Substituted for James Gray
(a) Leander Munsel	6.66	Private	Substitute for Wm. Payton
(b) Daniel Neele	6.66	Private	Discharged Oct., 1812
James Poteet	6.66	Private	
(b) William Payton	6.66	Private	Discharged Oct., 1812
(a) Roswell Phelps	6.66	Private	Substitute for Jos. Hilyard
Thomas Russell	6.66	Private	
(b) Robert Rutherford	6.66	Private	Discharged Feb. 9, 1813
Lewis Russell	6.66	Private	On command at Norton
William Russell	6.66	Private	
(b) Benjamin Ray	6.66	Private	Discharged Feb. 8, 1813
Thomas Roberson	6.66	Private	
John Russell	7.33	Private	Promoted Oct. 20, 1812 to Corp.
(b) Gilbert Stephenson	6.66	Private	Discharged Oct. 14, 1812
James Salmons	6.66	Private	On command
Bruce Stokes	6.66	Private	
John Stephenson	6.66	Private	
James Turner	6.66	Private	On extra duty
Sanders Witcher	6.66	Private	Discharged Oct., 1812

In compliance with general order bearing date January 13, 1815, the following details have been made from the 120th Regiment commanded by Captain Spurlock, February 24, 1815:

NAME	RANK	DATE OF COMMISSION	REMARKS
Burwell Spurlock	Captain	December 5, 1810	
John Hannon (?)	Ensign	April 12, 1813	
Achilles McGinnis	Lieutenant	April 12, 1813	
William D. Morris	Lieutenant	May 11, 1811	
Henry Love	Ensign	July 5, 1813	
Nimrod Johnston	Sergeant		
Isaac Stallings	Sergeant		
Isaac Brewer	Sergeant		
William Ferguson	Sergeant		
Edward Franklin	Sergeant		

NAME	RANK	DATE OF COMMISSION	REMARKS
Daniel Douthard	Corporal		
William Elkins	Corporal		
John Newman	Corporal		
William McComas	Fifer		
Joseph Henceley	Drummer		
William Hite	Private		
Eugene Roop	" "		
Mark Russel	" "		
William Stewart	" "		
William Paine	" "		
Joseph Dean	" "		
James Arthur	" "		
James Wilgus	" "		
John Burns	" "		
Jonathan Peyton	" "		Substitute
Ransom Dials	" "		
William Parsons	" "		
John Stephenson	" "		Substitute
Elisha McComas	" "		
John Wallace	" "		
Champin Napper	" "		
——— Parsons	" "		
Burton Cummeans	" "		
William Chapman	" "		Sick
Levi Vanhoose	" "		Substitute
John Bartram	" "		
Sires Damuel (?)			
James Preachard	" "		
Henry Hampton	" "		Substitute
Samuel Davis	" "		
John Ferguson	" "		Substitute
Rudolph Hoover	" "		
John Gilkeson	" "		
John Stokes	" "		
Thomas Gilkeson	" "		
John Smith	" "		
Anthony Hampton	" "		
Benjamin Ward	" "		
Daniel Witcher	" "		
Johnathan Grayham	" "		Substitute
Jacob Staley	" "		Substitute
Jeremiah Stephens	" "		
John Howard	" "		
John Chapman	" "		
John Peyton	" "		
Joseph Reece	" "		Substitute

MUSTER ROLLS 531

NAME	RANK	DATE OF COMMISSION	REMARKS
Thomas Swan	Private		
Philip Wince	" "		
Henry Helverson	" "		
James Brammer	" "		
Milken Ansil	" "		Substitute
David Stephenson	" "		Substitute
Joseph Wheeler	" "		
Philip Maile	" "		Substitute
Dabner Overstreet	" "		
Abraham Smith	" "		
James Becket	" "		
Newton Holt	" "		
Henry Mawry	" "		
James Brammer	" "		
Joseph Brammer	" "		
Andrew Guinn	" "		
John Hays	" "		
Levi Morris	" "		
John Cooper	" "		
William Stanley	" "		
George Hanley	" "		
Daniel Elkins	" "		
James Hager	" "		
Robert McNeely	" "		
Michael Hager	" "		
Thomes Demprey	" "		Sick
James Elkins	" "		Deserted
Richard McNeely	" "		Deserted
Thomas Chapman	" "		
James Moore	" "		
Emly Miller	" "		Absent
William B. Davis	" "		
William Swearingen	" "		
George Hensly	" "		Absent
John O. Dear	" "		Absent
Joseph Markman	" "		Deserted
Elijah Hensley	" "		Absent
Zachariah Blankenship	" "		Absent
John Berry	" "		Absent
William Ferrel	" "		Substitute
George Thompson	" "		Absent
Thomas Smith	" "		Substitute
Valentine Hatfield	" "		Absent
Samuel Dean	" "		

"I do hereby certify that the above remarks are correct.
Benj'n Brown."

"I do hereby certify that the list of men above detailed was under my command agreeable to general orders from the 24th of February, 1815, until the 7th day of March, 1815. I do also certify that they were furnished with rations, transportations by me for said time.— Given under my hand this 4th day of April, 1815.

> Burwell Spurlock
> Commandant of the detachment from the 120th Regiment, Virginia Militia."

"I, Geo. W. Summers of Kanawha County, Va. do hereby certify that the distance from Cabell Court House, Va. to the Great Falls of the Kanawha River, Va. the Road now travelled between those points, is seventy six miles—by the road as it was used in 1815 it was somewhat further, from two to three miles perhaps, By the River route going down the Kanawha and thence down the Ohio to Guyandotte it would be to Cabell C.H. about one hundred and forty three miles.

> Geo. W. Summers,
> April 18, 1859."

"I, Jonathan M. Bennett, Auditor of Public Accounts of Virginia hereby certify that the within is a true copy from a paper filed in this office. Given under my hand at the Auditor's office in the City of Richmond, Va. the 30th day of November, 1859.

> J. M. Bennett."
> Pension Office
> Dec'r. 19th, 1859

"The third Auditor reports "No evidence of Captain Spurlock's command, Virginia Militia, War of 1812.—From the testimony of Mr. Summers and Captain Spurlock (the latter on file in the claim of James Wilgus, No. 281,557) two days travel has been established."

> (Signature not legible)

"Examined by the Commissioner of Pensions this 20th day of Dec'r. 1859. B. Hood"

The seal of the pension office appears in two places on this roll one bearing date April 28(?) 1859, and the other December 15, 1859.

The foregoing roll, together with the several certificates was filed in the Pension Office December 15, 1859. It was used as a basis of pension claims of the various men whose names appear thereon as

MUSTER ROLLS 533

evidenced by notations which appear on the original roll but are not copied here.

CONSOLIDATED MUSTER ROLL OF CAPTAIN E. W. McCOMAS COMPANY C

The 11th Infantry Army of the United States, commanded by Colonel Ramsey, from the 11th day of April, 1847, when last mustered, to August 15, 1848, when the company was discharged.
All enlisted for the period of the war.
Name, rank, when, where and by whom enlisted, and remarks.
Elisha W. McComas, Captain
  (b) On furlough, number and date of order or by what authority not known.
  (c) Absent on sick furlough, order number and date unknown.
Joseph Samuels, Second Lieutenant
  (b) On furlough, authority number and date of order unknown.
Wm. W. McComas, First Sergeant, March 15, Barboursville, Captain McComas
  (b) Left sick at Perote Castle about October 4, 1847. Discharged on surgeon's certificate December 9, 1847.
James M. McComas, Second Sergeant, March 22, Barboursville, Captain McComas
  (b) Left sick at Jalapa about October 1.
  (c) Land warrant forwarded to Barboursville.
Robert A. Alexander, Third Sergeant, April 19, Ripley, Captain McComas
  (a) Later shown as Private.
Spottswood Hughes, First Corporal, March 19, Barboursville, Captain McComas
  (b) Died in the City of Mexico, December, 1847.
(1) Hiram Appleby, Private, June 23, Clarksburg, Lieutenant Samuels.
John Bias, Private, March 27, Barboursville, Captain McComas
  (a) Promoted to Corporal.
  (b) Left sick at Jalapa, date unknown. Discharged December 28, 1847 at V. C.
(1) John G. Batten, Private, June 21, Clarksburg, Lieutenant Samuels
  (b) Died at Vera Cruz, September 10, 1847. (E, November 1, 1847).
(1) Benj. W. Butcher, Private, June 27, Clarksburg, Lieutenant Samuels
  (b) Died at Perote October 24, 1847 of diarrhoea.
(1) Peter Black, Private, May 29, Barboursville, Captain McComas
  (b) Died at Puebla, date unknown (E, October 12, 1849).

---

(1) Indicates that name appears for first time on the Muster Roll of July 1, 1847—September 1, 1847.
(2) Indicates that name appears for first time on the Muster Roll of June 31, 1847 December 31, 1847.
(a) This notation appears on the Muster Roll of July 1, 1847—September 1, 1847.
(b) This notation appears on the Muster Roll of June 31, 1847—December 31, 1847.
(c) This notation appears on the Muster Roll of January 1, 1848—August 15, 1848.
  * Indicates transfer to Company E 11th Infantry as shown on the Muster Roll June 31, 1847—December 31, 1847.

*(1) Simon Boardman, Private, July 2, Wheeling, Captain McComas
(1) Gordon Brumfield, Private, April 3, Mason Township, Captain Mc-
Comas
    (b) Left sick at N. Bridge, September 1, Discharged December 30, 1847
at Vera Cruz.
Henry Brammer, Private, March 22, Barboursville, Captain McComas
Milton Burgess, Private, April 4, Logan Court House, Lieutenant Samuels
James C. Cabeen (Calreen), Private, April 22, Ripley, Captain McComas
    (c) Land warrant forwarded to Norwich, Ohio. Reassigned to C Company, for duty 11th of June, 1848, by order of Colonel Ramsay, having been temporarily assigned to F Company for duty by order of Major Hunter, January 1, 1848.
    (a) Shown as Lt.
    (b) Left sick at Puebla about December 4th.
Henry S. Cunningham, Private, April 30, Ripley, Captain McComas.
    (b) Died at Vera Cruz, October 12.
(1) William Cunningham, Private, May 20, Point Pleasant, Captain Mc-
Comas
    (b) Left sick at Puebla, December 4.
*(1) Andrew J. Campbell, Private, June 20, Wheeling, Captain McComas
*Basil C. Dewese, Private, April 19, Ripley, Captain McComas
(2) George R. Davidson, First Lieutenant
    (b) On furlough by authority of Major General Butler, date of order not known.
*(1) George W. Duff, Private, June 21, Clarksburg, Lieutenant Samuels
Andrew Dotson, Private, April 26, Barboursville, Captain McComas
James E. Darby, Private, May 10, Barboursville, Lieutenant Samuels
Henry Emerson, Private, March 20, Barboursville, Lieutenant Samuels
*Andrew J. Ferrell, Private, May 10, Barboursville, Lieutenant Samuels
    (b) Left sick at Puebla, December 4th.
(1) James Farrow, Private, October 4, Williamsburg, Captain Campbell
*(1) David Fife, Private, May 23, Point Pleasant, Captain McComas
    (b) Left sick at Puebla December 4th.
*(1) Andrew Fulton, Private, May 20, Point Pleasant, Captain McComas
    (b) Left sick National Bridge, date unknown.
*John G. Goff, Private, April 17, Jackson County, Captain McComas
    (b) Left sick Vera Cruz, date unknown.
*Daniel Harmon, Private, April 6, Barboursville, Captain McComas
    (a) Sick in hospital at Camp Begaira.
    (b) Left sick at Vera Cruz, date unknown—Pension 6/22/04 Slip 2355-883.
*Gilbert B. Harvey, Private, April 22, Ripley, Captain McComas
    (b) Left sick at Jalapa, November 9th.
David T. Hill, Private, April 22, Ripley, Captain McComas
    (a) Sick in hospital at Camp Begaira.
    (b) Died at Vera Cruz, November 9th (E 10 July 48).
(1) Albert G. Haymond, Private, July 3, Clarksburg, Lieutenant Samuels
    (b) Died at Vera Cruz, September 11th.

MUSTER ROLLS

(1) Elizah Hight, Private, July 3, Wheeling, Captain McComas
  (a) Sick in hospital at Camp Begaira.
  (b) Left sick at National Bridge, date unknown. Died November 27, 1847 at New Orleans Barracks.
(1) James W. Huff, Private, June 21, Clarksburg, Lieutenant Samuels
  (b) Died at Vera Cruz, date unknown (E. November 1, 49).
(1) John H. Howard, Private, June 18, Wheeling, Captain McComas
(1) Jacob Hoffman, Private, July 5, Wheeling, Captain McComas
  (a) Left sick in hospital at Camp Begaira.
  (b) Absent without leave. Supposed to have been killed by guerrillas.
(1) James Hogg, Third Sergeant, May 20, Point Pleasant, Lieutenant Samuels
(1) John H. Hummel, Private, June 26, Wheeling, Captain McComas
  (a) Sick in hospital at Camp Begaira.
*(1) Ephriam Ice, Private, July 13, Wheeling, Captain McComas
  (a) Left sick at Brazir, August 10, 1847.
  (b) Left sick at National Bridge in September.
*Garland Jarrell, Private, April 6, Boone Court House, Lieutenant Samuels
  (b) Left sick at National Bridge, date unknown. Died in Mexico.
George Jarrell, Private, April 10, Chapmansville, Lieutenant Samuels
  (b) Left sick at National Bridge, date unknown.
*(1) James Jackson, Private, June 24, Wheeling
  (b) Left sick at Puebla, date unknown.
(1) Michael P. Knopp, Private, May 20, Point Pleasant, Lieutenant Samuels
  (a) Sick in hospital at Camp Begaira.
  (b) Left sick at Vera Cruz, date unknown. Discharged on surgeon's certificate December 16, 1847.
(1) Henry Kriling, Private, June 19, Wheeling, Captain McComas
William Lucas, Private, April 19, Logan Court House, Lieutenant Samuels
  (a) Sick in hospital at Camp Begaira.
(1) Elias G. Legg, Private, May 31, Barboursville, Captain McComas
  (a) Sick in hospital at Camp Begaira.
  (b) Left sick at National Bridge, date unknown. Transferred from C to F 11th Infantry.
(1) John W. Little, Private, June 12, Wheeling, Captain McComas
Henry Manor, Private, April 22, Lonsville, Lieutenant Samuels
  (a) Left sick at New Orleans August 3, 1847.
John McIntosh, Private, April 23, Ripley, Captain McComas
  (b) Left sick at Vera Cruz, date unknown.
Isaac W. Meadows, Private, April 6, Boone Court House, Lieutenant Samuels
  (a) Left sick at Vera Cruz August 14, 1847.
  (b) Died at Vera Cruz, date unknown—20th August, 1848, (E. May 8, 48).
Hamilton C. McComas, Private, May 11, Cabell Court House, Captain McComas
  (b) Left sick at Vera Cruz, date unknown. Discharged September 21, 1847.
James Ursley Paine, Private, April 23, Logan Court House, Lieutenant Samuels

(a) Left sick at Brazir August 10, 1847.
(b) Left sick at Point Isabel, August 15.

J. Andrew Perry, Private, April 4, Logan Court House, Lieutenant Samuels
(a) Later a corporal.

James Parsons, Private, April 26, Barboursville, Captain McComas
(a) Left sick at Newport Barracks, July 27, 1847. Died August 9, 1847
(b) Left sick at Vera Cruz, date unknown. Died 9th August, 1847 at Newport Barracks.

*Marquis De L. Parsons, Private, April 22, Ripley, Captain McComas
(b) Left sick at Jalapa, date unknown.

Marion Powell, Private, March 15, Barboursville, Captain McComas

(1) Collin W. Peden, Private, June 11, Wheeling, Captain McComas
(a) Sick in hospital at Camp Begaira.

(1) Joseph Pelky, Private, June 22, Wheeling, Captain McComas

(1) Samuel B. Prunty, Private, July 8, Clarksburg, Lieutenant Samuels
(b) Died November 2.

(1) George Pack, Private, June 2, Barboursville, Captain McComas
(b) Left sick at Vera Cruz, date unknown.

Josiah Randels, Private, May 15, Barboursville, Captain McComas
(a) Left sick at Vera Cruz, August 14, 1847.
(b) Left sick at Vera Cruz, August 4.

(1) Randolph Robey, Private, May 29, Ripley, Lieutenant Samuels
(b) Died at Perote, date unknown (E. 6 July 49).

(1) John Rodgers, Private, June 22, Captain McComas
(b) Died at Puebla, date unknown (E. November 26, 49).

(1) W. A. Ramsey, Private, June 17, Wheeling, Captain McComas
(b) Left sick at National Bridge, date unknown.

(1) Peter A. Reidi, Private, June 28, Wheeling, Captain McComas
(b) Left sick at Vera Cruz, date unknown.

David Shelton, Private, April 12, Barboursville, Captain McComas

James A. Stuart (Stewart), Private, April 14, Ripley, Captain McComas
(a) Sick in hospital at Camp Begaira.

(1) Jacob Smith, Private, June 4, Barboursville, Captain McComas

(1) John Sindledecker, Private, June 17, Wheeling, Captain McComas

(1) Mitchell Stone, Private, June 5, Guyandotte, Lieutenant Samuels
(b) Left sick at Perote, date unknown. Died December 31, 1847 at Perote, Mexico.

(1) Nathaniel Smith, Private, June 6, Barboursville, Captain McComas
(b) Left sick at Perote, date unknown. Died December 21, 1847 at Perote, Mexico, of dysentery.

Oliver Stewart, Private, April 14, Jackson County, Captain McComas

(2) William H. Scott, Second Lieutenant, Present commanding company

Richard Taylor, Private, April 10, Logan Court House, Lieutenant Samuels

Abner Vance, Private, April 4, Logan Court House, Lieutenant Samuels
(a) Left sick at New Orleans, August 3, 1847.

(1) George W. Venim, Private, June 15, Wheeling, Captain McComas

(1) Alexander Vinson, Private, July 5, Wheeling, Captain McComas
(b) Died September 26, 1847 at Vera Cruz.

MUSTER ROLLS 537

Jonathan Ward, Private, April 19, Barboursville, Captain McComas
  (a) Left sick in hospital New Orleans, August 2, 1847.
James M. Workman, Private, April 14, Barboursville, Captain McComas
Ephriam Warrick, Private, April 22, Logan Court House, Lieutenant Samuels
  (b) Left sick at Puebla, date unknown.
(1) John T. Waggoner, Third Corporal, May 20, Point Pleasant, Captain McComas
(1) Joseph Wynn, Private, June 23, Clarksburg, Lieutenant Samuels
  (b) Died at Vera Cruz, September 11, 1847.
(1) Jacob Wyker, Private, June 12, Wheeling, Captain McComas
(1) David Wilson, Private, June 19, Wheeling, Captain McComas
  (b) Left sick at Perote, date unknown.
Ezekiel L. Young, Private, April 26, Barboursville, Captain McComas
  (b) Left sick at Vera Cruz, date unknown.

CONSOLIDATED MUSTER ROLL OF CAPTAIN GEORGE W. CHAYTOR'S

COMPANY F

11th Regiment of Infantry Commanded by Albert C. Ramsey
from December 31, 1847, to August 15, 1848

All enlisted for the period of the war.
Name, rank, when, where and by whom enlisted, and remarks.
George W. Chaytor, Captain.
  (a) Left Vera Cruz for the United States on furlough for two months. Date, number of order unknown.
C. P. Evans, First Lieutenant.
P. Lofland, Second Lieutenant.
  (a) Left Vera Cruz for the United States on furlough. Date, number of order unknown.
(1) John A. Bayard, Second Lieutenant.
Wiedman Forster, First Lieutenant.
  (a) In the United States by what authority unknown.

✓ ✓ ✓ ✓ ✓

The following list contains only the names of persons from the State of Virginia as taken from the above captioned Muster Rolls.
James C. Cabeen, Sergeant, April 22, Ripley, Captain McComas.
  (a) Left Puebla December 4, 1847.
  (b) Temporarily assigned for duty as Sergeant to F Company, from C, 11th Infantry, by order of Major John F. Hunter, January 1, 1848. Joined on March 9th and has performed the duties of Sergeant since

---

(1) Indicates that name appears for the first time on the Muster Roll of April 30, 1848—August 15, 1848.
(a) This notation appears on the Muster Roll of December 31, 1847—February 29, 1848.
(b) This notation appears on the Muster Roll of April 30, 1848—August 15, 1848.
* Indicates the men transferred from C Company to this (F) Company, January 1, 1848.

538 CABELL COUNTY ANNALS AND FAMILIES

that time. Transferred June 11, 1848, to C Company by order of Colonel Savage.
*Robert A. Alexander, Private, April 19, Ripley, Captain McComas.
Henry Emerson, Private, March 20th, Barboursville, Captain McComas.
  (a) Discharged by Surgeons certificate of disability at the City of Vera Cruz, December 26, 1847. Died in the city of Mexico, January 30, 1848.
*John H. Howard, Private, June 18th, Wheeling, Captain McComas.
  (a) On detached service with first brigade in Mexico.
*John H. Hummel, Private, June 26th, Wheeling, Captain McComas.
*Michael P. Knopp, Private, April 6, Boone Courthouse, Lieutenant Samuels.
  (b) Absent left sick in hospital at Vera Cruz, date unknown.
*Henry Kriling, Private, June 19th, Wheeling, Captain McComas.
*Elias G. Legg, Private, May 31st, Barboursville, Captain McComas.
  (b) Absent left sick at National Bridge, date unknown.
*William Lucas, Private, April 19th, Logan Courthouse, Lieutenant Samuels.
  (b) Sick in quarters in Mexico, January 5, 1848.
Patrick McDonnelly, Private, April 14th, Fredericksburg, Lieutenant Seddon.
John McIntosh, Private, April 23d, Ripley, Captain McComas.
  (a) By reason of surgeon's certificate of disability, discharged at the City of Vera Cruz, December 26, 1847.
(1) John McClune, Private, January 6th, '48, Wheeling, Lieutenant Clutter.
  (b) Joined from regimental depot April 25, 1848,
James Payne, Private, May 14th, Fredericksburg, Lieutenant Seddon.
George Payne, Private, April 22d, Fredericksburg, Lieutenant Seddon.
*Normal Powell, Private, March 15th, Barboursville, Captain McComas.
  (b) Sick in hospital.
*George Pack, Private, June 2d, Barboursville, Captain McComas.
  (b) Absent left sick at Vera Cruz, date unknown.
*James Parsons, Private, April 26th, Barboursville, Captain McComas.
  (b) Absent sick at Point Isabel, August 6, 1847. Died, August 9, 1847, at New Port, Kentucky.
*James W. Payne, Private, April 23d, Logan Courthouse, Lieutenant Samuels.
  (b) Absent left sick in hospital Point Isabel, August 6, 1847.
(1) John Patterson, Private, January 15, '48, Wheeling, Lieutenant Clutter.
  (b) Joined from regimental depot, April 25, 1848.
    Absent without leave, July 12, 1848, at New Orleans.
(1) Samuel S. Paul, Private, January 18, 1848, Wheeling, Lieutenant Clutter.
  (b) Joined from regimental depot April 25, 1848.
  Absent without leave, July 12, 1848, at New Orleans.
*(1) Josiah Reynolds, Private, April 23d, Logan Courthouse, Lieutenant Samuels.
  (b) Absent. In hospital at Vera Cruz, August 4, 1847.
*William A. Ramsey, Private, June 17th, Wheeling, Captain McComas.
  (b) Discharged at New Orleans, March 15, 1848, by reason of surgeon's certificate of disability.
*Peter A. Redie, Private, April 28th, Wheeling, Captain McComas.
  (b) Absent left in hospital at Vera Cruz, August 4, 1847.

MUSTER ROLLS 539

*Mitchell Stone, Private, June 5th, Guyandotte, Lieutenant Samuels.
  (b) Died at Perote, December 31, 1847.
(1) John Simpson, Private, April 16th, Spottsylvania, Lieutenant Seddon.
  (b) Sick in quarters.
Lawrence P. Skinner, Private, April 6th, Fredericksburg, Lieutenant Seddon.
  (b) Discharged at New Orleans, March 9, 1848, by reason of surgeon's certificate of disability.
*Abner Vance, Private, April 4th, Logan Courthouse, Lieutenant Samuels.
  (b) Absent left sick in New Orleans, August 3, 1847. Died September 13, 1847, at New Orleans barracks.
Samuel I. Wallace, Private, April 3d, Fredericksburg, Lieutenant Seddon.
  (b) Left in hospital at Vera Cruz, July 2d, 1847. Discharged at New Orleans February 29, 1848, by reason of surgeon's certificate of disability.
James Wilkinson, Private, April 18th, Fredericksburg, Lieutenant Seddon.

THE BORDER RANGERS, COMPANY E

(Eighth Virginia Cavalry, C.S.A., from Cabell County)

Made up from two rolls, one found in *Hardesty Encyclopedia,* the second made by the late Cameron L. Thompson.

*Indicates name or rank as shown on the Thompson roll that were not on the Hardesty roll.

Albert G. Jenkins (afterwards general), Captain.
Henry C. Everett, First Lieutenant.
*George W. Holderby, First Lieutenant.
Alexander H. Samuels (killed at Lee Courthouse, Virginia, 1863), Second Lieutenant.
*John E. Thompson, Second Lieutenant.
W. R. Gunn, Orderly Sergeant.
Robert Stribbling, First Sergeant.
*Dan Ruffner, Second Sergeant.
*Lemuel Wilson, Third Sergeant.
Isaac Ong, Third Sergeant.
*B. A. Wolcott, Fourth Sergeant.
*Henry C. Poteet, First Corporal.
John Thompson, First Corporal.
J. B. Dodson (captured at Prices Creek and taken to Camp Chase), Second Corporal.
*Thomas Noel, Second Corporal.
J. D. Sedinger, Third Corporal.
*Joseph Wilson, Third Corporal.
*L. L. Love (killed at Lee Courthouse, Virginia), Fourth Corporal.
James Wellington (drowned at Logan Courthouse, West Virginia), Fourth Corporal.

PRIVATES

*P. P. Baker (died).
John Bandy.
Frederick Baumgardner.

Henry Baumgardner (killed at Jonesville, Virginia, 1863).
*James Baumgardner (surrendered at Appomattox).
John Baumgardner (died in prison at Camp Chase).
John Beckwith *(killed in action).
*P. L. Belchen.
*M. A. Bias.
Francis M. Bing.
*Jake Black (enlisted in Monroe County).
*Ben Blankenship (wounded in action).
David Bowen.
William Boyd.
William Bramlett.
James Bridgman *(died).
James Brown.
J. A. Buckner.
*George Burnsides.
James Canterbury.
William Canterbury.
A. H. Chapman *(died).
John Chapman (killed in a skirmish in Putnam County, West Virginia, 1863).
*Sylvester Chapman.
Braden Childers.
Lewis Childers.
*Theodore Cook.
*Joseph Collier (killed in action)
*James Corns.
*John Cox.
*Ferdinand Crowder.
*D. W. Dabney.
Abraham Davis.
Joseph Davis.
*Samuel Davis.
*John Deal (killed in action at Moorefield).
*J. N. Dennison.
*Jesse B. Dodson.
*Thomas Dodson.
Thomas W. Dodson.
Edward Doyle (killed in action in Giles County, Virginia).
*Edward Doyle (killed at Wolf Creek).
George Eggers.
*Cyremus Emmons (captured and sent to Camp Chase).
Cyrus Emmonds.
John S. Everett *(surrendered at Appomattox).
Edward Ferguson.
Harvey Ferguson (died in Tazewell County, Virginia, 1862).
Jefferson Ferguson.

Joseph Ferguson (wounded in leg at Buckhannon in 1862).
Samuel Ferguson.
Thomas Ferguson.
Nelson Fletcher.
*Thad W. Flowers (captured at Wolf Creek and discharged from Camp Chase).
*Charles Golden.
George Golden.
Henry Golden.
*William Golden
*Allen Green (killed, Winchester, September 19, 1864).
*E. S. Guthrie (wounded in battle).
Edward Guthrie (wounded in thigh at Point Pleasant, West Virginia).
*John Guthrie (killed in battle).
William Gwinn * (wounded in Virginia).
John Hampton (wounded in head in Shenandoah Valley, Virginia).
A. A. Hanley.
Benjamin Hanley.
*E. Hannon.
*E. H. Hannon.
George Hannon.
Ephriam Hannson.
Archibald Harrison.
Thomas Harrison.
*Albert Harwood.
*E. Harwood.
*DeKalb Hawes.
George A. Heath (wounded in arm at Jonesville, Virginia).
Leo Hendricks.
*Lewis Hendrick.
*William Hengar.
*Byrd Hensley (wounded).
William Hensley.
Dr. James Hereford.
*D. D. Holderby (died).
Dudley Holderby (died near Abingdon, Virginia, 1862).
Robert Holderby (killed in action near Salem Virginia, 1863).
*William Holderby.
*Watt Hogg.
Pat Hoshell.
*Joseph Hundley (killed in action).
Cab. Hughs.
*Jeff Jenkins.
Thomas J. Jenkins.
Dr. Wm. Jenkins.
John T. Johnson (chaplain of the regiment).
S. N. Keenan.
*Charles Kelley.

*Jack Kelley.
Harvey Kelly.
James Kelly.
John Kelly.
*A. C. Kennedy.
Doc. Kennedy.
*W. S. Kinsolving (wounded).
William Lacy.
James Lambert.
John Lloyd.
*Albert Long (killed in action, Guyandotte, West Virginia).
John Love (committed suicide while in the service).
John E. Love.
Leonidas Love (killed at Jonesville, Virginia, 1863).
*John W. Loyd.
*John Lynch.
*Charles McCallester (wounded, Lee Courthouse, Virginia).
Malcomb McCollister.
Lafayette McCorkle.
H. McGinnis.
Ira J. McGinnis.
John McGinnis.
*L. H. McGinnis (died).
Leonidas McGinnis.
John M. McMahon (accidentally shot and killed near Lewisburg, 1861).
James Martin.
*U. H. Martin (wounded, Lee Courthouse, Virginia).
Uriah Martin.
*Henry Maupin (killed in action).
*John Mayrs (wounded).
Jesse Meeks (killed at Wymals Mills, Lee County, Virginia, 1863).
Gordon Midkiff.
Jackson Miller.
James Miller.
John Mitchell.
*John M. Mitchell (captured and sent to Camp Chase).
Frank M. Moore.
*W. B. Moore (died).
Wilson B. Moore.
George Morris.
Henry Morris.
*John Morris.
Joseph Morris.
Thomas Morris (wounded at Hurricane Bridge, West Virginia, March 28, 1863; captured and died in prison).
Albert Neale (killed in action at Point Pleasant, West Virginia, March 30, 1863).
Allen Neale (killed at Guyandotte in 1862).

*Henry Newman (wounded).
*Robert Noel (wounded, discharged from Camp Chase).
Rhoderick Noel.
Thomas Noel.
James Nowning.
*Isaac Ond (died).
*John W. Ong (discharged from Camp Chase).
*Walter Osborne.
Adolphus Page.
John Paine (killed at Hurricane Bridge, West Virginia, March 28, 1863).
*Marion Parrish.
*John Payne (killed at Hurricane).
Benjamin Pennybaker.
*Berry Pennybacker.
George Pennybaker (taken prisoner on Mud River in 1864).
James Pennybaker.
John Pennybaker.
Mounts Pennybaker.
William Pennybaker.
*John Peyton (died).
Greene Pine (shot in shoulder by a citizen near Twelve Pole River, 1863).
*Lewis Pine (killed in battle).
James Poindexter.
H. C. Poteet (captured at Howell's Mills, West Virginia, September 6, 1863).
*John C. Pope.
Samuel Pratt.
Alexander Preston.
William Preston.
*F. M. Rawson (died).
Peter Razer *(surrendered at Appomattox).
Josh Rece.
Warren Rece.
*Joseph L. Reece (wounded).
A. G. Ricketts (killed at Broad Ford, Holstein River, Virginia, November, 1863).
L. C. Ricketts *(surrendered at Appomattox).
*Ed. Robinson (surrendered at Appomattox).
Thomas Roffe.
William Roffe.
Archibald Rowsey.
John Rowsey.
Daniel Ruffner (killed by a citizen at Bristol, Tennessee, 1863).
*Albert G. Russell (surrendered at Appomattox).
*George Russell (died).
William Sands.
*H. M. Scott (died).
Harvey Scott.

Charles Seamands (missing in action in Virginia, never heard of afterwards).
*Charles Seamonds (killed in battle).
Sampson Seamonds.
H. H. Sexton (wounded somewhere in Virginia).
*Joseph Shealer (killed in action).
David Shelton.
George Shelton * (died).
*James Shelton (wounded).
James E. Shelton.
John Shelton.
Monroe Shelton (killed near the Tennessee line).
Charles Shoemaker * (surrendered at Appomattox).
*Sampson Simmons (surrendered at Appomattox).
Charles Simonson
William Simonton * (surrendered at Appomattox).
*Albert Smith (captured and surrendered at Camp Chase).
Charles Smith.
David Smith.
*M. C. Smith (died in hospital).
Mark Smith.
Washington Smith (wounded in leg at Jonesville, Virginia, 1863).
Walter K. Solven.
Hurston Spurlock.
Samuel Spurlock.
*Charles Stevenson.
*Hansford Stewart (killed in action).
*James Stewart (died in hospital).
*Joseph Stewart (wounded).
*Robert Stubling.
*George W. Summers (died in hospital at Salem, Virginia).
Sylvester Summers, *Bugler * (surrendered at Appomattox).
Henry Swann.
Joseph Swann.
John Tasson.
Harvey Templeton.
James Thompson.
Thadeus Thompson.
Dr. Robert Timms.
Joseph Tinsley (wounded at Seven Pines, Virginia).
William Tinsley.
Edward Vertegan * (surrendered at Appomattox).
George Vertegan * (surrendered at Appomattox).
James Vickers.
John Vickers.
Frank Vinson.
Lafayette Vinson.
Samuel Vinson.
*Sam S. Vinson (surrendered at Appomattox).

MUSTER ROLLS 545

Walter Walton.
G. D. Warren.
*Guil Warren (surrendered at Appomattox).
*William Wesson (died at Tazewell Courthouse).
John White.
*Ben Wilkinson.
Beverly Wilkinson.
*William Wilkinson.
William E. Wilkinson.
A. M. Williams.
*Arthur Williams (discharged from Camp Chase).
John Williamson (wounded in leg somewhere in Virginia).
Charles Wilson.
*Charles M. Wilson (surrendered at Appomattox).
Harvey Wilson (killed somewhere in Virginia).
Lemuel Wilson (wounded in Virginia).
*Oliver Wilson.
P. A. Wolcott.
William Woodrum.

After A. G. Jenkins was made colonel of the regiment, J. M. Corns was made captain of the company. When Jenkins was made brigadier general, Corns was made colonel of the regiment. W. R. Gunn was made captain of Company D, Eighth Regiment.

OFFICERS OF 2D INFANTRY, HUNTINGTON

Lieutenant Colonel George S. Wallace, October 1, 1910-May 9, 1916.

Major C. C. Hogg, Medical Department, August 11, 1900-May 1, 1916. (Lieutenant Colonel, May 2, 1908-March 14, 1911.)

Major James E. Verlander, August 11, 1900-December 31, 1911.

Major I. H. Sabel, January 1, 1901-December 27, 1909.

Major Thomas B. Davis, June 27, 1910-February 4, 1915.

Major Heber H. Rice, J.A.G.D., October 30, 1914. Reported for duty under call of President, June 26, 1916. Mustered out March 24, 1917. Called into World War service, April 2, 1917.

Major Herbert C. McMillen, June 15, 1915. Mexican Border service, mustered out March 24, 1917. Called into World War service, April 2, 1917.

COMPANY G, 2D INFANTRY, HUNTINGTON

Mustered February 27, 1892.

Captain I. H. Sabel, commanding, January 4, 1897-January 1, 1901.

Captain Thomas B. Davis, commanding, January 1, 1910-June 27, 1910.

Captain Fred W. Lester, commanding, December 29, 1910-February 14, 1913.

Captain Valkey W. Midkiff, commanding, February 14, 1913. Mustered in United States service for duty on Mexican Border, July 2, 1916. Mustered out with regiment, March 24, 1917. Called into World War service, April 2, 1917.

COMPANY H, 2D INFANTRY, HUNTINGTON

Authorized October 1, 1899. Mustered October 17, 1899.
Captain Fred W. Lester, commanding, October 1, 1899-June 27, 1910.
Captain Herbert C. McMillen, commanding, June 27, 1910-June 15, 1915.
Captain Austin M. Sikes, commanding, June 15, 1915-October 1, 1916, when transferred to Headquarters Company, 2d Infantry.

COMPANY I, 2D INFANTRY, HUNTINGTON

Mustered August 13, 1899.
Captain I. J. Davies, commanding, September 15, 1900-May 31, 1903.
Captain James L. Graham, commanding, July 12, 1903-April 1, 1907.
Captain George S. Wallace, commanding, April 2, 1907-October 1, 1910.
Captain Ira J. Barbour, commanding, October 1, 1910. Mustered in United States service for duty on Mexican Border, July 13, 1916. Mustered out with regiment, March 24, 1917. Called into World War service, April 2, 1917.

ROSTER COMPANY F, 2D INFANTRY, MILTON

Organized April 15, 1893. Disbanded January 31, 1906.
September 25, 1893: Captain M. L. Howes, First Lieutenant B. L. Neville, and Second Lieutenant W. O. Wills.
July 20, 1894: Captain D. L. Irwin, First Lieutenant B. L. Neville, and Second Lieutenant D. T. Field.
June 12, 1895: Captain D. L. Irwin, First Lieutenant Benjamin L. Perry, and Second Lieutenant W. J. Emery.
October 1, 1896: Captain D. L. Irwin, First Lieutenant Benjamin L. Perry, and Second Lieutenant F. L. Kinnaird.
January 1, 1898: Captain D. L. Irwin, First Lieutenant Benjamin L. Perry, and Second Lieutenant F. L. Kinnaird.
1899-1904: Captain B. L. Perry, First Lieutenant Lawrence L. Wilson, and Second Lieutenant Bennett V. Smith.
In 1904 Smith was succeeded by F. L. Kinnaird.

BAND, 2D INFANTRY, HUNTINGTON

Band mustered out May 19, 1901. Band reorganized June 18, 1903.
Edmund Lindemann, chief musician, discharged, January 15, 1900.
Lewis S. Sievers, chief musician, February 6, 1900-May 19, 1901.
Rhinehart A. Sang, October 26, 1903-.
James E. Ebersole, July 17, 1906-April 4, 1907.
Frank Bader, January 25, 1908-September 2, 1908.
Fred E. Waters, September 2, 1908-.

HEADQUARTERS COMPANY, 150TH INFANTRY, HUNTINGTON

Organization authorized June 23, 1923. Federally recognized June 24, 1924.
Captain August C. Reinwald, commanding, June 24, 1923-July 25, 1925.
First Lieutenant Arthur B. Snedegar, commanding, July 25, 1925-December 11, 1925.
Captain John Esque, commanding, December 11, 1925-May 13, 1926.

Captain James T. Worley, commanding, May 14, 1926-June 15, 1927.
Company mustered out at Huntington, June 15, 1927.

HEADQUARTERS, 3D BATTALION, 150TH INFANTRY, HUNTINGTON

Federally recognized December 4, 1923.
Major Ira J. Barbour, commanding, November 2, 1923-.

HEADQUARTERS COMPANY, 3D BATTALION, 150TH INFANTRY, HUNTINGTON

Organization authorized May 28, 1923. Federally recognized June 7, 1923.
First Lieutenant Henry A. Ackerman, commanding, April 18, 1923-February 8, 1924.
First Lieutenant George E. Pollard, commanding, February 8, 1924-.

MEDICAL DEPARTMENT DETACHMENT, 3D BATTALION, 150TH INFANTRY, HUNTINGTON

Federally recognized June 14, 1927.
Captain Robert S. Van Metre, commanding, June 4, 1927-.

COMPANY I, 150TH INFANTRY, HUNTINGTON

Organization authorized March 4, 1924. Federally recognized March 4, 1924.
Captain Charles F. Burrill, commanding, March 4, 1924-May 9, 1929.
Captain Arthur F. Stewart, commanding, May 9, 1929-.

COMPANY K, 150TH INFANTRY, HUNTINGTON

Organization authorized October 8, 1924. Federally recognized October 10, 1924.
Captain Cecil N. Rogers, commanding, October 8, 1923-May 9, 1925.
Captain Harley H. Thompson, commanding, May 9, 1925-February 27, 1926.
Captain Winston W. Murrill, commanding, February 27, 1926-February 1, 1928.
Captain Henry C. Cox, commanding, February 1, 1928-.

MEN COMMISSIONED FROM THE FIRST TRAINING CAMPS, 1917

Fred Adams, Second Lieutenant George Raymond Ayers, Lieutenant McKinley Ballard, Second Lieutenant Raymond Lee Beuhring, Second Lieutenant Owen M. Blackwood, Second Lieutenant Emil Brown, Second Lieutenant Joseph R. Brown, Second Lieutenant Stanley C. Butler, Second Lieutenant John H. Christian, Captain L. H. Cort, First Lieutenant John Curtis, Second Lieutenant Henry Winters Davis, C. Derbyshire (not commissioned. Enlisted and afterwards Brigade Sergeant Major), Second Lieutenant W. Verlin Dial, Second Lieutenant Burmah C. Dusenberry, Second Lieutenant Hubert S. Ellis, First Lieutenant Charles E. Frampton, Captain Luther O. Griffith, Second Lieutenant Daniel Irvin Hager, Second Lieutenant Clyde W. Hague, First Lieutenant Samuel Davidson Hall, Second Lieutenant G. H. Harbour, Major T. M. Hays, First Lieutenant Hubert G. Heinisch, Lieutenant Rex Hersey, Lieutenant Clay Hite, First Lieutenant Earl C. Jameson, Second Lieutenant C. E. Jaynes, Captain Wallace W. Johns, Second Lieutenant Frank

Johnson, First Lieutenant E. Macon Jones, Second Lieutenant V. W. Knapp, First Lieutenant Andrew Lawson Kouns, Second Lieutenant Calvin Land, First Lieutenant C. G. Leach, Second Lieutenant O. E. LeBlanc, Second Lieutenant Fred S. Loar, Captain W. T. Lovins, Second Lieutenant B. J. Lubin, Second Lieutenant K. B. Lutz, First Lieutenant Ben C. McComas, Second Lieutenant Guy Middleton, Second Lieutenant J. C. Miller, Lieutenant D. M. Moore, Second Lieutenant G. L. Morrow, First Lieutenant Rolland Mossman, Captain T. West Peyton, Lieutenant W. B. Poindexter, Second Lieutenant Robert O. Poole, First Lieutenant John R. Ramsey, First Lieutenant James B. Rich, Captain William A. Ritchie, Captain Clark E. Sloan, Second Lieutenant W. L. Snedeker, Captain Charles W. Strickling, Second Lieutenant Fred A. Strother, First Lieutenant Charles Irving Thornburg, Captain Harold B. Tyree, First Lieutenant F. C. Wallace, First Lieutenant Alfred Whittaker, Second Lieutenant Price Williams, and First Lieutenant E. E. Winters, Jr.

MEDICAL OFFICERS 1917-1919
DOCTORS AND DENTISTS

Arthur E. Bays, Oscar Biern, R. M. Bobbitt, C. M. Buckner, Captain H. L. Crary, B. J. Cronin, W. M. Dickerson, First Lieutenant Thomas Dugan, Captain Claude Gautier, First Lieutenant Earl B. Gerlach, Captain John Shackelford Gibson, Jr., First Lieutenant Herbert E. Guthrie, Major Henry D. Hatfield, First Lieutenant W. Warden Heald, Captain James Oscar Hicks, F. C. Hodges, First Lieutenant I. J. Kail, H. W. Keatley, First Lieutenant I. R. LeSage, Captain Joseph W. Lyons, Captain Lon C. Morrison, Major Walter W. Points, Captain Carl C. Prichard, Major J. C. Schulz, Captain Edward E. Shafer, Captain James F. Van Pelt, Captain Walter E. Vest, A. H. Whittaker, First Lieutenant Robt. J. Wilkinson, C. W. Wise, and Captain Guy Yost.

CABELL COUNTY'S HONOR ROLL
1917-1919

"Yes, give me the land where the battle's red blast
Has flashed to the future the fame of the past;
Yes, give me the land that hath legends and lays
That tell of the memories of long vanished days;
Yes, give me a land that hath story and song!
Enshrine the strife of the right with the wrong!
Yes, give me a land with a grave in each spot,
And names in the graves that shall not be forgot"

*Killed in action.   **Died of wounds.

**Tolbert Adkins
*Albert Agnew
Herbert W. Arthur
**Robert Bailey
*Raymond R. Beckett
Henry H. Bellomy
Granville Boswell

Isaac Landis
Albert G. Lenz
Robert C. Little
*Maryland McCloud
*Fred McKenny
Lyle F. Mahan
Claude V. Mankin

Frank E. Burnett
John L. Callicoat
Lorrid A. Carr
*Marean S. Carter
Clark Chester
**George L. Church
Robert E. Clark
Laurence J. Condon
Henry C. Copley
William B. Corn
Albert Chase Cox
Henry Crabtree
Jesse E. Cradic
Clifford L. Crawford
**Henry Winters Davis
Thedford Davis
*Walter Verlin Dial
Frederick A. Duncan
*Curtis Alexander Dye
*Andrew E. Effingham
*Pearl Elliott
*Leroy Ferguson
Delbert Fisher
John Foster
Ernest C. Fullerton
Ernest A. Gary
**Vickers Hall
*Clyde C. Handley
Roy Clarence Harless
Russell Hatchett
*Chester A. Holley
Ottus D. Jackson
*Azell M. Jenkins
*Charley Jones
John H. Kale
Lee Keyser
Walter Keyser
Ralph I. Lambert

Esom M. Meadows
Kenneth M. Meadows
*Oscar E. Mefford
Jack A. Morrisey
Letson B. Morrison
Raymond E. Neal
Clayton M. Newman
Farris P. Nixon
David S. Noble
Halsey Notter
Harry B. Osborne
Mark M. Payton
**Justice Pine
Ezra Porter
Alvie F. Pummell
Alva C. Reynolds
*John Rigney
Lawrence F. Romano
*Wedsell Ross
Robert L. Royse
William Scarberry
William A. Schafer
*Sam Shachtmaister
Earl W. Shank
Dolphus Simpson
Henry T. Simpson
Layton F. Slayter
Orbie Smith
*Roy Staton
**Charlie A. Stewart
Moss French Stone
Bronson Ewing Summers
Harold A. Trevillian
Herbert Watts
Ora H. Watts
Harold V. Weathers
James B. White
Herbert J. Witzgall

INDEX

A

Abbott, Angeline M., 346.
Abbott, Darwin E., 186, 209, 210, 215, 242, 247, 259, 323, 344, 345, 346, 347.
Abbott, Elizabeth Driggs, 346.
Abbott, Harriet, 347.
Abbott, Leonore, 347.
Abbott, Mae, 347.
Abbott, Mary, 347.
Abbott, Mason D., 346.
Ackerman, Henry A., 108.
Adams, Betty, 186.
Adams, Elizabeth Scales, 482.
Adams, Eloise Page, 469.
Adams, Joel N., 469.
Adams, H. M., 141, 210.
Adams, Mary Ann, 383.
Adams, N. S., 120, 327.
Adams, Robert, 117, 482.
Adams, Sarah Stratton, 383.
Adams, W. W., 279.
Adams, William, 383.
Adkins, Chapman, 491.
Adkins, Hezekiah, 286, 287.
Adkins, Jeremiah, 195.
Adkins, John, 72.
Adkins, Leatha Spurlock, 491.
Adkins, Nancy, 400.
Advertiser (newspaper), 205, 210, 436, 510-11.
Agnew, E. H., 111.
Ahern, Daniel, 295.
Alderman, R. H., 164.
Aldermanic school law, 130.
Alderson, Grace Walton, 509.
Alderson, J. Coleman, 509.
Alderson, John, 286.
Alexander, Lucy Vernon, 421.
Alford, John B., 40, 42, 81.
Algoe, William, 149-50.
Allegiance, oaths of, 37-8; changed, 47.
Allen, J. E., 159.
Allison, J. J., 141.
Altmeyer, Henry B., 294, 347.
Altmeyer, Jacob, 347.
Altmeyer, John, 347.
Altmeyer, Martha Quinn, 347.
Amos, Nancy, 490.
Amsden, Hannah, 405.
Anderson, C. N., 228.
Anderson, E. G., 228.
Anderson, George K., 509.
Anderson, Helen, 509.
Anderson, Joseph, 294, 334, 468.
Anderson, Marguerite, 509.
Anderson, Martha Walton, 509.
Anderson, William B., 228.
Archer, Francis Mather, 233, 347.
Archer, Frank Mather, 348.
Archer, Irma Knight, 349.
Archer, Richard Mather, 348.
Archer, Richey, 233.
Archer, Robert L., 92, 96, 102, 141, 270, 315, 348.
Archer, Robert Lamley, 348, 349.
Archer, Thomas, 233, 348.
Ardery, E. D., 110.
Argus (newspaper), 226.
Armstrong, C. C., 261.
Arnold, Gertrude, 483.
Arnold, Marie, 503.
Arthur, George, 322.
Arthur, Morris, 322.
Ashworth, L. J., 241-2.
Aspinwall, William H., 297.
Atkinson, George W., 193.
August, Dorothy Laidley, 370, 429.
August, Robert Mumford, 370, 429.
Ayres, G. R., 65.
Ayres, Myrtle, 460.

B

Baer, Peter, 237.
Bailey, George, 389.
Bailey, Ora Frampton, 389.
Baines, Alys, 352.
Baines, Dunbar, 352.
Baines, Harriet Laidley, 352.
Baker, Enoch, 193, 243, 244.
Baker, J. C., 172.
Baker, L. W., 461.
Baker, Lady Taylor, 501.
Baker, Mary Handley, 461.
Baker, R. M., 501.
Baker, Thomas Taylor, 501.
Ball, Linie Kilgore, 422.
Ball, J. S., 323, 324.
Ballard, Louise Smith, 515.
Ballinger, Absolom, 319.
Banks, W. H., 91, 102, 103, 258.
Banks, 203, 209.
Barber, Beuhring Hulverson, 372.
Barber, Curtis Crowell, 371.
Barber, Daniel Brown, 372.
Barber, Daniel Newman, 372.
Barber, Edith Naismith, 372.
Barber, Elizabeth Brown, 371.
Barber, Florence, 371.
Barber, Florence Crowell, 371.
Barber, James Brown, 371.
Barber, James David, 372.

Barber, Lawrence Graham, 371.
Barber, Lucy, 371.
Barber, Lucy Brown, 371.
Barber, Sarah Couch, 371.
Barber, Thomas Maxfield, 371.
Barber, Timothy Lawrence, 371.
Barber, Timothy Naismith, 372.
Barbour, Ira J., 94, 106, 108.
Barboursville, W. Va., 316-21; established, 316.
Barboursville college, see Morris Harvey college.
Barboursville seminary, see Morris Harvey college.
Barker, Nettie Kilgore, 423.
Barkla, Clarence S., 93.
Barlow, B. F., 241.
Barnum, W. H., 186, 205.
Barr, J. C., 309.
Barrett, Andrew, 22.
Barrett, Emma, 461.
Barrett, Harvey, 133.
Barrington, Francis G., 400.
Bartram, Rebecca, 481.
Bascum, Henry B., 299-300.
Bastianelli, Adrian, 354.
Bastianelli, Barbara, 354.
Bastianelli, Harry, 354.
Bastianelli, Louise Hawkins, 354.
Bastianelli, Raphael, 354.
Batts, Thomas, 2.
Baumgardner, Al, 252.
Baumgardner, J. B., 41.
Baumgardner, Jacob, 331.
Baumgardner, Molly, 425.
Baumgardner, Stella, 425.
Bayer, Ira P., 61.
Bayless, John C., 308.
Baylous, E. L., 195.
Beach, S. C., 243.
Beale, John M., 240, 334, 336.
Beams, Clara, 388.
Beams, Clarissa, 389.
Beardsley, A. J., 64, 167.
Beatty, Nancy, 353.
Beckett, Penina, 404.
Beebe, James C., 123.
Beeber, C. C., 272.
Belk, J. Blanton, 309.
Belknap, Priscilla Alden, 456.
Bell, Homer, 241.
Bellemere, Mary M., 432.
Bennett, E. A., 89, 244.
Berkeley, Ida Morris, 460.
Berkeley, T. J., 325, 460.
Bernheim, R. B., 193.
Beswick, Sam, 205.
Beuhring, Anna Maria, 351.
Beuhring, Dorothea Sandman, 354.

Beuhring, Edgar Francis, 354.
Beuhring, Emma, 353.
Beuhring, Emma Adelaide, 351.
Beuhring, F. G. L., 20, 22, 29, 118, 150, 152, 316, 318, 328, 349-51.
Beuhring, Fannie Miller, 353.
Beuhring, Frances, 354.
Beuhring, Frances Dannenberg, 351.
Beuhring, Frances E., 450.
Beuhring, Frederick, 354.
Beuhring, Frederick Konig Dannenberg, 351.
Beuhring, Harold Earl, 355.
Beuhring, Henry, 354.
Beuhring, Lee Davis, 354.
Beuhring, Lilian Huff, 355.
Beuhring, Louisa Mayer, 351, 353, 428.
Beuhring, Lucille, 354.
Beuhring, Mame Hovey, 354.
Beuhring, Mary Louisa, 354.
Beuhring, Nancy Slater, 354.
Beuhring, Nora Belle, 354.
Beuhring, Ora Peyton, 354.
Beuhring, Raymond, 354.
Beuhring, Robert, 355.
Beuhring, Victor, 355.
Beuhring, Virginia Elenor, 354.
Beuhring, Walter Dannenberg, 355.
Bexfield, Richard, 135.
Biagi, Pete, 239, 240.
Bias, George, 253.
Bias, R. S., 42.
Bias, Rolland, 155.
Bickers, William, 152.
Bickmore, Emma Brown, 372.
Bickmore, John Franklin, 372.
Bickmore, Judith, 372.
Bickmore, Norine King, 372.
Bickmore, Thankful, 372.
Biern, E., 215, 306, 307.
Biern, Sam, 307.
Biernbaum, James, 242.
Bierne, Emanuel, 234.
Biggs, George N., 64, 106, 228, 240, 250.
Biggs, William, 306.
Bill of rights, 97.
Billingsly, Morris, 163-4.
Billups, Bessie Ratcliff, 356.
Billups, Bunia, 355.
Billups, Burt, 356.
Billups, Clara Frazier, 356.
Billups, Dora, 355.
Billups, Ella, 356.
Billups, Emma Sipple, 356.
Billups, Fred, 356.
Billups, George, 355.
Billups, Harold E., 356.
Billups, Ida, 355.

Billups, John L., 355.
Billups, John S., 356, 357.
Billups, Margaret Frances, 356.
Billups, Mary Frances, 356.
Billups, Mary Wellman, 355.
Billups, Samuel, 355.
Billups, Sarah, 355.
Billups, Virginia, 356.
Bingham, Jack, 244.
Birke, Daisy Gideon, 395.
Birke, Sol, 395.
Bishop, Thomas R., 223.
Black, Adam, 100.
Blackwell, Alice Virginia, 481.
Blackwood, Fannie Morris, 461.
Blackwood, Helen, 461.
Blackwood, J. L., 137.
Blackwood, James Harvey, 461, 516.
Blackwood, Kate, 516.
Blackwood, Owen, 461.
Blackwood, R. L., 246.
Blackwood, Sallie Morris, 461.
Blair, Frank S., 360.
Blake, A. G., 240.
Blake, John M., 155.
Blake, Martha, 384.
Blaney, Marian, 461.
Blenko, W. H., 340.
Blenko, William, 340.
Bloss, James, 71.
Bloss, Valentine, 71.
Blume, E. W., 163.
Blundon, Edgar P., 86.
Bock, E. L., 224.
Boggess, Thomas N., 88, 233, 261.
Boldt, Charles, 259.
Bond, Katherine, 440.
Bond issues, 57.
Booker, Cynthia, 491.
Boone, Daniel, 399.
Boone, John, 93.
Boone, John W., 184, 207.
Booten, Cassia Spurlock, 491.
Booten, Rebecca, 491.
Booten, Reuben, 491.
Boreman, Arthur I., 37.
Borheim, Mose, 306.
Bossinger, H. C., 209, 223, 301, 303.
Bostick, Jency Scales, 357, 482.
Bostick, Manoah, 20, 22, 71, 74, 97, 316, 357, 409, 439, 482.
Boult, Isaac, 98.
Bourne, Virginia, 379.
Bovie, Frederick, 421.
Bovie, Frederick Morgan, 421-2.
Bovie, Lucy Alexander, 421.
Bovie, Marilla, 421.
Bovie, Mercy, 421.
Bowden, Sidney, 27.

Bowe, Lat, 355.
Bowe, Sarah Billups, 355.
Bowen, Dyke, 48, 119.
Bowen, Hugh 20, 242.
Bowers, Albert S., 298.
Bowles, W. H., 167.
Bowlin, Virginia Southard, 419.
Boxley, C. A., 189, 210, 236, 248.
Boyd, Lelia, 516.
Boyer, F. D., 289, 290.
Boyer, W. R., 151, 152, 153.
Brackman, Jim, 240.
Bradford, Cora, 352.
Bradshaw, Edmund D., 358.
Bradshaw, Elizabeth Goewey, 358.
Bradshaw, Ennis Wood, 358-9.
Bradshaw, Franklin, 358.
Bradshaw, George D., 266, 357-8.
Bradshaw, Grace Devine, 358.
Bradshaw, J. E., 357, 358.
Bradshaw, James, 358.
Bradshaw, Jenny Jewell, 357, 358.
Bradshaw, John, 358.
Brady, James J., 215, 295.
Brame, Susanna, 439.
Brammer, Mary, 410, 466.
Brandebury, H. A., 167, 189-91.
Brandenbury, Ida Haning, 249.
Bratton, Allen F., 88.
Braxton, Patty, 392.
Brazie, Henrie W., 88.
Breslin, John G., 201, 223.
Brinker, D. H., 322.
Brinker, Frances Beuhring, 354.
Brinker, W. E., 354.
Bristol, Florence, 469.
Broh, Adolph, 359.
Broh, Belle, 359.
Broh, Dan, 359.
Broh, Dorothy, 360, 395.
Broh, Eph, 359.
Broh, Evelyn, 360.
Broh, Fannie Moses, 360.
Broh, Harry L., 359, 360.
Broh, Herman L., 360, 395.
Broh, Ida Gideon, 360, 395.
Broh, Jettie Rose, 359.
Broh, Julius, 237, 269, 306, 359.
Broh, Lillian, 359.
Broh, Mayme, 359.
Broh, Mike, 237, 306, 359, 360, 395.
Broh, Rose, 359.
Broh, Ruth, 360.
Broh, Sidney, 359.
Bronson, Lillian, 377.
Bronson, S. C., 403.
Brooke, W. M., 264.
Brooks, Merton H., 201, 231, 297.
Brown, A., 141.

Brown, Agnes, 353.
Brown, Annie Dickinson, 372.
Brown, Benjamin, 20, 118, 150, 165, 308, 338, 363-4, 482.
Brown, Benjamin Beuhring, 372-3.
Brown, Ceres, 150, 364, 366, 371.
Brown, Charlotte Helen, 361.
Brown, Dorothy Rardin, 361.
Brown, Douglas Baker, 360.
Brown, Douglas Walter, 360-1, 363.
Brown, Eleanora Dannenburg, 372.
Brown, Elizabeth, 371, 409, 479.
Brown, Elizabeth Newhall, 373.
Brown, Elizabeth Newman, 363.
Brown, Elizabeth Woodbridge, 371.
Brown, Emma Matilda Seales, 372.
Brown, Flo Glidden, 363.
Brown, George, 363.
Brown, George Newman, 363, 364, 397.
Brown, Gertrude Woodbridge, 373.
Brown, Henry, 20, 326, 331, 362, 363.
Brown, Hester Newhall, 373.
Brown, J. C., 309.
Brown, J. M., 197.
Brown, J. N., 307, 309.
Brown, James Frederick, 353, 370-3.
Brown, James Henry, 18, 100, 353, 363-9, 428.
Brown, James R., 114.
Brown, Jean Morgan, 371.
Brown, Jennie Woodbridge, 371.
Brown, John E. Williams, 361.
Brown, John W., 167.
Brown, Josephine, 366.
Brown, Kathleen, 434.
Brown, Lee C., 360.
Brown, Leon G., 210.
Brown, Louisa Beuhring, 353.
Brown, Louise Beuhring, 371.
Brown, Lucille Ravencroft, 372, 434.
Brown, Lucy, 371.
Brown, Lynda Potter, 361.
Brown, Margaret, 372.
Brown, Mary Dickinson, 372.
Brown, Mary Harrison, 400.
Brown, Mary Lindsey, 360.
Brown, Mary Williams, 361.
Brown, Matilda Scales, 308, 364, 482.
Brown, Maxfield, 363.
Brown, Owen M., 434.
Brown, R. T., 164.
Brown, Richard, 118, 150, 338, 363-4.
Brown, Ruth Dannenberg, 371.
Brown, Sallie Lewis, 372.
Brown, Samuel, 299.
Brown, Sarah, 497.
Brown, Sarah Hampton, 363, 397.
Brown, Sarah Haney, 364.
Brown, Thomas R., 364.
Brown, Vesta, 118, 364, 427.
Brown, Virginia, 353, 369, 428.
Brown, Walter Lindsey, 146, 361.
Brown, William, 363.
Brown, William Campbell, 363.
Brown, Wirt, 336.
Brownsville, W. Va., 338.
Brumfield, William, 74.
Bryan, John, 69, 376.
Bryan, Nancy Lillard, 376.
Bryan, Nancy Spurlock, 496.
Bryan, Nimrod, 496.
Bryan, Silas L., 376.
Bryan, T. J., 246, 496.
Bryan, William Jennings, 50, 69, 231, 244, 376.
Bryant, John, 286.
Bryant, Nancy, 286.
Buck, C. M., 193.
Buck, Lillian Laidley, 352.
Buck, William, 352.
Buckholtz, William, 323.
Buckley, Nancy, 484.
Buckner, James A., 149.
Buckner, Joseph A., 376.
Buckner, Laura, 376.
Buckner, Olga Handley, 149, 376.
Buffington, Addison J., 63.
Buffington, Addison T., 461.
Buffington, Amanda, 373.
Buffington, Ann Cline, 373.
Buffington, David, 373.
Buffington, S. Stanard, 87, 167, 184, 373.
Buffington, Edna Morris, 461.
Buffington, Elenor Lane, 429.
Buffington, Eliza Stanard, 373.
Buffington, Florence, 375.
Buffington, Garland, 48.
Buffington, Henry, 42, 170.
Buffington, James, 98, 117, 373, 429.
Buffington, James H., 170, 373.
Buffington, Joel, 373.
Buffington, John, 170.
Buffington, John N., 42, 117, 166, 170, 203, 311, 312, 373.
Buffington, Jonathan, 4, 9, 373.
Buffington, Julia Garland, 375.
Buffington, Lou Garland, 306, 373.
Buffington, Louise Laidley, 427.
Buffington, Mary, 373.
Buffington, Mary Holderby, 415.
Buffington, Mary Jane, 373.
Buffington, Nancy Scales, 373, 374, 482.
Buffington, Peter Cline, 36, 42, 86, 99, 152, 170, 172, 173, 177, 203, 226, 236, 237, 328, 373.

INDEX

Buffington, Rebecca, 373, 479.
Buffington, Richard, 373.
Buffington, Ruth, 373.
Buffington, Susan, 373, 416.
Buffington, Susanna, 373.
Buffington, Thomas, 3-4, 9, 63, 68, 373, 398, 457, 479.
Buffington, Thomas C., 415.
Buffington, Thomas J., 117, 166, 224, 299, 300, 326, 330, 373.
Buffington, William, 3, 20, 62, 97, 98-9, 117, 150, 303, 327, 328, 357, 373, 374, 482.
Buffington, William Henry, 373, 427.
Buford, William E., 380.
Bugbee, Fred W., 111.
Bukey, Rodolphus, 329.
Bull, W. H., 174, 229.
Bullock, T. J., 184, 223, 248, 290.
Bumgardner, *see* Baumgardner.
Bunch, Zack,, 277, 278.
Burdette, Alexander, 375-6.
Burdette, Archibald, 375.
Burdette, Elizabeth Yates, 149, 376.
Burdette, Frank L., 376-7.
Burdette, Franklin L., 377, 456.
Burdette, Frederick, 375.
Burdette, Giles, 375.
Burdette, James, 375.
Burdette, James Roberson, 376.
Burdette, Jane Scott, 375.
Burdette, John, 375.
Burdette, Laura Buckner, 376-7.
Burdette, Lewis, 183.
Burdette, Mary Hill, 375.
Burdette, Mary L. Hill, 375-6.
Burdette, Richard, 375.
Burdette, Robert J., 375.
Burdette, Samuel, 375.
Burdette, Sarah Cornwell, 375.
Burdette, Thomas, 375.
Burdette, William, 375, 377.
Burdette, Willie Hardwick, 376.
Burgess, Alice, 495.
Burgess, Amelia, 495.
Burgess, Catherine, 495.
Burgess, Charity, 495.
Burgess, Charlie, 452.
Burgess, Clara Ferguson, 452.
Burgess, Emily, 405.
Burgess, G. G., 495.
Burgess, George Roberts, 452, 495.
Burgess, John B., 495.
Burgess, Leonora, 495.
Burgess, Martha Spurlock, 495.
Burgess, Octavia, 495.
Burgess, Sarah, 495.
Burgess, Strother, 495.
Burgess, Susan Margaret, 495.

Burgess, Virginia, 495.
Burgess, William, 495.
Burke, Thomas J., 90, 140, 175, 180, 201.
Burke, Wilbert M., 295.
Burks, Alice, 496.
Burks, Helen Laidley, 427, 497.
Burks, James, 497.
Burks, Lewis H., 170, 172, 304, 305, 334, 469, 497.
Burley, James, 125.
Burnett, Charles J., 311.
Burns, A. C., 167.
Burns, B. B., 251.
Burrill, C. F., 108.
Byrd, Hazel, 425.
Byus, Lillie, 489.

C

Cabell, William H., 5, 10.
Cabell county war memorial association, 270.
Cabell school, 143.
Cackley, R. M., 276.
Caldwell, J. L., 209, 333-4, 377.
Callahan, Robert D., 301.
Camden, Johnson N., 274.
Cammack, Bertha Haworth, 407.
Cammack, C. W., 234, 407, 408.
Cammack, Essie Haworth, 407.
Cammack, Grace LaFerre, 249.
Cammack, Howard Haworth, 408.
Cammack, John Henry, 90, 207, 234, 289, 290, 407.
Commack, Ruth, 377, 408.
Camp, T. W., 259.
Campbell, Charles William, 199, 246, 247, 269, 361, 377-8, 438.
Campbell, Elizabeth J., 297.
Campbell, Eugene M., 203.
Campbell, Jennie Eloise, 377, 438.
Campbell, Jennie Ratliff, 377.
Campbell, Lillian Bronson, 377.
Campbell, Mary Johnson, 377.
Campbell, Nan, 377.
Campbell, Robert D., 377.
Campbell, Rolla D., 137, 408.
Campbell, Ruth, 377.
Campbell, Ruth Cammack, 377, 408.
Campbell, T. B., 297.
Capehart, Sam, 41.
Carlile, John S., 419.
Carnegie Library, 143-4.
Carper, Margaret, 370, 428.
Carroll, James T., 100.
Carroll, John S. P., 88.
Carroll, Thomas, 293, 331.
Carson, R. F., 106.
Carter, Chester, 109.

556 INDEX

Carter, George W., 287.
Carter, J. C., 250.
Carter, John, 243.
Carter, John D., 287.
Cartmill, David, 17.
Cason, P. A., 223.
Casto, Gertrude, 502.
Cater, Daniel, 440.
Cater, George, 440.
Cater, Henson, 440.
Cater, Mima, 440.
Cater, Sallie, Love, 440.
Catlett, Alexander, Jr., 22.
Cavendish, William H., 17.
Cemeteries, 68-9.
Central City, W. Va., 322-4.
Central land company, 170-1, 210, 224, 267, 298, 314.
Chadwick, Cynthia, 439.
Chadwick, U. S., 144.
Chaffin, William, 195.
Chafin, Mary, 508.
Chafin, Richard, 508.
Chafin, Sarah Harvie, 508.
Chambers, Harry, 223, 315.
Chambers, J. H., 305.
Chandler, Thomas, 72.
Chapman, Alex, 83.
Chapman, Andrew I., 98.
Chapman, Cadwallader, 97, 98.
Chapman, Elizabeth Parker, 415.
Chapman, Fanny Holderby, 410.
Chapman, Floyd S., 272, 358.
Chapman, George, 98, 415.
Chapman, John, 42.
Chapman, Lucy Morris, 459.
Chapman, M. V., 322.
Chapman, Mabel E., 353.
Chapman, Philemon, 410.
Chapman, Susan Ann, 414, 415.
Chapman, T. L., 281.
Chase, Glenn E., 256.
Chase, L. C., 139, 140.
Chase, Owen G., 88, 201, 301.
Chenoweth, Virginia, 352.
Chesapeake & Ohio railroad, 125, 170, 201, 205, 251, 256.
Chesterman, A. D., 140.
Chesterman, James D., 159.
Childers, Samuel A., 37, 100.
Childs, Susanna, 439.
Chilton, Hezekiah, 286.
Chilton, William E., 51, 286.
Chinn, Lucy, 461.
Christy, Howard Chandler, 147.
Christy, J. C., 215.
Church, J. W., 46, 207.
Churton, Daniel, 264.
Civil war, *see* War Between the States.

Clap, Thomas, 489.
Clapp, Annie Love, 440.
Clapp, George, 440.
Clark, Abraham, 421.
Clark, Donald, 507.
Clark, H. S., 297.
Clark, Henry, 151.
Clark, James, 323.
Clarke, James Beauchamp, 159, 311.
Clark, Lyda, 379.
Clark, Mary Vinson, 507.
Clark, Mercy Marie, 421.
Clark, Rhoda M., 297.
Clark, Samuel F., 98.
Clark, Silas M., 43.
Clark, W. L., 135.
Clarke, Frank, 335.
Clarke, Peter, 327, 328, 331.
Clarkson, Bradford, 369.
Clarkson, John, 329.
Clarkson, John B., 79-81, 82.
Clarkson, John N., 42.
Clarkson, Mary Laidley, 369.
Claughton, Richard A., 152, 156.
Clay, George B., 258.
Clendenin, George, 453.
Clendinin, Sophia, 453.
Clendenin, William, 453.
Cline, Ann, 373.
Clingenpeel, C. C., 253.
Clymer, Mary, 70.
Coale, Elizabeth Holderby, 415.
Coale, Samuel, 415.
Coalter, John, 5, 10, 11, 17.
Cobbs, R. A., 312.
Cocke, W. J., 90.
Cockrell, J. K., 112.
Coe, S. S., 174.
Cogbill, Jack, 287.
Cole, Ann, 474.
Cole, Charles W., 91, 103, 104.
Cole, W. E., 111.
Cole, W. H., 143.
Collier, Caroline H., 478.
Collier, Jo, 79.
Collins, Prudence Bently, 501.
Collins, Tom, 213.
Commercial (newspaper), 228.
Compulsory education, 136.
Conklin, John F., 110.
Conley state forest nursery, 169.
Conner, Anna, 517.
Conner, Charles, 75.
Connor, R. M., 103.
Conrad, Jane, 421.
Constitution of 1872, 48.
Cook, J. J., 290.
Cook, Rufus, 170.
Cooley, Frances Vinson, 509.

INDEX

Cooley, W. T., 509.
Copen, C. E., 108.
Copley, W. H., 37.
Copper, Anna, 421.
Corbly, Lawrence J., 159.
Cord, John, 299, 300.
Cornwell, Edmund, 375, 377.
Cornwell, John J., 94.
Cornwell, Sarah, 375.
County government organized, 10-15, 17-22; districts, 29; poor farm, 30; reorganization, 43; reorganization (1872), 48.
County unity bill, 137.
Courthouse established, 10-15, 22; rebuilt, 27.
Courts, criminal, 59; domestic relations, 61.
Cowden, W. K., 103.
Cox, Albert E., 379.
Cox, Elizabeth, 286.
Cox, H. McP., 379, 425.
Cox, Henry Clay, 108.
Cox, James, 70, 286, 287.
Cox, John, 379.
Cox, L. H., 250, 259.
Cox, Martha Kyle, 425.
Cox, Maude, 379.
Cox, Maxine, 425.
Cox, Norman W., 290.
Cox, Pauline, 425.
Cox, Pearl, 379.
Cox, R. L., 250.
Cox, Sarah White, 378.
Cox, William, 378.
Cox, William T., 379.
Coxey's army, 103, 335.
Cranston, Earl, 303.
Crawford, A. J., 322.
Crawford, C. C., 447.
Crawford, Fannie Maupin, 447.
Crawford, Lizzie, 322.
Crawford, Rachael, 503.
Crawford, W. T., 223.
Crawford, William, 330.
Creel, Elizabeth A., 26.
Crider, J. L., 231, 301.
Crockett, Asher, 72.
Crockett, Mary Spurlock Harrison, 492.
Crockett, Sylvester, 492.
Croft, S. M., 305.
Crom, Adam, 72.
Crooks, Clara M., 402.
Crooks, James M., 402.
Crowder, E. H., 95.
Crowell, Florence, 371.
Crozet, Claude, 338.
Crum, Sam J., 356.

Crump, George, 485.
Crump, Richard, 326.
Crump, Susan Seamonds, 485.
Crump, William, 499.
Cullen, E. P., 93.
Cullen, George, 89-90, 207, 233.
Cullen, George T., 93.
Culloden, W. Va., 325.
Cummings, Charles, 64.
Cunningham, John S., 125.
Currie, A. L., 309.
Curtis, Annie, 454.
Curtis, Betty Martin, 448.
Cyrus, Elijah, 287.

D

Dabney, David W., 167, 334.
Daley, Mary Love, 442.
Daley, Robert H., 442.
Dameron, Jane, 444.
Damron, Joseph R., 239.
Damron, Mary, 507.
Damron, Oeneaferus, 72.
Damron, Pauline, 425.
Damron, Samuel, 507.
Damron, Sarah, 420.
Damron, Vashti Jarrell, 507.
Dandelet, Tom, 162.
Dannenberg, Frances Eleanora, 351.
Dannenberg, Dorothea Konig, 351.
Dannenberg, Eliza Konig, 351.
Dannenberg, Frederick, 351.
Darlington, James Henderson, 379.
Darlington, Julian Trueheart, 379.
Darlington, Kitty Pemberton, 379.
Darlington, Kitty Scott, 379.
Darlington, Lyda Clark, 379.
Darlington, Urban Valentine Williams, 95, 164, 305, 379-80.
Darlington, Virginia Bourne, 379.
Darnall, Emma Holderby, 415.
Darnall, Harry H., 415.
Daughters of the American Revolution, Buford chapter roster, 380-3.
Davidson, C. M., 263.
Davies, Evan J., 207, 209.
Davies, Oley, 207.
Davis, Aileen, 441.
Davis, B. T., 209, 224, 272.
Davis, Cary N., 361.
Davis, Daniel, 71.
Davis, Frances Miller, 354.
Davis, Henry Winters, 96, 354.
Davis, Ilicia Wheeler, 392.
Davis, J. P., 470.
Davis, John, 354.
Davis, Lloyd A., 114.
Davis, Mary Beuhring, 354.

558 INDEX

Davis, Nannie Seamonds, 485.
Davis, Paul Dannenberg, 354.
Davis, Rebecca A. E., 491.
Davis, Samuel, 88.
Davis, Thomas B., 92, 104, 105, 107, 207.
Davis, V. B., 242, 305, 485.
Davis, Walter, 242.
Deadman, Sarah, 71.
Dean, Esther, 480.
Dean, F. E., 400.
Dean, Herman P., 263.
Dedman, Samuel, 384.
Dedman, Sarah, 384.
De la Geneste, Marie Therese Clothilde Raison, 453.
Delebar, Ruth H., 388.
Denelsbeck, Dave, 259.
Derbyshire, Henry, J., 223, 314, 315.
Derton, Elizabeth, 25.
Devine, Grace, 358.
Dew, Amy Meek, 452.
Dew, Jack, Carlos, 452.
Dew, John, 300.
Dial, Walter V., 96.
Dick bill, 104.
Dickerson, J. Q., 377.
Dickerson, Noah, 466.
Dickerson, Ruth, 466.
Dickey, C. C., 425.
Dickey, Ham., 186.
Dickey, Nellie Kyle, 425.
Dickinson, Annie, 372.
Diehl, G. W., 164.
Diehl, H. T., 265, 266.
Dills, Ethel Walton, 509.
Dills, Grace Walton, 509.
Dills, Tunis, 509.
Dimick, M. C., 210, 281.
Dingess, Peter, 97.
Dingess, Sarah Ann, 512.
Dingess, William Anderson, 512.
District public school system, 133.
Dober, Paul, 239.
Dodson, Jesse, 79.
Dohrman, Arnold Henry, 437.
Donaldson, Newton N., 309.
Donella, S. C., 174.
Doolittle, Ambrose L., 63, 497-8.
Doolittle, E. S., 184, 229, 246, 247.
Doolittle, Edward, 50, 56, 57.
Doolittle, Ellen, 497.
Doolittle, F. L., 215, 229, 267.
Doolittle, L., 229.
Doolittle, Sarah Brown, 497.
Dougherty, John, 487.
Dougherty, Kate, 487.
Douglas, Henry Taylor, 127.
Douglas, J. P., 60.

Douglas, Stephen A., 394.
Douglass, John S., 314.
Douglass, William H., 287.
Douthat, David Greiner, 383.
Douthat, Mary Ann Adams, 383.
Douthat, Mary Eleanor Polly Yost, 383.
Douthat, Mary Jane Wells, 383.
Douthat, Robert, 383.
Douthat, Robert William, 383.
Douthat, Roxie Salmon, 384.
Douthat, Rudenz Sharp, 383-4.
Douthitt, Edward F., 234.
Douthitt, William, 81, 83.
Dovel, Esther, 432.
Dovel, Isaac C., 432.
Dovel, Mary C. E., 432.
Downer, W. S., 287.
Downey, Thomas, 295.
Downtain, J. G., 436.
Doyle, J. T., 447.
Doyle, Lucy Maupin, 447.
Drake, Peter, 213.
Driggs, B. P., 223, 346.
Driggs, Elizabeth B., 346.
Droddy, Margaret, 456.
Drown, Benjamin, 20.
Drummond, W. E., 215, 249, 268.
Dubois, Anna Maria, 409.
Dudley, Peyton, 236.
Duerson, W. R., 236.
Dugan, Mat W., 335, 336.
Duncan, James, 422.
Duncan, Mary Kilgore, 422.
Duncan, W. W., 304.
Dundas, Henry, 286.
Dundas, John, 62, 149.
Dundas, Sarah, 420.
Dundas, Thomas, 286.
Dunkle, Henry C., 150.
Dusenberry, C. C., 42, 210, 290.
Dusenberry, W. C., 335.
Dusenberry, William F., 135.
Duval, Isaac Harden, 88.
Duval, Sophia, 432.
Dwyer, T. W., 295.
Dwyer, Tim, 295.

E

Earls, Shelby, 337.
Early, John, 304.
Earp, Eunice Virginia, 465.
Eastman, Elisha J., 287.
Edler, Marie Kyle, 425.
Edler, Sherl, 425.
Edmunds, John Venable, 353.
Edmunds, Juliette Eskew, 353.
Edmunds, Paul G., 353.
Edmunds, Polly Gray, 353.

INDEX

Education, compulsory, 136.
Education in Cabell county, 130-41, 143, 147-50, 154-65.
Eisenmann, Andrew, 295.
Ekin, Elizabeth A., 440.
Elder, C. S., 322.
Elder, W. D., 241.
Elliott, Ellie Crawford, 389.
Elliott, John Francis, 389.
Elliott, Malcolm, 110.
Elliott, Permele Crawford, 389.
Ellis, Anna, 143.
Ellis, Kate, 143.
Emmons, A. S., 172.
Emmons, C. D., 224, 228, 231, 270, 315.
Emmons, Delos W., 139, 140, 170, 172, 184, 201, 203, 224, 373, 468.
Emmons, J. Alden, 210, 239.
Emmons, James, 120, 327.
Engelman, William, 88.
English, Thomas Dunn, 87.
Ensign, Anna, 410.
Ensign, Ely, 184, 187, 205, 210, 215, 246, 251, 312, 314, 315, 410, 479.
Ensign, Henry M., 209, 347.
Ensign, John W., 199, 315.
Ensign, Mae Abbott, 347.
Enslow, A. J., 139, 172, 184, 201, 233, 312.
Enslow, C. R., 167, 187, 249, 250.
Enslow, Edward B., 102, 233, 236, 272.
Enslow, Frank B., 179, 215, 233, 245, 246, 281, 312, 315.
Enslow, R., 141.
Episcopal church, see Protestant Episcopal Church.
Eppinger, Dora, 394.
Erskine, Russell, 229.
Eskew, Agnes Brown, 353.
Eskew, Garnet Laidlaw, 353.
Eskew, J. G., 353.
Eskew, John, 94.
Eskew, Juliette, 353.
Eskew, Juliette Laidley, 353.
Eskew, Juliette Shrewsbury, 353.
Eskew, Mary Lovell, 353.
Eskew, Nancy Beatty, 353.
Eskew, Roderick Koenig, 353.
Estes, Joel, 286.
European war, 1914-1918, 94-6; Selective service act, 94-5.
Evans, A. H., 322.
Evans, Dorsey, 241.
Evans, Hunter, 322.
Evans, T. L., 241.
Evans, Tom, 241.
Everett, Betty, 423.
Everett, C. F., 389.
Everett, Carrie, 386.
Everett, Charles, 170.
Everett, Chattie, 386.
Everett, Elizabeth Moore, 386.
Everett, Fannie, 386.
Everett, George S., 386.
Everett, Hallie Call, 386.
Everett, Henry, 42, 77, 83.
Everett, Henry Clay, 81, 86, 121, 279, 281, 328, 334, 386, 468.
Everett, James, 42.
Everett, Jennie, 83.
Everett, John, 20, 22, 71, 131, 286, 303, 384.
Everett, John F., 386.
Everett, John S., 42, 156.
Everett, Laban T., 386.
Everett, Mary, 460.
Everett, Naomi, 143.
Everett, Nathaniel, 98, 286.
Everett, Nettie Summerson, 386.
Everett, Peter, 42, 48.
Everett, Rebecca Frampton, 389.
Everett, Richard T., 95, 335, 386.
Everett, Sarah, 286.
Everett, Sarah Dedman, 384.
Everett, Sarah Woodson, 384.
Everett, Stella Wilson, 386.
Everett, Talton Woodson, 81, 152, 384-5.
Everett, Virginia, 386, 474.
Everett, William, 386.
Ewing, Thomas, 202.
Excelsior fire company, 177-9, 183.

F

Fallom, Robert, 2.
Farr, John S., 322.
Fay, Louise, 406.
Feazel, Everett, 100.
Feazel, William E., 100.
Federman, M. J., 266.
Feinstein, Abraham, 307.
Ferguson, Charles W., 156.
Ferguson, David P., 40.
Ferguson, Ella Harrison, 400.
Ferguson, J. M., 156.
Ferguson, James H., 25-6, 37, 42, 43, 44, 46, 47, 154, 492.
Ferguson, Mary Yenthus, 26.
Ferguson, Milton Jamison, 42, 318, 444, 490.
Ferguson, William, 25.
Fesenmeier, Andrew J., 323.
Fesenmeier, J. F., 323.
Fesenmeier, M. W., 323.
Field, Florence Laidley, 352.
Field, Frank, 352.
Field, Martha Archer, 499.
Field, Staunton, 152, 153, 154.

INDEX

Field, Susan Green, 499.
Field, Thomas, 499.
Field, Virginia, 352.
Field, Virginia Chenoweth, 352.
Fisher, Delbert, 94.
Fisk, Harvey, 297.
Fitzgerald, E. M., 41.
Fitzgerald, Gwendolen, 371.
Fitzgerald, Jean Banks, 371.
Fitzgerald, Louise Brown, 371.
Fitzgerald, Oscar Penn, 371.
Fitzgerald, T. H., 289.
Fitzpatrick, Herbert, 361.
Fitzpatrick, J. B., 314.
Fleming, A. B., 210.
Flesher, Andrew, 35.
Flick, amendment, 46.
Flickenstein, Joe, 233.
Flodding, G. A., 213.
Flodding, Paul, 239.
Floyd, John B., 281.
Floyd, Nell, 405.
Follansby, James T., 300, 304-5.
Fonerton, W. H., 152.
Fontaine, E., 125.
Fontaine, Mary Byrd, 352.
Forgey, Burrell E., 213.
Formation, 10-15.
Forsinger, Harriet Abbott, 347.
Forsinger, J. W., 347.
Forth, John, 100.
Foster, 212.
Foster, Bradley Waters, 170, 184, 201, 215, 231, 267, 346, 385, 386-8.
Foster, Joseph, 151, 318, 387.
Foster, Joseph S., 387.
Foster, Mary Huntington, 314, 387.
Foster, Sarah Holman, 387.
Foulk, Wilson M., 143, 144.
Fowler, George, 264.
Fowler, Sarah, 430.
Fox, Emma, 502.
Fox, John, 53.
Fox, Milo P., 110.
Frampton, Albert C., 388.
Frampton, Anna Martin, 388.
Frampton, Charles E., 96, 388.
Frampton, Clara Beams, 388.
Frampton, Clarissa Beams, 389.
Frampton, David, 388.
Frampton, David W., 102, 323, 388.
Frampton, Ephriam, 170, 388.
Frampton, Hiram, 389.
Frampton, Horace, 388.
Frampton, Isaac, 388, 389.
Frampton, James, 388.
Frampton, James Robert, 388.
Frampton, James Mann, 388.
Frampton, John, 388.
Frampton, John M., 388.
Frampton, Martin, 388.
Frampton, Nancy Woods, 388.
Frampton, Ora, 389.
Frampton, Peyton G., 388.
Frampton, Rebecca, 388.
Frampton, Rebecca Jane, 389.
Frampton, Ruth Delebar, 388.
Frampton, Sarah Mann, 388.
Frampton, William, 388.
France, Daniel, 97.
Francis, David Livingston, 389.
Francis, James Draper, 389.
Francis, John Elliott, 389.
Francis, Kate Dean, 389.
Francis, Permele Crawford, 389.
Francis, Permele Elliott, 389-90.
Frank, Ben, 360, 395.
Frank, Dorothy Broh, 360, 395.
Frantz, Dorothy Aleen, 354, 500.
Frazier, Clara, 356, 489.
Freeland, E. H., 223.
Freeman, Blanche, 390.
Freeman, Bridges, 390.
Freeman, Charles Wilkerson, 390-1.
Freeman, Fae Preston, 391.
Freeman, Maria Hagan, 390.
Freeman, Richard Valery, 390.
Freezell, W. E., 328.
Freutel, Bill, 223.
Freutel, Julius, 42, 43, 81, 334.
Frick, Omar T., 264, 265.
Friedman, Jake, 234, 236, 306.
Friedman, Julius, 236, 307.
Fry, Charley, 335-6.
Fry, Edmund, 191.
Fry, Emma, 335-6.
Fry, Ida, 335.
Fry, Joshua, 5.
Fudge, Harriet Louisa, 504.
Fuller, Elizabeth Page, 470.
Fuller, F. D., 226, 315.
Fuller, Sylvester, 470.
Fullerton, Nancy, 422.
Fullerton, William, 20.

G

Gaefe, Minnie, 420.
Gallaher, Ann, 391.
Gallaher, Drusilla Wright, 391.
Gallaher, Eliza, 391.
Gallaher, George, 391.
Gallaher, Georgella, 391.
Gallaher, James, 100, 118, 150, 326, 391, 420, 471.
Gallaher, John, 391.
Gallaher, Mary Johnston, 391, 420.
Gallaher, Sarah, 391.
Gallaher, Thomas, 391.

INDEX

Gallaher, William, 391.
Gallaher, Willie, 391.
Gallick, Joseph R., 144, 239, 272, 281.
Gardner, America, 415.
Gardner, Eliza, 453.
Gardner, Elizabeth, 308.
Gardner, Emily, 454, 480.
Gardner, Joseph, 316, 453-4.
Gardner, Marie Therese, 453.
Gardner, Mary, 481.
Garland, Anna Lyle, 229.
Garland, Julia L., 375.
Garland, Lou, 373.
Garland, T. S., 226, 229, 236, 305.
Garlic, Winnie, 430.
Garner, James A., 223, 237.
Garred, Joseph, 111.
Garrett, James, 100, 402.
Garrett, John, 100, 377.
Garrett, Nancy, 491.
Gas, 66-7.
Gaule, Mary, 250.
Gazette (newspaper), 229.
Germer, E. G., 282.
Gibson, Ann Wingerd, 392.
Gibson, Anna, 392.
Gibson, Catlett, 393.
Gibson, Charles Dana, 147.
Gibson, E. St. Pierre, 394.
Gibson, Elizabeth Shackelford, 393.
Gibson, Eustace, 48, 89, 179, 209, 245, 246, 393, 394, 485, 515.
Gibson, Frances Bodine, 392.
Gibson, Howard, 103, 394.
Gibson, Ilicia Davis, 392.
Gibson, Isaac, 392, 393.
Gibson, James Davis, 392.
Gibson, John, 141.
Gibson, John Shackelford, 314, 392, 393.
Gibson, John T., 228.
Gibson, Jonathan Catlett, 393.
Gibson, L. M., 256.
Gibson, Lee, 394.
Gibson, Mary Leadbetter, 392.
Gibson, Mary W. Shackelford, 393.
Gibson, Mattie Lackland, 394.
Gibson, Minor Winn, 393.
Gibson, Morrell Sanford, 393.
Gibson, Patty Braxton, 392.
Gibson, Philip Pendleton, 393.
Gibson, W., 179.
Gideon, Blanche, 395.
Gideon, Carolyn, 395.
Gideon, Daisy, 395.
Gideon, Dave, 228, 307, 395.
Gideon, Dora Eppinger, 394.
Gideon, Dorris, 395.
Gideon, Ida, 360, 395.
Gideon, Lillian Gottschalk, 395.
Gideon, Ray, 395.
Gideon, Sam, 50, 51, 89, 141, 179, 181, 184, 186, 209, 210, 228, 247, 267, 268, 306, 307, 394-5.
Gideon, Simon, 395.
Gideon, Sylvan, 395.
Gideon, William, 395.
Gideon, William H., 395.
Gilkerson, Leander, 42.
Gill, J. M., 221, 223.
Gill, William, 64.
Gillenwaters, James, 71.
Gillette, Frances, 462.
Gillock, Clara Belle, 423.
Gilmore, Charles, 104.
Givin, Byrne, 370.
Givin, Nelle Brown, 370, 428.
Givin, Virginia Laidley, 370, 428.
Givin, William Byrne, 428.
Gladstone, Robert T., 103.
Gladstone, W. S., 209, 312.
Godby, George, 121.
Goewey, Elizabeth, 358.
Gohen, C. M., 323.
Gohen, James A., 127, 210.
Goodwin, H. W., 428.
Goodwin, Virginia Laidley, 428.
Gordon, H. C., 195, 301.
Gottschalk, Lillian, 395.
Gould, J. R., 223.
Graham, J. L., 105.
Graham, John G., 147.
Graham, John T., 486.
Grammar, Carl E., 314.
Grandia, June, 146.
Grant, William L., 88.
Grant township, 44.
Graveyards, 68-9.
Gray, James, 287.
Gray, W. I., 328.
Green, E. M., 224.
Green, V. M., 250.
Greenbottom, Grant, 5-7.
Grimes, George, 135.
Grover, E. W., 167.
Grubb, James, 277.
Guinn, *see* Gwinn.
Guyandotte, W. Va., 326-36; incorporated, 327.
Gunn, W. R., 77.
Guthrie, L. V., 168.
Gwinn, Anne, 422.
Gwinn, C. E., 210, 267, 417.
Gwinn, D. B., 64.
Gwinn, Em, 460.
Gwinn, Essie Hall, 396.
Gwinn, Hettie Kilgore, 422.
Gwinn, John, 422, 516.
Gwinn, Lola, 516.

562 INDEX

Gwinn, O. E., 64.
Gwinn, R. E., 396.
Gwinn, Susan Jenkins, 417.
Gwinn, W. W., 64.

H

Hagan, Maria, 390.
Hagen, Fred W., 298.
Hagen, H. B., 215, 226, 267, 305.
Hagen, Julian W., 146, 281.
Hagen, Mary Buffington, 170, 373.
Hagen, William H., 47, 48, 51, 139, 140, 170, 172, 203, 209, 373.
Hager, Betty Maupin, 447.
Hager, John, 447.
Hager, Robert, 34.
Hale, Charles, 253.
Hale, Naomi, 442.
Hale, O. W., 298.
Hall, Charles Henry, 150, 239, 395, 396.
Hall, D. A., 396.
Hall, Eliza Neff, 396.
Hall, Elizabeth, 481.
Hall, Elizabeth Radford, 395.
Hall, Essie, 396.
Hall, G. H., 289.
Hall, Henry, 395.
Hall, Lillian Moore, 396.
Hall, Luna Bernice, 396.
Hall, Madge Pancake, 470.
Hall, Mary Matthews, 396.
Hall, Matthew S., 396.
Hall, Mildred Louise, 396.
Hall, Robert, 395.
Hall, Ruel W., 396.
Hall, Samuel B., 396.
Hall, Sarah Ann, 395.
Hall, Vivian H., 396.
Hall, William Dixon, 395, 396.
Hall, William Hadder, 395.
Haller William, 223.
Hallock, Harriet Prentice, 455.
Hallock, Joseph, 455.
Hallock, Susan Prentice Ensign, 455.
Halstead, Laurence, 111.
Hambilton, M. N., 301.
Hamer, T. J., 205, 221.
Hamilton, Frederic R., 159.
Hamilton, T. S., 306.
Hampton, Anthony, 439.
Hampton, Elizabeth, 439.
Hampton, G. W., 163.
Hampton, Anthony, 398.
Hampton, Cary Henry, 397, 398.
Hampton, Henry, 117, 165, 331, 397, 410, 416, 480.
Hampton, Joan, 396.
Hampton, John, 397.
Hampton, John W., 398.

Hampton, Malinda Shortridge, 397.
Hampton, Oliver, 397.
Hampton, Sarah, 363, 397.
Hampton, Susanna Love, 439.
Hampton, Thomas, 396-7.
Hampton, W. H., 314.
Hampton, Wade, 397.
Hampton, William, 396, 397, 398.
Handley, Alex, 502.
Handley, Caroline, 503.
Handley, Charles, 461.
Handley, Charles W., 440.
Handley, Claude E., 460.
Handley, Clifton, 461.
Handley, Elizabeth Love, 440.
Handley, Frank, 440.
Handley, Frank A., 461.
Handley, Fred G., 460, 461.
Handley, Gladys, 461.
Handley, Gordon, 460.
Handley, Grace Johnson, 461.
Handley, Ida Josephine, 461.
Handley, John, 503.
Handley, Kate Wahrheit, 460.
Handley, Laura McMasters, 460.
Handley, Leonidas B., 440.
Handley, Marian Blaney, 461.
Handley, Marion L., 440.
Handley, Mary, 308, 461.
Handley, Mary Morris, 460.
Handley, Olga, 149.
Handley, Ona, 440.
Handley, Robert, 308.
Handley, Sallie, 461.
Handley, Stella, 460.
Handley, Virginia F., 502.
Haney, Hansford, 98.
Haney, Sarah, 364.
Hanley, Calvert, 449.
Hanley, Eliza McCormick, 449.
Hanley, Isaac, 449.
Hanley, John, 170.
Hanley, Lee, 449.
Hannan, Charles W., 63.
Hannan, Esom, 399, 456.
Hannan, John, 20, 63, 100, 118, 133, 398-9.
Hannan, Miriam Morris, 456.
Hannan, Thomas, 4, 73, 100, 398.
Hannon, see Hannan.
Hansford, Sarah, 459.
Harahan, W. J., 221.
Harber, Charlie, 490.
Harber, Sarah, 489-90.
Hard, William F., 300.
Harder, Charlotte Brown, 361.
Harder, Charlotte Van Slyke, 361-3.
Harder, Judith Glidden, 361.
Harder, Philip Bradley, 361.
Harding, B. B., 102.

INDEX

Harding, Buck, 247.
Hardwick, Joel, 287.
Hardwick, Willie Ann, 376.
Harmison, F. J., 226.
Harmon, Thomas, 286.
Harper, W. H., 175.
Harriman, J. P., 479.
Harriman, John, 459.
Harriman, Marian Russell, 479.
Harriman, Nancy Morris, 459.
Harris, Josephine, 503.
Harris, W. P., 221.
Harrison, Allen, 186.
Harrison, Benjamin, 399.
Harrison, Calvin, 492.
Harrison, Charles O., 400, 401.
Harrison, Ella, 400.
Harrison, Eugenia, 400.
Harrison, Flora, 400.
Harrison, Greenville, 41.
Harrison, L. E., 400, 401.
Harrison, Mary, 400.
Harrison, Mary Spurlock, 492.
Harrison, Nancy Adkins, 400.
Harrison, Nannie Trent, 400.
Harrison, Orin, 400.
Harrison, Otis, 399.
Harrison, Ruth Taylor, 399.
Harold, Ira O., 335.
Harshbarger, Clara Crooks, 402.
Harshbarger, David, 62, 401, 402, 483.
Harshbarger, George W., 65, 401.
Harshbarger, Harrison M., 402.
Harshbarger, Hattie L., 402.
Harshbarger, Ira J., 65, 67, 401, 402.
Harshbarger, J. H., 95, 305, 403.
Harshbarger, John, 40, 65, 400, 402-3.
Harshbarger, Maude, 402.
Harshbarger, Nancy, 483.
Harshbarger, Peter, 402.
Harshbarger, William, 402.
Hartzell, Enos, 322.
Harvey, Clayte, 226, 236.
Harvey, Emma F., 501.
Harvey, Harry C., 212, 226, 248, 267, 304, 305.
Harvey, Morris, 163.
Harvey, Robert T., 226, 272.
Harvey, Thomas H., 48, 50, 67, 245, 246, 250, 337, 355, 445, 485, 498, 501, 507.
Harvey, W. J., 264.
Harvey, William, 245.
Harveytown, W. Va., 337.
Harvie, John, 508.
Hassman, William, 221.
Hatch, A. S., 296-7.
Hatfield, Adam, 404.
Hatfield, Alonzo, 404.

Hatfield, Bert, 404.
Hatfield, Dorothy, 405.
Hatfield, Elias, 403.
Hatfield, Emily Burgess, 405.
Hatfield, Elizabeth, 403.
Hatfield, George, 404.
Hatfield, H. D., 403.
Hatfield, Hannah, 404.
Hatfield, Hazel, 403.
Hatfield, Henry, 404.
Hatfield, Homer Whitesel, 405.
Hatfield, J. G., 404, 485.
Hatfield, J. T., 172.
Hatfield, James Benjamin, 405.
Hatfield, Joe, 404.
Hatfield, Kemp, 174.
Hatfield, Lou, 404.
Hatfield, Lucinda, 404.
Hatfield, Lulu Susan, 405.
Hatfield, Martha, 404.
Hatfield, Mary Lou, 405.
Hatfield, Mary Inez, 405.
Hatfield, Mary Seamonds, 404, 485.
Hatfield, Mona Pauline, 405.
Hatfield, Moses, 404.
Hatfield, Nell Floyd, 405.
Hatfield, Ola Alberta, 405.
Hatfield, Penina Beckett, 404.
Hatfield, Robert Pearl, 405, 485.
Hatfield, S. C. Bronson, 403.
Hatfield, Thomas, 316.
Hatfield, William Moses, 405.
Hatton, Solomon, 40.
Hawes, C. M., 144, 250, 442.
Hawes, Effie Ewing, 446.
Hawes, Hubert A., 114.
Hawes, Minnie Love, 442.
Hawes, Sarah Jane, 446.
Hawes, W. J., 446.
Hawk, Sam. A., 203, 221, 247.
Hawkins, Anna White, 354.
Hawkins, Betty Hanbury, 354.
Hawkins, Edward Donald, 354.
Hawkins, Elinore, 354.
Hawkins, Fred, 354.
Hawkins, Fred Marshall, 354.
Hawkins, Howard Burke, 355.
Hawkins, Irene, 354.
Hawkins, Irene Kelly, 354.
Hawkins, John, 354.
Hawkins, John Howell, 354.
Hawkins, John Lee, 144, 231, 267, 290, 354, 500.
Hawkins, John Marshall, 355.
Hawkins, Louise Beuhring, 354.
Hawkins, Marshall, 354.
Hawkins, Mary Howell, 354.
Hawkins, Mary McGregor, 355.
Hawkins, Nannie Lee, 354.
Hawkins, Nora Beuhring, 354.

564 INDEX

Hawkins, Thomas, 286.
Hawkins, Virginia Beuhring, 354.
Hawkins, Virginia E., 500.
Hawkins, Virginia White, 354.
Haworth, Alice, 406, 408.
Haworth, Alma, 407.
Haworth, Bertha Luella, 406.
Haworth, Clarence Everett, 240, 246, 281, 406.
Haworth, George, 406.
Haworth, Hannah Amsden, 405, 408.
Haworth, Harriet Vinton, 249, 406.
Haworth, James Rogers, 406.
Haworth, John, 406.
Haworth, Louise Fay, 406.
Haworth, Samuel Milton, 405, 406.
Haworth, Samuel Vinton, 406.
Hawte, Jane, 514.
Hay, C. C., 102.
Hay, Strother S., 103.
Hayden, Horace E., 311.
Haynes, Mrs. Dr., 215.
Haynie, Henry, 97.
Hays, "Pres," 219.
Hays, T. McK., 51, 95, 270.
Hayslip, Okey, 335.
Hayslip, Sam D., 327, 334.
Hayslip, Thomas J., 43, 46, 81, 83, 156, 157, 328.
Hayslip, Cary B., 88.
Hedrick, Ann, 475.
Heffley, George R., 61, 303.
Heffner, J. F., 219.
Heidt, *see* Hite.
Helverson, Nancy Holderby, 410.
Henderson, Joe, 276.
Henderson, W. B., 108.
Hendricks, Eugene Russell, 305.
Henley, Cal, 243.
Hennon, John, 335.
Hennon, Sam, 334.
Hensford, Calvary Morris, 456.
Hensford, Charles, 456.
Hensley, John, 64.
Hensley, Malinda, 463.
Herald (newspaper), 210, 240, 395, 406, 436.
Hereford, Elizabeth, 316.
Hereford, Frank, 46.
Hereford, James, 167.
Hereford, Sallie Handley, 461.
Hereford, W. D., 461.
Herman, Fred W., 110.
Herndon, Ann, 463.
Herndon, Elizabeth, 286.
Herndon, G. F., 312.
Herndon, James T., 287.
Herndon, Valentine, 63, 286, 287.
Herrenkohl, A., 167.

Hersey, Frank L., 89, 247, 281, 334.
Hersey, Rex, 146.
Hewitt, A. M., 377.
Hewitt, D. E., 303.
Hewitt, Ruth Campbell, 377.
Heydt, *see* Hite.
Heyl, Kenneth, 114.
Hiatt, A. J., 303.
Hickman, Al., 322.
Hicks, George W., 88.
Hider, John, 221.
Hiezey, John, 496.
Hiezey, Philip, 496.
Higgins, A., 347.
Higgins, E. N., 252.
Higgins, Leonore Abbott, 347.
Hill, A. N., 328.
Hill, Arthur M., 277.
Hill, Dan, 221.
Hill, Elizabeth Lively, 376.
Hill, James, 376, 377.
Hill, Mary, 375.
Hill, Mary Lively, 375.
Hill, Richard, 375.
Hill, Roy, 195.
Hilliard, John, 63.
Hiltbruner, Jacob, 329, 331.
Hilton, Glen, 233, 234.
Hilyard, Elizabeth Morris, 456.
Hilyard, Joseph, 456.
Hinchman, Adam, 404.
Hinchman, Martha Hatfield, 404.
Hindman, William L., 18, 26, 44, 46.
Hinerman, D. O., 441.
Hinerman, Harry H., 441.
Hinerman, Joyce Helene, 441.
Hinerman, Margaret Miller, 441.
Hinerman, Margie Ann, 441.
Hinerman, Mary Love, 441.
Hinerman, Muriel Helen, 441.
Hinerman, Sallie Love, 441.
Hines, Michael, 294.
Hite, Addie C., 154, 409.
Hite, Anna Dubois, 409.
Hite, Anna Ensign, 410.
Hite, Charles, 410.
Hite, Edward, 410.
Hite, Elizabeth Brown, 409.
Hite, Elizabeth Johnson, 410, 419.
Hite, Fannie, 410.
Hite, Frank W., 409, 410.
Hite, Gertie, 410.
Hite, H. C., 410.
Hite, Jacob, 117, 409, 482.
Hite, John B., 327, 328, 334, 409-10.
Hite, John W., 20, 120, 154, 303, 327, 328, 450.
Hite, Jost, 409.
Hite, Kate, 154, 410, 450.
Hite, Mary Brammer, 410.

INDEX

Hite, Mary Scales, 117, 409, 427.
Hite, Olive, 460.
Hite, Sally Scales, 482.
Hite, Sarah Scales, 409.
Hite, William, 117, 303, 409.
Hite, William F., 187-9, 300, 410.
Hoard, Arma Spurlock, 491.
Hoard, Charley, 491.
Hodge, John, 355.
Hodge, Virginia Lovell, 355.
Hodges, Thomas E., 102, 103, 159.
Hogg, C. .C., 91, 167, 215.
Hogsett, E. L., 290.
Holanbey, James, 97.
Holderby, Abner, 415.
Holderby, Absolom, 20, 410, 415, 447.
Holderby, Addie Hite, 154, 409, 415.
Holderby, America Gardner, 415.
Holderby, Areanna, 410.
Holderby, Areanna Lane, 410, 429.
Holderby, Columbia Stewart, 415.
Holderby, Dudley Drake, 415.
Holderby, Edward S., 172, 184, 415.
Holderby, Eliza, 410, 450.
Holderby, Eliza Priscilla, 415.
Holderby, Elizabeth Parker, 415.
Holderby, Emma, 415.
Holderby, Fannie, 410.
Holderby, George, 154.
Holderby, George S., 42.
Holderby, George Williams, 77, 83, 409, 415.
Holderby, Hallie Valentine, 415.
Holderby, James, 20, 117, 150, 153, 331, 397, 410, 411, 415, 416, 429.
Holderby, Lucy, 415.
Holderby, Lucy Wright, 415.
Holderby, Mahaley, 415.
Holderby, Martha E., 447.
Holderby, Mary Phenton, 415.
Holderby, Nancy, 410.
Holderby, Priscilla Pendleton, 410.
Holderby, Rebecca, 415.
Holderby, Rebecca Hoskinson, 415.
Holderby, Robert, 42, 151, 153, 303, 327, 410, 412-4, 415, 425.
Holderby, Robert S., 415.
Holderby, Sadie, 415.
Holderby, Susan, 303.
Holderby, Susan Chapman, 414, 415.
Holderby, Susan L., 415.
Holderby, T. E., 415.
Holderby, William, 72, 331, 410, 415.
Holderby, William P., 170, 410, 415.
Holderby, William Robert, 415.
Holderby, Willie Mae, 415.
Hollandshead, Jacob, 421.
Hollanshead, Jane Conrad, 420.
Hollandshead, Matilda Jane, 421.
Hollenbeck, George, 117, 410, 416.

Hollenbeck, John, 117, 416.
Hollenbeck, Martin, 415, 416.
Holloway, Sarah Ricketts, 474.
Holloway, William, 474.
Holman, Sarah K., 387.
Holroyd, John D., 287.
Holstein, Allen I., 100.
Holstein, J. W., 167.
Holswade, Georgella Gallaher, 391.
Holswade, J. F., 197, 224.
Holswade, W. H. H., 210, 224, 391.
Holt, Fannie, 515.
Holt, John Herriman, 59, 193, 215, 246, 247, 371, 377, 515.
Holt, Rush Dew, 437.
Holton, Forbes, 259.
Homrich, H. J., 242.
Honaker, Ray, H., 114.
Honshell, Gus, 215.
Hood, E. E., 210.
Hooe, Anne Frances, 478.
Hoof, J. H., 166.
Hoover, W. G., 289.
Hope, Matilda, 447.
Hoskinson, Rebecca, 415.
Hospital, established, 215-7.
Hounshell, David S., 44.
Hovey, Elken Thornburg, 502.
Hovey, Mame, 354.
Hovey, W. M., 502.
Hovey, William, 25.
Howard, Ann, 149.
Howard, H. R., 156.
Howell, A. C., 322.
Howell, Armistead B., 63.
Howell, Herbert L., 96.
Howes, M. L., 103.
Hoyt, John Lewis, 298.
Hubbard, Dana, 435.
Hubbard, Nath, 223.
Huddleston, Capt., 81.
Huff, Frank, 233.
Huff, Lilian, 355.
Huff, William, 326.
Huffman, J. W., 323.
Hughes, Belle Vinson, 506.
Hughes, James A., 507.
Hughey, Lillian Laidley, 352.
Hughey, William, 352.
Hull, James, 416.
Hull, Martin, 118, 373, 416.
Hull, Susan Buffington, 373, 416.
Humphrey, Elias, 287.
Humphreys, Andrew W., 434.
Humphreys, Eliza, 434.
Humphrey's Leonidas W., 434.
Humphreys, Mary E., 434.
Humphreys, Rose I., 434.
Humphreys, William J., 434.
Humphries, Lulu M., 476.

INDEX

Hunt, Rachael, 466.
Hunter, Charles W., 223.
Hunter, Henry, 17.
Huntington, Collis P., 125, 170, 171, 201, 209-10, 212, 213, 224, 267, 268, 296-7, 332-3, 387, 468.
Huntington, Harriet S., 387.
Huntington, Mary Lenora, 387.
Huntington, W. Va., 170-200; incorporated, 172; form of government, 172; police, 174; board of health, 175; water supply, 175; fire department, 175-9, 184, 207; charter amended, 186, 187, 193, 197; new charter, 199-200; political disturbances, 187-200.
Huntington state hospital, 168.
Hutchinson, Edward, 352.
Hutchinson, Elizabeth Love, 440.
Hutchinson, George W., 89.
Hutchinson, L. H., 281.
Hutchinson, R. L., 290.
Hutchinson, Virginia Field, 352.
Hutchinson, William, 253.
Hutson, John, 72, 73.
Hyman, Abe, 272.
Hyman, Miriam, 147.
Hyman, Sol, 272.
Hysell, James H., 88, 155.

I

Independent (newspaper), 201, 226.
Ingalls, George H., 221.
Ingalls, M. E., 50.
Ingersoll, F. M., 183.
Ingles, Mary, 2.
Ingram, George P., 207, 234.
Irwin, D. L., 103.
Isbell, L. D., 61, 246, 514.

J

Jack, R. A., 226.
Jacobs, F. H., 298.
Jaeger, Otto, 260.
James, Jesse, 180.
James, William, 141.
Jarrell, Boyd, 59.
Jarvis, George, 234.
Jarvis, John H., 207, 234.
Jefferson, Thomas, 130.
Jenkins, Albert Gallatin, 42, 77, 79, 82, 86, 87, 318, 319, 329, 417-8.
Jenkins, Charles McNutt, 417.
Jenkins, D. J., 66-7, 417.
Jenkins, Edith, 509.
Jenkins, Elizabeth Leete, 417.
Jenkins, Eustatia A., 417.
Jenkins, G. R., 417.
Jenkins, George, 419.
Jenkins, Grace, 417.
Jenkins, Harry W., 91.
Jenkins, Henrick A., 417.
Jenkins, Herman, 279, 281.
Jenkins, James Bowlin, 419.
Jenkins, Jennette A., 417.
Jenkins, Julia M., 417.
Jenkins, Julia Reed, 417.
Jenkins, Laura P., 417.
Jenkins, Margaret Virginia, 419.
Jenkins, Marguerite, 509.
Jenkins, Marshall L., 509.
Jenkins, Nellie Walton, 509.
Jenkins, Susan Holderby, 415, 417.
Jenkins, Susan M., 417.
Jenkins, Thomas J., 42, 63, 415, 417.
Jenkins, Virginia Bowlin, 419.
Jenkins, Walter, 509.
Jenkins, William A., 42, 119, 166, 167, 416, 417.
Jenkins, William G., 417.
Jenks, George A., 487.
Jenks, I. C., 104.
Jesse James robbery, 180.
Jewell, Jenny Linn, 357, 358.
Jimison, R. E., 277.
Johnson, Albert Lee, 441.
Johnson, Elizabeth A., 410.
Johnson, Flora Smith, 515.
Johnson, G. A., 170.
Johnson, George W., 448.
Johnson, Grace, 461.
Johnson, J. W., 305.
Johnson, Mary Catherine, 377.
Johnson, Mary Hinerman, 441.
Johnson, Mary McKendree, 448.
Johnson, Red, alias Charles Kitchen, 253.
Johnson, Sam W., 100, 391.
Johnson, Sampson, 100.
Johnson, W. H., 111.
Johnson, W. L., 170.
Johnson, Walker, 422.
Johnson, William, 100.
Johnston, Abner, 420.
Johnston, Albert, 420.
Johnston, Ann, 420.
Johnston, Archibald, 420.
Johnston, Bell, 420.
Johnston, Benjamin, 419, 420.
Johnston, Benjamin Franklin, 420.
Johnston, David E., 377.
Johnston, Eliza Kilgore, 420, 422.
Johnston, Emily, 420.
Johnston, Fannie, 420.
Johnston, Ida Sikes, 489.
Johnston, Isaac, 118.
Johnston, J. E., 281.
Johnston, James, 239, 308.
Johnston, John, 419.
Johnston, John L., 419.

INDEX

Johnston, Martha, 308, 420.
Johnston, Martha Logan, 419.
Johnston, Mary, 420.
Johnston, Mary Elizabeth, 391, 419.
Johnston, Mary Kennett, 420.
Johnston, Mary McCormick, 420.
Johnston, Melinda Kennett, 420.
Johnston, Minnie Gaefe, 420.
Johnston, Napoleon Bonaparte, 420.
Johnston, Pattie Taylor, 420.
Johnston, Rebecca Martin, 420.
Johnston, Sam, 489.
Johnston, Samuel Berry, 420.
Johnston, Samuel W., 118, 135, 422.
Johnston, Sara, 419.
Johnston, Sarah Damron, 420.
Johnston, Sarah Dundas, 420.
Johnston, Thomas, 420.
Johnston, William, 419.
Johnstone, Anne Frederick, 352.
Johnstone, Anni Laidley, 353.
Johnstone, Florence Mildred, 353.
Johnstone, Fred, 352, 353.
Johnstone, Grace Pugh, 353.
Johnstone, Lillian Laidley, 352.
Johnstone, Lynn, 353.
Johnstone, Mildred, 353.
Jones, Bob, 250.
Jones, E. Valentine, 312.
Jones, Frances Morris, 458.
Jones, John A., 144, 240, 281, 458, 459.
Jones, Levi, 187.
Jones, M. A., 177.
Jones, Richard Lord, 73.
Jordan, Eliza Gallaher, 391.
Jordan, Emma, 422.
Jordan, Jack, 277.
Jordan, John P., 135.
Jordan, Melinda Kilgore, 422.
Jordan, Robert, 422.
Jordan, Thomas Lee, 118, 391, 422.
Joy, Thomas, 43.
Justice, B. H., 325.

K

Kahler, Garnett Page, 469.
Kahler, W. F., 335.
Kahler, William F., 469.
Kahn, Lee, 306.
Kail, Adam, 421.
Kail, Andrew Jackson, 421.
Kail, Anna Copper, 421.
Kail, I. J., 137, 420-1.
Kail, Jane Hollandshead.
Kail, Joe, 421.
Kail, Julia Lindsay, 421.
Kail, Marilla Bovie, 421.
Kail, Mary, 421.
Kail, Matilda Hollandshead, 421.

Kail, Samuel Goodhue, 421.
Kail, Samuel Palmer, 420, 421.
Kearney, John J., 323.
Kearney, John P., 323.
Keating, John, 323.
Keck, Robert, 352.
Keck, Virginia Laidley, 352.
Keefe, William, 231.
Keeler, Anne Love, 442.
Keeler, David, 442.
Keeler, Harry, 442.
Keeler, Jane, 442.
Keenan, A. J., 53, 83.
Keenan, Clay N., 93.
Keenan, P. H., 331.
Keenan, Patrick, 20.
Keeney, Alma Haworth, 407.
Keeney, Alonzo T., 407.
Keeton, Justine, 484.
Keller, B. F., 193.
Keller, J. L., 120.
Kelley, Irene, 354.
Kelly, A. E., 253, 256.
Kelly, Heath, 236.
Kelly, Samuel, 152.
Kelly, Walter, 458.
Kelner, Lester, 306.
Kendle, C. W., 144, 261, 263.
Kennedy, Andrew, 294.
Kennett, John, 209, 229, 231.
Kennett, Mary Jane, 420.
Kennett, Melinda, 420.
Kenny, W. J., 159.
Kerr, A. H., 260.
Keyser, Andrew, 432.
Keyser, Arden P., 490.
Keyser, Dave Neal, 405.
Keyser, Esther, 432.
Keyser, Hester Spurlock, 491.
Keyser, Homer Lee, 405.
Keyser, James P., 491.
Keyser, Lois, 405.
Keyser, Lucile, 405.
Keyser, Lulu Hatfield, 405.
Keyser, Mona, 405.
Keyser, O. F., 405.
Keyser, Peggy Ruth, 405.
Kibbie, J. A., 301.
Kilgore, B. V., 423.
Kilgore, Betty Everett, 423.
Kilgore, C. W., 223, 423.
Kilgore, Clara Gillock, 423.
Kilgore, Eliza, 420, 422.
Kilgore, George, 422.
Kilgore, Hettie, 422.
Kilgore, Hettie Sanders, 422.
Kilgore, J. C., 423.
Kilgore, J. E., 423.
Kilgore, Jeremiah, 422.
Kilgore, Julia, 422.

Kilgore, Linie, 422.
Kilgore, Margaret McCormick, 449.
Kilgore, Martha, 422, 460.
Kilgore, Mary, 422.
Kilgore, Mary McCormick, 422-3.
Kilgore, Melinda, 422.
Kilgore, Nancy Fullerton, 422.
Kilgore, Nettie, 423.
Kilgore, Polly, 422.
Kilgore, Robert, 423.
Kilgore, Thomas, 20, 32, 326, 422.
Kilgore, Thomas W., 422-3, 449.
Kimbrough, Irene, 441.
Kinard, Mary, 460.
Kincaid, T. A. B., 324.
Kincaide, John, 420.
Kincaide, Martha Johnston, 420.
King, Carrie, 461.
King, E. J., 223, 224.
King, Norine, 372.
King, W. W., 301.
Kinney, G. R., 258.
Kinzer, J. W., 223.
Kirby, David, 164.
Kirk, George W., 242.
Kirk, J. S., 179.
Kirkpatrick, M. L., 66.
Kitchen, Charles, 253.
Kline, Thomas B., 245, 311.
Kneff, Ella, 140.
Knight, A. L., 349.
Knight, F. A., 336.
Knight, Irma Louise, 349.
Knight, John, 135.
Konig, Dorothea Louisa, 351.
Konig, Eliza, 351.
Konig, Frederick, 351.
Kuhn, W. S., 279.
Kump, H. G., 147.
Kyle, B. E., 425.
Kyle, Cecil, 425.
Kyle, Earl, 425.
Kyle, Edmund, 37, 48, 83, 119, 246, 424-5.
Kyle, Edmund Kelly, 425.
Kyle, Frank, 425.
Kyle, Hazel Byrd, 425.
Kyle, Ilda Montgomery, 425.
Kyle, Jemima Belle, 425.
Kyle, Marie, 425.
Kyle, Martha, 425.
Kyle, Mary Ann, 424.
Kyle, Mary Sophia, 425.
Kyle, Molly Baumgardner, 425.
Kyle, Nancy Shy, 425.
Kyle, Nellie, 425.
Kyle, Ona, 425.
Kyle, Robert, 423-4.
Kyle, Robert Thompson, 425.
Kyle, Roy, 425.
Kyle, Sarah West, 425.
Kyle, Sophia Thompson, 423.
Kyle, Stanard, 425.
Kyle, Stella Bumgardner, 425.
Kyle, Tate Russell, 425.
Kyle, Thomas, 42.
Kyle, Violet Thompson, 425.
Kyle, William, 425.
Kyle, William Galbraith, 425.

L

Lacey, Hugo, 312.
Lackland, Mattie, 394.
Lacock, Edward F., 102.
Lacy, Martha Jane, 478.
Laidlaw, see Laidley.
Laidley, Addie C., 409.
Laidley, Albert, 35-6, 64, 83, 118, 153, 170, 364, 427.
Laidley, Alberta, 364, 427.
Laidley, Amacetta, 427.
Laidley, Amelia Jo, 352.
Laidley, Anna, 352.
Laidley, Anna Beuhring, 351-2.
Laidley, Annie, 353.
Laidley, Bradford, 352.
Laidley, Bradford Dannenberg, Jr., 352.
Laidley, Clarence, 352.
Laidley, Cora Bradford, 352.
Laidley, Dick, 352.
Laidley, Dorothy Osborn, 370, 429.
Laidley, Douglas Scales, 370, 429.
Laidley, Eliza, 427.
Laidley, Elsie, 352.
Laidley, Emma Louisa, 352.
Laidley, Fannie Smith, 353.
Laidley, Florence, 352.
Laidley, Frances, 352.
Laidley, Frances Amelia, 352.
Laidley, Fredrick Alexander, 352.
Laidley, George, 154, 352.
Laidley, George Summers, 352, 427.
Laidley, Gladys Lanham, 352.
Laidley, Hannah Tamplin, 352.
Laidley, Harriet Corinne, 352.
Laidley, Helen M., 427, 497.
Laidley, Isabella, 409.
Laidley, James Grant, 427.
Laidley, James L., 425, 427.
Laidley, James Madison, 351-2.
Laidley, Jane Stewart, 425.
Laidley, Janet Scales, 370, 429.
Laidley, John, 20, 22, 24, 25, 33, 40, 71, 117, 133, 150, 151, 152, 153, 155, 170, 210, 303, 311, 316, 328, 363, 364, 366, 409, 425, 480.
Laidley, John B., 245, 246, 427.
Laidley, John James, 352.
Laidley, John W., 409.

INDEX

Laidley, Josephine, 352.
Laidley, Josephine Wilson, 352.
Laidley, Julia Rooke, 352.
Laidley, Juliette Shrewsbury, 353.
Laidley, Lillian, 352.
Laidley, Lillian Bradford, 352.
Laidley, Louise, 427.
Laidley, Lucy, 370, 428.
Laidley, Madelon Dannenburg, 370, 429.
Laidley, Madison Monroe, 353.
Laidley, Margaret, 352.
Laidley, Mary Beuhring, 352.
Laidley, Mary Elizabeth, 352.
Laidley, Mary Fontaine, 352.
Laidley, Mary Hite, 409.
Laidley, Mary Louisa, 369, 428.
Laidley, Mary Rogers, 352.
Laidley, Mary Rowena, 352.
Laidley, Mary Walton, 154.
Laidley, Rooke, 352.
Laidley, Salina C., 409.
Laidley, Sallie, 427.
Laidley, Sarah Osborne, 425.
Laidley, Theodore Beuhring, 370, 428.
Laidley, Thomas, 71, 425.
Laidley, Thomas M., 427.
Laidley, Ulysses, 427.
Laidley, Vesta Brown, 364, 427.
Laidley, Virginia Amacetta, 370, 428.
Laidley, Virginia Beuhring, 352.
Laidley, Virginia Brown, 369, 428.
Laidley, William Dannenberg, 352.
Laidley, William Sydney, 329, 332, 369, 370, 415, 427-8, 429.
Laidley case, 209-10.
Lallance, C. N., 233.
Lallance, John B., 233.
Lallance, M. F., 233.
Lallance, Margaret, 233.
Lallance, R. S., 233.
Lanahan, Alice Mary, 429.
Landing, John A., 282.
Lane, Areanna, 416, 429.
Lane, Eleanor, 429.
Lang, Christian, 435.
Lang, *see also* Long.
Langdon, Alice, 466.
Langdon, Elijah, 466.
Langfitt, S. E., 290.
Lanham, Gladys, 352.
Lattin, Charles, 29.
LaTulle, Victor, 294.
Law, Harriet Bell, 442.
Lawson, Ernest C., 114.
Lawton, J. W., 260.
Layne, Alice Lanahan, 429.
Layne, Carney M., 429.
Layne, Elizabeth White, 430.
Layne, Elmore, 430.

Layne, Eric L., 430.
Layne, Ernest, 430.
Layne, Garrett A., 430.
Layne, J. M., 184, 210.
Layne, Nancy Ellen, 429.
Layne, Nancy Ellen Truesdell, 429.
Layne, Nelson, 430.
Layne-Drummond, Ora, 430.
Layne, Robert, 430.
Layne, Sarah Fowler, 430, 431.
Layne, Stanley A., 430.
Layne, Thomas, 294.
Layne, William M., 429, 430.
Layne, Woodson, 430, 431.
Lea, John W., 312, 314.
Leadbetter, Mary, 392.
Lee, Fitzhugh, 221.
Lee, James M., 141, 143.
Lee, John, 286.
Leete, Elizabeth, 417.
Leftwich, F. C., 95.
Leftwitch, L., 306.
Lehman, M., 395.
Lehman, Ray Gideon, 395.
Lenoir, M. L., 479.
Lenz, George, 253.
Leonard, J. W., 112.
Le Sage, Flora Harrison, 400.
Le Sage, Francis J., 432.
Le Sage, Isaac Richard, 431-2, 434.
Le Sage, J. C., 186, 432.
Le Sage, Joseph A., 432.
Le Sage, Jules, F. M., 432.
Le Sage, Mary Bellemere, 432.
Le Sage, Mary Dovel, 432.
Le Sage, Mary Humphreys, 434.
Le Sage, Michael, 432.
Le Sage, Sophia Duval, 432.
Le Sage, William Dovel, 434.
Leslie, John, 72.
Lester, Fred W., 91, 103, 104, 106, 107.
LeTuttle, Victor, 331.
Levy, Joe, 306.
Lewis, A. M., 314.
Lewis, C. D., 396.
Lewis, Vergil A., 299, 399, 456, 457.
Lewis, Virgil, 130, 131, 132, 133, 299.
Lewis, Vivian Hall, 396.
Liggins, James (colored), 141.
Lightburn, 321.
Lillard, Elizabeth, 69, 376.
Lillard, John, 377.
Lillard, Nancy, 69.
Lillard, Thomas, 377.
Lincoln, Abraham, 394.
Lindbergh, Anne (Morrow), 203.
Lindemann, Edouard, 103.
Lindsay, Julia, 421.
Lindsey, Mary, 360.
Liquor licenses, 32-3.

Lloyd, J. H., 65.
Logan, Martha, 419.
Long, Al, 79.
Long, Ann Louise, 438.
Long, Ann Ratcliff, 438.
Long, Bernice Taylor, 500.
Long, Carolyn Westcott Whittington, 438.
Long, Cora Thompson, 437.
Long, Edward Christian, 435.
Long, Edward Harvey, 437, 439.
Long, Eloise Campbell, 438.
Long, Hilda Sheets, 439.
Long, Huey P., 437.
Long, Jennie Campbell, 377, 438.
Long, Jo-Harvey, 438.
Long, John Ratcliff, 438.
Long, John W., 500.
Long, Joseph, 435.
Long, Joseph Harvey, 246, 435-7.
Long, Luther Thompson, 437-8.
Long, Margot Maxwell, 438.
Long, Mary, 502.
Long, Mary Rebecca, 438.
Long, Paul Walker, 377, 437, 438-9.
Long, Phoebe Frazier, 438.
Long, Robert Dunbar Campbell, 438.
Long, Suzanne Hamilton, 438.
Longworth, Nick, 121.
Love, Agnes, 439.
Love, Allen, 100, 439.
Love, Anna Virginia, 441.
Love, Anne, 442.
Love, Annie, 440.
Love, Betty Jane, 441.
Love, C. A., 422.
Love, Charles, 70, 286, 439.
Love, Charles Henson, 440.
Love, Charles Marion, 342, 441, 442.
Love, Cynthia, 286.
Love, Cynthia Anne, 441.
Love, Cynthia Chadwick, 439.
Love, Daniel 27, 29, 286, 287, 439, 442.
Love, Ed, 422.
Love, Edward K., 441.
Love, Edward S., 440.
Love, Eliza, 286, 460.
Love, Eliza Morris, 460.
Love, Elizabeth, 286, 440.
Love, Elizabeth Ann, 439.
Love, Elizabeth Ekin, 440.
Love, Elizabeth Hampton, 439.
Love, Elizabeth Susan Frances, 440.
Love, Elizabeth Wardrop, 440.
Love, Ella, 441.
Love, Ella Skeens, 440.
Love, Erwin, 441.
Love, Eula, 441.
Love, F. Henson, 440.
Love, Francis Marion, 440.

Love, H. E., 439.
Love, Harry, 440.
Love, Helen Frances, 441.
Love, Irene, 441.
Love, Irene Kimbrough, 441.
Love, J. M., 223, 311.
Love, Jennie, 440, 442.
Love, John, 422, 441.
Love, John Allen, 439.
Love, John Erwin, 441.
Love, Katherine, 440.
Love, Katherine Bond, 440.
Love, Katherine McCleary, 440.
Love, L. L., 441.
Love, Lacy, 441.
Love, Leah Margaret, 439.
Love, Leonidas Louis, 441.
Love, Lewis A., 441.
Love, Llewellyn, 440.
Love, Lucretia Creth, 165.
Love, Lucy Temple, 442.
Love, Marian, 441.
Love, Mary, 439, 441.
Love, Mary Moore, 442.
Love, Mary Sweetland, 441.
Love, Minnie, 442.
Love, Minnie Moore, 441.
Love, Myrtle Steele, 440.
Love, Naomi, 442.
Love, Naomi Hale, 442.
Love, Peter E., 439.
Love, Richard, 440.
Love, Roland, 441.
Love, Sallie, 441.
Love, Sallie Virginia, 440.
Love, Samuel A., 441-2.
Love, Shelby Jackson, 440.
Love, Stuart Moore, 442.
Love, Susan, 286.
Love, Susanna, 439.
Love, Susanna Brame, 439.
Love, Susanna Childs, 439.
Love, Theodotius Alphonso, 441.
Love, Thomas Jefferson, 440.
Love, Virginia Stuart, 441.
Love, Washington Lafayette, 440.
Love, William, 286, 287, 439.
Love, William A., 286, 439, 460.
Love, William Liggon, 440.
Lovell, Betty Lewis, 355.
Lovell, Emma Beuhring, 355.
Lovell, Frances Beuhring, 355.
Lovell, Frederick Beuhring, 355.
Lovell, Howell, 355.
Lovell, Howell Lewis, Jr., 355.
Lovell, Mary Louisa, 355.
Lovell, May Rogers, 355.
Lovell, Virginia Lee, 355.
Lovet, H. T., 246, 251, 483.
Lovinus, A. G., 290.

Lowe, A. A., 297, 312.
Lowe, J. M., 312.
Lowe, Willis, 253.
Lowell, Benjamin Franklin, 372.
Lowell, Charles, 372.
Lowell, Mary Brown, 372.
Lowry, John, 233.
Lowther, M. P., 175.
Lunsford, Gordon, 289, 290.
Lusher, Fannie, 481.
Lusher, Irwin, 120.
Lusher, Johnson, 100.
Lusher, Sarah J., 485.
Lust, W. A., 289.
Lyon, Elizabth Harriet, 443.
Lyon, George Marshall, 442-3.
Lyon, Harriet Bell Law, 442.
Lyon, Marshall Allen, 442.
Lyon, Mary, 442.
Lyon, Natalie Sutherland, 443.
Lyon, Virginia Berkeley, 443.
Lyon, Theeta Searcy, 443.
Lyon, Virginia Sutherland, 443.
Lyons, Mary C., 334.
Lyons, W. A., 205.
Lyons, W. H., 91, 93, 102, 103, 221, 247, 249.

M

McAllister, Richard, 30.
McBride, W. G., 113.
McCain, Elizabeth Seamonds, 485.
MacCallister, E. M., 191, 246.
MacCallister, Josephine Morris, 461.
McCallister, Thomas, 98.
MacCallister, Wiliam, 461.
McCarty, John, 298.
McCarty, John Temple, 417.
McCleary, Katherine, 440.
McClintock, John D., 154, 308, 309.
McClung, J. D., 286.
McClung, Mary Jane, 292.
McClung, W. D., 168.
McCoach, J. M., 263.
McComas, A. C., 448.
McComas, Areanna Holderby, 410.
McComas, B. Curtis, 448.
McComas, Ballard, 100.
McComas, Benjamin J., 448.
McComas, Betty Curtis, 448.
McComas, David, 18, 447, 448.
McComas, Elisha W., 17, 20, 22, 27-9, 72, 74, 75, 76, 97, 99, 131, 316, 318, 326, 327, 410, 447-8.
McComas, George H., 246.
McComas, George J., 448.
McComas, Irene, 87, 448.
McComas, Isaac, 100.
McComas, James, 133, 448.
McComas, John, 72, 447.
McComas, Matthew, 448.
McComas, Rufus F., 448.
McComas, William, 27, 34, 97, 492.
McComas, William W., 318, 448.
McConihay, Ira T., 462.
McConihay, John, 462.
McConihay, Mary Morris, 462.
McConnell, Lucy B., 453.
MacCorkle, Alexander M., 166.
MacCorkle, W. A., 166.
McCormack, see McCormick.
McCormick, Armistead, 449.
McCormick, Charles, 449.
McCormick, David, 449.
McCormick, Eleanor, 449.
McCormick, Eli, 448.
McCormick, Eliza, 449.
McCormick, George, 449.
McCormick, Hester, 449.
McCormick, Isaac, 449.
McCormick, James, 423, 448, 449.
McCormick, Jane, 449.
McCormick, Jemima, 448.
McCormick, Joe, 243, 449.
McCormick, John, 308, 449.
McCormick, Levi, 20, 98, 449.
McCormick, Margaret, 449.
McCormick, Mary, 420, 422-3.
McCormick, Moses, 449.
McCormick, Patsy, 449.
McCormick, Sarah, 449.
McCormick, Walstein, 449.
McCown, W. B., 276.
McCoy, Anna Wiatt, 515.
McCoy, S. E., 514, 515.
McCue, W. W., 263.
McCullough, F. F., 48, 501.
McCullough, P. H., 65, 99, 152, 166, 170, 304, 318, 364, 501.
McCurdy, Azel, 195.
McDermitt, George M., 322.
MacDonald, Angus W., 371.
MacDonald, Elizabeth Brown, 371.
McDonoghan, Father, 294.
McDowell, Bennette B., 425.
McDowell, Henry, 425.
McDowell, John, 425.
McDowell, Marie Watts, 425.
McDowell, Pauline Damron, 425.
McDowell, Rachael Tompkins, 425.
McDowell, Valentine, 425.
McGinnis, A. B., 167, 303, 450, 502.
McGinnis, Achilles, 98.
McGinnis, Allen A., 20, 410, 450.
McGinnis, B. D., 40, 41, 46, 60.
McGinnis, Betty, 353.
McGinnis, Edmund, 20, 22, 131, 236, 416, 449-50.
McGinnis, Eliza Holderby, 303, 410, 450.

McGinnis, Elizabeth Thornburg, 502.
McGinnis, Eloise, 353.
McGinnis, Emma Beuhring, 353.
McGinnis, Ira J., 39, 40, 77, 209, 246, 353, 377, 450.
McGinnis, Ira J., Jr., 353.
McGinnis, James, 20, 449-50.
McGinnis, John B., 98, 99, 148.
McGinnis, John W., 303.
McGinnis, Kate Hite, 450.
McGinnis, Lyle, 353.
McGinnis, Mabel Chapman, 353.
McGinnis, Phyrus, 449, 450.
McGinnis, Sarah P., 450, 502.
McGlathery, Bertha, 503.
MacGregor, Ida Handley, 461.
McGregor, Mary, 355.
MacGregor, R. R., 461.
McGuire, W. C., 95.
McIntosh, George C., 229.
McIntosh, George R., 229.
McIntosh, R. E., 179.
McKeand, James, 422.
McKeand, Julia Kilgore, 422.
McKendree, Aaron F., 30, 99.
McKendree, Fannie, 461.
McKendree, George, 87, 168, 322, 448.
McKendree, Irene McComas, 448.
McKendree, Mary, 448.
McKendree, R., 120.
McKendree, William, 30, 490.
McKernan, *Father*, 294.
McLaughlin, Emma, 476.
McLaughlin, George Minor, 476.
McLaughlin, Hernando Ridgeway, 223, 476.
McLaughlin, James A., 476.
McLaughlin, Katherine Rolfe, 476.
McLaughlin, Lulu Humphries, 476.
McLaughlin, Mary Sue, 476.
McLaughlin, Nathan M., 88.
McLeod, R. M., 311.
McMahon, Emma, 334.
McMahon, J. R., 265.
McMahon, John, 79.
McMahon, William, 465.
McMaster, Josephine, 509.
McMasters, Laura, 460.
McMillen, A. J., 308, 481.
McMillen, America Samuels, 481.
McMillen, Archibald James, 408.
McMillen, Dolly, 480.
McMillen, Egede C., 408.
McMillen, Essie Haworth, 408.
McMillen, Herbert C., 94, 103, 104, 106.
McNeil, Dennis, 290.
McNeill, Asa, 484.
McNeill, Dolores Pearl, 484.
McNeill, Nancy Buckley, 484.

McNulty, Herman C., 96.
McNutt, Alexander, 416.
McNutt, Jeanette G., 416.
McNutt, Rachael Grigsby, 416.
McPherson, Joel, 125.
McWhorter, Henry C., 88.
McWilliams, R. W., 50.
Madison, James (Rev.), 141.
Madison, L. B., 304.
Maier, William, 146.
Maine, *Mrs.*, 149.
Mallory, Joseph E., 221, 245.
Mallory, S. F., 152.
Mallory, Sarah, 221.
Mallory, Victoria B., 221.
Mann, F. N., 264.
Mann, Jane, 388.
Mann, Sarah, 388.
Mansfield, America F., 99.
Mansfield, Columbia L., 99.
Mansfield, John Fletcher, 99.
Mansfield, Joseph Jefferson, 99, 318.
Mansfield, Joseph Jefferson, Jr., 99.
Mansfield, William L., 99.
Marchetti, Frank, 239, 240.
Marcum, Emma Wellman, 445.
Marcum, Fannie Williams, 462.
Marcum, James H., 246, 462.
Marcum, J. Roy, 446, 486.
Marcum, Jane Dameron, 444.
Marcum, John S., 246, 444-5-6, 485, 486.
Marcum, Joseph, 63.
Marcum, Lace, 246, 445, 486.
Marcum, Martha, 446.
Marcum, Stephen, 444.
Marcum, Thomas D., 444.
Marcum, W. W., 48, 50.
Marlin, John, 487.
Marlin, Kate Dougherty, 487.
Marlin, Silas J., 487.
Marr, B. W., 231, 249.
Marshall, Martha, 376.
Marshall, Norman F., 314.
Marshall academy, *see* Marshall college.
Marshall college, 33, 44, 132, 135, 140, 149, 150-63, 165, 240, 270, 304, 307, 308, 309, 311.
Marston, R. B., 137.
Martin, A. P., 265.
Martin, Anna Barbara, 388.
Martin, Annie E., 446.
Martin, Dorothy Maxine, 446.
Martin, George, 156.
Martin, George B., 364.
Martin, Joseph A., 446.
Martin, Rebecca, 420.
Martin, William Marshall, 245, 446.
Mason, C. R., 125.

INDEX 573

Mason, George, 130.
Mason, George W., 151, 409.
Mason, Mary, 154.
Mason, Salina C. Laidley, 153, 154, 155, 409.
Mather, Cotton, 348.
Mather, Francis Louise, 348.
Mather, Increase, 348.
Mather, Oscar, 321.
Mather, Richard, 348.
Mather, V. W., 209.
Mathews, Alice Haworth, 408, 409.
Mathews, David E., 57, 60, 187, 246, 408-9.
Mathews, H. E., 102, 212, 281.
Mathews, John, 17.
Mathews, R. A., 203, 210.
Mathews, S. V., 242.
Matthews, Mary Ann, 396.
Matthews, Sam, 396.
Maupin, Albert B., 166, 447.
Maupin, Alice, 140, 447.
Maupin, Betty, 447.
Maupin, Beverly W., 447.
Maupin, Chapman W., 447.
Maupin, Fannie, 447.
Maupin, Henry B., 22, 99, 166, 415, 447.
Maupin, Lucinda Smith, 447.
Maupin, Lucy, 447.
Maupin, Martha Holderby, 447.
Maupin, Margaret, 447.
Maupin, Matilda Hope, 447.
Maupin, Mildred, 447.
Maupin, S. A., 447.
Maupin, Shelby, 447.
Maupin, Thomas, 446-7.
Maupin, William L., 447.
Mauze, J. Layton, 309.
Maxon, Sarah, 479.
May, C. W., 409.
May, W. F., 65.
Mayo, M. L., 167.
Mays, James, 98.
Meade, William, 72.
Medley, J. F., 152, 303.
Mee, C. B., 311.
Meehling, Charles P., 53.
Meehling, Matilda, 53-5.
Meek, Amy Kirk, 450, 452.
Meek, Charlie Burgess, 452.
Meek, Edward, 450.
Meek, Howard Ferguson, 452.
Meek, John Burgess, 452.
Meek, John Henry, 419, 450-2.
Merrill, Emma E., 498.
Merrill, Joseph C., 88.
Merritt, Jane, 308.
Merritt, Larose, 71.
Merritt, Melchor, 287.

Merritt, Thomas J., 39, 40.
Merritt, William, 17, 40, 326.
Meshel, Fred, 324.
Methodist church, 299-306.
Methodist Episcopal church, 300-3.
Methodist Episcopal church, South, 303-4.
Mexican war, 75-6.
Meyerson, Ed, 306, 359.
Michie, Thomas, 485.
Michie, T. L., 246, 394.
Middleton, J. E., 102.
Middleton, Lillian, 488.
Midkiff, Solomon, 29.
Midkiff, Valkey W., 94, 107.
Militia system, 97-101.
Millender, C. F., 205, 210.
Miller, Annie Curtis, 454.
Miller, Belle H., 453.
Miller, Bessie, 454.
Miller, Catherine Wiseman, 453.
Miller, Charles F., 453.
Miller, Charles H., 163.
Miller, Christian, 453.
Miller, Christian S., 453.
Miller, Dollie, 454.
Miller, Eliza Gardner, 453.
Miller, Erskine, 229.
Miller, Eugenia, 149, 454.
Miller, Fannie, 353, 474.
Miller, Florence G., 453, 454.
Miller, Florence Tice, 454.
Miller, Frederick, 163, 452.
Miller, G. D., 305, 453.
Miller, George F., 29, 56, 209, 210, 215, 236, 246, 250, 305, 451-3, 454.
Miller, H. H., 81, 120, 152, 327, 328, 329, 502.
Miller, Hannah C., 453.
Miller, J. C., 258.
Miller, J. G., 120.
Miller, Jacob, 303, 327.
Miller, James I., 453.
Miller, James S., 46.
Miller, John, 453.
Miller, John C., 96.
Miller, John W., 88, 454.
Miller, Joseph S., 40, 48, 453, 454.
Miller, Josephine, 366.
Miller, Lavalette, 454.
Miller, Lee, 454.
Miller, Leonore, 503.
Miller, Lucy McConnell, 453.
Miller, Margaret, 453, 502.
Miller, Margaret Ann, 441.
Miller, Mary, 453.
Miller, Mary Samuels, 453, 481.
Miller, Mary Shelton, 453.
Miller, Mayme, 471.
Miller, R. H., 336.

INDEX

Miller, Samuel A., 44.
Miller, Sophia Clendenin, 453.
Miller, Thomas F., 454.
Miller, William Clendenin, 27, 29, 120, 453, 454, 480.
Mills, grist, 61-5.
Milton, W. Va., 340-1.
Minor, Ann, 482.
Miser, A. J., 89.
Mitchell, Arthur P., 175, 186.
Mitchell, E. T., 139, 170, 172, 186.
Mitchell, Fred O., 109.
Mitchell, Isaac H., 172, 174, 175, 181-3.
Mittenthal, Meyer, 266.
Molter, Adolph, 233.
Molter, Conrad, 233.
Molter, Lewis, 233, 236.
Molter, William C., 233.
Moncure, J. D., 311, 312.
Monroe, C. A., 309.
Montgomery, Ilda, 425.
Mooney, Jim, 242, 243.
Moore, Aaron, 329.
Moore, C. P. T., 455.
Moore, Addie Marion, 454.
Moore, Elizabeth, 386.
Moore, Frederick, 22.
Moore, Harriet Prentice, 455.
Moore, Isabella Laidley, 409.
Moore, James E., 96.
Moore, Joseph Hallock, 455-6.
Moore, Laban T., 294, 472.
Moore, Lillian, 396.
Moore, Lou, 149.
Moore, Martin, 149.
Moore, Mary T., 500.
Moore, Minnie Elizabeth, 441.
Moore, Priscilla Belknap, 456.
Moore, Samuel Everett, 149.
Moore, Sarah Everett, 149.
Moore, Stella, 500.
Moore, Thomas Waterman, 249, 409, 454-5, 456.
Moore, Vincent Morgan, 454.
Moore, William, 500.
Moore, William B., 20.
Moore, Wilson B., 42, 83.
Morehead, J. A., 260.
Morgan, Daniel, 98.
Morris, Abigail Scales, 457.
Morris, Addison Ferd, 461-2.
Morris, Albert, 461.
Morris, Albert A., 461.
Morris, Anna, 460.
Morris, Arthur A., 460.
Morris, Benjamin, 458, 459.
Morris, Beauregard, 461.
Morris, Calvary, 98, 456.
Morris, Carrie King, 461.
Morris, Carroll, 458, 459.

Morris, Charles, 461.
Morris, Charles K., 42, 422, 460.
Morris, Charlie R., 460.
Morris, Edmund, 17, 70, 286, 316, 326, 456, 457, 459.
Morris, Edna, 460.
Morris, Edna E., 461.
Morris, Edward, 97, 286, 461.
Morris, Electra Spurlock, 491.
Morris, Eliza, 460.
Morris, Eliza Love, 460.
Morris, Elizabeth, 456, 458, 459.
Morris, Elizabeth Stipes, 456.
Morris, Ellen, 460.
Morris, Em Gwinn, 460.
Morris, Emma Barrett, 461.
Morris, Eugene, 461.
Morris, Eva, 461.
Morris, Fannie, 460, 461.
Morris, Fannie McKendree, 461.
Morris, Fenton, 459, 505.
Morris, Florence, 462.
Morris, Frances, 458, 495.
Morris, Frances Simms, 459.
Morris, George, 461.
Morris, Gertrude, 462.
Morris, Gouvernor, 311.
Morris, Grace Smith, 249.
Morris, Guy Leland, 460.
Morris, Harry, 461.
Morris, Helen Russell, 461, 479.
Morris, Henry, 458, 459.
Morris, Ida, 460.
Morris, James, 461.
Morris, James E., 462.
Morris, James R., 42, 461, 479.
Morris, John, 22, 63, 70, 100, 133, 286, 325, 456, 458, 459-60.
Morris, John O., 460.
Morris, Joseph, 461.
Morris, Joseph W., 42, 460, 461, 479.
Morris, Josephine, 461.
Morris, Joshua, 458, 459.
Morris, Lena, 460.
Morris, Leonard, 458, 459.
Morris, Letha, 460.
Morris, Letha Richardson, 460.
Morris, Levi, 456, 458, 459, 491.
Morris, Lucy, 459.
Morris, Lucy Chinn, 461.
Morris, Margaret, 286.
Morris, Margaret Droddy, 456.
Morris, Martha Kilgore, 422.
Morris, Mary, 459, 460.
Morris, Mary Everett, 460.
Morris, Mary Jane, 462.
Morris, Mary Kinard, 460.
Morris, Mary Rebecca, 460.
Morris, Mary S., 462.
Morris, Mildred, 460.

INDEX 575

Morris, Miriam, 456.
Morris, Myrtle Ayres, 460.
Morris, Nancy, 459.
Morris, Olive Hite, 460.
Morris, Russell, 462.
Morris, Russell Love, 460.
Morris, Sallie, 461.
Morris, Sallie Spurlock, 496.
Morris, Sarah Hansford, 459.
Morris, Sarah Russell, 460, 479.
Morris, Sidney, 461.
Morris, T. H., 259.
Morris, Thomas, 459.
Morris Thomas Asbury, 70, 97, 98, 148, 299, 300, 456-8, 482.
Morris, Thomas L., 461.
Morris, Walter T., 461.
Morris, William, 456, 458, 459, 495, 496.
Morris Harvey college, 163-4.
Morrison, Ann Ward, 463.
Morrison, L. C., 95, 167.
Morrison, Malinda Hensley, 463.
Morrison, Nancy, 463.
Morrison, P. H., 463.
Morrison, Sallie, 491.
Morrow, Anne, 203.
Morrow, Dwight, 159.
Morrow, James E., 159, 203, 309.
Morrow, John, 480.
Moses, Fannie, 360.
Moss, C. D., 167.
Moss, Randolph, 167.
Moss, V. R., 42.
Mossman, Dan A., 210, 212, 239, 241, 253.
Mowers, Elden B., 315.
Mulcahy, Timothy, 294.
Mullen, Hugh, 294.
Mullinix, W. M., 301.
Murphy, Frank, 167.
Murphy, James, 167, 334, 336.
Murray, E. A., 223.
Murrill, Edwin L., 108.
Muster rolls (1812-to date), 528-49.
Myers, B. R., 104.
Myers, John D., 167.

N

Naglee, Benjamin, 462.
Naglee, Ellen, 462.
Naglee, Frank, 462.
Naglee, Hannah, 308, 462.
Naglee, Joseph, 308, 462, 512.
Naismith, Edith, 372.
Napier, P. H., 452.
Nash, America Payne, 462-3.
Nash, Ann Herndon, 463.
Nash, Charles A., 189, 249.
Nash, Clifton, 463.
Nash, Ethel, 463.
Nash, Frances Gillette, 462.
Nash, Gus, 463.
Nash, Herbert G., 503.
Nash, James, 463.
Nash, James J., 462.
Nash, John, 462.
Nash, Josephine Thornburg, 503.
Nash, Nancy Morrison, 463.
Nash, T. Henry, 30, 51, 195, 463.
Nash, Thomas Jefferson, 462-3.
National defense act, 107, 109, 112.
Neal, Albert Gallatin, 464.
Neal, Alice E., 464.
Neal, Alice Langdon, 466.
Neal, Andrew Dickinson, 464.
Neal, Bernard Gale, 466.
Neal, Charles Henry, 464.
Neal, Elliott, 466.
Neal, Eunice Earp, 465.
Neal, George Ira, 51, 102, 186, 187, 199, 217, 246, 247, 290, 341, 463-4, 465.
Neal, Irene, 465.
Neal, James, 464.
Neal, John M., 464.
Neal, Joseph Guthrie, 466.
Neal, Leonard B., 93, 466.
Neal, Malinda Newman, 464.
Neal, Margaret Ann, 465.
Neal, Mary Brammer, 466.
Neal, Susan Witten, 465.
Neal, Thomas J., 466.
Neal, Thomas Witten, 466.
Neal, Virginia, 465.
Neal, William Elmer, 93, 465.
Neal, William Leonard, 466.
Neff, Eliza E., 396.
Neff, G. W., 318, 319.
Neff, Henry Clay, 396.
Neff, Hiram Ellis, 396.
Neff, Jacob, 396.
Neff, Jane M. Ellis, 396.
Negley, James, 118.
Nelson, Alex C., 415.
Nelson, Betty Jane, 508.
Nelson, C. P., 508
Nelson, James, 312.
Nelson, Lucy Holderby, 415.
Nevill, B. L., 103, 465.
Neville, Margaret Neal, 465.
Newall, Nettie, 146.
Newberry, Jeff, 258, 306.
Newcomb, James F., 295.
Newcomb, W. H., 86, 141, 228, 303.
Newhall, Hester M., 373.
Newman, Bettie, 306-7.
Newman, Elizabeth, 363.
Newman, Harry, 236.
Newman, Joseph, 224, 287.

576 INDEX

Newman, Malinda, 464.
Newman, Mit, 65.
Newman, Peyton, 26.
Newman, Russell, 464.
Newman, Sarah Harbour, 464.
News, The (newspaper), 435-6.
Newspapers, 201, 205, 210, 226, 228, 229, 240, 435-6.
Nicholson, George J., 261.
Nicholas, Wilson Cary, 5.
Nickel, Katherine, 482.
Nickell, Iva Morton, 476.
Nickell, James Minor, 476.
Nickell, Mary McLaughlin, 476.
Nickell, Morton Carol, 476.
Norman, James, 77.
Northcott, Elliott, 186, 199, 246, 247.
Northcott, G. A., 215, 236, 237, 241, 250, 315.
Norvell, George W., 258.
Norvell, John E., 95.
Nouning, James, 149.
Nowery, Annie Wilson, 517.
Nowery, C. H., 517.
Nowery, Jo, 517.
Nowery, Margery, 517.
Nurnberger, Jemima Kyle, 425.
Nurnberger, William, 425.
Nutter, Olin C., 137.

O

Oakley, C. M., 223.
O'Brien, Gordon, 246.
Odd Fellows, 203.
O'Dell, Robert, 290.
Ohev, Sholom, 306-7.
Ogden, Herschel C., 435.
Ohlinger, Ella, 516.
Ohlinger, Henry, 516.
Old field school, 130, 138.
Oil, 66-7.
Oley, John Hunt, 86, 89, 140, 141, 172, 201, 209, 311, 312, 314, 466-7-8.
Oley, Rachael Hunt, 466.
Oley, Simon Van Antwerp, 466.
Ona, W. Va., 342.
O'Neal, R. P., 294.
O'Neil, R. L., 250.
O'Neill, Tom, 207, 234.
Oney, James K., 141, 179, 184, 186, 210, 249, 251, 391.
Oney, Robert T., 203.
Oney, Willie Gallaher, 391.
Ong, Elizabeth, 26.
Ong, Isaac, 77, 303, 331.
Ong, John, 331.
Oppenheim, Samuel, 307.
Origin, 1-7; original survey, 3; first settlers, 4, 8-9.
Osborne, Alice Stevens, 366.
Osborne, Anna Matilda, 366.
Osborne, Benjamin Brown, 366.
Osborne, Ethan Brown, 366.
Osborne, James Robert, 366.
Osborne, John, 366.
Osborne, Josephine, 366.
Osborne, Josephine Brown, 366.
Osborne, Josephine Miller, 366.
Osborne, Maria Mitchell, 366.
Osborne, Mary Elizabeth, 366.
Osborne, Robert, 366.
Osborne, Sara Josephine, 366.
Osborne, Sarah, 425.
Osborne, Sydney, 366.
Osborne, Virginia Alberta, 366.
Osborne, Virginia Wolgamuth, 366.
Overstall, Eliza Russell, 479.
Overstall, Fred, 479.
Owens, Bob, 335.
Owens, William, 514.

P

Pack, Blanche Freeman, 390.
Pack, James A., 390.
Page, Eloise, 469.
Page, Florence Bristol, 469.
Page, Garnett, 469.
Page, George S., 279, 281, 334, 386, 468-9.
Page, J. H., 334.
Page, Mann, 468.
Page, Nighbert Smith, 469.
Page, Pearl, 469.
Page, Robert, 468.
Page, Thomas Nelson, 393.
Paine, Ann, 470.
Paine, Betsy Russell, 479.
Paine, Charles, 148.
Paine, Charles Wesley, 470.
Paine, Elizabeth Russell, 469.
Paine, Ella, 470.
Paine, Fannie, 470.
Paine, Geoffrey, 470.
Paine, Henry B., 470.
Paine, John, 470.
Paine, Sarah, 470, 480.
Paine, Sid, 470.
Paine, Thomas, 470.
Paine, Uriah, 82.
Paine, William, 117, 148, 165, 303, 456, 469, 470, 479.
Palmer, A. B., 140, 301.
Palmer, T., 179.
Palmer, T. C., 301.
Pancake, Daniel Jefferson, 470.
Pancake, Ella Teays, 470.
Pancake, Isaac, 470.
Pancake, John Teays, 470.
Pancake, Kenna, 470.
Pancake, Madge, 470.
Pancake, Mary Taylor, 470.

INDEX 577

Pancake, Paul Clinton, 470.
Pancake, Stella, 470.
Paris, Treaty of, 1763, 2.
Parker, Allen, 112.
Parker, Granville, 36, 328.
Parker, Nancy Russell, 479.
Parker, R. M., 244.
Parker, Samuel, 479.
Parker, Walter M., 137.
Parrish, James, 42.
Parsons, C. F., 177, 201, 231, 297.
Parsons, H. Chester, 89, 297, 298, 344, 345, 346.
Parsons, Nellie C., 297.
Parsons, W. E., 231.
Parsons, Warren J., 344.
Patton, Jacob Harris, 151.
Paul, Hugh, 397.
Paxton, John C., 86.
Payne, America, 462.
Peabody funds, 141.
Pearsall, Jennie, 488.
Peck, John N., 151.
Peirce, Jesse Pindell, 298.
Pendleton, Edmund, 393.
Pendleton, Priscilla, 410.
Pennybacker, John M., 170, 209-10.
Pennybacker, N. H., 201.
Pennybacker, Sarah H. G., 209-10.
Pepper, R. H., 167.
Perry, B. L., 103.
Peterkin, George W., 312, 314, 392.
Peters, Ceres Samuels, 481.
Peters, David, 481.
Peters, Ethel, 481.
Peters, William L., 329.
Peterson, James J., 246, 436.
Petit, N. C., 229.
Pettis, Charles S., 164.
Pew, Mary Love, 441.
Pew, Shelba Glenn, 441.
Pew, W. C., 441.
Peyton, Albert H., 94.
Peyton, Angus Eugene, 371.
Peyton, Briscoe W., 371.
Peyton, Henry, 71.
Peyton, Homer, 71.
Peyton, James Frederick Brown, 371.
Peyton, Jennie, 474.
Peyton, Katherine Woodbridge, 371.
Peyton, Ora, 354.
Peyton, Ruth Brown, 371.
Peyton, T. W., 25, 102, 245, 247, 445, 486, 502.
Phelps, John M., 88.
Phelps, Joseph M., 88.
Phelps, Minerva Parke, 478.
Phelps, Nettie M., 478.
Phelps, Oliver, 88.
Philippine insurrection, 92-3.

Phillipson, David, 307.
Physicians, first in Cabell county, 165-7.
Pickering, G. L., 197.
Pierpont, Francis H., 35, 36.
Pierson, J. W., 306.
Pilcher, C. T., 223.
Pine, Albert, 64.
Pine, Alexander, 471.
Pitman, Arthur Loring, 353.
Pitman, James Eskew, 353.
Pitman, Mary Eskew, 353.
Plymale, A. G., 322.
Plymale, John, 42.
Poage, Ann Gallaher, 308, 391.
Poage, Anna, 471.
Poage, Edgar, 471.
Poage, George B., 152, 471.
Poage, Harry, 170.
Poage, James Harvey, 118, 135, 152, 172, 184, 203, 308, 328, 391, 449, 471.
Poage, Jemima McCormick, 308, 449, 471.
Poage, Josiah B., 151, 308, 453, 471.
Poage, Mary Miller, 453.
Poage, Mayme Miller, 471.
Poage, R. C., 391, 471.
Poage, Sarah, 471.
Poage, Sarah Gallaher, 391, 471.
Poage, William, 118, 308, 471.
Poindexter, C. W., 336.
Poindexter, Carl, 335.
Poindexter, Chal, 335.
Point, W. W., 384.
Polan, Evelyn Broh, 360.
Polan, Harry, 360.
Pollard, Fannie Johnston, 420.
Pollard, George E., 108.
Pollard, John, 420.
Pollock, L. A., 252.
Polsley, D. N., 156.
Porter, Bill, 334.
Poteet, Henry, 163.
Poteet, Henry C., 42.
Potter, Lynda Jeanne, 361.
Potts, J. N., 90, 234, 236, 287, 290, 407.
Powell, J. B., 151.
Powell, R. G., 110.
Powell, William H., 319.
Pratt, William P., 88.
Presbyterians, 307-9.
Preston, Fae, 391.
Prettyman, Wesley, 301.
Price, William, 98, 120.
Prichard, Edward, 354.
Prichard, Frances Davis, 354.
Prichard, Fred C., 165.
Prichard, K. C., 215.
Prichard, Lewis, 165.

578 INDEX

Prichard, Louise Beuhring, 354.
Prichard, Thomas J., 167, 215.
Prichard school, 165.
Prickett, W. B., 219.
Priddie, B. L., 102.
Prindle, R. S., 144.
Procter, Lydia M., 297.
Prohibition, 32-3.
Protestant Episcopal church, 309-15.
Public school sytsem, 133-4, 150.
Pugh, Grace, 353.
Purcell, Charles W., 448.
Purcell, Margaret McComas, 448.

Q

Quillan, John, 405.
Quillan, Mona Hatfield, 405.
Quirk, Thomas A., 180, 294, 471-2-3.

R

Rader, J. E., 167, 215.
Radford, Elizabeth, 395.
Radio station WLBH, 109.
Ragland, Nick, 223.
Raine, Anna Laidley, 352.
Raine, Anne Laidley, 352.
Raine, Edwin E., 352.
Ramey, R. E., 114.
Ramsdell, Z. D., 125.
Randall, E. B., 297.
Randall, E. E., 297, 301.
Randall, Sarah E., 297.
Randall, T. B., 297.
Randolph, Mary Morris, 460.
Rardin, Dorothy Ann, 361.
Ratcliff, Ann Louise, 438.
Ratcliff, Bessie, 356.
Ratcliff, George F., 89, 377.
Ratcliff, John, 438.
Ratcliff, William, 494.
Ratcliffe, John F., 226, 355.
Ratliff, Jennie, 377.
Ratliff, Nancy Frazier, 377.
Rau, John, 250.
Ravencroft, Lucille, 372.
Ray, Isiah, 135.
Reaser, H. C., 282.
Rece, Abia, 20, 286.
Rece, Allen, 70, 286, 287.
Rece, Edmund, 27.
Rece, Edmund C., 100.
Rece, Edna Morris, 460.
Rece, Elizabeth, 286.
Rece, John Calvin, 286, 287.
Rece, Mary, 286.
Rece, Milton, 340.
Rece, Morris, 287.
Rece, T. Heber, 460.
Rece, W. L., 290.
Reece, Warren P., 42.

Reed, Julia M., 417.
Reinwald, August C., 94, 108.
Restored government of Virginia, 35;
    constitutional convention, 36-7.
Revolution, Soldiers of, 70-3.
Reynolds, Gertrude Morris, 462.
Reynolds, James, 319.
Reynolds, James J., 462.
Rice, Harold A., 137, 147.
Rice, Heber H., 94, 107.
Richardson, Billy, 223.
Richardson, Frank H., 60.
Richardson, Letha, 460.
Richeson, Joseph, 377.
Richey, Emily Mather, 348.
Richmond, Alice N., 473.
Richmond, George, 474.
Richmond, J. L., 473-4.
Richmond, Lelia Snyder, 474.
Richmond, W. A., 473.
Ricketts, A. G., 92, 474.
Ricketts, Charles H., 91-2, 102, 474.
Ricketts, Cora, 474.
Ricketts, Ed. Merrill, 474.
Ricketts, Eleanor Compton, 474.
Ricketts, Elijah, 81, 474.
Ricketts, Ella, 474.
Ricketts, Fannie Miller, 474.
Ricketts, G. R., 474.
Ricketts, George Henry, 474.
Ricketts, Girard C., 152, 166, 242, 331, 474.
Ricketts, Jennie Peyton, 474.
Ricketts, Joe, 474.
Ricketts, John E., 474.
Ricketts, John G., 474.
Ricketts, Lucien C., 48, 81, 87, 311, 445, 474.
Ricketts, Sarah Eleanor, 474.
Ricketts, Virginia Everett, 306, 474.
Ridenour, Lester, 91.
Riggleman, Leonard, 164.
Ritter, C. L., 251, 269.
Ritz, Mary Billups, 356.
Ritz, Oliver, 356.
Roach, Leon L., 112.
Road system, 115-20.
Roberts, Columbus, 286.
Roberts, Isaac, 72.
Roberts, Jones, 100.
Roberts, Thomas, 72.
Rockwell, Eva Morris, 461.
Rockwell, Frank S., 461.
Roe, L. M., 205.
Roffe, Charles L., 42, 99, 152.
Roffe, Lewis, 27.
Rogers, C. N., 108.
Rogers, David, 36.
Rogers, Ella, 485.
Rogers, Emma Holderby, 415.

INDEX

Rogers, James H., 415.
Rogers, John, 326.
Rogers, Mary, 352.
Rogers, May, 355.
Rogers, Phillip, 289.
Rogers, W. C., 328.
Rolfe, Agnes Love, 439
Rolfe, Ann, 476.
Rolfe, Augusta, 476.
Rolfe, Charles L., 475.
Rolfe, Charles R., 223, 476.
Rolfe, Ida, 476.
Rolfe, Ingram, 439.
Rolfe, Katherine, 476.
Rolfe, Mary Ruffner, 475.
Rolfe, Sue, 476.
Rollins, Adonijah W., 88.
Romer, I. B., 266.
Rooke, Julia, 352.
Rose, Gettie, 359.
Rose, Solomon, 359.
Roseberry, Flora Ann, 514.
Roseberry, John, 514.
Rosebury, A. J., 281.
Rosenheim, W. S., 212.
Ross, Hall, 191.
Ross, Robert, 42.
Roster of officers and soldiers (1812-to date), 528-49.
Roster of officials, 522-7.
Rouse, J. H., 81, 82-3, 166.
Rowe, Bunia Billups, 355.
Rowe, Mat, 355.
Rowe, W. D., 167.
Rowland, George, 167, 175.
Roy, Joseph E., 296-7.
Royal, W. W., 305.
Rucker, Mary Love, 439.
Ruff, R. H., 164.
Ruffner, Ann Hedrick, 475.
Ruffner, Charles, 475.
Ruffner, Daniel, 475.
Ruffner, Joseph, 475.
Ruffner, Mary E., 475.
Ruffner, Mary Jackson, 168.
Ruffner, Mary Steinman, 475.
Ruffner, Peter, 475.
Russel, Albert, 478.
Russel, Albert Lacy, 476, 478.
Russel, Anne Hooe, 478.
Russel, Caroline Collier, 478.
Russel, John Hooe, 203, 209, 210, 215, 229, 231, 251, 278, 281, 312, 476, 478.
Russel, Martha Lacy, 478.
Russel, Mary Ellen, 478.
Russel, Minerva Phelps, 478.
Russel, Nettie Phelps, 478.
Russell, Albert, 470, 480.
Russell, Alice, 480.
Russell, Benjamin Henry Harrison, 480.
Russell, Betsy, 479.
Russell, Daniel, 479.
Russell, Dolly McMillan, 480.
Russell, Don, 267.
Russell, Edmund, 480.
Russell, Eliza, 479.
Russell, Elizabeth, 469, 480.
Russell, Elizabeth Brown, 479.
Russell, Esther Dean, 480.
Russell, Frank, 479.
Russell, Hallie Everett, 386.
Russell, Helen M., 461, 479.
Russell, Henry Clay, 386.
Russell, Henry Louis, 480.
Russell, Hugh Everett, 386.
Russell, Hugh L., 386.
Russell, Jeffrey, 72, 117, 479, 480.
Russell, John, 117, 373, 479.
Russell, M. Lenoir, 479.
Russell, Marian, 479.
Russell, Mark, 20, 73, 81, 97, 117, 131, 326, 391, 427, 479-80.
Russell, Nancy, 479.
Russell, Patty, 479.
Russell, Phillip, 480.
Russell, Polly Dean, 480.
Russell, Rebecca Buffington, 373, 479.
Russell, Romaine, 479.
Russell, S. M. E., 83.
Russell, Samuel Mark (minister), 331.
Russell, St. Mark, 152, 303, 480.
Russell, Sarah A., 460, 461, 479.
Russell, Sarah Dean, 480.
Russell, Sarah Maxon, 479.
Russell, Sarah Paige, 470.
Russell, Sarah Paine, 480.
Russell, Tate, 425.
Russell, Theodore, 480.
Russell, Thomas A., 479.
Russell, Thomas Lewis, 479.
Russell, Wesley, 480.
Russell, William, 479.
Rust, Hattie, 516.
Rutherford, Robert, 72, 480.

S

Sabel, I. H., 91, 103, 104, 105.
Saint Cloud, W. Va., 344.
Salmon, Joel Kellogg, 46, 384.
Salmon, Martha Blake, 384.
Salmon, Roxie Orelia, 384.
Salt Rock, W. Va., 343.
Sample, James T., 184.
Sampson, Alice Maupin, 447.
Sampson, George, 223, 447.
Samuels, A. H., 77, 481.
Samuels, America, 481.
Samuels, Ceres, 481.

INDEX

Samuels, Emily Gardner, 453, 480.
Samuels, Fannie Lusher, 481.
Samuels, Henry J., 18, 88, 99, 156, 157, 311, 318, 328, 481.
Samuels, James, 397.
Samuels, John, 20, 120, 131, 133, 150, 316, 427, 454, 480, 481.
Samuels, Joseph, 75, 76.
Samuels, Lafayette, 481.
Samuels, Mary, 480.
Samuels, Mary Eugenia, 453, 481.
Samuels, Mary Garden, 481.
Samuels, Nettie, 481, 502.
Samuels, Rebecca Bartram, 481.
Samworth, Alice Blackwell, 481.
Samworth, Elizabeth Hall, 481.
Samworth, F. W., 276, 481.
Samworth, Fred W., 481.
Samworth, Henry, 481.
Samworth, Leonard, 481.
Samworth, Robert, 481.
Sanborn, Chester, 143.
Sanborn, L. D., 175.
Sanborn, Paul H., 114.
Sanders, Anne Gwinn, 422.
Sanders, Hettie, 32, 422.
Sanders, Martha, 32.
Sanders, Sampson, 20, 24, 32, 63, 120, 316, 420, 422.
Sanders, William, 422.
Sandman, Dorothea, 354.
Sandridge, Justine Keeton, 484.
Sandridge, Reubens, 484.
Sands, H. V., 167.
Sang, R. A., 103.
Sartin, Lucy, 430.
Saul, J. R., 277.
Sault, Ste. Marie, 1.
Saunders, E. T., 167.
Saunders, Mike, 318.
Saunders, Nida, 146.
Savage, John, 2-3, 380.
Savage grant, 2-3, 300, 518-521; owners, 521.
Sayre, Howell Lovell, 355.
Sayre, J. William, 355.
Sayre, Mary Lovell, 355.
Sayre, Wilhelma, 355.
Scales, Abigail, 299, 457, 482.
Scales, Ann Minor, 482.
Scales, Elizabeth, 482.
Scales, James, 482.
Scales, Jency, 357, 482.
Scales, Mary, 482.
Scales, Mary Frances, 481.
Scales, Mary Scales, 482.
Scales, Matilda, 364, 365, 482.
Scales, Nancy, 373, 482.
Scales, Nathaniel, 71, 118, 299, 364, 481.
Scales, Noah, 20, 97, 326.
Scales, Peter, 427, 482.
Scales, Sally, 482.
Scales, Sarah, 409, 482.
Scanlon, Timothy S., 184, 210, 212, 236, 247, 267, 295.
Scheneburg, John B., 135, 294.
Scherr, Arnold C., 482, 483.
Scherr, Barbara, 482.
Scherr, Betty, 482.
Scherr, Gertrude Arnold, 483.
Scherr, Harry, 452, 482.
Scherr, Joseph, 483.
Scherr, Katherine Nickel, 482.
Scherr, Rosa Wall, 482.
Schonthal, Dez. C., 252, 307.
Schonthal, Joseph, 252, 307.
School system, 130-8.
Schroeder, J. Bert, 470.
Schroeder, Stella Pancake, 470.
Scorill, Miss, 151.
Scott, Anna Pauline, 484.
Scott, Anna Whitten, 484.
Scott, Catherine Sullivan, 375.
Scott, Dolores McNeill, 484.
Scott, Flora, 140.
Scott, Hugh Bartlett, 484.
Scott, James, 375.
Scott, Jane, 375.
Scott, Leah Love, 439.
Scott, Paul W., 246, 247, 483-4.
Scott, S. M., 439.
Scott, S. W., 303.
Scott, Sanford, 331.
Scranage, George, 201, 202.
Seamonds, Alfred, 470, 485.
Seamonds, Andrew J., 485.
Seamonds, Ann Paine, 470.
Seamonds, Charles, 485.
Seamonds, Elijah G., 484-5.
Seamonds, Elizabeth, 485.
Seamonds, Ephriam, 484.
Seamonds, "Gal," 485.
Seamonds, George R., 485.
Seamonds, Jim, 485.
Seamonds, John, 485.
Seamonds, Kate, 485.
Seamonds, Lucy, 485.
Seamonds, Maggie, 485.
Seamonds, Mary, 485.
Seamonds, Mary M., 404, 485.
Seamonds, Nancy Harshbarger, 485.
Seamonds, Nannie, 485.
Seamonds, P. H., 485.
Seamonds, Randolph M., 485.
Seamonds, Sarah Lusher, 485.
Seamonds, Susan, 485.
Seamonds, Susie L., 485.
Seamonds, William, 485.
Seamonds, William H., 404, 485.

INDEX

Seamonds, William R., 485.
Searcy, Theeta Carrington, 443.
Seashols, John, 165.
Seashols, Lucretia Love, 165.
Sebaugh, F. D., 263.
Sebrell, John P., 462.
Sebrell, Mary Morris McConihay, 462.
Secession, Ordinance of, 34-5.
Sedinger, James D., 79, 331, 334, 335.
Sedinger, Stoney, 335.
See, Elizabeth Morres, 458.
Sehon, Edmund, 240, 241, 315.
Seiber, W. M., 295.
Seiber, William, 322, 323.
Serey, James, 286.
Selby, A. D., 141.
Sexton, Schuyler, 177, 223.
Shackelford, Elizabeth Pendleton, 393.
Shackelford, John, 393.
Shafer, J. S., 144.
Shank, Bob, 58.
Sharitz, Seldon, 191.
Shaw, D. Blain, 164.
Shawkey, Morris P., 159.
Shearer, J. M., 309.
Sheets, Calvin, 354.
Sheets, Elinore Hawkins, 354.
Sheets, Hilda, 439.
Shelley, George L., 454.
Shelley, Lavalette Miller, 454.
Shelor, Daniel, 383-4.
Shelor, Elizabeth, 383.
Shelor, Lawrence, 384.
Shelor, William, 383-4.
Shelton, Anna Poage, 471.
Shelton, Anthony, 453.
Shelton, Charles, 42.
Shelton, Henry W., 99, 100, 101.
Shelton, Jerome, 99, 100.
Shelton, John, 42.
Shelton, Joseph R., 471.
Shelton, Mary M., 453.
Shepherd, Ella Rogers, 485.
Shepherd, Thomas B., 485.
Shepherd, Thomas Rogers, 246, 290, 445, 485-6.
Sheppard, John A., 251.
Shinn, Asa, 299.
Shively, John W., 267.
Shoffstall, Arthur Marlin, 488.
Shoffstall, Arthur Scott, 255, 256.
Shoffstall, Elizabeth Jane Harmon, 486.
Shoffstall, Jennie Pearsall, 488.
Shoffstall, Josiah, 486-8.
Shoffstall, Lillian Isobel, 488.
Shoffstall, Lillian Middleton, 488.
Shoffstall, Mary Jane, 488.
Shore, George L., 103.
Shore, Robert, 103, 203, 205.
Short, Dudley, 355.
Short, Marion, 355.
Short, Samuel, 20.
Short, Wilhelma Sayre, 355.
Shortridge, Elizabeth Love, 439.
Shortridge, George, 397, 398.
Shortridge, Malinda, 397.
Shy, Ben, 485.
Shy, Mary Seamonds, 485.
Shy, Nancy, 425.
Sievers, Lewis S., 102.
Sights, Godfrey, 42.
Sikes, Austin M., 94, 106, 489.
Sikes, Clara Frazier, 489.
Sikes, George H., 489.
Sikes, Glenn Austin, 489.
Sikes, Helen Louise, 489.
Sikes, Herbert A., 489.
Sikes, Ida M., 489.
Sikes, Janet N., 489.
Sikes, John J., 488.
Sikes, Levi, 488.
Sikes, Lillie Byus, 489.
Sikes, Mamie K., 489.
Sikes, Maude, 489.
Sikes, Minerva Williams, 489.
Sikes, Robert, 489.
Sikes, Thomas, 89, 174-5, 179, 322, 488-9.
Silver, Abba Hillil, 307.
Simmons, Calwellsy, 42.
Simmons, John, 74, 98, 326, 489.
Simmons, Mary Frances, 166-7, 509.
Simmons, Polly Kilgore, 422.
Simmons, Rachael, 501.
Simmons, William, 422, 489, 509.
Simms, A. M., 286, 287.
Simms, Frances, 459.
Simms, Henry C., 141, 179, 184, 245, 246, 249, 251, 267.
Simon, Ethel Peters, 481.
Simons, Lewis, 108.
Simple, John, 98.
Simpson, John, 143.
Sipple, Emma, 356.
Skeens, Ella, 440.
Skelton, Amie, 249.
Skinner, Leonard, 88.
Slater, Nancy Lee, 354.
Sliger, Thomas J., 205.
Sloan, Humpy, 335.
Sloan, J. M., 309.
Smiley, Samuel, 74, 98.
Smith, A. E., 468, 515.
Smith, Amanda, F., 99.
Smith, Ballard, 17.
Smith, Benjamin, 509.
Smith, Benjamin H., 150.
Smith, C. W., 245.
Smith, Crawley, 329.

582 INDEX

Smith, D. B., 290.
Smith, D. I., 40, 46, 48, 51, 52, 180, 209, 246, 300, 334, 427, 453.
Smith, Dan Veron, 146.
Smith, Dave, 223.
Smith, David, 300.
Smith, Dudley D., 300.
Smith, Ed, 300, 332.
Smith, Elizabeth, 509.
Smith, Emily Cordelia, 469.
Smith, Emmet, 515.
Smith, Eugene, 352.
Smith, Fannie, 353.
Smith, Flora, 515.
Smith, G. T., 265.
Smith, Hannah Miller, 453.
Smith, J. M., 41.
Smith, James, 77.
Smith, John, 98, 331.
Smith, L. Roy, 272.
Smith, Lizzie, 143.
Smith, Louise, 515.
Smith, Lucinda, 447.
Smith, Luther, L., 509.
Smith, Mark, 509.
Smith, Mary Walton, 509.
Smith, Nicholas, 334.
Smith, Percival S., 120, 300, 327, 328.
Smith, Richard, 509.
Smith, Robert, 515.
Smith, Sallie Wiatt, 515.
Smith, Tom P., 515.
Smith, Warren C., 515.
Smith, Wiatt, 335, 336, 515.
Smith, William G., 88.
Smith, Winifred, 515.
Snider, Earl Bailey, 370, 429.
Snider, Janet Laidley, 370, 429.
Snider, John Andrew, 370, 429.
Snider, William Sydney Laidley, 370, 429.
Snow, C. P., 212.
Snyder, Lelia Burgess, 474.
Solter, H. C., 415.
Solter, Sadie Holderby, 415.
Southworth, A. S. J., 441.
Southworth, Aileen Davis, 441.
Southworth, Andy F., 90, 184, 223, 243, 290.
Southworth, Louis Sweetland, 441.
Southworth, Mary Love, 441.
Spalding, George R., 110.
Spanish-American war, 91-2, 103.
Spence, T. E., 261.
Spencer, Dollie Miller, 454.
Spencer, Earl, 454.
Spencer, John W., 88.
Spencer, W. S., 51, 463.
Spilman, H. E., 66.
Spillman, B. D., 91.

Spitler, M. M., 323.
Sproul, Hazel Hatfield, 403.
Sproul, J. R., 403.
Spurlock, Abigail, 491.
Spurlock, America, 492.
Spurlock, Arma, 491.
Spurlock, Burwell, 42, 491, 492-5, 512.
Spurlock, Cassandra, 491.
Spurlock, Cassia, 491.
Spurlock, Charles, 496.
Spurlock, Cynthia Booker, 491.
Spurlock, Daniel, 98, 119, 496.
Spurlock, Electra, 491.
Spurlock, Frances Morris, 495.
Spurlock, Francis A., 491.
Spurlock, George, 496.
Spurlock, Hester Ann, 491.
Spurlock, Hurston, 42, 491.
Spurlock, Jeff, 496.
Spurlock, Jesse, 20, 22, 131, 489-90, 491.
Spurlock, John S., 496.
Spurlock, Leander, 491.
Spurlock, Leatha, 491.
Spurlock, Levi, 491.
Spurlock, Martha Ann, 495.
Spurlock, Mary, 492.
Spurlock, Mero, 491.
Spurlock, Milton, 491.
Spurlock, Nancy, 496.
Spurlock, Nancy Amos, 490.
Spurlock, Nancy Garrett, 491.
Spurlock, Bebecca Booten, 491.
Spurlock, Rebecca Davis, 491.
Spurlock, Roxanna, 491.
Spurlock, Sallie, 496.
Spurlock, Sallie Morrison, 491.
Spurlock, Sanders, 491.
Spurlock, Sarah Harber, 489-90.
Spurlock, Stephen, 490-1.
Spurlock, Stephen Marshall, 491.
Spurlock, Wesley, 491.
Spurlock, William, 97, 98, 491, 495.
Staats, Charles P., 503.
Staley, Alice Burks, 496-7.
Staley, Calvin, 496.
Staley, Daniel, 496.
Staley, Elizabeth, 308.
Staley, Jacob, 496.
Staley, Michael, 496.
Staley, Joseph, 496.
Staley, Mary, 501.
Staley, Stephen, 496.
Staley, W. M., 186.
Stanard, Eliza Jane, 373.
Starcher, Clare, 442.
Starcher, Elizabeth, 442.
Starcher, Jennie Love, 442.
Starcher, Robert, 442.
Stark, Graham, 405.

Stark, Lois Keyser, 405.
Starr, William C., 88.
State normal school, 154-63.
State university, 135.
Statts, Coleman A., 377.
Statts, Nan Campbell, 377.
Staunton, E. W., 375.
Staunton, Florence Buffington, 375.
Steel, William, 68, 72.
Steele, Myrtle, 440.
Steele, N. E., 277.
Steele, William, 299.
Steinman, Mary, 475.
Stenger, J. W., 294.
Stephens, John, 72, 73.
Stephenson, Calvary, 470.
Stephenson, Mary Paige, 470.
Stephenson, Vint, 329.
Sterling, W. D., 143.
Stern, Cornelia Anne, 370, 428.
Stern, Elizabeth Jane, 370, 429.
Stern, Jo Lane, 370, 428.
Stern, Josephine Lane, 370, 428.
Stern, Lewis Henry, 370, 428.
Stern, Louise Beuhring, 370, 428.
Stern, Lucy, Laidley, 370, 428.
Stern, Margaret Carper, 370, 428.
Stern, Virginia Laidley, 370, 429.
Sternberger, Leon, 306.
Stevens, Alice Waugh, 366.
Stevens, Leo, 277.
Stevens, Pat, 112.
Stevenson, Bernice, 500.
Stevenson, James, 500.
Stevenson, Jerusha, 500.
Stevenson, John, 72.
Stevenson, John B., 96, 199, 268, 278, 347.
Stevenson, Mary Abbott, 347.
Stewart, A. F., 189, 223.
Stewart, Burgess, 303.
Stewart, Columbia A., 415.
Stewart, Ella Billups, 356.
Stewart, George, 253.
Stewart, H. O., 287.
Stewart, J. F., 151.
Stewart, J. L., 356.
Stewart, Jennie, 64.
Stewart, Robert, 148, 287.
Stipes, Elizabeth, 456.
Stoddard, Hattie, 311.
Stokes, Miranda, 400.
Stokey, William P., 110.
Stookey, A. E., 464.
Stookey, Alice Neal, 464.
Storrs, James H., 297.
Stowaser, Henry, 163.
Stratton, Edward, 383.
Stratton, John Hampton, 383.
Stratton, Mary Ann Turner, 383.

Street railways, 274-6.
Stribling, Robert, 77.
Stringer, Mary, 503.
Strupe, Melchor, 70.
Stuart, Arthur S., 108.
Stuart, Herbert, 108.
Stuart, John, 501.
Stuart, Thomas F., 167.
Stuart, Virginia, 441.
Stuart, Virginia Taylor, 501.
Stump, J. L., 167.
Sutphin, James G., 210.
Suitor, J. K., 85, 121, 191, 247, 334.
Suitors test act, 38; repealed, 47.
Sullivan, C. M., 152.
Sullivan, Peter, 72.
Summers, Amacetta Laidley, 427.
Summers, George W., 18, 29, 101, 150, 318, 427.
Summers, H. E., 363.
Summers, Lewis, 17.
Summerson, Ann Wayne, 465.
Summerson, Charles H., 53, 334, 386, 465.
Summerson, Charles W., 329.
Summerson, Nettie, 386.
Sutherland, Howard, 443.
Suydam, Abraham, 311.
Swann, Benjamin, 286, 287.
Swann, Ethel, 517.
Swann, Fred, 405.
Swann, Freda, 405.
Swann, Jane, 405.
Swann, Jimmy, 405.
Swann, Louise, 405.
Swann, Mary Hatfield, 405.
Swann, P. H., 167, 328.
Swann, Patty Lou, 405.
Swann, Ralph, 405.
Swann, Robert, 405.
Swann, Rosalie, 405
Swann, T. A., 517.
Swann, Thomas, 287.
Swann, William, 405.
Sweetland, Mary Hester, 441.
Swint, John J., 295, 347, 471.
Switzer, Clymer, 497.
Switzer, E. C., 149.
Switzer, Ellen Doolittle, 497.
Switzer, Emma Merrill, 498.
Switzer, Henry, 497.
Switzer, Jonathan, 63, 149, 497.
Switzer, Nathan, 497.
Switzer, Ona Handley, 440.
Switzer, Rufus, 92, 149, 199, 246, 268, 269, 497, 498-9.
Switzer, Vera, 497.
Switzer, Virginia, 497.
Symington, J. H., 298.

T

Talbott, Patrick, 165.
Talley, C. C., 223.
Tanner, J. C., 223.
Tamplin, Hannah, 352.
Tarlton, Sarah, 71.
Tate, Lee, A. D., 305, 306.
Tauber, Bernhardt, 241, 334.
Taylor, Anne, 400.
Taylor, Bernice, 500.
Taylor, Bernice Stevenson, 500.
Taylor, Bill, 207.
Taylor, Charles Henry Kennon, 354, 499.
Taylor, Charles Trueheart, 95, 168, 189, 215, 500.
Taylor, Dorothy Frantz, 354.
Taylor, Elinore, 354, 501.
Taylor, Harvey Carter, 354, 500, 501.
Taylor, Harvey Carter, Jr., 354.
Taylor, James, 499.
Taylor, Jane, 500.
Taylor, John, 223, 400, 501.
Taylor, John Wallace, 354.
Taylor, Kennon, 501.
Taylor, Lady, 501.
Taylor, Margery, 501.
Taylor, Maria Trueheart, 499.
Taylor, Marjery Trueheart, 354.
Taylor, Martha Field, 499.
Taylor, Mary Martha, 470.
Taylor, Miranda Stokes, 400.
Taylor, Nancy, 500-1.
Taylor, Nancy Beuhring, 354.
Taylor, Nannie Hawkins, 354, 500.
Taylor, Pattie, 420.
Taylor, Powhatan, 500.
Taylor, Ruth Frances, 399, 400.
Taylor, Stella Moore, 500.
Taylor, Thomas Wallace, 60-1, 90, 195, 197, 245, 499-500.
Taylor, Virginia, 501.
Taylor, Wallace, 500.
Taylor, William, 500.
Teachers, 147-50.
Teays, Ella Hatcher, 470.
Teays, James Stephens, 470.
Teays, Thomas, 470.
Telgener, Emil, 135.
Templeton, C. Foster, 94, 106, 107.
Terrell, C. H., 223, 303.
Terwillinger, Charles, 502.
Terwillinger, Roberta Thornburg, 502.
Thackston, Eugenia Miller, 149, 454.
Thackston, Benjamin H., 51, 141, 149, 151, 159, 453, 454.
Thom, Alfred E., 308.
Thom, Mary, 308.
Thomason, J. D., 253.

Thompson, A. F., 261.
Thompson, Addison, 259.
Thompson, C. L., 515.
Thompson, C. W., 305.
Thompson, Cameron L., 90, 246, 311, 314, 315.
Thompson, Cora Hildeth, 437.
Thompson, Hannah Niblack, 437.
Thompson, Harley H., 108, 109.
Thompson, Henry Arnold, 437.
Thompson, J. E., 276.
Thompson, John, 79.
Thompson, John K., 193.
Thompson, Philip Rootes, 25.
Thompson, R. N. B., 100.
Thompson, Samuel R., 33, 157.
Thompson, Sophia, 423.
Thompson, Violet, 425.
Thompson, William, 135.
Thompson, William Rootes, 51, 246.
Thompson, William T., 59-60, 246.
Thornburg, A. M., 289.
Thornburg, Addie, 503.
Thornburg, Bailey, 481.
Thornburg, Bertha McGlathery, 503.
Thornburg, Caroline Handley, 503.
Thornburg, Catherine, 503.
Thornburg, Charles, 502.
Thornburg, Charles Irvin, 503.
Thornburg, Charles William, 306, 335, 503.
Thornburg, Claude, 502.
Thornburg, Collins T., 503.
Thornburg, E. H., 503.
Thornburg, Elizabeth, 502.
Thornburg, Ellen E., 502.
Thornburg, Emma, 501.
Thornburg, Emma Fox, 502.
Thornburg, Ephriam, 501.
Thornburg, George E., 320, 502.
Thornburg, Gertrude Casto, 502.
Thornburg, H. M., 287.
Thornburg, H. O., 336, 501.
Thornburg, Hezekiah, 501, 503.
Thornburg, Howard, 502.
Thornburg, J. L., 64, 305, 471, 502.
Thornburg, James Harvey, 503.
Thornburg, John, 502.
Thornburg, John D., 503.
Thornburg, John Griffin, 502.
Thornburg, John W., 119, 450, 501, 502.
Thornburg, Josephine, 503.
Thornburg, Josephine Harris, 503.
Thornburg, Leonore Miller, 503.
Thornburg, McCullough, 503.
Thornburg, M. S., 48, 501, 503.
Thornburg, Margaret Miller, 453, 502.
Thornburg, Marie Arnold, 503.

INDEX

Thornburg, Mary, 502.
Thornburg, Mary Long, 502.
Thornburg, Mary Samuels, 481.
Thornburg, Mary Staley, 501.
Thornburg, Mary Stringer, 503.
Thornburg, Moses, 481.
Thornburg, Nancy Wilson, 502.
Thornburg, Nettie Samuels, 481, 502.
Thornburg, Norma Wright, 503.
Thornburg, Paul L., 503.
Thornburg, Prudence Collins, 501.
Thornburg, R. Starr, 94, 501.
Thornburg, Rachael, 501.
Thornburg, Rachael Crawford, 503.
Thornburg, Rachael Simmons, 501.
Thornburg, Robert E., 502.
Thornburg, Roberta, 502.
Thornburg, Ruth, 503.
Thornburg, Sarah McGinnis, 450, 501.
Thornburg, Solomon, 20, 22, 27, 120, 501, 502.
Thornburg, Thomas, 22, 43, 47, 99, 133, 156, 157, 318, 320, 321, 328, 453, 501, 502, 503.
Thornburg, Victoria, 503.
Thornburg, Virginia Handley, 502.
Thornburgh, Thomas Bailey, 502.
Thornton, Grayson D., 66.
Thurman, Turner, 26.
Tice, Florence, 454.
Tiernan, Amand Buffington, 373.
Tiernan, Michael, 373.
Tims, Robert, 167.
Tinsley, J. G., 258.
Titus, I. R., 197, 209.
Titus, W. P., 179.
Tobacco production, 65-6.
Todd, John G., 259.
Tomlinson, W. H., 46.
Tompkins, Rachael, 425.
Toney, Fred, 324.
Toney, James, 99.
Toney, Jesse, 97, 462.
Trent, Nannie B., 400.
Trent, W. W., 400.
Trice, Cora, 143.
Trippe, Harry M., 110.
Truesdell, Christopher Columbus, 430.
Truesdell, Columbus, 430, 431.
Truesdell, James, 430, 431.
Truesdell, Nancy Ellen, 429.
Truesdell, Sarah Williams, 430.
Trueheart, Charles Scott, 499.
Trueheart, Maria L., 499.
Trueheart, Virginia Crump, 499.
Tueck, Oscar, 213.
Turley, James, 71.
Turner, C. W., 195.
Turner, Mary Ann, 383.
Turner, Scott, 186.
Turner, Thomas, 100.
Turner, Tom C., 181-3.
Turner, William, 81, 86, 88.
Turney, R. W., 223.
Tyler, Roger, 146.
Tyler, Roger S., 315.
Tynes, Achilles James, 504.
Tynes, Buford Cleveland, 504-5.
Tynes, Harriet Fudge, 504.
Tyree, Frank H., 189, 191, 247.

U

Ullman, W. A., 261.
Ulmon, W. A., 234.
Unconditional union convention, 37.
Underwood, E. M., 172.
Underwood, Enoch, 20, 27.

V

Vaich, H., 466.
Valentine, Hallie, 415.
Valentine, John W., 129, 226, 228, 250, 268.
Vallandingham, P. A., 137.
Van Bibber, C. O., 240.
Vancleve, H. C., 221.
Vandiver, James H., 33.
Van Fleet, A. F., 103.
Van Metre, Robert S., 108.
Varnum, Ann Cole, 474.
Varnum, Leander, 474.
Vaught, S. K., 152.
Veitegures, Edward G., 83.
Verlander, James E., 91, 102, 103, 104, 105.
Verlander, James W., 207, 229, 295.
Via, H. O., 229.
Vickers, R. E., 167, 215, 217, 251.
Vinson, Bennett Clay, 166-7, 509.
Vinson, Betty Nelson, 508.
Vinson, Charles C., 509.
Vinson, Clara Grace, 509.
Vinson, Fannie, 422.
Vinson, Frances V., 509.
Vinson, Ida Belle, 506.
Vinson, James, 507.
Vinson, James A., 509.
Vinson, Josephine, 507.
Vinson, Lindsay T., 506.
Vinson, Lulu Maud, 509.
Vinson, Lynn Boyd, 507.
Vinson, Mary, 507.
Vinson, Mary Chafin, 508.
Vinson, Mary Damron, 507.
Vinson, Mary Simmons, 166-7, 509.
Vinson, Polly, 505.
Vinson, Rhoda Sperry, 507.
Vinson, Samuel Sperry, 505-7.
Vinson, Taylor, 506, 507-8.
Vinson, Tennessee, 507.

INDEX

Vinson, W. S., 233, 393.
Vinson, William, 507, 509.
Vinson, William Sampson, 509.
Vinson, Zachary Taylor, 246, 250, 274, 507, 508.
Vinton, Harriet, 406.
Virginia, colony, organized, 1.
Virginia state government, division of, 34-6.
Vose, Charles L., 263.

W

Wade, T. S., 163.
Wagoner, Mary, 383.
Wahrheit, Kate, 460.
Waldron, William H., 92, 96, 112, 209.
Walker, Aaron, 297.
Walker, Charles E., 496.
Walker, Charles Swann, 297-8.
Walker, Marion, 335.
Walker, Matthew, 512.
Walker, S. L., 105.
Walker, William Parkinson, 207, 286, 287-8, 290.
Wall, J. O., 139, 167, 172, 174, 175, 201.
Wall, Rosa L., 482.
Wallace, C. M., 234.
Wallace, Champe C., 510.
Wallace, Charles Irving, 510.
Wallace, Elizabeth, 510.
Wallace, Frances, 510.
Wallace, Frances Gibson, 392, 510.
Wallace, George, 510.
Wallace, George E., 226.
Wallace, George Seldon, 51, 60, 92, 94-5, 105, 106, 107, 112, 392, 510.
Wallace, H. A., 282-3.
Wallace, Hugh, 510.
Wallace, Jesse, 510.
Wallace, John, 510.
Wallace, Margaret, 510.
Wallace, Maria Sclater, 510.
Wallace, Peter, 510.
Wallace, Porter W., 148-9, 510.
Wallace, Taliaferro, 510.
Wallace, Thomas, 510.
Wallace, Washington, 510.
Wallace, William, 510.
Wallace, William F., 179, 226, 228.
Walsh, David, 294.
Walter, E. H., 42.
Walton, Clara Vinson, 509.
Walton, Daniel Porter, 509.
Walton, David, 509.
Walton, Elsie, 509.
Walton, Ethel Vinson, 509.
Walton, Frances Richmond, 509.
Walton, Francis Henry, 509.
Walton, Grace Maud, 509.
Walton, John, 509.
Walton, Josephine McMaster, 509.
Walton, Lawrence Johnson, 509.
Walton, Martha, 509.
Walton, Martha Allen, 508.
Walton, Mary, 154, 509.
Walton, Mary Martha, 509.
Walton, Nellie, 509.
Walton, Thomas, 509.
Walton, Vinson Oliver, 509.
Walton, William, 508-9.
Walton, William Bennett, 509.
Walton, William O., 489, 508, 509.
Wambaugh, Eugene, 112.
War between the states, 77-90.
War of 1812, 74.
Ward, Ann, 463.
Ward, Evermont, 25, 26, 47, 53-5, 377, 444, 514.
Ward, George, 22.
Ward, Jeremiah, 24, 286, 409.
Ward, Margaret, 286.
Ward, Robert C., 103.
Ward, Thomas, 17, 22, 97, 343, 448.
Wardrop, Elizabeth, 440.
Ware, Felix H., 201, 203.
Warner, A. W., 245.
Warner, C. J., 152.
Warren, G. D., 83.
Warth, H. C., 61.
Waterways, 120-4.
Watt, H. E., 279.
Watters, H. C., 425.
Watters, Mary Kyle, 425.
Watts, C. W., 241, 263.
Watts, Marie, 425.
Waugh, Eustatia Jenkins, 417.
Waugh, L. V., 242.
Waugh, Pembroke, 417.
Wayne, Tom, 105.
Weaver, William J., 287.
Webb, H. G., 224.
Webb, Joe, 223.
Webb, Nancy, 511.
Webb, Paul L., 108.
Webb, R. T., 164.
Webb, Robert, 511.
Webb, Susannah, 511.
Webb, Thomas J., 180.
Weiler, Frank, 265.
Weiler, James J., 265.
Welch, C. S., 241.
Welch, W. T., 207.
Wellington, Noah, 300, 303.
Wellington, Taylor, 247, 334.
Wellman, Bennett, 511.
Wellman, Betty Gene, 511.
Wellman, Clyde Anderson, 510.
Wellman, Emma, 445.
Wellman, Hope, 355.

INDEX 587

Wellman, Ida Billups, 355.
Wellman, John, 511-12.
Wellman, John D., 445.
Wellman, Laban T., 512.
Wellman, Mahala Scott, 512.
Wellman, Martha Ann Walker, 510.
Wellman, Martha Edkins, 445.
Wellman, Mary Eleanor, 511.
Wellman, Mary Frances, 355.
Wellman, Mary Werth, 511.
Wellman, May Mulligan, 511.
Wellman, Nancy Webb, 511.
Wellman, Robert, 512.
Wellman, Robert Lee, 510.
Wells, Abner, 383.
Wells, Debora Sidwell, 383.
Wells, Elizabeth Shelor, 383.
Wells, Erna, 143.
Wells, Herb, 335.
Wells, Job Sidwell, 383.
Wells, L. W., 446.
Wells, Martha Marcum, 446.
Wells, Mary Jane, 383.
Wells, May, 446.
Wells, O. H., 336.
Welsh, Thomas, 167, 175.
Wentz, Pomp, 121.
Werninger, A. W., 212, 237, 239, 252.
Werninger, John Walter, 294, 296, 347, 512-13.
Werninger, Rebecca, 512.
Werninger, William, 512.
Werth, Cora Cornelia Minter, 511.
Werth, John, McRae, 511.
Werth, Mary Virginia, 511.
West, Samuel, 299.
West, Sarah, 425.
West Virginia, admission to Union, 37; organization of government, 36-38; constitution of 1872, 48; railroads authorized, 125; state university 135.
West Virginia asylum, 168.
West Virginia colored children's home, 168.
West Virginia home for aged and infirm colored men and women, 168.
West Virginia industrial home, 168-9.
West Virginia normal industrial school for colored orphans, 168.
Wetzel, D. D., 167.
Wetzel, Daniel, 114.
Wetzel, William B., 88.
Whalen, M. J., 263.
Whaley, K. V., 82, 83.
Wheeler, Joseph C., 82, 88, 331.
Wheeling conventions, 34-5, 36, 37.
Whieldon, W. W., 305.
Whitaker, Annie Dickinson, 372.
Whitaker, Benjamin Brown, 372.

Whitaker, Brown, 372.
Whitaker, Edward A., II, 372.
Whitaker, Sallie Brown, 372.
White, A. B., 346.
White, A. G., 83.
White, Anna, 354.
White, David, 430, 431.
White, Elizabeth Jane, 430.
White, Henry F., 137.
White, I. C., 402.
White, Sarah, 378.
White, Winnie Garlic, 430.
Whitney, A. M., 120, 327, 331.
Whitteker, Emma Laidley, 352.
Whitteker, Eugene Smith, 352.
Whitteker, Grace Williams, 352.
Whitteker, Henry, 352.
Whitteker, Keith, 352.
Whitteker, May, 352.
Whitteker, Robert, 352.
Whitten, Anna, 484.
Whittington, Carolyn Wescott, 438.
Whittington, Emma Jean, 438.
Whittington, Wescott, 438.
Wiatt, Anna Maria, 515.
Wiatt, Fannie Holt, 515.
Wiatt, Flora Roseberry, 514.
Wiatt, Francis, 513.
Wiatt, George, 514.
Wiatt, Hawte, 513-4.
Wiatt, Henry, 513.
Wiatt, John, 514.
Wiatt, John Robert, 514.
Wiatt, John William, 514.
Wiatt, Sallie, 515.
Wiatt, Susan Turner, 515.
Wiatt, Thomas, 514.
Wiatt, Thomas Andrew, 32, 245, 246, 498, 514.
Wiatt, William Owen, 141, 226, 515.
Wickham, William C., 125.
Wigal, Austin, 223.
Wigal, John, 141.
Wightman, William M., 304.
Wigmore, J. H., 112.
Wilcoxen, C. F., 103.
Wiles, Leon S., 255, 498.
Wiley, Rankin, 474.
Wiley, S. P., 189.
Wiley, Sarah Ricketts, 474.
Wilkinson, D. E., 40.
Wilkinson, John S., 39, 40, 46.
Williams, Arthur, 460, 462.
Williams, E. E., 95, 247, 483.
Williams, Ed, 53.
Williams, Ellen Morris, 460.
Williams, Fannie, 462.
Williams, Flora Glidden, 361.
Williams, Grace, 352.
Williams, John, 430, 431.

INDEX

Williams, John E., 361.
Williams, Lucy Sartin, 430.
Williams, Mary Glidden, 361.
Williams, Minerva J., 489.
Williams, Sarah, 431.
Williams, William, 462.
Williamson, Bob, 129.
Willington, James M., 79.
Willis, Anna Gibson, 392.
Willis, J. M., 392.
Willis, Paul H., 164.
Willis, W. O., 103.
Wilson, Anderson, 516.
Wilson, Anna Conner, 517.
Wilson, Anna Scott, 484.
Wilson, Annie, 517.
Wilson, Asa L., 287.
Wilson, David, 515-6.
Wilson, Ella Ohlinger, 516.
Wilson, Ethel Swann, 517.
Wilson, Etta, 517.
Wilson, Fred, 517.
Wilson, Goodrich A., 309.
Wilson, Hattie Rust, 516.
Wilson, Henry Anderson, 516.
Wilson, J. H., 517.
Wilson, James, 17, 20, 100.
Wilson, James Hiram, 516.
Wilson, John T., 244.
Wilson, Josephine, 352.
Wilson, Kate Blackwood, 516.
Wilson, L. L., 516.
Wilson, Lelia Boyd, 516.
Wilson, Lola Gwinn, 516.
Wilson, M. Jack, 516.
Wilson, Nancy, 502.
Wilson, Neal, 517.
Wilson, Robert, 64.
Wilson, Stella, 386.
Wilson, Stephen, 97.
Wilson, T. W., 386.
Wilson, Thomas Dale, 484.
Wilson, Walter, 516.
Wilson, William, 25.
Wing, Abner W., 318.
Wingerd, Ann Sophia, 392.
Wintz, Phil, 62.
Wirtenbaker, Charles, 396.
Wiseman, Catherine, 453.
Witcher, Abram, 326.
Withington, William, 297.
Witten, Philip, 466.
Witherspoon, W. L., 255.
Witcher, Vincent A., 42.
Witcher, Daniel, 326.
Witcher, Jeremiah, 29, 39.
Witcher, John S., 39, 43, 44, 46, 87-8.
Witcher, Sanders, 326.
Witten, Ruth Dickerson, 466.
Witten, Susan, 465.

Witzgall, Chris, 294.
Wolcott, August S., 327.
Wolcott, L. M., 328.
Wolcott, R. B., 229.
Wolf, Benjamin, 306.
Wolf, Bettie Newman, 306-7.
Wolford, James, 42.
Wolgamuth, Virginia E., 366.
Wood, Emily Johnston, 420.
Wood, Ennis, 358-9.
Wood, George C., 420.
Wood, Horatio H., 30, 39, 99.
Wood, John, 146.
Wood, Matthew L., 290, 292-3.
Wood, Warren, 102, 197.
Woodbridge, Jennie M., 371.
Woodley, Oscar I., 159.
Woodruff, William E., 318, 319.
Woods, Nancy Mann, 388.
Woodson, Sarah, 384.
Woodson, Tarleton, 384.
Woodward, Sylvester, 17.
Woodworth, A. H., 209.
Woodyard, Adam, 378.
Woomeldorff, James, 376.
Workman, R. W. Alderson, 156.
World war, see European war, 1914-1918.
Wormeldorff, Dan, 53.
Wotherspoon, W. L., 486.
Wright, Catherine, 308.
Wright, Clarence L., 145.
Wright, Drusilla, 391.
Wright, Edward, 415.
Wright, Edward B., 35, 37, 391.
Wright, Flora, 181.
Wright, John G., 331.
Wright, John W., 152.
Wright, Lucy, 415.
Wright, Norma Mildred, 503.
Wright, Sam, 207.
Wright, William O., 135.
Wriston, U. G., 233.
Wyatt, C. R., 246.
Wyatt, Sarah Sloan, 249.
Wyley, Henry, 183.
Wylie, R. D., 323.
Wyllie, H. R., 264.

Y

Yarrington, J. D., 223.
Yates, C. A., 242.
Yates, Elizabeth, 149, 286, 376.
Yates, Elizabeth Lillard, 376.
Yates, George, 376.
Yates, Martha Marshall, 376.
Yates, Michael, 376.
Yates, Richard, 377.
Yates, William P., 26, 69, 286, 287, 376, 377.

York, Dora Billups, 355.
York, J. F., 355.
York, John Y., 356.
Yost, Henry, 383.
Yost, Mary Eleanor Polly, 383.
Yost, Mary Wagoner, 383.
Young, A. C., 175, 177.
Young, David, 299.
Young, O. E., 177.

Z

Zeller, H. A., 96, 252, 270.
Zenner, Henry, 357.
Ziegler, Jacob, 236, 306.
Ziegler, John L., 83, 398.
Zihlman, A., 259.

www.ingramcontent.com/pod-product-compliance
Lightning Source LLC
Chambersburg PA
CBHW020630300426
44112CB00007B/75